POWER
WARS

Also by Charlie Savage

*Takeover: The Return of the Imperial Presidency
and the Subversion of American Democracy*

POWER WARS

INSIDE OBAMA'S POST-9/11 PRESIDENCY

CHARLIE SAVAGE

Little, Brown and Company

New York   Boston   London

Little, Brown and Company
Hachette Book Group
1290 Avenue of the Americas, New York, NY 10104
littlebrown.com

First Edition: November 2015

Little, Brown and Company is a division of Hachette Book Group, Inc. The Little, Brown name and logo are trademarks of Hachette Book Group, Inc.

The publisher is not responsible for websites (or their content) that are not owned by the publisher.

The Hachette Speakers Bureau provides a wide range of authors for speaking events. To find out more, go to hachettespeakersbureau.com or call (866) 376-6591.

ISBN 978-0-316-28657-2

LCCN 2015942263

10 9 8 7 6 5 4 3 2

RRD-C

Printed in the United States of America

For my sons, William and Peter

[The Bush-Cheney administration] puts forward a false choice between the liberties we cherish and the security we demand. I will provide our intelligence and law enforcement agencies with the tools they need to track and take out the terrorists without undermining our Constitution and our freedom.

— Senator Barack Obama, presidential campaign address on national security policy, August 1, 2007

I think the American people understand that there are some trade-offs involved....I think it's important to recognize that you can't have a hundred percent security and also then have a hundred percent privacy and zero inconvenience. You know, we're going to have to make some choices as a society.

— President Barack Obama, responding to the disclosure that the National Security Agency was systematically collecting records about Americans' domestic phone calls in bulk, June 7, 2013

Contents

POWER
WARS

A Note on Sources and Quotations

This history of national-security legal policymaking in the Obama administration is primarily based on my interviews with more than 150 current and former government officials, many of whom I spoke with on multiple occasions. Where possible, I cite these officials by name. Most of them agreed to speak with me on "background" rules, meaning that I would not identify them as sources of particular information. I sought to corroborate accounts by cross-referencing their memories and claims with multiple witnesses.

Power Wars also quotes internal government documents that are not, as of this writing, available for public scrutiny. Where possible, I cite publicly available sources, including leaked or declassified documents, congressional testimony, oversight reports, court files, memoirs, and contemporaneous news articles.

Finally, this book contains dialogue from private conversations and meetings. I use italicized text to signal remarks that have been reconstructed, from memories or notes, in approximate form. This practice extends to reconstructed dialogue I have drawn from former officials' memoirs, witnesses' testimony about previous events, and other journalists' work.

Selected Members of the Obama National Security and Legal-Policy Team

Keith Alexander — National Security Agency director, 2005–2014

James Baker — Justice Department intelligence counsel, 2001–2007; associate deputy attorney general, 2009–2011; Federal Bureau of Investigation general counsel, 2014–

David Barron — Justice Department Office of Legal Counsel acting assistant attorney general, 2009–2010

Robert Bauer — White House counsel, 2010–2011

Preet Bharara — United States attorney for the Southern District of New York, 2009–

Joe Biden — vice president, 2009–

Dennis Blair — director of National Intelligence, 2009–2010

John Brennan — White House counterterrorism adviser, 2009–2013; Central Intelligence Agency director, 2013–

Lanny Breuer — Justice Department Criminal Division assistant attorney general, 2009–2013

Valerie Caproni — Federal Bureau of Investigation general counsel, 2003–2011

John Carlin — Justice Department National Security Division assistant attorney general, 2013–

Ashton Carter — secretary of defense, 2015–

James Clapper — undersecretary of defense for intelligence, 2006–2010; director of National Intelligence, 2010–

Hillary Clinton — secretary of state, 2009–2013

James Cole — deputy attorney general, 2011–2015

James Comey — Federal Bureau of Investigation director, 2013–

Gregory Craig — White House counsel, 2009

James Crawford — Joint Chiefs of Staff legal counsel, 2007–2011

Rajesh De — National Security Agency general counsel, 2012–2015

Martin Dempsey — chairman of the Joint Chiefs of Staff, 2011–2015

Mary DeRosa — National Security Council legal adviser, 2009–2011

Thomas Donilon — White House deputy national security adviser, 2009–2010; national security adviser, 2010–2013

Brian Egan — National Security Council legal adviser, 2013–

Neil Eggleston — White House counsel, 2014–

Daniel Fried — State Department envoy for Guantánamo closure, 2009–2013

Robert Gates — secretary of defense, 2006–2011

Glenn Gerstell — National Security Agency general counsel, 2015–

Richard Gross — Joint Chiefs of Staff legal counsel, 2011–

Chuck Hagel — secretary of defense, 2013–2015

Avril Haines — National Security Council legal adviser, 2011–2013; Central Intelligence Agency deputy director, 2013–2015; deputy national security adviser, 2015–

Todd Hinnen — Justice Department National Security Division deputy assistant attorney general (and sometimes acting head), 2009–2011

Eric Holder — attorney general, 2009–2015

Jeh Johnson — Department of Defense general counsel, 2009–2012; Homeland Security secretary, 2013–

James Jones — White House national security adviser, 2009–2010

Nathaniel Jones — Justice Department National Security Division counsel to the assistant attorney general, 2009; National Security Council director for counterterrorism, 2009–2012

Elena Kagan — solicitor general, 2009–2010

Neal Katyal — principal deputy solicitor general (and sometimes acting head), 2009–2011

John Kerry — secretary of state, 2013–

Edwin Kneedler — deputy solicitor general, 1993–

Harold Koh — State Department legal adviser, 2009–2013

Caroline Krass — National Security Council deputy legal counsel, 2009–2010; Justice Department Office of Legal Counsel principal deputy assistant attorney general (and sometimes acting head), 2011–2014; Central Intelligence Agency general counsel, 2014–

David Kris — Justice Department National Security Division assistant attorney general, 2009–2011

Martin Lederman — Justice Department Office of Legal Counsel deputy assistant attorney general, 2009–2010

Michael Leiter — National Counterterrorism Center director, 2007–2011

Paul Lewis — Defense Department envoy for Guantánamo closure, 2013–

William Lietzau — National Security Council deputy legal adviser, 2009–2010; deputy assistant secretary of defense for rule of law and detainee policy, 2010–2013

Robert Litt — Office of the Director of National Intelligence, general counsel, 2009–

Loretta Lynch — United States attorney for the Eastern District of New York, 2009–2015; attorney general, 2015–

Neil MacBride — United States attorney for the Eastern District of Virginia (and chairman of the Terrorism and National Security Subcommittee of the Attorney General Advisory Committee), 2009–2013

Mark Martins — Justice-Defense detainee-policy task force codirector, 2009; Office of Military Commissions chief prosecutor, 2011–

Denis McDonough — foreign policy adviser to Senator Obama, 2007–2008; National Security Council chief of staff and head of strategic communication, 2009–2010; deputy national security adviser, 2010–2013; White House chief of staff, 2013–

Mary McLeod — State Department principal deputy legal adviser, 2010– (and acting head, 2013–)

Daniel Meltzer — deputy White House counsel, 2009–2010

Lisa Monaco — associate deputy attorney general, 2009–2011; Justice Department National Security Division assistant attorney general, 2011–2013; White House counterterrorism adviser, 2013–

Robert Mueller — Federal Bureau of Investigation director, 2001–2013

Michael Mullen — chairman of the Joint Chiefs of Staff, 2007–2011

Janet Napolitano — Homeland Security secretary, 2009–2013

Barack Obama — president, 2009–

David Ogden — deputy attorney general, 2009–2010

Matthew Olsen — Justice Department National Security Division deputy assistant attorney general, 2006–2009; Guantánamo detainee-review task force director, 2009; associate deputy attorney general, 2010; National Security Agency general counsel, 2010–2011; National Counterterrorism Center director, 2011–2014

Leon Panetta — Central Intelligence Agency director, 2009–2011; secretary of defense, 2011–2013

David Petraeus — United States Central Command commander, 2008–2010; International Security and Assistance Force in Afghanistan commander, 2010–2011; Central Intelligence Agency director, 2011–2012

Stephen Preston — Central Intelligence Agency general counsel, 2009–2013; Department of Defense general counsel, 2013–2015

Benjamin Rhodes — foreign-policy speechwriter to Senator Obama, 2007–2008; deputy national security adviser for strategic communications and speechwriting, 2009–

Susan Rice — ambassador to the United Nations, 2009–2013; White House national security adviser, 2013–

John Rizzo — Central Intelligence Agency principal deputy general counsel (and often acting general counsel), 1998–2009

Kathryn Ruemmler — principal associate deputy attorney general, 2009; deputy White House counsel, 2010–2011; White House counsel, 2011–2014

Virginia Seitz — Justice Department Office of Legal Counsel assistant attorney general, 2011–2013

Clifford Sloan — State Department envoy for Guantánamo closure, 2013–2014

Robert Taylor — Department of Defense deputy general counsel, 2009–

Karl Thompson — Justice Department Office of Legal Counsel acting assistant attorney general, 2014–

Donald Verrilli Jr. — associate deputy attorney general, 2009–2010; deputy White House counsel, 2010–2011; solicitor general, 2011–

Michael Vickers — undersecretary of defense for intelligence, 2011–

Andrew Weissmann — Federal Bureau of Investigation general counsel, 2011–2013

Brad Wiegmann — Justice-Defense detention-policy task force codirector, 2009; principal deputy assistant attorney general, Justice Department National Security Division, 2009–

J. Douglas Wilson — interrogation and transfer-policy task force director, 2009; and assistant United States attorney for the Northern District of California

Lee Wolosky — State Department envoy for Guantánamo closure, 2015–

Sally Yates — deputy attorney general, 2015–

PART I

OBAMA'S 9/11

1

The Captive

1. Aboard Flight 253

It was about half past eleven on December 25, 2009 — a quiet Christmas morning. The administration of President Barack Obama, the constitutional lawyer who had risen to power on a message of change from the tumultuous era of President George W. Bush's "global war on terror," was not yet a year old. The new president was vacationing in his native Hawaii, and his national security legal-policy team were scattered to their own homes as an event that would reshape their story began to unfold.

Around ninety-two hundred feet above the surface of the earth, Northwest Airlines Flight 253, an Airbus A330 bound from Amsterdam to Detroit, approached the border between Canadian and American airspace. Inside, one of the two hundred and ninety people aboard, a Nigerian passenger named Umar Farouk Abdulmutallab, stood up from seat 19A, next to the window looking out onto the aircraft's right wing.[1] Three days earlier, the young man — a banker's son who had studied in Britain and was fluent in English — had marked his twenty-third birthday. Now, he was preparing to die.

Abdulmutallab rummaged through the carry-on bag stashed in the overhead bin a row behind his seat, found a Ziploc of toiletries, and carried it down the aisle to the bathrooms at the rear of the plane.[2] Inside one of the cramped compartments, he methodically washed his face, brushed his teeth, and dabbed on cologne.[3] Then, considering himself purified, he walked back to his seat, past dozens of the strangers whom he intended to kill.

Abdulmutallab believed he was about to commit an act of jihad and martyrdom. This would be "retaliation," in his word, for the United States' support of Israel in its "killing of innocent and civilian Muslim populations in Palestine," as well as for America's "killing of innocent and civilian Muslim populations in Yemen, Iraq, Somalia, Afghanistan and beyond, most of them women, children, and noncombatants."[4] The innocent passengers on the plane who would die if his suicide bombing was successful were nearly all noncombatants too, and they included many women and children. But Abdulmutallab dismissed them all as "collateral damage" in a war between the United States and Islam.[5] It was a misuse of the term, since he was deliberately targeting them and a civilian aircraft. But the term was also heavily loaded from its frequent invocation by the American government in its excuses for the civilian casualties that resulted incidentally from its missile strikes targeted at Islamist militants — when the United States acknowledged those strikes and bystander deaths at all.

At 11:38 a.m., Flight 253 was passing over Lake St. Clair, which lies along the international border northeast of Detroit, and was about nine thousand feet above the ground. Muttering to a nearby passenger that he did not feel well and wanted to sleep a bit before they landed, Abdulmutallab slumped back in his seat and draped a thin airline blanket over his head and body. Concealed beneath it, he said his final prayers to himself and then pulled down his cargo-style pants.

His underwear, which he had been wearing for days, was curiously bulky — like a toddler's pull-up Pampers. But the extra padding was not intended to absorb. Sewn into pouches were packages of chemicals known by the abbreviations TATP and PETN, the latter a prime ingredient in plastic explosives. The idea, conceived by a bomb maker in Yemen, was to ignite a chemical fire that would detonate the TATP, which would in turn trigger a far more powerful PETN blast — a compound bomb that used no metal parts and so was undetectable at a routine airport-security checkpoint. The plane would be blown open in midair.

Abdulmutallab unwrapped the tape from a plastic syringe, inserted its tip into the seam around the TATP pouch, and pushed the plunger.

2. Change and Continuity

At that moment, six time zones to the west, the dawn had not yet broken over the highly guarded Hawaiian compound where Obama and his family were staying. Campaigning for the Democratic Party's presidential nomination, then–Senator Obama had sharply criticized many of the national security policies that Bush and Vice President Dick Cheney had put in place following the terrorist attacks of September 11, 2001. Claiming that a president's power as commander in chief trumped legal constraints in wartime, the Bush-Cheney administration had authorized Central Intelligence Agency interrogators to torture detainees in secret overseas prisons. It had declared that the Geneva Conventions did not protect wartime prisoners captured in Afghanistan, some of whom it held without trial at the American navy base at Guantánamo Bay, Cuba. It had directed the National Security Agency to wiretap on domestic soil without the court orders required by the Foreign Intelligence Surveillance Act (FISA). In the campaign and in his early days as president, Obama had vowed to chart a new course.

"To overcome extremism, we must also be vigilant in upholding the values our troops defend, because there is no force in the world more powerful than the example of America," Obama had said a year earlier as part of his first address to a joint session of Congress, in February 2009. "And that is why I have ordered the closing of the detention center at Guantánamo Bay and will seek swift and certain justice for captured terrorists, because living our values doesn't make us weaker. It makes us safer, and it makes us stronger. And that is why I can stand here tonight and say without exception or equivocation that the United States of America does not torture."[6]

But if Obama's words had seemed clear, his actions proved to be murky. In his first weeks as president, Obama had already started to assemble an ambiguous record on the security state he had inherited from Bush. He banned torture — but his new CIA chief said the agency would continue to use extraordinary rendition, the practice of seizing terrorism suspects and transferring them to the custody of third countries for questioning outside the criminal process, relying on diplomatic assurances that they would not be mistreated. He promised greater transparency — but his Justice Department had already twice reasserted the state secrets privilege to block pending lawsuits, one involving CIA torture practices and the other challenging the National Security Agency's warrantless surveillance program. He ordered the prison at Guantánamo closed — but his cabinet nominees had testified in their confirmation hearings that it was, nevertheless, lawful for the military to imprison al-Qaeda suspects without trial under the laws of war. He closed the CIA's black-site prisons — but the CIA's drone strikes in Pakistan had continued. And he halted Bush-era military commission trials at Guantánamo — but he left the door open to potentially reviving them after an overhaul of the rules, and he later did just that. In short, having promised *change,* the new president seemed to be delivering something more like a mere adjustment — a *right-sizing* — of America's war on terror.

As Obama's team was still drafting that first address to a joint session of Congress in early February 2009, I called the White House and said I was planning to write about what appeared to me to be a surprising degree of continuity between Obama's emerging national security legal policies and those he had inherited from Bush. I asked if I could speak with someone about it. Obama's new White House counsel, Greg Craig, invited me to his office in the West Wing. I had first met Craig in the summer of 2008 at a launch party for a book about the CIA torture program, *The Dark Side: The Inside Story of How the War on Terror Turned into a War on American Ideals,* by Jane Mayer of the *New Yorker.* With a shock of white hair, a ruddy face, and an energetic manner, Craig had been President Bill Clinton's defense lawyer during the Monica Lewinsky impeachment scandal, but his first love was foreign policy and national security issues. When many people had thought Senator Hillary Clinton was a lock for the 2008 Democratic presidential nomination, Craig was among those who broke with the Clintons to become an early and senior campaign adviser to Senator Barack Obama. He had hoped to be made secretary of state, but when Obama gave Clinton that job, Craig ended up as White House counsel instead. During the transition, he had been a key force in drafting Obama's executive orders banning torture, directing the CIA black-site prisons to close immediately and the military prison at Guantánamo to close within a year.

Our appointment was for the afternoon of February 13 — a brisk, sunny, windy day. I walked down from the *New York Times'* Washington Bureau office past the statues and trees of Lafayette Square to the White House visitors' gate on Pennsylvania Avenue, which has been closed to vehicles since the Oklahoma City bombing in 1995. Outside the fence, nine protesters wearing orange prison-style jumpsuits and black hoods stood with signs reading *Shut Down Guantánamo* and *Free the Uighurs*, a reference to some Chinese Muslims at the military prison who had been brought to Guantánamo by mistake and were stuck there because there was no good place to send them. Several months later, the Obama administration would badly mishandle an attempt to find a solution for the Uighur problem, damaging Craig's standing in the White House.

Inside the West Wing, a press aide ushered me up winding stairs to Craig's corner office. Denis McDonough, the chief of staff and head of strategic communications for the National Security Council, joined us. McDonough had been Senator Obama's top foreign-policy adviser and would later be his fourth White House chief of staff. But as we sat around a coffee table, he let Craig do most of the talking. Craig made no apologies for any disconnect between the expectations created by Obama's campaign rhetoric and his early governing decisions. He told me how during the transition after the election, the incoming Obama team had visited the CIA and spent extensive time talking with incumbent managers of Bush-Cheney administration intelligence and military programs. They were going to be slow, careful, and deliberate before enacting changes, he said. The Obama team's decision-making process about what to do with the counterterrorism structures Bush had bequeathed to them, he added, was not "shoot from the hip. It is not bumper sticker slogans."[7]

Following the interview, I drafted a story reporting that despite the early flurry of high-profile executive orders on issues like torture, "the Obama administration is quietly signaling continued support for other major elements of its predecessor's approach to fighting Al Qaeda," which was "prompting growing worry among civil liberties groups and a sense of vindication among supporters of Bush-era policies."[8]

The *Times* printed the story on an inside page, but it attracted widespread attention on the Internet thanks in part to a lengthy column written about it by Glenn Greenwald, then a prominent *Salon* blogger on civil liberties and secrecy issues. I had corresponded with Greenwald since 2006, when he took an interest in articles I had written about Bush's use of signing statements to claim a right to bypass new laws; in 2013, Greenwald would evolve from a commentator into a journalist after the former intelligence contractor Edward Snowden leaked him archives of top secret documents about surveillance programs. Back in February 2009, Greenwald highlighted my story as interesting but respectfully disagreed with my analysis, writing: "While believing that Savage's article is of great value in sounding the right alarm bells, I think that he paints a slightly more pessimistic picture on the civil liberties front than is warranted by the evidence thus far (though only slightly)."[9] But six months later, Greenwald had changed his mind: "In retrospect, Savage was right and I was wrong about that: his February article was far more prescient than premature," he wrote in July 2009.[10]

Indeed, what Obama's recalibration would add up to was subject to wildly divergent early interpretations. As Obama's first year wound on, some Bush-Cheney administration veterans, notably Cheney himself, focused on what had changed. They accused Obama of not really believing the country was at war with al-Qaeda and said he was making the country less safe. But other conservatives and Republicans focused on what had stayed the same. They crowed that Obama had vindicated the Bush-Cheney administration, revealing that much of the Democratic criticism of the previous president — including Obama's own campaign rhetoric — had been empty partisanship.

On the other end of the spectrum, some liberals and Democrats also focused on those things that had changed. While celebrating Obama's departures from Bush policies, they also tended to accept what was staying the same, changing their minds about policies they had opposed when Bush instituted them because Obama now said those policies were necessary and they trusted him more. But other liberals, like the American Civil Liberties Union, pointed to the places of continuity and accused Obama of betraying his promises. An anti-Obama left began to take shape, denouncing Obama for institutionalizing and normalizing aspects of the Bush-era security state by creating bipartisan consensus over what had previously been subjects of dispute. This movement would join forces with libertarians on the right, as the anti–Big Government sentiments that had been quiet under Bush reemerged within the Republican Party now that a Democrat was president.

None of these views, of course, reflected what Obama and his legal team understood themselves to be doing. During my early meeting with Craig, Obama's top lawyer insisted that the new administration's early signs of caution about changing some Bush policies should not be interpreted as meaning that Obama had embraced Bush's view of his powers or the world.

"We are charting a new way forward, taking into account both the security of the American people and the need to obey the rule of law," Craig said. "That is a message we would give to the civil liberties people as well as to the Bush people."

3. The Underwear Bomb

Ten months after that meeting, when Abdulmutallab injected the chemicals into the bomb hidden in his underwear, Mike Zantow was sitting just behind him in row 20.[11] For the past decade, Zantow had been working abroad as a military contractor for DynCorp International, supervising the repair of U.S. Air Force equipment being used in Iraq and Afghanistan. He was now returning home to visit his sick mother. Zantow later recalled that he had heard a "large pop" like a "very large firecracker." It was not immediately clear where the sound had come from. The whole plane grew quiet as everyone tried to figure out what was happening. Then, after about half a minute, the passenger sitting next to Abdulmutallab cried out, *Hey, dude, your pants are on fire!* A flight attendant hurried up to investigate and the man reiterated, *This guy's pants are on fire!* Zantow looked over the seat back and saw smoke rising from Abdulmutallab's "lap area between his legs." The Nigerian man appeared numb and displayed no awareness of what must have been searing pain.

The passengers pulled the passive Abdulmutallab out of the seat — Zantow grabbing his right arm — and laid him flat on his back on the floor of the aisle, exposing the burning and bulky underwear. As people screamed in panic and confusion throughout the aircraft, several passengers tried to smother the flames on his body, one of them using a hat, but the chemical fire needed no oxygen and blazed on.

Finally two flight attendants, Lamare Mason and Richard Cho, grabbed fire extinguishers and sprayed Abdulmutallab and the area around seat 19A. The fire went out. The two attendants pulled up the still-unresisting Abdulmutallab and walked him, in a headlock and shuffling with his pants around his ankles, to the front of the aircraft, where they sat him down in seat 1G, removed his pants and shoes, and covered him with a blanket as the pilot began a steep emergency landing into Detroit Metropolitan Airport.

It was 11:44 a.m. Just moments had passed since the pop and fireball. Eight minutes later, the plane was on the ground in Detroit. As it sat on the tarmac, Customs and Border Protection officers came on board to investigate what they had been told was a firecracker incident. They found instead a man who was naked from the waist down, his thighs and genitals severely burned. Holding the barefoot Abdulmutallab under the armpits, they helped him stagger off the plane toward a Customs holding cell, the blanket still wrapped around him. The young Nigerian appeared to be in shock from the physical pain and adrenaline rush mixed with sheer surprise at finding himself still alive.

A clue to Abdulmutallab's passivity and mind-set may be found in his later statement to FBI interrogators that in his view, the fact the bomb had failed to detonate "was merely evidence that it was not his time to die." God, he decided, likely wanted to purify him further before he would be ready for martyrdom; the event, therefore, had turned out to be a "possible test of patience imposed on him by God."[12] Yet Abdulmutallab was remarkably candid as they walked away from the 289 people he had attempted to kill, the agents later told their law enforcement colleagues.

What's going on? one of the Customs agents, Marvin Steigerwald, asked him. *What were your intentions on the flight?*

To bring down the airplane, Abdulmutallab replied.

Who are you involved with?

Al-Qaeda.

Where did you get the device?

Yemen, in the Middle East.

Who are you involved with? Steigerwald again asked.

I'm with al-Qaeda, Abdulmutallab again replied.

4. Obama's Ambiguous First Year

The war against al-Qaeda in the first year of Obama's presidency confounded easy pigeonholing. As the months unfolded, Obama and his legal team added check marks on both the "change" and "continuity" sides of the ledger of how they were dealing with the conflict, drawing criticism from both the Left and the Right. The president's team, pincered from both flanks by accusations and condemnations about his continuity and about his changes, rejected each side as cynical and wrong in its own way.

Dismaying liberals, Obama had refused calls for a "truth commission" to investigate Bush-era torture and surveillance programs, saying the country should look forward and not back, and Attorney General Eric Holder declined to launch a criminal investigation into CIA torture techniques that the Bush Justice Department had approved as legal. But, dismaying conservatives, Holder did reopen criminal investigations into instances of torture and detainee abuses that had gone beyond Justice Department guidance; his critics said he was on a witch hunt and would make the agency risk-averse, endangering the country.

Bush had deemed three American terrorism suspects—two of whom were U.S. citizens and one, a Qatari who was arrested while lawfully in the United States on a student visa and so qualified as American for legal purposes—"enemy combatants" and placed them in indefinite military detention without charges. One was still in a military prison when Obama took office, and the new administration quickly transferred him to the criminal justice system for prosecution before a civilian court, making clear that there would be no more military detention for Americans. But Obama also fought efforts by foreigners imprisoned without trial at Bagram Airfield in Afghanistan to win the right to bring habeas corpus lawsuits challenging their wartime detention. Otherwise identical prisoners being held without trial at the Guantánamo prison had those rights thanks to a 2008 Supreme Court ruling, which Senator Obama had praised at the time.

In June, the administration transferred a Tanzanian Guantánamo detainee, Ahmed Ghailani, to the Southern District of New York to face trial for his role in al-Qaeda's bombings of American embassies in Africa in 1998. Following that, in November, Holder announced that Khalid Sheikh Mohammed, also known as KSM, and four other high-level Guantánamo detainees accused of aiding the 9/11 attacks would also be brought to New York for trial before a civilian court rather than a military commission. Civil liberties advocates cheered this decision as restoring the rule of law, but many Republicans decried it as returning to a pre-9/11 mindset of dealing with terrorism as crime, not war. Even some Democratic officials from New York, who had not been told ahead of time, worried about the security implications of a trial in a federal courthouse in Manhattan. But that same day, Holder also approved reviving the military commissions system in order to prosecute several other detainees, including Abd al-Nashiri, a Saudi accused of helping to engineer the bombing of the USS *Cole* in 2000. By endorsing tribunals as a legitimate alternative venue for prosecuting terrorism cases, the administration muddied the principle it was trying to establish — why not then use them for KSM too, allowing the trial to be held at Guantánamo? — and helped cement a continuing role for them.

Meanwhile, tensions arose within the new Obama team. Craig repeatedly clashed over tactics and priorities with Obama's first White House chief of staff, Rahm Emanuel, and was forced out by the end of the year. Other members of the Obama legal team, while sharing similar worldviews, found that even they disagreed about crucial details, like how much contact with al-Qaeda was necessary to make someone eligible for indefinite detention without trial and what kinds of charges were legitimate for tribunals.

It was around this time that a senior member of the Obama legal team told me that governing had turned out to be more complicated than criticizing from the private sector or campaigning. The lawyer noted that the administration had taken over in the middle of Bush's mess, which constrained their policy choices — it was not like they were starting with a blank slate on the morning of September 12, 2001, able to put in place what they saw as the "right" policies. They could not un-invade Iraq and un-torture prisoners, for example. Indeed, they found themselves wardens to some detainees at Guantánamo who could not be prosecuted because the government had obtained its evidence against them through torture or because they were not linked to any specific terrorist attack. Yet the solution suggested by some liberals and human rights activists — release those who could not be charged — was hard to swallow. It seemed genuinely likely to the Obama officials that some of those detainees might kill innocent people if freed. Going forward, there would be no additional such prisoners because the Obama team was not going to torture anyone and because anti-terrorism laws had been expanded after 9/11 to cover more types of activity. But that left unresolved the dilemma of finding a responsible disposition for those it had inherited.

This official urged giving the administration more time to slowly turn the ship of state toward where it should have been headed in the first place. But that Christmas there arose a great storm.

5. First Responders

Andy Arena, the head of the Federal Bureau of Investigation's Detroit field office, felt his cell phone buzz as he was out in his driveway discarding boxes from a morning spent unwrapping presents. It had been the first Christmas in years that his extended family had gathered together. Now, interrupting the family day, an assistant was texting him.

Hey, boss, there's been a disturbance on an incoming flight. Possibly a passenger lit a firecracker.

Arena texted back: *Get me more facts on that.*

Back inside his house, he told his wife he was going to run out to the airport, which was about a fifteen-minute drive away.

"People have asked me about that, why not wait to find out more?" Arena later said. "The answer is twenty-two years of experience. Something in my gut told me this was not right. Something just didn't sound right."

Arena had worked his entire career as an FBI agent after graduating from law school in 1988, taking charge of counterterrorism programs for the Detroit field office, six months before 9/11. After the terrorist attacks, he was promoted to chief of the international terrorism operations section at FBI headquarters, then, a year later, elevated to be a top counterterrorism aide to FBI director Robert Mueller. In 2007, Arena took over the Detroit office, returning to the metropolitan area where he had been born and raised. Now, as he barreled toward the airport, Arena called Jim McJunkin, the head of the FBI's counterterrorism division. One thing you learn in the FBI: you don't want your bosses seeing something on CNN they didn't already know about.

McJunkin was at his home in a Washington, DC, exurb in Northern Virginia. His family had just finished a late Christmas brunch, he and his wife savoring the fact that their children were old enough now to let them sleep in, and they were moving into the living room to open presents. Arena quickly filled McJunkin in. Arena would remember the conversation as short and basic. McJunkin said they discussed in some detail what would happen when Arena arrived at the airport. *Make sure the other agencies with roles in air security and counterterrorism are alerted and kept up to speed with developments. Isolate the passengers. Isolate the luggage. Keep the plane locked up so that an evidence team can go through it. Make sure we talk again before you make any decision about when and how to interview the suspect.*

McJunkin then called his boss, Art Cummings, a top official at the FBI's national security branch. During the workweek, Cummings lived on a twenty-three-foot sailboat in Annapolis, Maryland, which cost him only $3,500 a year in slip fees and allowed him to work long hours without uprooting his wife and teenage kids from their home in Richmond, Virginia. But he was home for Christmas, a turkey was in the oven, and guests were coming for dinner. He would not be able to share it; Cummings grabbed his go-bag, already packed with toiletries and a change of clothes for just such an emergency, and headed north on Interstate 95 to Washington. On the way, he talked to McJunkin again; the FBI was fighting off efforts by other agencies, particularly the Department of Homeland Security, to interrogate Abdulmutallab. A decade into the war on terrorism, the FBI had deep experience in national security intelligence interrogations, and Cummings was determined to keep control of it. He placed a series of other calls, including one to Mueller, who told him to make sure John Brennan, Obama's top counterterrorism and Homeland Security adviser in the White House, was in the loop.[13]

Cummings also called Michael Leiter, the director of the National Counterterrorism Center, a clearinghouse for terrorism-threat information. Energetic and sarcastic, Leiter was a former navy pilot and a former president of the *Harvard Law Review* — a prestigious position he had held nine years after a young Barack Obama had had it. Leiter later became a federal prosecutor and then a staffer on a presidential commission that made recommendations for reforming the intelligence community after it had inaccurately concluded that Iraq had weapons of mass destruction. In 2007, Bush put Leiter in charge of the National Counterterrorism Center. Soon after, Leiter had briefed Senator Obama about terrorism-policy matters, at which time he made a pitch for having the government put greater emphasis on countering the ideology that radicalizes people and turns them into terrorists. Obama liked what he heard and kept Leiter in place after he took over the White House. Leiter helped run the weekly "Terror Tuesday" afternoon meetings at the White House Situation Room in which President Obama and his national security team — the heads of military, intelligence, and cabinet agencies — focused on high-level counterterrorism-policy issues. Throughout his first year in office, Obama listened attentively at these briefings but tended to say little, Leiter told me. Protecting against terrorism was important, but it was one ball among many being juggled. Others included winding down the war in Iraq and sending a surge of additional ground troops to Afghanistan in an effort to fix the war there, trying to pull the economy of its banking crisis free fall, confirming a new Supreme Court justice, and — the top domestic-policy goal — enacting legislation for a sweeping overhaul of the nation's health-insurance system.

When his phone rang that morning, Leiter was painting the basement steps of his Northwest Washington, DC, home. He was Jewish, so there were no presents, but he had plans to join the family of his new girlfriend — and future wife — for Christmas dinner. Now, he carefully put down the brush so the white paint would not spill and picked up the phone. Cummings told him there was a report that someone on a Detroit-bound international flight had tried to set fire to a plane or had set off firecrackers. The early details were sketchy, but, Leiter later said, "Art and I had gone through enough of those that you know which ones sound silly and which ones sound real. This one didn't sound silly."

Leiter jumped into his gray Acura and headed across the Potomac River to the National Counterterrorism Center, located in one of the two main buildings at an office park called Liberty Crossing. The other building housed the Office of the Director of National Intelligence, another bureaucratic creation of the post-9/11 reform era, intended to be a single head of the other sixteen spy agencies in the United States government. From the street, the complex is anonymous; at the entrance, there is only a large sign reading *1500 Tysons McLean;* a driveway disappears in a curve behind trees and a knoll that hides the armored gates, lurking guards, and other security measures designed to prevent unwanted visitors from reaching the parking lot. But viewed from above, there is nothing subtle about Liberty Crossing: the footprint of the two buildings creates a gigantic *L* and *X.*

Because al-Qaeda had a history of attacking in waves, the first priority for Leiter was to figure out whether there were other planes about to be bombed. At that moment, there were 128 flights in the air heading to the United States from Europe. Within ninety minutes of the attack, the Federal Aviation Administration notified all the pilots to take special precautions. At airport screening areas in North America and in Europe, new security measures were swiftly put into place, including more intrusive screening of carry-on luggage and passengers' bodies and the deployment of bomb-sniffing dogs and behavioral specialists in plainclothes to search for signs of trouble.[14] Then the focus shifted to Abdulmutallab himself — and just what had gone so wrong.

6. Withholding the Miranda Warning

When Arena reached the Detroit airport, he was dismayed. The plane should have taxied to a special hangar used for hijackings, in case there was a bomb — or other bombers — on board and to keep the passengers and luggage isolated to preserve potential evidence. Instead, it had taxied right up to the terminal, and a gate bridge had been extended to it. The passengers had all gotten off the plane. While their carry-on luggage was still in the overhead bins, the checked bags had been offloaded. The passengers were still there; several hundred people milled around. The toilet tank had been emptied, losing, it would turn out, some of the bomb-related packaging material Abdulmutallab had flushed as he was getting ready for the attack.

Adding to the chaos, a bomb-detection dog sweeping the checked luggage signaled a hit. The agents immediately evacuated that part of the terminal, herding the mass of passengers away and trying to keep them together and not let them talk with others before they could be interviewed. Meanwhile, Arena later recalled, two more inbound flights from Amsterdam had reported disturbances on board.

FBI agents searching the plane found the package of the intended primary charge, PETN, behind seat 13B. The badly scorched plastic explosive had fallen, unnoticed, out of Abdulmutallab's ankled pants as the flight attendants were hustling him forward. At the time, federal officials offered the public only oblique explanations of why the bomb had failed, suggesting there had been some kind of unspecified design flaw. According to Arena, there were two hypotheses that seemed most plausible to investigators, both stemming from the numerous days leading up to the attack that Abdulmutallab had been continuously wearing the device as underwear. One was that the chemicals needed be tightly packed to be effective, and they had likely loosened up. The other was that the device had soaked up days of sweat, and the moisture had interfered with the intended chemical reaction.

But the blaze had been enough to burn Abdulmutallab badly. Steigerwald, the Customs agent, had quickly decided to get him to the University of Michigan hospital, which has a top trauma and burn center and is located in Ann Arbor, a short drive west of the airport. Arena sent two experienced agents along with him to keep tabs on events and talk to the would-be bomber if it became possible. One of the accompanying agents, Timothy Waters, was a counterterrorism supervisor in the field office and ex-military; as a bureau agent, he had spent time overseas doing battlefield interrogations. The other, Theodore Peissig, was the head bomb expert for the field office. They joined Steigerwald to watch as Abdulmutallab was given high doses of the painkiller fentanyl so his burns could be debrided and dressed.[15] The damage to Abdulmutallab's genitals was grotesque.

Boss, there is nothing worse we could do to this guy — waterboarding, nothing, Waters told Arena.

Meanwhile, Arena and McJunkin discussed over the phone an issue that would erupt into intense and sustained political controversy: whether and when to read Abdulmutallab the Miranda warning. Arena and McJunkin agreed at that stage that the agents should not read the warning to him before asking questions.[16] Cummings had emphasized the same thing to McJunkin in their early phone calls.

The warning comes from a 1966 Supreme Court case, *Miranda v. Arizona.* It arose during a time of growing concern that the police might be coercing poor and uneducated prisoners into incriminating themselves, contrary to their Fifth Amendment rights, or, worse, inducing false confessions. The liberal Warren Court ruled that for a suspect's statements in police custody to be admissible as evidence, he must first have been informed that he had rights to remain silent and have a lawyer present. Contrary to popular belief, there was no requirement that police give the warning before asking questions, but if they did not, the suspect's answers could not be used in court. And in a 1984 case called *New York v. Quarles,* the more conservative Burger Court had carved out an exception to *Miranda.* The *Quarles* rule allowed prosecutors to use as courtroom evidence any answers a just-arrested suspect gave to police in response to questions about immediate threats to public safety — in that case, where in a convenience store the suspect had hidden his gun — even if he had not yet been informed of his rights.[17]

By then, Abdulmutallab had been in custody for several hours, so there was a risk in questioning him without first reading him the warning. If he confessed, a defense lawyer would surely argue that the *Quarles* window had closed, and a judge might throw out the confession. Still, under the circumstances, it seemed likely that a judge would still deem his statements to fall within the public-safety exception. And even if

the judge ruled them inadmissible, they had plenty of other evidence —
eyewitnesses on the plane, the remnants of the bomb, including residue
on the suspect and on the seats and passengers around him, and his
burned lap. The priority was to find out who sent him and, especially,
whether other bombings were imminent.

"We had to assume he wasn't the only attacker in the air," McJunkin
said. "We had to assume there were other planes still flying with bad
guys on them, and the chances were good if they were all trained and
equipped and instructed by the same group — we didn't know who they
were yet — there would be knowledge in his head about who they were
and where they were. We clearly had a *Quarles* exception, and we
decided to go ahead and do the initial interview without Miranda."

The FBI thought it was aggressively pushing the envelope by withholding the Miranda warning. But soon the Obama administration
would find itself accused of not going far enough.

7. Unconnected Dots

Meanwhile, in Washington, national security officials were frantically
trying to understand what was happening. The nerve center of the effort
was Liberty Crossing, where Leiter was soon joined by McJunkin. The
staff members there struggled to set up a secure video teleconference in
the main conference room at the National Counterterrorism Center,
which had a dozen television screens. But the technology was glitchy,
and for ninety minutes they were unable to get everyone on the same
video conference call. Moreover, most of the other agencies — including
the White House, Central Intelligence Agency, Department of Defense,
Department of Homeland Security, Transportation Security Agency,
and National Security Agency — were represented at first only by the
low-level officials who happened to be on duty on a holiday morning.

Soon more senior officials, including John Brennan, Obama's top
counterterrorism adviser at the White House, replaced them. A career
intelligence professional who projected confidence, Brennan, then fifty-

five, had grown up in New Jersey and joined the CIA out of college. Earlier in his quarter-century career, he served as station chief in Riyadh, where he developed close personal ties to the Saudi intelligence agency. Rising quickly, he returned to Washington and became a daily briefer to President Clinton. During the first term of the Bush-Cheney administration, he had been chief of staff to CIA director George Tenet, then served as the first director of the newly created National Counter-terrorism Center. Brennan left the government in 2005 and ended up becoming a top adviser on counterterrorism issues with Obama's presidential campaign. Once elected, Obama wanted to make Brennan his CIA director, but liberals saw Brennan as tainted by his association with the agency during the period in which it had established secret prisons and tortured al-Qaeda suspects. In a sign of the influence that rights groups had at the start of Obama's presidency, he bowed to that furor and instead made Brennan his top counterterrorism adviser in the White House, a position that did not require Senate confirmation. (In 2013, after winning a second term, Obama installed Brennan at the helm of the CIA after all.)

That Christmas Day, after getting to the White House, Brennan took control of what became a daylong, continuous secure teleconference. Information trickled in. As it became clear that there had been a bomb, analysts pulled the flight manifest and began running variant spellings of Umar Farouk Abdulmutallab through their databases, trying to dig up whatever they could — who he was, where he came from. After they learned that he had been a student in England for several years, they got Scotland Yard on the phone.

Soon, a more troubling cascade of information began. In the preceding weeks, intelligence agencies had picked up rising "chatter," meaning vague indications that lacked explicit details, that some kind of terrorist attack was coming from the Yemen branch of al-Qaeda, dubbed al-Qaeda in the Arabian Peninsula (AQAP). But analysts had assumed it would be an operation in the Middle East.* Now, the CIA reported that

---

* See chapter 6, section 1.

its files showed that on November 18, Abdulmutallab's father had walked into the American embassy in Nigeria and told the CIA station chief that he was concerned about his son, who had become an increasingly radical Muslim and was now in Yemen.[18] At that time, a CIA official had entered Abdulmutallab's name in a large database used to track basic tips about terrorists, but no one had nominated him for the terrorist watch lists. That step might have subjected him to extra physical scrutiny when passing through security at the airport in Amsterdam or even prevented him from boarding a flight to the United States. Because of a misspelling of Abdulmutallab's name, the State Department did not realize he had an active multi-entry visa to travel to the United States — Abdulmutallab had visited Texas in 2008 — and so his visa had not been revoked. The CIA had also written a biographical report on Abdulmutallab after hearing his father's account, but it did not distribute the report to the wider intelligence community. And by day's end, the NSA reported to the teleconference that it had found in its raw databases of intercepted communications discussions among members of AQAP about a Nigerian.*

8. Read Him Miranda

For Obama's critics, the most important thing about the episode was not why the government had failed to detect the plot and to prevent Abdulmutallab from boarding the plane in the first place, but the decision to deliver the Miranda warning to the captive suicide bomber that Christmas night. This became a key political flashpoint, establishing a pattern for recurring partisan battles over the handling of newly captured terrorism suspects. But the full story of how that happened — who made the decision, why, and how it played out — has never been reported until now.

Back in Michigan, the primary nurse treating Abdulmutallab, Julia

---

* See chapter 6, section 1.

Longenecker, told the FBI agents that he seemed to be tolerating the painkillers and appeared lucid and oriented. The FBI agents went into the room to talk with him. Abdulmutallab told them he had gone to Yemen hoping to join in jihad and had met a man named Abu Tarek. After spending days in a house talking about Islam, he went on, they agreed Abdulmutallab would carry out an attack. Tarek also supposedly gave him the underwear bomb and told him how to use it. Abdulmutallab also reported his travel patterns and said he had been sent alone and was not aware of any other attackers. They spoke for about fifty minutes, and then the doctors took Abdulmutallab in for surgery.

So many officials from Washington were dialing Arena's cell phone seeking updates that he could not place outgoing calls, and he eventually traded phones with one of his aides so he could talk. He told McJunkin what the agents told him Abdulmutallab had said. The agents believed the prisoner was lying about some events but telling the truth about other things. Officials were starting to see that the other inbound planes were not having problems, which dovetailed with Abdulmutallab's claim to be the sole attacker. Both of the disturbances on the inbound planes from Amsterdam had turned out to be just rowdy behavior by drunken passengers, and the bomb-sniffing dog that had found something in the luggage taken off Flight 253 had apparently been reacting to strong-smelling spices that a man from India had packed in his luggage. But when CIA analysts started checking files regarding the other things Abdulmutallab had said, they came up empty. There was no intelligence about any terrorist-linked figure in Yemen who used the name Abu Tarek.

"We ran it by the CIA analysts — all the lights are on, everyone is fully engaged — and everybody is basically shaking their heads, 'This doesn't make any sense,'" McJunkin said. "That was the sum total of his non-Miranda interview."

As Abdulmutallab underwent emergency surgery on his severely burned groin, the FBI had to decide how it would approach its next interview with him. The question was when the immediate threat to public safety had passed and, with it, the window in which law enforcement investigators could question a suspect without informing him of his Miranda rights and presenting him to a magistrate judge. It has never been reported who gave the order. It became routine for Holder's critics to say that *he* did it, or at least that it was an ideological decision by the Obama administration. That is false. McJunkin, a career FBI official, made the decision, he and other officials told me.

It wasn't an easy choice. Arena said he recalled arguing to FBI headquarters that the agents would be justified in squeezing in another round of pre-Miranda questioning after Abdulmutallab woke up from surgery. Still, as the hours passed, it became clear that Abdulmutallab hadn't been lying about being the only would-be attacker that day. The Department of Homeland Security had identified every aircraft that took off around the same time as the Detroit-bound flight from Amsterdam, and all landed safely. The exception to the Miranda rule applied only to questions about immediate threats to public safety, and those threats appeared to have passed.

McJunkin said that he spoke to Cummings about the issue without resolution, but that he had the most extensive discussions with Sharon Lever, a career prosecutor in the Justice Department's National Security Division who had worked on many terrorism cases. Lever was with him that day at Liberty Crossing and was keeping the head of the division, David Kris, in Boston at the time, up to speed.

Officials familiar with their deliberations said that Lever and McJunkin discussed several concerns. At that point, they did not yet know for sure what it was that had caught fire in Abdulmutallab's underwear. He had said it was a bomb, but the lab would not be able to provide an analysis of the charred remnants corroborating that account until the next day. Moreover, it was not clear that the statements from the fifty-minute intelligence interview would be deemed admissible; the question of whether the public-safety exception could be stretched even that long was untested, with the added problem that the suspect had been on narcotic painkillers when he made most of those statements. It was possible that Abdulmutallab would name conspirators, which might be "a whole lot of people inside the United States," McJunkin said. There was an outside risk that a judge might suppress such a statement and the information derived from it if he or she decided that the agents had delayed reading the suspect his rights for too long after the immediate public-safety concerns had dissolved. A judge might even throw out the entire case on grounds that the government had conducted itself outrageously. That latter concern, in hindsight, would look less realistic, but in the immediate high-pressure moment, it was among the things they talked about. Lever took the position that the bottom line was, he might give the FBI a useful statement, and why should they risk losing it?

The prospect of losing a key piece of evidence, McJunkin said much later, "was an outside shot, but as we were making the decision, we've got a terrorist who flew in a fully loaded commercial aircraft and tried to blow it up over Detroit. It was a big deal, a big case. We don't want to make a silly mistake and have the whole thing come crumbling down."

McJunkin decided to give the order.

Read him Miranda, he told Arena.

The other government officials participating in the secure video conferences — including those from the White House, the Pentagon, and the CIA — were working to unravel the backstory of the plot and deal with the fallout. As part of that, the question turned regularly to what was next in Detroit. McJunkin told me he said to them that "we were going to proceed just like any other investigation," which he said meant "we were going to read Miranda and see what we could get out of him." No one objected. Nor did anyone suggest transferring Abdulmutallab into military custody instead, on the theory, later embraced by many Republicans, that Abdulmutallab would have become more willing to provide information if he were held at Guantánamo without a defense lawyer.

Still, there was some dissent within the FBI. Arena, who corroborated McJunkin's account, recalled that he did not immediately agree with the instruction but eventually acquiesced.

"Basically it was Washington's decision that we need to go back in and we need to Mirandize him," Arena told me. "Personally, I argued against it at first. I told him we didn't need it. 'Well, the exigency is passed.' That's fine; I still don't need this information to prosecute. But the decision was made: 'Go back in there and use a clean team.'"

A "clean team" is a new set of interrogators who have not participated in the first round of questioning and don't know the details of
what the defendant said earlier. The use of a clean team is supposed to
make it harder for a defense lawyer to argue that defects with the first
interrogation tainted statements made during the follow-up interrogation. Arena picked a counterterrorism supervisor in his field office,
John Schalt, and another counterterrorism agent to go in that evening
around nine, when Abdulmutallab woke up from surgery. The plan,
Arena said, was to make small talk — *How ya doing?* — establish a rapport, if possible, and then eventually and casually advise him of his
rights so that it would not be disruptive to the flow of conversation. But
as soon as the agents walked in, it was plain that Abdulmutallab's window of cooperation, such as it was, had already closed.

"He was rocking in the bed, he was praying, and he looked at them
with a stone-cold look and said something to the effect that 'I'm going to
kill you,'" Arena said his agents had reported. "They knew right there —
one of the agents told me, 'Boss, he got his jihad back on.' There was no
way in hell he was going to talk to us. I think what happened was, obviously the adrenaline wore off, he realized 'I screwed up, I'm not with the
seventy-two virgins, I'm in a burn center with the FBI, I'm screwed.' So he
reverts back to 'You're the enemy. I'm not going to tell you anything.'"

The agents attempted to chat with Abdulmutallab anyway, but it was
going nowhere. They then read him the Miranda warning and had a
magistrate judge brought in for an initial presentment hearing. Nine
hours had passed since his arrest.[19] It would be weeks before he started
talking again.

9. The Accusation

On Christmas Day, in the first twelve hours after Abdulmutallab's
attack, the government and the media focused their attention on immediate operational concerns. The first phones to ring were those of
national security professionals, each a part of the permanent govern-

ment that exists largely out of the sight of ordinary voters and persists through changes in administrations. Over the next weeks, however, a political furor would envelop the failed attack. For Obama and his politically appointed national security team, the entire episode became the functional equivalent of the 9/11 terrorist attacks, which had transformed the Bush-Cheney administration. The result of the stomach-churning near miss of a mass murder over American soil and its political fallout would have profound implications for Obama's legal policy, hardening his administration's approach to counterterrorism. The ambiguous, ambivalent balance of the first year tilted; Obama's policy choices that departed from Bush-era programs dwindled, and those that continued — or even expanded — Bush-era programs rose, from a fierce campaign of drone strikes whose targets would include an American citizen to the perpetuation of a sprawling and voracious surveillance apparatus.

Surveying Obama-era counterterrorism policies, a range of people across the ideological spectrum would voice, with escalating intensity, what became a defining accusation not just of the moment, but of the entire presidency: *Obama was acting like Bush.*

2

Acting Like Bush

1. Post-9/11 Presidential Power

As the government has grappled with one terrorist crisis after another since 9/11, tremendous power and pressure have descended on the executive-branch lawyers charged with handling national security issues. Remarkably few of these attorneys, in either the Obama administration or the Bush-Cheney administration before it, came up professionally as trained specialists in national security law. Law schools barely taught that subject before 9/11, and its substance has evolved rapidly since then. Classes on the topic are now more widely available — but often, the professors teaching those classes turn out to have learned about it on the job as Bush or Obama administration officials.

For example, Andrew Weissmann, who taught one such class at the New York University School of Law, was the FBI's general counsel from 2011 to 2013, a position that left him well versed in national security issues. But that was a twist in his career; he had previously been a white-collar-criminal prosecutor on the task force that went after Enron. Weissmann told me that as a field, national security law lacks the deep history of other areas of the law, subjects that eminent professors at law schools spend their lives studying, exploring every nuance and permutation. Indeed, before 9/11, he said, just one of the FBI's thirty units of lawyers was devoted to national security issues — about ten to twelve people. Within a year after 9/11, that number had ballooned to about a hundred and ten people; similar expansions happened at "Main Justice," the department's headquarters across Pennsylvania Avenue from the FBI building, and elsewhere.

"People were just being grabbed —'You're now a national security lawyer,'" Weissmann said. "People were learning on the fly, on the job. It was all very new."

Adding to the sense of flux, domestic and international law had largely been written with the problems of the nineteenth and twentieth centuries in mind, and the twenty-first century presented unforeseen circumstances. The laws of war were designed for traditional contests between well-organized nation-state armies clashing on literal battle-fields, or for civil wars within a single country. Now they are being applied to an armed conflict against a transnational, loose-knit network of zealots who move from country to country, and which lacks a leader who can sign a peace treaty and make everyone on his side stop fighting. Surveillance laws and Supreme Court precedents interpreting Fourth Amendment privacy rights were written for an era of analog data and networks that kept most domestic communications on domestic soil and most foreign communications abroad. Now they are being applied to the Internet era, where fiber-optic data roams freely across lines of national sovereignty and jurisdictional control, domestic and foreign communications are commingled everywhere, and digital technology has made dragnet collection, storage, and analysis feasible on a massive scale. Interpreting and applying national security law to such turbulent and rapidly changing conditions has created an unending series of novel dilemmas. Often, even identifying what the legal rule *is* is subject to a range of viewpoints, and there is little prospect that a court will ever definitively resolve the question because it is very difficult for anyone to establish the legal standing to file a lawsuit about it.

The most fraught issues that have consumed American national security and foreign affairs since 9/11 — Guantánamo, torture, drone strikes and other targeted killings, surveillance, secrecy, executive power, and the balance between collective security and individual rights — all have a profound legal-policy dimension. Together, they raise the question of what it means to obey the rule of law in a twenty-first-century conflict. National security legal policy occupies an indistinct space between what *should* be done and what *can* be done. Interagency legal debates, often playing out behind closed doors, set the parameters for what policymakers may choose to do, at least in theory. But in practice, if the lawyers say it is permissible to take some disputed action that might, even marginally, reduce the risk of a terrorist attack, policymakers find it very difficult not to take that action. Moreover, if the lawyers say something is legal, government officials who act on that advice are safe from prosecution — even if the legal theories are later discredited and withdrawn. The flip side of this power is that if the lawyers say a particular disputed action is illegal, a government official takes extreme bureaucratic, political, and legal risks if he ignores them and does that thing anyway. As a result, the legal debate sometimes substitutes for the policy debate, and by the time voters find out what the government is doing in their names — if they ever find out, that is — the course has long since been charted.

Executive-branch lawyering thus carries momentous consequences for the safety of the country, for human rights around the world, and for America's continuing experiment in self-government. But in this twenty-first-century conflict against terrorism, especially, legal theory is malleable. Where the law is ambiguous, government lawyers make policy in another way: they decide which interpretations of the law are reasonably available and which are not. They can be caught between wanting to maximize flexibility for their president and wanting to make their advice conform to a principled worldview, especially when that advice is secret and so not subject to the check of public scrutiny. In matters of national security, the line that separates policy and politics from law has grown blurry. In the years after 9/11, Senator Obama and a cadre of Democratic lawyers who later became his administration's legal team were withering in their criticism of the Bush-Cheney legal team. The Democrats portrayed the Republican executive-branch lawyers as having illegitimately signed off on extreme and implausible legal pronouncements in order to facilitate unwise and illegal actions like torturing terrorism suspects and wiretapping without warrants. After Obama's rise to power in 2009, it became his administration's turn to confront questions about legal constraints and terrorism risks — and undergo scrutiny for how they decided to answer.

2. Cheney's Push to Expand Executive Power

The importance of national security legal policy for a post-9/11 American government came into urgent focus in June 2004, about two months before a young Illinois state senator named Barack Obama attracted national attention with a keynote speech before the Democratic National Convention. It was then, amid controversy over photographs of torture at the Abu Ghraib prison in Iraq, that secret Justice Department memos interpreting anti-torture laws extremely narrowly were leaked. The memos set off a political debate that would have been unthinkable in America a few years earlier, but mass murder on the scale of 9/11 had been unthinkable a few years earlier too. The following year, Senator John McCain, the Arizona Republican and former prisoner of war in Vietnam, proposed legislation to make clear that torture was illegal. Vice President Dick Cheney lobbied Congress not to pass it, or, if they did, to include an exception for the Central Intelligence Agency. President George W. Bush threatened to veto any bill containing McCain's proposal, even though Bush had not vetoed anything in his first five years as president. But in December 2005, Congress approved McCain's proposal so overwhelmingly that it had the votes to override any veto easily. Bush invited McCain and the press into the White House to acknowledge that McCain had won the debate and that Bush would accept this limitation, and it looked like the story was over.

Except it wasn't over. The night Bush signed the bill — the Friday before New Year's Eve, when few were still in town and paying attention — he appended a signing statement to it. A signing statement is an official document, published in the *Federal Register*, in which a president declares how he will interpret a new law and instructs his subordinates in the executive branch to interpret the statute in the same way. This signing statement told government interrogators to interpret the torture-ban provision in a manner consistent with the president's powers as commander in chief and as head of the "unitary executive" branch.

The next week, I called the White House to ask what this meant. Did it mean the president could lawfully override the torture ban and authorize interrogators to use techniques that would otherwise violate the new statute? A press aide put me on the phone with a White House lawyer, who spoke to me on the condition that I would not print his name. The lawyer said the answer to my question was yes. The Bush-Cheney administration thought the statute was binding in general, but if some particular instance arose in which the president decided that it conflicted with what was necessary for national security, he could lawfully override it.[1]

If that view of the president's constitutional powers was true, then that whole yearlong debate with McCain had been irrelevant. It didn't matter what Congress said the rules should be, because in the end, the president got to write his own rules. I wrote the only mainstream media article about that signing statement. Two months later, I was the only reporter to pay attention to a similar reservation Bush put on a bill to reauthorize the USA Patriot Act, the surveillance law. This statement claimed a right to bypass new oversight provisions Bush had agreed to accept as a deal to end a Senate filibuster and get the bill passed. The two stories got a big response, and my bureau chief and editor, Peter Canellos, suggested that I take some time off from regular reporting to figure out what was going on with Bush's signing statements more broadly.

By then, though we reporters had been paying no attention to them, Bush had issued signing statements for more than one hundred bills, cumulatively challenging more than seven hundred and fifty provisions of new statutes he had signed into law — more than all previous presidents combined had done. It wasn't clear how many of the statements were merely threats and how many were actually carried out, especially in national security matters, where what the government does is secret. But, deciphered, the statements were a road map to the implications of the expansive constitutional theories of executive power underlying them — theories that were also being employed in other, secret memoranda.

And there were reasons to believe that Bush was willing to act on his theories. These included the emerging revelations that his administration had authorized a torture program at the Central Intelligence Agency and a warrantless-wiretapping program at the National Security Agency. Both were based on the philosophy that the actions of the commander in chief could not be constrained by statutes and treaties.

As I dug deeper, it became clear to me that the signing-statements story, as interesting as it was, was just the proverbial tip of the iceberg — merely the most visible of many related developments all in play simultaneously. Each was pushing in the direction of limiting the power of Congress and the courts, increasing government secrecy, and otherwise concentrating more unchecked power in the upper levels of the executive branch. By talking to current and former Bush-Cheney administration officials, I learned that the push to establish a presidency that was beyond the reach of limits imposed by Congress was coming primarily from Cheney. I went hunting for the roots of this agenda in Ann Arbor, Michigan, the home of the Gerald R. Ford Presidential Library, where the National Archives houses box after box labeled *Richard Cheney Files.* They revealed a pattern in Cheney's history that had gone unremarked upon during the presidential campaign, when the media portrayed him as a calming and moderating voice of experience and wisdom. He had long been a consistent advocate of expansive presidential powers. This inclination traced back to the Ford administration, when Cheney had been White House chief of staff after the Watergate scandal and the Vietnam War and during the Church Committee investigation into intelligence abuses.

It was from that vantage point in the 1970s that Cheney witnessed a key moment for executive power: the effort by Congress to reassert control over an executive branch that in the first three decades of the Cold

War had grown into what the historian Arthur Schlesinger Jr. dubbed an "imperial presidency."[2] Following World War II, the United States military had not demobilized as it had after previous conflicts. Instead, large standing armies remained deployed in bases around the world. This meant presidents could order them into major combat operations without needing to ask Congress to raise them. Spy agencies created for the short-term exigency of defeating the Axis powers took root and evolved into permanent new clandestine intelligence forces — the CIA and the NSA — that gave presidents secret means by which to carry out covert acts of warfare and surveillance. At the same time, the consolidation of the New Deal's administrative state expanded the executive branch's regulatory reach over domestic life.

All this, mixed with the constant threat of nuclear war with the Soviet Union, fueled a tremendous expansion in the powers of the executive branch and a diminishment of the roles of Congress and the judiciary. The presidency had seized escalating powers, from Truman's unilateral decision in 1950 to take the country into the Korean War without congressional authorization to pervasive domestic spying on political opponents under presidents of both parties. Executive power had slipped loose from the constraints the Framers of the Constitution had intended when they established a democracy to replace the British monarchy, Schlesinger argued.

In the mid-1970s, Congress awoke. From the late Nixon administration through the Carter administration, lawmakers tried to restore checks and balances on the executive branch. They enacted — sometimes by overriding presidential vetoes — a series of laws intended to regulate the exercise of presidential power. From the vantage point of the Nixon and Ford administrations, this did not look like a necessary constitutional correction. The Nixon and Ford teams believed that strong presidential powers were natural and appropriate given the complexities and dangers of the modern world and that the post-Vietnam and post-Watergate reforms, by encroaching on the rightful and necessary powers of the commander in chief, threatened to weaken the United States as a whole.

Cheney emerged from the Ford administration with a lifelong mission. He wanted to refight the battles of the 1970s, reducing the power of Congress and the courts and restoring the power of the presidency to the levels it had enjoyed during his career's formative years. As a member of Congress from Wyoming, he became the Reagan administration's chief defender during the Iran-contra scandal, pushing the view that the law the administration had violated by funneling aid to anti-Marxist rebels in Nicaragua was an unconstitutional constraint on the president's power to conduct foreign affairs. As secretary of defense in the Bush-Quayle administration, he urged President George H. W. Bush not to seek congressional authorization for the Gulf War, contending that he, as commander in chief, had the constitutional power to attack Saddam Hussein's forces in Iraq and Kuwait on his own.

The first President Bush rejected Cheney's counsel and went to Congress for authorization anyway. But Cheney would have far more influence over Bush's son, President George W. Bush, who had been governor of Texas but lacked his father's deep experience in foreign policy and national governance. Especially in the younger Bush's first term, Cheney's life experiences and policy agenda guided their administration on matters important to him.

One of Bush's associate White House lawyers, Bradford Berenson, later told me that on January 21, 2001, the day after Bush's inauguration, the new White House counsel, Alberto Gonzales, talked about a goal to expand presidential power. Long before 9/11, Gonzales had laid out a mandate for the new administration's legal team: to seek out opportunities to protect and expand presidential power with a goal of leaving the office stronger than it had been when they arrived. It is important to emphasize that this aspect of their agenda was not partisan; their ambition was a permanent expansion of executive authority, especially in matters of national security, not just for themselves but for all future presidents, including Democrats.

In January 2002, Cheney took ownership of this agenda in an interview on ABC's *This Week*.[3] He acknowledged that he had long sought to reverse the "unwise compromises" after Watergate that served to "weaken the presidency." He complained that in the thirty-four years since he had come to Washington, he had "repeatedly seen an erosion of the powers and the ability of the president of the United States to do his job." And he disclosed that he had counseled Bush to join in his effort to shift the balance of executive power, invoking the same metaphor that Gonzales had used at the first meeting of the Bush-Cheney administration's legal team:

"One of the things I feel an obligation on — and I know the president does too, because we talked about it — is to pass on our offices, in better shape than we found them, to our successors," Cheney said.

3. The Bush-Cheney Legal Team

An armed conflict against a shadowy, transnational network of terrorists raised many novel legal problems about issues like detention, interrogation, and surveillance. After 9/11, the Bush legal team considered options for solving each of those problems, and Cheney often pushed the administration to select those options that relied on aggressive theories that a president, as commander in chief, has the power to lawfully override statutes and treaties.

Cheney said little in meetings with other officials, reserving his advice for private one-on-ones with the president. When the legal team deliberated, Cheney acted through his top lawyer, David Addington. A smart, sarcastic former CIA official who became a lawyer amid the post–Church Committee reforms, Addington had linked up with Cheney as a Republican staffer during the congressional investigation into the Iran-contra affair. Now, with Cheney's clout behind him and a forceful personality of his own, Addington wielded enormous influence in the Bush interagency legal-policy deliberations. Jack Goldsmith, a Justice Department lawyer who clashed with him, wrote in his memoir that when a proposed policy conflicted with federal statutes, other officials suggested going to Congress and seeking legislation to adjust the law, but Addington viewed such a step as a betrayal. "Why are you trying to give away the president's power?" he demanded.[4]

This bureaucratic pressure was aided by an ally in the Justice Department's Office of Legal Counsel. That office, which was once obscure, exercises extraordinary power. By statute, the attorney general is the top legal officer of the United States and can issue opinions that are binding on the rest of the executive branch. In the mid-twentieth century, as the government grew larger and more complicated, the attorney general delegated that power to what became the Office of Legal Counsel. (The attorney general or the president can still override its legal conclusions.) By the final three decades of the twentieth century, it had grown into a node of particular influence inside the executive branch.

Before 9/11, the Bush-Cheney team had installed a University of California, Berkeley, law professor named John Yoo in the Office of Legal Counsel to handle the then-sleepy portfolio of national security matters. As an academic, Yoo had made a name for himself by advancing idiosyncratic theories of presidential power, such as the thesis that the Framers had wanted the president to be far more like a king in terms of war powers than most legal scholars believed. Because Yoo was a key Justice Department official after 9/11, his theories had real-world consequences. Citing his own scholarly articles as authority, Yoo penned one secret memorandum after another claiming that the president, as commander in chief, had the constitutional authority to lawfully take actions that were seemingly prohibited by federal statutes and treaties.

In an administration filled with officials who were determined to prevent another 9/11-scale attack — or, failing that, to at least avoid being blamed afterward for not having done all they could — the repeated assertion of this philosophy in Justice Department memos kept the brakes off. General Michael V. Hayden, who led the NSA on 9/11 and later took over the CIA, was fond of saying that in carrying out intelligence activities, "I had a duty to play aggressively — right up to the line. Playing back from the line protected me, but didn't protect

America. I made it clear I would always play in fair territory, but that there would be chalk dust on my cleats. Against a merciless enemy, we fight hard. I don't apologize for that. But we fight within our laws."[5] The catch was that the Bush legal team's secret memos defined what those legal limits were—and weren't. And Cheney, seeing the long view, pushed to establish principles of executive power even when that tactic meant paying a political price in the short term. For example, he fought to avoid making public his energy-policy task force's papers, which looked terrible as a matter of politics, but resulted in a Supreme Court victory giving the executive branch greater secrecy powers.

This is the strategy that unites and explains the Bush-Cheney administration's actions, especially in its crucial first term. It was *in the business of creating executive-power precedents.*

For example, it wiretapped without warrants—not by asking Congress to amend the Foreign Intelligence Surveillance Act to permit such eavesdropping, but by relying on secret memos asserting that FISA could not bind a president's hands in wartime. It pulled the nation out of the Anti-Ballistic Missile Treaty and set aside the Geneva Conventions when handling prisoners captured in the Afghanistan war—not by asking Congress, whose Senate had ratified those treaties, to terminate or override them in light of new circumstances, but by asserting that a president could nullify, disregard, or reinterpret treaties on his own. It established military commissions for prosecuting terrorism suspects outside of the regular civilian court system—not by asking lawmakers to enact a statute authorizing an alternative war court system, but by asserting that a commander in chief could create tribunals at his own discretion.

By taking actions that relied on the greatest possible assertions of unilateral presidential power to bypass statutory and treaty constraints, the administration converted their assertions into historical fact. It was circular logic: a president had done certain things based on these theories, and since he had done them, those theories must be true. There were occasional setbacks, most notably when the Supreme Court ruled in 2006 that Bush needed Congress to change federal law to establish military commissions. But for all the controversy some of those moves engendered at the time, Cheney's project largely succeeded. Most of those precedents were never definitively rebuked, and so they are now part of American history. They are forever available to cite as authority by any future president who feels the need, in emergencies real or claimed, to act unilaterally, to keep things secret, or to defy a statutory or treaty constraint.

4. Two Critiques of Bush: Civil Liberties and the Rule of Law

As the Bush-Cheney administration pressed its agenda of expanding executive power, the people who would one day be members of the Obama administration's legal team were critiquing them from the sidelines. The record of their responses to the Bush moves helps explain a recurring disconnect in the debate over whether the Obama administration acted like Bush once in power. Obama's continuity with the outlines of many of the policies he inherited from the second Bush term — indefinite detention of Guantánamo detainees, military commissions, drone strikes, warrantless surveillance — surprised many observers on both the left and the right. Yet the Obama team protested that their actions were consistent with what they had always thought and said, vehemently rejecting accusations that they were hypocritically behaving like the previous administration they had criticized.

To compare Bush's and Obama's actions, it's necessary to separate out two very different strands of criticism of the Bush-Cheney administration's policies and practices that arose while Bush was still in power. The first was a *civil liberties* critique: the problem was the counterterrorism policies themselves, because the government should not have the power to take certain actions, like torturing prisoners, prosecuting people before military courts with fewer protections than regular courts provide, and wiretapping an American's phone calls without a judicial order. The second was a *rule-of-law* critique: the problem was not the policy but the legal process supporting it, because the president should not have the power to disregard statutes, such as those barring torture or requiring a court order to wiretap an American's phone calls. These two strands of criticism were interwoven for the first and middle part of the Bush-Cheney administration and could often be found merged in variations of a recurring indictment: *Bush was violating civil liberties and the rule of law.*

But a pattern emerges when one looks back at how the future Obama legal team responded to Bush's legal-policy controversies at the time. Like many Democrats, they objected to much of what Bush did. But with only a few exceptions, like torture, they were far more likely to criticize Bush for violating the rule of law than for violating civil liberties. To most of them, acting like Bush, at least in the national security sphere, meant the president, as commander in chief, behaving as if he were essentially above the law. They tended to say less about any parallel problems from an individual rights and privacy perspective, leaving others to make that point at various events during the Bush era.

There is an important difference between the two critiques: Congress can cure or greatly diminish any rule-of-law problems with controversial practices like warrantless wiretapping or military commissions by enacting legislation to authorize them. But the only way to cure civil liberties problems with those policies is for the government to stop engaging in them.

A particularly illuminating example of a Bush-era uproar fueled by both civil liberties and rule-of-law concerns began late in 2005 when the *New York Times* revealed that Bush had authorized the NSA to wiretap on American soil without the court orders seemingly required by the Foreign Intelligence Surveillance Act.[6] For many of Bush's critics, the civil liberties and rule-of-law problems with that program stood side by side. But nearly all the concerns voiced by those Democrats who later joined the Obama legal team focused on Bush's alleged lawbreaking — not on the parallel claim that the program violated privacy rights.

One man who criticized the NSA program was David Kris, who would later be Obama's first appointee to lead the Justice Department's

National Security Division. A former prosecutor, Kris had worked as a national security official in the Justice Department in the early years of the Bush-Cheney administration, before leaving government in 2003. Three years later, the *Times* disclosed the warrantless surveillance program, and Bush defenders argued that wiretapping without warrants in wartime had ample historical precedent. Kris thought that argument missed the point entirely. In an e-mail to a top aide to Gonzales that later became public, Kris made a polite but devastating observation: all the historical examples they were citing came from before 1978, when Congress enacted the warrant law for national-security wiretaps.[7] Soon after, Kris testified before the Senate Judiciary Committee that it was "essentially impossible" to interpret the law as the Justice Department was doing.[8] But Kris did not say, as so many others in that era claimed, that warrantless surveillance violated individual rights; instead, he offered lawmakers suggestions about legislation to modify the statute and legalize the program.

Kris was not alone among future Obama officials in critiquing Bush's surveillance program primarily from a rule-of-law vantage point. In February 2006, the American Civil Liberties Union sponsored a town-hall event about the surveillance revelations called "Freedom at Risk: Spying, Secrecy, and Presidential Power." One of the panelists was Anthony Romero, the ACLU's executive director. He raised concerns about executive lawbreaking, but he also warned darkly that the government might wiretap political dissidents, saying, "It does send chills up one's spine." But another panelist was Mary DeRosa, who became Obama's top lawyer for the White House's National Security Council. When it was her turn to speak, DeRosa quietly offered a very different critique. She said she actually agreed "with many of the arguments that the [Bush] administration makes to support the program. I think terrorism is a grave threat; it is a different kind of intelligence challenge than what we've faced in the past. It requires some types of new technology and information, and more domestic intelligence than previously." What she disagreed with, she stressed, was that Bush had done it unilaterally rather than by working with the other branches. "I might be okay [with] the type of surveillance they're conducting, but it needs to have oversight, particularly with the new kinds of intelligence challenges. It needs checks, oversight, and transparency to the degree possible by Congress and the public."[9]

Meanwhile, the revelations had prompted a flood of litigation against the NSA and the telecommunications companies that had secretly provided the agency with access to their customers' private information without warrants. A federal district court judge ruled that the program was illegal in a lawsuit brought by the American Civil Liberties Union. When the government asked an appeals court to overturn that ruling, a lawyer named Donald Verrilli wrote a friend-of-the-court brief denouncing Bush's theory that the program was legal as "flouting the statutory directives of Congress as well as the Fourth Amendment." The program was dangerous to individual liberties, he said, but for a particular reason: it bypassed congressional regulation and court oversight.[10] Verrilli would later join the Obama administration as a top national security aide in the deputy attorney general's office, rising to deputy White House counsel and then solicitor general. In the meantime, Congress enacted a law authorizing the warrantless surveillance program and bringing its general administration under the oversight of an intelligence court. In 2012, a new legal challenge to it, also brought by the American Civil Liberties Union, reached the Supreme Court, and Verrilli defended the program with equal gusto, stressing that there were no rule-of-law problems with it anymore.[11]

5. "No More Ignoring the Law When It Is Inconvenient"

No lawyer was more important to Obama's legal team than Obama himself, a commander in chief who had once taught constitutional law at the University of Chicago. Obama's famous 2004 Democratic National Convention speech included a line supporting civil libertarians who worried that a provision of the USA Patriot Act that permitted the FBI to get business records could be used to root through library circulation lists.* "We worship an awesome God in the blue states, and we don't like federal agents poking around in our libraries in the red states," he said. As a United States senator two years later, in May 2006, Obama voted against confirming Bush's nominee for CIA director, Hayden, because in his previous role as NSA director, Hayden had put in place the warrantless-wiretapping program. Obama explained his vote as stemming from a desire "to send a signal to this administration that even in these circumstances, even in these trying times, President Bush is not above the law. No President is above the law." Obama's remarks flicked at concerns about civil liberties, but he criticized the president primarily for failing "to reach out to Congress to tailor FISA to fit the program" that had been put in place.

"There is no one in Congress who does not want President Bush to have every tool at his disposal to prevent terrorist attacks — including the use of a surveillance program," Obama said, adding, "We do not expect the President to give the American people every detail about a classified surveillance program, but we do expect him to place such a program within the rule of law and to allow members of the other two coequal branches of government — Congress and the judiciary — to have the ability to monitor and oversee such a program."[12]

When he ran for president, Obama often subtly channeled questions about civil liberties into attacks on Bush for violating the rule of law. At one campaign event, for example, a voter asked Obama about the Patriot Act. His response focused the crowd's attention not on the counterterrorism powers Congress had approved but on the ones Bush had put in place unilaterally. "Most of the problems we have had in civil liberties were not done through the Patriot Act. They were done through executive order by George W. Bush," Obama said. "I taught constitutional law for ten years. I take the Constitution very seriously. The biggest problems that we're facing right now have to do with George

---

* In the Senate, Obama cosponsored a bill to tighten limits on how the FBI could use the provision, but when it failed, he voted in March 2006 to reauthorize the Patriot Act anyway. This provision later became the claimed basis for the NSA's secret bulk phone records program.

Bush trying to bring more and more power into the executive branch and not go through Congress at all. And that's what I intend to reverse when I'm president of the United States of America."[13]

Obama's focus on the rule of law — his siding with the faction that believed that *acting like Bush* meant a president overriding statutory constraints — dovetailed with the views of his closest campaign advisers. In the summer of 2007, Obama delivered a major speech laying out his national security philosophy at the Woodrow Wilson International Center. He declared that when he became president, he would "reject torture without exception," and, in a rapid-fire sequence, he promised to "close Guantánamo, reject the Military Commissions Act, and adhere to the Geneva Conventions."[14]

Obama's line rejecting the Military Commissions Act sounded dashed off. But it was the product of intense internal deliberations among his campaign legal-policy advisers that amounted to foreshadowing. During the preparations for the Wilson speech, I was later told by participants, some of Obama's advisers had wanted him to simply "reject military commissions" — period. But then Jeh Johnson intervened.

Tall, polished, and imperturbable, Johnson was a trial attorney who had been general counsel to the air force in the Clinton administration but signed on early to help Obama raise campaign funds. He would go on to be Pentagon general counsel in Obama's first term and Homeland Security secretary in his second. Johnson had a proud family history: his grandfather was a prominent sociologist and president of Fisk University; his uncle was one of the Tuskegee airmen, the famous squad of African American pilots in World War II. Johnson himself attended Morehouse College and then Columbia Law School, became a federal prosecutor and then the first black partner at the law firm of Paul, Weiss; he also served as chairman of the New York City Bar Association committee that rated judicial nominees.

Johnson was interested in foreign and legal policy, and back in the presidential campaign he helped Senator Obama with both. As Obama and his team were preparing for his big 2007 national-security policy speech, Johnson told Denis McDonough — a key Obama senatorial aide who later became one of his top national security advisers and then White House chief of staff—that it would be a mistake for the presidential candidate to rule out tribunals without leaving himself any wiggle room. Johnson argued that Obama needed to maintain a degree of policy flexibility for when he became the commander in chief and confronted unforeseen sticky situations. He also pointed out that in 2006, after the Supreme Court had struck down Bush's first version of tribunals and the Republican-led Congress passed the Military Commissions Act to reestablish them, Obama had voted for the Democrats' alternative version of the bill. The Democrats' version included more defendant protections but nonetheless still authorized military trials. Therefore, if Obama precluded tribunals in all forms, he'd be moving to the left of his own previous position and that of many Senate Democrats who had supported that bill, including Hillary Clinton, Carl Levin, who was now the Senate Armed Services Committee chairman, and even Ted Kennedy, the outspoken liberal.

Johnson's arguments prevailed, and instead of rejecting *military commissions* in his Woodrow Wilson Center speech, Obama rejected only the *Military Commissions Act of 2006.* The difference was subtle, leaving the impression among casual listeners that he opposed *any* use of tribunals. In fact, he left the door open to using a different version of tribunals authorized by a different law.

To be sure, some of Obama's rhetorical blasts at Bush touched on civil liberties concerns: "This administration acts like violating civil liberties is the way to enhance our security. It is not."[15] But when Obama detailed what he meant beyond his absolute rejection of torture, his specific complaints and promises were heavily tilted toward fixing the legal process. "That means no more illegal wiretapping of American citizens," he said. "No more national security letters to spy on citizens who are not suspected of a crime. No more tracking citizens who do nothing more than protest a misguided war. No more ignoring the law when it is inconvenient. That is not who we are. And it is not what is necessary to defeat the terrorists. The FISA Court works. The separation of powers works. Our Constitution works."

The parsing was careful too. It sounded like a wholesale rejection of Bush policy outcomes, but it was really just about making sure the legal foundation was solid. *Lawful* surveillance programs, meaning those authorized by Congress and subject to the FISA Court's oversight, were fine.

All this culminates in the second helpful model for determining whether Obama acted like Bush. If one takeaway is that the Bush-Cheney legal team was consciously seeking to expand presidential power as an ideological end in itself, a key point to understand about the Obama legal team is that they were trying to fight al-Qaeda while adhering to what they saw as the rule of law. President Obama and most of his people appeared in practice to care somewhat more about civil liberties than President Bush and most of his team. But the Obama team was not, and never had been, the full-throated civil libertarians that Senator Obama had allowed and encouraged his supporters in the Democratic primary campaign to think — and his opponents to fear — they would be.

The crucial insight that arises from this model is that by the time Obama inherited the presidency, many controversial post-9/11 policies had a much stronger legal basis than when Bush first created them. Over the years, the courts had become more involved in overseeing the fates of detainees and surveillance practices, giving judicial blessing to formerly unilateral policies. The Bush-Cheney administration moderated its interrogation practices and accepted a Supreme Court ruling that the Geneva Conventions protected terrorism detainees. And Congress passed the Military Commissions Act, the FISA Amendments Act, and other laws that adjusted federal statutes to bring them into alignment with what Bush had been doing.

Senator Obama's campaign rhetoric rarely reflected these evolving legal facts. The 2007–2008 Democratic primary campaign was in part a contest to see who could attack Bush the most vigorously, and Obama designed his message to make liberal voters cheer. Consistently, Obama framed his criticism of Bush in ways that led casual listeners to conclude that he opposed Bush's programs altogether, when in fact a close reading shows that he was often attacking the way Bush had put them into place unilaterally back in his first term.

As a result, in January 2009, the new administration inherited a series of programs that many voters thought he viewed as inherently wrong and was promising to change. But most of the rule-of-law problems with them had actually already been fixed, even though civil liberties complaints about the post-9/11 security state remained fervent.

6. The Executive-Power Survey

What the next president did with the newly enhanced powers and precedents he or she inherited from Bush could be pivotal for the future of American-style democracy. But in 2007, as I watched the early primary season, I was frustrated to see that the campaign rhetoric about presidential power was often so vague that it could mean anything or nothing. And I was annoyed to see that the television journalists entrusted to moderate presidential debates weren't asking the right questions — really, *any* questions — about the topic. After hearing me groan once too often, my wife, Luiza, suggested that I just ask the candidates the questions I wanted them to answer myself.

In the fall of 2007, at the *Boston Globe,* I developed a questionnaire on executive-power issues and submitted it to the top six presidential candidates of both parties. It asked pointed questions about what they believed the scope and limits of their constitutional powers would be, should voters entrust them with the presidency. The survey ranged over such issues as conducting warrantless surveillance and torturing prisoners in defiance of statutes, attacking another country without congressional authorization, using signing statements to claim a right to override new laws, holding American citizens without trial as enemy combatants, bypassing human rights treaty restrictions, and withholding information from Congress under a claim of executive privilege.

The Obama campaign was an early and enthusiastic participant, and Obama's willingness to answer my questions pressured reluctant

Democratic rivals — notably two frontrunners at the time, Senators Hillary Clinton and John Edwards — to do so as well. The other three Democratic candidates — Senators Joe Biden and Chris Dodd, and New Mexico governor Bill Richardson — needed little coaxing to provide answers.

On the Republican side, Representative Ron Paul and Senator McCain were also early and enthusiastic participants, and Governor Mitt Romney eventually joined in as well. Paul and McCain appeared to be interested in these issues on a personal level and answered many of my questions themselves in phone interviews, while Romney had a well-organized campaign with legal-policy advisers who were capable of drafting written answers for the governor to mull over, adjust, and endorse. The mere fact that the other major GOP candidates aspiring to the throne — former New York mayor Rudy Giuliani, former Arkansas governor Mike Huckabee, and former senator Fred Thompson — chose not to answer the questions seemed revealing in its own way.

Because he went on to win the White House, Obama's Q&A would prove to be of enduring interest. As with the Wilson Center speech, the first draft of Obama's answers to the survey was sketched out by Ben Rhodes, a policy adviser and speechwriter, with oversight and direction from Obama's top campaign legal-policy advisers, Johnson and Greg Craig. Obama then reviewed, revised, and authorized the final answers, making them his own.

In many cases, the pattern held: Obama blasted Bush policies but primarily in terms of his acting outside an accepted legal framework. "The creation of military commissions, without congressional authorization, was unlawful (as the Supreme Court held) and a bad idea," Obama said, adding that he would "only authorize surveillance for national security purposes consistent with FISA and other federal statutes."[16] Obama didn't point out that by then Bush had, however reluctantly, later obtained congressional authorization for tribunals and for a warrantless-wiretapping program.

Obama also said he would obey anti-torture laws and limit American officials to using techniques approved in the army field manual on interrogation — a set of standard rules written to comply with the

Geneva Conventions — and declared that the president had no power to hold American citizens as enemy combatants. Those answers comported with his later behavior in office. But some of Obama's other answers clashed with his later actions as president, including his endorsement, in the survey, of robust limits on when a president could bomb another country without congressional authorization, withhold documents under executive privilege, and use signing statements to bypass the intent of Congress.

At the conclusion of the questionnaire, Obama said that it was important for all would-be presidents to lay out their understanding of the limits they were bound to obey before voters decided whom to entrust with those powers.

"These are essential questions that all the candidates should answer," the senator said. "The American people need to know where we stand on these issues before they entrust us with this responsibility — particularly at a time when our laws, our traditions, and our Constitution have been repeatedly challenged by this Administration."

7. Foreshadowing

As Bush's second term progressed, he sought to place his surveillance programs on a firmer legal footing. The Bush-Cheney administration had persuaded Congress — now under Democratic control — to pass the Protect America Act in July 2007, thereby authorizing the warrantless surveillance program. But the bill was a temporary fix — it expired after six months — and no one was happy with it. The White House wanted a more permanent solution allowing the program to keep going, and it wanted Congress to include retroactive legal immunity to the telecommunications companies that had assisted the NSA, killing the lawsuits against them. Civil libertarians did not want the program to continue, and many liberals were opposed to retroactive immunity, arguing that it would remove any incentive for such companies to say no if the government again asked them to facilitate illegal spying.

All the Democrats in the primary seeking their party's nomination, including Obama, voted against the Protect America Act, but the issue was not settled. That fall, as the Iowa caucuses neared, Congress began working on its replacement, which had a far less flamboyant name: the FISA Amendments Act. When it turned out that the bill would include a provision granting retroactive legal immunity to the telecoms, Dodd jumped in front of the Democratic pack and won praise from the "netroots"—tech-savvy liberal and libertarian bloggers and opinion leaders—by announcing that he would filibuster it. Liberal bloggers mounted a campaign to pressure the other Democratic contenders to do likewise, and the Obama campaign soon put out a statement matching Dodd's promise: "To be clear: Barack will support a filibuster of any bill that includes retroactive immunity for telecommunications companies," said Obama campaign spokesman Bill Burton in a statement.[17] Civil libertarians cheered.

Obama went on to win the Iowa caucuses. But once Clinton rebounded to win the New Hampshire primary, the two settled in for a long duel. In late February 2008, Dodd dropped out of the race and endorsed Obama, who issued a lengthy statement praising Dodd and making a play for the civil libertarians whom Dodd had sought to rally. "I've been proud to stand with Senator Dodd in his fight against retroactive immunity for the telecommunications industry," Obama said. "Secrecy and special interests must not trump accountability. We must show our citizens — and set an example to the world — that laws cannot be ignored when it is inconvenient."[18]

That tone stretched into June, when Obama finally secured enough delegates to clinch the Democratic nomination and turned toward the general election. In July, the Senate brought the FISA Amendments Act to the floor. Obama voted for an amendment that would have stripped the immunity provision, but it was defeated thirty-two to sixty-six. Then Obama, instead of filibustering the final bill as he had promised to do, voted to bring it to an up-or-down vote and then voted in its favor. (Clinton, by contrast, voted to filibuster the bill and voted against the final passage.)

Obama was attacked from both the left and the right as a flip-flopper and a cynical politician.[19] Explaining his conduct, Obama said he knew some of his supporters would be disappointed with his vote, but he also defended the importance of surveillance programs so long as they were legally authorized and under oversight by judges: "In a dangerous world, government must have the authority to collect the intelligence we need to protect the American people. But in a free society, that authority cannot be unlimited. As I've said many times, an independent monitor must watch the watchers to prevent abuses and to protect the civil liberties of the American people. This compromise law assures that the FISA Court has that responsibility.... Given the choice between voting for an improved yet imperfect bill, and losing important surveillance tools, I've chosen to support the current compromise."

He also reminded his supporters that even if they were angry with him over this matter, they surely did not want to cast their votes for his Republican opponent.[20] And he promised to do a top-to-bottom review of surveillance and privacy policies once he took office.

Many civil liberties and privacy advocates, while disappointed in Obama's vote, remained convinced that he was one of them. Around October 2008, when the polls suggested strongly that Obama would be the next president, one such advocate, Kate Martin — the director of the Center for National Security Studies, a civil liberties advocacy organization — came to the Dirksen Senate Office Building. She was meeting with two future members of the Obama administration: DeRosa, who was then Senator Patrick Leahy's national security counsel on the Senate Judiciary Committee staff, and Suzanne Spaulding, a former CIA lawyer and former Democratic staffer on the House Intelligence Committee.

Spaulding and Martin were preparing written submissions in connection with a subcommittee hearing chaired by Senator Russ Feingold, Democrat from Wisconsin, on "Restoring the Rule of Law"— meaning, what should happen after Bush left office — and they wanted to consult with DeRosa. Martin expressed enthusiasm about what the coming change would mean for privacy issues: *It's going to be so great to have an administration I agree with.*

But DeRosa, drawing on her experience as national security official in the Clinton administration, saw things differently. *You won't be as happy as you think. You'll find plenty to criticize on privacy issues,* she said.

8. Obama and the "War" on Terrorism

Obama's invocation of the need for robust but legally authorized surveillance programs in a dangerous world dovetails with his approach, and that of most members of his future legal team, to perhaps the most fundamental question that faced the United States after the 9/11 attacks. It was whether what Bush liked to call the "global war on terror" — counterterrorism efforts beyond the invasion and occupation of Afghanistan — was, for legal purposes, a literal *war* or just a metaphor for rallying public support behind a difficult effort, like the "war on drugs" or the "war on poverty."

Some liberals and many civil libertarians and international legal scholars rejected the notion that there could be such a thing as an armed conflict with a transnational terrorist group rather than a nation-state. In their view, al-Qaeda was a criminal gang — a particularly dangerous one, to be sure, but more akin to a band of pirates or an international drug-trafficking cartel than to Nazi Germany or North Vietnam.

The answer to this question has profound consequences. If the war model is wrong, then a host of wartime measures based on individuals' presumed membership in al-Qaeda — like detaining suspected adversaries indefinitely and killing them in situations when they do not present an imminent threat — are illegal. Police are not allowed to imprison criminal suspects without trials or gun them down if they are not about to hurt someone.

Conservative critics of Obama, seeking to portray him as soft on terrorism, frequently accused him of failing to understand or believe that the country was at war. They said he wanted to return to a pre-9/11 mentality of dealing with al-Qaeda as exclusively a law enforcement problem.

It was true that Obama and his legal team preferred to use law enforcement tools to handle terrorism matters in some contexts, avoiding the use of military force on domestic American soil and choosing to prosecute terrorism cases in the civilian court system. But these political attacks were not a description of the world as it was. Obama clearly accepted that the United States was at war with al-Qaeda and its allies, an armed conflict Congress had authorized in 2001 and the Supreme Court had endorsed in a 2004 wartime detention case. The Obama team did not think that this war ended because Bush gave way to Obama on January 20, 2009. As a result, in the team's legal-policy view, the powers available only to a nation that was literally at war remained in the government's toolbox — and Obama would use them with vigor, angering his liberal critics.

Indeed, Obama was no dove and never had been. In October 2002, when he was a state senator, he gave a speech against Bush's coming invasion of Iraq — a speech his campaign would make famous by using it as a cudgel against Clinton, who had voted to authorize the invasion — but Obama still managed to make clear he was not a pacifist. "Let me begin by saying that although this has been billed as an anti-war rally, I stand before you as someone who is not opposed to war in all circumstances," Obama said. "After September 11, after witnessing the carnage and destruction, the dust and the tears, I supported this administration's pledge to hunt down and root out those who would slaughter innocents in the name of intolerance, and I would willingly take up arms myself to prevent such tragedy from happening again. I don't oppose all wars."[21]

In Obama's first year as president, he twice articulated a broad philosophy for fighting a war against al-Qaeda while respecting the constraints of law. The first key moment confirming this thinking came at a speech at the National Archives in May 2009 in which he defended his decision to retain military commissions and indefinite detentions to critics on the left while clarifying his support for obeying the laws of war — including treating enemy prisoners humanely — to critics on the right. "We are indeed at war with al Qaeda and its affiliates," Obama said. "We do need to update our institutions to deal with this threat. But we must do so with an abiding confidence in the rule of law and due process; in checks and balances and accountability."[22]

And on December 10, 2009, Obama traveled to Oslo to receive the Nobel Peace Prize, an honor even White House officials privately conceded was awkwardly premature at best. Obama chose in his acceptance speech to defend "just war," arguing that at times nations found "the use of force not only necessary but morally justified" to prevent the deaths of innocent people at the hands of foes like Nazi Germany or al-Qaeda, enemies who would never lay down their arms through negotiations and could be defeated only militarily. Still, Obama said, there were right and wrong ways to fight, and he was determined to conduct the continuing war against terrorism within the rules and standards that governed the use of force lest American "actions appear arbitrary and undercut the legitimacy of future interventions, no matter how justified ...

"Even as we make difficult decisions about going to war, we must also think clearly about how we fight it," Obama added. "Where force is necessary, we have a moral and strategic interest in binding ourselves to certain rules of conduct. And even as we confront a vicious adversary that abides by no rules, I believe the United States of America must remain a standard bearer in the conduct of war. That is what makes us different from those whom we fight. That is a source of our strength."[23]

9. The Role of Law

Just as the teams running the first two post-9/11 presidencies applied very different conceptions of the rule of law to the armed conflict against al-Qaeda, they also sharply contrasted in another way: the *role* of law in shaping their deliberations and governance.

As a matter of both style and substance, the Bush-Cheney administration had an unlawyerly approach to government. Bush and Cheney were CEOs, not lawyers, by experience and nature. Bush's leadership style was to be, as he confidently described himself, "the decider," and he trusted his instincts, acting with dispatch and without extensive deliberations and without second-guessing himself afterward. "I'm not a textbook player, I'm a gut player," Bush once said.[24] Cheney was a masterful bureaucratic player, manipulating and sidestepping normal governing processes in order to steamroll or circumvent internal dissent and push through the policy changes he desired. Moreover, many of the lawyers they surrounded themselves with — at least, the members of the inner circle who were told what was going on in the first years after 9/11 — embraced such sweeping views of executive power that the law was not a factor. They dispatched every hard problem with the same easy answer: the president could do whatever he deemed necessary to protect national security.

This governing style contributed to both strengths and weaknesses. Responding to the crisis, the Bush-Cheney policymakers were able to rapidly put in place programs and policies that dramatically altered governmental institutions and departed from traditions. Critics said the Bush-Cheney administration did not fully think through counterarguments and potential risks before acting, and as a result it could be reckless. But, for better or for worse, Bush was also decisive. His administration could move and get things done.

If the Bush years can be caricatured as government by cowboy, energetic but shooting from the hip, the Obama era was government by lawyer, methodical and precise — sometimes to a fault.

Lawyerliness suffused the Obama administration. During the transition, Tom Donilon — a practicing lawyer who came in as Obama's deputy national security adviser, taking the immediate lead on legal-policy matters — designed a National Security Council decision-making process that would ensure wide consultation of lawyers from different agencies. Donilon told me he had received "direct advice from one of my predecessors" in the Bush-Cheney administration about the importance of having the right people vet issues fully. Donilon declined to say whom, but Bush's first national security adviser, Condoleezza Rice, wrote in her 2011 memoir about interagency breakdowns in which Cheney and Addington had circumvented Rice and her National Security Council legal adviser John Bellinger, as well as other top national security officials at the State, Defense, and Justice Departments. She cited in particular an episode in November 2001 in which Cheney placed a draft order establishing military commissions in front of Bush, and Bush had signed it, even though she "had not even seen" it.

"The interagency process exists to ensure that all perspectives are represented so the President gets a comprehensive look at the potential impact of his decisions," Rice wrote. "Perhaps a more thorough review would have brought to the surface some of the procedural challenges that led the Supreme Court to halt the tribunals in 2006. We will never know for sure, but that is why the vetting of controversial ideas is important."[25]

Seeking to avoid that kind of dysfunction, the Obama team revived the *interagency national security lawyers group,* a bureaucratic institution from the 1990s that the Bush-Cheney administration had essentially dismantled. The lawyers group was an elite council of the top lawyers from each of the core national security–foreign policy agencies. These included the Pentagon general counsel, the uniformed legal adviser to the Joint Chiefs of Staff, the State Department legal adviser, the head of the Office of Legal Counsel, and the top lawyer for the Office of the Director of National Intelligence (and sometimes the CIA). The National Security Council legal adviser chaired the lawyers group while serving two bosses — Obama's White House counsel and his national security adviser. The group routinely met in the Situation Room to debate highly fraught national security legal-policy issues. It provided advice to the policymakers at each stage in the bureaucratic process, taking assignments from them and presenting legal issues in high-level meetings. Operating alongside the hierarchy of policy-makers, it set the framework within which a decision could be made — such as, for example, whether killing a particular terrorism suspect was permissible. This structure gave the lawyers the first shot at many decisions, and they remained to address any wrinkles that arose.

"We learned from the Bush administration," Donilon said. "There were real, severe process failures in the Bush administration that led to poor decisions, in my opinion. I was determined to make it better in this administration. Number one, as the national security adviser, as the deputy, I insisted on bringing the consideration of legal issues into the [National Security Council] process, which it had not been during the Bush administration. To be fair, they were under tremendous time pressure. We had the ability to do it right."

Lawyerliness shaped Obama's governance as a matter of style and thought, not just process. Obama was a lawyer and a law teacher, not a CEO, and he chose many other people with law degrees — including his vice president, the secretaries of key cabinet departments and agencies, and several of his White House chiefs of staff — to be members of his team. This was important, because lawyers are trained to think in very particular ways. When analyzing a problem, they try to identify all the issues and grapple with the strongest arguments against their own position. They demand good writing. They attempt to keep options open as an end in itself. They prize rigorous adherence to process. They consider it a judicial virtue to move incrementally and stay within the narrow facts at hand.

In the Obama White House, legal ways of analyzing problems disciplined deliberations. In one Situation Room policy meeting about Syria in February 2013, Jake Sullivan, the newly installed top national security policy adviser to Biden — and a Yale Law School–trained former Supreme Court clerk — was struck by the tenor of the conversation. After the meeting, he turned to Lisa Monaco, Obama's top counterterrorism policy adviser — and a former federal prosecutor — and marveled at how central the discussion of legal questions seemed to be to every facet of policymaking. For her part, Monaco later told me that she had observed even some of the nonlawyers in internal policy debates pick up the lawyers' approach.

"They search for precedent, articulate policy in terms of frameworks," Monaco said. "You end up having operators who never went to law school, but the legal issues keep recurring and so they get used to them and even raise them themselves."

This approach had its own weaknesses. If the Bush administration sometimes seemed reckless, the Obama administration sometimes seemed paralyzed, grappling with a problem from all sides and then putting it off to be taken up again at the next meeting. As Obama weighed — and weighed — dilemmas like whether to send a surge to Afghanistan or arm the so-called moderate rebels in Syria, critics like Cheney accused him of dithering and indecision.[26] And Obama could seem detached and analytical to a fault. In his memoir, Leon Panetta, Obama's former CIA director and defense secretary, wrote that Obama's caution was "not a failing of ideas or of intellect.... He does, however, sometimes lack fire. Too often, in my view, the president relies on the logic of a law professor rather than the passion of a leader."[27]

But a lawyerly mind-set to government policymaking also has advantages. It meant that the administration, though it made its share of mistakes, was cautious and deliberate. It thought through all the reasons *not* to take a proposed action before acting and made sure that every part of the government that had an interest in a matter was given a chance to weigh in. It was willing to revisit a previous decision in light of new evidence.

And as a matter of legal substance, this mind-set ensured that a full range of views was thoroughly aired. Whenever there was a legal angle — even soft law or shades-of-gray law, like norms of international behavior — the Obama team took it very seriously. This does not mean that legal considerations dictated every decision. But as Abram Chayes, the top State Department lawyer during the Kennedy administration, wrote in a classic memoir about the Cuban missile crisis, an administration that wants to legitimize its actions with legal arguments finds that legal concerns organize and mold its deliberations, even when military, diplomatic, and political considerations are also important to the ultimate outcome.

"The requirement of justification suffuses the basic process of choice," Chayes wrote. "There is a continuous feedback between the knowledge that the government will be called upon to justify its action and the kind of action that can be chosen."[28]

Many accounts of presidents' national security and foreign-policy records pay scant attention to the role of law and the influence of executive-branch lawyers. This is an omission in any era. But Obama's governance, in particular, cannot be seen clearly without looking at it through a legal lens.

"Virtually every issue we faced had significant legal issues — many of first impression," Donilon said, using the term for a matter a court has never addressed and that therefore has no binding precedents to guide its outcome. "We never had a meeting that didn't include the legal adviser to the National Security Council or her assistant. My own training as a lawyer was essential to my ability to function as national security adviser because the legal issues were so pervasive and because the president and the vice president were lawyers and addressed these legal issues rigorously."

10. The Obama Legal Team on Christmas

Back in 2008, when Obama was moderating his tone on national security for the general election, not all of his future legal-team members were ready to take that step with him. In June 2008, Eric Holder gave a speech at a conference of the American Constitution Society, a liberal legal network. He denounced the Bush-Cheney administration for having led the country astray after 9/11, away from its "commitment to the Constitution and to the rule of law," and declared that "we owe the American people a reckoning."[29]

Holder would go on to be one of the most liberal members of the

Obama cabinet. In November 2009, he announced that Khalid Sheikh Mohammed and four other former CIA prisoners who were accused of aiding the 9/11 attacks would be brought from Guantánamo to New York and tried by a federal civilian court rather than a military tribunal. His decision came as a surprise to elected Democrats in New York, who were unhappy about it due to security fears surrounding such a trial, but it seemed that the turbulence would subside over time.

A month later, at his home in Northwest DC, Holder took out his iPhone and snapped a photograph of a tantalizing Christmas turkey, hot from the oven and not yet carved; several months later, he would show me the picture during an interview, a reminder of a moment in time just before the world had changed.

When the house phone rang that Christmas Day, Holder was complimenting his wife, Sharon Malone Holder, on how good the bird looked. Their teenage son picked up the line. An official with the Justice Command Center — a secure compound on the sixth floor of the department's headquarters, one of many places around Washington where national security officials are on duty twenty-four hours a day — asked to speak to the attorney general. Holder was connected to David Kris, the assistant attorney general in charge of the Justice Department's National Security Division.

Kris was on the line from Cambridge, Massachusetts, where he, his wife, Jody, and their two children were visiting Kris's father. They had decided to go to an early matinee at the theater in Harvard Square, and the lights had just gone down when Kris's cell phone had buzzed. He slipped out to a stairwell behind the seats and took the call. It was Art Cummings at the FBI with the initial report of some kind of incident on an inbound plane to Detroit. Kris dialed other numbers and was shushed a couple of times by disgruntled patrons. He missed the whole movie, which starred Meryl Streep and Steve Martin and was called *It's Complicated.*

Now, Kris told Holder what he had learned in his initial calls. Details were still sketchy and Kris said he would get back to him; they stayed in regular contact throughout the day as Kris provided updates. "[Holder] was very engaged and very thoughtful and interested in understanding details and knowing exactly what was going on and making judgments, and this is not easy to do in a fast-moving, complicated environment plagued by uncertainty and the typical fog of war that attends one of these fast breaking events," Kris later told me.

Litt, the top lawyer for the Office of the Director of National Intelligence, was also in New England. A former federal prosecutor in the Southern District of New York with a close-cropped gray beard and a dry sense of humor, Litt was a rare official who had gained deep experience with national security legal policy before 9/11; during the Clinton administration, he was a senior Justice Department official for matters like surveillance and covert-action reviews. After 9/11, he was a rare Democrat who defended Bush's decision to create military commissions to prosecute terrorists, telling *Newsday* in late 2001 that "the idea of holdings tribunals is a good one." But his reasoning was subtle; he argued that keeping terrorism cases out of the regular civilian criminal justice system would prevent the Supreme Court and Congress from approving rules that would undermine protections for ordinary criminal defendants, adding that as the tribunal rules were written, "We should try as much as we can to replicate military or civilian courts."[30]

Now, six months after the Senate had confirmed him to return to government, Litt and his wife, Deborah, were at their Vermont lake house. Litt would spend much of his vacation week on the phone or answering e-mails dealing with the fallout from the attempted attack, but he did not come back to DC right away. The immediate problems were operational, matters for career national security officials to handle; the legal-policy issues would come to center stage later.

The story was similar for Mary DeRosa, the top lawyer for the National Security Council. She was home in Northwest DC with her husband, Peter Bleakley, their seventeen-year-old son, Nicky, and her parents when news of the attempted bombing spread. DeRosa decided not to cancel her flight to Los Angeles the next day, but she was back in Washington by New Year's Eve as the broader issues heated up.

Also in Northwest DC, David Barron, a Harvard Law professor

serving as acting head of the Justice Department's Office of Legal Counsel, was with his wife, Juliette Kayyem, and their three young children at a neighbor's Christmas party. For the first few days after the bombing attempt, Kayyem, a top Department of Homeland Security official, was busier than her husband was. But Barron's professional life and reputation were soon consumed by the consequences of the attack.

The White House counsel's seat was in flux on Christmas. Obama's first counsel, Greg Craig, who had pushed so hard to close Guantánamo, had formally announced his resignation in November and was transitioning out; his successor, Robert Bauer, Obama's former personal lawyer and the top lawyer to his presidential campaign, was transitioning in. The skinny on Bauer was that he was smart, politically savvy, and less likely than Craig to use his role to advance a policy agenda in national security deliberations; he lacked significant experience in post-9/11 issues. Married to Anita Dunn, Obama's first White House communications director, who had stepped down two months earlier, Bauer was at his home in the DC suburb of Chevy Chase, Maryland, on Christmas. He would soon attend his first Situation Room meeting, chaired by John Brennan, to go over the fallout from the underwear-bomb attack.

Stephen Preston, the CIA's top lawyer, was at his home in Northwest DC too. Preston had been a senior lawyer in the Department of Defense and general counsel of the navy during the Clinton years. He and his wife, Mary, had just opened presents with their twelve-year-old daughter and ten-year-old son. When he heard the news, he was struck: the United States had just been attacked, and it had been years since that happened.

Five days later, a suicide bomber blew up a CIA base in Khost, Afghanistan, killing nine people, including seven CIA operatives. Preston knew one of them personally and had an even more visceral reaction.

"The fight for me seemed more real, more immediate, and more personal after those holiday attacks," Preston later told me.

*   *   *

Meanwhile, in Montclair, New Jersey, Jeh Johnson was trying not to brood. After the campaign, Obama had made Johnson the Pentagon general counsel, which meant it was his job to sign off on targeted killing operations by the Joint Special Operations Command in places like Somalia and Yemen — a task for which little about being air force general counsel back in the 1990s had prepared him. A week before Christmas, amid a surge in vague chatter that al-Qaeda's Yemen branch was planning some kind of attack, Johnson had approved a cruise-missile strike on a suspected terrorist camp. It had gone wrong due to incomplete intelligence, and ended up killing several dozen women and children in addition to the militants who were its intended targets. Johnson had watched the carnage play out on live surveillance video and was shaken.*

While Johnson had moved into a town house in Washington's Georgetown neighborhood for his new job at the Pentagon, he had kept his larger home in the New York suburbs. His wife, Susan DiMarco — a former dentist who had grown up across the street from him on Cottam Hill in Wappingers Falls, New York[31] — was living there while their children finished high school. Montclair remained a calmer world, the place where the stakes of the decisions he made were lower. Throughout the Bush-Cheney years, for example, Johnson had donated to fundraising drives for Newark's public radio station, WBGO, and was permitted once or twice a year to "host an hour." He would bring his own CDs and play his favorite rhythm and blues artists — Sam Cooke, Otis Redding, Aretha Franklin, the Dells, Smokey Robinson, the Whispers, Gladys Knight, and Jackie Wilson. Now, after the bad strike, Johnson had left Washington to rejoin his family in Montclair for Christmas and tried to impose on himself a news blackout for the holidays. It was about to be pierced.

Harold Koh, Johnson's counterpart at the State Department, had also left Washington for Christmas and was back at his home in New

---

* See chapter 6, section 1.

Haven, Connecticut, with his wife, Mary-Christy, a legal-aid lawyer for veterans, and their two children. Koh had a powerful personality but walked with a slight limp, the result of being afflicted with polio as a child. He was the son of a South Korean diplomat who had been granted asylum in the United States after a military coup; his parents had been the first two Asian Americans to teach at Yale University. Koh had gone to Harvard College and Harvard Law School, clerked for Supreme Court Justice Harry Blackmun, and then worked as a low-ranking lawyer in the Office of Legal Counsel during the Reagan administration. Later, as a human rights lawyer, he had helped sue the Clinton administration over its treatment of Haitian refugees, then gone to work for it as the State Department's top human rights official. As a professor and then dean of Yale Law School, his classes on international human rights and even on civil procedure were known for awakening idealism in a generation of Yale Law School students. He had also become an early and vocal opponent of the Bush-Cheney administration's national security legal policies after the 9/11 attacks, picking apart Bush's international law case for war in Iraq for his students and later organizing litigation to challenge Bush's policy of holding prisoners without charges or judicial review.

Johnson and Koh became poles in the Obama legal team, even though both were Democrats and had similar political views. Indeed, both had publicly criticized Bush legal-team members over their approval of torture, each saying that government lawyers had a duty to be more than instruments of policymakers, willing to bless whatever their clients wanted. "Sometimes a lawyer has to say, 'You just can't do this,'" Johnson had said in December 2004.[32] In congressional testimony a few days later, Koh made a similar observation. "If a client asks a lawyer to do something which is flatly illegal, the answer is 'no.' It's not, 'Here's how we can justify it,'" he said.[33]

But Johnson, a professional litigator, and Koh, an academic, had very different approaches to being a government lawyer. Johnson viewed his role primarily as representing a client—the secretary of defense—

which meant adapting to the client's policy mind-set and rigorously marshaling facts to achieve a conclusion that dovetailed with what his client wanted to accomplish, so long as that conclusion was reasonable. By contrast, Koh, a scholar by background, was used to thinking about law and policy for himself, not for a client. No evidence emerged of any significant disconnect between his views and the policies pursued by his boss, Secretary of State Hillary Clinton, but he operated with a freer rein. And Koh also brought a different emphasis to what it meant to obey the rule of law — a difference that would fuel some of the most important internal debates over national security legal policy during the Obama era. Koh saw the core mission of his career as promoting "a lawful U.S. foreign policy" through the lens of human rights law.[34]

As a result, more than most other members of the Obama administration legal team, Koh kept a foot in the camp of what I'm calling the civil liberties faction, and he was less deferential to or satisfied by statutes enacted by Congress if he saw them as undermining rights. In internal deliberations, this philosophy prompted him to take more liberal positions than his colleagues on some questions, like what limits international law might impose on the president's power to conduct drone strikes. But the same view led him to take more executive-power-friendly positions than his colleagues on others, like how to respond when Congress sought to block Obama's efforts to wind down the Guantánamo prison and to prosecute the 9/11 case in regular civilian court.

That Christmas, back in New Haven, Koh turned on his television and saw the news. Moments later, a message came in on his BlackBerry from the State Department Operations Center.

Six time zones to the west, Obama was staying with his family in a rental house in his native Hawaii. They were singing carols when a military aide interrupted the president to say that his top counterterrorism adviser, Brennan, was on the phone about an urgent matter.[35]

Just a few weeks earlier, in his Nobel Peace Prize acceptance speech, Obama had said: "Where force is necessary, we have a moral and strategic interest in binding ourselves to certain rules of conduct. We lose ourselves when we compromise the very ideals that we fight to defend. And we honor those ideals by upholding them not when it's easy, but when it is hard."[36]

Things were about to get harder.

3

Things Fall Apart

1. First Political Fallout from the Christmas Attack

As the United States absorbed how close the underwear bomber had come to bringing down an airliner over Detroit, a wave of fear swept across the country. Republicans pounced, seeking to portray the Obama administration as feckless and weak. And they had early help: On December 27, Homeland Security secretary Janet Napolitano made a politically tone-deaf remark to CNN, saying that "the system worked" because the response to the attack had been swift. By the next morning she was explaining that she understood that the system had, obviously, failed miserably up until that point. But her gaffe helped politicize the crisis.

Meanwhile, Obama received a briefing behind closed doors about what was happening and ordered reviews of what had gone wrong. But he went golfing the next day in Oahu, and made no public statement about the incident for several days. On December 28, he told the public that Napolitano, John Brennan, and Eric Holder were "monitoring" the situation. Then, while he talked about what had gone wrong and the reviews he had ordered, he incorrectly described the attack as the work of an "isolated extremist."[1] The young administration immediately learned a lesson. Ben LaBolt, a White House spokesman at the time, told me that henceforth the rule was "if anything significant happened, the president goes out more quickly" and would be seen to be personally handling it in a detailed way.

But the criticisms were not just about bad optics and gaffes. Republicans had seethed during Obama's campaign and his first year in office when he condemned the Bush-Cheney administration for overreaching in the war on terror. Now, Obama looked vulnerable. "People suspended judgment and wanted to let [Obama] play his hand," said Karl Rove, the former top political adviser to Bush. But the Christmas bombing attempt "has caused doubts about how he is handling this to bubble to the surface."[2] The attacks were led by Cheney, who said on December 30, "We are at war and when President Obama pretends we aren't, it makes us less safe."[3]

Republicans and conservative media outlets like the evening Fox News programs began to hammer that message. And in liberal Massachusetts, where Scott Brown, a Republican, was widely expected to lose to Democrat Martha Coakley in a special election to fill the Senate seat left vacant by Ted Kennedy's death, the accusation that Obama was not tough enough against terrorists became a campaign issue. On January 4, 2010, Brown said Obama should have deemed Abdulmutallab an enemy combatant and taken him to Guantánamo for interrogation rather than handling him in the civilian criminal justice system.[4]

To see how the message performed, a Brown campaign pollster added this question to internal campaign-strategy polls: "On the issue of dealing with accused terrorists, for whom would you vote for U.S. Senate if you knew that Scott Brown believes that accused terrorists should be treated as enemy combatants and face military justice [and] Martha Coakley believes that accused terrorists should be provided constitutional rights and tried in civilian courts?" The results were overwhelming: respondents backed the position described as Brown's 61 percent to 29 percent.[5] In the closing days of the campaign, Brown made it into a core closing argument for why Massachusetts should send a Republican to Washington. In his final debate with Coakley, Brown blasted her for supporting a civilian trial for Khalid Sheikh Mohammed.

"To think that we would give people who want to kill us constitutional rights and lawyer them up at our expense instead of treating them as enemy combatants to get as much information as we can under legal means — it just makes no sense to me, and it shows me that you don't quite understand the law when it comes to enemy combatants versus terrorists for United States citizens," he said.[6]

National Republicans, too, were starting to use the episode to press for advantage. On January 8, twenty-two Republican lawmakers sent Obama a public letter decrying the fact that the Obama administration was handling Abdulmutallab in the criminal justice system instead of sending him to Guantánamo. They noted that the administration was keeping military commissions to prosecute suspects like Abd al-Nashiri, accused of masterminding the *Cole* bombing. The lawmakers zeroed in on the apparent lack of a compelling reason for why Abdulmutallab or KSM would get a civilian trial while al-Nashiri faced a tribunal.

"It creates the impression that terrorists are rewarded with the full panoply of rights and privileges of an American if they attack defenseless civilians at home, but not if they attack our government or military interests abroad," the letter read. "This will only further incentivize terrorists to attack our Homeland."[7]

2. First Policy Fallout from the Christmas Attack

At first, the Obama administration shrugged off the politics of Napolitano's gaffe and Cheney's broadsides to concentrate on substance: what had gone wrong, and what to do about it. Its focus on Yemen also intensified. Days before the Abdulmutallab attack, the United States had already carried out two cruise-missile strikes aimed at al-Qaeda in the Arabian Peninsula.* On January 2, General David Petraeus, the leader of the United States military's Central Command, which oversees forces in the Middle East and Afghanistan, visited the president of Yemen, Ali Abdullah Saleh, at his palace in Sanaa. While a diplomatic cable recounting the meeting does not explicitly mention the Christmas bombing attempt, the increased attention the Obama administra-

---

* See chapter 6, section 1.

tion was putting on security issues in Yemen was palpable. Petraeus opened the meeting by telling Saleh he was requesting that the United States more than double the security assistance given to Yemen to fight al-Qaeda in the Arabian Peninsula — from the $67 million in 2009 to $150 million in 2010. In addition, he said, Obama had decided to provide intelligence to Yemen to help its ground operations against al-Qaeda.[8]

Meanwhile, back in Washington, the Obama administration had begun scrambling to recalibrate. At the Terrorist Screening Center, the part of the FBI that determines who goes on various terrorist watch lists, officials significantly relaxed the criteria for putting someone on the no-fly list, which prevents people from boarding airplanes in the United States or flying into American airspace; the list would undergo rapid expansion.[9] When the full Justice Department policymaking team reconvened around January 3, even Holder, the champion of civilian trials and arguably the most liberal member of Obama's cabinet, told his subordinates that it was time to rethink all kinds of terrorism-related policies, he recalled in an interview the following month. *Things have changed,* he told them. *It's a new day.*

The fact that Abdulmutallab had not talked since the FBI had read him the Miranda warning was not yet public. But as the Brown campaign rhetoric showed, the administration's decision to handle him in the criminal justice system was already fodder for political attacks. Even as Obama's team defended itself in public, it was privately wringing its collective hands. At one point, David Kris asked Jeh Johnson whether the Department of Defense would like to take custody of Abdulmutallab from the Justice Department and prosecute him in a military commission. According to persons familiar with the matter, Kris was not so much suggesting that he thought it was a good idea but rather checking whether there was any disagreement within the government as to how to proceed. Johnson demurred, noting that it was an academic question since there was at that point a policy against adding any detainees to the Guantánamo inmate population and there was nowhere else set up to handle tribunals; in any case, by then, Abdulmutallab was already being dealt with in the criminal justice system. He told Kris that since they had him, they should stay the course. The issue was raised again at a January 5 meeting in the Situation Room led by Obama himself. According to a letter Holder later sent to Congress in response to Republican demands that Abdulmutallab be transferred to military custody, at that meeting, "no agency supported the use of law of war detention for Abdulmutallab, and no agency has since advised the Department of Justice that an alternative course of action should have been, or should now be, pursued."[10]

At that meeting, as my colleague Scott Shane reported, Obama grimly asked his team to imagine how the world would have been different had the bomb exploded. The consequences of such an event were not hard to envision. It would be the worst mass murder on American soil since 9/11, with at least 289 innocent people dead. The air-transit system would be in turmoil, and the already frail economy would receive a massive blow. An even greater wave of fear would sweep the vulnerable nation. Critics of Obama's move away from Bush-Cheney policies like torturing prisoners would feel vindicated, and the attempt to wind down the post-9/11 land wars in the Muslim world could collapse. "Part of his point was that the pressure on us would be to do a lot more in Yemen," Ben Rhodes, the deputy national security adviser, said. "Everything we were trying to do to scale back military involvement in the region would have been reversed."[11]

The meeting also focused on the myriad ways the massive post-9/11 security apparatus had failed. Obama, one participant told me, announced to his cabinet in a stern tone — one that struck this official as unnatural — that such a sequence of missteps must never happen again. Implicitly threatening to fire people if it did, Obama used a legal term that refers to situations in which a defendant is automatically held responsible for any damages or losses without any need for a plaintiff or prosecutor to prove fault, intention, or negligence.

It's strict liability now, he said.

After that meeting, Obama emerged from the Situation Room and spoke to the press.[12] Part of his remarks were a summary of what had gone wrong—the intelligence community, in hindsight, had had enough information to recognize that Abdulmutallab should not be allowed to board a plane to the United States but had failed to connect the dots in time. That, he said, was unacceptable, and changes were being made to reduce the risk that clues to a future attack would go overlooked.

Other things were tightening up, too—some visible, some not. In his public remarks, Obama announced an open-ended moratorium on the repatriation of any more Yemeni detainees. This dealt a staggering blow to his goal of closing the prison at Guantánamo Bay, because half the remaining prisoners there were Yemenis. Yemen clearly presented a real-world, legitimate security problem. But Obama's decision to impose an inflexible ban on transferring inmates there, no matter how strong the case for releasing a particular Guantánamo detainee, was driven by the politics of the moment.

Later that same month, an interagency task force Obama had appointed to review the cases of each of the detainees at the prison completed its yearlong work. Its report recommended transferring most of the lower-level Yemenis. The report was meant to lay the political and policy groundwork for a final push to wind down the Guantánamo prison in a responsible way. But in the new atmosphere, the administration did not release the report or hold a rollout in Congress to explain the findings.

That same day, January 5, Holder sent a classified letter to three Democratic senators that the public would not learn about for nearly four years. The senators had been urging the administration to declassify a secret legal interpretation crafted by the Bush-Cheney administration. The government was using it to justify dragnet collection by the National Security Agency of records about Americans' phone calls and e-mails. The provision used for phone call records, a part of the Patriot Act, was coming up for reauthorization, and the senators argued that it was important for democratic debate that people understood the government believed it could be used for bulk collection.

But in the post-Abdulmutallab environment, there was no appetite for greater transparency about intelligence programs aimed at uncovering terrorists. Holder told the senators the legal theory would remain classified. As a result, one of the most domestically intrusive measures of the vast surveillance state that Obama had inherited from Bush — and kept in place, as will be detailed in a later chapter — stayed secret, building up pressures that would not be released until an enormous leak by a former NSA contractor in 2013.[13]

The reformist side of Obama's national security legal policy was starting to crack. The political pressure on it would only increase.

3. The Law Enforcement Approach in Action

After Abdulmutallab emerged from surgery and ceased cooperating, the FBI field office in Detroit had not sat on its hands. Andy Arena, the leader of the Detroit field office, consulted with the CIA and sent two agents — one a counterterrorism specialist, the other a street-gang agent known for his interpersonal skills and ability to cultivate sources — to Nigeria. They spent several days getting briefed on all the information the intelligence agencies were developing, flew on January 1 to Lagos, the large port city, and eventually moved on to the Nigerian capital, Abuja. They visited Abdulmutallab's school, met with his relatives and known friends and associates, ate dinner at his house, played with his nieces and nephews, and assessed his family. One of the agents, Mike Connelly, later recalled that Abdulmutallab had "a tremendous extended family. They had a great amount of national pride and pride in their religion. They were shocked at what he had done."[14]

Abdulmutallab's father, a wealthy banker, had sent his son to expensive private schools around the world. But the young man had become interested in radical Islam at an early age. He and his father experienced a rift in their relationship. The FBI agents persuaded several relatives — his uncle, mother, and two sisters — to fly to Detroit on January 17 and meet with Abdulmutallab but decided not to bring his father.[15]

"They were embarrassed and they were mad, and they wanted to help the U.S. government," Arena said. "It's almost like they had to restore the family honor. They honestly did want to help us."

By now, Abdulmutallab had been out of the burn center for several weeks and was being held in the Federal Correctional Institution, Milan, in a special unit apart from the general inmate population. Arena recalled telling Abdulmutallab's uncle, who considered himself an Islamic scholar, not to debate with his nephew but rather just talk to him about his family back home and how they missed him. A few days after they arrived, the family went in to speak with Abdulmutallab for the first time, taking him a candy bar. The uncle ignored Arena and lectured his nephew on his misdeeds.

But the relatives also urged Abdulmutallab to cooperate for his own good. His defense lawyer negotiated a deal with federal prosecutors under which the talks were considered part of negotiations over a potential plea deal. Under the so-called proffer letter, anything Abdulmutallab said could not be used directly as evidence against him in a trial — even though it would still be useful intelligence — unless he later changed his story on the witness stand. When Connelly went in to question Abdulmutallab, the agent was able to talk in detail about his family and his life in Nigeria, proving that he had actually met with them and received the family's stamp of approval — a crucial step in building rapport.

The gambit worked. Several weeks after clamming up, Abdulmutallab started talking again. His words would have enormous consequences. But the administration initially kept secret that it had persuaded him to cooperate so that it could follow up on his information without alerting his associates. And meanwhile, the political uproar continued to swell.

4. The Shock Wave of Brown's Victory

On January 19, Brown won the special election to fill the "Ted Kennedy" Senate seat. The Republican's victory was an extraordinary upset. It took the Democrats' majority in the Senate from a filibuster-proof sixty votes to fifty-nine, giving Republicans the ability to block up-or-down votes on some legislation and all executive-branch and judicial nominees. With the midterm election ten months away, the GOP win in deep blue Massachusetts was stunning.

The shift did more than cast doubt on Obama's ability to advance his legislative agenda, which included his signature effort to overhaul the nation's health-insurance system. A year after his inauguration with overwhelming Democratic control of Congress, it was suddenly conceivable that he would end up as a failed one-term president. Some pundits saw it as a sign of the strength of the Tea Party movement that had erupted in opposition to Obama's stimulus plan and health-care bill, even though Brown represented the moderate faction of the Republican Party and Massachusetts voters already had mandatory health insurance under Romneycare, so Obamacare would not affect them much. Other pundits saw it as a sign that the continuing weakness in the economy, which was still struggling in a great recession resulting from the 2008 financial crisis, would damage Democrats in 2010 as much as it had helped them in 2008. But as GOP leaders gleefully focused on what had happened, Brown's political advisers told them their polling data showed that the terrorism issue — his attacks on dealing with terrorists as ordinary criminals instead of as enemy combatants — had helped Brown more than any other.

"It really tested through the roof," pollster Neil Newhouse told *Politico*'s Josh Gerstein, adding that Republican candidates nationally should take heed: "If voters in Massachusetts are telling us that, and it's one of the more liberal states in the country, I can only imagine where Ohio, Pennsylvania or Colorado voters might be on something like this." Eric Fehrnstrom, a Brown campaign strategist, told reporters in Boston on the night of the election, "National security was a more potent issue than health care, based on the polling we saw, on dealing with terrorists as ordinary criminals versus enemy combatants."[16]

At first, the White House had dismissed the Republican attacks on the handling of Abdulmutallab as the usual Beltway partisan noise; instead of focusing on good-faith criticism related to matters of genuine policy substance — *How had the United States government failed to connect the dots? What should be fixed to ensure that did not recur?* — political opponents were lapsing into opportunistic demagoguery. After all, there was no legal process for taking someone arrested on United States soil — where the Constitution applies to everyone, citizen or not — putting him in military custody, and shipping him to an overseas base. Every terrorism suspect arrested inside the United States during the Bush-Cheney administration — including Richard Reid, who had attempted to blow up a transatlantic flight with a shoe bomb in December 2001 — had been charged in the civilian law enforcement system. Even the two terrorism suspects arrested inside the United States whom Bush eventually placed in military detention, including the U.S. citizen Jose Padilla, had initially been Mirandized and charged using law enforcement procedures. From the top of the White House to the FBI's Detroit field office, officials believed that what their critics were arguing the government should have done had never been a real-world option.

"We were criticized — 'Why did the FBI in Detroit let a bunch of farmers do this interview?'" Arena said later. "There was no one better qualified in the country — they were good agents. I couldn't wait for some 'high value' team to get up there. Why didn't I turn him over to the military? I'd turn him over to the military any time the military showed up, but what the hell was I supposed to do — the nearest military post was the recruiting station down on Jefferson by the Chinese restaurant. What the hell was I supposed to do? I had to act, and quickly."

But the fallout drove home that whether or not it was fair, the politics of national security had real-world consequences. And it was about to get worse.

5. Mirandizing Terrorists Becomes a Political Issue

On January 20, the day after Brown's victory, a Republican senator leaked a fact from the ongoing investigation just as that fact was becoming obsolete: Abdulmutallab had not said a word to interrogators after he was read the Miranda warning. This notion added a razor's edge to the Republicans' previous complaints, in which they had linked the handling of Abdulmutallab in the criminal justice system to Holder's increasingly unpopular decision to prosecute KSM and the other 9/11 defendants in a civilian courtroom.

At a Senate Homeland Security Committee hearing, the ranking Republican, Senator Susan Collins of Maine, pressed the administration witnesses — Michael Leiter, Janet Napolitano, and the director of national intelligence, Dennis Blair — to say whether they personally had been consulted about the decision to charge Abdulmutallab in civilian court; all of them said they had not been. Collins also remarked, as if in passing, "We know that those interrogations can provide critical intelligence, but the protections afforded by our civil justice system, as opposed to the military tribunal system, can encourage terrorists to lawyer up, to stop answering questions. And indeed, I'm told that with Abdulmutallab, once he was Mirandized and received civilian lawyers, that's exactly what he did. He stopped answering questions."[17]

At that same hearing, Blair made further headlines by saying that a specialized High-Value Detainee Interrogation Group (HIG), a newly created team the Obama administration had established to question significant terrorist captives, not ordinary FBI agents on the scene, should have made the decision about whether to use criminal law enforcement procedures on Abdulmutallab. Later that day, Blair's office issued a statement walking this back; in fact, the group was not yet operational. But the seeming admission of fault by Blair, combined with Collins's disclosure that Abdulmutallab had stopped talking after being Mirandized, led Republicans to begin refining their attacks. They accused the Obama administration of endangering national security because of its supposed ideological commitment to viewing terrorism as a crime rather than an act of war.

"We remain deeply troubled that this paramount requirement of national security was ignored — or worse yet, not recognized — due to the administration's preoccupation with reading the Christmas Day bomber his Miranda rights," wrote several Republican senators, including the Senate minority leader, Mitch McConnell, and John McCain, Obama's 2008 opponent, on January 27.[18]

As the Obama administration defended itself, two rival descriptions of what had happened emerged—one by the critics and one by the White House—and competed for the public's brains and hearts. Both were false; the truth was complicated and did not fit into an easy political attack or political defense.

Republicans claimed that Abdulmutallab had stopped talking *because* the FBI told him he had a right to remain silent; they wanted the public to think that the terrorist would have kept cooperating and providing valuable intelligence if only the Obama administration had not been driven by its liberal ideology to inform him of his rights. This was not true; Abdulmutallab had *already stopped talking* before he was read the Miranda warning, and the decision had been made by McJunkin, a senior career FBI agent, following consultations with Arena, Art Cummings, and Sharon Lever, all also career officials—not by Obama political appointees.

But in rebutting the accusation, the White House was misleading too. Its account left the impression that the decision to Mirandize Abdulmutallab had been a pragmatic response to his changed behavior, implying that if Abdulmutallab had resumed talking after he woke up from surgery, he would not have been Mirandized. This was not true either; the White House account omitted the fact that the FBI had *already made the decision* to read him the warning as a matter of legal philosophy and tactics before anyone knew that his attitude had changed.

Years later, Arena still fumed about the whole mess. Democrats, he said, "didn't stand tall. They weren't strong. They were kind of waffling back and forth—'what do we do?'" And Republicans, he said, twisted the facts about a national security issue for political gain.

"To this day it pisses me off," Arena said.

6. The KSM Trial Plan Collapses

By late January, the Obama administration was in full retreat. Among the casualties left on the battlefield was Holder's plan to prosecute the 9/11 case in civilian court. Had the administration moved decisively to bring KSM and the other four detainees to New York and arraign them after Holder's announcement the previous November, the wheels would have been irreversibly in motion already. Instead, the intended defendants had remained at Guantánamo, a dangling target.

Now, Ray Kelly, commissioner of the New York City Police Department, came up with a heavy-handed security plan for the trial — steps no high-profile terrorism trial before or since has remotely required — that would all but shut down Lower Manhattan and cost as much as one billion dollars. Soon after, New York mayor Michael Bloomberg, who had initially endorsed Holder's trial plan, withdrew his support for it, as did key Democrats in New York's congressional delegation.

On January 29, at 2:30 p.m., Obama presided over a bitter National Security Council meeting in the Roosevelt Room. It was clear to all in the meeting that the 9/11 trial was not going to happen in Manhattan.[19] But Obama, Biden, Holder, Brennan, and Harold Koh still wanted to do it in a civilian court — perhaps a special trial convened at a federal prison in Otisville or at Stewart Air National Guard Base. Other cabinet members were not so sure.

At the end of the meeting, Obama read aloud a transcript of Judge William Young's statement at the 2002 sentencing hearing for Reid, the would-be shoe bomber. The Bush-Cheney administration had handled his case using civilian criminal justice system procedures without controversy, and he was serving a life sentence at the federal supermax facility in Florence, Colorado. Holder and Koh had each brought copies of the transcript to give the president.

Obama quoted Young telling the shoe bomber that he was "not a soldier in any war. To give you that reference, to call you a soldier, gives you too much stature." And the judge had lauded the use of regular courts to deal with the terrorist, saying that it showed the American system of freedom would endure because the way the United States treated the bomber was a measure of its own liberties.

"Why can't I give that speech?" Obama asked in frustration after reading it, and he walked out of the room without another word, according to journalist Daniel Klaidman.[20]

Days later, McConnell delivered a blistering speech to the conservative American Enterprise Institute denouncing the decision to hand Abdulmutallab "over to a lawyer after a fifty-minute interview" and linking that decision to the Obama administration's closure of the CIA prisons and preference for civilian courts. "Treating terrorism as a law enforcement matter is precisely the attitude that kept us from seeing this threat when we should have," he said. "Reverting to it now is not only dangerous, it's potentially disastrous."[21]

In a question-and-answer period following his prepared remarks, McConnell candidly acknowledged the political advantages of hammering away at the issue, citing Brown's victory.

"If this approach of putting these people in U.S. courts doesn't sell in Massachusetts, I don't know where it sells," McConnell said, adding: "You can campaign on these issues anywhere in America."[22]

7. Abdulmutallab Fingers an American Citizen

A gulf had opened between the premise of the political debate and what was happening in the real world. The FBI's interrogation strategy had worked, and Abdulmutallab was providing a wealth of intelligence information about the people he had encountered, the places he had been, and the training he had received.[23] The FBI relayed that information to the CIA and the NSA, which corroborated parts of what he was saying and followed up on other parts as active intelligence leads. He dropped his Christmas Day story that he had been sent by a mysterious terrorist named Abu Tarek, whom no one had ever heard of. Now his story was different. It became clear that Abu Tarek was a composite of several people who were familiar to counterterrorism analysts.[24] Some details he had attributed to "Abu Tarek" matched what he now said had been the actions of Ibrahim al-Asiri, a notorious bomb maker for al-Qaeda in the Arabian Peninsula who had implanted a bomb in his own brother's rectum and sent him on a failed mission to kill a top Saudi counterterrorism official. Other parts of Abdulmutallab's account about Abu Tarek matched what he now said had been the actions of Anwar al-Awlaki, an English-speaking radical Muslim preacher in Yemen who had been born in New Mexico and was a United States citizen.

The raw transcripts of Abdulmutallab's interviews remain secret. But significant details of his account are contained in unclassified court filings, and neither he nor his defense team challenged their accuracy. Abdulmutallab told the FBI that he had started listening to online recordings of al-Awlaki's lectures and reading his writings as far back as 2005. In August 2009, when Abdulmutallab was a graduate student living in Dubai, he decided to join the cause. He flew to Yemen and began visiting mosques, asking random strangers if they knew al-Awlaki. Eventually, an intermediary took his cell-phone number and gave it to al-Awlaki, who sent him a text asking him to call. Abdulmutallab did so, and al-Awlaki instructed him to write an essay explaining why he wished to get involved in jihad and why he wanted the preacher's guidance.

Abdulmutallab said he spent several days working on the essay; al-Awlaki apparently found it satisfactory. Abdulmutallab was told to get into a certain car, which then drove him through the desert to a house. Al-Awlaki was there. Abdulmutallab would spend three days talking with al-Awlaki and two other men about martyrdom and jihad. "Awlaki told defendant that jihad requires patience but comes with many rewards," said a Justice Department court filing drawn from his January-to-April interviews. "Defendant understood that Awlaki used these discussions to evaluate defendant's commitment to and suitability for jihad. Throughout, defendant expressed his willingness to become involved in any mission chosen for him, including martyrdom — and by the end of his stay, Awlaki had accepted defendant for a martyrdom mission."

Abdulmutallab said he was then taken to another house in Yemen where he met al-Asiri, the bomb maker. After further discussions about jihad, al-Asiri came up with the plan for a martyrdom mission to bomb an airplane, and al-Awlaki signed off on it. Abdulmutallab was given a two-week crash course at an al-Qaeda in the Arabian Peninsula training camp. While he was generally kept isolated from other members of the group, he met some he would tell the FBI about. One of them was another American citizen, Samir Khan, who helped put out an online English-language propaganda magazine called *Inspire* with articles about jihadism, including one called "Build a Bomb in the Kitchen of Your Mom."

While Abdulmutallab's training and indoctrination unfolded, he said, al-Asiri built the underwear bomb, ultimately giving it to him in person and having him practice pushing the syringe that was supposed to lead to its detonation. Meanwhile, al-Awlaki instructed Abdulmutallab to make a martyrdom video, to be released after the attack, explaining who he was and why he had carried out the operation. The court filing asserted that al-Awlaki made the arrangements for a "professional" camera crew and helped Abdulmutallab write the statement.

Al-Qaeda in the Arabian Peninsula would later dribble out clips from this session in various lengthy propaganda videos. In late 2012, it made public an excerpt showing a very young-looking Abdulmutallab wearing a white shirt and a white cap sitting before a dingy wall, an AK-47 on his left, the black flag of al-Qaeda on his right. Abdulmutallab rocked back and forth constantly, alternating between looking at the camera and rolling his eyes slightly up and then down at his lap. Abdulmutallab spoke in Arabic, at least for that excerpt, and addressed "my Muslim brothers in the Arabian Peninsula," to whom he said, "You have to answer the call of jihad because the enemy is in your land, along with their Jewish and Christian armies."[25] In December 2014, AQAP made public another several-second clip showing Abdulmutallab standing between al-Awlaki and Nasir al-Wuhayshi, the leader of the terrorist group. This was the first time al-Awlaki and Abdulmutallab were seen in the same frame.[26]

The Justice Department said that al-Awlaki left it up to Abdulmutallab to choose the flight — so long as it was a United States airliner — and the date of the attack. But the cleric told him not to travel directly from Yemen to Europe. Abdulmutallab ultimately departed Yemen for Ethiopia, traveled to Ghana, returned to his native Nigeria, and only then flew to Amsterdam, where he boarded the flight to Detroit.

Al-Awlaki's "last instructions" to Abdulmutallab, according to the court filing based on his interrogations, "were to wait until the airplane was over the United States and then to take the plane down."

As Abdulmutallab started cooperating, the Justice Department and the FBI took satisfaction in their success. The interrogators had used rapport-building, not torture. They had harnessed family pressure premised on his relatives' understanding that Abdulmutallab was being treated humanely. They had enlisted the defense lawyer as an ally in helping Abdulmutallab see that it was in his interest to cooperate because he might receive more favorable treatment; they dangled the prospect of his being housed for the rest of his life under conditions more comfortable than those in the supermax prison in Florence, Colorado. All these proven, law enforcement–style techniques persuaded a committed jihadist to provide valuable intelligence to the American government. The question of whether Abdulmutallab needed to be sent to a military or intelligence facility had remained a topic of internal discussion throughout January. But when political advisers to Obama saw how much he was talking, it settled the argument: using the civilian law enforcement system, not the military, to handle terrorists on domestic soil *worked*.

How things looked outside the executive branch was another matter.

8. "We Need a Commander in Chief, Not a Professor of Law"

The Obama administration, as noted, did not immediately reveal that Abdulmutallab was actively cooperating; because he was providing actionable intelligence that could be used for strikes or arrests abroad, officials wanted it kept confidential. The secrecy allowed Republicans who didn't know the reality to press forward with the narrative that Abdulmutallab *would* be talking if he was placed in military custody and that Obama was refusing to do so for ideological reasons, therefore endangering the country—a theme hammered home in conservative media outlets.

McJunkin, the FBI official who had made the call to read Abdulmutallab the Miranda warning, came home around nine o'clock one evening after working another fifteen-hour day, and one of his sons said he had just watched the Fox News talk-show host Bill O'Reilly attack the decision to Mirandize the suspect as idiotic. This recollection appears to match O'Reilly's February 2 show, in which O'Reilly called Obama out for "three strikes" on his terrorism policies—the closing of the Guantánamo prison, which was "not working out," the civilian trial for KSM, which was "falling apart," and "botching the interrogation of the underwear guy—unbelievably dumb." O'Reilly added: "This is just common sense. When you have foreign killers stalking America, you don't treat them like embezzlers. You isolate the terrorists and extract as much information from the person as possible. You're not going to defeat terrorism with Miranda rights. Again, why does President Obama not know this?"[27]

McJunkin was infuriated. In "just a few weeks," using the criminal justice process, they had flipped a suicide-bomber who had a hostile, jihadi mind-set to one who was efficiently spilling out "accurate intelligence" that they were handing over to the intelligence community for action. To him, it was stupidity for O'Reilly to argue that just as good, let alone better, results would have been achieved if Abdulmutallab had instead been thrown into a military brig without a defense lawyer to tell him it was in his own best interests to talk and with harsh optics that would have kept his family from interceding, too.

"It offended me and I haven't watched Fox News since," McJunkin said. "They really didn't know what the hell they were talking about."

McJunkin was mad at Democrats, too—"they needed to grow a pair of balls"—and such frustrations were growing on the left as well. On February 1, administration officials had secretly briefed senior members of Congress, including Senator Kit Bond of Missouri, the ranking Republican on the Intelligence Committee, about what they were learning from Abdulmutallab. At a hearing the next day, Bond nevertheless excoriated a panel of senior national security officials over the FBI's reading Abdulmutallab the Miranda warning, even though Bond knew he was now cooperating. At the end of the hearing, the chairwoman, Senator Dianne Feinstein, Democrat from California, took matters into her own hands, just as Senator Collins had done in leaking from the dais that Abdulmutallab had stopped talking. Feinstein told CIA director Leon Panetta and FBI director Robert Mueller that it was her understanding that Abdulmutallab "has provided valuable information" and that "the interrogation continues despite the fact that he has been Mirandized." They said she was correct.[28]

Feinstein had disclosed a very vague fact, but the Obama administration — fuming over the false impressions that the conservatives' attacks were giving — seized on it as an excuse to say far more. That afternoon, the White House assembled a background briefing for reporters to lay out the whole sequence, beginning with Abdulmutallab's Nigerian relatives. Officials revealed that "he has been cooperating for days" and portrayed the results as a vindication of their decision not to put him before a military interrogator.

"I keep scratching my head," one senior administration official said at the briefing. "People with no experience and apparently less knowledge about the case and the issues involved have made this a cause célèbre, as though there was some type of strange practice or action that took place here, when it's consistent with all the practices of the previous administration as well as what was promulgated by the former president."[29]

In his blistering speech at Heritage the next day, McConnell offered rebuttals to the critique of Republican attacks. It was true that the Bush-Cheney administration had prosecuted foreign terrorists in civilian courts, he acknowledged, but "it was wrong to do so. The enemy in this fight is adaptable. We must be too." And, addressing the revelation that Abdulmutallab had been cooperating with interrogators, he suggested that the captive would have done so from the start, without any gap, but for the Miranda warning. The White House, he said, had "leaked information aimed at rehabilitating and justifying the administration's mishandling of the Nigerian bomber. Yet despite their best efforts, the fact remains that all the intelligence he possessed concerning the locations, training techniques, and communications methods of al-Qaeda in Yemen is perishable. Yemeni forces needed that information on December 25th, not six weeks later. Meanwhile, the American people are left to wonder whether, in place of interrogations, their safety depends on terrorists having families who can persuade them to talk."[30]

Three days later, the 2008 Republican vice-presidential nominee, Alaska governor Sarah Palin, drew enthusiastic applause with a more populist version of this narrative in a speech she gave before a Tea Party convention. "There are questions we would have liked this foreign terrorist to answer before he lawyered up and invoked our U.S. constitutional right to remain silent," she said, adding: "To win that war, we need a commander in chief, not a professor of law standing at the lectern."[31]

John Brennan had had enough. On February 7, he went on NBC's *Meet the Press* and revealed that on Christmas night, he had briefed McConnell and Bond, along with their top Republican counterparts in the House, John Boehner and Pete Hoekstra, and told them that Abdulmutallab was in FBI custody. They knew, Brennan said, that the criminal justice process includes Mirandizing suspects and presenting them to magistrate judges, where their rights are read to them again. "None of those individuals raised any concerns with me at that point. They didn't say, 'Is he going into military custody?' 'Is he going to be Mirandized?' They were very appreciative of the information." Brennan made clear that he saw the political attacks that had unfolded the following month as contemptible.

But a partisan line had been engraved. The Brown victory, and the polling data behind it, had created a new policy plank for the Republican Party platform: terrorism captives should be handled exclusively by the military. A few Bush-Cheney administration veterans with counter-terrorism expertise tried to carve out a pragmatic middle ground, arguing that sometimes the criminal justice system was a more effective tool for persuading terrorists to cooperate and ensuring their incapacitation later, but their voices were drowned out. For the remaining years of the Obama administration, whenever a terrorism suspect — whether he was arrested inside the United States or brought to the country from abroad — was charged in the civilian justice system, congressional Republicans accused Obama of being soft on terrorism.

9. Obama's Approach to Counterterrorism Hardens

The experience of the Christmas Day attack — both the frightening specter of what had almost happened on its watch and the brutal political backlash driven home by Brown's upset Senate victory — profoundly hardened the Obama administration's attitude toward counterterrorism policy.

A reverberating change in attitude started from the top. Obama had always respected Brennan. But now, as Brennan used his counterterrorism bona fides on Sunday-morning TV shows to aggressively push back against Republicans' attacks and defend using law enforcement tools on domestic soil while other Democrats cowered, he became a far more central and influential player, a man to whom Obama looked for guidance.[32] The president was not alone; at the Justice Department and elsewhere, more liberal members of the Obama legal team, I was told, began to see Brennan as their hero.

Before the Christmas attack, Obama's top political adviser, David Axelrod, had not attended the weekly Terror Tuesday policy meetings, Michael Leiter recalled. Now, tellingly, he started coming.

And Leiter, briefing Obama on terrorism matters, observed a visceral difference. Obama had been deeply engaged in war-on-terror issues throughout 2009, but mostly in terms of cleaning up problems he'd inherited from Bush. On actual counterterrorism operations,

Obama had been attentive but largely passive, in receive mode — just taking in the information. Now, he changed to active mode, pushing back and questioning his briefers: *Why are we doing this? How are we doing this? Is there anything else we should be doing? Do you need anything more from me?*

"Terrorism and the threat to the homeland went from a theoretical concern to something that the president understood could shape the course of his presidency," Leiter told me. "The president suddenly understood that in an instant, people could still be killed inside the United States by al-Qaeda and that such an event could have catastrophic political consequences for the rest of his agenda....Obama was much more engaged in blocking and tackling."

The consequences of the Christmas attack would ripple for years. Obama's moratorium on repatriating Yemenis was a crippling blow to his effort to close the Guantánamo prison, but at the end of 2010, the changed politics of terrorism issues prompted the still Democratic-controlled Congress to deliver the coup de grâce, barring the government from bringing any detainee into the United States for prosecution or continued detention.

Meanwhile, even as the administration publicly defended the decision to Mirandize Abdulmutallab, the White House counsel, Bob Bauer, led an internal review that seriously considered changing the criminal justice system's interrogation rules protecting the rights of newly arrested suspects. The effort eventually failed, but participants later marveled at how the post-Christmas atmosphere had led them to get so far down its path.

At the National Counterterrorism Center, the Christmas bombing settled an argument. Leiter had been pushing to allow the center to make its own copies of huge databases assembled by other parts of the government that contained information about Americans who were not suspected of terrorism. The ingestion would allow the center to use Big Data–style analysis to search for terrorists on domestic soil. Other agencies — notably the Department of Homeland Security — were resisting, citing privacy concerns. But the consensus that the system had possessed the dots to stop Abdulmutallab but had failed to connect them shifted the debate. It took two more years to work out the details, but the center won.

Indeed, even years later, the searing memory of the near miss led to what was arguably an overreaction to a leak, even by the standards of what by then had already become an unprecedented campaign of going after unauthorized disclosures of secret information. In May 2012, the Associated Press reported that counterterrorism officials had disrupted a plot by al-Qaeda in the Arabian Peninsula to blow up a plane with a new-and-improved underwear bomb. National security officials were furious that someone had told the AP about the bomb and launched a leak investigation. As part of that case, the Justice Department secretly, and without advance notice, subpoenaed a vast trove of telephone records showing the calling records of AP journalists, including some who had nothing to do with the story. When the sweeping subpoena was disclosed, it prompted bipartisan criticism in Congress.

But the most significant policy fallout from the Christmas attack was Obama's decision to deliberately kill al-Awlaki, an American citizen, in a drone strike. Even Bush had not signed off on the deliberate killing of a United States citizen without a trial. And notwithstanding the extraordinary precedent this established for state power and individual rights, the Obama administration would fight for years to keep the basic facts and legal analysis about its action secret from the public.

PART II

WAR IN THE TWENTY-FIRST CENTURY

4

Look Forward, Not Back
(Captives 2009)

1. The Executive Orders

"We need to look forward as opposed to looking backwards," President-Elect Barack Obama said. "My general belief is that when it comes to national security, what we have to focus on is getting things right in the future as opposed to looking at what we got wrong in the past."[1]

As a senator and candidate, Obama had sharply criticized President George W. Bush's handling of captives in what Bush called the "global war on terror." Asserting a right to bypass the Geneva Conventions, Bush had imprisoned people without trial or judicial review at the American naval base at Guantánamo Bay; had permitted interrogators to use torture; and had established military commissions, which gave defendants fewer rights than civilian trials did, to prosecute accused terrorists. Some of the problems with those policies had already been fixed by the end of the Bush years; the CIA torture program, for example, had essentially ended, and after the Supreme Court ruled that Bush's first military commissions system was illegal because it lacked congressional authorization, Congress had enacted a law to authorize them. As Obama prepared for his inauguration, his instinct was to quickly fix any remaining problems and move on rather than getting bogged down in recriminations. But like so much else about governing in the post-9/11 age, this would prove far easier said than done.

Obama's transition legal-policy team developed a sweeping package of executive orders that they thought would finish turning the corner. The team included Greg Craig, who went on to be White House counsel, and three law professors: David Barron of Harvard and Marty Lederman of Georgetown, who would run the Justice Department's Office of Legal Counsel, and Daniel Meltzer of Harvard, who became Craig's deputy. Under the orders the team drafted, Obama would bar the CIA from operating long-term black-site secret prisons, restrict all official questioners — even those with the CIA — to those techniques listed in the army's field manual on interrogations, and direct the military to close the Guantánamo prison within a year. Obama also decreed internally that no newly captured detainees were to be brought there in the interim — that there would be no *Obama Wing* at Guantánamo, as he put it — though the public orders did not mention that.

"It was explicit," Craig later told me. "I remember him saying so: 'No one new is going to Guantánamo.' I think it might have been very early — during transition."

Obama's orders did not, however, say anything about whether to keep or jettison military commissions. Secretary of Defense Robert Gates, whom Obama kept on from the Bush-Cheney administration, asked the military judges overseeing tribunals at Guantánamo to pause so the new administration could carry out a 120-day policy review. The pause included pretrial hearings in the death-penalty case against Khalid Sheikh Mohammed and four other accused accomplices in the 9/11 attacks. The previous December, KSM had announced in the Guantánamo courtroom that he and the others wanted to plead guilty and dispatch with the rest of the proceedings, and the military judge was still wrestling with whether to let them do so.[2] Now, a resolution would have to wait. Years later, as the 9/11 case bogged down in political conflict and seemingly endless dysfunction, the fact that the government had not seized the moment when the defendants were on the verge of pleading guilty without a trial would look, in hindsight, like a mistake.

Obama and his legal team thought their set of detainee policies would be seen as bipartisan. Bush had set a goal of closing the prison too, and by the time he left office, only 242 of the 780 men he had brought there remained. In his 2010 memoir, Bush would write: "While I believe opening Guantánamo after 9/11 was necessary, the detention facility had become a propaganda tool for our enemies and a distraction for our allies. I worked to find a way to close the prison without compromising security."[3] Obama's Republican opponent in the 2008 campaign, John McCain, had fought the Bush-Cheney administration to end torture and told Iowa voters that to combat anti-Americanism in the world, "one of the things I would do the first day I'm president of the United States is close Guantánamo Bay. I would close it and move those prisoners to Fort Leavenworth. It has become a symbol, which is very bad for America."[4]

At eleven o'clock on the morning of January 22, 2009, President Obama sat at his desk in the Oval Office in front of Vice President Biden and sixteen retired generals and admirals and described the orders to assembled reporters before signing them.

"There we go," Obama then said, looking pleased.[5]

The orders also created three interagency task forces. Two were forward-looking. One would determine what the country's policy should be regarding interrogation and transfers of prisoners to other countries. A second would determine how the United States should detain its terrorism captives in the future.

A third task force would review the files on each of the remaining detainees at Guantánamo and recommend what to do with him. It could choose one of four options for every legacy captive: transfer to the custody of another country, release, prosecute, or employ some other "lawful means" of disposition.

Few observers that day picked up the significance of that euphemistic last category. It could mean only one thing: Obama and his team of lawyers were leaving open the possibility that they would continue holding some men in indefinite detention without trial.

Under the international laws of war, an armed force may detain enemy fighters without trial until the end of hostilities, to prevent their return to the battlefield. Many European allies believed that the fight against al-Qaeda was not war, making the detentions at Guantánamo illegal in their view, but it was settled that within the American legal system, they were lawful. After 9/11, Congress had enacted an Authorization for Use of Military Force, or AUMF, against the perpetrators of the attacks, and in 2004 the Supreme Court had ruled that the president's war powers under the law included the authority to hold al-Qaeda and Taliban captives in such law-of-war detention.[6]

But some people remained deeply uncomfortable with the implications of that idea. The intent of law-of-war detention, a long-standing part of customary international law enshrined in the Geneva Conventions, was to create a humanitarian alternative to slaughtering captured enemies to keep them from posing a future threat. But the rule was written for traditional wars between nation-state armies, whose soldiers stop fighting and go home when their leaders surrender or sign peace treaties, thereby making it safe to release wartime prisoners. The rule was not written for a conflict against a non-nation-state network of religiously motivated terrorists that might never come to a definitive end. From one perspective, applying the detention rule to this twenty-first-century struggle twists its humanitarian origins. It raised the prospect of imprisoning people for life without trial and based only on their associations. From another point of view, just because a legal rule produces harsh results when applied in a new context does not necessarily mean it is invalid.

2. Dilemma of the Yemenis

As the new Obama administration tackled the problem of closing Guantánamo fast, it confronted the largest policy obstacle to achieving that goal: the Yemenis. Al-Qaeda's active presence in Yemen and the country's weak central government had made Bush officials reluctant to repatriate Yemeni detainees. As a result, while lower-level detainees from other countries had left Guantánamo, Yemenis who posed an equivalent or even a significantly lesser risk had stayed behind. They became the largest bloc remaining there — some 99 of the 242 captives that Obama had inherited.

Closing Guantánamo meant dealing with the Yemenis. And it would fall to Matt Olsen, a career national security prosecutor, to disillusion the new political masters of the executive branch about just how hard resolving their fates was going to be. An earnest, youthful-looking, but shrewd lawyer from North Dakota, Olsen had become the acting head of the Justice Department's National Security Division when Bush's political appointees resigned upon Obama's inauguration. In the final years of the Bush-Cheney administration, Olsen had participated in the effort to legalize the NSA's surveillance programs.* Now, the new attorney general, Eric Holder, selected him to lead the Guantánamo detainee-review task force. In late February 2009, as Olsen's team was still setting up shop at a nondescript but secure office building in a Northern Virginia suburb of Washington, DC, he drove to the White House for his first meeting on the topic.

John Brennan, Obama's counterterrorism adviser, and Mary DeRosa, the National Security Council lawyer, asked Olsen to look at a group of about twenty Yemeni detainees who had strong ties to Saudi Arabia. The Saudis had created a rehabilitation program for Saudi citizens who got involved with Islamist extremism but who had not committed serious acts of terrorism. It involved holding them in comfortable custody, bringing in religious leaders and family members to talk them out of their militant religious views, and setting them up with wives and jobs in order to reintegrate them into peaceful society. Brennan's idea was that if the Saudis put the Yemenis through the same program, the risk that they would engage in terrorism after their release would be lower than if the United States just dropped them off in the chaotic Yemeni society.

The Bush-Cheney administration had already repatriated most of the Saudis from Guantánamo, and the rehabilitation program had been successful in reducing recidivism. But it wasn't perfect; underscoring

---

* See chapter 5, sections 10, 11, and 14.

the risks, on January 23, a video posted to jihadist forums had featured a former Guantánamo detainee repatriated to Saudi Arabia in 2007. The video described him as the number-two leader of a new Yemen-based affiliate of al-Qaeda that called itself al-Qaeda in the Arabian Peninsula.

Olsen asked his colleagues to dig into the intelligence files about the Yemenis with strong Saudi ties. But the news was not good.

"It was clear to us that many of them had troubling pasts and were not good candidates for transfer, at least at this early stage," Olsen later told me. "I let the White House know the results of our preliminary review of Yemenis. I knew this was not going to help advance the process, but saw my role as being an honest broker and shielding the review process from the politics on all sides."

There was another problem. During the transition, some members of the Obama team had assumed that most Guantánamo detainees who were too dangerous to release could be prosecuted, save for a few who had been tortured, which made the evidence against them tainted. (For example, six days before Obama's inauguration, the top official overseeing Bush's military commissions system had said in an interview that a Saudi detainee at Guantánamo, believed to have been the intended twentieth hijacker on 9/11, could not be charged because the official had concluded that he had been "tortured."[7]) But Olsen's task force, which included aggressive federal prosecutors eager to bring cases, soon found that many detainees were untriable for a different reason: they were not linked to any specific terrorist plot, and there was no crime to charge them with.

This was exclusively a legacy-detainee problem. There is a federal statute that makes it an offense just to be involved with a terrorist group, a crime termed *providing material support for terrorism*. But as originally written, the law applied only to Americans. In late October 2001, as part of the Patriot Act, Congress expanded it so that it would apply to the actions of non-Americans abroad too. But the Constitution does not permit Congress to retroactively criminalize something, so the statute could not be used to prosecute, for example, a Yemeni who had provided support to al-Qaeda by attending one of its training camps in Afghanistan in early 2001 and who had not done anything else concrete before being captured.

In late February and early March, Olsen met on several occasions with officials working on detainee issues at the White House National Security Council, including DeRosa and her deputy, Caroline Krass, and at the Justice Department, including Barron and Lederman. Olsen said they pressured him for specific numbers, and while he resisted providing them, he did predict that "we were likely to have more than a few detainees who would fall into the law-of-war category, perhaps several dozen. This was contrary to the expectations of some, especially those who had not been inside the government working on these issues."

It was rapidly becoming clear that closing Guantánamo was not going to be as simple as the incoming Obama team had assumed. As Olsen went back to work, Brennan traveled to the Middle East. On March 15, he visited King Abdullah of Saudi Arabia, presenting the monarch with a letter from Obama about the dilemma of the Yemeni detainees. The king suggested an alternative idea for reducing the risk of letting them go: Why not implant electronic chips in the detainees' bodies, allowing their movements to be tracked? This had been done with horses and falcons, he said.

"Horses don't have good lawyers," Brennan replied.[8]

3. Fighting Habeas Rights at Bagram

With far less political and media attention, Obama also inherited six hundred detainees in a prison built from an old hangar at Bagram Airfield in Afghanistan—far more than at Guantánamo. Conditions at Bagram were more grim and secretive than at Guantánamo. One wing, the Bagram TSF—for "temporary screening facility"—was essentially a black-site prison for the military where officials held and interrogated prisoners captured in Special Operations raids without notifying the

Red Cross about them.⁹ Obama's team would work to improve conditions at Bagram, but it would also try to prevent court oversight of what the government did there.

Like Guantánamo, Bagram had evolved into an accidental long-term prison; the military had not anticipated that the war would last as long as it did, and the infrastructure, both legal and physical, was inadequate for the role it was playing. Late in the Bush years, Pentagon detention-policy officials like Sandra Hodgkinson and Mark Stamilio had started making plans to build a modern prison to hold the detainees; it opened late in 2009 at the edge of the air base under the rebranded name Parwan. By the time the Obama team took over, Hodgkinson and Stamilio were also developing procedures for review boards that would periodically examine whether a long-term detainee still needed to be held or could be released, and on Obama's watch these were put into practice in the field. Human rights groups would criticize the review boards' rules as too stacked against detainees, but they were an improvement over what had come before. In connection with those changes, officials told me, the Red Cross got its first walk-through of the black-site wing in 2009 and gained regular access to it around 2010.

But the brand-new Obama team also battled to prevent judicial review of whom the United States was detaining without trial at Bagram, under what conditions, and on what basis. This was a shocking development at the time and one of the earliest signs of a disconnect between the expectations created by Obama's campaign rhetoric and the reality of how he governed.

The battle focused on a lawsuit on behalf of several Bagram detainees. The plaintiffs said that, unlike most of the prisoners there, who had been captured in raids and battles inside Afghanistan, they had been arrested in other countries and brought by the United States government to the war-zone prison. They contended that they were not part of al-Qaeda and wanted to challenge the evidence before a judge. In June 2008, the Supreme Court had ruled that detainees the United States had brought to the Guantánamo prison were entitled to habeas corpus hearings, and the Bagram plaintiffs contended that they had the same rights.[10] During the campaign, Senator Obama had praised the 2008 ruling about Guantánamo detainees, saying it meant "we are going to live up to our ideals when it comes to the rule of law."[11] But late on Friday, February 20, the Justice Department filed a court brief saying that Obama's administration was sticking with Bush's view about Bagram detainees: they had no right to bring habeas corpus lawsuits.[12]

On April 2, federal district court judge John Bates, a George W. Bush appointee, disagreed. He ruled that three non-Afghans at Bagram, captured elsewhere, had a right to hearings, writing that Obama's claim to the contrary "resurrects the same specter of limitless executive power the Supreme Court sought to guard against" in the 2008 Guantánamo ruling.[13] The administration appealed Bates's ruling.

In interagency deliberations at the Justice Department's secure command floor, not everyone was so sure that Bates was wrong. For example, Barron and Lederman noted in those discussions that the ideals Obama embraced as a candidate would seem to mean that detainees captured outside of the war theater, at least, should get judicial review.

But the military did not want to open the door to "judicializing" war-zone prison operations. It found a strong ally in the Justice Department official overseeing the deliberations: Neal Katyal, a Georgetown law professor serving as the new deputy solicitor general. He took the position that there was a principled legal distinction between Guantánamo and Bagram.

Guantánamo was a unique place. There are many American military bases on foreign soil. But allies host most of them and retain some say over what happens there. By contrast, in the aftermath of the Spanish-American War, Cuba signed a lease in 1903 giving the United States perpetual control over Guantánamo, and ever since Castro's Communist revolution, the two governments had had no diplomatic relations. Lawyers for Guantánamo detainees had argued at the Supreme Court that these facts meant the United States was effectively the only sovereign power over the base. But Bagram Airfield was on the sovereign soil of an American ally, Afghanistan.

For Katyal, championing this argument seemed like a role reversal.

During the Bush-Cheney administration, he had argued before the Supreme Court on behalf of a Guantánamo detainee, winning a landmark 2006 ruling that not only struck down Bush's first military commissions system but established that humane-treatment requirements in the Geneva Conventions protected captive terrorism suspects.[14] Now, Katyal would personally argue before an appeals court that Obama had the power to hold detainees at Bagram, even those captured outside Afghanistan, with no rights to hearings. But to Katyal, there was no contradiction: he believed both legal stances were accurate descriptions of the scope and limits of detainee rights.

Phil Carter, who succeeded Hodgkinson as the top detainee-policy official at the Pentagon in 2009, told me that the key to understanding the administration's Bagram litigation policy was realizing that every day Special Forces were going out and capturing new terrorism suspects. Bagram was the only wartime prison accepting new captives, whether from Afghanistan or, hypothetically, some other country incapable of holding them itself, like Yemen or Somalia. The administration was cautious about making a move in court that could have unintended consequences for future operations.

The ongoing wars were "like a specter hanging over all the discussion of policy," Carter said.

4. The Last American-Soil Enemy Combatant

Even as they wavered on the rights of indefinite detainees in the Afghan war theater, Obama and his legal team remained true to their ideals that American terrorism suspects should be handled exclusively by the civilian criminal justice system — not the military.

One of the most controversial things Bush had done after 9/11 was claim a right to hold *United States persons* — which means American citizens as well as noncitizens on American soil, who also have constitutional rights — in military detention without trial or access to lawyers. He had held three United States persons he deemed to be terrorists as enemy combatants. One was Yasser Hamdi, an American citizen captured in Afghanistan fighting with the Taliban. The second was Jose Padilla, an American citizen arrested in Chicago and accused of plotting attacks for al-Qaeda. And the third was Ali Saleh Kahlah al-Marri, a Qatari citizen on a student visa who was arrested in Peoria, Illinois, and accused of being an al-Qaeda sleeper agent. The question of whether the Constitution really permits a president to do such a thing divided the courts and legal commentators across ideological lines.

In June 2004, by a five-to-four vote, the Supreme Court upheld the detention of citizens captured fighting for the enemy on a foreign battlefield. But the majority also rejected Bush's claim that he had plenary power to hold Hamdi. They said the prisoner had a right to a lawyer and some kind of hearing to ensure that Bush's accusations about him were accurate. (Despite having told a lower court that Hamdi was too dangerous even to be permitted to talk to a lawyer, in October 2004 the Bush-Cheney administration chose to release him into Saudi Arabia.) The court also said its decision was limited to those facts — captured while fighting the United States on a battlefield where war was still being waged. That meant the more fraught question of Americans arrested on domestic soil remained unresolved. Two appeals courts reached opposite conclusions about whether Padilla's detention was constitutional, and in 2006, before the Supreme Court could resolve the issue, Bush transferred Padilla to the criminal justice system for a trial.

The Bush team had justified holding Padilla incommunicado for "enhanced" interrogation by saying they wanted him to become psychologically dependent on his questioners, and letting him talk to a defense lawyer would interrupt that process. Bush policy alarmed even many conservatives who were generally strong supporters of executive power. Supreme Court justice Antonin Scalia was among the four justices who dissented in *Hamdi;* he maintained that citizens accused of aiding the enemy in wartime should instead be given a criminal trial for treason. In 2007, the conservative former attorney general under

Reagan, Ed Meese, told me that while he thought most of Bush's post-9/11 policies had been lawful and appropriate, he did "have concerns about U.S. citizens being held as enemy combatants."

Several future members of the Obama legal team were involved in litigation challenging Bush's detention of Padilla without due-process rights, and many on the left thought *Hamdi* had been wrongly decided. In December 2007, when I surveyed presidential candidates about their views on executive power, one question was "Does the Constitution permit a president to detain U.S. citizens without charges as unlawful enemy combatants?" Obama's answer was "No. I reject the Bush Administration's claim that the President has plenary authority under the Constitution to detain U.S. citizens without charges as unlawful enemy combatants.... The detention of American citizens, without access to counsel, fair procedure, or pursuant to judicial authorization, as enemy combatants is unconstitutional."[15]

When Obama and his legal team took office, one United States person — al-Marri — was still being held as an enemy combatant in the naval brig in Charleston. The previous summer, the federal appeals court in Richmond, known as the Fourth Circuit, had ruled, six to five, that it was constitutional for Bush to imprison al-Marri in law-of-war detention if the accusations that he was helping al-Qaeda were true. (It also said he was entitled to a better opportunity to challenge the accusation than he had received to date.)[16] Al-Marri's appeal of the closely divided Fourth Circuit ruling was now pending before the Supreme Court.

The new Obama team shut the whole thing down fast. Obama's January 22 actions included a memo directing a review of al-Marri's case. Holder announced on February 27 that al-Marri had been indicted in civilian court for providing material support to al-Qaeda.[17] The Supreme Court vacated the Fourth Circuit's ruling and dismissed the matter as moot, leaving a cloud of legal uncertainty over whether a president could do the same thing to other United States persons deemed to be terrorist supporters.[18] Obama's act terminated the policy of holding people arrested inside the United States in indefinite military detention. But preventing a definitive Supreme Court decision about whether that was constitutional. That left a vacuum for what became, after the attempted Christmas bombing, a recurring political debate over how newly captured terrorism suspects should be handled.

Al-Marri pleaded guilty. He admitted that he had conspired with KSM to carry out al-Qaeda operations inside the United States and that he had used fraudulently obtained credit cards. He also admitted that he had searched for information about cyanide poisons on his computer and bookmarked information about dams, waterways, and tunnels in an almanac.

Prosecutors asked for fifteen years. At al-Marri's sentencing hearing, the commander of the brig testified that al-Marri had been well behaved. A federal judge sentenced him to eight years, taking into account the five he had already served in military custody, much of it in solitary confinement. The government agreed not to return him to military detention after he served out his sentence,[19] and after credit for good behavior, al-Marri completed his sentence and was repatriated to Qatar in January 2015.

5. The Path to Keeping Military Commissions

On March 1, three weeks after he was confirmed as the new Pentagon general counsel, Jeh Johnson convened an unusual meeting at the conference room of the Pentagon visitors center. He had invited the civilian official overseeing the military commissions system, its chief prosecutor, the top Judge Advocate General officers of the military services, and defense lawyers for detainees. His goal was to come up with some quick improvements to the tribunal rules.

Secretary of Defense Gates had asked the military judges to hold the cases in adjournment for 120 days, but they wouldn't wait forever. Nor would the family members of victims of the two major terrorism cases involving half a dozen former CIA prisoners now held at Guantánamo: the 9/11 attacks and the October 2000 bombing of the *Cole*, which had killed seventeen sailors.

Already, in February, one military judge had refused to go along with Gates's request. He had simply dismissed the *Cole* case, although the charges could be refiled. And the day after that dismissal, Obama had had an emotional meeting with relatives of victims of the two attacks. One participant, John Clodfelter, whose son died in the *Cole* bombing, later told me he was "about ready to bite bullets" when he went to the White House.

"I asked the president, 'Why is it taking so darn long? Back here in Virginia, when someone is charged with something, they are before the judge the next day. It's been like fourteen years!'" he said. "The president told me, 'Mr. Clodfelter, I want to know what is going on, versus what is supposed to be going on.' He had good intentions."

Obama had also told the families that he was determined to "ensure that those who are guilty receive swift and certain justice within a legal framework that is durable."[20] He asked for their patience as his team reassessed the tribunals.

But it was already clear they were going to need more time. Johnson had called the meeting to come up with changes Gates could make administratively to the tribunal rules. His idea was they could use the changes to show the military judges—and the families—they were making progress, and buy another extension.

The meeting came up with five improvements, including tightening the rules of evidence to exclude all statements obtained by the use of cruel treatment and giving defendants greater latitude to select defense lawyers. That was the new administration's first step down the path of fixing, not dropping, commissions.

6. Seeds of the Senate Torture Report

Obama may have wanted to look forward, not back, when it came to torture, but other powerful government officials thought there was a pressing need to get to the bottom of what had happened. On March 5,

2009, the Senate Select Committee on Intelligence voted fourteen to one to launch an oversight investigation into the CIA's detention and interrogation of terrorism suspects during the Bush-Cheney administration. The bipartisan vote set in motion the most searching and critical look at intelligence abuses since the Church Committee investigation of the 1970s.

The committee's action traced back to a December 2007 *New York Times* story exposing the fact that the CIA — defying instructions from agency lawyers and the White House — had destroyed videotapes of detainee interrogations, including waterboarding sessions.[21] The Senate committee had launched a limited oversight investigation into the tapes' destruction, and in early 2009, staffers completed a classified report suggesting that detainees at the agency's secret black-site prisons had been treated far worse than lawmakers had been told in briefings. That led the top Democrat and Republican on the committee, Dianne Feinstein and Kit Bond, to launch the more comprehensive oversight probe.

The newly confirmed CIA director, Leon Panetta, told employees that in response, he was creating a "Director's Review Group for Rendition, Detention, and Interrogation" to be the Senate investigators' point of contact, assemble historical data, and "formulate coordinated positions on the complex, often controversial, questions" that defined the now-defunct program. He tapped Peter Clement, a senior official from the agency's intelligence directorate.[22]

"The Chairman and Vice Chairman of the Committee have assured me that their goal is to draw lessons for future policy decisions, not to punish those who followed guidance from the Department of Justice," Panetta said. "That is only fair."

There remained the question of how the investigation would unfold. Feinstein told Panetta that the committee was prepared to issue a subpoena for access to unredacted classified information — meaning documents without the black censoring lines covering up sensitive items, such as the true names of agency personnel, communications between the agency and other governments and other parts of the American government, and the locations of the black-site prisons.

Rather than engage in protracted litigation over such a sweeping demand for the most sensitive operational documents in the CIA's possession, Panetta worked out an unprecedented arrangement with Feinstein. The CIA would provide access to the unredacted documents to the cleared committee investigators, but they would have to come to a CIA-leased building in Northern Virginia to access them. A copy of the documents would be placed on a CIA-controlled computer network created for the purpose, called RDINet for rendition, detention, and interrogation. The Senate staff would have their own partition of a shared network drive on which to save copies of documents in which they were interested and write their own notes and report drafts, which would be deemed congressional, not CIA, records.

The CIA eventually paid about $40 million in taxpayer dollars to lease the space, build RDINet, and pay contractors with Centra to review millions of documents before making them available to the Senate investigators.[23] (RDINet would also be used for other purposes, including a Justice Department investigation.)

Panetta struck this deal unilaterally, without White House authorization. That fact would lead to a blowup over the question of documents in the CIA's possession that showed direct interactions with the Bush-Cheney White House, and so might be subject to executive privilege, but that had already been placed into RDINet and shown to Senate staffers.* Panetta also asked Clement to conduct his own review of the documents being turned over to the committee in batches and produce weekly case reports summarizing what they showed. In 2014, the legislative staffers' use of a flaw in RDINet to acquire these documents, which came to be known as the Panetta Review, would lead to a confrontation of nearly constitutional-crisis proportions between the CIA and the Senate.†

---

* See chapter 9, section 6.
† See chapter 10, section 13.

7. Keeping Indefinite Detention

The same Thursday that the Senate announced its torture investigation, March 5, Obama summoned to the Oval Office many of his top legal advisers from the White House and the Justice Department. The topic was terrorism and detention-case issues, including the need to answer an uncomfortable question posed by Judge Bates. In addition to the Bagram case, Bates was also overseeing several pending habeas lawsuits filed by Guantánamo detainees, and he wanted to know — by the following Friday — if Obama thought he had the power to keep detaining people without trial, and if so whether his standards were any different than the Bush-Cheney administration's. Bates wasn't willing to grant any extension. For the young Obama administration, the decision about whether to keep indefinite law-of-war detention was one in which, as Amy Jeffress, a national security aide to Holder, told me, "the legal process drove the policy process."

Olsen's warnings that his task force would likely put dozens of detainees into the untriable and unreleasable bucket now had policy implications. Had there been only a handful of such hard-case prisoners, as Obama's transition team had hoped, Obama might have sought some other imperfect disposition option for them — perhaps even letting them go and keeping them under surveillance — in order to shut down indefinite detention. But *dozens* of such detainees were far too many to release. For such a sizable bloc, the government decided that it needed to keep law-of-war detention powers available.

But telling Bates so quickly exactly how much involvement with al-Qaeda was sufficient to make someone a detainable enemy raised a risk of unintended consequences. For example, they might draw the line too narrowly, and only later realize that they had made a mistake because they had not thoroughly studied what the government had to stop doing under any new standard. It also seemed too hard to quickly craft such a complicated thing and get everyone comfortable with it. Justice Department officials, including Jeffress, Barron, and Lederman, proposed meeting Bates's deadline by telling the judge that for now, as a placeholder, the Obama administration was sticking with the Bush-Cheney administration's theory of who was detainable, leaving open the possibility that it would come to a different view later. But at the Oval Office meeting, which lasted almost two hours, Obama balked at waiting to make changes.

A particular concern was that the Bush legal team had claimed that the president not only had power granted by Congress in the AUMF to detain al-Qaeda members, but he also independently had *inherent* and *exclusive* power to imprison people he deemed to be enemies. This unwritten authority was implied by his constitutional role as commander in chief and could not be constrained by Congress, they asserted. Obama wanted to drop any mention of inherent power and refer only to the wartime authority granted by Congress. His overriding concern was to build in some limits on the powers he was claiming.

I don't think it makes sense for me alone to decide, just because I'm president, who should be detained, Obama said at one point. *I'm not comfortable exerting that authority.*[24]

Notwithstanding the deadline pressure, Obama told the Justice Department to go back and work on it.

Barron and Lederman convened the relevant lawyers for a seventy-two-hour crash exercise. Working through the weekend, they drafted a twelve-page brief laying out a revised theory of wartime detention powers.[25] The following week, they held a marathon series of intensive meetings with lawyers and officials from the Pentagon, the State Department, and intelligence agencies to make sure everyone could live with their handiwork.

On one level, the brief sounded more constrained than the Bush-era versions. They did not make any reference to inherent commander-in-chief power, though they did not disclaim it either. They also added the word *substantial* to the sort of support for the enemy that might make someone detainable. They dropped the phrase *enemy combatant*, which the Bush legal team had used but which did not exist as a meaningful term in international law, and paid greater respect to the notion that

Obama's wartime powers had to be interpreted in light of the international laws of war.

On another level, the power for Obama they were claiming remained sweeping. Obama, they wrote, had authority under the AUMF to detain not just members of al-Qaeda or the Taliban but also *associated forces* fighting with them against the United States or its partners. Obama could detain not only people who were *part of* such enemy forces but also people who *substantially supported* them. And this power, they wrote, was "not limited to persons captured on the battlefields in Afghanistan." But the details, they cautioned, still needed to be worked out.

Before filing the brief, Barron and Lederman quietly consulted Harold Koh, the Yale Law School dean who would soon become the top lawyer at the State Department. Koh had spent years fighting presidential claims that courts had no power to review executive-branch actions to imprison foreigners at Guantánamo. In 1993, he led a lawsuit challenging the Clinton administration's detention of Haitian refugees at the naval base. These Haitians were stranded in indefinite limbo. They qualified for refugee status and so could not be returned to Haiti. But they tested positive for the virus that causes AIDS and so the government did not want to bring them into the United States. The Justice Department back then had urged a judge to throw out the case, asserting that it had no jurisdiction over foreigners held on Cuban soil. Koh and his cocounsels won a ruling that the judiciary *did* have power to hear lawsuits brought by the Haitian detainees, but the government offered a deal: rather than appeal, it would let Koh's clients into the United States in exchange for having the ruling vacated.[26] Koh took the deal, helping his clients at the cost of preserving Guantánamo as a legal black hole. A decade later, when Bush opened a wartime prison there and claimed courts had no jurisdiction to oversee it, Koh and others started from scratch to challenge that notion.

Obama was about to nominate Koh for the State Department job, but consulting Koh at this moment was touchy; the Senate had not confirmed him to wield government power.[27] Now, three and a half months before his confirmation, Koh blessed Barron and Lederman's reasoning; he particularly liked language that Obama's war powers should be interpreted "consistent" with the law of armed conflict, which implied that international law imposed limits on those powers.

The Obama team's definition of who could be detained under the Authorization for Use of Military Force resolution came to be known as the March 13 Standard. It essentially defined whom the United States believed itself to be at war with, drawing lines around the amorphous, loose-knit al-Qaeda network. As a result, it became a point of recurring reference for Obama's war against al-Qaeda in ways that extended far beyond Guantánamo litigation. When the government deliberated about whom it could detain without trial in Afghanistan or aboard a ship, or when it debated whether it could lawfully kill somebody in a drone strike or commando raid, the March 13 Standard framed those questions.

Obama's legal team expressed pride about the limitations on his power they had built in, as compared to the broader claims of authority made by the Bush team. But their bottom line was the same: the war against al-Qaeda was a real war, law-of-war detention was legitimate in that armed conflict, and Obama would use that power when he needed to. Accepting the definition in another Guantánamo habeas case, Judge Reggie Walton observed that Obama's refinements to the scope of presidential detention powers struck a "distinction of purely metaphysical difference" from Bush's definition and "appear to be of a minimal if not ephemeral character."[28]

In hindsight, Jeffress largely agreed. "The new definition didn't change much — it was philosophically different, but the outcome was similar," she said. "The idea was to put it in place and revisit it later, but the revisiting didn't happen."

It was true, insofar as Guantánamo went, that the new standard changed little in practice. But when the detainee-review-board process got going at Bagram Airfield in late 2009 and early 2010, its members used the March 13 Standard there, too — and officials said it resulted in the release of many Afghans who were being held for intelligence purposes but did not meet the new standard.

Several of Obama's top advisers from this period told me that he did not believe he had committed to keeping indefinite detention at this point. He was acknowledging only that there was a legally defensible argument for holding some Guantánamo detainees without trial for the time being. And indeed, throughout the spring and into the summer of 2009, he continued to wrestle with whether he would keep using it.

But in hindsight, Obama's promise to close Guantánamo suffered a grievous wound at this moment. One way to empty the prison would have been philosophically pure: prosecute or release every detainee. But Obama's plan was messier: he would move some of those men to a different location and continue to imprison them without trial — continuing the main policy that had made Guantánamo notorious and hence worth closing. Obama would remain determined to fulfill his vow in the most literal sense, making pragmatic public arguments that the prison in Cuba was too expensive to operate and was a poisonous symbol that fueled anti-American sentiments, making allies less willing to work with the United States and helping terrorists recruit new members. But after his March 13 Standard embraced indefinite detention as legitimate, he could not argue that the wartime prison should be closed to end any ongoing injustice and restore the rule of law.

8. Quashing an After-Action Review

By April 2009, the issue of how the Obama team was dealing with the legacy detainees was becoming politically poisonous. That month, the administration declassified and made public a set of Bush-era legal memos in which Justice Department lawyers had approved as lawful certain torture techniques.* Conservatives like Dick Cheney denounced

---

* See chapter 9, section 4.

Obama for damaging national security, while liberals renewed their calls for an investigation to provide historical accountability for what the United States had done. One proposed model they liked was the Truth and Reconciliation Commission that South Africa had established after the abolition of apartheid; perpetrators of human rights violations could testify about what they had done in exchange for amnesty from civil liability or criminal prosecution.

Obama had already made clear that he did not want a lengthy investigation of public servants who had thought they were protecting the country. But Admiral Mike Mullen, the chairman of the Joint Chiefs, pointed out to Greg Craig that after major operations, the military performs an "after-action report," looking at what went wrong and what went right. Maybe the government should do something similar about its response to 9/11. The idea was to satisfy the need for a historic accounting, reframed in a neutral rather than accusatory way.

Craig told me that he directed an aide, Michael Gottlieb, to prepare a policy paper laying out a proposal. The paper included substantial research into the history of comparable blue-ribbon commissions in the past and made the case for an after-action report. It also identified a list of prominent, above-the-fray individuals who could serve as potential commission members, such as Sandra Day O'Connor, the retired Supreme Court justice, Tom Keane, the former Republican governor of New Jersey and cochair of the 9/11 Commission, and Abner Mikva, the former federal appeals court judge and Clinton White House counsel.

After reading Gottlieb's paper, Obama changed the topic of a National Security Council cabinet meeting scheduled for the next day in order to talk about it. Most of the participants assembled in the Situation Room an hour early for a pre-meeting, and Craig handed around Gottlieb's paper. The conversation, according to Craig, was very positive.

Then the president walked in. He said he had thought about it some more, and was concerned that the mere creation of a commission, even if styled as an after-action review, would be seen as a partisan exercise: Obama going after Bush.

Now, one by one, everyone who had liked the idea ten minutes earlier reversed course and told Obama he was right. Craig was left to make a last pitch for why it would work.

Mr. President, give me two minutes to make the case. This would be good for the country. There would be ways to shield it from political attacks, such as having serious Republicans on it, and making sure there were no preordained conclusions. Maybe it would come out and say that what Bush did saved lives.

Obama, however, had made up his mind.

9. Keeping Military Commissions

Obama had decided to keep indefinite detention for the time being and not to investigate CIA interrogations. Meanwhile a third question was looming: whether to keep military commissions as an available venue for prosecuting terrorists. The answer started to take shape on April 24, when Obama convened a meeting in the Situation Room on detention issues. Sitting between Craig and Biden, Obama heard updates from the leaders of each of the three task forces established by his executive order. Matt Olsen, for example, told Obama that it seemed likely that his detainee-review task force would determine that many dozens of detainees were neither prosecutable nor releasable.

Olsen's warning bled into the update from the detention-policy task force, which was led by Brad Wiegmann, the top deputy at the Justice Department's National Security Division, and Colonel Mark Martins, the head of international and operational law for the Army Judge Advocate General's Corps. At that stage, their task force was concentrating on two issues: where to move the remaining detainees when the Guantánamo prison closed, and what to do about military commissions, including the pending cases that were currently paused. Coming out of the meeting, participants understood that making a decision about whether to keep commissions had moved to the front burner.

A focus of the discussion, and the wider debate, was an irony that is sometimes lost in the arguments over tribunals. Critics see military commissions, which have more flexible rules of evidence than civilian courts, as a sham process—a way for the government to ensure a conviction. But the evidence against some detainees, gathered under battlefield conditions, would be admissible *only* under tribunal rules. For that group, the choice was not where they would receive a trial, but whether they would receive a trial at all—or just stay in indefinite detention without any defined sentence and perhaps forever. From that perspective, keeping commissions would reduce the number of law-of-war detainees. The question, however, was whether that group was sizable enough to drive such a major policy decision.

In early May, ahead of a principals committee* meeting on tribunals, Craig sent a memo, drafted with help from his aide Trevor Morrison, saying that the Obama administration should jettison commissions. The memo argued that it was not worth entrenching a system that human rights advocates loathed as second-class justice just to prosecute a few hypothetical detainees. Following the meeting, the counsel's office also drafted a neutral decision memo for Obama laying out three options and saying where each agency stood.

The first option was to ask the military judges to extend the pause in the existing cases and say that the administration was going to seek major reforms to the tribunals' rules through legislation. The second was to ask for another extension in the cases without committing to keeping military commissions. The third was to abandon tribunals and let the cases shut down, as Craig wanted to do.

Of the top advisers to Obama, only John Brennan, the counterterrorism adviser, strongly agreed with Craig, officials told me. His argument was that Obama was going to have to have a difficult conversation

---

* Most interagency executive-branch policymaking happens at the level of the *deputies committee,* the number-two officials from relevant departments and agencies. Their disagreements are resolved by the *principals committee* of cabinet-level secretaries and agency directors. Those questions on which the principals cannot agree are resolved by the president. When the president chairs a cabinet meeting on security issues, the people sitting around the table are the same ones as at a principals committee, but it is called a *National Security Council* meeting. Separately, the national security and foreign-policy officials at the White House are called NSC staffers.

with the country about the need to keep a system of indefinite, preventive detention and that it was not worth doubling down on that by keeping commissions too.

The State Department argued for the second option: not to make any decision now. But most of the other key voices — the Defense Department, the CIA, the Office of the Director of National Intelligence, and even the Justice Department — thought it made more sense to keep commissions available as an option. A strong force arguing for that outcome was Martins, the co-head of the detention-policy task force. He was deeply immersed in the legal issues and potential reforms to the Military Commissions Act.

Craig and Brennan faced an uphill fight. As noted, back in 2006, Obama had voted for a bill that would keep military commissions. The arguments that keeping them would maintain his flexibility and be a bipartisan gesture seemed persuasive.

Obama checked the box on the decision memo to reform but keep military commissions. The White House would formally announce his decision on May 14.

As events unfolded, it became clear that the Obama legal team's not-yet-made decision to prosecute KSM and the other 9/11 defendants before a civilian court was damaged at this moment. There were two philosophically pure approaches to prosecuting terrorism cases: give *everyone* a regular trial before a traditional civilian court, or prosecute *everyone* before a military commission. But Obama and his team had again chosen a middle-ground, have-it-both-ways tack that they saw as pragmatic but that was ideologically muddled and so left them vulnerable to criticism from both flanks.

Civil libertarians and human rights advocates did not like military commissions, even after the overhaul, and accused Obama of entrenching a two-tier legal system in which weaker cases would receive second-class justice. To rebut those attacks, Obama and his aides insisted that after the 2009 reforms, the tribunals system was now a fair venue. But accepting commissions as legitimate opened up an attack from the right: If there was no problem with tribunals, what was the point of ever using civilian courts for terrorism cases? Republicans increasingly came to argue — especially after the Christmas bombing — that *all* terrorism cases should be handled by the military at Guantánamo and *any* use of regular civilian courts for terrorism cases was weak and raised unnecessary risks.

10. Turbulence in the Effort to Close Guantánamo

In May, conservative Republicans attacked Obama after word leaked that he was planning to release several Guantánamo detainees onto American soil. As soon as that plan came under criticism, the administration swiftly abandoned it. The rocky political moment prompted Obama to deliver a speech at the National Archives that became a touchstone for future legal-policy deliberations. The uproar also led the Democratic-controlled Congress to impose the first legal restrictions on his power to transfer detainees.

To many close observers of Guantánamo issues, the detainees the administration was preparing to release inside the United States were particularly sympathetic because they had been brought to the prison by mistake but were now stuck there. They were the ethnic Uighurs, Chinese Muslims who had fled to Afghanistan to escape oppression by the Communist government. Several had learned to fire guns in Afghanistan, but they were not part of al-Qaeda and their enemy was the Communist government in Beijing, not the United States. The Bush-Cheney administration had conceded in court that they were not enemy combatants, and a federal district court judge had ruled that the United States had no lawful authority to keep them in prison and had ordered them freed. But the Uighurs could not be repatriated because China might abuse them, and China was pressuring other countries not to resettle them, so they remained locked up.

The administration had decided to resettle two of the men — the best English speakers — in a Uighur immigrant community in Northern Virginia under close monitoring, hoping that demonstrating that the

United States was willing to resettle a few of them on its own soil would help persuade other countries to take in other Uighurs. Craig was a champion of this plan, and in accounts of his later ouster from the administration, he was blamed for the political problems it caused. But it was his bureaucratic rival, White House chief of staff Rahm Emanuel, who chaired the April 14 principals committee meeting at which the decision to move forward was made by consensus.

When he found out about the plan, Representative Frank Wolf, the Republican congressman from the Virginia district where the Uighurs were to be released, launched a high-profile protest. He sent a public letter to Obama on May 1 declaring that "the American people cannot afford to simply take your word that these detainees, who were captured training in terrorist camps, are not a threat if released into our communities."[29] He delivered a floor speech on May 4 warning that "these terrorists would not be held in prisons but they would be released into your neighborhoods."[30] Other Republicans joined in. Former Speaker Newt Gingrich linked the Uighurs to 9/11.

Emanuel, according to the *Washington Post,* pulled back the plan; the heat was an intense distraction at a time when the White House was trying to get major legislation through Congress.[31] The Uighurs who had been bound for Virginia instead went to Bermuda, found jobs, and got married; while they lacked passports and could not travel, they lived quietly thereafter.[32] In June 2009, Representative Dana Rohrabacher, a California Republican and anti-Communist, denounced his colleagues for using the Uighurs as political ammunition. "No one on the Republican side was arguing facts," he said. "I am ashamed of the leadership of my party."[33]

On May 21, Obama and Cheney delivered dueling speeches. Obama explained his national security legal policies in front of the Constitution at the National Archives, and the framework he laid out — including preferring regular civilian trials for terrorism cases where possible, but keeping military commissions as a backup option — became a touchstone for internal administration debates in the coming years. Meanwhile, Cheney criticized Obama's policies at the American Enterprise Institute, a conservative think tank.

Cheney focused on an area where his policies contrasted most with Obama's: inflicting suffering on terrorism suspects to make them talk against their wills, which Cheney would not call *torture*. He blasted Obama for releasing the enhanced-interrogation memos and ending the CIA program: "No moral value held dear by the American people obliges public servants ever to sacrifice innocent lives to spare a captured terrorist from unpleasant things."

Cheney's critique was complicated by the fact that his own administration had already essentially terminated the CIA torture program, over Cheney's objections, by the end of Bush's time in office. Still, another of his swipes was an interesting analysis of the difference between rhetoric and actions, a point that would later become a theme for Obama's liberal critics.

"It's one thing to adopt the euphemisms that suggest we're no longer engaged in a war," he said. "These are just words, and in the end it's the policies that matter most. You don't want to call them 'enemy combatants?' Fine. Call them what you want — just don't bring them into the United States. Tired of calling it a 'war?' Use any term you prefer. Just remember it is a serious step to begin unraveling some of the very policies that have kept our people safe since 9/11."[34]

However, at the National Archives, Obama insisted that he did see the conflict as a war, but a war that must be waged with rules:

"We are indeed at war with al Qaeda and its affiliates," he said. "We do need to update our institutions to deal with this threat. But we must do so with an abiding confidence in the rule of law and due process; in checks and balances and accountability.... The decisions that were made over the last eight years established an ad hoc legal approach for fighting terrorism that was neither effective nor sustainable — a framework that failed to rely on our legal traditions and time-tested institutions, and that failed to use our values as a compass." This, he said, was now going to change.

Many media commentators portrayed the speeches as opposites. Tonally, that was true. But as a matter of policy substance, it was striking how far Obama had already shifted from the expectations of change created by his campaign: explaining his plan to close Guantánamo, he endorsed military commissions and indefinite law-of-war detention.

"There remains the question of detainees at Guantánamo who cannot be prosecuted yet who pose a clear danger to the American people...who, in effect, remain at war with the United States," he said. "I am not going to release individuals who endanger the American people."[35]

Obama promised to work with Congress to develop legal rules and procedures for holding those detainees. But interbranch relations on detainee issues were souring.

After the Uighurs flap, even Democrats began to suspect the administration had not thought through its plan. In late May and June, Congress was completing work on a war-funding bill. Overwhelming bipartisan majorities rejected an administration request for eighty million dollars to help close Guantánamo. They also approved imposing restrictions on the transfer of Guantánamo detainees: no public funds could be spent to release Guantánamo detainees inside the United States, and the executive branch had to notify Congress and then wait for a period before it could import any to domestic soil for the purpose of prosecution or continued imprisonment. The waiting period also applied to transfers to other counties.[36]

It was extraordinary for Congress to restrict the commander in chief's ability to make operational decisions about where and when to transfer wartime prisoners. Bush would not have stood for it. But Obama was loath to make Bush-like claims about his war powers, and he wasn't planning to close the prison before the limits expired on September 30. Maybe he could get Congress not to include the language in the next cycle. So Obama acquiesced—and rather than letting the restrictions expire, Congress continually renewed and strengthened them.

In retrospect, the Uighurs moment was the first serious political stumble for the administration's national security legal policy—the moment when it became clear to all that Obama's government was not going to sail along and close Guantánamo. It also foreshadowed the toxic politics of detention that would spill over in the aftermath of the Christmas attack. Later, Obama's team would realize that the president and his advisers had made a major political miscalculation. By retreating in the face of the first congressional resistance rather than standing up to Wolf about the Uighurs and challenging the transfer restrictions, Obama signaled to Congress that he could be pushed around on Guantánamo issues.

Obama himself, looking back in 2015, said his original mistake had come even earlier. Asked what he would do differently if he could go back to his first day in office, Obama said he would have ordered every Guantánamo detainee transferred to a different prison immediately instead of declaring he was going to do so and then not acting on that policy right away.

"I think I would have closed Guantánamo on the first day," Obama said. "I didn't because at that time, as you'll recall, we had a bipartisan agreement that it should be closed; my Republican opponent had also said it should have been closed. And I thought that we had enough consensus there that we could do it in a more deliberate fashion. But the politics of it got tough and people got scared by the rhetoric around it. And once that set in, then the path of least resistance was just to leave it open, even though it's not who we are as a country. It is used by terrorists around the world to help recruit jihadists. So instead, we've had to just chip away at it, year after year after year. But I think in that first couple of weeks we could have done it quicker."[37]

11. A Hidden Tribunals Debate

The only publicly visible work of Obama's detention task force was a preliminary report issued on July 20 and signed by its cochairs, Wiegmann and Martins.[38] It defended a limited role for military commissions. Attached was an unsigned, two-page document, negotiated between Kris and Johnson, that listed considerations for deciding whether prosecutable detainees should go before a civilian court or a tribunal. The takeaway was that there should be a strong preference for using regular courts but exceptions could be made to use military courts instead if there were "compelling factors," such as if the military had a special interest in the crime—the *Cole* bombing was an obvious example—or if civilian trial rules raised "legal or evidentiary problems."[39]

Behind the scenes, the task force had been doing much more. It convened a series of influential working groups on a range of topics, including how best to shape the Military Commissions Act of 2009. Their research and analysis informed several deputies committee meetings, convened by Tom Donilon, the deputy national security adviser, to work through which rule changes the administration would endorse in negotiations with Congress. They covered issues such as whether to copy the civilian justice system's approach to handling classified information (yes), whether the law should have a sunset clause that made it expire if Congress did not reauthorize it (no), and whether to codify a rule that statements obtained by cruelty—not just torture—should be banned (yes).

As these deliberations unfolded, Martins flooded the interagency task force with briefing slides and memos, and he ended up getting into a lively debate with Barron that has never been reported. They disagreed about whether involuntary statements made by the accused on the battlefield, at the moment he was captured or soon afterward, should be admissible as evidence against him in a commission trial—foreshadowing the enormous controversy that would break out over reading Miranda warnings to terrorism suspects following the Christmas attack.

The debate between Martins and Barron pitted the tribunals' fairness against their utility. A tenet of human rights is that people should not be punished for statements they were forced to utter. But no one expects combat troops shouting questions at enemy captives after a firefight—a highly coercive atmosphere—to tell prisoners they do not have to answer. If a newly captured foe, a gun in his face, pointed beneath the floorboards and said, *my bombs are hidden there,* could that later be used as evidence? Barron thought such statements had to be excluded from commissions, while Martins thought an exception should be made to permit them to be used as evidence. Other officials within the Pentagon, including Vice Admiral Bruce MacDonald, the top Judge Advocate General officer in the navy, were also pushing for a rule permitting involuntary statements made at the point of capture to be used.

Barron developed his argument in a series of Office of Legal Counsel writings that remain secret. Because Guantánamo was to be closed, his inquiry worked from the premise that any future tribunals would take place on American soil. In a May 4, 2009, memo, according to people who have read it, he concluded that American courts would likely rule that commission defendants had Fifth Amendment rights — including protection from self-incrimination.

Barron zeroed in on the involuntary statements issue in follow-up memos dated May 22 and June 3. Reviewing one hundred years of court-martial precedents, he warned that courts would overturn guilty verdicts from trials in which involuntary battlefield statements — even ones that proved to be reliable and true — had been used as evidence.

But on July 9, Martins sent Barron a memo taking sharp issue with that analysis. Barron may have been the head of the elite Office of Legal Counsel and a tenured Harvard Law School professor, but Martins was arguably the most scholarly Judge Advocate officer in modern times. He had graduated first in his class at West Point, studied at Oxford as a Rhodes Scholar, and attended Harvard Law School, from which he graduated in 1990, a year ahead of Obama; the two men had worked together on the *Harvard Law Review.* Martins had been thinking about military commissions for a long time; in 1996, he published a law-journal article reflecting on the problem of establishing tribunals without making them vulnerable to accusations of "victor's justice."[40] Unlike Barron, Martins had downrange field experience: he had served as the top military lawyer in Iraq to the commanding generals in that war, General George Casey and then Petraeus; his work included overseeing the task force that cleaned up detention operations after the Abu Ghraib scandal.

Now Martins raised concerns about whether the safety of troops "conducting dangerous missions on distant battlefields" would be compromised if they had to take steps to make sure anything new captives said was voluntary, and he argued that it was "unprecedented" to impose a voluntariness standard for statements of the accused in military commissions. On July 29, he sent Barron a draft legislative provision permitting involuntary battlefield statements to be used if military judges found them reliable and if their admission would serve the "interests of justice."

On August 5, Barron responded that while he recognized the importance of the security of troops in combat, the solution was to use such statements for intelligence and keep them out of court. His analysis, he said, was "limited to the legal question," and there was no support in the relevant precedents for a "battlefield exception" to the self-incrimination rule.

Martins was unpersuaded — as was Congress. Peter Levine, Carl Levin's top Democratic staff lawyer on the Senate Armed Services Committee, incorporated the battlefield-exception provision into the final version of the new Military Commissions Act. And Obama signed the bill that October, leaving it to tribunal prosecutors and judges to decide whether to risk using such evidence.

That same month, the military promoted Martins from colonel to brigadier general and deployed him to Afghanistan. Petraeus, now the head of the Central Command, wanted Martins to lead an effort to detoxify detention operations at Bagram on the eve of a surge of troops that would quintuple the number of wartime prisoners the United States held there.

At the time, Martins thought his work with military commissions was finished. But the tribunals system he had helped Obama overhaul would later draw him back in, transforming his career.

12. A Temptation to Entrench Gitmo-Style Policies

As the shape of Obama's law-of-war detention policy for Guantánamo prisoners came into view, a new question arose over how he should go about formally establishing it. This was a process that carried major implications: was the power to hold people without trial something Obama was using reluctantly and an exception that would fade away over time, or was he fully embracing it and institutionalizing as a normal counterterrorism tool for the twenty-first century? Two poles in that debate were Harold Koh and Senator Lindsey Graham, Republican from South Carolina.

The detention policy crystallized at a principals committee meeting in the Situation Room on July 14. Prisoners who could be neither prosecuted nor released would be moved out of Guantánamo, which officials still assumed would soon close, and taken to a different prison, subject to three overarching rules: (1) they would be held if they met the March 13 Standard, (2) federal courts would make that decision, and (3) parole-like periodic review boards would, at intervals, reexamine each man to determine if it remained necessary to keep holding him or if he could now be transferred. But the consensus raised a new question: How should Obama create this framework — by seeking a statute from Congress, issuing an executive order himself, or having the military issue a lower-profile regulation? In his National Archives speech, Obama had promised to work with Congress on establishing standards for indefinite detention. But after the Uighurs fight and the transfer restrictions, his administration had grown wary of Congress on terrorism-detainee issues. They had begun to see Congress as a place where partisanship and demagoguery crowded out serious and nuanced policymaking about terrorism issues. The cabinet was leaning toward recommending an executive order.

But Obama remained queasy about holding people in prolonged preventive detention. He wanted to know what Koh, whom the Senate had just confirmed as Clinton's top legal adviser at State, thought. Essentially Obama was using Koh as a sounding board to see how the international law, human rights, civil liberties, and academic communities might react if he issued such an executive order.

In late July, Koh came to the Roosevelt Room and sat across a conference table from Obama and Biden, surrounded by White House legal, political, and policy aides. Koh told Obama the decision was an early defining moment of his presidency, and he strongly urged Obama not to issue an executive order, let alone sign a law.

There might be no happy solution for some of the legacy Guantánamo detainees, Koh argued, but rights groups would forgive Obama for continuing to hold a few Bush-vintage cases in indefinite detention. They would not forgive him if he entrenched a permanent state of affairs in which the United States asserted that it had the power to keep snatching more people it saw as dangerous, far from any battlefield, and holding them in preventive detention. There should be no future need for law-of-war detention outside of active war zones, Koh said, because there was no reason to think the United States would take custody of anyone whom it could not prosecute. The United States was helping allies build up their own detention capabilities. Federal statutes like the material support law had been expanded to cover noncitizens abroad. Torture had been abandoned, so evidence would not be tainted.

Koh thought Obama should use low-profile military regulations to set up periodic review boards. He argued that a higher-profile executive order would signal comfort with the power to hold people in indefinite detention and create bureaucratic pressure to make that system the default for future captures. Instead of winding down Bush's global war on terror, Koh warned, Obama risked joining the ranks of men like Earl Warren, Hugo Black, and William O. Douglas — liberal legal heroes whose historical standing was tarnished by the fact that they supported the internment of Japanese Americans during World War II.

But whereas Koh worried about institutionalizing indefinite detention for future captives, Graham wanted to do just that. On August 5, 2009, shortly after Koh's meeting with Obama, Graham produced a one-page summary of a proposal for the administration, which he titled "Key Elements of a Guantánamo Detainee Disposition Plan." This document, which has never been reported, laid the groundwork for a year of on-again, off-again negotiations over a proposed grand bargain on detainee policies that went far beyond whether the prison in Cuba would stay open.

Graham urged making military commissions "the rule, not the

exception" for prosecuting terrorists, reversing the policy that Obama's detainee task force had just established. He argued that mixing wartime and civilian legal systems would create "chaos" if a civilian court acquitted someone like KSM on a technicality and the prisoner was then moved back into indefinite law-of-war detention, and he contended that it signaled — falsely, in his view — that tribunals were second-class justice. Graham also wanted to regularize indefinite detention for terrorists captured in the future. He proposed, among other things, setting up a new "FISA-like 'National Security Court' made up of sitting District Court judges appointed by the Chief Justice." It would hear habeas corpus petitions and make sure the detainee was indeed part of al-Qaeda, as well as a parole-like system of periodic review to see if a detainee still posed a threat or could be safely released.[41]

"Preventive, wartime detention is lawful and necessary," he wrote.

Graham had credibility. He had helped McCain fight the Bush-Cheney administration over torture. He did not demagogue about the Uighurs, and he criticized his fellow Republicans who did that instead of finding constructive solutions for a serious and difficult problem. And he supported closing Guantánamo. But in Graham's view, the United States needed a fully functional wartime prison *somewhere* — one that complied with the Geneva Conventions but allowed newly captured al-Qaeda suspects to be interrogated in military custody.

"The way I look at it, the war against al-Qaeda, the war on terror, is going to go on for a long time," Graham later told me. "We need a rational system here."[42]

Over the next year or so, Graham, negotiating primarily with Rahm Emanuel, offered a deal: If the White House would endorse his plan, he would provide some Republican support for legislation to move the Guantánamo detainees to a prison on domestic soil, giving skittish Democratic moderates political cover to go along too.

Emanuel wanted to take the deal, close Guantánamo, and move on. More liberal voices, like Craig, Holder, and Koh, contended that such a victory would be Pyrrhic, given the price Graham was asking: entrenching and expanding indefinite detention and military commissions.

Emanuel countered that during the campaign Obama had promised to close Guantánamo, but he had not promised a civilian trial for KSM. Besides, one out of two was better than none.

What's our North Star here? Emanuel asked repeatedly at cabinet meetings.

13. *Just Keep Plugging Away at It*

The heat, political and literal, was rising. It was August 11 — a sweltering day during the time of year when Congress flees swampy Washington for a monthlong recess. On talk radio and at town-hall meetings across the country, the Tea Party movement was rising to power inside the Republican Party. At 4:45 p.m. that Tuesday, Donilon convened a deputies committee meeting to talk about closing Guantánamo. With Obama's deadline less than six months away, they needed to find a replacement prison to hold the harder cases, at least for an interim period.

One option they discussed that day was a maximum-security prison in Standish, Michigan, that the state was about to close. But William Lynn, the deputy secretary of defense, said that early estimates of what it would cost to make necessary upgrades were daunting: as much as $400 million. It would likely cost just a fourth of that to use some existing Department of Defense prison, making it a more realistic choice; they could find the money in funds Congress had already appropriated for general purposes and not have to ask for new money.

Still, every option had shortcomings. The Pentagon's preference was the Charleston naval brig, but its closest airfield was eight miles away along a city road. Camp Pendleton in California had the best overall security, but its prison did not meet the CIA's standards for isolating the highest-level detainees. McCain's campaign-era idea of Fort Leavenworth would require buying up nearby land to expand fencing as well as moving maximum-security inmates already held there to someplace else. The list went on.

Donilon asked the Pentagon to take a closer look at Charleston and Pendleton and scheduled another deputies meeting to look at options for reducing the number of detainees who would need to be transferred onto domestic soil.

The follow-up meeting convened at 4:00 p.m. on August 17. One part of the ninety-minute agenda was an update from Dan Fried, the State Department envoy negotiating transfers. He had been traveling the world seeking homes for about forty detainees who were approved for transfer but who could not be repatriated. France had already taken a detainee. Ireland, Italy, Portugal, and Spain had each agreed to take one or several. Nine other nations were leaning toward taking some.

Then the meeting turned to a briefing by Matt Olsen, who had written a nine-page memo for the deputies summing up the status of the task-force review. Never made public, it was filled with blunt talk.

The task force had now gone through all the detainees and reached agreements on the easy ones, preliminarily recommending ninety-two for transfer and forty for prosecution. But that left the other hundred and nine, which included fifty-seven Yemenis and twenty-two Afghans. His memo and presentation boiled down to one question: *Should we accept more risk?*

Early on, Olsen later said, he had decided that the task force would require unanimity among the six participating agencies to release any detainee. His reason was that sooner or later, one of the former prisoners would do something bad, and the risk of finger-pointing was severe if one of them had objected to releasing him.

"Unanimity was critical to the integrity of the process," Olsen said. "There had been a lot of prior disagreement over the detainees, and we were committed to drive toward consensus if at all possible."

But the task force was now at an impasse about how to sort through the hundred and nine still-uncategorized detainees due to two issues.

The first was whether to use the likelihood that a detainee would win his habeas lawsuit as a factor in deciding if he should be released. Justice Department litigators were having trouble proving that detainees had sufficient connection to al-Qaeda to meet the March 13 Standard.

District court judges had ruled for the detainee in thirteen cases, and the government had conceded a loss in another eighteen. By contrast, it had won only eight. Many weak cases looked similar; the government could show that a detainee had stayed at an al-Qaeda-affiliated guesthouse and, sometimes, that he had attended a training camp, but judges had found those facts insufficient to show that a detainee was part of or substantially supported al-Qaeda. The disconnect illustrated the difference between intelligence and judicial standards for deciding if a proposition was true. As the defeats mounted, the Justice Department feared that its litigators' credibility to defend more solid cases was eroding and wanted the other weak cases moved to the release bucket. But the military and intelligence voices disagreed.

The other dispute concerned a group of detainees who clearly seemed to have been foreign fighters, but at the lowest level — rank-and-file al-Qaeda members who had gone to Afghanistan before 9/11 and helped the Taliban fight its civil war against the Northern Alliance but who were hardly KSM-style international terrorists, having no advanced training, expertise, or leadership roles.

The Bush-Cheney administration had released hundreds of such suspected foot soldiers, and while most had gone on to lead quiet lives, some had engaged in terrorist or insurgent activity afterward. Releasing the remaining low-level fighters would entail risk; a few would almost certainly cause problems if freed, but no one could reliably predict who. Yet they had all been held for about six years, and continuing to hold them forever would clash with the principles and policy goals Obama had laid out in the National Archives speech.

Olsen's message was that the task force had done as much as it could with the lowest-common-denominator standard for risk acceptance. It needed clear guidance from the members of the deputies committee if they wanted the group to change its approach; without that, Obama was going to end up with over a hundred detainees in indefinite detention.

Instead, the meeting ended in bureaucratic ambiguity.

Just keep plugging away at it, Donilon said.

14. The Interrogation and Rendition Task Force

The third captives-policy task force Obama had created in his early executive orders was assigned to review interrogation and transfer policy. Of the three, it received the least attention from the public and the press. Its leader was J. Douglas Wilson, a career prosecutor from San Francisco and the coauthor, with David Kris, of the book *National Security Investigations and Prosecutions*. Wilson completed a twenty-three-page final report on August 24, but the administration kept it secret, describing only selected elements of it in a lengthy press release.[43] I later read a copy, and it turns out that the press release omitted or obscured some important points.

Wilson's first major recommendation was to make permanent Obama's decision to limit all interrogators — including the CIA — to using the techniques listed in the army field manual. Even some people who opposed using torture criticized Obama's policy. Their argument was that there were surely other techniques that were lawful but that the manual did not list. Moreover, because the manual was publicly available and had no classified annex, adversaries could study it and know comprehensively what to expect if captured. The press release reported this recommendation, but it did not reveal that Wilson had asked the CIA and law enforcement agencies whether there were specific additional techniques they wanted permission to use and that no one had suggested any, an important fact to know for evaluating that criticism.

Wilson's second major recommendation was to create a High-Value Detainee Interrogation Group to question important terrorism suspects. This so-called HIG would be a mobile team of trained interrogators, subject-matter experts, analysts, behavioral specialists, and linguists drawn from multiple agencies but led by the FBI — not the CIA. It would prioritize collecting intelligence that could be used to prevent terrorist attacks rather than evidence that could be used in court if the two goals conflicted. Notably, the secret report provided no clear answer to what became the crucial question after the Christmas attack — whether and when to read a suspect the Miranda warning.

Wilson's final major recommendation was to keep transferring detainees to countries that might be hostile toward them so long as the receiving nation provides credible diplomatic assurances that it will not abuse them. These included prisoners handed over in covert-intelligence transfers, the CIA's practice of secretly transferring terrorism suspects to the custody of other governments' security services. This practice, sometimes called *extraordinary rendition,* had caused deep controversy during the Bush years because some of the detainees sent to places like Syria ended up getting tortured despite assurances that they would not be. Skeptics suggested that in some cases the whole process was a "wink-wink, nudge-nudge" exercise in outsourcing torture. Law enforcement transfers (deportations and extraditions) and military transfers (including repatriations of Guantánamo detainees) to countries with troubled human rights records could raise similar dilemmas.

Wilson's report detailed at length the arguments for ending the practice of relying on assurances, citing writings of human rights groups. The report made clear that the United States should not use renditions to outsource torture and included multiple pages of ways to improve assurances and monitoring of the humane treatment of transferred detainees. But in the end, the report rejected the idea of creating a blacklist of countries to which no detainee could be transferred, saying the executive branch should retain the power to evaluate whether assurances to treat people humanely were credible on a case-by-case basis. And it recommended keeping the same standard officially used by Bush (and Clinton before him) for deciding whether those assurances were credible: rendition was prohibited only when it was "more likely than not" — a greater than 50 percent chance — that the prisoner would be tortured.

"Particularly (but not exclusively) in the area of counterterrorism, transfers are an important tool for the United States in situations where U.S. prosecution or detention is not available, but where an individual may present a real danger or have significant intelligence value," the report said. It added: "Transfers facilitated by credible assurances may be preferable to the other options available to the United States — releasing potentially dangerous people (or declining to capture them in the first place), returning people to foreign governments without assurances against mistreatment, or trying to detain them indefinitely."

The press release did not say that this had actually been a central question considered by the task force: whether to keep or discard the CIA practice of making covert renditions of detainees to countries where they might be abused. Instead, it buried a passing reference to "transfers pursuant to intelligence authorities," listing it as one of seven types of transfers that existed, along with extraditions and deportations. It then described in detail various lesser recommendations for the United States to better live up to its obligations not to transfer a prisoner to torture, drawing attention away from the core policy choice that had just been made.

As of 2015, there remained little information available about how frequently the United States went on to use CIA-style renditions in the Obama years. As of this writing, there have not been the sort of specific and detailed allegations of outsourced torture that characterized the Bush years. The Obama administration did attract some controversy among lawyers for detainees by repatriating some lower-level Guantánamo prisoners to Algeria over their protestations that they feared abuse there. The United States received assurances from the Algerian government that they would not be abused.

One other piece of Wilson's report is worth noting. It relates to a controversy surrounding the proposition that Obama's order restricting all interrogators to army field manual–approved techniques blocked all forms of cruel treatment. The manual, which was last revised in 2006, contains an addendum — appendix M — that lists special procedures that can be used in the name of keeping a terrorism suspect separated from fellow prisoners. The stated purpose of appendix M is to prevent the captives from talking with one another in a way that might increase their resistance to interrogation, thus prolonging "the shock of capture" and fostering "a feeling of futility" while also ensuring that they could not work out cover stories.

Specifically, appendix M permits using blindfolds or blackout goggles and ear coverings (but not hoods) for "field expedient" separation when new captives must be physically proximate to one another. The manual asserts that these are not to be used to create the psychological distress associated with prolonged sensory deprivation, yet it permits using them for up to twelve hours at an initial interrogation site and allows the time to be extended with high-level permission. Longer-term physical separation — essentially solitary confinement — may last for up to thirty days, a period that can be renewed with permission but "must not preclude the detainee getting four hours of continuous sleep every 24 hours." The accusation is that these rules permit officials to employ both sensory and sleep deprivation, especially if a detainee was limited to four hours of sleep per day over weeks or months.[44] (One of the Bush-era CIA torture techniques was depriving prisoners of sleep for up to one hundred and eighty hours straight, which induced hallucinations and other types of physiological distress.)

In 2014, at a presentation before a United Nations Committee Against Torture, which monitors compliance with a global anti-torture treaty, an Obama administration delegation faced sharp questioning over appendix M. Brigadier General Rich Gross, the legal adviser to the Joint Chiefs, testified that the four-hour rule was "not a daily limit but rather a minimum standard. It is certainly not intended to mandate, for example, 30-days of separation with only 4 hours of sleep per day." He also argued that appendix M had to be interpreted in light of other rules in the manual requiring humane treatment and barring interrogators from using any technique they would not wish to see used on Americans. A member of the committee, Alessio Bruni of Italy, was unconvinced; he noted that the text of the rule allowed officials to keep suspects sleep deprived for long stretches and pointed out that sleep duration had no apparent connection to keeping detainees from communicating. He suggested that appendix M be deleted.[45]

In my many discussions with Obama-era officials, I have found no sign of any cynical conspiracy to leave the door open to torture when limiting interrogators to techniques in the field manual. But, of course, people might have been misleading me or ignorant of what was happening on the ground. In that light, it is interesting to see how Wilson's task force report, with the candor of not having been written for public consumption, handled the issue. It says only "Experienced interrogators believe that separation of a high-value detainee from other detainees is often essential to effective interrogation and that the U.S. government should maintain a detention capability that allows control of the detention environment to support intelligence collection."

The fact that Wilson's report did not spot appendix M as a potential loophole for inhumane interrogations suggests that there was no policymaker-level intention to use it that way, though it is not definitive proof. As of this writing, there is no public evidence that the government has ever invoked the minimum-sleep rule in appendix M during the Obama era. The available information remains incomplete.

15. Investigating Torture

The same day the government announced that Wilson had delivered his report on future interrogations and transfers policy, August 24, Holder announced that he was reopening criminal investigations into the CIA's treatment of prisoners held abroad during the Bush-Cheney administration. He assigned the task to John Durham, a career assistant United States attorney whom Bush's final attorney general, Michael Mukasey, had appointed in 2008 to look into the agency's destruction of videotapes of interrogations. Durham was still working on that investigation, so this amounted to expanding his mandate.

The preliminary review came with an important limit: Holder ruled out, from the start, pressing charges against CIA officials who had tortured within the limits approved as lawful by Bush-era Justice Department memos. Even though the Justice Department later withdrew and repudiated those memos, prosecutors could not charge a government official for taking an action their own department had assured them was legal at the time. The most important of those disputed memos were written by John Yoo, who had worked in the Office of Legal Counsel in the aftermath of 9/11. He was now back at his tenured position at the University of California, Berkeley, law school.

Holder said he had read new information that warranted reexamining cases that the department had closed without charges under the previous administration. The new information included a report from the CIA inspector general showing that interrogators had tortured detainees in ways that went beyond what Yoo had approved. (Examples included revving a power drill next to a prisoner's head — a form of mock execution — and waterboarding with greater frequency and ferocity than authorized.) He also cited a July 29, 2009, report by the Justice Department's Office of Professional Responsibility, the internal-ethics watchdog, looking into the conduct of Yoo and his supervisor, Jay Bybee, whom Bush had made a federal appeals court judge.

The ethics office report's contents were not yet public and its findings would not be official under Justice Department procedures unless a senior career official, David Margolis, decided to sign off on it. But the ethics office investigators, it would later emerge, had concluded Yoo and Bybee each committed professional misconduct by failing to provide "thorough, candid, and objective" analysis about what laws prohibiting torture really meant. It recommended referring them to their bar associations for sanction and reopening reviews of criminal investigations into detainees who had died in CIA custody.[46]

Although the Office of Professional Responsibility report was still at a preliminary stage, Holder had taken its advice about reopening investigations. His decision faced sharp blowback. Republicans accused the Obama administration of criminalizing policy disagreements and warned that it would make the CIA risk-averse, increasing the possibility of a terrorist attack. They were particularly critical of the fact that Holder had not personally read memos written by the career prosecutors during the Bush years explaining why they had closed various investigations without charges.

Holder's decision also ricocheted into the Senate Intelligence Committee's oversight investigation. Committee staff had only begun looking through millions of CIA documents on June 22, following lengthy negotiations about how they were to access them in RDINet, the special CIA computer network. Dan Jones and Alissa Starzak led the congressional study team, which spent the next six years working on the project; Starzak left after 2011 to work for the Pentagon general counsel's office.[47] It also included Evan Gottesman and Chad Tanner. They worked under the oversight of the committee staff director, David Grannis, and its general counsel, Michael Davidson, who retired midway through the project.

Current and former CIA officials now facing criminal jeopardy declined to be interviewed separately by these Senate staffers. Durham had sent a letter to the newly confirmed top CIA lawyer, Stephen Preston, advising that the agency should not force employees to talk to the oversight investigators. The reason was that the Supreme Court had ruled that when government officials were compelled to testify about a matter as a condition of employment, the actions they talk about can become immunized from prosecution.[48] In other words, government officials had a right to be free from self-incrimination too.

The committee reached out to the Justice Department and asked to coordinate witness interviews with Durham, but the prosecutor refused to meet with them, an Intelligence Committee staffer told me.

Because many important witnesses were unavailable, the Intelligence Committee decided that its investigation would rely on documents alone. Arguing that the report would never be definitive or fair if the Senate investigators could not interview the current and former CIA officials on whose work they were passing judgment, the Republican vice chair of the panel, Kit Bond, withdrew his support for the probe.

Holder's decision to expand the criminal investigation affected the Senate investigation in a second way. The CIA gave Durham's investigators access to the CIA files about the defunct program on the RDINet computer system in the same Northern Virginia building where the Senate staffers were reading them. In late February or early March 2010, Preston, the CIA lawyer, told the agency team charged with transferring files into the network to stop creating weekly case reports summarizing and assessing the most damaging parts of each batch — the documents that would later become known as the Panetta Review.

Durham had found out about the assessments and personally came to CIA headquarters to tell Preston to stop the agency from formulating after-the-fact judgments about what the now-historical documents showed. The problem, an official explained to me, was that it could complicate any later prosecution by the Justice Department if another part of the executive branch had produced an independent assessment of the actions of the agency personnel that made different judgments than the prosecutors had reached. Rather than restricting the weekly case reports to recounting facts only, Preston shut them down entirely. From that point on, the reports that the CIA team had already produced, marked *draft* and *deliberative work product,* essentially sat on a shelf on the agency side of the network.

Durham's investigators had unrestricted access to the documents, an official told me, but the Senate staffers, because they were from a different branch of government, were not supposed to be able to access those that were arguably subject to privilege. The CIA thought it had configured the computer system so that the weekly case reports would not be visible to the Senate staffers. But a technician made a mistake, one that would come to light only years later.

16. Papering Over the Yemeni Problem

After Tom Donilon told Matt Olsen to just keep plugging away at the hard problem of whether to release the Yemeni foot soldiers from Guantánamo, Olsen decided to try to get his question elevated to the principals committee. He went to Holder and his deputy, David Ogden. They agreed to back him, and on September 24, they distributed Olsen's memo, written for the deputies committee, to cabinet-level colleagues, along with a cover letter summarizing its arguments and recommending adopting the rules Olsen had asked for.

The principals committee, officials said, ended up giving Olsen one out of two: the task force was instructed to take into account, when deciding which detainees should be listed as transferrable, whether the evidence against them was so thin that they were likely to win a habeas case.[49] But the principals committee still provided no clear guidance on the other one: whether the task force should accept more risk when deciding whether to repatriate lower-level Yemenis.

Indeed, the Yemeni problem seemed intractable. While the task force agreed to recommend the transfer of a couple of dozen, a couple dozen others who struck them as slightly more risky remained a source of disagreement. As long as even one of the six agencies voted no, the detainee remained off the transfer list.

One day that fall, Olsen and Alan Liotta, the director for the Office of Detainee Affairs at the Pentagon, were standing outside the Saudi embassy. They had just met with some Saudi diplomats about a trip to examine the Saudi rehabilitation program. Liotta had an idea for making the problem go away: They could invent a new category for that second group of Yemenis called *conditional* transfers — they were recommended for release when security conditions in Yemen improved.

What this solution to the problem of the hard-to-categorize Yemenis meant was ambiguous. Those who thought the foot soldiers should be released interpreted it to mean they were approved for transfer. Those who thought they should not be released interpreted it to mean they were not approved for transfer, since Yemen continued to be a mess. In practice, as long as the policy remained that Yemenis would be only repatriated, not resettled, it just meant that they were standing in line behind the easier-to-release group — a line that was barely moving anyway.

17. The Outer Bounds of Detention Power

The efforts to decide the fate of every detainee — each of whom had his own life story and unique circumstances — were like pixels. Pulling back to the big picture, the Obama legal team thought of itself as showing that the United States could wage a war against al-Qaeda within legal limits. It did not accept the civil libertarian position that only law enforcement rules could apply to the threat of international terrorism, but neither did it act like Bush and Cheney in the immediate aftermath of 9/11 and suggest that the United States could wage a global war on terror unfettered by legal constraints. But it was one thing to proclaim in the abstract that they were restoring the rule of law. It was another thing entirely for the government to be prevented from doing something it wanted to do in some concrete and particular circumstance because the law barred it.

In the late summer of 2009, Koh and Johnson debated how to interpret international law and the limits of Obama's power. It was the first of many debates between the two top lawyers. This first flare-up centered on an Algerian detainee at Guantánamo who had been arrested in Bosnia. His name was Belkacem Bensayah. Intelligence analysts believed he had served as a kind of travel agent for Islamists who wanted to go to Afghanistan before 9/11, but they considered him a mere *supporter* of al-Qaeda, not *part of it;* he did not take orders from al-Qaeda and he had not sworn an oath of loyalty to Osama bin Laden.

During the Bush-Cheney administration, a judge upheld Bensayah's detention on the basis of the "direct support" he had provided to al-Qaeda. In September 2009, the case was due to be reviewed by a federal appeals court. The Obama legal team had to decide whether it agreed that he was detainable. Although its March 13 Standard said those who provided certain *substantial support* to al-Qaeda could be held in law-of-war detention, Bensayah raised a novel twist: he had been arrested half a world removed from the Afghan war theater.

On July 28, Lederman asked Koh and Johnson to submit views on the scope of Obama's power to detain people who provided substantial support to al-Qaeda or the Taliban but were not part of it. They produced rival memos that have never been made public.

Johnson sent a ten-page memo to Lederman on August 25. It argued that people who breach their duty of neutrality or become cobelligerents by providing substantial support to an enemy armed force are detainable under the law of war. The memo was sparse on legal analysis and consisted mainly of a list of twenty-one historical examples of persons who, the memo asserted, would have been subject to law-of-war detention as supporters, such as American trainers of South Vietnamese forces before the United States entered the war there, had the North Vietnamese captured the trainers.

Three days later, Koh sent a twenty-one-page memo addressed to both Barron and Lederman. The State memo was much denser, with detailed discussion of the Geneva Conventions. Its bottom line was that *some* civilian supporters of the enemy could be detained, but not *all* of them. Supporters who accompanied enemy forces in the field near the front lines, like mechanics, or who presented imperative security threats, might be detained for a period, but civilians who provided support "far from any battlefield…cannot be lawfully detained in accordance with the laws of war," it said. To Koh, distance made a legal difference.

In September, as the appeals court arguments in the Bensayah case neared, Barron invited Johnson and Koh to debate the question face-to-face in the Office of Legal Counsel conference room at the Justice Department. Lawyers from across the executive branch came to watch, lining the walls. Barron sat at the head of the table as the two reprised their arguments.

Afterward, the weekend before the arguments, Barron circulated a forty-two-page, unsigned, "non-final memo." It, too, has never been disclosed.

Barron essentially sided with Koh, writing that courts would likely view with "great skepticism" Johnson's argument that Congress had intended to provide the president "with such wide ranging powers," which, he said, "lack foundation in contemporary law-of-war principles or even, as best we can tell, in consistent historical or contemporary practice in conflicts bearing any resemblance to the current one."

But in a twist, the Obama team, despite having decided that the government's theory about why the man was detainable was probably wrong, did not let him go.

Instead, the Obama administration changed its theory about who Bensayah was, transforming him from a hard case to an easy case. The Justice Department told the court that it now believed that the nature of his assistance to al-Qaeda made him "functionally" a part of al-Qaeda, not a mere supporter after all, and so Obama could detain him on those grounds.

Poof. Just like that, the problem of whether someone like Bensayah could be detained went away. After countless hours of high-level officials wrestling with the hard legal issues raised by the case, the lawyers just shoehorned the facts into a different box so that the outcome was unchanged: Bensayah was detainable.

The episode raised a question about the difference between the Bush and Obama approach to executive-branch lawyering. If the end result was often the same — the president can do something specific he wants to do — does it make a difference if his lawyers got there by tossing off a five-page memo or by agonizing through a hundred-page memo? What is the difference between stretching and creatively interpreting statutes, treaties, and facts — like magically reformulating who Bensayah was — and just saying, *The rules weren't written for this situation and so don't apply, and the commander in chief gets to do whatever he wants*?

Over time, as the legal-policy problems got harder, critics as varied as civil libertarians on the left and former Bush lawyers on the right would increasingly identify this pattern. When I learned about and initially wrote of the Bensayah fight, a few months later, I spoke to John Bellinger, who had been the top lawyer at the National Security Council in Bush's first term and at the State Department in his second term, about Obama's approach to law-of-war detention. "I think the change in tone has been important and has helped internationally," he told me. "But the change in law has been largely cosmetic. And of course there has been no change in outcome."

Bellinger was one of several veterans of the Bush legal team who, with varying levels of sympathy and scorn, tended to highlight continuities in the Obama team's policy outcomes and downplay their changes.

Still, the Obama team made one notable change in this case. That same month — September 2009 — a federal district court judge, Gladys Kessler, asked the Justice Department to file a brief explaining its view of whether evidence obtained by torture should be admissible in habeas litigation. After an interagency scramble, the Justice Department told Kessler that, consistent with Obama's anti-torture policy and the administration's understanding of its obligations under the Convention Against Torture, "the government does not and will not rely upon statements it concludes were procured through torture in the Guantánamo habeas litigation."[50] Later, as things got harder, this promise would come under strain.* But in September 2009, dovetailing with its announced policy, the government withdrew a piece of evidence against Bensayah that the Bush administration had relied on at the federal district court level. The nature of it was redacted in later court records, but there was reason to believe it was a statement by Abu Zubaydah, one of the detainees the CIA had waterboarded, alleging that he had had phone calls with Bensayah in 2004 about passports.[51]

In July 2010, the court of appeals would rule that the evidence before the court, "viewed in isolation or together, is insufficiently corroborative" of the accusation that Bensayah was part of al-Qaeda.[52] The public version of the ruling, which was heavily censored, left it ambiguous whether the outcome changed because of the new theory or because of the removal of the torture-tainted evidence. It sent Bensayah's case back down to the federal district court for a do-over based on the new theory and a do-over submission of evidence.

18. Was Bush's Treatment of Padilla Clearly Illegal?

In the fall of 2009, to their exquisite discomfort, members of Obama's legal team found themselves in court defending John Yoo, the lawyer

---

* See chapter 7, section 10.

who embodied everything that they despised about the Bush-Cheney legal team. The question was how far to go.

The predicament arose because Jose Padilla, the former American citizen enemy combatant arrested in Chicago and interrogated in the Charleston naval brig for years, was suing Yoo. Padilla alleged that Yoo, in his Office of Legal Counsel memos about the scope of Bush's counterterrorism powers, had concocted false interpretations of the law, which in turn led the government to violate Padilla's constitutional rights. He cited his initial twenty-two months of incommunicado detention, during which he was not permitted to speak to a lawyer and claimed that he was subjected to extreme isolation, sensory deprivation, and other enhanced-interrogation techniques. It was a symbolic lawsuit; Padilla sought damages of just one dollar from Yoo, plus a declaratory judgment from the court that Yoo's theories were wrong and that the government's treatment of Padilla had been unconstitutional. Because Yoo was back at Berkeley as a law professor, Padilla sued him in the federal district court in San Francisco. The case was now pending before the appeals court based in that city, which is called the Ninth Circuit.

Normally, people cannot sue the government or individual officials for their official actions because of the doctrine of *sovereign immunity,* which comes from the ancient idea that you can't sue the king: the courts are not supposed to be used to harass or intimidate the people in power who are trying to run the country. Over time, Congress and the courts have punched holes in that shield protecting officials from liability for certain types of wrongdoing. But only some wrongs meet the criteria for a judicial remedy, and even if they do, if the defendant can show that it wasn't *clearly* established at the time that what he did was illegal, he remains protected by *qualified immunity.* Before Padilla could get his day in court, then, he had to establish that he had a right to be there.

Because he was being sued for his actions as a government official, Yoo was entitled to representation by the Justice Department. But after the Obama administration took over, he had opted for a private attorney, Miguel Estrada, a prominent conservative. Estrada told the court that it should dismiss the lawsuit. He made a technical argument: courts cannot hear lawsuits over official actions related to national security, because the concern over being sued would make government officials too risk-averse when acting to protect the country from foreign threats. But Estrada also made substantive arguments, including that Yoo was immune from the lawsuit because his legal analysis about Bush's power to handle terrorism detainees harshly might have been correct.

"Whether or not Padilla's treatment would have amounted to a constitutional violation in the criminal context, it is not clearly established even today — let alone from 2001 through 2003 — that harsh interrogation techniques are unconstitutional when they are applied to enemy combatants for the purpose of averting a terrorist attack," even in the case of a citizen, Estrada wrote.[53]

For institutional reasons, career officials at the Justice Department wanted the government to weigh in on their former colleague's behalf. Civil-division litigators proposed echoing both arguments Estrada was making. But to the Obama political appointees, Yoo was a legal pariah; they believed his writings about executive power were clearly false, and his memos had terribly tarnished the Justice Department. They did not want to make the argument that maybe it was not so clear that Yoo's legal theories were wrong.

Still, now they were in power, and they might get sued someday too.

The solicitor general, Elena Kagan, convened an internal debate both inside the Justice Department and among the interagency group. Kagan, according to a participant, said that since the Justice Department was not representing Yoo, they could leave Estrada to make the most aggressive argument — that maybe Yoo was right — and just put forward the technical argument that Padilla had no remedy regardless of whether Yoo had violated clearly established law.

But Johnson got Kagan to agree that this legal-policy decision applied only to this case. There was another, similar lawsuit pending in federal district court in South Carolina, where the brig in which the military had imprisoned Padilla was located. In that case, Padilla and his mother had filed a lawsuit against a large group of high-level Pentagon officials from the Bush era — including Donald Rumsfeld, the former defense secretary, and Jim Haynes, Johnson's predecessor as Defense Department general counsel — in their personal capacities, meaning over actions they had personally taken. Padilla was also suing the current defense secretary, Bob Gates, in his official capacity, meaning because he was the current occupant of that position, Padilla wanted an injunction against being returned to military detention if he ever got out of federal prison. The Pentagon, as an institution, had a far greater interest in that case, and Johnson wanted to keep open the option of making the more muscular set of arguments Estrada had used. Kagan agreed to keep an open mind.

On December 3, the Justice Department filed a brief asking the court to dismiss the case against Yoo on minimal, technical grounds: federal law created no right for Padilla to sue a government official in his personal capacity over wartime decisions, it argued, and it stopped there.[54]

But in July 2011, when Padilla's South Carolina lawsuit came before the appeals court, Kagan was on the Supreme Court. Ed Kneedler, a longtime career deputy solicitor general, handled the decision about what the Justice Department should say in that second case rather than a political appointee who was part of the Obama team. The reason was that almost everyone else was recused. For example, the newly confirmed solicitor general, Don Verrilli, had helped a group of retired generals file a friend-of-the-court brief seeking a court hearing for Padilla back in 2004, so he couldn't work on the issue.

The Obama administration had to file two briefs. One directly defended the current defense secretary. The other was a friend-of-the-court brief on behalf of Rumsfeld and other former officials. (The Bush-era officials also had private attorneys, Richard Klingler, who had been the National Security Council legal adviser in the second Bush-Cheney term, and David Rivkin, who had been a White House lawyer in the Bush-Quayle administration.) The question again was whether the Obama administration would say only that Padilla had no standing to file the lawsuit or if it would add that the former officials were protected by qualified immunity because it was not clearly established that treating him that way had been legal. Two officials familiar with the internal deliberations said that both draft briefs Kneedler intended to file argued, among other things, that it was not clearly established that a president could *not* lawfully place a citizen who was arrested on American soil and deemed to be a terrorist in military detention.

It was one thing to say that the Bush-era officials had reason to think that what they were doing to Padilla was lawful. They had made those decisions a decade earlier, before several important developments in the law that had clarified the right of terrorism detainees to be treated humanely. But it was another thing to suggest, as a means of blocking the request for an injunction, that the Obama administration, even now, thought a reasonable argument could be made that presidents had the power to treat a U.S. citizen arrested on American soil the way Bush had treated Padilla. When Avril Haines, who succeeded DeRosa as the top National Security Council lawyer, found out, she intervened. Under pressure, Kneedler removed the more sweeping argument from the second brief, the one defending the current defense secretary against the injunction request. When the Justice Department filed the final draft, it made no suggestion that the Obama administration was keeping the door open to holding citizens as enemy combatants.[55]

One way of looking at this was that it was a political appointee overruling a career official's decision. Another is that it was a narrowly averted ideological gaffe on the part of the administration. Had that argument stayed in the second brief, it might have been another standout moment in the pantheon of ways in which Obama could be accused of making a Bush-like claim, embarrassing the administration. Few would have understood or cared that Kneedler was a career official, not a political appointee; it would inevitably have been attributed to Obama.

In the end, making the argument proved to be unnecessary anyway. Both appeals courts found that the technical argument was sufficient grounds to dismiss Padilla's lawsuits.

A coda: Back in December 2009, the Obama legal team had reassured the court in its Ninth Circuit filing that the administration's support for dismissing Padilla's lawsuit against Yoo did not mean government lawyers could make false interpretations of the law with impunity. The Justice Department's brief stressed that *other* sanctions against such misconduct were available. It pointed to the Justice Department Office of Professional Responsibility's power to recommend bar discipline or even prosecution for Justice Department lawyers who abused their positions, and it noted that the ethics office had investigated Yoo for a not-yet-released report, suggesting that something big was coming.

But just a month later, the top career official in the Justice Department, David Margolis, overruled the ethics office's recommendation that Yoo and Bybee be referred to their bar associations for misconduct.[56] Margolis wrote that while the Bush lawyers' legal reasoning about torture had been flawed and showed "poor judgment," in his view it was not "knowingly or recklessly false or issued in bad faith." Margolis would also warn against losing sight of the grave sense of crisis that had pervaded the halls of government in the immediate aftermath of 9/11. Under Justice Department rules, he had final say.

19. The KSM Trial Decision

On November 13, 2009, Holder announced that KSM and the other 9/11 defendants would be tried in a regular civilian court in Manhattan.[57] At the same time, he approved letting the military prosecute five other detainees before a tribunal; the headline defendant for the military commissions system would be Abd al-Nashiri, the *Cole* bomber.

At a Senate Judiciary Committee hearing the next week, Holder was pressed to say what would happen if the 9/11 defendants were acquitted on a technicality; would they be freed? The real-world answer was the same regardless of whether prosecutors charged them in a civilian court or a tribunal: the United States government would keep them imprisoned under the laws of war. Critics who used that awkward fact to argue that any trial would be a pointless farce were wrong; a trial, in whatever venue, did serve a purpose — it gave officials the authority to put convicted prisoners to death. But Holder did not explain that. Instead, he gave a clumsy answer that fueled the sense that the trial would be for show only because the result was preordained.

"Failure is not an option," Holder said. "These are cases that have to be won. I don't expect that we will have a contrary result."[58]

Holder's decisions about where to try the two cases were both denounced and hailed on ideological grounds.

But he insisted then and afterward that his decision to hold the 9/11 trial in civilian court had been based on the specific evidence and his prosecutorial judgment that a successful outcome within the four corners of the legal case — convictions that would withstand appeal — was most likely in the civilian system. In explaining why it was appropriate to put the *Cole* case before a commission, Holder said there were "a variety of factors that went into it" but emphasized only one: it had been an attack on a military warship.

In fact, concerns about the evidence against al-Nashiri had been the overriding factor. Al-Nashiri, unlike KSM, maintained his innocence, and most of the evidence against him was circumstantial — for example, paperwork showing that he had rented the boat later used by suicide attackers to float their bomb up to the *Cole*. The most damning evidence against him was what other detainees had told interrogators about al-Nashiri; a former driver to Osama bin Laden, for example, told FBI agent Ali Soufan that he had heard al-Nashiri brag about his role in the attack.

That driver, Salim Hamdan, was now free in Yemen and unavailable to testify. But under military commission rules, the FBI agent could be called to the stand to tell the jury what the driver had recounted to him. This kind of testimony is called *hearsay*, or accounts of what people said outside of the courtroom, and in civilian trials it generally is not used as evidence because the Sixth Amendment gives defendants the right to confront their accusers in court. The military commission rules, however, permit it to be used if the judge deems it reliable.

Because the new tribunal system was legally untested, nobody could say for sure whether the Supreme Court would ultimately uphold a guilty verdict and death sentence against al-Nashiri in a tribunal, or if the court would instead overturn such a trial result on the ground that the looser rules of evidence made the system unconstitutional. But without that extra evidence, prosecutors feared that there might not be enough to bring any case against al-Nashiri. The choice, then, was whether to give him a trial at all, or hold him forever without charges.

Holder had decided to take the risk of using the tribunals system in the al-Nashiri case. But he saw a tribunal as unnecessary in the KSM case because the evidence there was cleaner. That evidence, it would turn out, included hundreds of hours of secretly taped conversations between KSM and the other accused 9/11 conspirators captured by hidden microphones in the prison yard of Guantánamo's Camp 7, where the former high-value CIA detainees were housed. What they said to one another about their roles in the attacks when they thought no one was listening would likely be admissible as voluntary confessions.[59]

At the White House, Emanuel, seeing the KSM trial issue as a political loser, overruled a plan for Holder to run an op-ed in the *New York Times* and appear on major Sunday talk shows defending his decisions, limiting him to an appearance on PBS's *NewsHour*.[60] But it was not clear how persuasive an unleashed Holder could have been. He did not want to provide public details of the evidence; the existence of KSM's taped conversations was classified, and it went against his prosecutor's instincts to give a road map to defense lawyers by advertising the centrality and vulnerability of the hearsay evidence against al-Nashiri and the untested tribunal rules. At his press conference announcing the decision, Holder asked for people to trust him.

"I have access to information that has not been publicly released that gives me great confidence that we will be successful in the prosecution of these cases in federal court," Holder said, adding: "To the extent that there are political consequences, well, you know, I'll just have to take my lumps, to the extent that those are sent my way. But I think if people will, in a neutral and detached way, look at the decision that I have made today understand the reasons why I made those decisions, and try to do something that's rare in Washington, leave the politics out of it and focus on what's in the best interest of this country, I think the criticism will be relatively muted. Having said that, I'm sure we'll hear a lot of criticism."[61]

The plan was to weather that criticism and just let the process work. In New York, a grand jury soon returned a sealed, eighty-page indictment against KSM.[62] But the administration did not immediately give notice to Congress after Holder's decision and move the 9/11 defendants to New York. This delay would prove to be a repeat of Obama's tactical mistake, back in January, of announcing that he was closing the Guantánamo prison but not immediately moving all the detainees out of it, creating time for political winds to shift.

20. The Calm Before

On November 18, Obama admitted publicly in television interviews what had become obvious: he would miss his self-imposed one-year deadline to shutter Guantánamo. Still, he expressed optimism that his administration would get the job done in the next year.[63] That same month, the White House settled on bringing the remaining detainees to a nearly empty maximum-security state prison in Thomson, a small town about a hundred and fifty miles west of Chicago in Obama's adopted home state of Illinois.[64] The Bureau of Prisons wanted to buy the facility anyway to ease federal overcrowding. In one of his last acts before leaving government, Phil Carter, the Pentagon detainee-policy official, visited the prison and concluded that the military could use a wing.

Olsen completed the Guantánamo detainee-review report and prepared to throw a party for his task force, with his own money, in a large Justice Department room generally used for press conferences; Holder and Brennan would attend. Though completed earlier, their report was formally dated January 22, 2010 — the anniversary of Obama's executive orders. It recommended holding four dozen men in continued law-of-war detention, prosecuting three dozen, and transferring the rest. The idea was to set up a final push to close the prison by giving the report a major rollout with Congress and in the media on January 22, explaining its careful and unanimous racking and stacking of the detainees. Meanwhile, the administration revived a Bush-era experiment of repatriating small batches of lower-level Yemenis. It had sent one man back in September, and when nothing went wrong, it repatriated six more on December 19, 2009. It seemed possible that the Yemeni problem could slowly but steadily melt away.

This was the atmosphere as Obama delivered his Nobel Peace Prize acceptance speech, defending war as sometimes "not only necessary but morally justified" in the face of threats to innocent life that could not be defeated through negotiations and nonviolent means, but stressing the need to fight such wars while "binding ourselves to certain rules of conduct."[65]

Obama had barred torture. The military was no longer holding any Americans as enemy combatants. The Guantánamo prison, he thought, would soon close. Although the military would continue to imprison some legacy detainees held without trial, their numbers would not grow. Holder's KSM trial decision was restoring the traditional justice system to primacy. While military commissions remained an option, Congress had reformed them, and they would be used rarely. If his campaign ideals about terrorism captives had run into pragmatic and political turbulence when faced with the realities of governing, the president still seemed basically on track to achieve what he had set out to do.

Obama left for Hawaii, and his legal team scattered. They intended to finish the job after Christmas.

5

Stellarwind
(Surveillance 1928–2009)

1. The Briefing

In June 2013, when a cascade of leaked top secret documents showed the world that Barack Obama had entrenched the post-9/11 surveillance state bequeathed to him by George W. Bush, several of Obama's advisers thought back to an afternoon some four and a half years earlier, shortly after their administration took office.[1] An important meeting with Obama was scheduled to begin in the Situation Room at half past noon on Friday, February 6, 2009. Officials who had been asked to participate gathered around the conference table waiting to brief the new president. They were there to tell him about secret surveillance programs, including the fact that the NSA was collecting Americans' domestic phone records in bulk. Obama was late.

Mary DeRosa, the top lawyer for the National Security Council, had organized the meeting. She and her deputy, Caroline Krass, were two of a small number of the new Obama legal team who already knew about the NSA programs that Bush had put in place after 9/11. DeRosa had been briefed about them in her previous role as the top intelligence lawyer on the Democratic staff of the Senate Judiciary Committee during the debate over the FISA Amendments Act. Krass had previously been a career lawyer in the Office of Legal Counsel, where she had worked on surveillance issues between 2004 and 2007. Now, DeRosa believed that it was urgent that the new president and the rest of his national security legal team understand what he had just inherited.

The timing was fraught. Two days earlier, *Politico* had published an interview with Dick Cheney. He warned that there was a "high probability" that terrorists would attempt a catastrophic attack on the United States in the coming years and said that he feared Obama's changes to the detention and interrogation policy the Bush-Cheney administration had left behind would make it more likely that such an attack would succeed.[2] Later that afternoon, a little before four o'clock, Obama was scheduled to meet with roughly forty family members of victims killed by al-Qaeda in the *Cole* bombing and on 9/11. It was sure to be an emotional meeting; many were upset that Obama had stopped the military commissions proceedings against Guantánamo detainees accused of aiding the two attacks.*

When Obama reached the Situation Room, his jaws were working a piece of nicotine gum. He went around the table shaking hands with everyone who had been waiting for him. Many were holdovers from the Bush years, such as the directors of the National Security Agency and the Federal Bureau of Investigation, Keith Alexander and Robert Mueller, and the agencies' top lawyers, Vito Potenza and Valerie Caproni. Obama sat at the head of the table, the new attorney general, Eric Holder, on his right, and the new White House counsel, Greg Craig, on his left.

Holder began the meeting, saying he was just coming up to speed on the programs; the Senate had unanimously confirmed him at the start of that week. But Benjamin Powell, the holdover general counsel for the Office of the Director of National Intelligence, did most of the talking. Alexander and Matt Olsen, a career Justice Department intelligence official who was then briefly serving as the acting head of its National Security Division, occasionally jumped in to expand on an explanation about a legal or technological point. Passing around handouts labeled *Top Secret* with markings for signals intelligence, Powell described NSA

---

* See chapter 4, section 5.

surveillance and data-collection activities Bush had instituted after 9/11, code-named Stellarwind. The program began in October 2001, bypassing a statute that required the government to get court orders when wiretapping on American soil. Bush's lawyers had said his power as commander in chief trumped the congressional law. But it had evolved over time, and each of its three components was now rooted in a congressional statute and had court oversight.

Obama already knew about the warrantless surveillance program, whose existence was public: the NSA had wiretapped the content of Americans' international phone calls without the warrants required by the Foreign Intelligence Surveillance Act, or FISA. Now, he learned about two additional activities that the Bush-Cheney administration had never declassified. The NSA had also been systematically collecting Americans' domestic *metadata* — both phone and e-mail records showing who contacted whom. Each day, in response to secret court orders, major phone companies were turning over fresh batches of their customers' calling records, and devices implanted on Internet backbone routers were harvesting header information from e-mails as they flowed past. The agency used the data for *contact-chaining*, or analyzing social links between people in search of hidden associates of known terrorism suspects.

This was something quite different than the warrantless-wiretapping program. Warrantless wiretapping involved surveillance that *targeted* specific individuals who might have connections to terrorism. The still-secret programs Obama learned about now, by contrast, involved *dragnet* collection of everybody's data — the communications logs of hundreds of millions of Americans who were suspected of no wrongdoing. True, the two bulk records programs did not involve listening to private conversations. But an observer can potentially infer intimate details about people's lives — their extramarital affairs, political and religious affiliations, contacts with abortion clinics or doctors specializing in AIDS or cancer treatment, and more — from these records.

Powell emphasized that the programs were rooted in an interpretation of a statute that judges on the Foreign Intelligence Surveillance

Court, or FISA Court, had approved. The congressional intelligence oversight committees knew about them too, so all three branches were on board, he said. Moreover, the FISA Court had imposed strict back-end rules limiting access to the data to mitigate the front-end privacy invasion; analysts could not root around, willy-nilly, in the records or use them for routine criminal investigations. They could query the storehouse only if they decided that the phone number or e-mail address they were starting with met a standard of reasonable, articulable suspicion of a connection to terrorism. They could scrutinize other people's records no further than three links from the suspect. And the data had to be destroyed after five years.

This was a glowing description of a rules-based program. However, just days before Obama's inauguration, the Justice Department had learned that the NSA was systematically violating these rules. The agency was also using the data as an alert system, telling analysts whenever someone using a phone number they were interested in placed or received a call. The alert numbers did not meet the very limited standard the court order imposed for dipping into the databases.[3] Olsen had told Judge Reggie Walton of the FISA Court about the discovery, and in a classified ruling on January 28, Walton said that he was "exceptionally concerned about what appears to be a flagrant violation" of the court's orders, one that was "directly contrary to the sworn attestations of several Executive Branch officials" about how the data was used.[4] Walton had demanded to know by February 17 why he should not refer those officials, including senior NSA executives, for criminal charges and shut the bulk phone records collection down.

In the White House briefing, Powell now told Obama that the NSA had not been strictly obeying the FISA Court's rules, which had angered a FISA Court judge.

This was a pivotal moment. The new president could have responded to the judge's concerns by shuttering the government's dragnet collection of Americans' data the instant he learned about it.

The degree to which Obama understood that the security state was implicitly asking him to decide whether to keep or jettison the program is unclear. Powell and the other briefers never explicitly teed up the question as a choice for Obama to make. In the same breath that they disclosed the problem, they explained that they were already fixing it. They stressed that there was no evidence of deliberate abuse; it was just a compliance problem stemming from the technical difficulty of retrofitting a preexisting program to judicial orders superimposing rules on it. And Alexander and other officials at the meeting emphasized that the program was a critical tool for protecting against terrorist attacks, one that might have prevented 9/11 had it been in place earlier — a claim that would face scrutiny after the program came to light in 2013.

Obama pointed to Holder on his right and Craig on his left.

I'm comfortable with what you're telling me, but I want my lawyers to take a look, he said.

The Obama advisers who were familiar with the dragnet because they worked on surveillance issues in the Bush years were not alarmed by the programs. They viewed them as useful in guarding against terrorism and, in their current forms, rooted in statutory authorization and overseen by judges. The newly informed advisers, Craig and Holder, were already busy with other, public controversies that put them at odds with the national security bureaucracy, including battles over what to do about Guantánamo and the legacy of the CIA's torture program. Moreover, Craig was a former public defender and Holder was a former prosecutor, so both were well aware that in 1979, the Supreme Court had ruled that Fourth Amendment privacy rights do not cover logs of phone calls.[5] While that case involved phone records of one criminal suspect — not everyone in the country — the legal reasoning behind the precedent did not turn on the volume of the calling data in question. Craig told me that he recalled thinking, after the meeting, that the constitutional issues "had been settled by the Supreme Court years ago" and that "there had been progress made in the introduction of court supervision," which he felt to be of "singular importance." To Craig, the issue was how to get the phone records program to work within the court's rules, not whether to shut the program down.

"It appeared to be a problem of compliance, not a problem of philosophy or principles," he said, adding: "It did not appear to me to be a rogue program. It was something for DOJ to take care of."

On February 17, Olsen and Alexander filed court papers urging Walton not to shut the program down.[6] The NSA was terminating the alert-list feature, they said, and launching an end-to-end review of both bulk records programs to find and fix any other problems.

Soon after, Holder reassigned Olsen to lead the review of Guantánamo detainees and named Todd Hinnen, a former chief counsel to Senator Joe Biden who had just become the new administration's first politically appointed deputy at the National Security Division, as its new acting head. Hinnen moved into an office behind door 7339 on the seventh floor of the Justice Department, the entrance to a secured warren where officials worked with highly classified information. His office had windows facing the department's interior courtyard. He had decorated the room only with a few photographs of his newborn daughter.

Throughout February and March, knocks on Hinnen's door brought fresh news of problems uncovered by the review. The e-mail records program turned out to have the same alert-list problem as the phone records program. The NSA was sharing raw data, which had not yet had privacy protections to mask innocent Americans' information applied, more widely than permitted, both inside the agency and with outsiders like the FBI, the CIA, and the National Counterterrorism Center.[7] Judge Walton observed that the privacy rules the court imposed for handling the data had "been so frequently and systemically violated that it can fairly be said" that the safeguards, a "critical element" for obtaining the FISA Court's legal blessing for the program in the first place, had "never functioned effectively."[8]

But the problems trickled into view over time, and the administration dealt with each in turn. It never revisited Obama's initial decision to keep and fix it.

"It's very hard to walk away from what has been determined to be a lawful intelligence tool that the intelligence community says is crucial to national security," Hinnen told me. "At the end of the day, the job was not to decide what the intelligence community needed. Our job was to help them bring the tool they said they needed up to conform with the rule of law."

2. The Snowden Revelations

The secret would hold for three more years. During that time, a few Democratic lawmakers who knew the secret began raising cryptic alarms that something was amiss with how the government was interpreting the Patriot Act, but no one could figure out what they were talking about. Then, on the evening of June 5, 2013, Glenn Greenwald, then best known as a civil liberties blogger, published a leaked FISA Court order on the website of the *Guardian*. The order required a Verizon subsidiary to hand over to the NSA, on an ongoing basis and for ninety days, "all call detail records or 'telephony metadata'" for calls with one or both ends in the United States, "including local telephone calls."[9] There had earlier been press reports that the NSA, as part of the post-9/11 Bush programs, had engaged in bulk collection of phone or e-mail records. But the claims had never been confirmed. Seeing the top secret FISA Court order made it real.

At a congressional hearing the next month, the chairman of the House Judiciary Committee, Representative Bob Goodlatte, Republican from Virginia, told Bob Litt, now the top lawyer for the Office of the Director of National Intelligence, that he was surprised that the secret had been kept for so long.

"Did you think a program of this magnitude — gathering information involving a large number of people involved with telephone companies could be indefinitely kept secret from the American people?" Goodlatte asked.

"Well," Litt replied, "we tried."[10]

By then Greenwald and several other journalists, including the documentary filmmaker Laura Poitras and Barton Gellman of the *Washington Post*, had begun publishing one NSA secret after another.

Edward J. Snowden, an intelligence contractor, came forward in Hong Kong and identified himself as having been the one who leaked the archives of classified documents. He then tried to travel to South America via Russia, only to have the United States government revoke his passport, stranding him in Moscow. Over the course of 2013, the journalists who had received Snowden's documents, eventually working with colleagues, relentlessly marched through a list of NSA programs and capabilities.

More revelations came from investigative articles by journalists who, even though they generally did not have access to the unpublished Snowden documents, were able to ask the right questions in the midst of a spike in internal government chatter about surveillance. In addition to these uncontrolled and unauthorized disclosures, the government declassified huge amounts of information about the limits on NSA programs, including internal NSA directives and an entire body of FISA Court precedents. The Obama administration did this in part because it was seeking to explain and defend the oversight and rules around the operational capabilities Snowden had exposed. It also did this in part because outsiders were pushing it to be more open. These pressures included Freedom of Information Act lawsuits. Privacy groups filed some of these cases, and I also filed several lawsuits with the *Times* lawyer David McCraw, resulting in the disclosure of thousands of pages of documents.

The first two secrets from Snowden's troves that the journalists decided to divulge involved electronic-spying activities on domestic soil: the bulk phone records program and the existence of Prism, an FBI-NSA system for collecting foreigners' e-mails from web-based providers like Yahoo, Microsoft, and Google under the FISA Amendments Act. Most of the disclosures that followed revealed astonishing surveillance capabilities and hacking activities overseas, where domestic statutes largely did not apply, as well as efforts to weaken encryption and implant back doors in network equipment sold around the world. One document, the so-called black budget, showed that in 2013, United States taxpayers had spent $10.8 billion on NSA surveillance and cyber-activities, up 53 percent since 2004. A program that included the NSA as well as the surveillance and code-breaking parts of the military services had employed some thirty-five thousand federal officials.[11] It became clear that twenty-first-century technology coupled with a virtually unlimited budget in the post-9/11 era were helping to grow the American government's global surveillance arm into a leviathan. It was also clear that the surveillance story, even more than other areas of national security legal policy, was really one single narrative that spanned the Bush-Cheney and Obama administrations. And it had significant roots in hidden events that took place long before 9/11.

In the chapter that follows and continuing in chapter 11, I piece together fragments of recently revealed information (and fill in some remaining gaps in the mosaic with my own new reporting) to form the first coherent public history of American surveillance policy in the contemporary era. To really understand the decisions that faced Obama, it is necessary first to know how the technology developed and how surveillance powers accumulated — largely in secret — for decades leading up to his administration.

3. The Road to FISA

Over the previous three decades, consumer electronics have undergone astonishing advances, from the first primitive home computers to Internet-enabled smartphones. During that period, the public sometimes caught half-submerged glimpses suggesting that the government's electronic-spying capabilities were becoming more powerful, too. These glimpses provided fodder for speculation ranging from educated guesses to wild conspiracy theories, but there was a deficit of hard facts. Now, all this newly available information has made it possible for the first time to understand the story of how surveillance technology — and attempts to impose or remove legal controls on it — developed behind closed doors over the past two generations.

Long-distance communications by wire arrived in the nineteenth

century, and the government quickly discovered that it could eavesdrop on telegraph and telephone signals by tapping copper transmis-
sion lines. But for generations, Americans struggled with the implications
this new technology had for the right to privacy in a free society. The
Supreme Court initially decided that Fourth Amendment privacy
rights did not protect people's conversations when they were intercepted on a phone line away from their homes or offices, then reversed
itself four decades later. Similarly, Congress initially banned criminal
investigators from using wiretapping, then reversed itself and established procedure for the police and the FBI to get wiretap warrants
from a judge.[12] The questions raised by wiretapping were hard enough
in the area of criminal law but became even more complex in matters of
intelligence. Presidents have long claimed inherent power to wiretap
for national security purposes, and they have repeatedly pressed against
apparent legal limits on that power.

Those unresolved questions came to a head in 1975, when Congress's
Church Committee uncovered decades of domestic-surveillance abuses
under presidents of both parties. The National Security Agency, a military spy outfit that had grown out of World War II code breakers, for
decades had worked with Western Union to collect a copy of every telegram entering or leaving the United States. Its computers used a watch
list with the names of hundreds of Americans to pull out their tele-
grams for analysts to scrutinize. The FBI, too, working with the telephone monopoly known as AT&T or Ma Bell, had eavesdropped on
domestic political opponents of those in power, including lawmakers,
journalists, labor union leaders, antiwar activists, and civil rights advocates. The claimed justification for these practices was national security: the government was looking for signs of Soviet-controlled
Communist subversive influences. But people were particularly outraged to learn that the FBI had spied on the Reverend Martin Luther
King Jr. and attempted to use embarrassing information about his personal life to blackmail or discredit him.

In response to these revelations, Congress, working with the Ford
and Carter administrations, developed a law to regulate electronic

surveillance for national security purposes: the Foreign Intelligence Surveillance Act of 1978. FISA required the government to obtain a warrant from a special new court in order to tap a wire on domestic soil, with the narrow exception of private circuits used exclusively by foreign embassies to communicate with their home governments. The FBI would need to persuade this new FISA Court that the person it was targeting was an agent of a foreign power. These rules were the "exclusive means" by which the American government could lawfully carry out surveillance covered by FISA.

Behind the scenes, the NSA and the FBI launched a new program in 1978 to handle their engineers' shared work with communications companies in carrying out FISA orders to conduct national-security surveillance. This program was code-named Blarney.

Basically, the techniques FISA now regulated encompassed routine, FBI-style wiretaps of people on American soil. But matters became far more complicated when it came to the more sophisticated, powerful, and generally secret capabilities of the NSA and Americans' international communications — those with one end on domestic soil and one end abroad. Even in that analog era, the agency was conducting some vacuum-cleaner collections of communications in bulk around the world. While FISA barred the NSA from such dragnet collection on domestic wires, it left almost untouched the two favorite methods used by the NSA in that era to eavesdrop on Americans' international communications — intercepting communications-satellite signals and tapping undersea cables from the international seabed.[13]

These other activities, which FISA did not regulate, were subject instead to rules imposed by the president. Ford issued the first such executive order, Carter replaced it, and then Reagan replaced Carter's with yet another one, called Executive Order 12333. Subsequent presidents chose to modify 12333 rather than replace it, so that remains the name of the executive branch's internal rules for intelligence activities.[14]

But technology was changing fast. Very quickly this arrangement began to erode, setting the stage for what happened after 9/11.

4. Transit Authority

In 1984, federal antitrust regulators broke up the Ma Bell telephone monopoly. Its long-lines division, which operated long distance and international phone calls, became AT&T Communications. It eventually had to compete with other network operators, like MCI and UUnet. But AT&T remained a dominant player in running equipment that made the communications network function. Among other things, it leased space on its lines to other phone companies to resell to their customers, who likely did not realize they were still using AT&T lines. In 1985, the NSA launched a corporate partnership program with the new AT&T, code-named Fairview.[15]

Meanwhile, in the mid-1980s, fiber-optic lines — bundles of super-thin glass tubes through which information is carried in pulses of light — emerged as a new method to transmit information over long distances, displacing copper coaxial lines and communications satellites.

The first transatlantic fiber-optic cable became operational in late 1988 and the first transpacific one in 1989.[16] Both were joint projects of international consortiums. AT&T was the American partner and operated the cable landing stations on American soil.

The arrival of the new technology presented an opportunity and a challenge for the NSA. For technical reasons, it is harder to tap fiber-optic cables from the middle, deep under the waves, than it is to tap coaxial cables that way. To intercept messages from a fiber-optic line, it was easier to collect them at one end or the other — where the cable head emerged from the ocean and plugged into a network hub. But the same collection from a wire that was unregulated if performed on the international seabed seemed to be covered by FISA's warrant rule if performed on American soil. Moreover, there was no need for a company to know about any clandestine operation to send a submarine to attach equipment to a cable in the middle of the ocean floor. But a company needed to know and cooperate about equipment installed in its buildings.

In 1987, the Reagan administration secretly began drafting a bill to change FISA "to meet a need created by technological advances," according to a 1990 Justice Department memo.[17] However, the Bush-Quayle administration decided to shelve it. Justice Department and NSA officials feared that Congress might add new restrictions to FISA if lawmakers opened up the statute for reforms. The officials preferred no public debate about changing technology and surveillance capabilities—and about what wiretapping laws, intentionally written to be hard for ordinary people and adversaries alike to understand, really permitted.

"It should also be noted the proposed amendment to FISA to resolve the NSA problem…is certain to be written in such enigmatic terms that only those who have been briefed in executive session will understand them," wrote Mary Lawton, then the top Justice Department intelligence official, in the 1990 memo. "This is bound to create speculation in the media about what is really intended and probably deepen suspicion that something sinister is going on. This will be hard to counter in public."

Even without changing the statute, however, the executive branch's legal team came up with a partial work-around. It permitted the NSA to intercept, on U.S. soil and without going through FISA's procedures for court wiretap orders, communications that both originated and terminated overseas—for example, if someone in Iran called someone in France and the call transited across the American network. Such foreign-to-foreign communications, they said, counted as purely foreign for legal purposes no matter where the government intercepted them. Thus, even when collected on domestic soil, they were regulated only by 12333 rules, not FISA rules. The name for this secret new power to employ a form of warrantless surveillance on domestic soil was *transit authority.*

Transit authority was mentioned in several internal NSA documents published in the first two years following the Snowden leaks. But it has been poorly understood. I have learned additional details that have never been reported about what it is, where it came from, and what its significance is.

A government official familiar with this period told me that the Reagan-era executive-branch legal team decided that it was lawful to ignore FISA for surveillance of foreign-to-foreign communications as they crossed U.S. soil. They concluded that a close parsing of the artfully worded FISA text showed that Congress had placed no statutory restrictions on the president's ability to spy on purely foreign communications. Moreover, the Constitution's Fourth Amendment did not cover foreigners who were located abroad. In the absence of any legal restrictions, they considered the president to have inherent authority to collect such signals intelligence. Still, they knew what they were doing was edgy. They asked the White House for a memo signed by Reagan and addressed to the attorney general and the secretary of defense. In this memo, Reagan stated that he understood and agreed that the NSA did not need FISA warrants to collect transiting foreign-to-foreign communications on domestic soil, meaning only 12333 rules applied.

Intelligence officials asked each subsequent president to re-issue a version of this memo, keeping the authority current as technical details continued to evolve. Obama would sign his version reconfirming the transit program in January 2012,[18] apparently because a network company wanted a fresher reassurance before it would agree to do something additional under the program; the details of this, and why it was not until the end of Obama's first term that he signed it, remain unclear.

Back in the spring of 1988, after receiving Reagan's memo, Deputy Secretary of Defense William Taft and Attorney General Edwin Meese signed a new "Classified Annex to Department of Defense Procedures Under Executive Order 12333."[19] The annex formally established transit authority. The government did not disclose this change to the public.

The invention of transit authority led to the modern relationships of cooperation between the NSA and American telecommunications companies. Participating firms identified network switches that were relaying foreign-to-foreign communications — just phone calls at first, but later Internet traffic — and installed surveillance equipment on them for the NSA. This took place in a near vacuum of law; it appeared that no statute *prevented* a company from doing this, but it appeared that none empowered the government to *compel* a company to do this, either. If FISA did not apply to foreign-to-foreign messages, then the FISA Court had no jurisdiction to issue orders compelling firms to provide them. Instead, companies cooperated voluntarily, responding to appeals to patriotism, the prospect of regulatory troubles and difficulty in securing government contracts if they made the wrong enemies, payment for their trouble, and promises to keep it all secret. This created a different kind of relationship between the government and those firms captured years later by a phrase in an internal NSA guide leaked by Snowden. When visiting AT&T facilities, it said, NSA personnel should be polite. It noted, "This is a partnership, not a contractual relationship."[20]

The executive branch gave them classified letters assuring them that it was legal, which they filed away.[21] Still, the NSA lawyers, according to several people familiar with the surveillance law and policy from this era, were cautious. Some fiber-optic switches commingled both purely foreign messages and some international messages that terminated in the United States. Those were initially off-limits because FISA makes it a felony punishable by five years of imprisonment if a government official wiretaps a private message to or from an American on domestic soil without a warrant.[22]

Over time, however, technology and the rules governing it continued to develop. The NSA and private-sector corporations developed a series of boxes that could sit on a switch and filter traffic crossing it, identifying those that were purely foreign and routing a copy of only those to the NSA's processing system. This innovation helped increase the amount of transiting communications the agency was able to collect while further deepening the cooperative relationship between the network companies and the agency.[23] Still, for various technical reasons, that solution did not work for all intermingled streams. One example is easy to understand. In the late 1990s, free web-based e-mail services

like Yahoo Mail became popular with users around the world, including terrorists. When users abroad logged in and sent e-mails to other
foreigners abroad, their messages often flowed to and from Yahoo servers on American soil. A transit authority filtering system looking for
foreign-to-foreign messages can easily spot a phone call between a person in Tehran and a person in Paris. But if the same Iranian used Yahoo
to send an e-mail to the same Frenchman, the system would be confounded. Crossing a network switch, it looked like two one-end-
domestic messages — one from Tehran to California when the Iranian
sent it, and another from California to Paris when the Frenchman
retrieved it. That made it off limits.

In short, transit authority gave the NSA easy access to huge amounts
of foreign traffic. But from the agency's perspective there was even more
that was tantalizingly just out of reach.

5. The Pre-Millennium Threat

There was another problem: volume. As the 1990s Internet revolution
unfolded, the quantity of communications data flowing around the
global fiber-optic network became massive. Because fiber-optic data
flows at the speed of light, the distance between points does not matter.
Data gets routed where the network pipe is the least congested, even if it
has to travel much farther to reach its destination. The United States,
which invented the Internet, had a huge head start in laying down fiber
cables. Its pipe was so large that it became the central hub of the global
network. (By 2002, less than 1 percent of worldwide Internet band-
width was between two regions that did not include the United States,
according to a leaked NSA document.[24])

As ever more people communicated online, the NSA could go fishing through ever larger portions of the world's messages — including in
its own backyard. But its systems were gagging. It needed to modernize
in order to take advantage of this abundance of riches. The agency
began developing experimental new systems for processing intercepted

communications and data in bulk. One of the most advanced projects was the brainchild of a team of NSA cryptographers and computer scientists, led by William Binney and Ed Loomis. They developed an experimental cluster of systems code-named Thinthread. Other NSA programs relied on collecting as much raw signal data as possible and sending it to the agency's headquarters, where it was later processed in search of interesting communications. In other words, Fort Meade got the entire haystack and only then went looking through it for needles. As Binney and others explained it to me, the conceptual innovation of Thinthread was to do more of the processing at the collection point so that it would send less worthless clutter back to Fort Meade. The Thinthread system decided whose content was likely to be worth collecting in part by automatically analyzing bulk metadata — graphing people's social relationships, financial transactions, and other life activities to identify new potential targets based on their emerging links to known targets. It was a system to be used abroad on foreigners' data, which FISA did not regulate.

In late 1999, ahead of the millennium celebrations, intelligence arose suggesting that a terrorist attack inside the United States was imminent. The NSA held high-level discussions about a proposal to turn on part of Thinthread — and to permit metadata records logging Americans' international communications to be fed into Thinthread's link-analysis component. The hope was that it might uncover any sleeper cells on domestic soil by finding links to known terrorism suspects abroad. The question was whether doing this was lawful.

Binney believed it would be. He and Loomis had built a privacy-protecting feature that could be used for domestic data. The system would encrypt Americans' communications records, substituting a code for each phone number and e-mail address so that the identities of the people involved would be unknowable to human eyes while still allowing computers to analyze the links for suspicious patterns. Their idea, Binney told me, was that FISA Court judges would accept their algorithm's conclusions that someone was suspicious as probable cause and issue an order permitting the NSA to unmask that particular suspect's identity and associated data for further investigation. Ultimately, he hoped the FISA Court would agree to automate that approval.

Robert Deitz, the NSA general counsel at the time, did not agree that this would be lawful. Deitz told me his office had come across a memo from the operations people describing this proposal, the last line of which was something like *don't tell the lawyers*, and scheduled a meeting with operators who supported using Thinthread. They sat around a conference table in the office of the NSA director at the time, General Mike Hayden. Deitz sat next to Vito Potenza, who was then Deitz's deputy and would later attend Obama's briefing, and Kevin Powers, who was then the senior associate general counsel for the NSA's signal intelligence operations. Across the table were the operators who wanted to deploy Thinthread's data analysis component on Americans' records. Deitz told them that the idea was illegal under both FISA and Executive Order 12333. The problem was that the NSA would need to deliberately collect and retain Americans' data, whether encrypted or not, *before* it could be analyzed. The law banned that initial acquisition and storage, the NSA lawyers concluded, and the proposed encryption feature for masking the stored data would not retroactively make that first step legal.

To make sure the agency lawyers were right, Hayden sent Powers to the Justice Department intelligence oversight office that interacts with the FISA Court, then run by Frances Townsend, who later became the top White House counterterrorism and homeland security adviser to Bush. Her office at the Justice Department agreed that collecting logs of the communications of Americans who had not been individually approved for targeting by the FISA Court was illegal, and that encrypting the data did not solve that underlying problem, according to several officials and a leaked draft NSA inspector general report.[25]

From talking to many people with different vantage points on this fight, I believe that this basic account is not in dispute. What is in dispute is whether the lawyers were *right* that the Thinthread proponents were pushing the NSA to do something before 9/11 that would have violated FISA. These proponents, who are not lawyers, did not agree with the lawyers' analysis; Binney told me that he and the other Thinthread proponents were frustrated that the NSA and Justice Department rejected their idea without even going to the FISA Court to see what a judge thought.[26] This dispute is a notable complexity in the history of this era because several of them later became known as whistleblowers and denounced their former agency for conducting surveillance after 9/11 that violated FISA.

In any case, the NSA did not deploy Thinthread ahead of the millennium celebrations. The intelligence warnings were correct: al-Qaeda was plotting to detonate a bomb at Los Angeles International Airport on New Year's Eve, it turned out. Fortunately, on December 14, when the would-be terrorist tried to cross the Canadian border with a massive bomb hidden in his car, a suspicious Customs agent caught him and thwarted the plot.

Twenty months later, the United States was not so lucky.

6. Stellarwind

After 9/11, there was a tremendous fear that there might be additional al-Qaeda sleeper cells lurking inside the United States and plotting additional attacks. Determined to do whatever could be done to stop them, the Bush-Cheney administration decided to release the NSA from FISA limits. Rather than asking Congress to change the law, however, Bush claimed he had the power to override it in secret.

The changes began in September 2001. On his own authority, Hayden instructed the NSA's overseas-based and satellite-based collection services to focus on links carrying international phone calls and e-mails between the United States and Afghanistan. They vacuumed up every communication in bulk. Such systematic collection of one-end-domestic communications was extremely aggressive. But Deitz opined that it was legal because the NSA was not targeting any specific American and the interception was not taking place on a wire inside the United States, so it fell outside FISA's rules.

"We were looking at every interpretation that we could revisit to see what we could do arguably legally," Deitz told me. *Arguably*, he said, meant there was a legal interpretation that could justify it and was not off the wall, even if it was not the most persuasive theory.

The NSA kicked around two other ideas. One was loosening the restrictions on transit authority, apparently so that Internet communications streams that were *mostly* foreign-to-foreign, but had some one-end-domestic messages mixed in, could still be sucked in under permissive 12333 rules rather than restrictive FISA rules. They also revisited the pre-millennium threat idea of using Thinthread's analysis system on Americans' data. But Deitz said no to both proposals; FISA was not "flexible" enough to permit this, in his view.[27]

Loomis, another Thinthread proponent, later recalled being frustrated that the NSA lawyers still considered their idea illegal.

"It was the NSA lawyers that responded to that suggestion, and they said that 'that's not in conformance with FISA,'" Loomis told an interviewer. "I wasn't going to argue with them at that point. This was three days after 9/11. The whole world is shocked. Here I'm trying to get them to use something, to use a provision that Reagan had put in place [in Executive Order 12333] for extenuating circumstances, and they ignored it."[28]

The problem with this idea is that a president can use an executive order to direct the government to do things in the absence of statutory regulation. But if Congress has enacted a statute that bars the government from doing something, an executive order cannot create an exception for extenuating circumstances. In other words, statutes trump executive orders.

Unless, that is, the statute is deemed to be unconstitutional. Then the statute is not law, just inconsequential words.

Hayden briefed George Tenet, the director of Central Intelligence, about his decision to start collecting U.S.-Afghanistan communications in bulk. Tenet relayed the information to Bush and Cheney in the

Oval Office. Cheney had a question, which Tenet relayed back to Hayden: *Could the NSA be doing anything more?*

Not within the NSA's existing legal authorities, Hayden replied.

A little later, Tenet called him back.

What could you do if you had additional authorities?

Hayden came to Cheney's office and told him how the agency could step up its hunt for terrorists if FISA were no obstacle. The NSA already had equipment in telecom hubs that functioned as chokepoints connecting the American network with the rest of the world. But because of FISA, they were only collecting transiting foreign-to-foreign messages. But if the NSA could go fishing for e-mails in data streams that had one end on domestic soil, the agency would be more likely to pick up a targeted terrorist's communications, such as foreign-to-foreign e-mails traveling to and from webmail servers on American soil. Moreover, they could pick up contacts between overseas suspects and anyone on American soil, which could be especially important in finding a hidden terrorist cell before it struck. In addition, the NSA could gather bulk metadata records about Americans' phone and e-mail records and use a Thinthread-style link analysis system to hunt for indirect links to suspects that might find hidden cells.

This proposal raised two questions. First, was this a good idea, in terms of the trade-offs between individual privacy and collective security? Second, if it was a good idea, what should the government do about the fact that FISA made it illegal?

With Ground Zero still smoldering, the administration hardly considered civil liberties. More interestingly, at that moment, Congress was preparing to pass, by overwhelming margins, the USA PATRIOT Act. The bill contained a grab bag of new and expanded law enforcement and surveillance powers the Justice Department had long coveted, and it made several changes to FISA. It would likely have been politically doable, in the post-9/11 atmosphere, to persuade Congress to add a section to the Patriot Act so that federal statutes would authorize, rather than prohibit, what the NSA was proposing to do.

One policy downside of going to Congress was that public discussion would draw attention to American surveillance capabilities. But there was another factor in play. The Bush-Cheney administration, dominated at that moment by Cheney and lawyers who thought like him, did not like the existence of FISA. They saw that law, and other post-Vietnam and post–Church Committee reforms, as unwise encroachments on presidential power. And they subscribed to a theory that the president, as commander in chief, had the constitutional authority to override such laws. They were ideologically opposed to going to Congress to adjust the law, because doing so would implicitly acknowledge a role for Congress in setting the rules.[29]

Now they had an opportunity to put their theory of presidential power into practice.

This was the root cause of years of agony over the surveillance and data-collection program: not going to Congress for help from the start. Everything that followed — years and years of bureaucratic infighting at the Justice Department and the White House, legal contortions by the FISA Court, roiling debates in Congress, and political controversies across two administrations — was about saving the program from its dubious legality. In the world of national security, once a program is up and running and has been relied upon, politicians, policymakers, government lawyers, and judges inevitably find themselves under tremendous pressure to keep it going. Officials who try to stop such a program put themselves in a difficult position, in terms of career risk and blame avoidance, because even if it is hard to point to any specific attack it thwarted in the past, it might prove crucial in the future: *The blood will be on your hands.* In the years that followed 9/11, executive-branch lawyers and FISA Court judges would repeatedly push the envelope to find ways to permit the various components of the program to continue, taking steps whose legitimacy would face harsh scrutiny once they were exposed.

Cheney's lawyer, David Addington, drafted a presidential authorization that purported to relieve the NSA of the need to obey FISA, even for purely domestic phone calls. Bush signed it on Thursday, October 4,

2001. Daniel Levin, then chief of staff to FBI director Robert Mueller and an aide to Attorney General John Ashcroft, recalled that a copy was "pushed in front of" Ashcroft that same day and he was told to sign it, certifying that it was legal, which he did.[30]

Hayden brought a copy of the order back to Fort Meade and showed it to Deitz, the NSA lawyer. The order contained no legal analysis, Deitz said — just what he called "thou shalts." Deitz said he wanted some time to consider it, went home, and "spent a sleepless night thinking about whether there was a theory by which this was lawful. I developed one, basically drinking my own bathwater — meaning I persuaded myself." On Friday, October 5, Deitz came back to work and told Hayden he thought the order was lawful. But Hayden still balked at one aspect. When Addington pointed out that the way it was written, the NSA could collect purely domestic messages, too, Hayden told Addington that the NSA would not do that. He limited the program to only those with one end abroad.[31]

Over Columbus Day weekend, an inner circle of about twenty veteran NSA officials, including from the Special Source Operations division that managed partnership programs with telecoms, were called at home and told to report for a special briefing on Monday to be conducted by Hayden and Deitz. Tenet steered $25 million in black-budget intelligence funding to the NSA, and the agency ordered fifty industrial servers to store and process the anticipated new data flow. The equipment arrived at Fort Meade with a police escort on October 13, the same day that Hayden sent three phone and network companies letters saying that Bush had authorized a set of collection activities based on his powers under Article II of the Constitution and that Ashcroft concurred that it was lawful.[32]

Levin told Ashcroft it was not fair that he had to bear all the weight of saying the program was legal, and the White House agreed to let another Justice Department official know about it: John Yoo, the Office of Legal Counsel lawyer who believed in sweeping presidential powers. Yoo completed a twenty-one-page memo on November 2 concluding that it was lawful. He asserted that Bush's power as commander in chief trumped FISA, that FISA was not written to cover national security situations anyway, and that the Fourth Amendment did not prohibit warrantless surveillance in a national security situation.[33] Other lawyers later criticized this analysis. Yoo did not mention the key Supreme Court ruling about the limits of presidential power to override statutes in war, a decision made in a Korean War case involving the seizure of steel mills. He also did not mention a provision of FISA that shows that Congress *did* write it to apply to wartime — the statute says the warrant requirement is waived for the first fifteen days of a war. But the conclusion of the highly classified memo was all that mattered. Remarkably, when Deitz asked to read it, Addington would not let him. The Bush-Cheney White House was asking the NSA to violate FISA but would not permit it to read the official legal justification.[34]

That Stellarwind violated FISA is well understood. An additional wrinkle is that it separately violated Executive Order 12333 and the Defense Department directives and regulations implementing that order. Just as the Bush-Cheney administration did not ask Congress to change FISA, it also did not rescind or modify 12333 and its related directives. The publicly available versions of Yoo's Stellarwind memo remain heavily redacted, but Senator Sheldon Whitehouse, Democrat from Rhode Island and a member of the Senate Intelligence Committee, obtained permission to declassify a conclusion from it on this topic: "An executive order cannot limit a President. There is no constitutional requirement for a President to issue a new executive order whenever he wishes to depart from the terms of a previous executive order. Rather than violate an executive order, the President has instead modified or waived" it.

"Think of it," Whitehouse said. The proposition "that executive compliance with executive orders is optional turns the *Federal Register* into a screen of falsehood, behind which lawless programs can operate in secret, notwithstanding Supreme Court case law since 1871 that a valid executive order has the force and effect of law."[35]

At this moment, the NSA's preexisting technological interfaces with the phone companies and its relationship of voluntary cooperation, forged with the creation of transit authority in the 1980s, became crucial. Three major network companies immediately began providing the agency with access to Americans' international phone calls.[36] Two of them were particularly important because they also offered access to international e-mail content. A later draft NSA IG report leaked by Snowden identified them only as Company A, which started providing e-mail content to the NSA as early as October 2001, and Company B, which started doing so in February 2002. The report identified their market shares, however, which corresponded to A being AT&T and B being MCI, according to Federal Communications Commission records.[37]

Separate from that post-9/11 program, the NSA's technology continued to improve for collecting transiting foreign-to-foreign Internet communications. An internal newsletter from September 2003 touted the rollout of a new system that it portrayed as a " 'live' presence on the global net." AT&T was the first partner to deploy the system, which in its first month provided 400 billion Internet metadata records, as well as the contents of "more than one million emails a day to the keyword selection system" at the NSA's Fort Meade headquarters. Another corporate partnership program, code-named Stormbrew, had not yet turned on that system. (That program appears to have involved both MCI and Verizon, which purchased MCI in 2006, and seems to have been a junior partner. It eventually provided bulk metadata, but only turned on the collection of bulk foreign-to-foreign e-mail content in March 2013.)[38]

By contrast, the Stellarwind program's content component, which sifted through one-end-domestic traffic, was a targeted program, not a bulk collection one. The NSA was collecting the communications of people it already suspected of links to terrorism, not indiscriminately grabbing all messages for keyword searching. From October 2002 until January 2007, the NSA *tasked*, meaning told the system to target some 37,644 phone numbers and e-mail addresses for warrantless content collection as part of Stellarwind. Of those, 8 percent were U.S. soil targets and 92 percent were foreign.[39] Still, it was incompatible with FISA's

requirement that the government obtain a warrant whenever it collected, from a wire and on domestic soil, a private message that had at least one end on domestic soil.

Binney, the NSA technical expert who helped design Thinthread, retired from the NSA in late October 2001 following a bureaucratic dispute over Hayden's decision not to use Thinthread to modernize the NSA's systems.* Binney said that while he was not invited to participate in Stellarwind, he heard enough from colleagues to figure out what was going on. He would later accuse the NSA of using, as part of Stellarwind, the bulk metadata–analysis system he had built for Thinthread —but stripping out the encryption feature he had designed to mask Americans' personal data. I asked Hayden why the NSA had not used any such privacy-protecting feature for its bulk data programs. He said that doing so would have made the programs more cumbersome while providing no legal or operational advantage.

"We had the president's authority to collect, and therefore, it then comes down to, 'Is this the best technical solution to the problem?'" Hayden said.

7. The FISA Court Starts to Evolve

The Bush-Cheney administration did not intend to tell the FISA Court about the fact that the NSA was no longer obeying FISA, and it did not brief James A. Baker, who had succeeded Frances Townsend as the chief intelligence lawyer at the Justice Department, about Stellarwind. (Baker became the FBI general counsel in Obama's second term.) But the FBI was putting information from the warrantless-wiretapping program into affidavits seeking ordinary FISA Court orders—which the government still used when collecting purely domestic messages of suspects on American soil—and Baker eventually figured it out. He insisted that, as an ethical matter, the FISA Court must be told where

---

* See chapter 8, section 1.

the information was coming from. When Baker refused to sign a wiretap application containing such information, Addington wanted Baker fired for insubordination. But eventually, in January 2002, the White House permitted him to tell the presiding judge on the court, Royce Lamberth, about the program. From then on, only Lamberth received applications containing information derived from the program.[40]

Before 9/11, under Lamberth, a Reagan appointee, the FISA Court had issued orders that frustrated the intelligence community by enforcing a strict separation between criminal and intelligence investigations.[41] This rule, known as "the Wall," prevented law enforcement officials managing ordinary criminal cases and intelligence officials involved in national security investigations from working closely together. The purpose was to uphold Americans' Fourth Amendment rights by preventing agents from gaming the system and obtaining intelligence wiretap orders, which have lower standards than criminal wiretap warrants, when the agents' purpose was really to gather evidence to put someone in prison.[42]

But one of the reasons the government had failed to dete_ and disrupt the 9/11 plot was that the CIA had not shared crucial i telligence with the FBI about two al-Qaeda suspects who the CIA kr.ew might have been in the United States. After 9/11, there was a widespread effort to encourage different parts of the government to share what they knew about al-Qaeda. Congress included a provision in the Patriot Act intended to tear down the Wall, and the Justice Department asked Lamberth to dismantle it. He lowered it some but refused to give the executive branch everything it was asking for.[43] But the Bush-Cheney administration appealed Lamberth's ruling to a special FISA Court of Review — the first such appeal since FISA had been enacted in 1978 — and in November 2002, it overturned Lamberth.[44]

Back in May 2002, Lamberth's ruling about the Wall was the end of an era — his seven-year term on the FISA Court was over the next day. Judge Colleen Kollar-Kotelly, a Clinton appointee who also served on the federal district court for the District of Columbia, succeeded Lamberth as the FISA Court presiding judge. The administration briefed

her about Stellarwind. She took over as the only judge who handled applications containing information derived from the warrantless surveillance program.[45]

As Lamberth was preparing to pass that torch, Baker submitted a revolutionary motion to the FISA Court. While the government made public Lamberth's ruling about the Wall, it kept this other litigation classified. The NSA considered it so important that an agency official listed it on a secret timeline of significant developments in the agency's legal rules between 1972 and 2010, making it one of only three FISA Court rulings to make the cut. But its existence would remain hidden from the public until 2014, when Poitras shared an archive of Snowden-leaked documents referring to legal issues with me, and she and I developed a *New York Times* story about them.[46]

The case arose on the classified docket as matter No. 02-431 and was informally called the "Raw Take Motion." It asked the FISA Court to substantially weaken FISA surveillance back-end rules that protected innocent Americans' privacy. These rules, called *minimization,* are a major part of why regular courts have found FISA to be constitutional even though it has lower standards than ordinary wiretaps. Previously, these rules required the FBI to delete irrelevant personal details before sharing information gathered in a FISA wiretap or search more broadly within the government. Such details include the names of, and information about, any innocent Americans who happened to communicate with the target of an investigation about an unrelated matter, meaning that the government invaded their privacy incidentally. The statute requires that nonpublic information about Americans "shall not be disseminated in a manner that identifies any United States person" unless his identity is necessary to understand or assess foreign intelligence.

In his motion to relax this rule, Baker argued that the regulation might lead to clues about al-Qaeda going overlooked. An FBI analyst listening to a wiretap might hear something that was important intelligence but he or she might not recognize it as such and so fail to share it with counterparts at the CIA or NSA who would understand its significance. Citing the 9/11 attacks, he wrote that the FBI should be able to share *everything* it picked up via FISA with those other two agencies.[47]

On July 22, Kollar-Kotelly and her colleagues secretly agreed to let the three agencies share the raw FISA information the FBI was gathering. Over time, the FISA Court would build on this precedent, extending and modifying the Raw Take orders. Toward the end of the Bush-Cheney administration, after Congress made the warrantless surveillance program a part of FISA, the court extended its permission for the agencies to share certain raw information gathered without a warrant, too.[48] And in 2012, it approved a Justice Department request to add a fourth agency to the sharing pool, the National Counterterrorism Center.* None of these relaxations of the rules were disclosed to the public.

8. The Hospital-Room Crisis

In March 2004, Stellarwind brought the Bush-Cheney administration to the brink of an election-year meltdown. The crisis was kept secret at the time, and the full story has not been reported.

The outlines became public later in the Bush years.[49] Turnover catalyzed it. In 2003, a new head of the Justice Department's Office of Legal Counsel, Jack Goldsmith, began raising legal doubts about aspects of Stellarwind. In March 2004, when it came up for a periodic reauthorization, Ashcroft was hospitalized and his new deputy, James Comey, was the acting attorney general. Based on Goldsmith's advice, Comey refused to recertify that Stellarwind was lawful.

Then, on the night of March 10, Bush's White House counsel, Alberto Gonzales, and chief of staff, Andrew Card, visited Ashcroft in his hospital room and asked him to override Comey and reauthorize the program. Ashcroft refused. Bush then reauthorized Stellarwind on his own, and nearly the entire top leadership of the Justice Department,

---

* See chapter 11, section 5.

including Mueller, the FBI director, threatened to resign. Bush backed off and agreed to certain changes that put it on a firmer legal footing, defusing the crisis. When this story came out, it cemented Comey's image as a champion of the rule of law, contributing to Obama's decision in 2013 to appoint him to succeed Mueller as FBI director.

Additional details about the bureaucratic fight dribbled out slowly over time, and the most fulsome account yet was contained in a Justice Department inspector general report I obtained via a Freedom of Information Act lawsuit in 2015. But the Obama administration has continued to censor as classified the substance of the dispute and the changes to the program Bush agreed to.[50] Because of leaks, we nevertheless know that one aspect of the fight concerned the legality of the bulk e-mail records program,[51] which Bush agreed to turn off for several months as part of his concessions.[52] But Goldsmith demanded more than one change before he would say the program was lawful.

What really happened, I was told by officials familiar with the matter, is that there were legal-policy fights over two different things, each of which was fraught in its own way. One was whether the NSA could keep operating the bulk e-mail records component, and the other was whether the NSA could keep using Stellarwind's content component against terrorism suspects who were not linked to al-Qaeda. The original program, as it existed from October 2001 to March 2004, could be used for investigations into *any* international terrorist threat — including ones that had nothing to do with 9/11, such as the Shiite terrorist group Hezbollah or the Iraqi intelligence service.

When he sat down to reanalyze Stellarwind, Goldsmith jettisoned the expansive theory of commander-in-chief powers Yoo had embraced. Instead, Goldsmith sought to root the program in the congressionally enacted Authorization for Use of Military Force against the perpetrators of 9/11, coupled with a less extreme understanding of commander-in-chief powers.

Goldsmith's new legal theory required the NSA to stop using Stellarwind's content component for counterterrorism purposes that had no connection to the 9/11 war. As of this writing, this contraction of the entire program remains largely hidden from the public history of this era.[53] But it was a major source of disagreements with Cheney, Addington, and others in the Bush White House in the hospital-room episode. The contraction had other consequences as well. After Bush accepted the new limitation, it led to the first analysis inside the executive branch of which groups counted as *associated forces* or *cobelligerents* with al-Qaeda, meaning those on the fringes that the NSA could still monitor under Stellarwind. The Obama administration's legal team would look at that question years later through the lens of who the military could lawfully detain and who the military or the CIA could lawfully kill.

After Bush reluctantly agreed to confine the use of Stellarwind to al-Qaeda, Goldsmith was willing to approve the warrantless content component as lawful, notwithstanding the fact that it was still inconsistent with the language of FISA. He invoked the president's wartime authority — an ambiguous combination of the power bestowed by Congress to fight al-Qaeda, and Bush's own constitutional powers as commander in chief to wage *that particular war,* the one Congress had authorized. Since spying on the enemy is a traditional aspect of warfare, he reasoned, Bush's war powers were sufficient to trump FISA's warrant requirement for the purpose of surveillance that targeted al-Qaeda communications. A year and a half later, when the warrantless-wiretapping component of Stellarwind came to light, the Justice Department released an unsigned white paper defending the program on those grounds. Many legal experts in surveillance law and constitutional law asserted that this rationale was still wrong and that the program remained illegal. Nonetheless, the 2006-era program and its legal justifications were significantly less radical than the previous incarnations.

That left the two bulk metadata dragnets. Goldsmith apparently concluded that the bulk phone records component was acceptable because the phone companies were already creating billing records showing whom their customers had called. FISA does not prevent the government from *accepting* business records turned over voluntarily by phone companies. The legal issue was instead focused on the phone companies. Other communications privacy statutes generally bar phone companies from *providing* customer records to the government without legal process, but there are exceptions. For example, companies can voluntarily give the government a customer's phone records in an emergency when someone is at risk of death or serious physical injury.[54] My theory is that the government expansively interpreted the al-Qaeda threat as a continuing emergency, permitting the Justice Department to tell the companies they could lawfully provide the records in bulk, but this is only speculation.

But the bulk e-mail records program was different. Internet data showing who e-mailed whom looks similar to phone records, but the way it gets created is very different. Network companies do not make records of e-mails for billing purposes; after an e-mail is transmitted across an Internet switch, it normally leaves no trace. To systematically create a set of such records, devices had to be installed on network switches to log what was crossing them.[55] The way Congress wrote FISA, this activity counted as the kind of "electronic surveillance" that was covered by the statute and so required individualized court orders even when the NSA did not bring the contents of those e-mails back to Fort Meade.[56]

This raises one last mystery: Why was Goldsmith willing to say that Bush's wartime powers could trump FISA for the content component but not the bulk e-mail records component? The answer, according to people who have read the unredacted version of his memo, was that the content component targeted the communications of specific enemies, while the e-mail records component involved indiscriminate domestic electronic surveillance of Americans. Goldsmith concluded that Bush's wartime powers could be stretched to encompass the former, but the latter went too far. The memo cited a passage from Justice Robert Jackson's concurrence in a famous 1952 Supreme Court case striking down President Harry Truman's order to seize steel mills during the Korean War, a seminal precedent about the scope and limits of executive power in war. Jackson allowed that there were occasions when the president could override a statute limiting his actions in war, but there were other occasions when the president could not. To help decide which was which, Jackson had emphasized a distinction between external actions affecting the conduct of a war abroad, and internal actions affecting Americans on domestic soil.[57]

9. Legalizing Bulk Data Collection

To avert the mass resignations, Bush reluctantly agreed to scale back Stellarwind's content component to al-Qaeda and to shut down the bulk e-mail records collection. But the idea was that Goldsmith would search for a legal way to restart the e-mail records program. He decided that the solution was to ask Kollar-Kotelly, the only FISA Court judge who knew about Stellarwind, to issue an order authorizing the NSA to harvest the data from Internet switches. Such an order would satisfy the FISA statute, so the program could be turned back on again. But it required persuading her to accept a stretched interpretation of the law.

In the spring and early summer of 2004, Justice Department and NSA lawyers came up with a creative legal theory for why FISA gave the court the power to issue such orders.

A provision in FISA says the government may get a court order to install a pen-register/trap-and-trace device, which normally means a device that records metadata about the incoming and outgoing calls of a particular phone line but not the content of those calls. To get such an order, investigators must show the court evidence that the data they are seeking is relevant to a counterterrorism or counterespionage investigation. The Bush legal team urged Kollar-Kotelly to apply the concept of a pen-register device to Internet technology and reimagine the word *relevant* so that instead of limiting what the government could collect, it would permit the NSA to collect records of *all* communications. This could be justified, they said, because the program needed to have the haystack of data about all e-mails in order to identify the needles of those e-mails that might reveal a hidden terrorist.[58] The government's ability to access that database would be limited to certain circumstances designed to ensure that humans would look only at data that was actually relevant to a terrorism investigation. Ashcroft, Comey, Goldsmith, Baker, and Philbin signed the classified application. So did two lower-ranking attorney advisers in the Office of Legal Counsel whose names were redacted when the government released it.[59] One of them was likely Caroline Krass, the future Obama legal team member. She worked in the Office of Legal Counsel at the time, and Comey told her about the secret of Stellarwind shortly after the hospital-room crisis so she could assist with surveillance issues.

Kollar-Kotelly secretly accepted the stretched relevance theory, issuing the order on July 14, 2004.[60] The Stellarwind bulk e-mail records component was reborn and henceforth was referred to in top secret documents as the FISA PR/TT program, for FISA's "pen register/trap and trace" provision, which supposedly authorized the court to issue such orders. The Obama administration later declassified her judicial opinion after the Snowden leaks. In it, she noted that in deciding to endorse the executive branch's idea, she relied on information from a briefing provided by several top Bush-era officials, as well as three officials who would also serve in government under Obama: Mueller, Baker, and John Brennan, who was then the director of a precursor to the National Counterterrorism Center.[61] Brennan's part of the briefing focused on the "current and near-term threats" posed by al-Qaeda that the program could help prevent. She offered no further details, but with its application the Justice Department had submitted to Kollar-Kotelly a heavily redacted memo[62] signed by Tenet. It warned that an al-Qaeda sleeper cell was likely planning to use weapons of mass destruction to carry out an attack inside the United States pegged to "US election politics," adding that "especially attractive" targets included the mass-transit systems of Boston and New York, the "host cities for the Democratic and Republican Party conventions."*

---

* There was no terrorist attack on the American election. The Senate Intelligence Committee's torture report, released in December 2014, discussed the primary

As part of the churn of this period, the FBI's new general counsel, Valerie Caproni, conducted a study of a sampling of all the counter-terrorism leads Stellarwind had generated for the bureau to pursue between 2001 and 2004, according to one of the classified inspector general reports that the *Times* and I obtained via our Freedom of Information Act lawsuits. She defined as *useful* those that made a substantive contribution to identifying a terrorist, deporting a suspected terrorist, or identifying a potential confidential informant. Just 1.2 percent of them fit that category. In 2006, she conducted a comprehensive study of all the leads generated from the content basket of Stellarwind between March 2004 and January 2006 and discovered that zero of those had been useful.[63]

Caproni decided to go back and do that second study because of James Risen and Eric Lichtblau, my future colleagues at the *New York Times*. A few months after the hospital crisis, they had learned that the NSA was wiretapping on American soil without warrants in contravention of FISA — the content component of Stellarwind — and by October 2004 they were preparing to publish a story about it. The Bush-Cheney administration persuaded the leaders of the *Times* to quash the story, claiming that the program was saving lives and assuring them the Justice Department had no doubt that it was legal. (The hospital-room crisis was still secret.) In 2005, Risen decided to publish the information himself in his upcoming book *State of War*. When the *Times* editors found out, to avoid being scooped by their own reporter, they ran a Risen-Lichtblau story about "warrantless wiretapping" in December 2005.[64] The article won a Pulitzer Prize and led to hearings and lawsuits. So that the government could defend itself, Bush declassified the existence of the warrantless-wiretapping component of Stellarwind and rebranded it the "Terrorist Surveillance Program." But his administration made clear there might be other activities that the president had not acknowledged, and he never declassified the bulk phone and

---

source of the intelligence behind the CIA's warnings that there was an al-Qaeda plot to carry out one. It turns out to have been dubious. See chapter 10, section 20.

e-mail records components, even after *USA Today* wrote in May 2006 that the NSA had collected phone records of millions of Americans.[65]

Even before this pivotal moment, the Bush-Cheney legal team had been mulling over ways to bring the other two components of Stellarwind under claimed statutory authority and FISA Court approval. The inspiration was its success in gaining court approval for the bulk e-mail data component and its alarm when it learned that the *Times* knew about the warrantless-wiretapping component. But the effort was not particularly urgent until the *Times* belatedly published its article and sparked lawsuits against the phone companies. As they dealt with that headache, the companies also grew uneasy about the legality of their still-semi-submerged practice of voluntarily handing over their customers' calling records without any legal process. They wanted to be legally compelled to do so, shielding them from potential liability.

The second-term Bush legal team — which included Gonzales, now the attorney general, and Steven Bradbury, the new acting head of the Office of Legal Counsel — decided to see if the FISA Court would agree to issue orders to the phone companies for the bulk phone data program. This time, they invoked a provision of FISA that permitted the FBI to get court orders for business records that were deemed *relevant* to a national security investigation. Congress had added that provision to FISA under section 215 of the Patriot Act. This provision had a similar standard as FISA's pen-register provision. To get a court order compelling a business to turn over relevant data about its customers, the Bush lawyers cited Kollar-Kotelly's secret 2004 opinion as precedent for interpreting "relevant" records as meaning "all" records if the purpose was to analyze possible links to hidden terrorists.

When the government declassified and released this application in 2013, all the names on it except Gonzales's were redacted. The others involved were Bradbury, Baker, and two aides to Bradbury at the Office of Legal Counsel — a top deputy, John Eisenberg, and Krass.

The Bush legal team filed its application regarding the bulk phone records program on May 23, 2006.[66] The next day, the FISA Court judge sitting in rotation that week, Malcolm Howard of the Eastern District

of North Carolina, issued terse orders to the phone companies requiring them to give the NSA all their customers' calling records—
including purely local calls, which had not been part of the original
Stellarwind—on a daily basis.[67] The Stellarwind bulk phone records
program was now reborn as the FISA BR program, for FISA's "business
records" provision.

Howard was a Reagan appointee who had fought in Vietnam, gone
to law school, and then worked as a federal prosecutor and a staff lawyer to President Nixon just before his resignation. He was the last of the
judges selected to serve on the FISA Court by Rehnquist before the
chief justice died in 2005. Strikingly, Howard did not write any opinion
explaining and memorializing his legal reasoning. He just ordered the
phone companies to turn over their records. Howard made his orders
expire in precisely eighty-seven days, on August 18, 2006. As it happened, August 18 fell on a Friday, the last day of a week that Howard
was again scheduled to be the judge on rotational duty. He therefore
ensured that *he*—not any of his ten colleagues on the FISA Court—
would be the judge who reviewed his own handiwork and decided
whether to extend the orders.

On August 18, as expected, the Justice Department formally applied
for an extension. Howard approved the orders that same day.[68] This
time, they would expire on November 15, 2006—a more regular-
looking ninety-day cycle. A different FISA Court judge, Frederick Scullin of the Northern District of New York, was on duty when it came up
for renewal. Faced with an active program that had now been operating
under the FISA Court's authority for half a year, Scullin reapproved the
orders.[69] Scullin, too, produced no opinion endorsing a theory for why
FISA gave him the legal authority to issue such sweeping orders. Nor
would his successors. It was not until August 2013, after the Snowden
leaks led the government to acknowledge the existence of the program—
and cast a harsh public spotlight on the FISA Court's role in facilitating
it—that a judge finally wrote an opinion laying out a legal rationale for
the orders the court had been issuing for the past seven years.[70]

One last point is worth noting. The statutory interpretation behind the two bulk programs after the FISA Court began blessing them may have been a stretch, but rooting the programs in a statute made them more powerful. FISA provided authority for investigating national-security threats in general, not just for fighting wartime enemies. Taking advantage of this broader mandate, at some point the Justice Department gained the FISA Court's approval to use the programs to hunt for operatives of the government of Iran and its associated terrorist groups like Hezbollah, not just for al-Qaeda cells.[71]

10. The Path to Legalizing Warrantless Surveillance

The FISA Court's decision to bring Stellarwind's bulk Internet and phone records components under its authority was another milestone in the court's own evolution. It not only once again secretly decided to re-interpret the law to grant government requests for greater spying powers. It also established broad rules within which an NSA program would operate. Compared to the more limited job of approving individual requests to spy on the communications of a particular suspect, this *programmatic* approval amounted to the court's embracing a policymaking role that was more like an executive supervisor than a judicial decision-maker. Its next step would accelerate this evolution further.

As the reaction to the *New York Times'* warrantless-wiretapping story continued to grow, the Bush-Cheney administration sought to bring the last part of Stellarwind, the content collection component, under the FISA Court's authority, too. At the time, pressures were mounting from all quarters. On August 17, 2006, in a case brought by the American Civil Liberties Union, a federal district court judge in Detroit, Anna Diggs Taylor, ruled that the warrantless-wiretapping program was likely illegal and issued an injunction ordering the government to shut it down.

"It was never the intent of the Framers to give the president such unfettered control, particularly when his actions blatantly disregard the parameters clearly enumerated in the Bill of Rights," she wrote.[72]

An appeals court would later overturn her decision for technical reasons.[73]

But that ruling was not handed down until July 2007, and in the interim, her judgment added urgency to getting the final remaining piece of Stellarwind on a more stable legal basis. There was also a fresh set of eyes on the problem. On September 30, 2006, the Senate confirmed Ken Wainstein, the U.S. attorney for the District of Columbia, as head of a newly created National Security Division inside the Justice Department. When he came to Main Justice, he brought with him Matt Olsen, a national security prosecutor from Wainstein's previous position. Olsen became Baker's successor in dealing with the FISA Court and would go on to be another important lawyer in the Obama legal team.

Soon after they arrived, Vito Potenza, now the NSA's top lawyer, briefed them about the full details of Stellarwind. Wainstein and Olsen also learned that at the Office of Legal Counsel, Bradbury, Eisenberg, and Krass had been kicking around theories for bringing the content component of Stellarwind under FISA Court orders too. Back in May 2006, the Justice Department had taken a draft of a memo to the FISA Court judges during their semiannual meeting, when they were all in Washington at the same time, for feedback. It put forth an unconventional interpretation of FISA that would purportedly permit the court to authorize a program of warrantless surveillance.[74] The judges were thinking about it. The new National Security Division's first task was to finish the job.

Three and a half months later, Gonzales announced in a letter to Congress that, following lengthy negotiations, on January 10, 2007, an unidentified judge on the FISA Court had issued what he portrayed as "innovative" and "complex" orders to bring the so-called Terrorist Surveillance Program under the court's authority.[75] That was the official end of Stellarwind; in internal documents, the content component was now called the Large Content FISA program.

But Gonzales did not publicly explain how FISA could possibly be interpreted as authorizing warrantless wiretapping. Adding to the mystery, later that year, the administration abruptly submitted a bill to Congress that would amend FISA to explicitly permit a warrantless-wiretapping program, suggesting that something had gone wrong with the solution Gonzales had announced with such fanfare. There was vague talk of a disagreement on the FISA Court that had created an intelligence gap. In August 2007, Congress enacted a short-term law, the Protect America Act, to permit warrantless wiretapping if it was aimed at foreigners abroad; the following year Congress enacted a more enduring version, the FISA Amendments Act.

From the outside, what happened in 2007 was inexplicable. How could the FISA Court have blessed a warrantless-wiretapping program? And what caused the Bush-Cheney administration to abruptly seek Congress's help instead after just a few months? Some of the story's pieces shook loose with the Snowden leaks. More came into public view in late 2014 and early 2015 with the release of redacted FISA Court files in response to two Freedom of Information Act lawsuits, one that I filed with the *Times* and one that the Electronic Frontier Foundation filed. But before this book, the full story of the Stellarwind endgame has still not been told.

It began on December 13, 2006. The Justice Department submitted a seventy-six-page motion[76] to the FISA Court. This was no ordinary wiretap application. The government wanted FISA orders permitting the NSA to carry out a warrantless surveillance program. Of course, it had already been doing that for five years, but now it wanted the court to say that it was legal—without any changes to the law by Congress. The idea was to reinterpret a word in FISA—*facility*—that had traditionally been understood to mean a phone number or an e-mail address. For regular FISA orders, after judges agree that a target is probably an agent of a foreign power, they authorize surveillance directed at the specific facilities the target uses to communicate. The executive-branch lawyers argued that *facility* could mean an entire gateway switch or cable head connecting the American communications network to the global network. Among the millions of people using it to communicate, some were probably al-Qaeda members, and the NSA could decide which of the messages flowing across it to keep. Specifically, they could decide whether particular e-mail addresses and phone numbers met a standard of suspicion suggesting they were being used by al-Qaeda. The government would periodically show the court a list of the phone numbers and e-mail addresses it had already placed under surveillance.

Somewhat audaciously, the Justice Department styled this proposal as fitting "comfortably" within the words and legislative intent of FISA. It was true that Congress, back in 1978, had contemplated instances where a switchboard for a corporation or building would have to be targeted, as in cases where there was no way to isolate a particular extension being used by a person of interest. But this was an exponential stretch of that idea.

On January 10, a FISA Court judge issued the order giving the executive branch most of what it wanted.[77] The judge was Malcolm Howard.

On the surface, this was a striking coincidence. There were eleven FISA Court judges, so it would seem that there was only a 9 percent chance that the same judge who had blessed the bulk phone records program happened to be sitting on weekly rotational duty again when the Justice Department presented its request. In fact, this was no coincidence. The Justice Department knew which FISA Court judges would be sitting which week.[78] Officials told me that Bradbury in particular had pushed hard to file the application on a week when Howard was sitting again.[79] This was *forum shopping*—strategically filing a lawsuit in the venue where you think you are more likely to win.

The move provoked an immediate response from the FISA Court; starting in January 2007, Kollar-Kotelly abruptly cut off the Justice Department's access to the advance roster of judges' duty weeks. The executive branch would no longer know ahead of time who would be sitting when, reducing its ability to game the system. But this administrative change, which has never been reported, came too late to prevent the administration from making sure it was Howard who got to decide whether to pronounce the warrantless-wiretapping program legal.

11. A Hidden Fight

Howard's embrace of the Bush-Cheney legal team's reinvention of FISA was deeply controversial among his colleagues on the FISA Court, leading to a hidden debate among the judges. Still, Howard had given the NSA only part of what the administration asked for. He issued an order accepting the Bush legal team's theory for surveillance targeting foreigners' phone numbers and e-mail addresses, including existing suspects and new ones that might arise.[80] But he did not *quite* accept their theory for targeting Americans. He wanted a slightly stricter regime for people on domestic soil. So, on that same day, Howard issued a second order that approved a lengthy list of specific domestic phone numbers and e-mail addresses that the NSA had already been monitoring. The order permitted the agency to keep eavesdropping on them. For new al-Qaeda suspects inside the United States, Howard signed off on a different system. The NSA could still regularly wiretap new people on domestic soil without waiting for advance court approval, he said. But to do it, the agency would use a provision in FISA that Congress reserved for "emergency" situations in which the government could submit a wiretap application after the fact for a retroactive finding that the standards had been met. Whenever there were suspicions that someone on American soil might be linked to al-Qaeda, that now constituted an emergency. Since the exception was now going to be the rule, Howard also approved a "streamlined" set of forms for the government to fill out when seeking retroactive approval.

As with his first order for the bulk phone records program the previous spring, Howard issued these extraordinary secret orders without writing any memorandum opinion analyzing the legal questions, evaluating the government's various arguments, or explaining why he had concluded that FISA could legitimately be interpreted as giving the FISA Court the authority to issue them.

This was the decision that prompted Gonzales's exuberant, but mysterious, announcement. But it provoked a convulsion inside the FISA Court that has never been reported. In addition to blocking Justice

Department access to the advance duty roster for the FISA Court, Kollar-Kotelly summoned all the judges to Washington for a special meeting in the secure-information facility at the Justice Department that served as a surveillance courtroom. The judges, including Howard, discussed whether his ruling was a legitimate interpretation of the law. There was very little support for what Howard had done, although the other judges' opinions differed about how much of what the government was asking for was permissible under other theories.

On March 21, 2007, the Justice Department applied to renew Howard's orders after they expired in April. The judge serving that week was Roger Vinson. He was another conservative, a former navy aviator appointed to the Northern District of Florida by Reagan. Chief Justice Roberts had placed Vinson on the FISA Court in May 2006, just as things were heating up. And in an April 3, 2007, opinion that dovetailed with the skepticism of most of the FISA Court judges, Vinson balked. He rejected the government's — and Howard's — reinvention of the term *facility* and its theory that FISA permitted executive-branch officials, rather than judges, to decide that probable-cause standards had been met. He sharply criticized the idea of routine after-the-fact judicial review of surveillance that had already commenced.

"The legislative history [of FISA] makes clear that the purpose of pre-surveillance judicial review is to protect the Fourth Amendment rights of U.S. persons," Vinson wrote. "Congress intended the pre-surveillance 'judicial warrant procedure,' and particularly the judge's probable cause findings, to provide an 'external check' on executive-branch decisions to conduct surveillance. Contrary to the intent of Congress, the probable cause inquiry proposed by the government *could not possibly* restrain executive-branch decisions to direct surveillance at any particular individual, telephone number or e-mail address" (emphasis in original).[81]

Vinson suggested that the Justice Department ask Howard to extend the expiration date of his orders to May 31 but made clear Howard could not go beyond that. At the Office of Legal Counsel, Bradbury had his staff draft a potential appeal to the FISA Court of Review so he could see what it would look like.[82] But at the National Security Division, Wainstein and Olsen pushed to submit legislation to Congress asking it to amend FISA to settle the problem, arguing that a new statute would be a far more stable and reliable solution. Wainstein prevailed. (At the White House, Gonzales summed up the mood as one of "disappointment" and said that the decision "confirmed our concern about going to" the FISA Court in the first place.[83]) In April, the Bush-Cheney administration submitted a bill to the House and Senate Intelligence Committees, which scheduled hearings. Now, the Justice Department lawyers begged Vinson to permit the warrantless collection to continue just a little bit longer so Congress could have time to act.

On May 31, 2007, in a move that showed how hard it is to be responsible for turning off a counterterrorism program — to accept the risk that if there is an attack, people will say *the blood is on your hands* — Vinson acquiesced. He gave the government what Howard had authorized minus just a bit. Vinson approved continued surveillance targeting a long list of phone numbers and e-mail addresses — both foreign and domestic this time — that were already being monitored. And, importantly, he approved a system whereby the NSA could routinely commence surveillance on new targets without delay and come to the FISA Court for after-the-fact approval — a major reversal from the principle he had voiced just the previous month. The court would make the retroactive finding that the legal standard had been met for every such target. To justify this, Vinson accepted yet another novel interpretation of the Patriot Act.

Eventually, Section 215 of the Patriot Act became notorious — that was the business-records one used for the bulk phone records program. But another provision was Section 206. It added to FISA so-called *roving wiretap* authority, permitting the FBI to swiftly follow a suspect who switches phones in an effort to thwart surveillance, coming back to the court later to tell the court which phone numbers it listened to.

Adopting a stretched interpretation of this provision — one that clearly Congress was not thinking about when it wrote it — Vinson said this roving-wiretap provision could be used systematically with *al-Qaeda* as the target rather than any particular *member* of al-Qaeda, thereby allowing the government to immediately start wiretapping a newly identified "al-Qaeda" phone number or e-mail address without first coming to the court for permission.

Vinson's decision to let the government continue to wiretap people without pre-surveillance judicial review provoked a new round of disagreements among his colleagues at the FISA Court. The judges had reconvened in Washington in May for their semiannual meeting, which is normally a mostly social affair. That spring, it was deadly serious. Many judges disagreed with what Vinson had decided to do — not because they were concerned about any impact on privacy rights, but because they did not think the statute could be legitimately interpreted that way. (This was another instance of focusing on a rule-of-law critique where others might make a civil liberties critique.) But the Justice Department had submitted the application to Vinson, and so he alone controlled it.

This extraordinary internal FISA Court dispute was reflected, but not explained, in a short opinion Vinson secretly issued on August 2, 2007.[84] It clarified what his May order had empowered the NSA to do. Over the summer, the Justice Department had come back before other judges sitting in rotation to seek retroactive approval for the new targets it had already placed under surveillance. Many justices — George Kazen, John Bates, Dee Benson, Nathaniel Gorton, Scullin, and Kollar-Kotelly — had balked. They found a hook to express their dissatisfaction with Vinson's approach: the roving provision says it is for granting permission to wiretap phone numbers and e-mail accounts that a suspect is going to use, but that are "unknown" at the time the government applies for the order. The judges demanded proof that the NSA had not known anything about the new targets' phone numbers or e-mail accounts back when the government had submitted its application to

Vinson invoking the roving-wiretap authority. This required the government to search through its files and attest that it did not previously have any information about those e-mail accounts or phone numbers.

In his August 2 opinion, Vinson insisted that it was acceptable for the NSA to use the roving-wiretap power to start targeting accounts it had already known about earlier, at the time of its application, so long as analysts had not completed the process of "connecting the dots" that al-Qaeda was indeed using them until afterward. He wrote that "it is appropriate to grant the government as much latitude in initiating surveillance as the statute can reasonably be construed to permit."

12. Upstream Internet Surveillance

Years later, several months into the revelations from the Snowden leaks, I asked a former government official whether everything affecting Americans' rights was now out or if there were more shoes left to drop. The person I was talking to made a cryptic comment about how there was something left that supposedly involved a form of *bulk content* collection. By talking to many other people, I eventually pieced together what this person may have been hinting at. It centered on a powerful and previously secret feature of wiretapping Internet switches — one that appears to have been evaluated for the first time in Vinson's April 3, 2007, opinion, although it was then classified.

Wiretapping e-mails is different than wiretapping phone calls. When a phone call is carried over a traditional phone network, all the audio data travels together on a circuit. It is therefore easy for interception equipment on a phone switch to identify calls involving a targeted phone number and duplicate only them, leaving everyone else's private conversations unmolested. But when an e-mail is transmitted over the Internet, it is broken apart like a puzzle. Each piece of the puzzle travels independently to a shared destination, where they converge and are reassembled. For this reason, interception equipment on a switch in the middle cannot grab only a target's e-mail. Instead, the wiretapper has to make a copy of *everything*. The cloned data — copies of all the puzzle pieces of millions of e-mails and other Internet messages — are temporarily stored in a buffer and filtered for *selectors*, identifiers like the e-mail address of a person who has been targeted for surveillance. Whenever the equipment finds a puzzle piece containing a targeted selector, it then sifts through the rest of the heap and finds all the other pieces associated with that message so that it can put the puzzle back together. Only then can the remaining, irrelevant puzzle pieces be deleted.[85]

This so-called *upstream* Internet surveillance has a side consequence of enormous power, one that the government strove to keep secret for years: it ends up collecting *all* e-mails containing whatever selector is used to filter the heap, no matter where in the messages it appears. Most of the time that selector will be in the "To" or "From" line in an e-mail header, because the government is usually looking for messages involving its target's e-mail address. But sometimes that filtering term is instead in the body of a message. If two other people are talking and one mentions a target's e-mail address — *You should send Joe a message at joe@email.com* — the system will grab that message, too.

In other words, under the FISA Amendments Act, American network companies, acting on behalf of the NSA, are systematically scanning and sifting the contents of all international e-mails sent to or from an American. At the end of that process, the companies are handing to the NSA copies of e-mails not only when Americans have been directly in contact with foreign targets, but also when they have merely mentioned those targets to someone else abroad — even though neither party to the communication was previously on the government's radar.[86]

The temporary cloning and sifting of everything that crosses a link, and this resulting ability to collect messages that are merely *about* the target, are features of upstream Internet surveillance that are simply alien to phone technology. It is also a particularly powerful tool for the

NSA. The Justice Department's original application to Howard, which the government later declassified due to overlapping Freedom of Information Act lawsuits by the Electronic Frontier Foundation and myself, made clear that it was a core advantage of Stellarwind.[87]

"Under the proposed method of conducting electronic surveillance, then, NSA will be in a position not only to learn information about the activities of its targets, but also to discover information about new potential targets that it may never have otherwise acquired," a declaration from an agency official explained.[88]

For this reason, applying legal terms and concepts that were developed for circuit-based phone networks to the Internet, which works very differently, raises profound, almost philosophical problems. Bringing upstream surveillance under legal rules like FISA and the Fourth Amendment brings up crucial questions: Did that initial step, in which everyone's message puzzle pieces were temporarily copied and sifted, but not stored permanently, amount to *bulk content surveillance*, a notion that is incompatible with the Fourth Amendment and its bar on unreasonable searches and seizures?

It is not clear whether the FISA Court has ever addressed this question. There is nothing about it in the unredacted portions of any of its rulings made public as of this writing. Privacy activists have separately been trying to get a court in the regular judicial system to address it. To date, the government has successfully killed those lawsuits without any such scrutiny by invoking the state secrets privilege.

There is an important catch. Some privacy advocates have suspected that telecoms were giving the NSA a copy of all the Internet data crossing its switches, and the government was doing the filtering and sorting. The Electronic Frontier Foundation, representing a group of AT&T clients, made that allegation in a court case in 2014. After the Obama administration reiterated the assertion that litigating that type of case would reveal state secrets, a judge largely dismissed the case in February 2015. But the judge said that he had been shown classified information and that the plaintiffs' description of upstream surveillance was inaccurate. He did not elaborate.

Later in 2015, the *Times* and *ProPublica* partnered on a joint story taking a look at AT&T and the NSA's relationship with the telecoms, using more Snowden documents provided by Laura Poitras. The documents showed that contrary to the privacy groups' suspicions, the NSA "typically" did not have "direct access" to the systems of network operators like AT&T and Verizon. Instead, the companies had done the filtering and sorting and provided the messages that the government believed it was permitted to collect.

"Corporate sites are often controlled by the partner, who filters the communications before sending to N.S.A.," one internal NSA presentation said, adding that this system sometimes leads to "delays" when the government sends new tasking instructions.[89]

By distilling the data into different categories, the firms enabled the NSA to bring different legal surveillance powers to bear on them. FISA required a warrant to collect a purely domestic message. When a foreigner abroad messaged an American, the FISA Amendments Act permitted the NSA to target that foreigner without a warrant. And FISA did not apply to foreign-to-foreign transiting communications, permitting the NSA to collect them in bulk without targeting anyone. If the different types of messages were all mixed together when the NSA received the traffic, it would have to use the most restrictive set of rules to avoid violating FISA by collecting a domestic message without a warrant.[90]

There was another question: Did Congress, in enacting FISA, really give the government the authority to collect messages, on American soil and without a warrant, between two people who were not themselves targeted and had previously done nothing to attract suspicion?

When Howard pronounced the upstream warrantless surveillance program to be compliant with FISA, he did not analyze most such questions. But in Vinson's April 2007 ruling, he did take the time to analyze the "about the target" question. He decided that it was acceptable. (Later that year, Kollar-Kotelly revisited the question, asking extensive written questions and holding a secret hearing devoted to the thorny topic. She, too, agreed it was acceptable.[91]) But when the question of enacting a bill to bless a warrantless-wiretapping program came before Congress, most lawmakers would have no idea that this aspect of upstream-style surveillance was part of what they were being asked to authorize.

13. The Protect America and FISA Amendments Acts

Even after the compromises of Vinson's May 31 order, NSA analysts had to spend a lot of time preparing paperwork necessary to show the FISA Court that probable-cause standards had been met. Resource limitations — there were only so many people, with only so many hours in the day, to fill out such paperwork — acted as a constraint on how many new targets the NSA could start wiretapping. The objections by Vinson's colleagues to retroactively approving new surveillance of e-mail addresses and phone numbers that the government had already known about before May caused further problems.

"After the 31st of May we were in extremis because now we have significantly less capability," Mike McConnell, then the director of national intelligence, recalled in an interview later in 2007.[92]

His words are more understandable now than they were at the time. The draft NSA inspector general report said that the number of phone and e-mail accounts the NSA was targeting under the program plunged, from eleven thousand in 2006 to three thousand. A once-classified Justice Department inspector general report, which the government released in response to another Freedom of Information Act lawsuit I filed with the *Times*, said that "the rigorous nature of the FISA Court's probable cause review of new selectors submitted to the various FISA Court judges following Judge Vinson's May 31, 2007, order caused the NSA to place fewer foreign selectors under coverage than it wanted to." That and other factors "combined to accelerate the government's efforts" to seek a legislative fix.[93]

In the spring and summer of 2007, the second-term Bush legal team urged Congress to rapidly approve the FISA reform bill.[94] Adding to the pressure, in July, the intelligence community issued a National Intelligence Estimate concluding that al-Qaeda was regrouping in the tribal regions of Pakistan and regenerating its ability to send suicide bombers onto American soil.[95] The Bush-Cheney administration also briefed lawmakers and key staffers of both parties about the full extent of Stellarwind in an effort to level with them. One of the important legislative staffers who was told these secrets and worked on developing surveillance-reform legislation was hired in April 2007 by Senator Patrick Leahy, Democrat from Vermont, to be the Senate Judiciary Committee's chief counsel for national security. It was Mary DeRosa, who a year earlier had said at the ACLU panel that she might be okay with Bush's warrantless-wiretapping program as long as there were greater checks, oversight, and transparency about it.* DeRosa would later be Obama's first legal adviser to the National Security Council and organized his February 2009 briefing on still-secret surveillance programs.

In August 2007, Congress passed a short-term reform bill, the Protect America Act, which changed the law so that it would permit, rather than forbid, what the government was already doing. It permitted the warrantless-wiretapping program to keep going so long as it only targeted noncitizens abroad. Leahy voted against it, as did all the major Democratic candidates seeking their party's presidential nomination — Barack Obama, Hillary Clinton, and Joe Biden among them.

The Protect America Act was temporary. When Congress replaced it in July 2008 with the FISA Amendments Act, the revised law had the same basic structure but two additional features. The 2008 law blocked lawsuits against companies that assisted the NSA with the Stellarwind program, in a hard-fought win for those companies and the intelligence community that depended on their cooperation. But it also made an important reform that protected privacy: it required the NSA, for the first time, to get an individualized FISA Court order if it wanted to

---

* See chapter 2, section 4.

deliberately target for surveillance an American located abroad. After the FISA Amendments Act, government insiders began to refer to the warrantless content program as "702" surveillance, after the section in the 2008 bill that authorized it.

The Protect America and FISA Amendments acts carved out a hole in FISA. They explicitly permitted the NSA and the FBI to collect the messages of noncitizens abroad, on American soil, and without individual court orders, even when those targets were communicating with Americans. While the domestic debate over this new statutory power for the government has focused on Americans' rights, it is also important to recognize that the NSA used it to gather purely foreign-to-foreign communications, too. It worked in parallel to transit authority: for those streams in which the government persuades itself that there will be no one-end-domestic messages, it uses transit authority, meaning it is permitted to collect content in bulk and do keyword searches to find new targets. For those intermingled streams, where foreigners may be talking mostly to other foreigners but occasionally an American will be the other party, the government uses the FISA Amendments Act, meaning it can only collect the content of specific targets. The bottom line was that to make it easier for the NSA to pick up its foreign targets' messages without getting a warrant on each one, Congress decided to let the government pick up international messages to and from Americans — incidentally, but inevitably — without a warrant, too.

In addition to solving its legal problems, the Protect America and FISA Amendments acts significantly expanded the NSA's power. Stellarwind was initially limited to foreign terrorist threats and then was contracted by Goldsmith to surveillance hunting for al-Qaeda specifically. But the new, congressionally authorized warrantless surveillance program could be used for *any foreign intelligence purpose*, encompassing topics like spying on foreign governments and international organizations, global military matters, trade and the global economy, international drug trafficking and other transnational criminal threats, and anything else that can be put into that extremely broad category. [96]

The enactment of the FISA Amendments Act was a signature lame-duck accomplishment of the Bush-Cheney administration. Many of the same Democrats who had opposed the Protect America Act, including Biden, Clinton, and Leahy, voted against the 2008 law too. But, as noted, there was one surprising flip: voting in favor of the bill was Senator Barack Obama, who had just secured the Democratic presidential nomination.*

14. Prism

There was another way in which the Protect America and FISA Amendments acts made the NSA far more powerful. Its Stellarwind program had been built on the deep and preexisting relationships between the NSA and the phone and network companies, which were willing to cooperate voluntarily with the agency because they had already been doing so for many years under the transit-authority program. After the Protect America Act, the rules changed. The government no longer needed to cajole and persuade companies to allow it to conduct warrantless surveillance on their systems. Instead, it could get sweeping FISA Court orders requiring companies to participate. This opened a new front: Silicon Valley.

It was already routine for the FBI to get court orders requiring new powerhouse tech firms like Google and Yahoo — companies that *used* the Internet to enable people to communicate, but did not *operate* the network itself — to turn over the contents of individual users' e-mail accounts stored on their servers. Usually, those were Americans who were the target of a criminal investigation. Now, the FBI's Engineering Research Facility at Quantico, Virginia, working with the NSA, built a system, code-named Prism, to collect foreigners' e-mails, chats, and log-in information from those firms without individualized orders. Although the NSA analysts decided which foreigners' accounts to

---

* See chapter 2, section 7.

request, the FBI administered the Prism system and interacted with the companies on behalf of the government. The creation of Prism led to an important legal battle with Yahoo that remained largely hidden from the public until years later, when the Obama administration declassified the litigation after the Snowden leaks.

Shortly after the enactment of the Protect America Act, Judge Reggie Walton of the FISA Court ordered Yahoo to begin providing warrantless access to whichever of its users' e-mail accounts that the NSA and the FBI identified as belonging to noncitizen targets located abroad. In late 2007, Yahoo secretly challenged the constitutionality of that order. This became the big test case; while Microsoft, which ran the popular Hotmail service, apparently had already started cooperating, the other major Internet companies watched to see what would happen with Yahoo.

When the litigation documents became public in 2014, they showed how difficult it could be to litigate before the FISA Court. Yahoo's lawyer Marc Zwillinger had not been permitted to see the procedures the NSA intended to employ to decide whether a user account met the standards for being targeted. Nor had he been allowed to read the safeguards for the information of Americans whose private messages were collected incidentally and without a warrant because they were talking to foreign targets. The company had to blindly argue to Walton that maybe those procedures were insufficient.

The Bush-Cheney administration contended that Yahoo had no standing to make those arguments in the first place—only its users could file a lawsuit, with the catch that none of the users whose communications Yahoo was forced to turn over would know about it. Walton rejected that idea and let Yahoo's challenge proceed, but on April 25, 2008, he issued a secret, ninety-eight-page legal opinion upholding his own order to Yahoo.[97]

Yahoo mulled filing an appeal, and it did not immediately begin complying. On May 9, Matt Olsen secretly asked Walton to impose a fine— $250,000 a day, a figure that would double every week—if Yahoo did not immediately begin turning over the e-mails of the NSA's foreign targets.[98]

The exponential math was rough: in fewer than fifteen weeks, the fine would exceed Yahoo's $35 billion market capitalization. On May 12, Yahoo surrendered and began feeding the targeted foreign users' data into Prism. Three months later, the FISA Review Court upheld Walton's finding that the Protect America Act was constitutional.[99] Prism became entrenched as a permanent new relationship between the American government and Internet firms.

The existence of the Prism system was the second major leak from the Snowden archives to be published. The initial reports about it in the *Washington Post* and the *Guardian* were overstated and created confusion. They said nine major Internet companies had given the NSA direct access to their servers of stored customer messages, where the private messages of hundreds of millions of American users resided.[100] If so, it would be a system that was ripe for abuse. But this turned out to be based on an apparent misunderstanding of an ambiguous phrase on a single slide in a leaked NSA presentation about Prism, and it was not corroborated by any subsequently published Snowden-leaked documents.[101] The companies insisted that they had not given the government a back door into their user data, and the Yahoo litigation, when declassified by the government the following year, showed that when the company had started cooperating with FISA Amendments Act orders, it did not involve giving the NSA direct access to its servers. Rather, the government gave Yahoo a list of foreign user accounts it wanted, and the company had worked down the list in order of priority to start providing the messages in them. [102]

But even though the initial accounts of Prism were inaccurate, the real-world Prism system was still an enormously powerful and important development. What was new about Prism was that it allowed the government to obtain *all the stored messages* in a newly targeted user's account right away. By contrast, the upstream system only enables the collection of new messages the target sends or receives after he comes to the NSA's attention, in dribs and drabs. By handing thousands of older messages from a new target to intelligence analysts right away, Prism permitted the government to look backward in time to see what the target had been saying and thinking for years. Prism also gave the government, in one go, the target's entire social network because years of metadata could be instantly scraped and analyzed.

As a result, the volume of intelligence generated via Prism soon grew to be far larger than upstream Internet surveillance. By October 2011, the government was collecting more than two hundred and fifty million Internet communications each year under the FISA Amendments Act, of which 9 percent came from the upstream system and 91 percent from the Prism system.[103] And by April 2013, the leading source of intelligence reports contributed by the NSA to Obama's daily briefing on national security and foreign affairs was material gathered via Prism.[104]

15. Erosion

Toward the end of the Bush-Cheney administration, the Justice Department and the Pentagon rewrote the executive branch's internal rules governing intelligence gathering to which FISA does not apply. It relaxed limits on protections for Americans' private communications and data that was incidentally gathered under Executive Order 12333 — that is, collection from a cable outside the territorial United States, from satellite signals, and from transit authority. One significant change was classified and the other was hidden in plain sight. Both belatedly came to light thanks to the Snowden leaks.

The classified change dropped an internal executive-branch rule against using Americans' metadata — logs of phone calls and e-mails — gathered under 12333 for the purpose of contact-chaining. Previously, when the NSA analyzed links between people using communications records gathered under 12333, it had to stick with foreigners' data; it could not start with an American's account, and if a chain hit an American's account, it had to stop, absent special high-level permission. Bob Gates, the secretary of defense, signed a document dropping this rule on October 19, 2007, and Attorney General Michael Mukasey signed it on January 3, 2008.[105] The public was not told about this; at the time even the technique of contact-chaining was considered classified. Under the new procedures, the NSA began a pilot program to use Americans' data gathered under 12333 for this purpose, and the Obama administration would make it a general practice.*

The hidden-in-plain-sight change laid the groundwork for the NSA to share raw communications intercepted under 12333 rules, allowing other agencies to root through them for their own purposes, just as the FISA Court's Raw Take rules permitted the FBI, CIA, and NSA to make their own copies of wiretapped conversations gathered under FISA rules. Previously, the executive order did not permit the NSA to share "signals intelligence" with other agencies until it had processed the information to apply privacy protections to any Americans' messages that were incidentally swept in, like deleting their names and irrelevant private information. But on July 30, 2008, Bush issued an executive order modifying 12333.[106] The executive order was sold to the press as merely cleaning up 12333 to add references to the newly created position of director of national intelligence, and few paid attention to it. But hidden in the new order's tortured syntax was a substantive change that went overlooked at the time: lifting the ban on the NSA disseminating raw signals intelligence with other agencies. Now, Bush said the NSA *could* share raw signals intelligence, including the incidentally collected Americans' messages, with other agencies, once the defense secretary and attorney general signed off on procedures for doing so.

The Bush-Cheney administration left it to its successors to develop such procedures.†

16. The Obama Team and the Stellarwind Legacy

In late March 2009, the Senate confirmed David Kris as the first head of the Justice Department's National Security Division for the Obama

---

* See chapter 11, section 2.
† See chapter 11, section 17.

administration. This brought one of the nation's foremost experts on what FISA means — and *doesn't* mean — up against the two massive bulk-metadata programs that relied on an unorthodox interpretation of the statute's word *relevant*.

As noted, Kris had been a career Justice Department national security official during the early years of the Bush-Cheney administration and had even testified in favor of the Patriot Act.[107] After the *Times* revealed the warrantless-wiretapping component of the program, Kris had criticized the Bush legal team's post-Goldsmith theory of why it was lawful.* Kris had also labored over a two-volume treatise, *National Security Investigations and Prosecutions* — a kind of manual for the philosophical and operational intricacies of rules that authorize and constrain government security powers. Lamberth, the former presiding judge on the FISA Court, wrote the preface to its second edition, calling it "the single best treatment of the topic I have ever seen."[108]

In his book, Kris devoted several chapters to unpacking and explaining each provision of the notoriously complex and inaccessible FISA statute, clause by clause. Nothing in his discussion of the business-records or pen-register provisions remotely suggested that Americans' phone call and e-mail metadata could be collected in bulk. After the Snowden leaks, Kris, who had stepped down from the government again, wrote an article about bulk collection suggesting that even he had been surprised to learn, back in 2009, about the government's secret interpretation of FISA to permit such indiscriminate vacuuming.

"It seems clear that the interpretation was not obvious, not something that would inevitably have occurred to an outside observer," Kris wrote, adding that "reasonable minds may disagree" as to whether the FISA Court was correct to accept the government's proposed legal interpretation.[109]

But by the time Kris was confirmed in 2009 and told about the programs, a series of FISA Court judges had been issuing orders accepting

---

* See chapter 2, section 4.

that interpretation for years, and Obama had already been briefed about the programs and had decided to mend, not end, them.

Kris joined his deputy, Todd Hinnen, in working to fix the problems the programs had in complying with the FISA Court's rules. And in the midst of those efforts, the Obama national security team experienced what they saw as a vivid demonstration of the importance of the surveillance and data-collection programs they had inherited. On September 6, 2009, somebody sent an encoded e-mail to an account associated with an al-Qaeda suspect in Pakistan. The NSA had been targeting the recipient account under the FISA Amendments Act warrantless surveillance program and intercepted the e-mail. The sender turned out to be an Afghan American living in Colorado. His name was Najibullah Zazi.

The discovery came just in time: Zazi and two friends, who had visited Pakistan the previous year and trained with al-Qaeda, were days away from carrying out a coordinated suicide bombing on New York City's subways. The NSA's bulk phone records program also made a minor contribution, helping investigators identify a previously unknown phone number used by one of Zazi's coconspirators. National security professionals considered the Zazi operation to be "one of the most serious terrorist plots against the homeland since September 11th."[110] The intelligence community had at times appeared to hype threats to bolster legislative or political support for its preferred policies.* But the Zazi plot showed that the 2007 national intelligence estimate about al-Qaeda regrouping in the tribal areas and regaining its ability to send attackers onto American soil, which had helped pressure Congress to pass the Protect America Act, had been accurate.

After the Snowden revelations, government officials would frequently point to the Zazi case as an example of the value of the warrantless surveillance and bulk phone records programs. Skeptics would note that the government did not need a warrantless surveillance program for that; it could have obtained a traditional FISA Court order to

---

* See, for example, chapter 10, section 20.

monitor the e-mail account associated with an al-Qaeda suspect in Pakistan. The rebuttal is that it takes so much more time and paperwork to justify a traditional FISA Court warrant that, for reasons of bureaucratic resources, the spy agency would target fewer total accounts if there were no FISA Amendments Act. Maybe the government would have monitored that account in that alternative universe, but maybe not.

17. Keeping the Patriot Act Interpretation Secret

Obama made one choice when he decided to keep each of the programs that developed out of Stellarwind. But there was another to make: whether to keep it a secret that the government had reinterpreted the law to permit itself to systematically collect things about Americans in bulk in the abstract. That final piece began to snap into place one day in the early fall of 2009, when Kris showed up at the office of Mark Agrast, a top deputy in the Justice Department's Office of Legislative Affairs. His arrival broke with department custom; usually people in "Leg Affairs" took the walk when there was something to talk about with a substantive or litigating part of the department. But Kris urgently needed their help.

Agrast's boss, Ron Weich, had sent a letter telling Congress that the Obama administration supported reauthorizing several expiring provisions of the Patriot Act, including section 215 — the FISA business-records provision on which the bulk phone records program was based.[111] Weich's letter had given no sign that the NSA was using the provision for a bulk domestic phone records program in addition to investigators' routine collection of specific records. Instead, it said only that the provision should be reauthorized because it "has proven valuable in a number of contexts" and that in practice, nothing supported the fears that the FBI would exploit it to collect "sensitive personal information on constitutionally protected activities, such as public library records."

It was imperative, Kris said, that the rest of Congress know how the government was really interpreting the statute before lawmakers cast their votes to reauthorize it. To get permission to brief all 535 of its members, Kris had had to battle intelligence agency officials, who feared it would result in the leaking of the program. But Kris prevailed. Now, he told Agrast that the administration needed to press the Intelligence Committees to alert the rest of Congress to the secret.

Agrast arranged conference calls with intelligence officials and drafted a letter to the leaders of the Intelligence Committees. The leaders in turn sent cryptic letters to their colleagues inviting them to come read a report on a topic of importance. The first public hint came on September 22, when Hinnen testified before a House subcommittee that in addition to the regular use of section 215, the Patriot Act provision "also supports an important sensitive collection program, about which many members of the subcommittee or their staffs have been briefed."[112] The next day, Kris used the same carefully worded statement in similar testimony before the Senate Judiciary Committee.

When the phone records program was revealed in 2013 and the government's secret interpretation of *relevant* came under fire, Kris's intervention became important. Among other things, defenders of the program maintained that when Congress had reauthorized section 215 of the Patriot Act in 2010, knowing how it was being used, that amounted to ratification of the interpretation and made it legitimate. Still, despite Kris's efforts, many lawmakers who voted to reauthorize section 215 — likely a majority of them — never heard about what the government had secretly interpreted it to mean; Kris would argue that the executive branch had done its part to offer the information to all members "even if they did not attend the briefings."[113]

Some of those members of Congress who did attend the briefings thought that the American people had a right to know how the government was interpreting the Patriot Act. In a November 2009 letter, three Democratic senators who knew the secret, Richard Durbin, Russ Feingold, and Ron Wyden, called on Holder to declassify the use of section 215 ahead of the Patriot Act reauthorization debate, saying "informed discussion is not possible when most members of Congress — and nearly all of the American public — lack important information."[114] In December, Wyden met with Biden to further urge disclosure, telling the vice president — his former Senate colleague — that the executive branch's secrecy surrounding the official interpretation of the law violated the American people's trust.[115]

But then came the attempted underwear bombing of the Detroit-bound plane on Christmas. In its aftermath, across a range of issues, those officials who argued for greater security powers and secrecy gained influence; those who argued for more openness and protections for individual rights and privacy became quieter.

On January 5, 2010, Holder wrote back to the senators and informed them that there was no appetite inside the executive branch for any declassification of the secret interpretation of the Patriot Act. The intelligence community maintained that if people knew that the law had been interpreted to permit bulk collection of business records about Americans, they might infer the existence of the secret phone and e-mail data programs specifically, so the information "must remain classified."[116] His letter was marked *Top Secret*.

Soon afterward, Congress passed an extension of the expiring Patriot Act provisions, including section 215, without changes. When the dust settled, Wyden wrote a classified letter to Holder expressing disappointment that the government would continue to hide a "significant discrepancy between what most Americans think is legal and what the government is actually doing."

But Wyden also said he would not make the information public.

"I am aware that as a member of Congress I could conceivably go down to the floor of the U.S. Senate and make public whatever information I see fit, but I believe it would be irresponsible of me to unilaterally disclose classified information in this manner," he wrote.[117]

6

Targeted Killing

1. Two Air Strikes in Yemen

Something was stirring in the badlands of Yemen.

In the run-up to Christmas in 2009, intelligence agencies detected activity by al-Qaeda in the Arabian Peninsula suggesting that the Yemeni branch of the terrorist network was in the end stages of preparing an attack on American interests. The chatter was alarming — but it was also vague.

"We thought it was going to be something in Yemen," Mike Leiter, then the head of the National Counterterrorism Center, told me years later. "So we surged resources for targeting in Yemen... to disrupt that 'something,' even though we didn't know what it was."

The government of Yemen's autocratic president, Ali Abdullah Saleh, exercised little control over the countryside, and the terrorist group had found a haven there. The United States had provided aid to Saleh since 2001, including stationing advisers at a joint operations center in the Yemeni capital, Sanaa, to share counterterrorism intelligence. In a July 2009 meeting with Obama's counterterrorism adviser, John Brennan, Saleh had granted the United States permission to attack al-Qaeda on Yemeni soil, so long as the Americans did not publicly acknowledge it. "Highlighting the potential for a future A.Q.A.P. attack on the U.S. Embassy or other Western targets, Saleh had said, 'I have given you an open door on terrorism, so I am not responsible,'" according to a leaked diplomatic cable.[1]

On December 16, 2009, the Pentagon hosted a secure video teleconference call to discuss a proposal to launch cruise missiles at three al-Qaeda targets. General David Petraeus, the leader of the U.S. Central Command, which oversees military operations in the Middle East, added the third proposed target at the last minute because evolving intelligence suggested a particular operative had just arrived at that location. Jeh Johnson, the Pentagon general counsel, approved the first two proposed strikes as lawful but blocked the third because too many civilians were nearby.[2]

One of the two strikes Johnson approved would later come under sharp scrutiny. It focused on a suspected al-Qaeda training camp at a rural site called al-Majala in the Abyan Province. The governor of Abyan later said that there was intelligence suggesting that a Saudi terrorist leader had brought twenty al-Qaeda members to the camp, including "a Pakistani expert in poisons and explosives."[3] At the briefing, an official told me, there was also discussion of a report that suicide vests had been stockpiled there. Throughout his tenure, Johnson watched surveillance aircraft video of every strike he had approved.[4] The next day, he was watching live in the Pentagon operations center as cruise missiles exploded amid tents and campfires, killing the people moving among them. He was shaken by the carnage, confiding to a friend, *If I were Catholic, I'd have to go to confession.*[5] This remark, which has been previously reported, has sometimes been misinterpreted as an expression of remorse about civilian casualties. But Johnson made it even before the unintended consequences became clear.

Those unintended consequences were severe. Killed along with fourteen militants, according to a Yemeni parliamentary investigation, were forty-one civilians.[6] Two days later, the deputy prime minister of Yemen told the American ambassador that "the civilians who died were largely nomadic, Bedouin families who lived in tents near the A.Q.A.P. training camp" and who "were poor people selling food and supplies to the terrorists."[7] They included fourteen women and twenty-one children.

The mass civilian casualties raised a distinction in targeting law. There are two main categories of killing in both war and self-defense. The *target* is the person the shooter is trying to kill or the building the bomber is trying to destroy. Under international law, the target must be a fighter or a valid military objective. Other members of the enemy who happen to be standing too close are not the target, but are classified as *enemy killed in action.*

Collateral damage refers to civilian bystanders who are killed incidentally. It is a war crime to target civilians, but collateral-damage killings are lawful within limits — even when the bystander deaths were not an accident because the shooter anticipated that their deaths would be a side consequence of pulling the trigger.[8] This aspect of targeting law, while permitting harsh results, comes with constraints: the attack, in war or in self-defense, must be necessary and proportionate. For example, it is clearly illegal to carpet bomb a residential neighborhood to kill one enemy soldier, even if he is a lawful target under normal circumstances. But when the intelligence behind a strike is bad and leads to many civilian casualties or when the intended target turns out not to be there, the antiseptic logic of collateral damage becomes particularly strained. It was not the *intention* of the United States government to kill forty-one innocent people at al-Majala. Nevertheless, by firing missiles from afar, the American government ran the risk of making a deadly mistake.

About a week after the al-Majala strike, the Pentagon convened another interagency video conference to discuss a new proposed strike in Yemen. Johnson had returned to his home in Montclair, New Jersey, for Christmas, leaving his career deputy, Robert Taylor, in charge, supported by Rear Admiral James Crawford, a one-star navy lawyer and the top legal adviser to the Joint Chiefs. Taylor approved the strike as lawful. On December 24, missiles launched from an American naval vessel slammed into a compound in Shabwa Province. This time there were no reports of civilian casualties. But the strike became controversial for a different reason.

In a statement, the Yemeni military, which falsely claimed that its own fighter jets had fired the missiles, asserted that the target had been a meeting of what was believed to be "scores of Yemeni and foreign al-Qaeda operatives" apparently plotting a response to the December 17 operations.[9]

Among those "presumed to be at the site," it said, were the top two leaders of al-Qaeda in the Arabian Peninsula. But also "presumed" present, it said, was Anwar al-Awlaki, a citizen of the United States.

2. The Radical Muslim Cleric

In life and in death, al-Awlaki was a pivotal figure in the history of Obama's national security legal policy.

Al-Awlaki's parents were living in New Mexico in 1971 when he was born, making him an American citizen. His father, Nasser al-Awlaki, was from a prominent tribe in Yemen and part of the country's ruling elite. After studying in the United States, Nasser moved his family back to Yemen, when Anwar was seven, and would go on to serve as agriculture minister in the Yemeni government and then as the head of two universities. Anwar al-Awlaki returned to the United States for college. He studied engineering in Colorado but became interested in religion and took jobs as an imam at mosques in San Diego and Northern Virginia. He also recorded a series of sermons that mixed religious scholarship with Western pop-culture references and marketed them to English-speaking Muslims.[10] At the same time, he led a hidden life, frequently visiting prostitutes.

In March 2002, al-Awlaki delivered a fiery sermon expressing anger at a recent FBI raid on Muslim organizations in northern Virginia. He also, as recounted in my colleague Scott Shane's book about al-Awlaki, *Objective Troy*, learned from an escort-service manager that the FBI had been watching him and was keeping a file on his visits to prostitutes — un-Islamic behavior that could ruin him.[11] Al-Awlaki abruptly moved to Britain, where his rhetoric became much more militant, and he returned to Yemen in 2004. Two years later, the Yemeni government arrested him; al-Awlaki blamed the United States for encouraging his detention. After his release in late 2007, he started a website where he posted hard-line sermons justifying jihadist violence against the West.

One enduring mystery is whether al-Awlaki became radicalized after 9/11 or whether he had been hiding his true ideology earlier. After 9/11, it emerged that two of the hijackers had attended his mosques, but that seems to have been a coincidence.

"We interviewed Awlaki after 9/11 on three separate occasions," Mark Giuliano, the head of the FBI's national security branch, later testified. "He identified one of the 9/11 hijackers as somebody he knew as to going to his mosque. We were never able to obtain a stitch of evidence that shows Awlaki knew beforehand about 9/11 or supported the 9/11 hijackers."[12]

But by the late 2000s, al-Awlaki's Islamist writings and recordings had begun regularly showing up in the homes of English-speaking Muslims arrested on terrorism charges. The U.S. government placed his website e-mail under surveillance and monitored thousands of messages sent to him, only a few of which he replied to. One person who reached out to al-Awlaki was Nidal Hasan, an American army major who was working on military-sponsored research about mental and medical issues related to military service by Muslim soldiers.[13]

Starting in December 2008, Hasan sent al-Awlaki a series of e-mails. Hasan's first message raised the question of whether incidents in which Muslim American soldiers killed fellow American soldiers in the name of Islam could be reconciled with the Koran. Hasan sent several other e-mails as well. Al-Awlaki ignored most of Hasan's messages. But he responded to the most innocuous one, in which Hasan suggested that al-Awlaki return to the United States to hand out a scholarship awarded in his honor; al-Awlaki declined the invitation.

In November 2009, Hasan went on a shooting rampage at Fort Hood, Texas, murdering thirteen people and wounding more than thirty others. Soon after, al-Awlaki praised Hasan on his website as a "hero" and a "man of conscience who could not bear living the contradiction of being a Muslim and serving in an army that is fighting against his own people."[14]

Al-Awlaki had not plotted with Hasan. But the fact that Hasan had reached out to him was, in hindsight, obviously significant. Media interest in al-Awlaki rose, and politicians and commentators speculated that the FBI had been timid about scrutinizing Hasan out of mis-guided political correctness. Kris, the head of the Justice Department's National Security Division, told me that counterterrorism profession-als did not see the shootings as a singular event. They arose in the midst of an extremely busy time, including the arrest in September of an Afghan American from suburban Denver who was plotting to bomb the New York subway system* and in October of a Pakistani American in Chicago who had helped plot the 2008 Mumbai terrorist attacks. Both of those cases, in contrast to Fort Hood, had involved major sur-veillance operations before the arrests.

Fort Hood was "more of a political controversy than an operational controversy," Kris said. "It's fairly isolated and entirely reactive and dealt with swiftly, and ends up in the military justice system."

Then came the December 24 air strike and the Yemeni statement naming al-Awlaki as one of the notable figures presumed present. Denying that his son was an al-Qaeda member despite his outspoken Islamist views, Nasser al-Awlaki told a reporter: "If the American gov-ernment helped in attacking one of [its own] citizens, this is illegal. Nidal Hasan killed thirteen people and he's going to get a trial. My son has killed nobody. He should face trial if he's done something wrong."[15]

3. The Christmas Eve Strike

None of the prominent figures named in the Yemen statement as "pre-sumed present" at the December 24 gathering died in the strike, if indeed they were even there. The next day came Abdulmutallab's attempted underwear bombing of the Detroit-bound airliner, clearing up what the intelligence concerning an imminent al-Qaeda in the Ara-bian Peninsula attack had been about. Soon, lawmakers who received classified briefings began dropping hints that the National Security Agency had found evidence that Abdulmutallab may have been in

* See chapter 5, section 16.

contact with al-Awlaki in Yemen.[16] But murkiness would remain about the December 24 strike and the period just after the Christmas attack. Two apparently incorrect notions have circulated that cloud accurate understandings of Obama's national security legal policy. Both involve when the government first decided to try to kill al-Awlaki.

First, several voices have claimed al-Awlaki was the December 24 strike's target. Jeremy Scahill's *Dirty Wars: The World Is a Battlefield* states that "the target was an American citizen" that day.[17] The Bureau of Investigative Journalism and the *Long War Journal*, each of which tracks counterterrorism strikes, also described the December 24 bombing as the first attempt to kill him.[18] Second, in early 2010, the *Washington Post* claimed that al-Awlaki was not the focus that day but was added to a military kill list in the final week of 2009.[19] If either was true, it would mean that the government decided it could intentionally target and kill an American without hard evidence that he was anything more than a propagandist, despite the First Amendment. It would also mean that the government had casually decided it could kill an American without first going through carefully lawyered deliberations.

I have concluded that both claims are wrong. I spoke to several dozen current and former officials who had an insider vantage point on counterterrorism operations in that era. In all these independent conversations with multiple people who were in a position to know, I have not found anyone who said he or she recalled a decision to target al-Awlaki in 2009. Many officials told me that circumstantial evidence had pointed to a possible connection between al-Awlaki and the Christmas attack. But it was only the detailed account given by Abdulmutallab when he started talking to his FBI interrogators in late January 2010* that convinced intelligence analysts that al-Awlaki had evolved from a mere propagandist into a person who played a specific, operational role in plotting terrorist attacks. This changed understanding, in turn, prompted the decision that he could and should be targeted.

---

* See chapter 3, section 7.

That does not mean that the possibility that al-Awlaki might be killed on December 24 was not discussed, but multiple officials told me that the top two al-Qaeda in the Arabian Peninsula leaders were the target of the strike and al-Awlaki was not. (It was not clear that al-Awlaki was actually there, and he never spoke in public about it, although a former Islamic militant from Denmark who later became disillusioned and worked for a Western intelligence agency claimed in a memoir that Awlaki had sent him an encrypted e-mail afterward saying: "Phew. Maaaaaan — that was close."[20]) Still, given the type of gathering it supposedly was and his role in the organization, there was a distinct possibility that he might be there. The discussion was framed like this: By virtue of his American citizenship, did al-Awlaki walk around with an iron dome around him, protecting not just himself but also the people near him, even if those nearby people were otherwise lawfully targetable? The lawyers decided that al-Awlaki did not walk around with such a dome. Had al-Awlaki been there and died that day, they would have considered him an "enemy killed in action" by virtue of his close ties to al-Qaeda, they said, not collateral damage like an innocent civilian bystander. But that does not mean the government believed, based on what it knew about him as of December 24 or even as of December 31, that if it spotted him off by himself it could lawfully kill him.

The *Post* source's claim that Special Operations put him on a list of terrorist suspects approved for killing in the final week of 2009 was also wrong, multiple officials told me. That article was garbled and the *Post* later formally retracted another part of it,[21] so this claim likely originated from the same questionable sourcing. One official said that intelligence analysts were growing more interested in al-Awlaki as attention to al-Qaeda in the Arabian Peninsula spiked after the Christmas attack and speculated that the *Post*'s anonymous source may have relayed an exaggerated understanding of that chatter. But in any case, the Joint Special Operations Command had no authority to approve an out-of-theater targeting by itself, and there was no interagency decision about targeting al-Awlaki that early, officials said.

In his memoir, Leon Panetta, then the CIA director, wrote that the

Obama administration's "national security staff had formally approved an effort to kill or capture Anwar al-Awlaki," with "final approval from the president," on Friday, February 5, 2010.[22] Prior to that decision, the Justice Department's Office of Legal Counsel had given oral advice that targeting al-Awlaki would be lawful. The *Times* and the American Civil Liberties Union later forced the government, in Freedom of Information Act lawsuits, to make public a seven-page Justice Department memo memorializing the Office of Legal Counsel's prior oral advice*; it was dated later in February, which dovetails with this sequence.

"The idea of targeting Awlaki was raised as early as 2007, in the Bush administration, and the answer was 'No we can't,'" Leiter said. "Only with Abdulmutallab — not even with Fort Hood — did we get the intelligence to support targeting him under our standards. That was in January 2010."

4. Sovereignty and Lies

On January 2, 2010, Petraeus visited Saleh at his presidential palace in Yemen to talk about the burgeoning campaign of American air strikes. An account of their conversation later became public in a leaked diplomatic cable.[†] It illustrated a difficulty in assessing one aspect of the legality of targeted killings away from hot battlefields: whether the use of force by the United States on another sovereign nation's soil is a violation of international law.

"Saleh praised the December 17 and 24 strikes against A.Q.A.P. but said that 'mistakes were made' in the killing of civilians in Abyan," the classified cable recounted.[23] The Yemeni president also brought up two of the prominent people who had been presumed present at the second strike, mentioning that "A.Q.A.P. leader Nasser Al Wahishi and extremist cleric Anwar Al Awlaki may still be alive." While he told Petraeus

---

* See chapter 9, section 20.
† See chapter 8, section 7.

that he would not permit American ground forces to participate in counterterrorism operations, the Yemeni president encouraged his American visitor to keep conducting the air strikes, saying: "We'll continue saying the bombs are ours, not yours."

That lie had long been suspected, but the leaked cable confirmed it. This had significant implications. In international law, it is illegal for one country to use military force "against the territorial integrity" of another sovereign country without the consent of the host government, the permission of the United Nations Security Council to go to war, or a legitimate self-defense claim. But sometimes a host government grants permission for such strikes without saying so publicly for domestic political reasons. It has been widely reported that Pakistan's government secretly granted permission for drone strikes in the ungoverned tribal areas even as it publicly condemned them; Yemen preferred to pretend that it had carried out the strikes itself.

From the outside it sometimes looked like the United States government might be violating those nations' sovereignty, even if it wasn't. By the terms of the diplomatic deals, the United States was unable to defend itself from those accusations except through veiled hints and winks so that "everybody knows" what is going on.

That such secret arrangements solve the legal problem does not, of course, make them seemly. They are most feasible with an antidemocratic ruler. Indeed, in the meeting with Petraeus, the frank backroom atmosphere prompted Yemen's deputy prime minister for defense, Rashad al-Alimi, "to joke that he had just 'lied' by telling Parliament that the bombs" had been deployed by Yemen's air force.

5. The First al-Awlaki Memo

Before the United States government launched an operation aimed at killing al-Awlaki, the Justice Department had to decide whether it would be lawful to kill an American citizen without a trial. It was suggested to me that an executive branch rule—probably a line in the covert finding memorandum that authorized the CIA to use lethal force against terrorists—required the attorney general to approve any operation that would target an American. Also, Johnson at the Pentagon and Stephen Preston, the top CIA lawyer, wanted the reassurance of a formal legal pronouncement before they would permit their agencies to carry out such a strike. The unprecedented question now fell to David Barron and Marty Lederman, the top officials at the Office of Legal Counsel: Was it lawful for the government to kill an American citizen without a trial?

Barron, then a youthful-looking forty-two, had a calm, seemingly ego-free manner. Lederman, then forty-eight, was animated and indefatigable. Both had been junior lawyers at the Office of Legal Counsel during the Clinton administration before becoming law professors at Harvard and Georgetown, respectively. In 2004, after the leak of the Bush-Cheney administration's torture memos, they had been among a group of Clinton legal-team veterans who signed a pointed and idealistic set of "Principles to Guide the Office of Legal Counsel." The document laid out a high standard for preventing executive-branch lawyering from becoming politicized.

"When providing legal advice to guide contemplated executive branch action, O.L.C. should provide an accurate and honest appraisal of applicable law, even if that advice will constrain the administration's pursuit of desired policies," the guide said. "The advocacy model of lawyering, in which lawyers craft merely plausible legal arguments to support their clients' desired actions, inadequately promotes the president's constitutional obligation to ensure the legality of executive action."[24]

Lederman had also become a prolific legal blogger, specializing in blasting the Bush legal team. In 2008, Barron and Lederman coauthored a book-length, two-part article for the *Harvard Law Review* examining the history of legal disputes over the powers of the commander in chief and statutes restricting his wartime actions. They concluded that the Bush view of a presidency that could not be constrained by Congress was "an even more radical attempt to remake the constitutional law of war powers than is often recognized."[25]

Neither was supposed to be in charge of the Office of Legal Counsel.

Obama had installed them as the top deputies and nominated a more senior lawyer, Dawn Johnsen, an Indiana University professor who had also briefly led it in the Clinton administration, to be its permanent head. The younger and less experienced Barron — he had been a rank-and-file attorney in the office during the Clinton years — was supposed to be her number two. Johnsen had been particularly outspoken in her criticism of the Bush-Cheney legal team, denouncing Yoo's torture memos and theories of executive power as "irresponsibly and dangerously false in a way that impugns OLC's integrity over time and threatens to undermine public faith in the possibility that any administration can be expected to adhere to the rule of law."[26] She had also written in favor of abortion rights. Conservative senators targeted her as too liberal, and she never received an up-or-down Senate floor vote.[27] Her absence left Barron, the principal deputy, as the Office of Legal Counsel's acting head, with Lederman as his number two. They were about to be tested by extraordinary circumstances and pressure.

The CIA determined that al-Awlaki had become an operational terrorist leader who was "engaged in continual planning and direction of attacks" on innocent Americans, as Barron later recited in a memo. This document eventually became public as a result of a Freedom of Information Act lawsuit I brought with my colleague Scott Shane and the *New York Times*, along with a similar, parallel case by the American Civil Liberties Union.* Al-Awlaki could not be tried since he was not in custody and the American legal system does not have trials in absentia. The CIA also judged that if he were to be located, his arrest would be infeasible, apparently based on several factors: Saleh's forces did not control the Yemeni countryside and Saleh would not let Americans operate on the ground. But it might be feasible to kill al-Awlaki from the air. The policymakers wanted to know whether they could lawfully take the shot.

Barron and Lederman accepted the CIA's conclusions about al-Awlaki as factual premises; the lawyers did not see it as their role to independently

---

* See chapter 9, section 8.

reconsider the evidence, especially at this rushed initial stage. Barron provided his first, interim, answer orally — yes, it would be lawful to take the shot. And then he and Lederman began drafting a memo fleshing out and recording their reasoning.

Based on the CIA-supplied assessments, they believed that al-Awlaki was a lawful military target, all else held equal. They then looked at several reasons why it might nevertheless be illegal to kill him, rejecting each in turn.

The first was a ban on *assassination*. Following the Church Committee's revelations about CIA links to Cold War–era killings of foreign leaders, President Gerald Ford issued an executive order regulating foreign intelligence operations. It banned "political assassinations." Presidents Carter and Reagan had replaced that order with their own versions, which dropped the word *political* for reasons that are unclear.[28] The Reagan order — Executive Order 12333, the same one that is so important for surveillance — remained in effect. It said: "No person employed by or acting on behalf of the United States Government shall engage in, or conspire to engage in, assassination." The order does not define what types of killings amount to assassinations. Neither does federal law.

There were, however, other executive-branch precedents to look to. In 1986, Reagan had signed a covert-action finding granting the CIA the power to take worldwide action against terrorism. This finding had been expanded over time through various so-called memoranda of notification. In 1998, the CIA proposed commissioning an Afghan tribal militia to attack Osama bin Laden's compound and kill him. According to the 9/11 Commission report, the Clinton legal team's position was that such an operation was consistent with the executive order banning assassination because "killing a person who posed an imminent threat to the United States would be an act of self-defense, not an assassination."[29]

On the day of the 9/11 attacks, the CIA's acting general counsel, John Rizzo, drafted a new memorandum of notification expanding the agency's covert authorities to go after al-Qaeda. Bush signed it on September 17, 2001, and the public learned of it through an anonymous senior official's leak to Bob Woodward a month later: "The gloves are off," the official said. "The president has given the agency the green light to do whatever is necessary. Lethal operations that were unthinkable pre–September 11 are now underway."[30] Rizzo later wrote in his memoir that among the powers Bush granted to the agency — and that therefore were seen as consistent, by definition, with the executive order banning assassination — was the power to take "'lethal action against members of al-Qaeda and any affiliated groups,' or words to that effect. We would hunt down and kill anyone in al-Qaeda, or acting under its direction or influence, involved in the 9/11 attacks or actively planning attacks on the homeland or on U.S. citizens anywhere."[31]

Although Bush's memo remains classified, officials told me certain additional details about it that have not been reported. Among them, the memo says that for the CIA to kill an al-Qaeda suspect under the authority granted by the finding, the agency's target must pose a "continuing and imminent threat." By contrast, the CIA had broader latitude to capture and imprison al-Qaeda suspects: to be eligible to be detained under the finding, a terrorist must meet the lower standard of being a "continuing and serious threat." In March 2002, the Justice Department's Office of Legal Counsel issued a still-classified memo "analyzing the assassination ban in Executive order 12333," according to court filings, but it has never been made public.[32] Reagan's original counterterrorism covert finding, as expanded by Bush's still-operative memorandum of notification and previous memos on the general topic of killings formed a backdrop for Barron and Lederman to evaluate whether killing al-Awlaki would violate the assassination ban. Whatever else was true, they concluded, it was well established that targeting an operational al-Qaeda leader who was actively involved in plotting attacks against Americans was not forbidden by the executive order banning assassinations.

"Killings in self-defense are not assassinations," Barron wrote.

Barron's analysis treated the word *assassination* as a term of art. But the word also has a plain-English definition, typically something like "the surprise killing of a prominent person for political reasons." Some people think targeted killings should be called assassinations too. In a later court ruling rejecting a lawsuit by al-Awlaki's father, Judge John D. Bates used that terminology, writing, "Can the Executive order the assassination of a U.S. citizen without first affording him any form of judicial process whatsoever, based on the mere assertion that he is a dangerous member of a terrorist organization?"[33] Elliot Ackerman, a former Special Operations Marine who became a CIA paramilitary officer in 2009 and helped plan drone strikes at militia leaders in Afghanistan and tribal Pakistan, would later write that he and some of his colleagues felt discomfort with the practice. It seemed like they were violating Executive Order 12333, a copy of which each had to sign upon joining the agency.

"Lawyers with the CIA and the administrations of George W. Bush and Barack Obama had drawn up semantic arguments carefully delineating the difference between a targeted killing and an assassination," he wrote in 2014. "But when the picture of the person you were trying to kill sat on your desk; when you watched the Predator strikes light up the night sky just across the border; and then, when you took that same picture and moved it into a file for archiving, it sure felt like an assassination."[34]

Killing al-Awlaki also raised constitutional problems. As a citizen, he was protected by the Bill of Rights. The Fifth Amendment bars the government from depriving a citizen of his life "without due process of law." The Fourth Amendment bars "unreasonable" seizures, which includes the use of excessive force by the government, as when the police kill someone without justification. Neither, Barron and Lederman concluded, would bar a strike targeting al-Awlaki. In light of the circumstances, they reasoned, all the process that he was due was a review by executive-branch officials of intelligence tying him to terrorism, and it was reasonable to kill him if that was necessary to bring an end to the threat to public safety he presumably posed.

They based this in part on a 2004 Supreme Court ruling—the *Hamdi* case—which said that an American captured on the battlefield in Afghanistan could be held without trial as a wartime prisoner, just like any other enemy fighter.[35] And the court had also held, in other contexts, that *due process* could mean different things depending on how heavily the public interest in collective security weighed against an individual's interest in not having the government take an action in error.[36] While al-Awlaki's presumed interest in not being mistakenly killed was as significant as it gets for an individual, the public interest in not having innocent people killed by an unarrestable terrorist was also profound. Moreover, in several Fourth Amendment cases, the Supreme Court had held that it was reasonable for police to use potentially deadly force to stop suspects who posed an immediate and substantial threat to public safety. These decisions included a 1985 case in which a police officer shot and killed a fleeing burglary suspect[37] and a 2007 case in which a deputy rammed a suspect's car to bring an end to a high-speed chase.[38]

"We do not believe al-Awlaki's citizenship provides a basis for concluding that he is immune from a use of force abroad," Barron wrote.

Barron signed the top secret document, addressed to Holder, on February 19, 2010. He and Lederman, the onetime scourges of Bush-era Office of Legal Counsel, had taken seven pages to approve killing an American citizen. And by April, they would realize they had overlooked something important.

6. The Targeting Law of 9/11

Buoyant and self-assured, Harold Koh climbed the podium in the ballroom of the Washington's Ritz-Carlton Hotel. It was March 25, 2010, and as the State Department legal adviser, Koh was set to deliver a keynote speech before the annual meeting of the American Society of International Law. Koh had been one of the outspoken liberal critics of the Bush-Cheney administration global war on terror from his position as dean of Yale Law School, decrying what he portrayed as its "claim that a War on Terror permits the commander in chief's power to be expanded into a wanton power to act as torturer in chief."[39] But Koh was not a pacifist; he believed the use of force to protect innocent life was both moral and legal under certain circumstances — including military interventions to stop atrocities. By the end of his speech, he had become the chief public defender of the legality of the Obama administration's targeted killing operations, even as he argued behind the scenes for placing greater constraints on them.

Koh's speech would highlight another major legal dispute over targeted killings — one that inflamed many international law scholars in Koh's audience. It centers on which body of international law regulates such killings. War zones are governed by the *law of armed conflict*, which has permissive rules for killing. On a battlefield, you may kill people who belong to the enemy force based on nothing but their status as part of the hostile group. It does not matter if they present no immediate threat — you may bomb their barracks as they sleep.[40] Unless they are surrendering, you may kill them even if it is possible to capture them alive instead.

By contrast, peacetime zones are governed by *human rights law*, which has more restrictive rules for killing. You may kill only in personal or national self-defense. The target must pose an *imminent* threat at that moment. And killing must be a last resort — if you can arrest the target to eliminate the threat he poses, you may not shoot him. These are essentially criminal justice rules; police officers may lawfully shoot a kidnapper who is pointing a gun at a hostage or at themselves. But if the kidnapper gets away and the police later spot him harmlessly sitting in a coffee shop, they may not summarily gun him down.

But dividing targeting law into these two categories is premised on twentieth-century situations. The twenty-first century has added some new twists. Terrorists planning transnational attacks on the United States and crossing borders hide in remote and ungoverned places. These are often far from traditional war zones where the United States has ground forces engaging in sustained armed combat — places that people sometimes call the *hot battlefield*. Without ground forces or a functional local government, there is no way to capture a terrorism suspect, but the rise of drones has made it increasingly possible to penetrate inaccessible regions and kill people from the air.

This new situation raises many legal disputes. But for targeting-law purposes, the primary disagreement comes down to whether literal imminence matters. The controversy is whether it is necessary for the alleged terrorist to be in the very end stages of a pending attack before it is lawful to fire a missile at him, or whether it is lawful to kill him whenever there is a fleeting opportunity to do so.

During the Bush-Cheney administration, the United States outraged many European allies and international law scholars by talking in extravagant terms about the "global war on terror," suggesting that the whole world was subject to battlefield rules. That was more rhetoric than action, but Bush did oversee the first armed drone strike in Yemen in 2002 and, later, many more in tribal Pakistan. His administration also occasionally used wartime-like powers outside of armed-conflict zones, including the military's detention of a handful of Guantánamo prisoners who had been arrested in Bosnia and the CIA's seizure, or kidnapping, in 2003 of a Muslim cleric off the street of Milan, Italy.

Senator Obama, the liberal constitutional lawyer, seemed to be against that worldview. His rhetoric was certainly less militant. But as president, Obama was in the midst of a major escalation of targeted killings away from recognized combat zones. There was only one known American air strike in Yemen under Bush, but in 2012 alone there were about forty-one strikes there.[41] In Bush's final year, the number of air strikes in tribal Pakistan jumped from the low single digits to about thirty-five. They continued to accelerate under Obama, peaking at about a hundred and seventeen in 2010.[42]

That same year, Philip Alston, the United Nations' "special rapporteur" (or top investigator) on extrajudicial, summary, or arbitrary executions, criticized the United States for being too secretive about its targeting policy and the details of whom it was killing, including civilian deaths. He accused it of being "the most enthusiastic and prolific proponent of targeted killings carried out in circumstances which sometimes appear to violate the applicable international law."[43] Criticism among international law scholars was rising that Obama, too, was invoking battlefield rules where they did not apply in order to justify what amounted to a campaign of extrajudicial executions or assassinations. And some political critics went further: Bush had taken much heat from the likes of Koh for overseeing an administration that tortured terrorism captives, but wasn't droning people more abhorrent?

"Surely killing people is worse than waterboarding them," declared William McGurn, a George W. Bush speechwriter turned *Wall Street Journal* opinion columnist.[44]

Like many liberals, Koh had come in uncomfortable with the idea of targeted killings. But after months of immersion in classified intelligence reports, he told his increasingly critical friends back at Yale that it was easier to take purist stances from the faculty lounge than from a position of responsibility. There really were people out there actively plotting to kill innocent Americans, as the Christmas 2009 attack vividly demonstrated, and the government was not going to just sit there and hope that the terrorists bungled it on their own. Koh also bristled at criticism that equated Obama's killings to Bush's torture. This was a common fallacy among commentators who do not understand law, but the difference between the two is huge: Torturing prisoners is *always illegal*, no matter what. In war or self-defense, if carried out in compliance with domestic and international law, killing is *permitted*.[45] A reason for this seemingly counterintuitive distinction is that a prisoner in custody poses no threat.

In late 2009, Koh began lobbying internally to make the speech at the international law conference defending Obama's policies about what he called "the Law of 9/11" regarding detentions, use of force, and prosecutions. Other lawyers on the national security team were also looking for a way to make a public statement asserting the lawfulness of the strikes. Preston, the CIA lawyer at the time, later recalled that after his confirmation in July 2009, "I could not pick up a newspaper or turn on a news broadcast without seeing erroneous references to 'illegal' U.S. Government counterterrorism operations overseas. Not fringe media, but mainstream press. Not isolated or occasional instances, but quite routine — as if it were conventional wisdom that the United States' use of lethal force in the armed conflict against al-Qaeda was 'unlawful.' For me, and others in the administration, this was deeply disturbing, and something had to be done about it."[46]

For those who felt that way, the willingness by Koh, the liberal human rights champion, to publicly defend the operations was great. (The downside for them, later on, was that Koh liked to remind people, during arguments over the legality of some proposed new wrinkle in which he was usually on the side of greater constraint, that he had gone out there and said what they were doing was legal.) Others in the intelligence community were hesitant about a speech because they were not sure if such topics could be discussed without disclosing classified information, and they were worried that Koh might, in his official capacity, pronounce that what the CIA had done under Bush was torture. The speech went through a heavy interagency vetting process; some portions were still being cleared for approval as he spoke, leading him to pause at spots to find the last-minute inserts. But the final version included a sweeping statement.

"It is the considered view of this administration — and it has certainly been my experience during my time as Legal Adviser — that U.S. targeting practices, including lethal operations conducted with the use of unmanned aerial vehicles, comply with all applicable law, including the laws of war," Koh declared. He added: "As a matter of international law, the United States is in an armed conflict with al-Qaeda...and may use force consistent with its inherent right to self-defense under international law.... A state that is engaged in an armed conflict or in legitimate self-defense is not required to provide targets with legal process before the state may use lethal force."[47]

Years later, the liberal lawyers of the Obama administration would find that their participation in counterterrorism policymaking — and targeted killing operations in particular — had made them suspect in the eyes of some on the left. The antiwar group Code Pink, for example, protested Obama's nomination of Barron to be a federal appeals court judge because he had written the memo clearing the way to kill al-Awlaki.[48] When Obama nominated Johnson to be secretary of homeland security, Code Pink gathered in front of his house in Georgetown and projected a documentary about drone strikes onto its exterior. (Johnson joined the protesters on the street for conversation and later invited them to visit him at his new government office.[49])

No one received rougher treatment than Koh. Liberal human rights advocates and international law specialists on the left who were angry with Obama for acting like Bush on some counterterrorism policies were particularly upset with Koh, too. Just as Obama had bestowed a gloss of bipartisan consensus on those Bush-like policies he continued, Koh had leveraged his history as a liberal human rights champion to vouch for what Obama was doing — including, in this speech, drone strikes, the Obama policy many liberals were most upset about.*

After leaving the State Department at the start of Obama's second term, Koh spent the 2014–15 academic year as a guest professor at New York University. A group of law students, alumni, and activists there organized a petition condemning his hiring. Citing his 2010 speech (and overstating his personal influence over internal policymaking), they accused Koh of "crafting and defending what objectively amounts to an illegal and inhumane program of extrajudicial assassinations and potential war crimes,"[50] and said he was no longer qualified to teach human rights. Their petition was prefaced with a Hannah Arendt quote about Nazi functionaries.

Numerous prominent law professors and human rights figures rallied to his defense with an "open letter in support of Harold Hongju Koh" that called the petition "patently wrong and unfair," arguing that he had actually been "a leading advocate for preservation of the rule of law, human rights and transparency within the Obama Administration, including on the drones issue."[51] In a *Washington Post* opinion column, Elisa Massimino, the president of Human Rights First, portrayed the activists as having mistaken an ally for an enemy and said they were demanding a purity of human rights advocates that would,

---

* See also chapter 12, part 5.

in practice, foreclose people with their mind-set from working in government on disputed actions, where decisions with real impact took place. She said Koh's 2010 speech had both "made the best case anyone could" but also "left a lot to be desired," stressing that her group was still not satisfied that the Obama administration's targeted killing program was consistent with the laws of war. But Koh, she said, had "forged progress behind the scenes on a range of issues, from military commissions and Guantánamo to transparency about drones.

"That wasn't the kind of work that made headlines, but it strengthened respect for human rights and reduced suffering," Massamino wrote. "If that makes Koh a sellout, we need more of them."[52]

7. Is the World a Battlefield?

When Koh made the unqualified statement in his speech that the Obama administration's targeting practices were legal, he invoked *both* armed-conflict law *and* self-defense law in the same breath, leaving it ambiguous as to whether alleged terrorists had to pose an imminent threat to be legally killed away from hot battlefields. During a question period after his main speech, Mary Ellen O'Connell, a University of Notre Dame professor of international law and an outspoken critic of targeted killings, rose to challenge Koh along lines that captured some of the disconnect and the criticism that would follow.

"What I'm hearing you say is that the Obama administration continues to see that there is such a conception as a global war on terror and I would just urge you to reconsider —" she began.[53]

"I didn't — I didn't say that, Mary Ellen," Koh interrupted.

"You believe that it's possible to target people —" she began again.

Koh continued: "I said a lot of things in my remarks. That's not one of the things I said."

Over time, what the Obama administration was saying — and not saying — about targeting terrorists away from traditional war zones became clearer. It focused on a complexity raised by the existence of ungoverned badlands. As noted, twentieth-century rules seemed to divide the world into two types of places: battlefields where armies were actively waging sustained combat, where the law of war applied, and everywhere else — normal places, where human rights law applied. But there is a third kind of space: badlands and failed states, where there is neither sustained combat nor a police force that can arrest people who are plotting terrorist attacks. Obama's human rights and international law critics believed that peacetime targeting rules should apply to regions in anarchy if they were not part of an active zone of armed conflict. After 9/11, and continuing into the Obama administration, the United States was shifting the default: if there was no active peacetime government controlling a space, then wartime targeting rules applied to enemies who went there.

Part of the ambiguity about what the Obama administration was saying stemmed from the fact that its own thinking was a muddle. Many Obama lawyers, including Johnson, were satisfied that armed conflict law followed the terrorists to ungoverned badlands, so that decisions about targeting were largely a policy issue, not a legal one. But some, especially Koh, wanted to place constraints on that power by overlaying human rights–law principles, raising the standards that had to be met. Meanwhile, the main policymakers on targeting decisions — Obama and Brennan — for reasons that had more to do with strategy than law, wanted to exercise restraint and strike only at highly threatening individuals, not just blast away at foot soldiers. As a result, what the United States was doing could be justified by either legal theory — except for the factor of whether imminence mattered. To overcome this hurdle, the administration floated the notion that significant individual al-Qaeda operatives who were essentially in the business of trying to attack the United States posed a *continuous and imminent threat*, and so could be targeted whenever spotted.

This idea was just beginning to emerge with Koh's speech, but Brennan would state it directly a year and a half later, in a keynote address at a Harvard Law School–Brookings Institution conference on the tenth anniversary of the 9/11 attacks. Brennan's speech, which had also gone through heavy editing by the interagency lawyers during the drafting process, was full of talk of respect for restraint.

"In practice," Brennan argued, the American approach to targeting "is far more aligned with our allies' approach than many assume.... Practically speaking, then, the question turns principally on how you define 'imminence.' We are finding increasing recognition in the international community that a more flexible understanding of 'imminence' may be appropriate when dealing with terrorist groups."[54]

And two months after Brennan's speech, the Justice Department completed an unsigned white paper on targeting issues — although it would not become public until leaked in January 2013, buffeting Brennan's confirmation to be CIA director* — that spelled out their idea in greater detail:

"The condition that an operational leader present an 'imminent' threat of violent attack against the United States does not require the United States to have clear evidence that a specific attack on U.S. persons and interests will take place in the immediate future," the white paper contended. "The threat posed by al-Qaeda and its associated forces demands a broader concept of imminence in judging when a person continually planning terror attacks presents an imminent threat, making the use of force appropriate."[55]

Many international legal scholars criticized this attempt to blend the two bodies of international law into a hybrid set of rules. Naz K. Modirzadeh, the director of the Harvard Law School Program on International Law and Armed Conflict, wrote in 2014 that the Obama legal team had taken positions on issues of lethal force, human rights, and armed conflict that "would have been surprising and disappointing to those same professionals back in 2002 when they began their battle against the Bush Administration's formulations of the 'Global War on Terror.'" She accused them of having "traded in strict fealty to international law for potential influence on executive decision-making." The result, she said, was the creation of "folk international law, a

---

* See chapter 9, sections 13 and 14.

law-like discourse that relies on a confusing and soft admixture" of multiple legal disciplines "to frame operations that do not, ultimately, seem bound by international law—at least not by any conception of international law recognizable to international lawyers, especially those outside of the U.S."[56]

Much of international law is malleable. It evolves with the customs and practices of states. If the United States ultimately fails to persuade the rest of the world to accept its innovation as a new norm in light of changing circumstances, Modirzadeh's portrayal will likely be how history remembers this era. If a consensus emerges that the modification makes sense in light of twenty-first-century terrorism and technology, such criticism may, in hindsight, appear to have been closed-minded and obsolete. Either way, it is a legitimate critique.

Some of Obama's critics went further, accusing him of believing, as some of Bush's rhetoric suggested, that the entire world was a battlefield. But that was wild overstatement. That would mean that the United States was asserting that it had a legal right to rove the globe and summarily gun down an al-Qaeda suspect on sight, even if the suspect posed no imminent threat at that moment and even if he was in a place where he could instead be arrested, like a café in Paris. While the Obama administration did push past some geographic limits of armed-conflict zones, it did not claim that battlefield-targeting rules applied inside normal countries with functioning governments and police— that is to say, the overwhelming majority of the world's landmass. Its elastic battlefield-style targeting rules covered only a few lawless spaces: rural Yemen, tribal Pakistan, the failed state of Somalia, and—later— chaotic regions of Syria and Libya.

"The United States does not view our authority to use military force against al-Qaeda as being restricted solely to 'hot' battlefields like Afghanistan" and maintains that international law permits it to take action without doing a separate self-defense analysis each time if or when "other governments are unwilling or unable to take the necessary actions themselves," Brennan acknowledged. But, he emphasized:

"That does not mean we can use military force whenever we want, wherever we want."[57]

8. The Second al-Awlaki Memo

In April 2010, the news broke that Obama's National Security Council had added al-Awlaki's name to the CIA's kill-or-capture list, prompting controversy that would jar Barron and Lederman into revisiting their legal analysis.

Some of the controversy was expected. For example, Glenn Greenwald, then best known as a civil liberties blogger, wrote — in boldface and underlined — that Obama had taken "a step beyond where even George Bush would go" by claiming a power "not merely to imprison, but to assassinate far from any battlefield, American citizens **with no due process of any kind**."[58] But the Obama lawyers had already secretly worked through why they thought killing al-Awlaki would not be an assassination or raise a Fifth Amendment due-process problem.

Another commentary, however, was a seeming stomach-dropper. On a blog for international legal scholars called *Opinio Juris,* Kevin Jon Heller, a Stanford-educated law professor based in Australia, pointed out that there is a federal statute that forbids Americans from killing other Americans overseas. "A CIA operative involved in the killing who is American is presumptively a murderer," Heller wrote. "Progressives can't have it both ways: if Bush could ignore the torture statute, Obama can ignore the foreign-murder statute; if Bush could not, Obama cannot."[59] In a significant omission, Barron and Lederman had not even addressed the existence of the foreign-murder statute.

They told their colleagues that now that there was more time, they needed to research and write a better memo. The decision sent anxiety through the national security establishment; Johnson and Preston sought and received reassurances that the first memo remained good law in the meantime, in case the United States found al-Awlaki before they finished. Over the next few months, they would produce dozens of drafts, and the replacement grew to six times the length of the original.

The foreign-murder statute was only one of the additional issues they addressed. But it was a particular problem. The domestic-murder statute covers only "unlawful" killings, so it was easy to say that killing an enemy in war or self-defense was lawful and so not murder. But the text of the foreign-murder statute contains no exceptions; on its face, it simply covers all instances in which any American kills any other American overseas. One solution was to say that Obama, as commander in chief, could override the statute in a national security context. But Barron and Lederman had written a massive *Harvard Law Review* article criticizing that theory and the Bush-Cheney legal team for embracing it. Another solution was to go to Congress and ask it to adjust the statute, but the whole thing was secret, and if they conceded that the statute mattered and then al-Awlaki was found before lawmakers acted, it would prevent a strike during that fleeting window of opportunity.

Prosecutors had almost never used the statute, so there was little precedent to examine. But Barron and Lederman found a 1997 case involving a woman charged with killing her child while in Japan.[60] Her defense lawyer argued that the foreign-murder statute was too blunt to be constitutional because on its face it outlawed all killings, even those that lacked criminal intent. But the judge had ruled that the foreign statute must be interpreted as implicitly incorporating all the exceptions of its domestic homicide counterpart.

"Congress did not intend to criminalize justifiable or excusable killings," the judge wrote.

It was just a federal district court case, but the 1997 ruling was a hook for Barron and Lederman: judicial authority to cite and echo. When government officials, acting with public authority, kill an enemy abroad in wartime or as a matter of national self-defense, they wrote, Congress did not intend to criminalize that act as murder. They had found a way to interpret the foreign-murder statute as posing no bar to a strike on al-Awlaki without invoking the sweeping theories of presidential powers to override statutes that they had previously denounced.

There was another sticky question: What if a civilian official at the CIA, not a soldier in uniform, pressed the button to fire the missile? This raised several even more esoteric legal issues,[61] and however Barron and Lederman worked through them, that section remained redacted when their longer memo was released in response to our law-suits. The bottom line was that the memo concluded that the Authorization for Use of Military Force was an independent legal basis for the CIA to target al-Qaeda members and that the foreign-murder statute would not apply to agency personnel participating alongside the military in that war, so long as their targeting obeyed the laws of armed conflict.

There was, however, an incredibly awkward coincidence that called into question the whole enterprise. In the spring of 2010, as Barron and Lederman were laboring away on the longer al-Awlaki memo, prosecutors at Guantánamo were preparing to open the first trial under Obama's revamped military commissions system. A Canadian detainee, Omar Khadr, was charged with "murder in violation of the laws of war."* Military prosecutors accused Khadr of throwing a grenade that killed an American soldier during a firefight in Afghanistan in 2002. Soldiers who fight in uniform for state armed forces are *privileged belligerents,* meaning they are permitted to kill in battle, as long as they obey the laws of war, and cannot be prosecuted as murderers. But the government maintained that it could prosecute Khadr for a war crime because he was an *unprivileged belligerent.*

The Pentagon had written that language for the Bush-era manual for military commissions and copied it into the Obama-era rewrite. Lederman glanced over it, recognized the profound disconnect, and raised internal alarms: How could the United States prosecute Khadr as a war criminal while simultaneously maintaining that civilian CIA drone operators, who are also unprivileged belligerents, were obeying the laws of war when they killed people?

The Pentagon scrambled to rewrite the manual, which delayed its

---

* See chapter 7, section 9.

publication until the cusp of Khadr's opening hearing. The new-look version said that a killing by an unprivileged belligerent was not an *international* war crime after all but could violate *domestic* laws against murder. The upshot for the CIA was that its drone operators were theoretically subject to prosecution in Pakistani or Yemeni courtrooms under those countries' domestic laws against murder—a remote possibility, given that they were working from satellite uplinks in Langley, Virginia, and that their identities were secret. But they were not war criminals and they were safe from prosecution in the United States.

Barron signed the second al-Awlaki memo on July 16, 2010. It was his last day before returning to Harvard; Lederman returned to Georgetown in September, though he continued as a contract consultant until February 2011. Four years later, Barron was confirmed as a federal appeals court judge just before the two al-Awlaki memos became public.

9. Why Wasn't al-Awlaki Indicted?

On October 29, 2010, acting on a tip from Saudi intelligence, bomb squads searched cargo planes during layovers in England and Dubai. They found two packages sent from Yemen, addressed to locations in Chicago and containing Hewlett-Packard laser printers. Terrorists had replaced the toner in the printer cartridges with plastic explosives and rigged them to explode just before the planes landed in the United States. Intelligence officials suspected that the same master bomb maker who had built the Christmas underwear bomb had designed the cartridge bombs. They also claimed to reporters that al-Awlaki was directly involved in this plot too.[62]

Several days later, in an unrelated case, the Yemeni government prosecuted al-Awlaki in absentia in a Yemen court for plotting to kill foreigners. But he was never indicted in the United States. The Justice Department, I was told, did prepare a draft criminal complaint against him so that it was in a position to swiftly file it in court as the basis of an extradition request were Yemen to arrest al-Awlaki, but that never happened. This presents a puzzle: If the evidence of his ties to the Christmas underwear-bomb plot and later the cartridge-bomb plot was strong enough to justify killing him, why was it not strong enough to charge him with conspiracy to commit terrorist attacks?

Part of the answer may be that the standard of proof for courtroom convictions is higher than for wartime intelligence conclusions; the criminal justice system is tilted more toward individual rights than national security. Notably, al-Awlaki did not publicly confess. In a February 2010 Al Jazeera interview, for example, he praised Abdulmutallab's attack and called him "one of my students" but denied that he had actually directed the underwear-bomb plot: "There was communication between us. However I did not issue a fatwa to [Abdulmutallab] for this operation."[63]

Still, Andy Arena, then the special agent in charge of the Detroit field office who oversaw the Christmas underwear-bombing attempt, said he thought al-Awlaki should have been indicted, "just like Osama bin Laden was charged out of New York" in 1998 after al-Qaeda's bombings of American embassies in Africa.

Officials told me different reasons for why al-Awlaki was not indicted. One official said there were parallel conversations between the Justice Department's National Security Division and the Pentagon and the CIA. Participants had differences of opinion about whether, if the government indicted al-Awlaki, that might create a "bad fact" for its belief that it was also lawful to simply kill him. A bad fact, legally, is something that creates a problem for your side's argument—a point the adversarial side will trumpet. It doesn't necessarily mean your side is wrong, but, at a minimum, it has to be addressed and explained away. Here, an indictment would have suggested that al-Awlaki was a criminal, not a wartime enemy.

But another official said that the reason was more strategic. The Supreme Court has ruled over a long line of cases that indicting a suspect activates his right to legal representation during his interactions with the government. Were al-Awlaki indicted and then later arrested, it would have been harder to hold him for a lengthy period of interrogation without a defense lawyer present for the purpose of gathering intelligence about any pending attacks. Using a criminal complaint instead of an indictment has its own drawbacks: complaints are usually accompanied by a lengthy and detailed affidavit by an FBI agent explaining to a judge why the government thinks someone committed a crime, and the defendant usually gains access to that affidavit ahead of any trial. Since an affidavit in al-Awlaki's case would need to discuss classified intelligence sources, the government was reluctant to risk filing it unless it proved to be necessary. Bin Laden, this person said, had been indicted in the 1990s when no one was thinking about these kinds of permutations yet; national security lawyering has developed extensively since 9/11.

From Arena's vantage point, crass politics may also have played a role: "I'm not living in the political world in Washington. If they would have indicted him criminally, it would have set off a firestorm on the Republican side: 'See, there you go again, treating this as a criminal problem.'"

10. Signature Strikes

On March 17, 2011, a CIA drone tracked a car in the mountainous tribal region of northwest Pakistan that borders Afghanistan. The agency did not know the names of the men in the car. Still, the men's activities seemed to bear the pattern of Taliban militants; according to some accounts, they were linked to a Pakistani Taliban leader in the area. Under American policy, this made the car eligible for a different category of targeted killing: a *signature strike.*

In the beginning of the armed-drone era, attacks by the CIA were limited to *personality strikes* targeted at specific, known individuals whom intelligence analysts have judged to be high-value terrorists. But in the final year of the Bush-Cheney administration, as al-Qaeda and the Taliban were regrouping in the Pakistani tribal areas, the standards for targeting militants there were relaxed under a secret deal with Pakistani president Pervez Musharraf. Two of my *New York Times* colleagues, Eric Schmitt and David Sanger, soon caught wind of this deal and published a description of it in February 2008. "Instead of having to confirm the identity of a suspected militant leader before attacking, this shift allowed American operators to strike convoys of vehicles that bear the characteristics of Qaeda or Taliban leaders on the run, for instance, so long as the risk of civilian casualties is judged to be low," they wrote.[64]

Other so-called patterns of life that could make people targetable for a signature strike clearly included being present in a suspected terrorist training camp or compound. But officials were secretive about the standards they used, and intelligence could be ambiguous; if a group of armed men were seen loading a large amount of fertilizer into a truck, were they planning to use it as a bomb or were they farmers? Nearly everyone in tribal Pakistan was routinely armed.

Signature strikes were the reason that the pace of American attacks in Pakistan started its rise in Bush's last year in office. When Obama became president, he was initially skeptical of their legitimacy, but security agencies persuaded him that they were valuable and should continue. One reason was *force protection* in what was effectively an extension of the battlefield: the low-level militants just across the loosely drawn border from Afghanistan were attacking American troops and then withdrawing again. Another was that the United States sometimes ended up killing high-value terrorists without realizing that they were among a group of suspected militants in its sights. By May 2010, the *Los Angeles Times* reported that "of more than 500 people who U.S. officials say have been killed since the pace of strikes intensified, the vast majority have been individuals whose names were unknown, or about whom the agency had only fragmentary information. In some cases, the CIA discovered only after an attack that the casualties included a suspected terrorist whom it had been seeking."[65]

But it was also easier to make mistakes when the agency was basing its targeting decisions on fragmentary information. The number of civilian casualties in Pakistan was mounting — although the exact figures were disputed, in part because the area was so dangerous that few independent reporters went there. Public anger at the United States among Pakistanis was soaring, and it spiked further in early 2011 after it turned out that Raymond Davis, an American who shot two Pakistani men he said were trying to kidnap him and was arrested by Pakistani police, was a CIA contractor.

That was the context as the car carrying the Taliban-linked men came into the sights of the CIA's remote-piloted aircraft. But the agency decided to wait and hit whomever the men contacted too.[66] The car pulled up to an open space near a village market where a group of several dozen men were apparently waiting to meet them. Now the CIA drones fired. Between twenty-six and forty-eight people were killed, according to varying accounts, and dozens more were injured. An American official would tell the *New York Times* that all were insurgents: "These people weren't gathering for a bake sale. They were terrorists."[67]

But local villagers and a Pakistani intelligence official told a very different story. The gathering had been a *jirga,* or meeting of tribal elders, to resolve a dispute concerning ownership of a local chromite mine. The Taliban, which effectively governed the region and taxed chromite mining, had sent members there to mediate the dispute. One of the dead turned out to be a top Taliban militia commander, but most of the casualties were local civilians who had come to talk about the mining dispute.

The Pakistani military chief, General Ashfaq Parvez Kayani, took the unusual step of publicly condemning the United States for the attack. "It is highly regrettable that a jirga of peaceful citizens, including elders of the area, was carelessly and callously targeted with complete disregard to human life," he said.

As new protests against the United States roared across Pakistan, the Obama administration reconsidered its signature-strike policy. Hillary Clinton and Mike Mullen, the chairman of the Joint Chiefs, had become increasingly skeptical of the CIA's methodology. After the

March 17 strike, Tom Donilon, now the national security adviser, and others at the White House questioned whether the agency should back off on signature strikes and return to focusing on specific high-level alleged terrorists, not foot soldiers.[68] In the end, the administration changed the rules to give the U.S. ambassador to Pakistan more opportunity to challenge proposed strikes and make sure that any disagreements between State and the CIA were vetted at a higher level.

The ethics and efficacy of targeting groups of people whose identities were unknown would remain controversial. In 2012, the Obama administration loosened limits on targeting in Yemen to permit strikes at presumed militants whose identities were unknown.[69] But it insisted, even internally, that it was not approving signature strikes there, instead coming up with a new term, *terrorist attack disruption strikes,* or TADS. The idea was that there had to be evidence of a threat to the United States.[70]

Whether that amounted to any real difference or was just rebranding to remove the taint that had been attached to the term *signature strikes* was less clear. But as Obama's first term wound down, his legal team began developing a new playbook that would tighten the rules again.

11. The Secret (bin Laden I)

I am about to read you into the biggest secret in Washington, said Mike Vickers, the undersecretary of defense for intelligence.

It was March 24, 2011. A few days earlier, Mary DeRosa, the top lawyer at the National Security Council, and Preston, the top CIA lawyer, had made a highly unusual trip to the Pentagon to see Johnson and Crawford, the top civilian and uniformed lawyers for the military. Meeting in Johnson's Pentagon office suite, DeRosa and Preston asked what they portrayed as a hypothetical question: *Suppose we found a very high-value target. What issues would be raised?*

Johnson and Crawford kicked around the abstract issues. Among other things, Johnson offered a note of policy apostasy. If someone like Osama bin Laden or his deputy Ayman al-Zawahiri was captured, Johnson said, *I'd make an exception to our policy not to add any new prisoners to Guantánamo.*

DeRosa and Preston left without explaining why they had come all the way to the Pentagon to ask such a question. The meeting had been awkward. Afterward, Preston and DeRosa talked it over. In fact, Preston had wanted to tell them why they were asking such questions. But the White House was holding the secret extremely close because of intense concerns about leaks. Now, Preston told DeRosa that he did not think it was productive to engage like that with colleagues who did not know. DeRosa took the message back to Donilon. Soon afterward, Vickers had told Johnson that they needed to talk about something. (Crawford was briefed separately.)

Vickers walked through a slide presentation showing the multiyear investigative trail leading to a mysterious, high-walled compound in Abbottabad, a military-garrison town thirty-five miles north of the Pakistani capital of Islamabad. Surveillance from the sky showed that a tall, thin man occasionally paced on the building's terrace. Intelligence analysts believed the pacing man might in fact be post-9/11 America's greatest enemy.

The hunt for Osama bin Laden has been much scrutinized. But the legal advice that helped shape Obama's decisions about what to do and that permitted the operation that killed the al-Qaeda leader to go forward despite several difficult legal problems has never been reported. That story adds another dimension to one of the most important national security events of the Obama presidency.

When Johnson next saw DeRosa, she murmured, *I know you got read into it.* It was a relief to have another top lawyer in the mix. Preston had learned first about what the CIA called "AC1," for Abbottabad Compound 1, around September 2010. Not long after, DeRosa had been told when the CIA briefed Obama, and for a long time they were the only two lawyers thinking about what could be an extraordinarily high-risk and legally edgy operation.

The Obama lawyers had little doubt that bin Laden was a lawful target; Congress had, after all, authorized the use of military force against the perpetrators of the 9/11 attacks, and as the leader of al-Qaeda, he was presumably always thinking of new ways to attack the United States. But the question of how to go after him raised a complex tangle of legal and policy dilemmas. They discussed the case over secure conference calls and in meetings in DeRosa's office, sometimes pulling each other aside after unrelated meetings to whisper updates while pretending to the rest of the administration that nothing was going on.

It was an extraordinary time. Many fraught issues were consuming the national security legal and policy teams at once. These included the fallout from Pakistan's arrest of the CIA contractor Raymond Davis and the bad signature strike on the chromite dispute meeting. There was, at the same time, huge controversy over Obama's decision to intervene militarily in Libya without congressional authorization and a swelling issue over whether the War Powers Resolution required him to pull out of the operation by May 20.* At one point after a tense meeting about Libya, a senior intelligence programs official at the National Security Council shook his head, privately telling one of the few lawyers who knew about Abbottabad, *All these people think that is the most important thing going on.* They had no idea.

For a long time, the inner circle of lawyers was just those four. Donilon was fearful of any leak that could cause bin Laden to get away again, and he limited as much as he could the number of people who were told the secret. Among the regular members of the interagency national security lawyers group, both Koh and Caroline Krass, who was now the acting head of the Justice Department's Office of Legal Counsel, were left out. Later Bob Bauer, the White House counsel; Charles Newman, an additional National Security Council lawyer working for DeRosa; and Robert Eatinger, a CIA lawyer working for Preston, were told the secret so they could help. But despite all the legal problems the operation involved, as late as April 28, a week out from

---

* See chapter 12, sections 4 and 5.

the raid, even Holder remained in the dark. At that point, Mike Leiter, the National Counterterrorism Center director, suggested bringing the nation's top law enforcement official into the legal deliberations.

I think the AG should be here, just to make sure, he told DeRosa.

That was a decision for Donilon and for Bauer. It was not clear why Holder's input was necessary, they said; Holder, as well as Mueller, the FBI director, were told to come to the White House on the following Saturday, one day before the raid, and were finally briefed, long after the legal issues had been settled.

12. Operation Neptune Spear (bin Laden II)

The administration explored several courses of action, which they referred to as COAs.

One course was to ask Pakistan to arrest bin Laden or conduct a joint raid on the compound with Pakistani security forces. But the United States did not trust the ISI, the Pakistani intelligence service, because elements of it had close ties to the Taliban. Heightening their suspicions, the CIA acquired intelligence suggesting that Mullah Omar, the fugitive leader of the Taliban, was being treated for an illness in the Aga Khan University Hospital in Karachi. In January 2011, the CIA director, Leon Panetta, confronted Pakistani President Asif Ali Zardari over the Mullah Omar intelligence, but nothing came of it, according to diplomatic files leaked to *The Washington Post* after it emerged that Omar likely died in a Karachi hospital in 2013.[71] The fact that bin Laden had been living for years in a suspicious-looking compound in Abbottabad, the heart of the Pakistani security establishment, was strong circumstantial evidence that ISI elements might have been helping him or at least knew he was there.[72] Obama was not willing to risk their tipping him off that the United States had located him.

Another course was an air strike. Obama's military advisers, including Gates and General James Cartwright, the vice chairman of the Joint Chiefs, favored this option. They argued that it was the least risky, and

Gates recalled the disaster when a helicopter bearing commandos went down in 1980 on a mission to rescue hostages in Iran. There were two variations of this plan.

One variation called for having B-2 stealth bombers drop thirty-two smart bombs, each two thousand pounds, to annihilate the compound. This would ensure the destruction of any bunkers beneath the compound. If bin Laden was inside, he would die. But all the women and children in his compound would die, too. And so would a lot of other people who had nothing to do with bin Laden: the compound was in the middle of a neighborhood. The tentative casualty estimate was fifty to a hundred people, "most of whom, of course, would be innocent civilians in a country with whom we were not at war," as Panetta later wrote.[73] Cartwright put it in more vivid terms: "That much ordnance going off would be the equivalent of an earthquake."[74]

People familiar with his lawyers' advice told me that the military advantage of killing bin Laden was so high that the lawyers — at that point, still just Preston and DeRosa — were prepared to deem as necessary and proportionate, and so legally justified, a significant number of civilian bystander deaths. But even if something was a legally available option, it didn't mean it was a good idea. Moreover, success would mean not just killing bin Laden but *verifying* that he was dead. The decision not to use heavy bombing, then, was both legal and political.

"There was, number one, the collateral-damage dimension," Donilon later told me. "Not only would there be noncombatants at the compound killed, there could be completely innocent people. That was a key factor in the decision. And all it would have bought us was a propaganda fight. Al-Qaeda would deny he had been killed, we would say he had been killed, and we'd not be able to settle it. And this goes back to number one, because they'd claim all the civilian deaths were a complete botching. We had a long discussion about collateral damage."

The other air-strike variation involved aiming a small missile from a special small drone at the pacing man. The missile was too tiny to hurt anyone else. But if it missed, there would be no second chance, and even if it hit its target, Pakistan might not give the United States direct access to the remains to conduct its own DNA test. Obama ruled out that option for policy reasons alone.[75]

A final proposed course of action was a raid by American forces. Advisers played around with two variations of this too: sending CIA operatives over the wall to snatch him, or sending in helicopter-borne SEAL Team Six commandos, which was more realistic. A raid would reduce the risk of civilian casualties and permit the United States to verify that bin Laden was there. But it raised other problems, including the possibility that the Americans would be killed or captured. Obama decided to take that risk: the commandos had to go in so they could bring out the body.

The daring raid was code-named Operation Neptune Spear, and it raised tremendous legal problems. As it moved from just one possible course of action, to a likely course, to the central plan, and as Crawford and Johnson were brought in, the lawyers worked through every significant legal issue that they could identify. In most of the operational planning sessions in the Situation Room — some led by Donilon, some by Brennan — DeRosa, as the National Security Council's legal adviser, was the only lawyer in the room. But as she answered questions, she was also relaying advice from her three colleagues. There was one key White House meeting, on April 12, 2011, at which the legal issues received a fuller airing. Preston attended this one. Following a briefing by then-Vice Admiral William McRaven, the commander of the Pentagon's Joint Special Operations Command, who had been working up a plan for a raid, Preston briefed the assembled officials about the major issues that Obama and the other policymakers needed to make decisions about, or at least be aware of. He marched through a set of slides he and DeRosa had prepared.

By the end of the planning for the raid, the four key lawyers were satisfied that, as they communicated to Obama and their principals, there was clear and ample authority for the use of lethal force under U.S. and international law. But several days before the first potential date on which the operation might take place, Preston called DeRosa and proposed that they prepare memos for the record about each of the major issues they had worked out and their resolutions. His reasoning was sobering.

We should memorialize our rationales because we may be called upon to explain our legal conclusions, particularly if the operation goes terribly badly, he said. *We won't have time to articulate them with any care after the fact, and we want to show that this was not post hoc rationalization. And it will further discipline our thinking, and confirm that there is consensus, to write it down.*

DeRosa had also said during the deliberations that they should be thinking about it from the perspective of a future congressional oversight investigation if things went wrong. She agreed that writing it all down was wise. Preston drew up a list of discrete questions and assigned them to various members of the group. They put together five short memos on classified laptops. Too closely guarded even for the classified e-mail system, they relied on trusted couriers of their own to hand-circulate the drafts — a curious echo of how bin Laden himself communicated to avoid surveillance.

Perhaps the biggest legal issue was Pakistani sovereignty. Pakistan had granted permission only for air strikes over the rugged tribal area adjacent to Afghanistan, and a raid involving ground forces who penetrated deep into its sovereign territory was a far different thing. International law appeared to require the United States to ask Pakistan to send its own security forces to raid the compound. But the risk that elements in Pakistan's government would tip off bin Laden was deemed to be too high for that. The four lawyers searched for a legal justification permitting a unilateral military incursion into Pakistani territory without its consent.

Though they all had developed the legal analysis together, the sovereignty problem was Johnson's specific task to write up. His memo invoked the idea that Pakistan was *unable or unwilling* to suppress the threat emanating from its soil, and thus its sovereignty could be violated lawfully by the United States under its right to national self-defense. The "unable or unwilling" exception is not universally accepted as customary international law. But the United States and a few other

Western countries have expanded the notion of self-defense to encompass this right to strike at a nonstate terrorist group operating inside the territory of a nation even if its government does not grant consent.[76]

In working through his research, Johnson drew upon a memo on "unwilling or unable" developed the previous September in Vancouver by the West Point Group, an annual meeting of national security lawyers from countries like the United States and various members of the European Union that face counterterrorism issues and also engage in international military operations. While many other countries and international legal scholars disagreed that there was an "unable or unwilling" exception, the West Point Group memo suggested that there was emerging acceptance that sovereignty could be overridden in such limited circumstances.[77]

Still, the doctrine's contours were undefined, and even by American standards, it was a novelty and a stretch to apply it to government-controlled territory in Pakistan *without even asking* for its government's help first to see if it was willing to raid the compound. Moreover, there was precedent for Pakistan's being able and willing to help, since Pakistani security forces had conducted many joint counterterrorism operations on its soil in the past.

But under the circumstances, the four lawyers concluded that Pakistan could be deemed unwilling or unable to suppress the threat posed by bin Laden, so its sovereignty rights could be overridden.

Some legal scholars disagree that this was the best interpretation of the law of sovereignty. Still, it might be a *colorable* or *legally available* claim, as lawyers like to say, meaning an argument that is not laughably off the wall. There was also a trump card. For all of Obama's focus on obeying international law, his legal team believed that Obama could decide to violate a *covert action* — a step to shape foreign affairs that the United States would not acknowledge international law as part of — as long as Congress had never incorporated the global rule into a domestic law. They revealed that view in early 2014, when Obama nominated

Krass to be the general counsel of the CIA and the administration cleared her to say this in a written answer to a question posed by the Senate Intelligence Committee.[78]

There was a limit to how useful covert cover was. If the Obama administration killed bin Laden, it was going to trumpet its accomplishment, and the secret would never have been possible to keep anyway. Obama also signed off on a plan for the commandos to fight their way out rather than be captured if the local police or Pakistani military arrived, and if that kind of gunfight erupted, it would be hard to cover up. But it was also possible that the SEALs would arrive at Abbottabad and kill people at the compound only to discover that the pacing man was not bin Laden after all, and then slip back out of Pakistan. In that case, the United States might be able to avoid acknowledging that it had violated Pakistani sovereignty, allowing both countries to pretend in public that it had never happened.

Preston spearheaded a memo about whether the executive branch must notify Congress ahead of time about a development under the covert finding authorizing the C.I.A. to go after Al Qaeda. A federal statute generally requires notice to the Intelligence committees or, in extremely sensitive situations, just the Gang of Eight — the top Democrat and Republican in each chamber and on each intelligence committee. The lawyers decided that the president could decide that the risk of any leak legally justified delaying notice until after the raid. But it later turned out that Panetta, the CIA director, had unilaterally briefed top lawmakers about the Abbottabad discovery anyway.[79]

(Separate from the five legal policy memos, there was also a legal memo about having Navy SEALs conduct the raid as a covert CIA-run mission. Although federal law permits other agencies to carry out covert actions, by tradition, only the CIA does so. Johnson prepared paperwork for Vickers and Gates to loan SEAL Team Six and their supervisors, up to and including McRaven, to the CIA as "sensitive support" for its mission.) From McRaven, the chain of command now ran up to Panetta and then to the president. McRaven's usual superiors, the

Special Operations combatant commander, Admiral Eric Olson, and Gates above him, were cut out.

Reality on the ground in Abbottabad would limit the administration's ultimate options; the secrecy option fell apart as soon as the SEALs arrived over the compound and one of their helicopters promptly crashed. No matter who turned out to be inside, there could be no plausible deniability afterward because they were going to leave an American helicopter behind. After the raid, Pakistan's government would protest the "unauthorized unilateral action," raging: "Such an event shall not serve as a future precedent for any state, including the United States."[80]

13. Kill or Capture (bin Laden III)

Before the raid, Preston, DeRosa, Johnson, and Crawford also grappled with whether it was lawful to tell the commandos to go in with the intention of killing bin Laden, rather than to try to capture him alive.

The law-of-war and lethal force question had been one of DeRosa's memos, and officials told me that it was, explicitly, a kill mission, with capture as a secondary and largely theoretical option. The lawyers concluded that bin Laden was a lawful military target and that using lethal force against such a target was acceptable under the laws of war so long as the commandos were prepared to accept any genuine offer by bin Laden to surrender. In any battle, it is a war crime to "deny quarter," meaning to kill an enemy who is surrendering and so no longer poses a threat. Panetta later wrote, "Assuming we found Bin Laden, we were prepared to take him prisoner, but we anticipated resistance and were prepared to capture him only if he conspicuously surrendered. This was a military raid, not an arrest."[81]

Still, the lawyers had told the White House that if bin Laden did surrender in a way that could be reasonably accepted, the SEALs would have no choice but to capture him alive. If that happened, one option was to take him to Guantánamo. But that would violate Obama's vow not to add to the detainee population there. Another was to bring him into the United States to face trial in New York, where he had been indicated in 1998. But controversy over security had already derailed Holder's plans to hold a 9/11 trial there for KSM and four other accused conspirators who were already in American custody.

Later, in 2012, Obama said that if bin Laden had been captured alive, Obama had personally been inclined to prosecute the al-Qaeda leader in a civilian court — which government officials often called an Article III court, because the judicial branch is established by Article III of the Constitution, as opposed to a court run by the military. "We worked through the legal and political issues that would have been involved, and Congress and the desire to send him to Guantánamo, and to not try him, and Article III," Obama said. "I mean, we had worked through a whole bunch of those scenarios. But, frankly, my belief was, if we had captured him, that I would be in a pretty strong position, politically, here, to argue that displaying due process and rule of law would be our best weapon against al-Qaeda, in preventing him from appearing as a martyr."[82]

It was true they had contemplated many scenarios, but they never actually picked one because no one expected bin Laden to get out alive. DeRosa wrote a memo about detaining bin Laden, but the only firm plan was to take him to a ship for interrogation and then figure out what to do next. (The lawyers also developed analysis about handling any other prisoners, but they did not record it in a memo because the final plan called for the SEALs to leave everyone else behind.)

One reason that they did not think bin Laden would live was that the SEAL Team expected to face resistance at the compound and were going in with killing him as their default option. Moreover, they knew that military rules of engagement for such an operation would narrowly construe what kind of surrender offer would count as feasible to accept. If bin Laden was trying to surrender amid a firefight but other al-Qaeda fighters around him were still shooting, the SEALS could shoot him alongside them anyway. The commandos also had to believe that any offer to surrender was genuine — and there was always the possibility he might be wearing a suicide-bomb vest under his clothes. In short, to be captured alive, bin Laden would more or less have to be discovered virtually naked, alone, on his knees, and with his hands in the air.

"If we had the opportunity to take bin Laden alive, if he didn't present any threat, the individuals involved were able and prepared to do that," Brennan said the day after the raid. "We were not going to put our people at risk. The president put a premium on making sure that our personnel were protected and we were not going to give bin Laden or any of his cohorts the opportunity to carry out lethal fire on our forces."[83]

The rules of engagement as relayed to the operators appear to have been somewhat less nuanced. In a 2012 memoir, one of the SEAL Team members recalled that a team of VIPs from Washington, led by Mullen, came out to the training site for a briefing and dress rehearsal. "Toward the end," he recalled, "a question was raised about whether or not this was a kill mission. A lawyer from either the Department of Defense or the White House made it clear this wasn't an assassination. 'If he is naked with his hands up, you're not going to engage him,' he told us. 'I am not going to tell you how to do your job. What we're saying is if he does not pose a threat, you will detain him.'"[84] (While Preston was on this trip, this speaker was most likely McRaven's top uniformed lawyer, not one of the administration lawyers.) And in a 2013 interview with *Esquire*, another SEAL Team member recalled a tacit understanding was that killing was the preferred outcome. "Everybody wanted him dead, but nobody wanted to say, Hey, you're going to kill this guy. It was just sort of understood that's what we wanted to do," he said.[85]

There are inconsistent accounts of how the raid unfolded; it was dark and chaotic and things moved quickly, and years later, members of the team would disagree about who took the kill shot.[86] But there are some basic lines of agreement. The SEALs stormed the compound and shot three adult males as they rapidly cleared each room. As two members of the team approached the third floor, a tall, thin man with a beard and close-cropped hair under a white cap was peering around a curtain covering a door. It was bin Laden. The point man fired from ten feet away—maybe striking bin Laden, maybe not—and the tall man disappeared back into the room. Two or three women ran out of the room, and the point man grabbed two women and shoved them aside, clearing a path and protecting his teammates had the women been wearing suicide vests. The second man rolled into the room. The accounts begin to differ here as to whether bin Laden was already down, shot in the head by the point man, or whether he was standing and the second man shot him in the head.[87] In any case, bin Laden was quickly down and dead or dying from a severe head wound as other SEAL members poured into the room and pumped additional rounds into his chest.

When the shooting was over, they found two weapons on a shelf in the room, but bin Laden was unarmed. There were no booby traps and no one was wearing an explosive vest. Bin Laden had neither resisted nor surrendered.

14. *What Would a Lawyer Have to Add at This Point?* (bin Laden IV)

A final legal-policy question the lawyers grappled with before the operation was what to do with bin Laden's corpse assuming the raid went off as planned and the commandos flew safely back out of Pakistan with the body. This memo fell to Crawford, the Joint Chiefs' lawyer.

National security officials strongly wanted a burial at sea to avoid creating a shrine for Islamist militants. The American navy has procedures for burying sailors at sea if they die on a vessel while it is deployed in wartime, and some veterans ask to be buried at sea. But doing that with bin Laden's corpse seemed incompatible with the laws of war. The Geneva Conventions say enemy dead killed in battle must be "honourably interred, if possible according to the rites of the religion to which they belonged" and "that their graves are…marked so that they may always be found."[88] It is generally obligatory in Islam to bury the dead in the ground, with their bodies turned toward Mecca. Islam does permit burial at sea, but only if there is not time to reach land — an anachronism in the modern era, when helicopters can fly between ship and land.[89]

Crawford's research focused on what became a crucial nuance: ultimately, it is not *offensive* to Islam to bury a Muslim at sea; it is religiously acceptable if necessary, not a desecration. But the lawyers knew this decision, like everything else about the operation, would be put under a microscope. Crawford said bin Laden's home country, Saudi Arabia, must be asked whether it wanted to take the corpse. If the Saudi government declined, there would be no other obvious land where the United States could bury bin Laden. Given the situation, the lawyers said that they could instead invoke Islamic permission for burial at sea.

After the raid, the military flew bin Laden's body to the USS *Carl Vinson* in the Arabian Sea. The United States asked the Saudi government if it wanted him back, and, as expected, it declined. So bin Laden's body was given some Muslim burial traditions — washed and wrapped in a weighted white shroud and given final prayers in Arabic by a military chaplain. It was then placed in a body bag with three hundred pounds of iron chains, placed on a table, and tipped over the rail.[90]

Around six o'clock on the Sunday morning of the raid, Johnson had planted a flat of impatiens on the side yard of his Georgetown town house and then donned a sport coat and casually told his family he needed to go to work and was not sure when he would be home. On his way he stopped by an Episcopal church in Georgetown and took Communion. Crawford attended mass at his Catholic church in a northern Virginia suburb of Washington and then had a similar conversation with his wife. Both converged on the Pentagon, where they would watch and listen to feeds from the raid in the operations center. DeRosa and Bauer were on hand at the White House Situation Room. Preston watched from the CIA's headquarters in Langley. He had packed an overnight bag with a toothbrush and a change of clothes and brought it with him, knowing that if the operation went bad they would be up all night and beyond. He and about a dozen officials watched in the CIA director's conference room, which served as a command center for Panetta to oversee the raid.

At the White House, Obama and his top aides and cabinet officials began in the big Situation Room, where technicians piped in an audio feed of the operation. But a closer-up video feed was playing only in the small Situation Room. When Obama realized he was missing the visual, he wanted to see it, but it would have taken three or four minutes for the technicians to take it down and bring it back up again on the big room's screen — and those were crucial minutes. Obama left to watch in the smaller antechamber, and a dozen or so senior officials followed him into the cramped room, where the White House photographer took a famous photograph of a grim-faced Obama and other senior officials staring at the off-camera screen, apparently moments after the helicopter had crash-landed. The lawyers quietly stayed behind in the main Situation Room.

When the second helicopter lifted with all the American commandos aboard, a cheer went up in Panetta's conference room. At the White House, people relaxed, especially after the helicopters safely exited Pakistani airspace. But they lingered to unwind. The highest-stakes national security decision of Obama's presidency had succeeded. While legal factors alone had not dictated the decision Obama made — military, diplomatic, and political considerations were intertwined, as they always are in national security policymaking — a serious engagement with legal issues had permeated and shaped the deliberations.

On the day of the operation, however, the lawyers' role was over. As the cabinet officials started to drift away from the Situation Room, Mullen remarked to Bauer, *You haven't said anything all day long.*

Bauer responded: *What would a lawyer have to add at this point?*

15. Drone Fallacies

In early May 2011, a few days after the bin Laden raid, the United States learned that al-Awlaki was hiding in the remote Yemeni village of Abdan. The United States had paused its strikes in Yemen a year earlier after a botched bombing killed a Yemeni government official, enraging

Saleh.[91] American and allied intelligence agencies used the lull to step up their efforts to penetrate al-Qaeda in the Arabian Peninsula. In the meantime, as one event after another kept linking back to al-Awlaki, he was a topic of conversation at multiple Terror Tuesday meetings, threat briefings, and National Security Council meetings. Obama "was very fixated on him," making it clear that he saw al-Awlaki as a high-value target, and he was "never uncomfortable with the notion of targeting Awlaki as a matter of policy," one participant in those deliberations said.

Now there was a tantalizing opportunity to take out a second top target within a week — one that would open a new phase in the secret war in Yemen: drone warfare.

Under Obama, remote-controlled aircraft were becoming the weapon of choice for strikes away from traditional battlefields. In part this is because he had far more of them to deploy than Bush had had — the technology was brand-new and it had taken time to ramp up production. But Obama was also enraptured by their potential for risk reduction. Conventional air strikes put American pilots — and sometimes Special Operations spotters on the ground — at risk. By contrast, if a drone crashed or was shot down, its pilot still went home for dinner. They also enabled operators to watch a target for a long period before unleashing a missile, which held out the promise of greater precision and fewer civilian deaths.

Skeptics noted that drones' theoretical precision relied on the quality of the underlying intelligence, which was sometimes spotty in places where the United States had no ground forces. And the drones' constant presence in the sky created a new kind of blowback. At a Senate hearing in April 2013, a Yemeni man who had studied in an American high school testified that a drone strike on his home village had turned his former neighbors against the United States in a way that propaganda by al-Qaeda in the Arabian Peninsula had failed to do. This happened even though there had been no collateral damage; the strike killed only its intended target. But the villagers were now terrified by the bolt of death and the buzzing of unseen predators in the sky. His friends, he said, had known about the United States mostly through "my stories of the wonderful experiences I had" here. "Now, however, when they think of America, they think of the fear they feel at the drones over their heads."[92]

These are important policy considerations in weighing the rise of drones, but they are not legal factors. In public debate, people sometimes conflate the legality of targeted killings with the use of drones. This is a fallacy. There are some weapons systems, like chemical and biological weapons, that are inherently indiscriminate — a cloud of poisonous gas or a virus is not controllable enough to be *targeted* — and are banned. But drones are not one of those systems, and so the use of a drone is legally irrelevant: killing someone with a missile from a drone is the same as killing him with a missile fired from a traditional manned aircraft, or with a bullet, or with a rock to his head; sometimes those are legal, and sometimes not. From a legal angle, the *killing* is what matters, not how the killing is done.

There is a more nuanced way of thinking about drone strikes and legal tensions. It flows from the insight that even though individual strikes from drones are surely on average more accurate and surgical than previous methods of aerial bombardment, drones have lowered practical barriers to carrying out bombings in remote areas. This means there are now more total strikes. The United States was killing more enemies, including devastating the upper ranks of core al-Qaeda in Pakistan. But it was also likely killing as many or more innocent bystanders due to its *overall decision* to have a drone program than it would have killed with yesterday's blunter but less frequently used technology. In this sense, the practical limitations of older technology acted like a shadow gloss on targeted killing law, imposing a de facto higher standard on when the trigger would be pulled. This is yet another example of twenty-first-century situations calling into question twentieth-century rules.

Now, in May 2011, the intelligence that al-Awlaki was hiding in Abdan ushered in the era of routine drone warfare in Yemen. The military sent both traditional fighter jets over Abdan and, for the first time, armed drones launched from a base in Djibouti. Beneath them was a truck in which al-Awlaki was riding.

The first missile missed al-Awlaki's truck. Clouds and dust from the explosion blocked the view from above as al-Awlaki jumped into another vehicle, which drove off in a different direction. The American drones continued to follow the first truck. They destroyed it but missed their intended target.[93]

According to a later account of the strike in al-Qaeda in the Arabian Peninsula's online magazine *Inspire*, al-Awlaki took shelter in nearby cliffs. The near miss *increased my certainty that no human being will die until they complete their livelihood and appointed time*, he said. *But*, he added, *this time eleven missiles missed its target but the next time, the first rocket may hit it.*[94]

When Obama's advisers brought him the news that the strike had missed its target, the president's response was clear: *Keep after it.*

16. Is the United States at War with al-Shabaab?

In the summer of 2011, a simmering debate inside the Obama legal team regarding another expansion of targeting powers came to a head. It centered on whether al-Shabaab, the Islamist group vying for control of Somalia, was an *associated force* of al-Qaeda and engaged in the same armed conflict. If it was, then the United States could hit al-Shabaab militants systematically, including blowing up training camps full of rank-and-file fighters. If it was not, then the United States could target only senior leaders of al-Shabaab who had strong ties to al-Qaeda as individuals or posed a specific threat.

The difference defined whether the United States was essentially at war with a dozen people in Somalia — or thousands. It could also serve as a precedent for what might become a forever war. As the original al-Qaeda waned and new Islamist groups arose, the lower the standards the United States set for linking them to the existing armed conflict, the less likely the 9/11 war would come to an end.

The concept of looping an associated force into an existing war is not a well defined part of international law. Notably, in 1941 and 1942, the Roosevelt administration sought separate declarations of war from Congress against Germany, Italy, Bulgaria, Hungary, and Romania, rather than simply deeming each of them an associated force of Japan and so part of the original war declaration on December 8, 1941. The lines separating one terrorist organization from another were blurrier than those separating nation-states, but defining the standard for deciding who was in and who was out raised many difficulties. The Obama administration settled on a three-part test, first articulated publicly by Johnson in a 2012 speech at Yale Law School: an associated force was (1) an organized, armed group that (2) aligned itself with al-Qaeda, and (3) entered the fight against the United States and its coalition partners.[95]

Whether al-Shabaab passed that test first surfaced as an issue for the Obama legal team in September 2009, when intelligence arose that a senior militant in the group, Saleh Ali Saleh Nabhan, was likely to be traveling along an isolated coastal road. Johnson signed off on a plan to send helicopters from a navy ship to strafe Nabhan's convoy. The operation raised discussion of whether al-Shabaab itself was targetable, but there was no need to resolve the question because Nabhan also had enough personal ties to al-Qaeda that he could be deemed part of it.

But the status of al-Shabaab had the potential to become very fraught because Somali American teenagers from Minneapolis were going to their ancestral homeland to help al-Shabaab fight a U.S.-backed Kenyan invasion. Koh decided to become an expert on al-Shabaab, studying intelligence reports and seeking briefings from outside experts. By Thanksgiving 2009, he had become convinced that it was not a single well-organized group but rather a network of several factions. One was led by a militant known as Ahmed Abdi Godane who had sworn allegiance to al-Qaeda and had transnational ambitions. Another was led by a militant known as Mukhtar Robow who instead had a parochial focus on controlling Mogadishu. Because of this fracturing, Koh argued that al-Shabaab as a whole was not an associated force of al-Qaeda.

Johnson, too, was thinking hard about its status. In January 2010, he produced a lengthy top secret memo concurring that al-Shabaab as a group was not an associated force. His focus was a different part of the test; there just was not enough evidence that al-Shabaab had joined the broader fight against the United States and its allies. The next month, Special Operations Forces proposed striking an al-Shabaab operative who was going to be traveling with more than a dozen other militants. Johnson stunned his Pentagon colleagues by blocking the strike. He explained that the entourage was so large that killing them would amount to targeting al-Shabaab as a group and that he was not satisfied that the group was an associated force of al-Qaeda and so subject to battlefield-targeting rules.

This was not just a conversation that played out between Koh and Johnson. It was an interagency matter, and at various levels Obama, Gates, Brennan, Barron, DeRosa, and many others were involved in sorting through it. But Koh and Johnson's dialogue was a particularly striking part of the deliberations. Koh later told Johnson that placing constraints on the military's ability to target al-Shabaab in general was his *finest moment*.[96]

Whether or not that was so, the moment would not endure. The military's joint staff—including its director and the J2 intelligence directorate and the J3 operations directorate—launched a lobbying campaign to convince Johnson that he was wrong, sending Special Operations leaders to brief him on the latest intelligence threats. It was a season of mounting concern; in July 2010, al-Shabaab bombed a soccer stadium in Uganda, its first attack outside of Somalia.

By the fall of 2010, Johnson and Koh started to diverge. The occasion, first reported by Daniel Klaidman, was a secure conference call to discuss a targeting list for senior al-Shabaab leaders. Brennan would make the decision, but DeRosa was canvassing the interagency lawyers for input. Johnson said the United States could lawfully kill both Godane and Robow. Koh agreed that the United States could target Godane, given his al-Qaeda ties, but pushed back about killing Robow. Koh argued that killing the leader of the faction who opposed fighting the

West was unjustified. DeRosa told Koh that she understood his "policy" objections and would convey them to Brennan. But Koh insisted that his objections were "legal": Robow's faction was not a cobelligerent with al-Qaeda, he maintained, so by law he was not part of the armed conflict, and there was no self-defense rationale for killing him, either. So that there could be no mistake, Koh spoke with emphasis: *For the record, it is my belief, as the State Department legal adviser, that this killing would be unlawful.*[97] Johnson and DeRosa later told colleagues that Koh had been over the top.

But in a twist to this dramatic scene that has not been reported, DeRosa never conveyed Koh's concerns to Brennan at the meeting where the final list was approved. Brennan already agreed with Koh on policy grounds and had no interest in killing Robow, so the dispute over whether doing so was legal never arose at his meeting.

Meanwhile, Johnson was having increasing doubts about his initially cautious position on al-Shabaab. Intelligence officials were making the case that there were elements of the group—not just individual leaders, but the militants in their faction—who were part of the external fight with al-Qaeda. In December 2010, Johnson asked an intelligence officer a semi-rhetorical question: *Am I being stubborn for the sake of being stubborn?* Deciding to revisit the problem with fresh eyes, he assigned an aide, Chris Fonzone, to draft a memorandum analyzing the issue.* In early 2011, Johnson announced that, based on current intelligence— where al-Shabaab leaders had trained, who they were communicating with, what plots they were discussing—he had decided the entire group qualified as an associated force after all. If policymakers wanted to launch signature strikes at al-Shabaab foot soldiers, Johnson would bless them.

Koh dug in. As 2011 unfolded, they traded a series of sharply contrary memos. The dispute was theoretical because in order to minimize blowback, the administration's counterterrorism strategy was to target only individual Somalis believed to be involved in specific terrorist

---

* Fonzone would later join the Justice Department's Office of Legal Counsel and then become the number-two lawyer for the National Security Council in Obama's second term.

plots on American interests. But if hitting al-Shabaab systematically was seen as a legally available option, there was always the chance that the war would expand.

In 2012, Johnson started to change his mind yet again. Intelligence indicated that splits within al-Shabaab were growing, again suggesting they were less a group than a cluster of disorganized, discombobulated factions. Indeed, in 2013, after both Johnson and Koh had left the administration legal team, Robow challenged Godane's leadership, and their factions broke into open combat with each other. Godane was killed in an American drone strike in September 2014. Even after that, the question of whether al-Shabaab could be treated as an associated force—if a policymaker wanted—was still unresolved.

In September 2011, amid this flux, I wrote an article that brought to public attention this internal debate about al-Shabaab.[98] By coincidence, the *Times* published it the same day that Brennan delivered his keynote address at the Harvard conference on the tenth anniversary of 9/11. During a question-and-answer session following Brennan's prepared remarks, someone asked him about the legal procedures that administration lawyers used when making targeting-policy decisions. He replied with a remarkable description of executive-branch lawyering on national security issues inside the Obama administration.[99]

"The interagency lawyers will get together to look at what is being proposed and then have that discussion, that is very rich, about whether or not what is being proposed is consistent with the law and consistent with best practice, or are we actually sort of now going in new areas and new directions," Brennan said. "...What we have now within U.S. government, at the insistence of the president and others, is that type of discourse among the lawyers. We want to make sure that we hear all the different views and perspectives. That provides us [with] a good sense of what those legal parameters are within which we can work."

But, Brennan went on, "I have never found a case that our legal authorities, or legal interpretations that came out from that lawyers group, prevented us from doing something that we thought was in the best interest of the United States to do....Can there be shifts [in the law]? Yes. And those shifts are affected whether we're attacked, you know, on 9/11, or in other types of threats and challenges to our system.... That's why a Harold Koh and a Jeh Johnson, when they get together and they talk about these things — they really want to wrestle it to the ground. Is there a right answer? Truth is elusive — as is 'right.'"

17. Killing Americans

Over the course of a scorching summer in 2011, the CIA had completed a new clandestine drone base in a remote stretch of desert in Saudi Arabia, adding to the remote-piloted firepower the United States could now project into Yemen. On the morning of September 30, 2011, four drones converged over a group of trucks in al-Jawf Province. Al-Awlaki was riding in one of them.

Alongside him was Samir Khan, a twenty-five-year-old naturalized American citizen from Pakistan who had also joined al-Qaeda in the Arabian Peninsula and produced its English-language online magazine *Inspire*. The administration had considered whether the United States could target Khan. But the intelligence indicated that he was only a propagandist without any operational role, and so they never decided that he met the standard.

Missiles blew their vehicle apart.

Without quite saying who had killed al-Awlaki, Obama hailed his death as "a major blow to al-Qaeda's most active operational affiliate."[100] But the United States government had killed not just one but two American citizens in that strike — one of whom it had not determined it could specifically target but who ended up dead anyway.

Meanwhile, al-Awlaki's oldest son, sixteen-year-old Abdulrahman al-Awlaki, was looking for his father. He was also an American citizen. Born in Denver in 1995, he lived in the United States until he was about seven. With his father on the run, the skinny teenager lived with his mother and grandparents in Sanaa. In early September 2011, Abdulrahman ran away from home, leaving a note explaining that he wanted to find his father. But, not knowing where al-Awlaki was, he took a bus to the wrong province, Shabwa.

Just after sundown on October 14, a military Special Operations drone operator fired a missile at a group eating food beside the road in Shabwa, killing about seven people. Abdulrahman was one of them. Intelligence officials said it was an unintended coincidence combined with bad intelligence — the target was an Egyptian al-Qaeda in the Arabian Peninsula operative named Ibrahim al-Banna, who turned out not even to be there, and they had not known the American teenager was present. If that is true, it was another demonstration that no matter how surgical a weapon drones are as compared to cruise missiles, the intelligence can still be unreliable — with deadly results.[101]

The al-Awlaki family issued a statement that criticized the United States for killing Anwar al-Awlaki but also acknowledged that he "got what he wanted" — martyrdom. But Abdulrahman, it said, was just a kid and was killed "unjustly and wrongly."[102]

No one was happy. At the Pentagon, for example, Johnson asked what had happened. The J2 intelligence staff tried to persuade him that Abdulrahman had been part of al-Qaeda in the Arabian Peninsula too, but Johnson was skeptical.

Come on, he's sixteen, Johnson said.

Still, two months later, a Yemeni journalist who had toured Abyan Province embedded with al-Qaeda in the Arabian Peninsula posted an article claiming that the teenager had decided to join the group to avenge his father's death, telling a local leader, "I hope to attain martyrdom as my father attained it" the very day before he was killed.[103] If that is true, that was consistent with his being present with a group of people that intelligence had indicated were militants, even if the part about Banna being among them had turned out to be wrong. But the incident remains murky.

Meanwhile, on November 16, the CIA carried out a signature strike against a group of suspected militants in tribal Pakistan. Among the dead turned out to be a twenty-three-year-old American citizen named

Jude Kenan Mohammad. The son of a Pakistani father and an American mother, he was a high-school dropout in Raleigh, North Carolina, who fell in with a group of Islamists at the local mosque. In July 2009, a federal grand jury indicted him along with a group of seven other men in what the FBI called the Triangle Terror Group and accused them of plotting terrorist attacks on U.S. soil and abroad.[104] The other seven men were convicted, but Mohammad was gone. He had gone to Pakistan, where he got married and, intelligence officials claimed, got involved with the original al-Qaeda and the Pakistani Taliban. Soon after the strike, his wife called his mother in North Carolina and said he had been killed, but the FBI kept him on its wanted list until the administration acknowledged his killing in 2013.[105]

What this means is that, remarkably, in the span of just six weeks, the United States government had killed four American citizens, even if only one was targeted.

The government is known to have killed one U.S. citizen under Bush: On November 5, 2002, in what is believed to be the first Predator drone strike outside a hot battlefield, the CIA blew up a car in Yemen carrying Abu Ali al-Harithi, an alleged senior al-Qaeda operative believed to have played a role in the *Cole* bombing. Killed alongside him was Kamal Derwish, an American from the Lackawanna suburb of Buffalo, New York. But Derwish was not the target. It was in deliberately targeting al-Awlaki that the United States on Obama's watch broke new ground.

Around the time that Mohammad was killed, I conducted a written survey of the major Republican presidential candidates about their views on executive power. By December 2011, I had received answers from Mitt Romney, Rick Perry, Newt Gingrich, Jon Huntsman, and Ron Paul. (Michele Bachmann and Rick Santorum did not answer the questions.) The first question I asked was: "Under what circumstances, if any, would the Constitution permit the president to authorize the targeted killing of a United States citizen who has not been sentenced to death by a court?"

Romney's campaign had a large national security law subcommittee with about a score of Bush-Cheney administration veteran lawyers to help craft his replies.*

"Due process permits the use of deadly force against all enemy combatants, including citizens, who engage in acts of war against the United States on behalf of an enemy of the United States," he wrote, adding: "My preference would be to capture, interrogate, and prosecute any U.S. citizen who has engaged in acts of war against the United States. But if necessary to defend the country, I would be willing to authorize the use of lethal force."[106]

The answers by all but one of the other Republican contenders dovetailed with Romney's. That meant the presidential-power precedent Obama had established had bipartisan consensus.

But the libertarian-leaning Paul, who answered for himself, disagreed, saying simply: "None."

18. A New Targeted-Killing Playbook

In Obama's initial years in the White House, the process for approving lethal operations had been relatively loose. When a particular opportunity arose, the national security lawyers and policymakers assembled in interagency meetings, usually over secure video teleconferences, for a briefing and deliberations. If the lawyers signed off on a particular proposed strike as lawful, it would commence almost immediately.

But over time, the process had become more formalized. Starting with al-Awlaki, but then expanding to foreign terrorists, the legal questions about targeting potential alleged terrorists often were ventilated even before they were located. Agencies nominated a particular terrorism suspect for consideration, and the National Counterterrorism Center developed short summaries of their lives and activities for discussion. Lawyers signed off in the abstract if they decided that the nominee met the legal standard of someone participating in the war Congress had

---

* See chapter 10, section 1.

authorized against the perpetrators of 9/11 — essentially, if he fell within the March 13 Standard developed in the context of the Guantánamo habeas litigation.*

But, as multiple officials explained it to me, media accounts that this constituted a "kill list" were oversimplified because no one was preapproved for targeting whenever the CIA or the military's Special Forces spotted him. Rather, if a terror suspect on the list was located, it raised new questions. Could he be captured? If his capture was infeasible but an airstrike was possible — as was typically the case in a place like tribal Pakistan or rural Yemen — the lawyers would convene again to consider the legality of a particular proposed operation, including factors like how many civilian bystanders would be put at risk. If there was consensus that a strike would be legal and a good idea, Obama's top counterterrorism adviser — Brennan in his first term, Lisa Monaco in his second — decided whether it made sense and, if so, gave the go-ahead. But if an agency director or cabinet official disagreed, the question went to Obama — a rule that grew out of the bad 2011 signature strike in Pakistan that Panetta and the CIA had carried out over the objections of Clinton and the State Department.

In early 2012, Obama was facing the prospect that he might lose reelection. He decided to institutionalize the targeted-killing procedures that had evolved over his three years in office so that he could hand it off to any successor. He also wanted to tighten up the standards for targeting.

"He would like to leave his successor with a sustainable approach, not open questions," Ben Rhodes later told me. "On drones and the direct action side, that means nesting it in clearly established guidelines."

Brennan coordinated the task, and Avril Haines, now the top lawyer at the National Security Council, implemented it. As amiable as Brennan was gruff, Haines was a former owner of a bohemian bookstore in Baltimore who had gone on to law school and specialized in international human rights. This led to a job in the State Department under Koh and then her move to the White House, where she earned a reputation for working deep into the night.[107]

---

* See chapter 4, section 7.

Haines helped Brennan develop a new "presidential policy guidance," a form of an executive order that codified a set of rules and procedures to govern killings away from hot battlefields. The text of the Presidential Policy Guidance was classified, but officials said it specified that a suspected terrorist must pose a "continuing and imminent threat" to *Americans*, not just to allies, to be targeted. Some military and intelligence officials had proposed a more elastic standard under which threatening "American interests" would be enough to make someone targetable, but Brennan and Haines had held the line. There also had to be "near certainty" that no civilians would be killed. Together, those rules seemed to bar signature strikes.

Haines toiled on the "playbook," the nickname for the new bureaucratic rules. Crucial minutiae filled it. Haines delved into the format of the EXORD — or execute orders — issued to operators ahead of each strike, tightening them up to reflect Obama's policy guidance. For example, their opening paragraphs were highly tailored to each target, but around the sixth paragraph, which specified which property could be hit, the CIA had created a boilerplate phrase that contained a potentially huge loophole — "and other personnel connected with it." Haines sought to identify and close such gaps, and she also combed through specialized annexes for each country in which drones operated.

It took more than a year to complete; after Obama won reelection, some of the time pressure eased. Obama signed the rules in May 2013, in connection with a major speech on security policy at National Defense University.* On the eve of announcing the new rules, Obama declassified the fact that the United States had indeed killed the four Americans back in the fall of 2011, ending the long period of awkward pseudo-secrecy about al-Awlaki.

Against that backdrop, officials said the new rules contained another feature of interest: in the future, if the United States government targeted an American citizen, the preference was for the military to carry out the killing. That way, it would be easier to discuss in public after-

---

* See chapter 9, section 16, and chapter 10, section 12.

ward than a covert CIA action. As important, they said the playbook called for a transition in which the CIA would give its drones to the Pentagon and return to focusing on gathering intelligence. Still, drone operations in tribal Pakistan — the center of the CIA's signature strikes — would keep playing by the old rules until American forces withdrew from Afghanistan.

In early 2013, Brennan left the White House to be the new CIA director, and Koh returned to Yale. Obama nominated Haines to succeed Koh at State, but in June he yanked back that nomination and instead appointed her as deputy CIA director, meaning she and Brennan would oversee how their new rules were used.

19. But Targeted Killings Continue

The changes Obama announced — and, in reference to the CIA, that were discussed by his officials on background — seemed momentous, in theory. How things played out in practice was more complicated.

On the one hand, the pace of strikes declined, suggesting that higher standards were making a difference.

On the other hand, reports of civilian deaths continued, calling into question the "near certainty" standard.[108]

And as the years passed, there was still no sign that the CIA was relinquishing its drones to the military. Among other factors, the Congressional intelligence committees were resisting letting that happen, which would mean giving up their own oversight clout to the armed forces committees.[109] Even inside the executive branch there was a strong impression that the CIA was better at targeted killing than the military's Special Operations, on measures ranging from the frequency of bad strikes in which civilians were killed to the quality of the nominations that each agency was putting forward for approval.

As Obama's presidency entered its final stretch, a handful of episodes showed how the United States was still struggling to find a stable policy about when and where it would carry out targeted killing operations.

To start with, consider the saga of Mohanad Mahmoud al-Farekh, another American citizen turned Islamist militant. Al-Farekh had been born in Texas but moved out of the United States as a child. He later attended college in Canada and became radicalized by watching videos of al-Awlaki's sermons, according to court filings. In 2007, he and two other men went from Canada to Pakistan, adopted the war-name Abdullah al-Shami, and received training by al-Qaeda in how to use roadside bombs and other devices to attack American forces in Afghanistan. There, it turned out, he met Najibullah Zazi and the two other men involved in the 2009 plot to bomb the New York City subway system. Zazi and the others later provided information about al-Farekh when they cooperated with the government as part of their plea agreements.*

The Obama interagency lawyers began talking about whether al-Farekh was targetable in late 2012, and the deliberations lasted two years. Policymakers at the CIA and the military's Central Command, which ran the war in Afghanistan, supported targeting him.[110] But the interagency lawyers group was not so sure.

One question they wrestled with was whether al-Farekh met the standards for targeting a citizen established by Barron's memo on al-Awlaki — a senior-enough operational planner whose capture was infeasible. Barron had said only that the characteristics al-Awlaki alleg-edly embodied were *sufficient,* not that those would be *necessary* for targeting some other citizen. But the lawyers group nevertheless treated those standards as loose requirements within which they could oper-ate. At the same time, they wrestled with whether the al-Awlaki analy-sis even applied in the Afghanistan-Pakistan war zone, or whether being in or near a hot battlefield and allegedly linked to operations to plant roadside bombs targeting American troops changed those stan-dards. The lawyers pressed for more information to ensure that his cap-ture was truly not feasible, and they argued about how Obama's policy guidance making it preferable to publicly acknowledge any citizen's

---

* See chapter 5, section 16.

killing factored in. While they talked, new bits of intelligence trickled in, and some of the new information took away from the initial analysis of who al-Farekh was, causing the lawyers to reconsider and look at everything again.

Along the way, the delays frustrated some officials in the national security bureaucracy. Hawks on the House Intelligence Committee, during a closed-door hearing in July 2013, grilled military and intelligence officials about why the government had not yet approved the targeting of al-Farekh.

We've never seen a bigger mess, the committee's Republican chairman at the time, Representative Mike Rogers of Michigan, is said to have declared at the classified hearing.[111]

When American scrutiny first descended on him, al-Farekh was in an inaccessible tribal area of Pakistan. But in 2014, the Pakistani military launched a push into that region, causing al-Farekh and other al-Qaeda militants to move. The United States lost track of him for a period, but in late 2014 intelligence arose that he was in a place where Pakistani security forces could capture him. The CIA tipped off the Pakistanis, who arrested him and interrogated him for several months. They then turned him over to the United States, which brought him to New York to face terrorism charges in civilian court.

The national security bureaucracy is a powerful force, and on many occasions the Obama team bent to its warnings that particular counterterrorism actions were necessary. This was a counterexample.

In January 2015, soon after al-Farekh was captured, there was another cluster of American deaths from drone strikes. A strike in tribal Pakistan killed Adam Gadahn; a thirty-six-year-old star of al-Qaeda propaganda videos, he had grown up in California, converted to Islam, joined al-Qaeda, and been indicted for treason and placed on the FBI's Most Wanted list. Another drone strike that same month, a signature strike targeting a suspected al-Qaeda compound, killed a less famous American citizen, Ahmed Farouq, who was allegedly the deputy leader of a branch of al-Qaeda in the Indian Subcontinent. The government said neither Gadahn nor Farouq had been approved for deliberate targeting, and it had not known that either of those men was present in the strike zones before firing the missiles.

Tragically, the same strike that killed Farouq also accidentally killed two Western aid workers whom al-Qaeda had been holding prisoner inside the compound: Dr. Warren Weinstein, an American USAID contractor who had been a hostage since 2011, and Giovanni Lo Porto, an Italian aid worker and a hostage since 2012. The government said it had not realized they were inside the compound either.

Back in 2013, Brennan had told Congress during his confirmation hearing that the United States should publicly acknowledge unintended civilian deaths from counterterrorism strikes. But that did not happen for at least the first two years of his tenure as CIA director.[112] Now the deaths of the Americans and Lo Porto prompted the administration to take the rare step of openly discussing a drone strike. Obama said he took "full responsibility for all our counterterrorism operations, including the one that inadvertently took the lives of Warren and Giovanni." He expressed "profound regret" and said that he had ordered a review. But the initial assessment, he said, was that the strike had been "fully consistent with the guidelines under which we conduct counterterrorism efforts in the region," given the prestrike intelligence, which included "hundreds of hours of surveillance" — apparently aerial video footage that would have shown people coming and going but not prisoners locked up inside.[113]

"It is a cruel and bitter truth that in the fog of war generally and our fight against terrorists specifically, mistakes, sometimes deadly mistakes, can occur," Obama said.

Finally, two other strikes in June 2015 suggested that the White House was quietly relaxing its own rules for targeting. The first was a CIA drone strike in Yemen that killed Nasir al-Wuhayshi, the leader of al-Qaeda in the Arabian Peninsula (and now also purportedly the No. 2 of core al-Qaeda). Although anonymous government officials told *Bloomberg View* in great detail that Wuhayshi had been the CIA's target,[114] presumably different anonymous government officials told the *Washington Post* that the CIA had been unaware of any "high-value target" in its sights before firing at a group of suspected militants, and only found out afterward that Wuhayshi was among the dead.[115]

The *Post* also reported that in 2015, after Hadi fled and Houthi rebels overran Sanaa, Obama eased limits on targeting in Yemen to permit attacks on clusters of presumed militants even when there was not a known high-value terrorist among them.

That sounded like signature strikes. Dovetailing with the *Post*'s reporting, an official told me in 2015 that the intelligence community had begun pushing for permission to "widen the aperture" of targeting permission in Yemen a year earlier. The argument was that their rhythm of strikes against al-Qaeda in the Arabian Peninsula was too slow given the danger it posed. Adding to the pressure, officials participating in the deliberations were told that the Yemeni president, Abdo Rabu Mansour Hadi, had privately said the United States was being too cautious.

The other June 2015 strike with legal-policy implications was a bombing by American F-15 jets of a compound in Libya. It was an attempt to kill Mokhtar Belmokhtar, an al-Qaeda–linked terrorist who had planned the 2013 seizure of an Algerian gas plant in which thirty-eight foreign hostages died. (Belmokhtar apparently survived.)[116] Libya's government issued a statement saying it had consented to the strike, although the government barely existed. Following the 2011 NATO air war that helped rebels topple its strongman leader, Colonel Muammar Gadhafi,* Libya had collapsed into anarchy, and a hotbed of al-Qaeda and Islamic State militancy. The broader significance was that Obama had opened a new front for American targeted killing operations away from traditional battlefields.

20. "Must Be Trusted"

Back in June 2012, Samir Khan's mother and Anwar al-Awlaki's father, Nasser, filed a federal lawsuit seeking unspecified damages over the two

---

* See chapter 12, sections 3 through 5.

fall 2011 Yemen strikes. It named several top military and intelligence officials who, it said, were responsible for organizing and directing them.

"The killings violated fundamental rights afforded to all U.S. citizens, including the right not to be deprived of life without due process of law," their complaint said.[117]

This was Nasser's second attempt to obtain judicial review. In 2010, he had filed a similar case seeking an injunction blocking attempts to kill his son, but a judge threw it out on the ground that he had no legal standing to file it.* Now, as executor of his son's and grandson's estates, there was no question that he had such standing. The lawsuit raised the possibility that a court would offer a definitive take on the al-Awlaki strike as a precedent for future citizen killings.

The Obama administration urged the judge, Rosemary M. Collyer, to dismiss the lawsuit without any such review. The Justice Department contended that if she even held a hearing to test the evidence that al-Awlaki had been a terrorist, it would interfere with executive-branch decisions about protecting national security in wartime.

In April 2014, Collyer threw out the case without an evidentiary hearing. She explained that executive-branch officials carrying out national security operations "must be trusted" to do the right thing, because even the prospect of a later lawsuit could make officials risk-averse and "hinder their ability in the future to act decisively and without hesitation in defense of U.S. interests."[118]

Nasser decided not to appeal, saying he had lost faith in the American justice system.[119]

Collyer's ruling, coupled with the earlier lawsuit's failure, meant courts would play no role, either before or after a strike, in reviewing decisions by presidents to kill American citizens deemed to be terrorists operating overseas — even away from hot battlefields.

---

* See chapter 9, section 1.

PART III

THE SECURITY STATE

7

Ratchet (Captives 2010–2011)

1. The Straw Man Plan for Future Captures

By the end of January 2010, the uproar following the Christmas underwear-bombing attempt had left Obama's national security legal policy in shambles, from the moratorium on repatriating Yemeni detainees from Guantánamo to the collapse of political support for trying KSM in a civilian courtroom in New York.[1] The criticism also featured a recurring accusation: Obama, having shuttered the CIA black-site prisons and forbidden the importation of any new prisoners to Guantánamo, had no plan for dealing with newly captured high-level terrorism suspects. Some critics began to maintain that he was just drone-killing terrorists he could have captured — sacrificing potential intelligence from their interrogations to avoid the headache. The administration strongly denied this. At his Harvard speech, for example, John Brennan, Obama's top counterterrorism aide, portrayed as "absurd" the suggestion "that we do not have a detention policy [and] that we prefer to kill suspected terrorists, rather than capture them....I want to be very clear — whenever it is possible to capture a suspected terrorist, it is the unqualified preference of the Administration to take custody of that individual so we can obtain information that is vital to the safety and security of the American people."[2]

Still, amid the political furor that followed the Christmas underwear-bomb attempt, the Obama legal and national security teams recognized that there was a gap in their detention planning. They knew what they would do if a terrorist was captured on American soil: use law enforcement procedures. ("Our military does not patrol our streets or enforce our laws—nor should it," Brennan said.) They knew what they would do if a terrorist was captured in the Afghanistan or Iraq war zones: put him in a military detention camp in one of those theaters. And they knew what they would do if an ally with a functioning and trustworthy security service captured a terrorist: leave him in that country's hands, rather than making the United States the world's jailor. But they had no ready-made plan for what would happen if the United States directly captured a high-value terrorist outside a war zone or needed to take custody of someone an ally could not handle. That had not happened on Obama's watch yet—there were no American ground forces in places like Yemen and tribal Pakistan, where air strikes were heating up, so captures were infeasible—but sooner or later it would.

Back in 2009, the detention-policy task force run by Brad Wiegmann and Mark Martins had looked at such issues. The public never heard about it, but their task force had produced a final report, which was dated January 22, 2010, stamped *classified,* and never announced or made public—more collateral damage in the political fight over the Christmas bombing attempt. It compiled many "lessons learned" from the first eight years of the 9/11 war. These included the takeaway that the longer you wait to prosecute someone after he is in custody, the more difficult it becomes; evidence goes stale and witnesses die or move somewhere where they can't be called to court. Therefore, it is smart to be thinking from the start about what you are going to do with a terrorism captive to lock him up for the long run in a legally stable way—including, potentially, if and when the 9/11 war came to an end.

But the report was not an operational document. Now, Tom Donilon, then still Obama's deputy national security adviser, directed the interagency policy and legal groups to come up with such a plan under the oversight of Brennan and Mary DeRosa, the top lawyer at the National Security Council. By mid-February 2010, Nate Jones, the Brennan aide, had compiled the interagency's views into a six-page draft plan entitled "Revised Detention Policy 'Straw Man' for Individuals Taken into Custody Outside of Iraq and Afghanistan." It would undergo many more drafts, but the documents have never been made public.

The paper's focus was what should happen when the United States took custody of a noncitizen terrorism suspect from a foreign government, or directly captured one through a unilateral operation in a place without a real government, like Somalia. By "straw man," they meant a dummy stand-in, a hypothetical captive whose handling they could assess with cool heads and without a crisis atmosphere. The basic idea they came up with was to start by holding such a person in a short-term screening facility, such as a nearby base or aboard a vessel. That period would last no longer than fourteen days. The National Security Council deputies committee would then decide what to do with him.

One option would be "intermediate-term" law-of-war detention. To qualify, such a prisoner would have to meet three criteria: 1) He must be detainable under the March 13 Standard interpreting the Authorization for Use of Military Force against al-Qaeda. 2) He must possess critical intelligence about current terrorist threats to the United States. And 3), he must pose a significant threat, such as by being a senior leader or a key facilitator, trainer, or recruiter. Under no circumstances would they bring anyone to Guantánamo. But at the time, there was another option: the temporary screening facility at Bagram Airfield.* To avoid having it called a black-site secret prison, they would acknowledge the facility's existence and notify the International Committee of the Red Cross about the prisoner.

For long-term disposition, the Obama team decided, the preference would be to transfer the foreign prisoner to another country if it could meet security and humane-treatment conditions. If that was impossible, the backup option would be prosecution in a federal court or continued law-of-war detention somewhere — they left that vague.

The Straw Man Plan became the subject of more than half a dozen meetings as 2010 unfolded and the interagency lawyers and operators

---

* See chapter 4, section 3.

came up with twists and variations on capture-interrogate-prosecute scenarios. The officials were forced to confront the pragmatic dimension of their ideas, such as who exactly would be on a ship where a detainee was brought, where the ship would be located, and how they could ensure that a prisoner could be prosecuted in a civilian court if that ended up being the choice. They were determined to wrestle with the issues completely and institutionalize clear, predictable procedures so there would be no ad hoc decision-making that would lead to trouble.

"I would chair these meetings and look around the room and there were some of the most important counterterrorism practitioners and legal scholars in the world around the room, debating," Donilon said. "It was a rigorous process where each of the pathways was carefully thought through, rooting it in legal and practical principles."

Finally, toward the end of 2010, they thought they were done. Donilon, whom Obama had promoted to succeed Jim Jones as the national security adviser in October, took the near-final Straw Man Plan to Obama. When Obama read through it and came to the section about long-term indefinite detention being an option, he balked.

We're not going to turn Bagram into Gitmo, Obama said, according to Ben Rhodes.

Obama ordered that section deleted. Another one of his aides told me that it was not clear if the president was saying he would never use long-term detention on a new captive, or if he just didn't want it enshrined in a policy document as a routinely available choice. A third aide maintained that Obama was clearly saying the United States would not use indefinite detention on any new captives. Either way, Obama was showing that his legal team, bent on keeping options available, had strayed in a direction he did not want to go.

2. *Democrats Get to Be President, Too*

As the Obama administration continued to reel, a debate broke out among his legal team over whether Congress had the constitutional power to block the president from prosecuting Guantánamo detainees, from low-level al-Qaeda foot soldiers to senior leaders like KSM, in civilian court. This debate, which has never been reported, was one of the clearest internal clashes of the two fundamentally different visions of what course correction was needed after the Bush presidency: Was the main problem that Bush had violated the rule of law, so Obama needed to take a more modest view of executive power to override statutes? Or was the main problem that Bush had trammeled human rights and civil liberties, so Obama needed to roll back those changes to American policy—even if it meant defying acts of Congress that impeded that goal?

With the banner of handling foreign terrorism suspects in the criminal justice system in political retreat, Lindsey Graham seized the moment to revive negotiations with the White House over a possible grand bargain on detainee policies. The senator met with Rahm Emanuel and Daniel Meltzer, the principal deputy White House counsel. Graham said he wanted Obama to send KSM back to a military commission and endorse a statute that would regularize indefinite law-of-war detention, including for al-Qaeda suspects captured in the future. In return, he again offered Republican support for a plan to close the Guantánamo prison by bringing the remaining detainees to a military prison on domestic soil.

Adding to his leverage, Graham also told the White House that he planned to file legislation barring the expenditure of funds to prosecute the 9/11 defendants in civilian court.

Just the previous November, the Democratic-controlled Senate had voted down an identical measure proposed by Graham. But now the politics seemed utterly transformed: a Republican had capitalized on the attempted underwear bombing to win Ted Kennedy's former Senate seat in deep blue Massachusetts, and even New York Democrats were rebelling against Holder's KSM trial plan.

Over the final weekend of January, David Barron, the Office of Legal Counsel head, quietly pounded out another unsigned, nonfinal white paper on Graham's not-yet-filed legislative proposal. It contained bad news for those who opposed Graham's proposal to give primacy to military commissions and to entrench indefinite law-of-war detention — people, that is, like Harold Koh, the State Department legal adviser.

The existence of this memo, entitled "Constitutional Issues Related to the Graham Amendment or Similar Legislation," has never been reported. In it, Barron wrote that a law barring the expenditure of funds on prosecuting the 9/11 case in regular court would be an "unprecedented attempt to foreclose the executive from pursuing otherwise available Article III prosecutions," that it "raises serious separation of powers policy concerns," and that it would "set a dangerous precedent." But despite all this, Barron concluded that such a statute would likely be a constitutional constraint on Obama's power. His reasoning was that Obama could still prosecute KSM in a military commission, and it is generally not unconstitutional for Congress to provide the executive branch with law enforcement tools that are less than what the president considers ideal.

Barron's not-quite-official opinion meant that if Obama wanted to strike the grand bargain with Graham, Obama could agree to sign a legal ban on any civilian trial for KSM as part of it. In other words, ironically, the legal opinion made it possible for Obama to reach a deal with Graham, but only by adopting a weak conception of the powers the Constitution gives the presidency in prosecutorial matters. At a meeting and in follow-up e-mails that were cc'd among many officials, Koh confronted Barron and accused him of being too timid about Obama's executive authority.

In full view of their colleagues, the two legal philosophers — Barron characteristically mild and cautious, Koh characteristically outspoken and self-confident, and both of them among the best legal minds of their generation — now dueled.

Koh pointed out that just the previous June, Barron had written that it was unconstitutional for Congress to block State Department officials from attending United Nations meetings chaired by state sponsors of terrorism, like Iran.* If *that* statute was an invalid encroachment on the

---

* See chapter 12, section 12.

president's power to conduct foreign affairs, Koh demanded, how could it now be legitimate for lawmakers to substitute their judgment for the president's exercise of core military, foreign policy, and prosecutorial functions when it came to trying KSM?

Barron countered that Congress had on *many* previous occasions used its funding powers to impose limits the executive branch did not like; that did not mean they were unconstitutional.

Koh cited a famous 1983 Supreme Court case showing that just because Congress had frequently done something in the past, it didn't mean it was constitutional to do that thing.[3]

Barron asked Koh why he was so sure his view was legally correct.

Koh, thirteen years Barron's senior, retorted that he had been working on these issues since the 1980s. Even though he, Koh, was known as a strong proponent of congressional power in foreign policy, he still thought there were constitutional limits on lawmakers' authority and maintained that the Obama team should not let their previous criticisms of Bush's overreach make them afraid to invoke legitimate theories of executive power.

There was no clear resolution to the debate about Graham's bill. But as time progressed, Koh repeatedly urged more aggressive use of executive power by Obama to roll back policies on detention that Bush had been able to put in place only because Bush, to say the least, was not meek about invoking unilateral presidential authority. Koh's internal push offered a counterpoint to the American Civil Liberties Union meme that Obama was acting *too much* like Bush; as Koh repeatedly argued in meetings: *Democrats get to be president, too.*

3. Power, Sought and Unsought (Gitmo Habeas Collapse I)

In Obama's first year, federal district court judges had repeatedly sided with lower-level detainees bringing habeas corpus lawsuits. They ordered the government to release prisoners against whom there was weak evidence of ties to al-Qaeda. As those rulings piled up, they created pressure inside the bureaucracy, where there were often disagreements about the risk posed by releasing particular detainees, to transfer out more lower-level prisoners. In this way, these losses by the executive branch in court added tailwinds to Obama's broad goal of closing the prison. The losses also made things easier politically: it was harder for skeptics of Obama's policy, including in Congress, to criticize the administration for releasing a detainee in response to a court order than if it was an executive-branch policy decision. At the same time, however, the Justice Department litigators working on individual cases naturally wanted to win them, and more risk-averse elements in the security bureaucracy did, too. As a whole, the Obama administration's approach was shot through with irony and ambivalence: it was arguing in court for a relatively broad scope of detention powers with its fingers crossed behind its back.

This game became far more complicated in 2010 for two reasons. First, because of the heightened political and bureaucratic scrutiny placed on Yemen after the Christmas attack and Obama's moratorium on repatriating any more detainees there, the administration took increasingly aggressive stances in court to defend Obama's power to keep holding Yemeni detainees, specifically, but the principles it established applied across the board. Second, the cases began reaching the Court of Appeals for the District of Columbia — a conservative-dominated court to which Obama would fail to appoint a single judge until his second term — and it did not play along. Every time the appeals court had an opportunity to rule against a Guantánamo detainee in a habeas corpus case, it did. Adopting a posture of deference to the executive branch, it instructed district court judges to tilt their interpretation of ambiguous evidence more sharply against the prisoners. The Supreme Court declined to hear further appeals by the detainees, leaving that constellation of rulings in place. Gradually, the appeals court hollowed out the Supreme Court's 2008 ruling establishing judicial review of executive-branch decisions about Guantánamo detainees. This withdrew district court judges as de facto allies to Obama's goal.

In retrospect, this shift began with a ruling in the appeals court's first substantive review of a Guantánamo detainee's habeas lawsuit, issued on January 5, 2010. The prisoner, a Yemeni named Ghaleb Nassar al-Bihani, was one of the unlucky few who had lost his case at the district court level. He had appealed, and the appeals court agreed that he was detainable. But Judge Janice Rogers Brown, a George W. Bush appointee, went further than simply saying the district judge had decided the case correctly. She used the opportunity to try to give Obama even more detention power than he wanted. First, the Justice Department had argued that the government should have to show by a *preponderance of the evidence* that the man met the definition of a detainable enemy, meaning it was at least 50.1 percent likely that he was al-Qaeda. Given the stakes, the detainee's lawyers argued for a higher standard of proof. Brown said the government's proposal was acceptable, and she invited the Justice Department to argue for an even lower standard next time — *some evidence* was enough, even if seemingly outweighed by countervailing evidence. Second, the Justice Department had said the court should interpret Obama's wartime detention powers consistent with, meaning *limited by*, the international laws of war. Joined by another Bush-appointed judge, Brown maintained that the government was wrong and international law did not limit the president's war powers.[4]

Inside the Justice Department, career litigators who were tired of losing one habeas case after another wanted to accept Brown's invitations to get more aggressive. They wanted to argue, in future cases, that a lower standard of proof was sufficient for the government to win and that the international laws of war did not constrain Obama's detention powers. Those steps would have made it easier for them to win. But Obama's political appointees would not let them. That February, I asked Holder about the unresolved debate, but he predicted, accurately: "I don't think we are going to deviate from our argument."[5] (Later, the full Court of Appeals upheld the outcome of that case but retracted Brown's reasoning about international law.[6])

This was a part of a pattern for Obama's detention policy: throughout his presidency, Obama came under constant pressure to expand his wartime detention powers, but he showed no appetite for doing so.

At the same time, however, the Obama legal team tried not to diminish the detention powers he already had. One example was lawsuits related to the Uighurs, the unfortunate Chinese Muslims the government had brought to Guantánamo by mistake and was having trouble getting rid of.* The litigation was complex but boiled down to whether courts could interfere with the executive branch's decisions about what to do with them. The Bush-Cheney administration had argued against the Uighurs' efforts to control what happened to them, and an appeals court had ruled against the detainees. The Obama administration in 2010 persuaded the Supreme Court not to review the matter. (The last Uighurs would depart Guantánamo in 2013.[7])

The Obama administration, as noted, also fought to prevent the courts from expanding Guantánamo-style habeas corpus rights to detainees at Guantánamo. On May 21, 2010, the appeals court overturned Judge Bates's April 2009 ruling and held that nobody at Bagram, not even those captured outside Afghanistan and brought there, were entitled to judicial hearings.[8] The decision, which was unanimous across an ideologically diverse panel of judges, vindicated the legal arguments of the deputy solicitor general, Neal Katyal, that Guantánamo and Bagram were very different places, legally speaking.† Still, during the presidential campaign, few would have predicted that a court ruling permitting the president to take captives to Afghanistan and imprison them there without any judicial review would be a victory for Obama.

Surveying those cases in the summer of 2010, Stephen I. Vladeck, an American University law professor, said that many of the ways in which Obama was accused of acting like Bush were only superficial. At the constitutional level, he noted, Obama was not making Bush's hallmark

* See chapter 4, section 10.
† See chapter 4, section 3.

argument that the commander in chief wielded unilateral powers that could not be constrained by acts of Congress or international law. But the stances the administration took in the Uighur and Bagram cases, Vladeck said, *did* deserve the Bush comparison: just like Bush, the Obama team had made arguments "in favor of effectively unreviewable executive detention" powers.[9]

4. *You and Me Both*

Don't ever come into this building and say that again or you will lose all credibility in your new job, DeRosa told Bill Lietzau.

This building was the White House. Lietzau's new job was deputy assistant secretary of defense for detainee policy. And the thing Lietzau should not say again was that he didn't think it made much sense to keep trying to close Guantánamo.

Lietzau played a central role in crafting detention policy for both the Bush and the Obama administrations without fitting comfortably into either. A Yale Law School graduate and uniformed lawyer in the Marine Corps, he was a specialist in international law. After 9/11, he helped Bush political appointees design military commissions but was aghast that the Bush-Cheney administration refused to call its captives prisoners of war and treat them accordingly. Lietzau came to oppose the use of military commissions but remained a strong believer in the notion that holding enemy fighters without criminal trials was a routine and legitimate part of warfare.

In Bush's second term, Lietzau had moved to Germany to serve as the staff judge advocate at the U.S. European Command under General James Jones. When Jones became Obama's first national security adviser in 2009, he brought Lietzau to work for him at the National Security Council. Lietzau was supposed to stay away from detainee policy, given his history, but in late 2009, Phil Carter stepped down as the Pentagon's top civilian detainee-policy official, and DeRosa asked

Lietzau, who was ready to leave the Marines, if he wanted the job. Others on the Obama team weren't sure about hiring him for the role, but then came the Christmas attack. At that point, his reputation as slightly more conservative on terrorism issues wasn't a detriment. Lietzau started at the detention-policy job on February 16, 2010. He later was part of a group that flew down to visit Guantánamo with newly elected Republican senator from Massachusetts, Scott Brown. Lietzau joked with Brown that he, Lietzau, had gotten his job only because of the underwear bomber.

You and me both, Brown replied, by one account.*

At Guantánamo, Lietzau received the official tour in which the military put a positive light on how it handled its business there, from the special secure courtroom built for tribunals to high-quality detainee health care. When he returned, he visited DeRosa at the White House and asked: *If we're now doing everything right at Guantánamo, then why close it? Why not try to change the world's perception of it instead?* It was then that DeRosa counseled him that it was unwise to question such a high-profile policy by the president.

Going forward, Lietzau would learn greater subtlety. For example, he once told me in an interview that the administration wanted to close the prison because it was costly and useful for enemy propaganda. But, he argued, people should consider that goal separately from its effort to develop "principled, credible and sustainable" law-of-war detention policies. When the two become linked, he said, "it sometimes feeds the implicit narrative that having detainees at Guantánamo is somehow inherently unlawful or immoral. But the Supreme Court has upheld wartime detention, which is the humanitarian alternative to killing in war. We want to close Guantánamo, but not because detaining in war is immoral."[10]

---

* Brown told me he remembered visiting Guantánamo with Lietzau and several other executive-branch officials soon after his election. He did not specifically remember this exchange but thought that he had probably responded with something phrased more seriously, like *I know what you mean. Terrorism certainly played a huge role in my campaign.*

Lietzau was not the only official at the Pentagon who quietly felt that way.

5. Curbing Miranda Rights

In public, the administration was stoutly defending the fact that the FBI had read the Miranda warning to the underwear bomber. But behind closed doors in the spring of 2010, the Obama administration was quietly harboring doubts. Its legal team seriously explored the idea of permitting the government to hold terrorism suspects arrested on domestic soil for a longer period without informing them they had constitutional rights to a lawyer and to remain silent and without presenting them to a magistrate judge for an initial hearing.

The new White House counsel, Bob Bauer, who had succeeded Greg Craig at the end of 2009, directed the effort to draft a potential bill curtailing the rights of newly arrested terrorism suspects. Don Verrilli, now a deputy to Bauer, drove the day-to-day process, telling the Justice Department he wanted a quick turnaround on ideas. Brennan and his aide Jones were also involved, but the process was primarily a legal exercise. It began with closely held White House meetings, but the agencies soon caught wind of it. Bauer invited interagency lawyers like David Kris, head of the Justice Department's National Security Division, and Valerie Caproni, the FBI general counsel, to participate.

They focused on two related issues. One was the "public safety" exception to Miranda that the Supreme Court had already recognized. It permitted the police to ask questions about immediate threats before informing a suspect of his rights, and prosecutors could still use the suspect's answers to those early questions as courtroom evidence.* The Obama team explored whether the government could stretch that exception period from a few minutes to hours or days in a terrorism case. The wrinkle was that the Supreme Court had created the Miranda

---

* See chapter 1, section 6.

rule and proclaimed that it derived from the Constitution itself. Congress cannot enact a statute that overrides the Constitution. But the Obama team thought that if Congress voiced its support in legislation for interpreting Miranda as permitting a lengthier public-safety period in terrorism cases, courts would be more likely to uphold it.

The other issue was presentment hearings. A federal rule of criminal procedure requires bringing newly arrested prisoners before judges for initial hearings "without unnecessary delay," which generally means within forty-eight hours, unless a prisoner waives the hearing. That, too, could interrupt the flow of an interrogation. Congress has the power to change criminal procedure rules. An initial draft of potential legislation would have permitted waiting seven days. But one morning, the interagency legal team awoke to find an e-mail Koh had blasted out around 3:00 a.m. pointing out that no other Western democracy allowed suspects to be held for more than four days without a hearing.[11] The draft proposal was scaled back to ninety-six hours.

On May 1, 2010, Faisal Shahzad, a naturalized U.S. citizen who had been trained by the Pakistani Taliban, tried to blow up a bomb hidden in a Nissan Pathfinder parked in Times Square. Fortunately, the bomb did not work. After his arrest, law enforcement officials questioned Shahzad for three or four hours under the public-safety exception — the longest such delay to date. After they finally read him the Miranda warning, he waived his rights and continued talking for almost two weeks.

Although the Shahzad interrogation was a success under existing criminal justice procedures, Republicans criticized the Obama administration for using them instead of placing Shahzad into military custody. Still, the administration decided it was in a position of strength to unveil its proposal to change those procedures. Eric Holder appeared on NBC's *Meet the Press* on May 9 and floated the idea.

"We're now dealing with international terrorists," Holder said, "and I think that we have to think about perhaps modifying the rules that interrogators have and somehow coming up with something that is flexible and is more consistent with the threat that we now face."[12]

Holder talked on TV only about Miranda, not presentment hearings, even though the latter was the real change Congress and the executive could make.[13] But both ideas fizzled immediately. Congressional Democrats wanted nothing to do with it, and Republicans thought it did not go far enough.

Instead of legislation, the administration acted on its own. On October 21, 2010, the FBI sent an unsigned, three-page memo to its agents about interrogating terrorism suspects. Holder told me about the existence of this memo in an interview two months later; while the government refused to make it public at that time, someone gave me a copy the following spring and I published its full text.[14] It instructed agents questioning "operational terrorists" to use "a significantly more extensive public safety interrogation without Miranda warnings than would be permissible in an ordinary criminal case," listing topics to explore, such as "the identities, locations, and activities or intentions of accomplices who may be plotting additional imminent attacks."[15]

Civil libertarians criticized the policy because it undermined Miranda rights and conservatives criticized it because terrorism suspects would still eventually get criminal justice procedures. Obama was also criticized for acting unilaterally instead of through Congress. The Obama team saw its approach as a rational compromise that took into account twenty-first-century threats without militarizing law enforcement on domestic soil. The lawyers were increasingly coming to believe that it was no longer possible to have a serious bipartisan conversation about counterterrorism policy with Congress. Some lawmakers had responded to the Times Square plot by pushing a bill that would empower the government to involuntarily strip American terrorism suspects of their citizenship, even though Supreme Court precedent makes clear that idea is unconstitutional.[16]

Years later, many members of the Obama legal team seemed to view the Miranda and presentment exercise with discomfort, embarrassed that they had so seriously explored trying to change the law in a way that put them to the right of Republican administrations. One claimed that Obama himself had recoiled when the idea was presented to him in the Oval Office. *What are you talking about?*

This episode illuminates an arguable downside to government policymaking by lawyers. The Obama legal team were busily developing options for their client to consider, which is generally what good lawyers do. But numerous members later insisted to me that they had been queasy about the implications of what they were doing. Holding people arrested on domestic soil incommunicado — that seemed like something two-bit dictatorships did. Barron remarked at one point to colleagues, *I can't believe we're doing this.* At another point, in a White House meeting, Caproni, who had been the FBI's top lawyer since 2003, pretzeled her body language into a physical manifestation of her discomfort at the questions they were exploring and blurted out, *Even the last administration never asked these questions.* Not everyone was ashamed; one told me that this had been "a bit of overreaching" and that there had been no enthusiasm for it, but the initial notion had been that by engaging with Congress on this topic, perhaps they could head off more drastic legislation. But Matt Olsen, who became a top national security official in the deputy attorney general's office in 2010, after the detainee review task force completed its work, expressed strong misgivings.

"It was not a good idea," Olsen later told me. "It warped decades of constitutional law and criminal procedure to address an issue that was politically driven, and it was a change for which there was very little hard evidence of any need."

6. Giving Up on Closing Guantánamo

By the middle of 2010, it was clear that while closing Guantánamo remained Obama's stated goal, it was fading as a priority. The White House would occasionally reiterate its position but put little political muscle behind such words on Capitol Hill. Nor did it intervene on behalf of the executive-branch officials trying hardest to carry out that policy in internal disagreements, such as whether to approve detainee resettlement deals negotiated by Dan Fried. One official explained the disconnect to me like this: "Guantánamo is a negative symbol, but it is much diminished because we are seen as trying to close it. Closing Guantánamo is good, but fighting to close Guantánamo is O.K. Admitting you failed would be the worst." Another official told me that the administration had done its part — its plan to move the remaining detainees to the empty prison in Thomson, Illinois, was ready to go — so Congress was to blame for the fact that the Guantánamo prison remained open. "The president can't just wave a magic wand to say that Gitmo will be closed," he said.[17]

In May 2010, the House and Senate Armed Services Committees approved versions of the annual defense bill. Both included provisions that would block the Thomson plan and impose strict new restrictions on detainee transfers.[18] Jones, Obama's national security adviser, responded with a letter to lawmakers stating that in his military judgment and that of several other flag officers, the continued operation of the prison endangered American troops by fueling anti-American sentiment.[19] Congress ignored him. Soon after, I spoke with Carl Levin, the Senate panel's chairman, who contrasted that mild protest to the Guantánamo provisions with the White House's "very vocal" threats to veto any bill that funded a particular fighter-jet engine that it opposed.

"The administration is not putting a lot of energy behind their position that I can see," Levin told me. "It's pretty dormant in terms of their public positions."[20]

Graham was frustrated at the paralysis from a different vantage point. His talks with the White House about striking a grand bargain on detainees had lapsed inconclusively. "We can't get anyone to give us a final answer," he told me around that time. "It just goes into a black hole. I don't know what happens."[21]

Against that backdrop, on June 24, 2010, the National Security Council deputies committee met in the Situation Room to discuss the future of military commissions. Pretrial hearings at Guantánamo had resumed against three detainees with charges pending from the Bush years. The first set to go to trial was Omar Khadr, the detainee accused of throwing a hand grenade during a firefight in Afghanistan that killed an American army sergeant.* Khadr was a Canadian who had been born into a family of radical Islamists that moved to Afghanistan before 9/11. At the time of the firefight, he was fifteen years old.

Prosecutors had charged Khadr with murder, spying, and planting roadside bombs. From a policy perspective, this was a public relations disaster. The last thing the Obama administration wanted, after laboring for a year to revamp and redeem military commissions, was for the system's flagship trial to be of a child soldier. Global coverage of Khadr's case was dominated by questions about whether bringing the case to trial at all was appropriate. The administration was hoping to avert the trial with a plea deal, opening diplomatic talks with Canada about transferring him to its custody as part of any arrangement. His defense team wanted to strike a deal, but negotiations had not borne fruit; Khadr claimed he hadn't thrown the grenade and, more sweepingly, that he should not be held responsible for activities adults had coerced him into doing. He had vowed not to plead guilty. But there were still six weeks to go — perhaps something could be worked out.

What the Pentagon really wanted to do was move forward with bringing new charges in more serious cases — especially a death-penalty case against al-Nashiri, the accused planner of the Cole bombing that had killed seventeen sailors. Bauer and DeRosa, according to a participant, agreed that new cases should proceed. Koh argued that any such charges should wait for a simultaneous announcement of a new civilian trial venue for the KSM case.

The other focus was where to hold future commission trials. The option favored by most officials present, including representatives from Defense and Homeland Security, was to resume cases at Guantánamo for the time being and move them to the prison at Thomson if that became possible. Bauer, however, observed that if they went that route, Guantánamo would become the default location and it would be much harder to relocate the trials. Koh argued for permitting limited, pretrial activity to resume at Guantánamo but preparing the Charleston naval

---

* See chapter 6, section 8.

base, including retrofitting a warehouse to be a courtroom, to hold the actual trials.

Because of the disagreements at the deputies level, the questions were kicked up to a principals committee meeting.

7. An Exception to the Moratorium (Gitmo Habeas Collapse II)

In the late spring and summer of 2010, two competing pressures began to push harder against each other. There were many Yemenis at Guantánamo against whom there was very weak evidence of ties to terrorism — a group the United States would have long since repatriated had they come from a more stable country. But because of Obama's moratorium on any more transfers to Yemen, the Justice Department had to defend Obama's legal power to keep holding the Yemenis with weak evidence. When federal district court judges ruled that it was not lawful for Obama to keep holding one of these prisoners, it raised the question of whether the administration should make an exception to the moratorium and let him go, or appeal the judgment and ask the Court of Appeals to interpret Obama's detention powers more expansively.

The sequence began on May 26, when federal district court judge Henry Kennedy "emphatically" ordered the Yemeni freed from Guantánamo.[22] The evidence before Kennedy against this man, Mohammed Odaini, was that he had been present at a Pakistani guesthouse when security forces raided it in March 2002. It was one of two guesthouses raided that night for suspected ties to al-Qaeda. Abu Zubaydah, a particularly important operative whom the CIA later waterboarded, was captured in the other one.

Odaini had been seventeen at the time. He maintained that he was a religious student and that the night of the raid had been his first visit to the guesthouse. Military officials had recommended his transfer in 2002, 2004, and 2007. Olsen's task force, internal records showed, had unanimously agreed he should go on June 24, 2009. But concerns about security in Yemen had kept him locked up. Now, Kennedy said the evidence was "overwhelming" that Odaini had no connection to al-Qaeda, declaring that imprisoning him for eight years "at such great cost to him has done nothing to make the United States more secure." It was a striking moment; for all the Obama administration's pride in coming up with the March 13 Standard for who was detainable and who was not, here was a judge saying they had nevertheless spent the next fourteen months imprisoning a man who did not even come *close* to meeting that standard.

The administration made an exception to Obama's moratorium on Yemeni repatriations and sent Odaini home on July 13.[23] Inside the interagency deliberations, the Justice Department reported that seventeen more Yemenis were also likely to win their lawsuits because the evidence against them was similarly thin. The repatriation, then, might end up being a precedent that could permit Obama to repatriate many low-level Yemenis despite the moratorium.

But the same day as that transfer, July 13, the appeals court reversed a judge's order to release yet another Yemeni detainee against whom the evidence was weak. In that case, the Justice Department had chosen to appeal rather than comply with the order—and the government won.[24] The two contrasting results became a focus a week later when Lieutenant General James Clapper, then the head of the Defense Intelligence Agency and Obama's nominee for director of national intelligence, came before the Senate Intelligence Committee for his confirmation hearing.[25]

At the hearing, Kit Bond, the Republican vice chair of the committee, criticized Obama's policy of trying to release low-level prisoners from Guantánamo. He began by saying, "We know the recidivism rate for Gitmo detainees is now above 20 percent."

It was true that some former Guantánamo detainees had engaged in terrorism or insurgent activity after their transfer. Still, to reach Bond's figure, two steps were necessary. First, Bond combined those the CIA considered *confirmed* to have done so with those analysts merely *suspected* of it based on unverified information, like a rumor passed on by a single source. Second, Bond conflated the 532 detainees transferred by the Bush-Cheney administration, which had struck diplomatic deals to repatriate large blocs to countries like Saudi Arabia and Afghanistan, with the sixty-six released during the Obama administration using the Olsen task force's individualized reviews. Of the Obama-era transfers, there were just two confirmed and three suspected.[26] Still, every release undeniably created some risk.

Bond then cited the recent appeals court ruling overturning the release order as showing that the government could and should appeal habeas losses. And he went on to reveal that someone had told him that the CIA and the DIA—Clapper's agency—"did not concur" in the administration's decision to transfer Odaini rather than appeal Kennedy's ruling.

This was a remarkable moment. Bond, the Republican, was reaching out to Obama's nominee and getting him to side with him in public against the administration's policy decision. The two did not elaborate on what the dispute about Odaini had been, but a participant in the deliberations later told me what it was. There was an additional piece of alleged evidence against Odaini that the government had not shown to Kennedy: a statement some other detainee, apparently arrested the same night, had made to interrogators shortly after he was subjected to some kind of torture or cruelty. I could not learn the details of what the abuse was, exactly how much time had passed between the abuse and the statement, or the specifics he said to interrogators. Leaked dossiers on some other Guantánamo detainees captured in the same raid alleged that the occupants of the two guesthouses may have been part of a cell planning to plant roadside bombs in Afghanistan,[27] although a leaked dossier on Odaini did not say that about him.[28]

Because the statement, whatever it was, was deemed to be tainted, the Justice Department had declined to use it as evidence in court, in line with its promise. Even with the statement included, the evidence against Odaini was weak. Olsen's task force had seen all the evidence in the government's files, including restricted files from the CIA black-site interrogations, and officials from all six agencies on the task force unanimously thought Odaini should be transferred. That did not mean they thought he should go to Yemen, however. Clapper's agency had wanted to appeal Kennedy's decision because they thought the suppressed evidence showed that releasing Odaini into a chaotic environment like Yemen was too much of a risk.

At the hearing, Clapper emphasized that repatriations were "something you have to watch very carefully in Yemen because their ability to monitor and then rehabilitate anyone is problematic at best." But, he added, decisions about transferring detainees were an interagency process "in which intelligence is an important, but not the only, input to that decision."

Bond sent a signal: "I assume you would not hesitate if the intelligence agencies' conclusions point to a different direction than the ultimate policy decision, that you would share your honest assessments with the oversight committee in our confidential deliberations."

"Yes, sir, I would," Clapper replied.

The very next day, Kennedy ordered the government to free yet another Yemeni detainee. This man's name was Adnan Latif. The decision about whether to release Latif or appeal that order would set in motion a chain of cascading calamities at Guantánamo.

8. One Last Push for a KSM Civilian Trial

The Obama team's internal tensions over their deteriorating Guantánamo policy came to a head on August 10 as Hillary Clinton pushed back against Bob Gates in a Situation Room principals committee meeting.[29] When Jones opened the meeting just after eleven that morning, Gates pushed hard for permission to get going on new military commission charges. Holder's KSM trial plan had collapsed more than half a year before, and the attorney general had made no progress on finding a new Article III trial venue. The Pentagon did not want to keep waiting for the Justice Department to get its act together.

We promised a revised process and we accomplished that, Gates said. *There's never a good time to move forward. We are not going to get approval to close Guantánamo. We can't kick the can down the road and hold them with no prospect for a trial. We should hold the trials where the detainees are.*

Clinton erupted.

It is a very difficult position, but if we do that we'd be throwing the president's National Archives speech into the trash bin, she said, and as she spoke she picked up her briefing papers for the meeting and dramatically threw them onto the floor. *We need to recognize that this would be giving up on closing Guantánamo and giving up on having a different process. We have done a very poor job of defending the president's strategy.*

Clinton continued to speak, laying waste to the White House political operation. There was no congressional strategy, she said. There was no clear public relations strategy. They had put Holder out there to announce the KSM case decision without follow-up, and forbidden him from engaging as the plan drew criticism. The mishandling of the situation had cost them dearly. Closing Gitmo was the principal argument they were making internationally that the United States was returning to the rule of law and holding itself to high standards. With this action, resuming military trials, they would be throwing up their hands in defeat. And if they continued to limp along, they could expect a well-orchestrated effort in Congress to attack the task force's determinations and to try to halt all Guantánamo transfers that fall. This would create serious foreign-policy concerns because of all the assurances they had made in foreign capitals across the world — promises to allies that had already done them favors by taking in detainees to help close it. They needed to defend the process with an aggressive and comprehensive legal and public relations strategy.

I realize how impossible this is, but we must take a strong stand and push, she said.

Holder jumped in, dittoing Clinton. He argued that if they went ahead with the Defense Department proposal, they would never close Guantánamo and restore the role of Article III courts. They had never tried to educate the public, to counter the arguments that you could not protect sensitive intelligence in civilian court or hold terrorists securely on domestic soil. It might not have been politically wise to choose Manhattan as the venue for the KSM case, he said, but no one had rebutted his arguments that civilian court could handle the 9/11 trial and made the most sense. He asked for ninety days more without any new military commissions trials to try to find a way to bring the KSM case in regular court.

It might be tilting at windmills, but it's worth it, Holder said. *Give me three months to come up with a plan.*

Janet Napolitano, the Homeland Security secretary, said she agreed with Clinton too. But Leon Panetta, the CIA director, was not so sure. He said it wasn't an either/or situation; moving forward with military trials was not walking away from the National Archives speech.

We've made our case, he said. *We have to recognize reality. We should proceed with trials. Speedy trial is one of our values too. We can go to Congress and try to get approval for Charleston at the same time, though I don't think we will.*

Clinton pointed out to Panetta that even though Republicans had blocked Obama's policy on an energy bill to reduce carbon emissions and a bill to reform the immigration system, nobody thought Obama had given up on those issues. If they mishandled Guantánamo, she said, everyone would think he had given up on it. She raised the specter of letting the commissions go forward full tilt and Obama issuing an executive order to govern indefinite detentions at Guantánamo, which would mean that *it's over.* Clinton said she disagreed with the extent of inherent executive authority claimed by Bush, but she did think Obama had some powers he wasn't using. There were things he could do; he could order prosecutions of detainees in Article III courts and live with the consequences.

Gates doubted that the White House wanted to get into a big fight over lifting the transfer restrictions in the next ninety days. But he said he had no problem waiting another few months. He just urged Holder to move on bringing some charges in Article III courts soon, later adding that Article III trials and commissions should be balanced and move together *like two wheels on a bicycle.*

Holder happily promised that by the end of September he would come up with a concrete plan for an Article III trial that they could go public with postelection. He told Gates it was fine to keep going with the three pending cases; everything else should hold.

We could be in trial right now with KSM and his buddies in New York, Holder added.

Panetta remained skeptical that waiting would make any difference.

I don't disagree with taking ninety days, Panetta said. *I just don't want us to kid ourselves.*

9. How to Avert a Trial

Two days later, on the first day of the military commission trial for Omar Khadr, the Canadian Guantánamo detainee and former child soldier, his military defense lawyer began coughing in court and then, reaching for some water, collapsed. He was taken to the base hospital on a stretcher.[30] It turned out to be complications from gallbladder surgery. The judge postponed the trial until late October. The unexpected reprieve offered the Obama legal team a new chance to avert the Khadr trial so that a case that made the government look better could instead be the first full use of the revamped tribunals system.

On August 18, Cynthia Hogan, the counsel to Vice President Biden, convened a meeting at the White House with several other interagency lawyers to confer about the path to closing Guantánamo. But no one from the Justice Department was invited — on purpose. Hogan said Obama wanted them to step up their public position that fall to keep Congress from imposing steeper transfer restrictions, and to dust off the Justice Department plan to prosecute the 9/11 case in civilian court. But the White House wanted Clinton and Gates, not Holder, to be out front in promoting this.

Obama also wanted to revive a political defense of his approach of using both Article III trials and the reformed military commissions based on case-by-case circumstances. But the problem with military commissions, Hogan said, was how to distinguish their process from that under the Bush years. The prospect of a Khadr trial compounded their public relations problem. Hogan said it would destroy military commissions because it looked so bad. The question was what steps to take to get a plea deal. But the White House's hands were tied because people in the executive office of the president were not supposed to talk to prosecutors about particular cases, to avoid any appearance of political interference.

That left Johnson, the top lawyer at the Pentagon. But he, too, was cautious about intervening, for instance by telling Captain John F. Murphy of the navy, the tribunals' chief prosecutor, that he really ought to take a softer line in plea-deal negotiations so they could avoid a trial. The problem was that an intervention by Johnson could be seen as *unlawful command influence*. This was a concept imported from the regular military courts-martial system. Trials of troops accused of crimes happen within the military hierarchy, rather than through an independent judiciary. But it is against the rules for a commander to use his or her power over subordinate officers handling a case to affect its outcome by saying things like, *I want you to throw the book at that private!* The Military Commissions Act, dating back to its 2006 iteration, contained a clause saying that it was illegal "to coerce, or, by any unauthorized means, influence" the judgment or actions of military prosecutors or the tribunals' civilian overseer.

Later that month, after picking up chatter about this internal hand-wringing, I wrote a front-page story about how the administration legal team was cringing at the spectacle of inaugurating the revamped system with the trial of a child soldier.[31] It also explored how Colonel Morris Davis, Murphy's predecessor as chief tribunals prosecutor, had suggested the command-influence provision to Congress in 2006. Davis had complained that Bush appointees, like Johnson's predecessor as Pentagon general counsel, William Haynes, had inappropriately pressured him to use evidence he considered tainted by torture. Davis, who had since retired, told me that the provision was never meant to block someone from urging a prosecutor to go easier on a defendant: "It's clearly not 'command influence' to do something favorable to the accused," he said. "The whole concept was the opposite of that."

Negotiations with Khadr resumed, and in October they finally struck a deal. The murder charge stayed in, but his prison sentence would be capped at eight years. Moreover, Khadr would be eligible for repatriation to Canada after just one year, and under Canadian law he would be eligible for parole after serving just a third of his sentence. Koh's office negotiated an exchange of diplomatic notes with the Canadian foreign ministry over the potential transfer, which they signed on October 23. Khadr pleaded guilty the next day.

On the day of the plea, Murphy told me that he had instructed subordinate prosecutors to "re-engage" Khadr's defense team about a plea deal in August. He would not say whether he had discussed the matter with Obama administration officials but insisted that his handling of the case was "my own independent decision alone" and "not the result of any political interference with the case."[32]

The Canadian government dragged its feet about taking Khadr back,[33] but in September 2012, he was finally transferred there to serve out the remainder of his sentence. In May 2015, he was freed on bail while trying to get all his convictions vacated, arguing that they were not international war crimes and so the tribunals never had jurisdiction over him in the first place.* Meanwhile, like Khadr, the other two detainees with leftover charges each had pled guilty without trials in exchange for guarantees of even shorter sentences.

At Guantánamo, it could be an advantage to be accused of doing something bad enough to be charged with a crime. A defined prison sentence was a ticket home. By 2013, the military repatriated the last of those three — Khadr to Canada, and the other two to Sudan. They left behind dozens of other prisoners who were not accused of doing

---

* See chapter 10, section 8.

anything chargeable and so remained stuck in law-of-war detention with no end in sight.

10. Tortured Evidence (Gitmo Habeas Collapse III)

After Judge Kennedy's scathing ruling ordering the government to release Odaini, the Yemeni Guantánamo detainee, the administration came under pressures to push harder to keep such lower-level Yemeni detainees locked up. In one such case, this led to an emotional internal dispute about using evidence that some officials believed was tainted by torture, and in another, it resulted in a fateful decision to file an appeal.

The dispute over using the evidence arguably derived from torture, which has never been reported, centered on another Yemeni who had been arrested in the same March 2002 raid on the Pakistani guesthouse as Odaini. The evidence against this man, Abdul Hakim Alhag, was similar; he too said he was a religious student, and their fellow guesthouse resident's torture-tainted statement, which the Justice Department had declined to use against Odaini, applied to him too. Alhag's leaked dossier, which was completed four years after the leaked dossier on Odaini and was far lengthier and more detailed, raised the possibility that the guesthouse residents were part of an intended roadside bomb-planting cell, and it said that additional information about him was available in a supplement that was classified at a higher level of secrecy.[34]

But the details of this evidence were apparently dubious: the six agencies on Olsen's task force had seen it and nevertheless unanimously agreed that Alhag was transferrable. Indeed, the United States had nearly transferred Alhag to Luxembourg earlier in 2010. But the resettlement deal fell apart after he made a comment to a visiting delegation from Luxembourg in July that suggested he might later decide to return to Yemen. Luxembourg told the United States it would have no legal power to stop him from traveling if he decided to go home. The intelligence community had taken the firm position that no detainee should go back to Yemen and argued that sending Alhag to Luxembourg, in light of his comment, would violate that policy. In mid-September 2010, Fried apologized to Luxembourg's minister of foreign affairs; the deal was off. With a hint of bitterness — they had been in negotiations about Alhag for nearly a year — the minister, Jean Asselborn, told a Luxembourg reporter that he thought the reason was political. Because of the Christmas underwear attack, he contended, the Obama administration was willing to let a detainee go back to Yemen only if a court ordered it, but not if the executive branch was responsible for making the decision.[35]

Alhag's case was also pending before Kennedy, so now the Justice Department had to defend Obama's power to keep holding him. A government brief laying out the evidence that Alhag was detainable was due on November 17, 2010. But Justice Department litigators, blistered by Kennedy's reaction to the extremely weak evidence they had presented in support of Obama's claimed power to detain Odaini, were balking at defending against Alhag's lawsuit unless they were permitted to use the torture-tainted statement. Tony West, the Justice Department Civil Division chief, cited an ethics rule that sanctions lawyers who make frivolous claims in courts, saying his litigators worried that they would run afoul of it if they told the judge Alhag was detainable based on the same evidence he had already rejected in the Odaini case.

At the State Department, Koh argued that using the statement would cross a fundamental moral red line, not to mention violate its promise not to use tortured evidence in court for the habeas cases.*

But declining to defend the government's right to keep holding Alhag — a step in habeas corpus litigation called *conceding the writ* — was seen as meaning letting him go, directly or indirectly, to Yemen. The intelligence community — now led by Clapper — opposed sending any more detainees there, saying it was an intolerable security risk. Bob

---

* See chapter 4, section 17.

Litt, Clapper's lawyer, contended that the government should defend Obama's right to keep holding Alhag. The intelligence community also suggested that enough time had passed between when the other detainee was abused and when he made the statement to an interrogator that the evidence had not really been obtained by torture and so was suitable for use in court.[36]

The three-way clash created a legal-policy trap from which there was no ideal exit. One of the three factions had to lose. In the end, the State Department was in the weakest position bureaucratically; the Justice Department "controlled the pen" — it was the agency that wrote the briefs and appeared in court — and national security concerns about Yemen, in the post–Christmas attack atmosphere and with Congress bearing down, held sway. The litigators used the disputed evidence to defend keeping Alhag locked up. This has never been reported: the filing was sealed and classified and thus invisible to the public.

The Alhag case illustrated a slowly boiling dynamic: Because Yemen was a chaotic mess, and because the Obama administration did not want to take the political hit of sending someone home to Yemen, it was making increasingly strained or edgy arguments about the scope of Obama's detention powers in order to defend against habeas cases where the evidence was weak. For a while, the lawyers seemed to be doing this with their fingers crossed that the courts would order the detainees freed anyway. But then the appeals court turned out to be determined to defer to the executive branch in such cases. Detainees stayed locked up, and Obama's detention power ratcheted up, even as his promise to close Guantánamo withered away.

The Alhag case never came to a conclusive end. After Alhag's legal team saw the information in the classified brief, they and Alhag made the decision to ask Kennedy to stay the proceedings indefinitely. The reason, according to people familiar with the matter, was that by then it was clear that the appeals court was ruling against detainees every time it could, and so even if Kennedy sided with Alhag, there was a high risk that he would be reversed. If the only way a detainee would get out was as a matter of executive-branch policy discretion, not by court order, their strategic calculation was that Alhag's chances were better if there was never any definitive judicial ruling that he was detainable.

That same logic began spreading among many habeas litigants around this time. Among them was Bensayah, the Algerian-Bosnian whose status as a mere "supporter" of al-Qaeda from afar had been the subject of the battle between Koh and Johnson the previous fall.* After the appeals court sent the case back to the district court for new consideration, Bensayah's legal team asked the judge to pause the case indefinitely. (Both Bensayah and Alhag spent additional years locked up but ultimately were transferred, Bensayah to Algeria in December 2013, and Alhag to the Eastern European nation of Georgia in November 2014.)

The gradual hollowing out of Guantánamo habeas corpus rights reached its apotheosis in the case of Latif, the Yemeni detainee Kennedy had ordered freed in August 2010, just one day after Bond's exchange with Clapper about Yemenis and appeals. Arrested by Pakistani police near the Afghan border in December 2001 and turned over to the Americans, Latif claimed that he was in the region to get free medical treatment from Islamic missionaries there, not to be a terrorist. He had sustained a traumatic brain injury in a car accident in Yemen in 1994 and had medical papers—and no weapon—on him when arrested. The evidence that he might instead have been an enemy fighter consisted of an intake form somebody had filled out when the Pakistanis turned him over. The form said he had told an interrogator that he had carried a weapon as part of an Arab militia that was helping the Taliban fight the Northern Alliance but had not fired a shot. Latif claimed this was a translation error or someone else's statement misattributed to him in the war-zone confusion. Kennedy said the form was not enough to prove that Latif was part of al-Qaeda because Latif had offered a plausible alternative story for what he was doing in the region. The military, he said, must release Latif.

The administration weighed its options. Odaini had set a precedent;

* See chapter 4, section 17.

they could use Kennedy's order as an excuse to repatriate Latif despite the moratorium and take the hit of criticism from Congress. After all, executive-branch officials had repeatedly recommended releasing him — at least twice by military intelligence analysts at Guantánamo during the Bush years and again by Olsen's task force at a meeting on July 8, 2009.

But on September 17, 2010, instead of obeying Kennedy's order and transferring Latif, the Justice Department filed an appeal. Every appeal has to be approved by the solicitor general. But there were no Obama appointees to make that call. Elena Kagan had just become a Supreme Court justice, and her principal deputy and acting successor, Katyal, was recused from Guantánamo litigation because of his work during the Bush years. So Ed Kneedler, the career deputy solicitor general, made the decision. An executive-branch lifer, Kneedler was a strong advocate of preserving executive flexibility. Still, there were times when there were legal-policy gaps between the Obama political appointees and Kneedler, and the White House cared enough about the issue to pressure Kneedler to get in line.* The Latif case was not one of those times.

A year later, in October 2011, an appeals court panel voted two-to-one to overturn Kennedy's order and restore Obama's power to imprison Latif. Writing for the majority, Janice Rogers Brown said the intake form was entitled to a "presumption of regularity," meaning its words had to be taken as true unless there was a good reason to think otherwise.[37] The dissenting judge, David Tatel, a Clinton appointee, argued that courts should not evaluate a record "produced in the fog of war" by a standard that essentially forced judges to accept any claim on a government document as accurate. He said the precedent gutted the Supreme Court ruling that detainees were entitled to a "meaningful opportunity" to contest the evidence against them.

The Supreme Court let it — and every other such ruling before it — stand without review. That was essentially the end of habeas corpus lawsuits as a route out of Guantánamo.

---

* See chapter 4, section 18.

11. The Ghailani Verdict

Back in October 2010, a civilian trial had opened for Ahmed Ghailani in the Manhattan federal courthouse. Prosecutors accused Ghailani of helping to orchestrate al-Qaeda's 1998 bombings of two American embassies in Africa, which killed 224 people. The Obama administration had transferred him from Guantánamo in 2009 for prosecution before a regular court, making his case a test of both security (there were no incidents, and life in New York was not disrupted) and the criminal justice system's ability to handle the complexities of prosecuting a former CIA black-site prisoner. The result was a win for the government as a matter of substance that looked like a loss as a matter of politics, ultimately sealing the fate of the plan to prosecute the 9/11 case in a similar venue.

During pretrial hearings, Judge Lewis Kaplan ruled that the five years Ghailani had spent in American custody before the government brought him to court did not violate his right to a speedy trial, given the circumstances. But the judge also ruled that prosecutors could not call as a witness a man who said he had sold explosives to Ghailani. The defendant had uttered the witness's name in connection with what Kaplan called "extremely harsh interrogation methods" at a secret CIA prison. (The details were redacted, although the Senate torture report later said Ghailani had been "subjected to extended sleep deprivation and experienced hallucinations."[38]) Kaplan cited the doctrine of *fruit of the poisonous tree*, meaning the evidence had derived from unconstitutional coercion and so he had to suppress it to protect Ghailani's constitutional right against self-incrimination.[39]

On November 17 — just after the midterm election in which Republicans retook the House of Representatives — a jury convicted Ghailani of one count of conspiracy to destroy American buildings and property. But, in a shocking and seemingly incoherent act, it acquitted him on 284 other charges — including murder counts for each victim who had died when the bombs destroyed the buildings.

Even the one conviction was enough for a potential life sentence. But media accounts understandably focused on the spectacle of the surprise acquittals, creating the impression that Ghailani had essentially won.

In the political sphere, critics portrayed the outcome as proof that Obama's and Holder's support for prosecuting terrorists in civilian court was folly. Their premise was that the acquittals stemmed from Kaplan's suppression of the witness testimony, evidence that would have been admissible in a military commission.

That analysis was easy to understand, politically potent, and almost certainly wrong. As Kaplan explained in a footnote to his opinion suppressing the witness testimony, it was "very far from clear" that a military commission judge would have deemed it admissible for two reasons: tribunal rules also barred torture-tainted evidence, and it was likely that courts would rule that Fifth Amendment rights applied in military trials too.[40]

In my view, there actually was a plausible argument to be made that the case would have turned out differently in a commission, but it was more complicated and less useful as political ammunition. It has to do with juries, not rules of evidence.

There were strong indications that what really happened with the Ghailani verdict was a compromise made with a holdout on the jury in order to avoid a mistrial: eleven jurors persuaded the twelfth to convict on one count in exchange for their agreement to acquit him on the rest. A few days before the verdict, one juror had sent Kaplan a grammatically garbled note asking to be excused: "At this point am secure and I have come to my conclusion but it doesn't agreed with the rest of the juror. My conclusion it not going to change. I feel am been attack for my conclusion."[41] But Kaplan had kept her on the panel.

The chances of an idiosyncratic holdout disrupting a military commission trial are lower. Tribunal juries are handpicked from ranks of active-duty commissioned officers, and under commission rules for noncapital cases, merely two-thirds must vote to convict. Civilian juries are essentially chosen at random from the much more varied population of registered voters, and civilian trial rules require unanimous guilty verdicts.[42]

Still, even though the jury had convicted Ghailani on just one charge, it was enough for the civilian criminal justice system to incapacitate him forever. In late January 2011, Kaplan sentenced Ghailani to life without parole. An appeals court later upheld the trial and its result, going out of its way to praise Kaplan for handling the difficult issues raised by the case fairly.[43]

12. The Guantánamo Transfer Restrictions

I'm tired of these issues, said Clinton.

You think I'm not? responded Holder.

It was January 7, 2011. After the Ghailani verdict, Congress — in its waning days under total Democratic control — took up the National Defense Authorization Act of 2011. The final version forbade spending money to transfer any Guantánamo detainees onto domestic soil for any purpose, including prosecution. The bill also imposed steep restrictions on the transfer of low-level detainees to other countries by requiring the secretary of defense to personally certify to Congress, thirty days ahead of any transfer, that the receiving country had met an extensive list of security conditions. Countries where even one former detainee had become a recidivist were ineligible to receive any more. In short, it would kill Holder's KSM trial plan — not that he had found a new civilian venue anyway — and it would severely limit Obama's ability to transfer away any more lower-level detainees.

Holder had sent an angry letter to Congress calling it "an extreme and risky encroachment on the authority of the executive branch to determine when and where to prosecute terrorist suspects" and warning that it would set a "dangerous" constitutional precedent.[44] When Congress ignored him, Obama's advisers weighed whether to issue a signing statement asserting that the transfer restrictions were unconstitutional.[45]

Barron, by then, had left government, but the Office of Legal Counsel, now under the temporary leadership of Jonathan Cedarbaum, remained in the mind-set of Barron's unofficial white paper eleven months earlier: it was skeptical that Obama's executive powers could trump a statute forcing him to use a military commission instead of civilian court for particular cases. And even if a legal justification to defy the restrictions could be constructed in theory, it seemed politically impossible to many in the White House that Obama would, at least at that moment in his presidency, close Guantánamo unilaterally and bring all the detainees to a prison on American soil. Democrats had just lost the midterm election and control of the House of Representatives, Obama was preparing to seek re-election, and his political advisers saw the issue as a loser.

Obama signed the bill on January 7, issuing a signing statement that denounced the restrictions as a bad idea as a matter of policy but claimed no constitutional power to override them.[46] That same day Obama's national security cabinet gathered again in the Situation Room for a two-hour meeting on finding a way forward with the Guantánamo policy, a meeting that opened with Clinton's and Holder's lament.

Gates told the group that it was time to finish the draft executive order governing Guantánamo detainees and resume military commissions. The prosecution team was starting to break up due to the long delays.

Clinton was still hoping to avoid rolling out commissions cases piecemeal apart from any sign of movement on closing Guantánamo. And why, she complained, was the military leading off with the "major mistreatment" cases? They needed to move the military commissions to the United States to mitigate the spectacle.

Holder said he agreed. Clinton turned to him. Why couldn't the Justice Department strike a plea bargain with some Guantánamo detainee? she asked. If there was a case ready for sentencing without any need for a trial, it would be a basis for objecting to the transfer restrictions as infringing on presidential authority.

We should be strong on this, she said.

Panetta asked whether plea bargains were possible in some case other than KSM's.

Someone wondered what Graham would think if they did that.

Bauer spoke up. He said Graham had called him and the senator said he liked the draft executive order. He was thinking about incorporating it into legislation he was drafting. Moving forward with military commissions, he added, would be warmly received by Graham.

But a little later in the meeting, Susan Rice, then the ambassador to the United Nations, abruptly injected a note of high despair about the whole Guantánamo situation.

This has become an international disaster, Rice said. *We have to protect the president.* Allies, she said, were telling her, "You people have lost your way, fallen from grace."

The principals committee meeting ended with no clear plan for what to do. On that day, there were eighty-nine men waiting on the recommended-for-transfer list. And for nearly three years, not one of them would leave Guantánamo — at least, not alive.

13. Giving Up on a Civilian Trial for KSM

Later in January 2011, the interagency lawyers gathered to make one last effort to figure out how to reassert Obama's commitment to restoring the primacy of Article III trials despite the ban on bringing Guantánamo detainees into the United States. Koh was still fighting, but many others were ready to give up in the face of the new federal statute.

We have been hobbled, observed Jim Cole, the deputy attorney general, according to a participant.

Kathy Ruemmler, whom Bauer had brought over from the Justice Department to be deputy White House counsel, thought the legal environment had become hopeless. She cited Barron's Office of Legal Counsel white paper.

We can't really challenge this, she said, referring to the transfer restrictions.

But Koh strongly objected.

OLC has not given an opinion, he declared. *A year ago, that white paper was not on this issue, and there was no interagency discussion. OLC has to draw lines so the president knows what his options are.*

Koh also argued that it was important to show that there was still movement toward prosecuting additional Guantánamo detainees to trial in Article III civilian courts. Everyone in the room was aware that the Ghailani case, despite the political hay that had been made of its bizarre mixed verdict, had actually been a success as a substantive matter. Denis McDonough, now the deputy national security adviser, said he was very sympathetic to what Koh was saying. So was Brennan.

We need to demonstrate a commitment to our system, Brennan said. *We need to make a full-throated defense of Article III courts.*

But Ruemmler, a former prosecutor, was skeptical about trying other Guantánamo detainees in civilian court, too. Many of the potential Guantánamo cases had stale witnesses and stale evidence, she said, as well as speedy-trial-rule problems.

Koh declared that they should just announce which detainees were going to be tried in an Article III court. The transfer restrictions' infringement on the speedy-trial rule would become a reason why the restrictions were unconstitutional, he proposed.

Johnson tried to slow things down. Moving the prisoners to the mainland on a military plane, the Pentagon lawyer said, would now be a "criminal" violation.

We need to see that analysis, Koh shot back.

But political reality was setting in. On March 7, 2011, Gates finally authorized the military commissions system to begin charging new cases. (Al-Nashiri, the accused *Cole* plotter, would be arraigned at Guantánamo in October.) That same day, Obama issued his long-delayed executive order establishing a system of parole-like hearings for Guantánamo detainees who were being held in indefinite law-of-war detention and not facing charges. The boards would periodically review whether national security still required imprisoning each man. The executive order had been under development in fits and starts since 2009. Avril Haines, DeRosa's deputy and eventual successor as the National Security Council legal adviser, had completed the work of drafting the order and driving it through the interagency process.[47]

At the same time, Obama issued a statement reiterating support for using civilian courts as "a key part of our arsenal in the war against al-Qaeda and its affiliate."[48] But his statement did not mention closing Guantánamo.[49]

The executive order was widely understood to be an acknowledgment that the Guantánamo closure policy was dead and that the prison would remain open for business indefinitely. Dismayed human rights groups also saw it as entrenching the idea that the United States government would imprison people without trial for the foreseeable future. "This is a step down the road toward institutionalizing a preventive-detention regime," said Elisa Massimino, president of Human Rights First.[50]

The centerpiece of Obama's order was its direction to create the parole-like periodic review boards. But there was little administrative urgency in carrying out Obama's order, in part because there was now little point in moving a detainee to the recommended-for-transfer category, since nobody from either group was going to be leaving under the new transfer restrictions. Interagency disagreements paralyzed the process of developing the boards for more than two years. A key sticking point was whether or how the boards should be shown evidence that suggested a detainee might be too dangerous to release, but that came from torture.*

One of the last remaining fragments of Obama's 2009-era policy for dealing with legacy captives was their hope to prosecute KSM in a regular civilian court. It toppled in late March. According to an account in the *Washington Post*, Holder called Obama and informed him that he was returning the 9/11 case to the military commissions system.

---

* See chapter 10, section 12.

Obama did not object and called it a pragmatic decision.[51] A few days later, on April 4, 2011, a grim-faced Holder announced publicly that the five alleged 9/11 conspirators would be tried before a tribunal at Guantánamo after all. Holder said he stood by his judgment that civilian court would work out better but acknowledged that Congress had made that impossible.

"We must face a simple truth: those restrictions are unlikely to be repealed in the immediate future," he said. "And we simply cannot allow a trial to be delayed any longer for the victims of the 9/11 attacks or for their families who have waited nearly a decade for justice."[52]

Rights groups like the American Civil Liberties Union, which had praised Holder's original trial decision as a restoration of the rule of law, expressed frustration that the administration had given in. New York–based Democrats who had come out against holding the trial in Manhattan in the fearful aftermath of the attempted Christmas attack said the decision was the right call. Republicans did too but focused their remarks on excoriating the administration for having ever tried to do otherwise.

14. A New Tribunals Prosecutor

At 7:00 p.m. on April 28, 2011, a group of highly influential national security law insiders from across the ideological spectrum converged at Nora, an upscale organic restaurant near DuPont Circle. Johnson had invited them to the private upstairs room for an annual dinner he hosted; guests over the years had ranged from Anthony Romero, the American Civil Liberties Union director, to Lindsey Graham, along with many current and former executive-branch officials from both the Obama and Bush-Cheney administrations. Guests at the 2011 dinner included Barron, now back at Harvard Law School, and Michael Mukasey, the former judge and Bush-era attorney general who had become an outspoken critic of Holder's handling of national security issues.

At the 2011 dinner, several participants told me, Johnson requested feedback on Guantánamo policy issues.

What am I doing wrong? What am I not hearing that I need to hear? he asked.

The conversation that ensued focused on the shortcomings of the military commissions system. It was now clear that KSM and the other 9/11 defendants were going to be prosecuted before a tribunal. Some of the guests were happy about that, and others were not, but the issue was settled; this was going to happen. And in light of that reality, there was pan-ideological agreement that Johnson needed to take serious steps to upgrade the prosecutors' office; no disrespect to the current military commissions prosecutor, reservist navy captain John Murphy, an assistant United States attorney in Louisiana, they said, but Johnson needed to bring in an A-team for what was coming. This view, dinner participants later recalled, united former officials as different in outlook as Barron and Mukasey.

Johnson had already been thinking about personnel issues; the previous month, he had named retired Rear Admiral Bruce MacDonald, the former top uniformed lawyer in the navy, the new overseer of the commissions system. Now Johnson started thinking about prosecutors.

Two years earlier, Johnson had picked then-Colonel Mark Martins to be the Pentagon's co-leader of Obama's 2009 detention-policy task force, where Martins had pushed hard to keep and strengthen military commissions.[*] As noted, in the fall of 2009, the military had promoted Martins to brigadier general and deployed him to Afghanistan to work on detention operations. His work included setting up periodic review hearings for the detainees at Bagram Airfield and overseeing the movement of some eight hundred prisoners out of the old prison built in a hangar and into the new sixty-million-dollar prison at the edge of the base, called Parwan.

By May 2010, Martins had, with help from Generals David Petraeus and Stanley McChrystal, moved out of detention operations. He led a

---

[*] See chapter 4, section 11.

newly created NATO Rule of Law Field Support Mission, which helped train Afghan police, courts, and prison guards. The hope was that NATO could eventually turn over more detention operations to the Afghan criminal justice system.

That was what he was still doing a year later when Johnson sent Martins a cryptic e-mail asking how he had liked his courtroom experience in his younger JAG days. Martins responded that he had loved it. On May 24, 2011, around 5:30 p.m. Afghanistan time, Martins was at his office in Kandahar when the phone rang. It was Johnson. He wanted Martins to come back to Washington and accept a new assignment: chief prosecutor of the Office of Military Commissions.

This request meant a significant sacrifice. Martins was widely expected to become *the* Judge Advocate General for the army, a three-star position. The military commissions chief prosecutor was a colonel's billet. And it would likely consume the remainder of Martins's time in the service. He could keep his one star but would never get a third.

Martins said yes.

15. Torture and bin Laden

At his 2011 dinner party, Johnson had also invited as a special guest Stephen Preston, the CIA lawyer, who arrived looking strained and rapidly gulped down two martinis. Three days later, on May 1, an American commando team under CIA control killed Osama bin Laden at his secret compound deep inside Pakistan, making it clear to all why Preston had seemed so stressed out.* (At Johnson's 2012 dinner, a calmer and more cheerful Preston returned, joking, *You can probably see that I'm looking much more relaxed, if you want to draw conclusions about whether there are any imminent major operations going on.*)

A crucial breakthrough in the hunt for bin Laden's hideout, it swiftly

---

* See chapter 6, sections 11 through 14.

emerged, had been identifying the courier who served as the al-Qaeda leader's link to the outside world. Former Bush-era officials felt vindicated, asserting that information gathered through the CIA torture (or, as they still called it, "enhanced interrogation") program was responsible for that breakthrough. "President Obama can take credit, rightfully, for the success today, but he owes it to the tough decisions taken by the Bush administration,"[53] John Yoo wrote. Although the torture program had essentially ended by the time he had become attorney general in late 2007, Mukasey went further, making a series of extremely important factual assertions in a high-profile opinion essay published by the *Wall Street Journal* under the headline "The Waterboarding Trail to bin Laden."

"Consider how the intelligence that led to bin Laden came to hand," Mukasey wrote. "It began with a disclosure from Khalid Sheikh Mohammed (KSM), who broke like a dam under the pressure of harsh interrogation techniques that included waterboarding. He loosed a torrent of information — including eventually the nickname of a trusted courier of bin Laden.... Another of those gathered up later in this harvest, Abu Faraj al-Libi, also was subjected to certain of these harsh techniques and disclosed further details about bin Laden's couriers that helped in last weekend's achievement."[54]

This asserted history, for which Mukasey cited no sources, was puzzling at the time. It was incompatible with what my colleague Scott Shane and I were hearing. Various officials told us that from one perspective, the intelligence trail had begun in 2002 when an allied government's intelligence service told the CIA the trusted courier's nickname, Abu Ahmed al-Kuwaiti, and his likely role as one of many al-Qaeda message carriers. From another perspective, the trail had begun in 2004, when the CIA recognized the courier's significance thanks to a breakthrough interrogation of a detainee named Hassan Ghul. Officials said Ghul had explained the courier's singular importance as bin Laden's remaining link to the outside organization. They also said, ambiguously, that Ghul had been both voluntarily cooperative and subjected briefly to some enhanced techniques that did not include waterboarding. But, we were told, KSM and Abu Faraj al-Libi never disclosed any real information about the courier; in fact, after Ghul's revelations, the CIA came to believe the two had been lying about him despite having been tortured, which the agency interpreted as indirect corroboration that he must be unusually important. In short, either what we were hearing from others was fabricated or a former attorney general of the United States was spreading blatant misinformation to the public.[55]

Three and a half years later, the Senate Intelligence Committee report on CIA torture, along with the rebuttal reports by Republican senators and the CIA, would expose Mukasey's claims as indisputably false.[56]

First, the report, citing and quoting extensively from contemporaneous CIA cables, showed that the CIA knew far more than anyone had realized about Abu Ahmed al-Kuwaiti in 2002, before the United States had tortured anyone. The government was already wiretapping phone and e-mail accounts associated with the man, and it already knew details about his age, physical appearance, and family that would later prove crucial to finding him. The CIA knew these things from information provided by an allied intelligence service based on its interrogation of a detainee in its custody. (It is, of course, entirely possible that this allied service had tortured that detainee.) The rebuttals to the Senate report did not question these facts; rather, they stressed that the information in CIA files was meaningless at the time because its importance was not yet recognized.

Second, the report said, Ammar al-Baluchi, KSM's nephew and one of his four codefendants in the 9/11 military commissions case, told the CIA in 2003 that Abu Ahmed al-Kuwaiti was a bin Laden courier. Al-Baluchi said this after he had been tortured in ways that did not include waterboarding. But this, too, was not a breakthrough that triggered recognition of his importance because al-Baluchi then recanted everything he had said during and in the immediate aftermath of the torture, and CIA analysts discounted it at the time. The rebuttals did not claim al-Baluchi's statement was any breakthrough in the investigation, although they pointed out that it became additional corroboration in retrospect, after the courier's importance was recognized.

Third, KSM did not provide Ahmed al-Kuwaiti's nickname, and Abu Faraj al-Libi did not provide further details about bin Laden's couriers that helped with the raid. Rather, when they were asked about Ahmed al-Kuwaiti, KSM said the man had retired, and Abu Faraj al-Libi denied knowing anyone with that name. He made up a false name for bin Laden's primary courier, for whom the CIA then fruitlessly hunted. The rebuttals stressed that once the CIA understood that Ahmed al-Kuwaiti was bin Laden's courier, the post-torture denials by KSM and Abu Faraj al-Libi became corroboration that he was a secret worth protecting. Thus, Mukasey's description of what KSM and Abu Faraj al-Libi had said was false.

Finally, the Senate report held that Ghul indeed provided the breakthrough — the "best" and "most accurate" information that Ahmed al-Kuwaiti was bin Laden's courier — and the rebuttals concurred that he was "a milestone" and "clearly…important." Strikingly, the report showed that Ghul did not provide the breakthrough information after being tortured. He had been captured by Kurdish forces in Iraqi Kurdistan in January 2004, and when U.S. forces came to take custody of him, he was sitting sipping tea in a safe house, not in a cell or handcuffed, and having a free-flowing conversation. In CIA custody, Ghul continued to be cooperative without being tortured: "He sang like a Tweetie Bird, he opened up right away and was cooperative from the outset," a CIA official told the inspector general later that year. Ghul explained that bin Laden was likely living in a house in Pakistan with Ahmed al-Kuwaiti serving as his link to the outside world, among other things. He spoke so much, and provided so much valuable information, that the CIA sent back twenty-one intelligence reports based on those conversations.

The agency then tortured him anyway, to see if he would say more. This turned out not to be so brief; they transferred him to a black site, shaved him, shackled him in stress positions, and kept him awake for fifty-nine straight hours, causing him to hallucinate and experience abdominal and back spasms, irregular heartbeats, and partial paralysis of his limbs, the Senate report said, citing CIA cables. The Senate report said he produced "no actionable information" following this treatment, and the agency later let him go free. The rebuttals argued that Ghul *did* provide additional information after this treatment. He had added that Ahmed al-Kuwaiti had delivered a letter from bin Laden to Abu Faraj al-Libi in 2002, a concrete detail that served to corroborate his earlier account.

The Senate torture report also showed that the movie *Zero Dark Thirty*, which purports to depict the hunt for bin Laden, had skewed what really happened in a way that increased the utility of torture. First, the movie showed a detainee named Ammar first being waterboarded — although the real Ammar al-Baluchi, KSM's nephew, was not — and then naming Ahmed al-Kuwaiti as a man who his "uncle" had said "worked for bin Laden" and who, when Ammar had met him a year earlier, had been carrying a letter from "the Sheikh."[57] Second, the movie also showed a detainee named Hassan Ghul being held in Pakistani custody telling a CIA interrogator that he had "dealt with the mukhabarat" — Arabic for "intelligence service" — and had "no wish to be tortured again," so he would cooperate. This fictionalized version of a post-torture Ghul then explains that Ahmed al-Kuwaiti "works for Faraj and bin Laden. He is his most trusted courier.... He brought me many messages from the Sheikh."[58]

We know, thanks to a Republican congressional investigation and a Pentagon inspector general report, that the CIA fed information to the screenwriter of *Zero Dark Thirty*.* The Senate report also cited internal CIA papers showing that in March 2011, two months before the bin Laden raid, the agency had already begun preparing a public relations campaign that would emphasize "the critical nature of detainee reporting in identifying bin Laden's courier." At a May 5, 2011, briefing to Congress, just after the raid, the CIA said Ghul had been subjected to enhanced interrogation and had provided top-tier information linking

* See chapter 8, section 19.

al-Kuwaiti to bin Laden, misleadingly suggesting that the crucial information came *after*, not before, the torture.

Mukasey had been out of government for more than two years by the time of the raid, so someone must have fed him the information he agreed to put his name behind—presumably Mukasey did not know that it was false—and deliver to the American people in the pages of the *Wall Street Journal*. I e-mailed Mukasey and asked how the column had come about in light of the information in the torture report. He did not reply.

Mukasey had concluded his *Wall Street Journal* column asserting that waterboarding led to bin Laden by calling for the criminal investigation into CIA interrogations, for which he blisteringly criticized Holder, to be shut down.

A month later, Holder announced that John Durham, the career prosecutor leading the investigation, had recommended closing, without any charges, his preliminary investigation into the treatment of nearly one hundred detainees whom the CIA had held in its overseas black-site prisons.[59]

But Durham was elevating two cases, both of which involved prisoners who died in the agency's custody, to full investigations.

16. A New High-Value Detainee

On June 28, 2011, Vice Admiral William McRaven, who had overseen the SEALs raid that killed bin Laden, came before the Senate Armed Services Committee for his confirmation hearing to be leader of the Special Operations Command.[60] Graham asked him what the United States would do if it captured a high-value terrorism suspect in a place outside of a war zone, like Somalia or Yemen. McRaven told him the military would initially hold the captive on a ship.

"What's the longest we can keep somebody on the ship?" Graham asked.

"Sir, I think it depends on whether or not we think we can prosecute that individual in a U.S. court or we can return him to a third-party country," McRaven replied.

"What if you can't do either one of those?" Graham asked.

"Sir, again, if we can't do either one of those, then we will release that individual," McRaven said. "I mean, that becomes the unenviable option, but it is an option."

Later in the hearing, McRaven and another general disclosed that the United States could not bring anyone captured outside of Afghanistan to Bagram anymore because the Afghan government had grown hostile to that practice. Guantánamo remained off-limits for new captives. McRaven said "it would be very helpful" to have a prison somewhere for the long-term detention and interrogation of new captures.

What the public did not know was that the discussion was not hypothetical. At that moment, the military was holding a Somali prisoner aboard a ship in the Indian Ocean — the first high-value terrorism suspect to come into American custody abroad for several years. His name was Ahmed Warsame. His fate would make him arguably the most important terrorism captive in the Obama era.

Navy SEALs snatched Warsame from a fishing skiff in international waters between Yemen and Somalia on April 19. He was a member of al-Shabaab, the Somali militant group. Al-Qaeda's affiliate in Yemen, al-Qaeda in the Arabian Peninsula, had been teaching him to build bombs and he was returning to Somalia to share that knowledge with his group. With him, he had a laptop computer and several thumb drives holding important intelligence.

The opportunity to grab Warsame had arisen suddenly. In line with the Straw Man Plan, the SEALs deposited Warsame in the brig of the USS *Boxer*. An interrogation team flew out to question him for intelligence purposes. They did not read him the Miranda warning, but they did not torture him either. Instead, they used only army field manual–approved techniques, officials said.

Back in the United States, Brennan convened a cycle of deputies committee meetings to figure out what to do with Warsame. The capture had raised a series of legal-policy problems.

The first was timing. The Straw Man Plan called for holding a new captive aboard a ship for no more than two weeks. But Warsame was talking freely to his interrogators about many topics, apparently including his recent contact with Anwar al-Awlaki, the rogue American cleric for which the United States was hunting. (The drone strike that just missed the elusive Awlaki in early May 2011* may have been linked to intelligence provided by Warsame.)

The administration did not want to interrupt the flow by moving Warsame.

But article 22 of the Third Geneva Convention prohibits the internment of wartime prisoners on ships. Reviewing the matter, Koh and James Crawford, the top legal adviser to the Joint Chiefs, concluded that the military could lawfully keep holding Warsame on the ship for the time being. Article 22, they found, was a reaction to the historical practice of warehousing prisoners of war in crammed and unhygienic floating prisons, like British "hulks" in eighteenth and nineteenth centuries. Temporarily holding Warsame while they found out more about what he knew, they decided, was a *transitional* activity and so did not count as *internment*, which connoted a long-term imprisonment. They also insisted that since the government had notified the International Committee of the Red Cross that Warsame was in its custody and on the ship, it was not a secret prison.

There was yet another problem. The Straw Man Plan said that one purpose of the initial two-week confinement was to determine whether the prisoner qualified for indefinite law-of-war detention. At the time, Koh and Johnson were arguing about whether al-Shabaab counted as an associated force of al-Qaeda and so fell under the Authorization for Use of Military Force as a group, as Johnson believed, or if only particular al-Shabaab members personally linked to al-Qaeda fell under it, as

---

* See chapter 6, section 17.

Koh believed.* Ultimately they concluded that Warsame was detainable under either legal theory, and they would remain studiously ambiguous about which they were relying on.

Still, the clock was ticking. Everyone knew that under international law, they could not keep floating Warsame around in military custody forever. Brennan focused the deputies meetings, which had settled into a weekly tempo, on potential disposition options.

Transfer to the custody of another country was problematic since Somalia and Yemen lacked functioning and reliable criminal justice systems. There was no other obvious foreign candidate. That meant the United States needed to keep him.

Justice Department officials who attended the meetings were initially reluctant to take Warsame. They included James Cole, the deputy attorney general via an Obama recess appointment, and Todd Hinnen, who had become the acting head of the department's National Security Division when David Kris stepped down in March. In one early exchange, Cole expressed skepticism that a case could be made against Warsame based on the available, admissible-under-civilian-court standards of evidence. Koh pushed back, pointing out that they had Warsame's computer and a witness who said Warsame was holding the computer when captured. But Cole argued that, given the rocky politics over any use of the civilian criminal justice system for cases involving foreign terrorists, the administration needed to be able to show that long-term military custody was not a viable alternative and so there was no choice.

To answer that question, Jeh Johnson researched the strengths and weaknesses of two military options — holding Warsame in long-term law-of-war detention without trial, or prosecuting him before a military commission. Each had drawbacks. Indefinite detention was a problem because the two American wartime prisons set up to handle such prisoners, Bagram and Guantánamo, were off-limits: as noted, the

---

* See chapter 6, section 16.

Afghan government did not want new out-of-theater detainees brought onto its soil, and the official policy was still that Guantánamo was being closed, not expanded. Prosecuting Warsame in a tribunal at Charleston or some other military base was also a problem because it raised serious legal risks. For the tribunals to have jurisdiction under the Military Commissions Act, prosecutors would likely have to prove that Warsame was part of al-Qaeda or that he had personally conspired to attack the United States or its coalition partners in some specific way.

There would be no such threshold problem with a civilian court. But the Justice Department's reluctance to charge Warsame in regular court came against the backdrop of recurring cycles of toxic politics over using the civilian criminal justice system for terrorism cases. Underscoring the political risks, in late May 2011, the Justice Department indicted two Iraqi men living in Kentucky. Prosecutors accused them of conspiring to send support to al-Qaeda's Iraq affiliate. In addition, there was evidence one of them had planted roadside bombs in Iraq in 2005 before coming to the United States as a refugee in 2009.

The Republican Senate leader, Mitch McConnell — who represented Kentucky — tore into Holder, saying that trying the men in civilian court would create the risk of terrorists attacking the courthouse in Kentucky in retaliation. He also said the men, though arrested on American soil, should be sent to Guantánamo for interrogation and prosecution before a commission.

Holder pushed back, saying civilian courts had handled hundreds of terrorism cases successfully, none of which had resulted in retaliatory attacks on courthouses, and characterized proponents of putting all terrorism cases in military hands as employing "fear-mongering" and "overheated rhetoric that is detached from history and from the facts."[61]

This time, Holder's plan to use the regular court system held, and the two Iraqis pleaded guilty in the Kentucky courthouse in December 2011 and August 2012. There were no security incidents. A civilian judge sentenced one to life in prison and the other to forty years. They quickly faded from public consciousness.[62]

17. The Hybrid Model

The Obama administration in mid-2011 finally developed a procedure for dealing with newly captured foreign terrorism suspects. It was a hybrid approach, starting with a period of interrogation for intelligence purposes, often in military custody, and then transitioning to prosecution before a civilian court. This approach grew out of its handling of Warsame and became a model for future captives — and a pillar of its national security legal policy.

The crucial moment in the Warsame interrogation came in mid-June, two months after his capture. The United States had learned much of intelligence value from him without using torture, but it was extremely unlikely that any court, military or civilian, would deem his self-incriminating statements to have been voluntary because he had made them in an inherently coercive environment: locked up for months in the brig of a warship, and without a defense lawyer. He was too significant a terrorist operative to simply release, and neither Somalia nor Yemen had governments that could be trusted to hold him. For a stable, long-term disposition to keep him locked up, they wanted a trial and a conviction, which meant they needed admissible evidence.

The Obama legal team was in uncharted territory. The Supreme Court had, over the years, permitted prosecutors to use certain evidence even though a defendant's constitutional rights had been violated at an earlier stage. The idea of this *attenuation-of-taint* doctrine was that government interrogators could take certain steps enabling them to obtain a knowing and voluntary confession from the defendant later on. But courts had recognized those rules in a completely different context.

"We had to figure out how that doctrine applied in a new situation that was utterly unforeseen by the courts that developed it," Hinnen told me.

The plan they worked out was to give Warsame a significant break from questioning — four days, during which the military flew a delegation from the Red Cross to the *Boxer* to visit him. They would then send in a different set of interrogators — a so-called *clean team* of FBI agents. They did not know what Warsame had said earlier. They would advise him of his Miranda rights and start over.

Hinnen also said they considered moving Warsame to a new boat to further emphasize that the situation was now different, but after the military explained how the security would work, they decided that changing his location would be counterproductive.

"A court was just as likely to find that taking a shackled prisoner in the dead of night onto the deck of one ship and transferring him over pitching seas to the deck of another ship further coerced the prisoner, as it was to find that it was among a number of factors that helped to restore his free will," he said.

Warsame waived his rights and continued talking to the clean team. They reread him the warning each morning, and the process repeated. By the end of the week, the administration was confident that it had obtained admissible confessions to a series of terrorism-related crimes. None were international war crimes that were clearly triable in a military commission: he had not been involved in any specific terrorist attack. But he could be charged in civilian court with domestic crimes that could yield a life sentence, like conspiracy to provide material support to a terrorist organization.

The clean-team interrogation had wrapped up by June 28, the morning of the Senate Armed Services Committee hearing with Graham and McRaven. The full Senate was also scheduled to hold a series of votes that day. As the Obama legal team was meeting in the Situation Room to decide Warsame's fate, an aide interrupted them and handed a White House notecard to McDonough. Scribbled upon it was *Cole 55– 42 confirmed.* Cole, a mere recess appointee to the role of deputy attorney general no longer, would frame the card and hang it in his office.

After the congratulations to Cole, the meeting turned back to a final plan for Warsame. They agreed to bring him to Manhattan for prosecution before a civilian court. Two days later, a grand jury returned a sealed indictment.[63] On July 3 the Justice Department took custody of him from the military and flew him to New York. The Obama legal team had improvised the hybrid military-criminal approach. The endless meetings to agonize over Warsame's disposition showed how hard it was to get rid of terrorism captives once the government took them, and it was not clear to participants at the time how it would turn out. But in this instance it had worked so well, in their eyes, that it became a standard blueprint. They saw it was the best of both worlds: a way for the government to have a period of intelligence interrogation while still using regular Article III courts for a stable, long-term disposition. The civilian system, after all, was continuing to march through one life sentence after another in terrorism cases — even as the military commissions system floundered.

In the years that followed, the Obama administration applied the Warsame model to several other terrorism suspects who were captured abroad away from traditional war zones. They included Ahmed Abu Khattala, an Islamist accused of leading the militia that assaulted the American consulate in Benghazi in 2012, and Abu Anas al-Libi, an accused al-Qaeda operative charged with participating in the 1998 Africa embassy bombings. Both were interrogated on an American ship and then charged in civilian court. There were also variations, like Abu Ghaith, a son-in-law of bin Laden, who was interrogated in Turkish custody for about a month in 2013, then extradited via Jordan directly into the American civilian court system.

The arrival of the Warsame model provided a way forward but it complicated familiar ideological arguments on both sides. Some conservatives and congressional Republicans repeated their views that the civilian courts should never be used for prosecuting foreign terrorists. But a number of Republicans with executive-branch national security experience broke partisan ranks and praised the Warsame model as a success that showed the value of letting counterterrorism professionals have the flexibility to choose Article III disposition. Among them was Ken Wainstein, who had been the first head of the Justice Department's National Security Division, and then the chief White House counterterrorism adviser, in the Bush-Cheney administration's second term.

"From the government's perspective, it's better to maintain options for custody and prosecution and in each case to select that option that best fits the needs of a particular case," Wainstein said.[64]

From the other direction, some liberals denounced the fact that the Obama administration had interrogated Warsame on a ship for two months without a Miranda warning. The *New York Times* editorial board (a separate organization from the newsroom), for example, said it showed Obama was "drifting toward establishing his own system of extralegal detention and tainted questioning."[65] But other liberals, like Tom Malinowski, then the Washington director of Human Rights Watch, said the government appeared to have "totally played by the rules here," because it had notified the Red Cross about Warsame and allowed it to visit him.[66]

"In the context of where we are politically, I'm really happy that they did this," Malinowski told me at the time. "One of the most important things it does is disprove the narrative that many people, including in the Pentagon, have been putting out there — that the U.S. government doesn't have detention options for these kinds of people because Obama won't send anyone to Gitmo. Actually, you can indict them and put them before a court, and that doesn't stop you from conducting an intelligence interrogation first."

18. Policy Success

As it turned out, there was never a need to test whether Warsame's clean-team statements were admissible; later that year, he would secretly plead guilty, and his sentencing was indefinitely deferred. In 2013, court papers were unsealed showing that he had continued to meet with the government every week for hours at a time, disclosing information about al-Shabaab and al-Qaeda figures including "high-level international terrorist operatives." He was so cooperative that prosecutors were considering putting Warsame and his family in a witness protection program and relocating them under new identities.[67]

Meanwhile, in September 2011, a trial judge upheld the admissibility of the self-incriminating statements by the would-be underwear bomber, Abdulmutallab, during the fifty-minute interrogation back on Christmas 2009, despite the fact that he had been on painkillers and had not been read the Miranda warning, as a "fully justified" use of the public-safety exception.[68] The administration saw the ruling as confirmation that its new legal policy was constitutional. (Abdulmutallab would plead guilty and be sentenced to life in prison.)

Bolstered by that ruling, the success of the Warsame policy, and the sense that killing bin Laden was a shield against accusations that it was soft on terrorism, the Obama administration began to display restored confidence in its legal policy about captives. While Congress had thwarted his legacy-prisoners policy by blocking the closure of Guantánamo, Obama was successfully pushing the American system for handling *newly captured* terrorism suspects toward something resembling normalcy or stability.

Going forward, Americans would not be held in military detention.

Foreigners arrested on American soil would not be held in military detention either.

Guantánamo remained open, but it was not growing. Non-Americans captured away from battlefields would not be brought there and placed in indefinite detention. If possible, they would instead be handled by the justice systems in the countries where they were caught or from which they were from. If that was not possible, the United States would either, in lower-level cases, permit them to go but use surveillance to keep an eye on them, or, in higher level situations, interrogate them for intelligence purposes and then build a criminal case against them in federal civilian court. Long-term indefinite detention was only for unwinding the difficult cases Obama had inherited, not for new captives.

Lawmakers would have different ideas, but for the moment, the issue was off the administration's daily meeting list.

"It is the firm position of the Obama Administration that suspected terrorists arrested inside the United States will — in keeping with long-standing tradition — be processed through our Article III courts," said

Brennan in a speech marking the tenth anniversary of 9/11. "As they should be. Our military does not patrol our streets or enforce our laws — nor should it. This is not a radical idea, nor is the idea of prosecuting terrorists captured overseas in our Article III courts. Indeed, terrorists captured beyond our borders have been successfully prosecuted in our federal courts on many occasions. Our federal courts are time-tested, have unquestioned legitimacy, and, at least for the foreseeable future, are capable of producing a more predictable and sustainable result than military commissions."[69]

8

The Leak Crackdown

1. The Leak Task Force

On April 15, 2010, the Justice Department announced that a grand jury had returned an indictment against a former National Security Agency official named Thomas Drake. Then just shy of his 53rd birthday, Drake was tall and cerebral, with an intense manner. He had come up in the intelligence world as an air force officer before joining the NSA. Now, Drake stood accused of serving as a source for a series of articles in the *Baltimore Sun* in 2006 about waste and mismanagement at the NSA, although the specific charges against him focused on mishandling classified documents.[1] The government claimed that Drake had set up an anonymous e-mail account to communicate with a *Sun* reporter, Siobhan Gorman, and that they had exchanged hundreds of messages. It said he had researched stories for the reporter by e-mailing NSA colleagues and accessing classified documents on the NSA network. And it said he had cut-and-pasted portions of classified documents into blank files, removed the classified markings, and brought home printouts. Prosecutors were threatening Drake with thirty-five years in prison.

"Our national security demands that the sort of conduct alleged here — violating the government's trust by illegally retaining and disclosing classified information — be prosecuted and prosecuted vigorously," Lanny Breuer, the head of the Justice Department's Criminal Division, said in a statement announcing the charges.

The Drake case came to exemplify an unprecedented Obama-era

criminal crackdown on leaks of national-security secrets. This development was a complete surprise. Many of the ways that the Obama administration turned out to be more hawkish than many had expected were, in hindsight, consistent with certain things Obama had said all along, such as his proclamation in 2002 that he was not a pacifist and was not against all wars, just dumb ones. But Obama had promised to protect whistleblowers and vowed greater transparency in government. Moreover, until Obama it was exceedingly rare for prosecutors to bring charges against people who provided classified information to the public without authorization. Yet on Obama's watch, the government would bring criminal charges in — as of this writing — three times as many leak-related cases as all previous presidents combined.

To begin sifting through what happened and why, the case against Drake is particularly illuminating because it developed during a moment of transition. The roots of the case traced back years before Obama took office, to an early 2006 decision by the Bush-Cheney Justice Department, shortly after the *New York Times* revealed the warrantless wiretapping component of the NSA's Stellarwind program, to set up a special task force dedicated to pursuing high-level leaks.

This was an innovation. The Justice Department's counterespionage section traditionally handled criminal referrals about leaks. But its longtime chief, a career prosecutor named John Dion, had a reputation for being reluctant to expend resources pursuing leak cases, according to former officials. His attitude was that there were foreign spies to chase instead, culprits in leak cases were hard to identify without going after reporters, and intelligence agencies often balked at declassifying the information necessary to hold a trial. So Attorney General Alberto Gonzales cut Dion out. Alice Fisher, the Criminal Division head, tapped Steven Tyrrell, a career prosecutor in the counterterrorism section, to lead the new task force. Tyrrell had experience working on major cases with classified intelligence angles, and his mandate was to move away from Dion's practice of deciding up front that no case could be brought. His team would instead gather all the facts before determining whether a trial was feasible. Part of the idea was that even if there were never any charges, an aggressive investigation could still serve as a deterrent to other would-be leakers.

The Justice Department gave the task force extraordinary resources to go after leakers: half a dozen prosecutors and about twenty-five FBI agents. It was particularly intent on finding the sources for the *Times'* warrantless surveillance story and several follow-up articles by the reporters who wrote it, James Risen and Eric Lichtblau. But its scrutiny eventually spilled out into other leaks, two of which became important in the Obama era.

The first other case concerned a different classified secret Risen had exposed: the existence of a Clinton-era CIA effort to sabotage Iranian nuclear research, dubbed Operation Merlin. The idea was to send a Russian scientist defector to sell flawed plans for a triggering device to Iran. Risen had tried to write that story in the *Times* in 2003, portraying the operation as reckless and botched and showing how its architects had been promoted despite its problems. But the Bush-Cheney administration insisted that the operation had not been botched and argued that exposure of the CIA method for disrupting the proliferation of nuclear weapons — using Russian scientist defectors to shop flawed blueprints — could result in the deaths of millions. The editors at the time killed the story.[2] A year later, Risen and Lichtblau had learned about the NSA's warrantless wiretapping program, but in October 2004 the administration persuaded the *Times* not to publish that one, either. Then Risen had written a book, *State of War,* which was to be published in early 2006. It contained a chapter about the warrantless wiretapping program and another chapter about Operation Merlin. Before the book came out, the *Times* decided to publish the NSA surveillance story after all, and Risen and Lichtblau went on to win a Pulitzer Prize. But the *Times* never published the Merlin story.

There was an obvious suspect for the leak about Merlin: Jeffrey Sterling, a former CIA official who had worked on that operation and later told congressional oversight staff that it had been botched, a portrayal that matched the book's account. In addition, Sterling had filed an employment lawsuit against the CIA alleging racial discrimination, but the government invoked the state secrets privilege to kill the lawsuit; Risen had written an article in March 2002 about the discrimination case, so he had a known tie to Sterling.[3] On January 28, 2008, prosecutors subpoenaed Risen to provide documents and testimony about his sources for the Merlin chapter to a grand jury. Risen resisted, setting up a momentous court fight over the First Amendment, which was still pending when the Obama team took over.[4]

Another leak case the task force worked on, which led to the Drake indictment, traced back to a dispute inside the NSA at the end of the Clinton administration about how to modernize the agency's surveillance system. One idea, called Thinthread, had been developed relatively cheaply and in-house.* The rival idea, called Trailblazer, was more ambitious in some ways but also far costlier, involving massive contracts to outside corporations. The NSA director, General Michael Hayden, had opted for Trailblazer. Three NSA officials who were proponents of Thinthread retired in October 2001 to start a private company aimed at harnessing similar technology for nonclassified uses, like hunting big data to find evidence of fraud. And in 2002, the three — along with a just-retired House intelligence committee staffer who agreed with them, Diane Roark — filed what they thought was a confidential whistleblower complaint with the Department of Defense inspector general. They alleged that the decision to go with Trailblazer had been a massive waste of taxpayer dollars, raising the possibility of corrupt dealings with outside contractors.

The whistleblowers' 2002 letter to the inspector general also said there was a senior NSA official still on the inside "who has significant knowledge regarding this whole matter, who is willing to come forward if necessary but would request full confidentiality."[5] That official was Drake, and he went on to help the inspector general. When the inspector general report was completed in late 2004, it portrayed Trailblazer

---

* See chapter 5, section 5.

as a fiasco that had wasted a staggering volume of money—but to the frustrations of the whistleblowers, it was also kept largely classified so the public did not know about it.[6] Around November 2005, Drake reached out to Gorman, the *Sun* reporter looking into mismanagement and overspending at the NSA.[7]

That December, the *Times* ran its NSA warrantless wiretapping story. Several months later, the *Sun* ran its series on NSA waste and mismanagement. The articles included a description of Thinthread, which, in the *Sun*'s telling, would have been a legal alternative to the illegal surveillance program that the *Times* had just (partially) exposed[8]— a striking clue about its likely sourcing. Back in 2000 and 2001, the Thinthread proponents had repeatedly insisted that it would be legal to use their system to mine data about Americans' communications. But this view was idiosyncratic and contested: NSA and Justice Department lawyers believed that it would be illegal to do that. Moreover, there was a link between some of them and concerns about Stellarwind: just before leaving the NSA, one of the Thinthread proponents, William Binney, had found out about the Stellarwind program, which appeared to use technology drawn from the Thinthread system and that he had helped design. He told Roark about it. Before she retired, Roark had tried without success to raise concerns about the Stellarwind program with several members of Congress, executive-branch officials, and judges.[9] But they did not put anything about Stellarwind in their whistleblower complaint because, Binney told me, it was outside the jurisdiction of the Defense Department inspector general and they did not want the watchdog's inquiry to get diverted away from investigating what they saw as corruption.

Now, the NSA's security and counterintelligence directorate told the Justice Department that the Thinthread proponents were persons of interest in the leaks to the *Sun*.[10] And in part because it was so remarkable to have two leaks in short order about NSA matters, investigators wondered if the same people were sources for both the *Sun* and the *Times*. "Whenever you find someone who has a penchant for talking to people outside the agency, you may have suspicions they might have been talking to more people outside the agency," one law enforcement official familiar with the task force's work later told me.

In July 2007, FBI agents working with the leak task force raided the homes of the people who had filed the whistleblower complaint, carting away computers and boxes of papers. Four months later, they searched Drake's home and office, too.[11] An affidavit for the Drake search warrant application, signed by the lead FBI agent on the warrantless wiretapping leak case, told a magistrate judge the investigative focus was finding the sources for the *Times'* warrantless wiretapping story. The affidavit also opened a window into just how intense the leak task force's work had become: at that point it had interviewed more than a thousand people, issued more than two hundred grand jury subpoenas for phone and e-mail records, and reviewed thousands of pages of documents — including the phone and e-mail records of about sixty people.[12]

Now, when the agents came to his home, Drake told me, he talked freely to them and acknowledged that he had given some information — which he insisted was unclassified — to the *Sun*. But the agents kept wanting to talk about the *Times* article instead.

"The focus of their investigation was finding any and all sources for Risen and Lichtblau, period, and it's quite clear they thought I was the source, there's no question," Drake said.

Drake's life was wrecked. On the same day the FBI raided his house, the NSA stripped him of his top secret security clearance and placed him on leave, beginning "the worst period of my life," he later said. The following year he resigned to avoid being fired and ended up working retail in an Apple store. But prosecutors never found evidence that Drake or the other critics of NSA waste and mismanagement had been sources for the *Times* about the warrantless wiretapping program, and Risen eventually stated that they were not.[13]

In April 2008, the FBI summoned Drake for a meeting at its secure facility in Calverton, Maryland. Tyrrell confronted Drake over the *Sun* articles, telling him he was likely facing Espionage Act charges that carried lengthy prison terms and urging him to hire a lawyer.

Prosecutors pressured Drake to plead guilty to a single charge and finger coconspirators. Drake refused. Sterling wouldn't cave either. And as they held out, Senator Barack Obama won the presidential election. His transition website featured a page portraying whistleblowing by executive-branch employees as an act "of courage and patriotism" that "should be encouraged rather than stifled." As part of his promised changes, he said he would strengthen protections for officials who exposed waste, fraud, and abuse of authority in government.[14]

Just as the Bush-Cheney administration prepared to relinquish control, it looked like there might be a breakthrough for the task force on its main assignment. In December 2008, a former Justice Department lawyer named Thomas Tamm publicly confessed to *Newsweek*'s Mike Isikoff that he had been a source for Lichtblau about the NSA surveillance program, describing how he had nervously called the reporter from a pay phone with a tip.[15] Tamm had worked in the Justice Department intelligence office that prepared applications for FISA Court wiretap orders. He had heard there was some kind of special NSA program that was generating information about Americans — information that was being used in certain wiretap applications, which were being shown only to the presiding judge of the FISA Court and none of the other judges.* Although Lichtblau later said he had many sources, Tamm's phone call apparently helped put him on the hunt; Risen was separately on the hunt through his own sources.

In an episode that has never been reported, on December 16, 2008, just a few days after the *Newsweek* issue hit the stands, Tyrrell sent a letter to Lichtblau's and Risen's lawyer, David Kelley — a former United States attorney in the first Bush-Cheney term, whom the *Times* had hired to represent its reporters. In the letter, Lichtblau recalled, Tyrrell demanded that Lichtblau provide information for the case or face a

---

* See chapter 5, section 7.

subpoena. It became clear that they wanted Lichtblau to confirm their suspicion that Tamm had been a person Lichtblau had described in his 2008 book, *Bush's Law*. The official had told Lichtblau that while he had not been "read in" to the classified details, he had heard enough to know there was a "closed program" involving the NSA that was testing the limits of executive power.[16] If Lichtblau did not talk, Tyrrell is said to have told Kelley, they would issue a subpoena to Lichtblau on January 19, 2009 — the day before Bush left office.

Lichtblau told me he never confirmed to prosecutors whether Tamm had talked to him, notwithstanding what was in *Newsweek*. But he had Kelley tell Tyrrell, as an informal "proffer" of information, that Tyrrell was wrong about who Lichtblau had been referring to in his book. Prosecutors never subpoenaed Lichtblau. (The Justice Department never threatened to subpoena Risen over the NSA story.)

In the spring of 2009, Tyrrell came to Breuer, his newly appointed Obama administration boss at the Criminal Division, and said that he planned to leave the Justice Department. His task force had brought no charges, but it had several open and well-developed investigations, albeit with still unresolved issues. Breuer had to decide what to do with the task force's half-completed work.

One solution would have been to quietly pass the leak task force's files to Dion at the counterespionage section, which had moved out from the Criminal Division in a late 2006 reorganization of the Justice Department and was now part of the new National Security Division. Dion's team might have done something with them, or it might not have. They were focused on other things, like tracking a ring of ten Russian sleeper agents. (The government arrested and deported the spies in 2010, following a multiyear investigation.)

But at the same time, Breuer was dealing with another management problem. He had just removed a top prosecutor in the Criminal Division, William Welch, from the position of chief of the public integrity section. A judge had ordered an investigation into the botching of a 2008 corruption trial of Ted Stevens, a Republican senator from Alaska, and as head of the section, Welch was among its subjects. Breuer believed the problems with the Stevens trial had not been Welch's fault, and the investigation would indeed end up exonerating him. But in the meantime, Welch could not keep running the section and needed something else to do.

Breuer solved both problems with one move. He assigned Welch, a man who was now seeking to vindicate his professional reputation and who had nothing else to focus on, to take over Tyrrell's leak task force investigations and resolve them. When Welch formally took control in November, he did so with gusto.

2. Unprecedented

As Obama took office, Drake and Sterling had reason to believe that despite all the scrutiny they had received, the investigations would be closed without charges, given the historical dearth of leak cases. But they were standing in front of a tsunami. By Obama's seventh year in power, he had overseen nine criminal cases involving unauthorized disclosures of government secrets for public consumption. By contrast, under all previous presidents combined, there had been just three such cases.

What happened? While there have been many new government secrets worthy of scrutiny in the years since 9/11, the explanation for the Obama-era surge cannot have been that there was just more leaking. There have always been unauthorized disclosures of information to the news media. It's how Washington works and has always worked. There are official announcements and press releases, there are tacitly sanctioned releases of information, and sometimes there are leaks by individual officials who do not go through the proper channels but want something newsworthy to reach the public. That is not to say the people at the top liked leaks, at least when they were not the ones making them. But in the past, when an official was suspected of leaking, it was handled differently. The official might find himself cut out of the loop and not invited to the key meetings. He might get a letter of reprimand in his file. He might even lose his security clearance and be fired. But it was virtually unheard of, until very recently, for the government to treat as a crime the unauthorized public disclosure of military and intelligence information.

Overnight, the rules changed. People were going to prison. The crackdown sent fear throughout the national security establishment. The result was that the normal give-and-take, even discussing routine things on background to make sure reporters understood them, became much more difficult. It may not have been obvious amid the deluge of secret diplomatic, military, and surveillance documents in the middle Obama years, but almost all of those came from just two leaks. Ordinary national security investigative journalism — the kind that can bring individual facts to light and keep the public informed in a more routine way — was placed into a deep chill.

Generally, we will never know what we do not know. But an exception and a case study is the NSA's bulk phone records program, since it eventually was revealed. In the spring of 2011, two Democratic senators on the Intelligence Committee, Ron Wyden and Mark Udall, began delivering vivid but oblique warnings that the government was secretly interpreting the Patriot Act in a twisted and outrageous way.* For two years, no reporter was able to figure out what was happening — not until Edward Snowden leaked archives of NSA documents. The first to be published was a FISA Court order showing that the NSA was collecting Americans' calling records in bulk. The government soon declassified related documents showing that the FISA Court had blessed a secret interpretation of Section 215 of the Patriot Act, which says the FBI may collect records "relevant" to a security investigation, as permitting the NSA to collect everyone's phone records for the purpose of analyzing links and hunting for hidden terrorists.

As one of the journalists who had tried to figure out what the senators were talking about before the Snowden leaks,† I believe that the

---

* See chapter 9, section 8, and chapter 11, section 6.
† See also chapter 9, section 7.

leak crackdown was the reason that I failed. I was eventually able to piece together that it involved non-content business records held by the telecommunications firms, but there I was stymied; it was beyond my imagination that the statute could be read as authorizing the government to systematically collect, store, and analyze all Americans' calling records in bulk.

After the Snowden revelations, I thought back to several conversations I had while on the investigative trail. I had talked to perhaps two dozen people who knew the secret. Any of them could have reminded me that *USA Today* had written an interesting article about the NSA and phone records back in 2006 that people had basically forgotten about.* Any of them could have suggested that I think harder about what *relevant* might mean. But no one did. Among the people I spoke with, some pretended not to know what Wyden and Udall were talking about but later turned out to have been deeply involved in the program. Others acknowledged knowing what it was but declined to help. One told me that its importance was wildly overblown — it increased the chances of detecting and thwarting a plot by maybe 1 percent, in this person's opinion — but wouldn't say what it was.

One conversation, in retrospect, was particularly memorable. It was with Michael Sussmann, the Perkins Coie lawyer and former Justice Department computer-crimes prosecutor who represented many phone and Internet companies in their dealings with law enforcement and intelligence agencies. I suspected Sussmann might know about the program given his clientele and expertise or at least might have some smart thoughts since he was immersed in surveillance law.

One afternoon in late July 2011, I dropped by Sussmann's office at Perkins Coie in downtown Washington to talk about several issues we were both interested in. At one point, I asked if he knew anything about the Patriot Act section 215 thing Wyden and Udall kept talking about. Sussmann was sitting next to his special Department of Defense–issued safe, where he was permitted to store classified documents. He pulled a

---

* See chapter 5, section 9.

paperback intelligence community sourcebook off his desk, flipped to a section that reprinted the Patriot Act, and read the relevant provision aloud to me. I listened, nodding, but when he was finished I did not feel any more enlightened than I had been before. Seeing that he was not going to tell me anything directly, I tried another route.

"Is there some interesting article or blog out there I should read?" I asked.

"There is," he said.

"Well, what is it?" I asked.

"I won't tell you," he replied.

We laughed but he was being serious, too. Sussmann made it abundantly clear that he was not going to assist me even indirectly. He said if I did figure it out and the FBI later gave him a polygraph and asked if he had helped me, he intended to be able to honestly deny responsibility. He had young children at home, he said, pointing to their pictures on his desk.[17]

After the Snowden leaks brought the secret of the Patriot Act bulk phone records program to the surface, it turned out that Sussmann was, personally, no fan of the program. In fact, back in 2009, when he was representing Sprint, he had gone so far as to draft a secret FISA Court challenge to the legality of the program, although Sprint ultimately decided not to file it.*

I learned about the aborted Sprint challenge in 2014 when the government declassified FISA Court litigation related to it. The government continued to censor the name of the company and its lawyer, and Sussmann would not confirm to me that it was him. He also, in granting me permission to publish this anecdote, emphasized that he would never reveal classified information to someone not authorized to receive it under any circumstances.

I, however, believe that his reticence — standing in for many other people I spoke with, and many others whom other reporters no doubt

---

* See chapter 11, section 2.

fruitlessly spoke with as well — exemplified the chilling effect engendered by the leak crackdown.

In normal times, leaks serve as a pressure-release valve for a particular classified fact like that, one for which there was an overriding public interest in disclosure notwithstanding the intelligence bureaucracy's insistence on keeping it secret. But the leak crackdown jammed the valve shut, so the pressure of surveillance-related secrecy continued to build until the Snowden explosion threw the secret of the bulk phone records program out into the open — along with hundreds of others.

On the surface, at least, this criminalization of leaks seemed to come out of nowhere. The question is whether the Obama administration made a deliberate policy decision to crack down on leakers or whether it just happened. Over the years, I asked many current and former senior officials in the Justice Department whether anyone remembered a particular meeting or memo in which Obama or Holder slammed his fist on the table and said, "There's too much leaking — get me some heads on pikes!" Consistently, they insisted to me that there had been none. "When we took office in January 2009, I don't think bringing a lot of leak cases was high on anyone's agenda," Matthew Miller, who was Holder's director of public affairs from the start of the Obama administration until July 2011, told me. "But then they came up one by one, and without anyone realizing it, we had set a record."[18]

Allowing for this explanation does not mean absolving Obama administration officials of any responsibility in what happened. Law enforcement officials on Obama's watch took several steps of unprecedented aggression when investigating and charging leak cases. These included, as this chapter will explore, equating leaking with treason, labeling a reporter a criminal coconspirator of a leaker, and fighting to the Supreme Court to clarify that the First Amendment contains no privilege for reporters to protect confidential sources. But the instinct that there must be an easy answer for why there were suddenly so many leak cases in the first place — that somebody decided to do that —

appears to be wrong. Instead, a constellation of factors changed how leak investigations played out.

One was atmospheric. Holder repeatedly faced questions in 2009 about the Justice Department's attitude toward unauthorized disclosures of national security secrets — in part, ironically, because he was supporting the enactment of a "media shield" law that would permit federal judges to quash subpoenas to reporters in some cases,[19] something most states have but the federal government does not. Over and over again, he assured lawmakers and intelligence officials that he would take leaks of classified information seriously.

Around that same time, the director of national intelligence, Dennis Blair, also asked Holder to streamline the handling of criminal leak referrals. Blair later spoke expansively about this moment, portraying a series of phone calls and meetings with Holder in which they discussed the need to hunt down leakers. "My background is in the Navy, and it is good to hang an admiral once in a while as an example to the others," Blair said. "We were hoping to get somebody and make people realize that there are consequences to this and it needed to stop."[20]

Blair stood apart from most Obama-era officials in seeming to want to take credit for the crackdown. But his pushing of the Justice Department to keep on top of leak referrals cannot be the explanation. For one thing, the department was already on a path to converting more referrals into charges: as of mid-2015, three Obama-era referrals regarding *ordinary* leaks, meaning disclosures of particular secrets, led to Espionage Act charges, but three Bush-era criminal leak referrals did so, too. (The complication is that prosecutors were only ready to charge two of the cases that came from Bush-era referrals after the administration turned over.) Two other cases that began on Obama's watch did not start off with a leak referral; the investigations ended up finding leaks by surprise. And the last two involved the new phenomenon of *bulk* disclosures of many thousands of classified documents at once by culprits whose identities were known almost immediately, which belongs in a category of its own.

Still, Blair's push reflected a general anti-leak atmosphere. Anger in Congress over leaks (there is no "pro-leak" caucus in Congress to impose a checking and balancing political force) pressed in the same direction. So did the pledges Holder had to keep making due to the debate over the media-shield legislation. Without there ever being a formal policy directive, the message trickled down through the bureaucracy that it was important to Holder that prosecutors make a good-faith effort to bring cases over significant leaks of classified information if it was feasible. Then, when prosecutors developed doable cases and sought permission to move forward with charges, Holder was unwilling to hit the brakes.

And suddenly, in a way that had never happened before, viable cases started popping up.

3. Leak Prosecutions Before Obama

Until very recently, it has not been a part of the American tradition for prosecutors to file criminal charges in cases where a government official has disclosed national-security secrets to the public without authorization.

An oddity of American law is that it is not technically a crime to disclose classified information just because it is officially secret. By contrast, England has an Official Secrets Act, which makes it a crime to leak or publish government secrets. [21] The United States, with its stronger constitutional tradition of protecting free speech and newsgathering, has never had an equivalent. Instead, Congress has specifically barred the disclosure of a few narrow slices of data, like the identities of covert agents and specifics about electronic surveillance techniques, but otherwise it is not a crime, per se, to disclose classified information without authorization.

But the American statute books do contain a law called the Espionage Act. It was passed during World War I, before the advent of the modern system for stamping documents as Secret or Top Secret, and so it makes no reference to classified information. But the dusty act makes it a felony to communicate information about the "national defense" to someone not authorized to receive it, if the information could potentially harm the United States or help a foreign adversary. While its title is about espionage, the wording of its provisions is broad and, viewed in isolation, not limited to spying. Nor is it limited to government officials with official access to secret information. In theory, the Espionage Act could be used against anyone who comes into possession of restricted information and decides either to keep it[22] or to pass it on to anyone who is not authorized to receive it, even the reader of a leak-based newspaper article who saves a clipping or tells a neighbor what it said. For this reason, the Espionage Act has long been thought unconstitutional in certain applications, and for most of its history, it was only rarely used against people who were not spies.

In recent years, generations after the law's enactment, the government has begun exploiting the loose wording of the Espionage Act to turn the statute into a de facto Official Secrets Act by wielding it against leakers and whistleblowers, if not (yet) against publishers. Calibrated for spies, the Espionage Act is a harsh weapon when wielded against leakers. It carries extremely long sentences, giving defendants an incentive to plead guilty without a trial in exchange for relatively reasonable prison terms. And if they instead opt to go to trial, the act does not permit defense lawyers to mount an affirmative whistleblower defense to juries — that is, urging them to find the defendant not guilty because the disclosure was in the public interest or because the defendant's intent was to enlighten Americans, not help the nation's enemies. In deciding guilt or innocence, a jury is told to consider only whether there was reason to think that the information *could* be used to harm the United States or advantage a foreign power — a standard that prosecutors argue is presumptively met if the accused leaker was a government official trained to protect information someone has stamped *classified*.

Nixon's Justice Department was the first to use the Espionage Act to go after leakers. In 1971, prosecutors indicted Daniel Ellsberg and

Anthony Russo for leaking the Pentagon Papers, a classified history showing how the government had repeatedly lied to the public about the Vietnam War. A judge threw out the indictments in 1973, however, citing government misconduct; Nixon's "plumbers" — so named because they were formed to plug leaks and eventually expanded their work to burglarizing the Democratic campaign headquarters in the Watergate complex — had broken into Ellsberg's psychiatrist's office to steal information to discredit him.[23]

A decade later, Reagan's Justice Department tried again, bringing Espionage Act charges against Samuel Loring Morison, a defense analyst accused of leaking classified satellite photographs of a Soviet shipyard to *Jane's Defence Weekly*. Morison was convicted at trial and sentenced to two years in prison. He appealed on free-speech grounds, but lost.[24] It was the first successful leak prosecution. It stood glaringly alone, eventually leading to a campaign to pardon Morison long after he had served his time. "What is remarkable is not the crime, but that he is the only one convicted of an activity which has become a routine aspect of government life: leaking information to the press in order to bring pressure to bear on a policy question," wrote Senator Daniel Patrick Moynihan, Democrat from New York, to President Clinton in 1998.[25]

Intelligence agencies objected to the pardon proposal. Then, in 2000, as Clinton was still mulling it over, the Republican-controlled Congress passed a bill that would make it a felony to leak any classified information, a clear legislative sanction for an American version of the Official Secrets Act. Clinton vetoed the bill, writing: "Although well intentioned, that provision is overbroad and may unnecessarily chill legitimate activities that are at the heart of a democracy."[26] Two months later, on his last day in office, Clinton pardoned Morison.

A few years later, in connection with the political furor over the failure to find weapons of mass destruction in Iraq, the Bush-Cheney administration appointed a special prosecutor, U.S. attorney Patrick Fitzgerald, to investigate the leak of CIA operative Valerie Plame Wilson's identity to the press. The case became fraught, especially after

Fitzgerald subpoenaed a *New York Times* reporter, Judith Miller, to testify about her sources; she initially refused to comply and was jailed for eighty-five days for contempt. Cheney's chief of staff, I. Lewis "Scooter" Libby, was indicted and convicted for lying to investigators about his contacts with reporters. But Fitzgerald closed the broader case without charging anyone with leaking secrets, including Richard Armitage, the deputy secretary of state, who admitted that he had been a source for the leak. (Bush later commuted Libby's prison sentence.)

The third leak case in American history developed around that same time. In 2005, the Justice Department charged a Pentagon analyst, Lawrence Franklin, under the Espionage Act for leaking classified intelligence about Iran to two lobbyists with AIPAC, the pro-Israel group. Prosecutors accused the lobbyists of passing the information on to journalists. They also accused Franklin of directly providing some information to "members of the media" but did not charge him with that.[27] Franklin pleaded guilty to a lesser charge and a judge initially sentenced him to twelve years in prison. In an unprecedented twist, the Justice Department also prosecuted the AIPAC lobbyists for further disseminating the secrets, even though they were not government officials who had signed confidentiality agreements and had not been entrusted with official access to secret information. But the trial judge issued skeptical rulings about that gambit, undercutting the prosecutors' case, and in May 2009, the Justice Department dropped the charges. While career prosecutors made that call, David Kris, who had been confirmed as head of the department's National Security Division five weeks earlier, accepted their recommendation, and Holder raised no objections.[28] A month later, the judge slashed Franklin's twelve-year prison sentence to just ten months in community confinement.[29]

The government's third attempt to criminalize leaking using the Espionage Act had sputtered out. With a Democrat in the White House, the path Nixon, Reagan, and Bush had tried to forge appeared to have reached an end. And while from the inside, the dismissal of the charges against the AIPAC defendants had happened organically, with little active influence from the new Obama administration political appointees, from the outside it looked like the change in administrations had resulted in a dramatic departure. The charges brought under the Bush-Cheney administration, with its aggressive anti-leak policy, had evaporated under the new Obama administration. For press freedom advocates, it seemed to herald a new era.

But something unexpected was about to happen instead.

4. The First Case: Leibowitz

Shamai Leibowitz was outraged by what he was hearing. An Israeli-born immigrant and former human rights lawyer known for outspokenly liberal views on the Israeli-Palestinian conflict,[30] Leibowitz in 2009 had become a contract Hebrew linguist for the FBI. He worked at the same secure bureau facility in Calverton where Tyrrell had confronted Drake a year earlier. His job was to translate intercepted conversations. And that April, believing that the public needed to know about an issue, Leibowitz gave classified documents to a blogger. For that act, he became the subject of the first leak case to be charged in the Obama era.

Leibowitz later told me about his last day of work in August 2009, when FBI agents had confronted him. "They said, 'We're searching your apartment right now, as we talk. We're searching your car.'" Leibowitz assumed it was an administrative matter, but he said his attorney later told him, "'This is a criminal investigation, there is a prosecuting attorney on your case,' and I realized this was way bigger."

Four months later, Leibowitz was arraigned. He pleaded guilty on the same day, accepting a twenty-month sentence. Unlike the leftover Bush-era cases, Leibowitz's prosecution was being handled by Dion's counterespionage section in the National Security Division, which put out a press release. "The willful disclosure of classified information to those not entitled to receive it is a serious crime," Kris said in a statement. "Today's guilty plea should serve as a warning to anyone in government who would consider compromising our nation's secrets."[31]

The nature of those secrets was a cipher to the public. Court documents said vaguely that Leibowitz had provided five documents pertaining to "communications intelligence activities" to an unidentified blogger, who published information derived from them, compromising sources. When a judge approved the sentence on May 24, 2010, he admitted that even he was in the dark: "I don't know what was divulged other than some documents, and how it compromised things, I have no idea."[32]

A blogger named Richard Silverstein, who is also critical of Israel's treatment of Palestinians, later told my colleague Scott Shane that the documents had been transcripts from wiretaps involving the Israeli embassy.[33] In the spring of 2009, Silverstein had claimed on his blog and in an online column for the *Guardian*[34] that Israeli diplomats and their American allies were waging a secret campaign to influence public opinion so Americans would support any preemptive airstrike by Israel against Iranian nuclear facilities. He feared that if Israel attacked Iran, "bloodletting and mayhem" would be the result. He cited "information I gathered from sources both public and not" as the basis for his claim about the alleged propaganda campaign.

While he would not comment on Silverstein's account, Leibowitz said his motivation was that "I believed that we were being led into an illegal and unconstitutional war by foreign agents. And war is a serious thing. So I basically revealed classified information because I was so troubled by what I was exposed to."[35]

And he told me that during plea negotiations, he had asked the prosecutor not to put out a press release, arguing that both sides had reasons to avoid drawing attention to the matter, but the Justice Department had insisted on announcing the case.

"They were so adamant to teach a lesson, to use me as a deterrent, that they compromised their own intelligence," he said. "Whatever was published was published. That's the government's fault. They could have kept my case pretty much hidden from public view if they wanted to."

After we understood what it was about, the Leibowitz case seemed to put in a new light comments that Bob Litt, the top lawyer for the Office of the Director of National Intelligence, had made during a panel discussion in November 2009. That was about five months after the Senate confirmed him, and a month before Leibowitz's arraignment and guilty plea. The unauthorized disclosure of classified information, Litt had said, "is obviously not a new problem or an easy problem to solve, and I think we all recognize that people are very concerned, both about overclassification and about ensuring the free flow of information to the public. Having said that, I have been in a number of briefings where people have been able to point to leaks of classified information that have caused specific and identifiable losses of intelligence capabilities — not just theoretical, but briefings where this appeared in the press and this target changed its behavior in that way. And this is something of great concern."[36]

Despite the press release, the swift plea deal and the lack of details ensured that the Leibowitz case attracted relatively little attention at the time. But in retrospect, the fact that he was even charged at all was significant — and was recognized as foreshadowing after more cases arose. Someone had been caught disclosing restricted information to the public without authorization, and the young Obama administration had not just fired him for it. It had sent him to prison.

5. The Second Case: Drake

That fall, Welch took control of the cases he had inherited from Tyrrell, and Holder let him move. The grand jury that Tyrrell had used to issue the original subpoena to Risen had expired, raising the prospect that the whole thing would go away. But in January 2010, Welch obtained Holder's permission to obtain a new grand jury subpoena seeking testimony from Risen against Sterling. Welch did not immediately issue the subpoena but used the permission to reopen negotiations with Risen's lawyers.

And in the meantime, Welch brought the second Obama-era leak-related case, obtaining the indictment against Drake. It charged the former NSA official with ten counts, including five violations of the Espionage Act for unauthorized retention of classified information.

The indictment was narrower than the one the leak task force had originally been planning. An earlier draft of the indictment prepared under Tyrrell, which Welch had mistakenly faxed to Drake's lawyer,[37] also contained charges that he had communicated classified information to the *Sun* reporter. But Welch had dropped that part. Welch had also decided not to charge the four other Thinthread supporters involved in the inspector general complaint, even though prosecutors clearly thought all of them were part of a group with Drake. Welch would later explain in court that it was hard to bring charges of conspiracy against the others in Drake's specific alleged offense—unauthorized retention of sensitive documents. Drake had admitted to the FBI that he had brought the documents home, but there was not good evidence that the others knew and had agreed that he would retain those documents.[38]

By then, Drake had run out of money to pay his lawyer and was represented by James Wyda, a federal public defender, and his deputy, Deborah Boardman. Wyda said his client had been "extraordinarily cooperative" with investigators and was "very disappointed that the process ended in criminal charges."[39]

Less than two weeks later, Welch moved again. On April 28, 2010, Risen received a new grand jury subpoena requiring him to testify before a grand jury in the leak investigation against Sterling. Through his lawyer, Joel Kurtzberg, Risen said he would not comply and would again ask a judge to quash it.

"He intends to honor his commitment of confidentiality to his source or sources," Kurtzberg said. "We intend to fight this subpoena."[40]

6. The Third Case: Manning

On May 7, 2010, Sergeant Paul Adkins, a supervisor at a forward operating base outside Baghdad in Iraq, was called into a classified information facility. A young, slightly built intelligence analyst from Oklahoma, Specialist Bradley Manning, had left the workstation and gone into a storage room. Inside, Adkins found Manning lying on the floor in a fetal position, "clutching his head as if he was in pain." At Manning's feet was a small knife, and Manning had carved the words *I want* into a chair. Within a month, the deeply troubled Manning became the third Obama-era leak defendant.

Adkins had been dealing with Manning's erratic behavior for months. At one point Adkins had removed the clip from Manning's gun, and he had recently received an e-mail from the soldier with the subject line "My Problem" and a selfie photograph of Manning dressed as a woman and wearing a wig. (Bradley Manning later became Chelsea Manning, declared a desire to undergo gender-reassignment surgery, and asked to be referred to henceforth by female pronouns.) Now, Adkins and Manning spoke for about an hour. Then, remarkably, Adkins returned Manning to finish out the shift because, as Adkins later explained at the trial, "there were tasks to do in regards to analyzing the threat" of Shia militias. For that same reason, Adkins never filed a report about the pattern of problems that might have prompted the military to remove Manning's security clearance and access to classified databases.

Later that same shift, Manning punched a female colleague in the face. When a higher-ranking officer found out, Manning was finally banned from the information facility. About to be dishonorably discharged and feeling isolated, Manning reached out over the Internet on May 21 to Adrian Lamo, a twenty-nine-year-old former hacker. In an online conversation over the next several days, Manning confessed to — or, rather, bragged about — having downloaded from a classified government computer network hundreds of thousands of military-incident reports from the wars in Iraq and Afghanistan, dossiers on Guantánamo detainees, years of diplomatic cables from American embassies all over the world, and war-zone videos showing the deaths of civilians.

Over the previous several months, Manning had uploaded these files to WikiLeaks, an antisecrecy organization whose website then solicited "classified, censored or otherwise restricted material of political, diplomatic or ethical significance." Operated by a transnational collective of computer specialists and using servers based in multiple countries, including Sweden and Iceland, the WikiLeaks website received and disseminated documents from and to anyone in the world with an Internet connection.

"God knows what happens now," Manning wrote to Lamo. "Hopefully worldwide discussion, debates, and reforms."[41]

Lamo turned Manning in. Arrested, charged within the court-martial system with violating the Espionage Act, and taken to a military base in Kuwait, a despairing Manning made a noose from sheets. Manning was placed on suicide watch and transferred to the Marine prison barracks at Quantico, where low-level officials housed the young soldier away from fellow prisoners and maintained austere prevention-of-harm conditions — like taking away Manning's clothing at night — even after a prison doctor said it was no longer necessary. This fueled allegations by Manning's supporters that the Obama administration was abusing the prisoner as a warning to others. Eventually, following an intervention by Jeh Johnson, the Pentagon general counsel, Manning was moved to Fort Leavenworth and better conditions to await trial.

7. Bulk Leaks

Over the course of 2010 and early 2011, WikiLeaks released the batches of the files Manning had uploaded to them. For most of them, Julian Assange, the leader of WikiLeaks, offered several traditional news outlets — including the *New York Times* — access in advance to the trove so they could put together reported articles and help people make sense of the raw documents. While the news outlets published selected documents in support of particular articles, WikiLeaks hosted the broader databases on its website. The revelations introduced the world to a new phenomenon: bulk leaks.

Some of the documents were individually newsworthy. The diplomatic cables, for example, recounted backroom deals kept hidden from the public and observations by American officials about corruption in places like Tunisia that some credited with helping to fuel the Arab Spring. Other insights arose only because the bulk publication of the documents enabled systematic analysis, including a finding that the number of documented civilian deaths in the Iraq War was likely as many as fifteen thousand more than those reflected in official government accounts.[42] Even after the initial burst, journalists like me found that the files continued to be a valuable resource to check when reporting on other topics, providing detail and nuance to help make sense of the world.

Critics of the leaking zeroed in on the fact that some of the war-log reports identified Afghan villagers who had helped NATO forces by providing information about Taliban insurgents. Mike Mullen, the chairman of the Joint Chiefs of Staff, said, "Mr. Assange can say whatever he likes about the greater good he thinks he and his source are doing, but the truth is they might already have on their hands the blood of some young soldier or that of an Afghan family."[43] American officials expended considerable time and resources getting some people named in the documents out of potential harm's way, but never identified anyone who had been killed as a result of the releases, testimony at Manning's 2013 court-martial showed.[44] Defense Secretary Bob Gates called worries about the impact on foreign policy "fairly significantly overwrought. The fact is, governments deal with the United States because it's in their interest, not because they like us, not because they trust us, and not because they believe we can keep secrets."[45]

At first, before it was clear that all of these documents came from the same source, Assange soaked up the fame or notoriety from these releases. It seemed as if WikiLeaks had many different sources inside the United States government and that its new model of journalism was the pivotal development. Eventually, it became clear that Manning was the source of all the high-profile releases and the true historic actor. Manning was the first to show how technology has enabled a new kind of leak that is far less frequent than the traditional, retail-scale disclosure of specific information, but far more consequential when it does occur: the wholesale-scale bulk disclosure of vast archives of docu-

These two never-before-published photographs show key early meetings about detention legal-policy issues by Obama and his legal team. At this March 5, 2009, meeting in the Oval Office, they thrashed out a court position on the scope of Obama's power to keep holding Guantánamo prisoners in indefinite law-of-war detention without trial.

At this April 24, 2009, meeting in the Situation Room, leaders of the three detention-related task forces briefed Obama about their progress, and it became clear that Obama needed to decide soon whether to keep military commissions. He opted to do so after working with Congress to overhaul their rules. *(Unreleased White House photos by Pete Souza; author's files)*

Selected members of Obama's national security legal-policy team

James Baker

David Barron

Robert Bauer

Valerie Caproni

John Carlin

James Cole

Greg Craig

James Crawford

Rajesh De

Mary DeRosa

Brian Egan

Neil Eggleston

(U.S. government photos, except Barron from Harvard Law School, Bauer from Perkins Coie, DeRosa from Chertoff Group, Eggleston from Dupont Photographers)

Selected members of Obama's national security legal-policy team

Richard Gross   Avril Haines   Eric Holder Jr.

Jeh Johnson   Neal Katyal   Harold Koh

Caroline Krass   David Kris   Martin Lederman

Robert Litt   Loretta Lynch   Mark Martins

(U.S. government photos, except Lederman from Georgetown University)

Selected members of Obama's national security legal-policy team

Mary McLeod

Daniel Meltzer

Lisa Monaco

Matt Olsen

Stephen Preston

Kathryn Ruemmler

Virginia Seitz

Karl Thompson

Donald Verrilli Jr.

Andrew Weissmann

Brad Wiegmann

J. Douglas Wilson

(U.S. government photos, except Meltzer from Harvard Law School, Ruemmler from Latham Watkins, Seitz from Sidley Austin, Wilson courtesy self)

In this never-before-published photograph from May 2008, the Foreign Intelligence Surveillance Court posed alongside senior Bush-Cheney national-security officials and Chief Justice John Roberts, who selects the judges who serve on the spy court. As part of a years-long effort to legalize each component of the post-9/11 Stellarwind program, the court secretly accepted novel interpretations of surveillance laws offered by the Justice Department.

Front row: Mike McConnell, director of national intelligence; Robert Mueller, FBI director; Michael Hayden, CIA director; Chief Justice John Roberts; Colleen Kollar-Kotelly, FISA Court presiding judge; Michael Mukasey, attorney general; Keith Alexander, NSA director. Back row: J. Patrick Rowan, Justice Department national-security division acting head; FISA Court judges Robert Broomfield, George Kazen, Reggie Walton, John Bates, Mary McLaughlin, James Carr, Nathaniel Gorton, James Zagel, Roger Vinson, Dee Benson, and Frederick Scullin. (Unreleased Supreme Court photo by Steve Petteway; author's files)

In 2013, the former intelligence contractor Edward Snowden handed an archive of top secret documents about the National Security Agency to journalists in this Hong Kong hotel room. Snowden's massive leak set off a debate about the government surveillance programs that Obama had inherited and kept, including judicial scrutiny and congressional reform of the bulk phone records program the FISA Court had secretly blessed. (Laura Poitras / Praxis Films)

In this frame taken from a propaganda video apparently produced by al-Qaeda in the Arabian Peninsula, Anwar al-Awlaki (left), a radical Islamist cleric, posed with Umar Farouk Abdulmutallab (center), a twenty-three-year-old banker's son from Nigeria, and Nasir al-Wuhayshi, the leader of AQAP. Abdulmutallab tried to blow up a Detroit-bound plane on December 25, 2009, with a bomb hidden in his underwear. *(Internet video)*

American drone strikes killed al-Awlaki in September 2011 and al-Wuhayshi in June 2015. Drone strikes away from hot battlefields, including in Pakistan and Yemen, sharply escalated under Obama. No targeted-killing operation attracted greater controversy than Obama's decision to intentionally kill al-Awlaki, an American citizen, without a trial. *(U.S. Air Force photo by Leslie Pratt)*

The Obama administration oversaw an unprecedented number of criminal cases against people accused of leaking government secrets to the public. The leak-related defendants included Thomas Drake (left), a former NSA official whose case traced back to the Bush-Cheney years, and Chelsea (then Bradley) Manning (middle), who gave archives of secret military and diplomatic documents to WikiLeaks. The Justice Department fought a legal battle to show that the First Amendment did not protect *New York Times* journalist James Risen (right) from being compelled to testify in the trial of a former CIA official accused of leaking to him, but prosecutors did not force him to take the stand. (*Drake courtesy self, Manning from U.S. Army, Risen from Bill Risen*)

Dozens of low-level detainees at Guantánamo were recommended for transfer but remained imprisoned for years because of troubled security conditions in their home countries. They included Adnan Latif (left), a Yemeni who committed suicide in 2012, and Jihad Ahmed Diyab (middle), a Syrian whose hunger strike drew scrutiny to the military's practice of force-feeding protesters. The Obama legal team divided over an appeals court case involving Ali al-Bahlul (right), a higher-level Yemeni detainee who had been convicted by a military commission on charges of conspiracy and providing material support for terrorism, neither of which is a war crime. (*Department of Defense photos, leaked by Manning*)

Obama's national-security legal policies faced congressional pressures from both directions. Republican senator Lindsey Graham (left) pushed Obama to make greater use of military-commission trials and to hold newly captured terrorism suspects as enemy combatants. Democratic senators Mark Udall (right, back) and Ron Wyden (right, front) pushed Obama to place limits on surveillance and make public secret legal memos about electronic spying and targeted killings. (*Senate photos*)

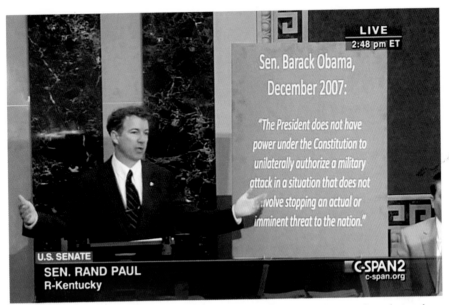

Sen. Barack Obama,
December 2007:

"The President does not have
power under the Constitution to
unilaterally authorize a military
attack in a situation that does not
involve stopping an actual or
imminent threat to the nation."

U.S. SENATE
SEN. RAND PAUL
R-Kentucky

C-SPAN2
c-span.org

In April 2011, Senator Rand Paul, Republican of Kentucky, criticized Obama for ordering the American military to carry out air strikes against Libya without prior congressional authorization. Paul noted that in 2007, when Obama was a senator and presidential candidate, he had told the *Boston Globe* that presidents do not have such power. *(Still frame from C-SPAN video)*

In August 2013, Obama was on the verge of unilaterally ordering, without congressional authorization, air strikes against Syria for using chemical weapons. But after a forty-five-minute walk through the Rose Garden, he gathered his aides in the Oval Office and told them he would go to Congress first. At that meeting, he said he agreed with what he had said to the *Boston Globe* in 2007 about war powers. *(White House photo by Pete Souza)*

ments by a single person. Its closest analogue was the leaking of the forty-seven-volume Pentagon Papers, although that was about one topic rather than countless ones. To achieve it, Ellsberg and Russo had to spend many hours photocopying some seven thousand pages and then physically carted the voluminous materials to a newspaper. Today, an official with computer savvy can systematically download hundreds of thousands of pages from a classified government server and instantaneously disseminate them over the Internet.

8. The Fourth Case: Kim

While unusual in that it was brought at all, the Leibowitz case had nevertheless been an easy one for the National Security Division's counterespionage section to prosecute. Leibowitz said he had taken no steps to cover his tracks when calling the recipient of his leaks and shipping documents to him. He also agreed to plead guilty soon after being confronted, meaning the FBI did not have to make any difficult decisions about subpoenaing the blogger to testify against his source, declassifying sensitive evidence for a trial, or even publicly identifying what the leak was and thereby implicitly confirming its authenticity. That same summer, the section was handed another leak referral that also proved to be relatively easy to solve. It became the fourth Obama-era case to be charged.

On June 11, 2009, a Fox News reporter, James Rosen, published an item on the Fox News website about North Korea. He reported that "U.S. intelligence officials have warned President Obama and other senior American officials that North Korea intends to respond to the passage of a U.N. Security Council resolution this week — condemning the communist country for its recent nuclear and ballistic missile tests — with another nuclear test." He also detailed three other steps North Korea intended to take but not announce, information the CIA had learned "through sources in North Korea." Rosen added that he was "withholding some details about the sources and methods by which American intelligence agencies learned of the North's plans so as to avoid compromising sensitive overseas operations in a country — North Korea — U.S. spymasters regard as one of the world's most difficult to penetrate."[46]

The unsurprising information about North Korea's plans itself was a "nothing burger," as one government official put it.[47] But the Fox News report nevertheless infuriated intelligence officials and the FBI threw resources into investigating it. The reason for the government's angry reaction, as officials later explained it to me, was that Rosen's report risked alerting North Korea to the existence of one of the United States' only intelligence sources inside its government. The information had leaked extremely swiftly; the CIA report had been disseminated to other parts of the American government the same day Fox News reported on its contents, court documents later showed. The short time between when the North Koreans came up with their plans and when they learned that the CIA already knew about them increased the risk that they would figure out that a particular person or communications link had been compromised, in which case that intelligence source would dry up.

Investigators following up on the leak referral came to scrutinize Stephen J. Kim, a State Department analyst who focused on arms issues related to North Korea. Kim was on a short list of people who had both received the report and had a known relationship with Rosen; in March 2009, a State Department press officer had asked Kim to speak to Rosen for a sanctioned briefing about North Korea.[48] When FBI agents came to his office in September and asked him about the story, Kim denied being a source for it.

In August 2010, Kim was indicted, becoming the fourth leak defendant of the Obama era. He would hold out longer than most accused leakers, draining his family's savings to pay legal fees,[49] but pleaded guilty in February 2014.[50] He agreed to serve thirteen months in prison; prosecutors had been threatening him with more than fifteen years if he went to trial.[51]

When the plea deal was announced, Kim's lawyer, Abbe Lowell, portrayed his client's actions as identical to "what so many government officials do every day in Washington." Calling the system for prosecuting leaks "broken and terribly unfair," in part because lower-level employees like Kim were charged with crimes while high-level officials "leak classified information to forward their agenda or to make an administration look good with impunity," Lowell urged Congress to modify the Espionage Act now that it was being used to prosecute leaks.[52]

"The act and its penalties are designed to punish traitors and spies — not State Department analysts answering questions from the media about their area of expertise," Lowell wrote.[53]

9. Electronic Trails

The way investigators identified Kim as the likely source of the North Korea leak is worth pausing over because it shows how technology cuts both ways. Technology makes the government much more vulnerable to the risk of a bulk leak, as Manning and Snowden demonstrated. But technology has also made it much easier for the government to successfully investigate leaks. It turns out that this is a major reason that leak referrals are more likely to lead to viable cases than they were even a few years ago, helping to explain the surge of cases that arose in the Obama era.

In a May 28, 2010, affidavit for a search warrant as part of the investigation, an FBI agent described how the bureau had come to suspect that Kim was the likely culprit. Audit trails in government databases, the agent said, showed that Kim had accessed the CIA report about North Korea on a classified database multiple times on the morning of the day Rosen published his article. State Department phone records showed that the phone in Kim's office had been used to place multiple calls to Rosen's phone on that same day. A database that logs when people enter and leave the State Department showed that both had left the building at almost the same time that morning and reentered twenty-five minutes later. A few hours after that, Rosen posted his article on the Fox News website, and then a twenty-two-second call was made from Rosen's phone to Kim's phone. The same types of data also allowed the FBI to rule out other potential suspects, the affidavit added: "So far, the FBI's investigation has revealed in excess of 95 individuals, in addition to Mr. Kim, who accessed the Intelligence Report on the date of the June 2009 article and prior to its publication." But only Kim had both accessed the report and had contact with Rosen on the date of the article's publication, it said.[54]

This is a case study for why leak referrals that were hopeless a generation ago are now increasingly becoming viable to investigate, usually without any need to threaten reporters with prison if they refuse to identify their confidential sources. Today, we all leave such detailed and permanent records of electronic trails that any ability to hide contacts between people from the government's eye is evaporating. Previously, if CIA officials opened the *New York Times* and saw an article containing a classified fact, they would routinely make a criminal referral to the Justice Department's counterespionage section. Law enforcement officials would respond with a basic question: "How many people had access to this fact?" If the CIA even knew, the answer could be overwhelming — something like "This list of a thousand people." That would effectively end the investigation; it was impractical to investigate such a haystack.

Increasingly, however, law enforcement officials can follow up with other questions: How many of those one thousand people looked at the report before it was leaked? Of those, who has sent or received e-mails on his work account or made or received phone calls on his office line or work-provided cell phone with the reporter who wrote the story? Very quickly, the FBI can narrow the universe of potential suspects down a group small enough that it is realistic to investigate each individual.

Its follow-up investigation will also rely on electronic trails. You have to be wiretapping someone ahead of time to eavesdrop on the contents of phone calls, but e-mails leave a record of what people said to each other and the FBI can get warrants for suspects' personal e-mail accounts in order to read them. It can subpoena their credit card records to see where they were having dinner or traveling on a given day. It can seize their hard drives and see whether they contain evidence of communications, even recovering data the suspect tried to delete.

With these data-driven advantages, the FBI can increasingly identify the likely culprit and send agents to interview him. And if this person initially denies having been in contact with the reporter, as may be natural in a moment of surprise and panic, prosecutors can use the electronic trails to add an open-and-shut charge of making false statements, which carries another five years. By threatening the suspect with decades in prison under the Espionage Act and waiving such circumstantial evidence, prosecutors can persuade a defendant to plead guilty in exchange for a sentence of just a year or two, sidestepping any need for a trial and the problems of compelling a reporter to testify or declassifying evidence. As a result of all this, when referrals are made and investigators look into a leak, they are increasingly able to bring the case in for a landing.

This is not something that Bush or Obama created, and it is not something that a future president could change even if he or she wanted to. The new technological reality simply happened to arrive at the same time as the post-9/11 wars fostered a surge in government secrets and secrecy, meaning more to leak about and more sensitivity to those leaks.

Some technology enthusiasts argue that encrypting e-mails is the answer. But while encryption can make it harder for the government to snoop on the contents of conversations, it remains difficult to mask the fact that two people have sent e-mails to each other without additional steps. Moreover, taking such steps can even be counterproductive: a government official who begins using technologically sophisticated measures to hide his communications is putting up a red flag that he may be trying to conceal something. Even after the 9/11 wars fade, if they ever do, data trails will remain, with profound consequences for the future of investigative journalism.

10. The Fifth Case: Sterling

As powerful as it has been, the arrival of Big Data has some limits. It cannot solve leaks based on diffuse sourcing, when reporters piece together a mosaic of tidbits after talking to dozens of officials in such a way that no individual can really be said to be the leaker. And circumstantial evidence of contact may not be enough to win a conviction if a defendant refuses to plead guilty — like Sterling was refusing to do.

Even though prosecutors obtained data showing that Risen and Sterling frequently communicated,[55] Welch claimed he needed Risen's eyewitness testimony because the data did not indicate what they had talked about. The Justice Department narrowed the scope of its subpoena. Tyrrell had wanted to force Risen to identify his source about Operation Merlin directly. But Welch told Judge Brinkema that he wanted to force the journalist only to explain "the where, the what, the how, and the when" that he had learned about Merlin, using pseudonyms like "Source A" in lieu of names. (Welch still wanted to force Risen to talk directly about what Sterling had told him in connection with the earlier article about his discrimination lawsuit against the CIA).[56] Still, there would be no limits on how deep Welch could go in grilling Risen within those parameters, and when married up to data about his contacts and movements, the answers to such questions might still prove who his sources had been or otherwise help prosecutors. Risen continued to refuse to comply with the subpoena, and so the prospect remained that he would be jailed for contempt.

On November 24, 2010, Judge Brinkema quashed the grand jury subpoena to Risen, saying that the Justice Department did not need his testimony to indict Sterling. Still, she said, the analysis might be different if the case went to trial because the government would need to meet a higher standard of proof to convict Sterling.[57] It was a novel ruling,[58] but Welch decided not to appeal it. On December 22, 2010, at Welch's request, a grand jury indicted Sterling on seven Espionage Act charges.[59]

But the lowering of press-freedom tensions over the case was brief. It soon emerged that the government had put Risen under intense scrutiny in other ways. In February 2011, a court filing by Sterling's lawyers discussing evidence prosecutors had revealed to the defense in "discovery" included "various telephone records showing calls made by the author James Risen. It has provided three credit reports—Equifax, TransUnion and Experian—for Mr. Risen. It has produced Mr. Risen's credit card and bank records and certain records of his airline travel."[60]

The brief did not say when the government had obtained the records, whether in the Obama era or the earlier Bush phase. Justice Department rules said prosecutors could issue subpoenas to journalists for their testimony or to phone companies for a journalist's call records only if the information sought was essential and the government could not obtain it in another way. They also said the attorney general had to personally sign off, and generally required notifying a reporter within ninety days if his phone records had been subpoenaed. Risen received no such notice. It remains unclear whether the prosecutors obtained Risen's phone records directly or had gotten the relevant ones by subpoenaing Sterling's records. (Such rules did not apply to other kinds of personal records for journalists, like credit card reports.)

But there was no doubt that Holder had personally approved the next step. On May 17, 2011, Welch subpoenaed Risen again, this time to testify at Sterling's trial. Risen again vowed to go to prison rather than comply.[61]

11. "We Had Lost"

In the spring of 2011, as Drake's case moved toward trial, Jesselyn Radack, a whistleblower advocate with the Government Accountability Project, helped him develop a media campaign to increase public pressure on the Obama administration over what it was doing.

Drake cooperated for a ninety-two-hundred-word scathing look at the case in the *New Yorker* by Jane Mayer, who was famous for her exposés of the Bush-era CIA torture program.[62] The TV newsmagazine *60 Minutes* aired a profile of Drake entitled "U.S. v. Whistleblower Tom Drake."[63]

"Why do you think you were charged under the Espionage Act? That's pretty rare," Scott Pelley, the *60 Minutes* correspondent, asked at the conclusion of its segment.

"To send a chilling message," Drake replied.

"To whom?" Pelley asked.

"To other whistleblowers, to others in the government, not to speak up or speak out. 'Do not tell truth to power. We'll hammer you,'" Drake said.

Inside the Holder Justice Department, officials who considered themselves liberals squirmed. And as public scrutiny mounted, prosecutors and the defense were fighting over what secret evidence could be used at the trial.

The dispute centered on the Classified Information Procedures Act. Enacted in 1980, its purpose is to mitigate the problem prosecutors disparage as "graymail," in which criminal defendants claim that they need to discuss secret information in open court. It allows the government to discuss particular facts with substitutions—like saying "Intelligence Collection Activity A" instead of detailing a classified surveillance program, for example. The judge weighs whether government requests to use substitutions would infringe on the defendant's constitutional right to a fair trial.

Closed-door hearings over classified evidence in the Drake case stretched from April to June 2011. Much remains sealed. But according to people familiar with the case, a series of problems arose for the government. It turned out that Mike Hayden, the former NSA director, had given background briefings to reporters containing some of the same supposedly classified information Drake was being prosecuted for mishandling. There were also disputes about whether particular information was really classified and whether the agency could use substitutions for *unclassified* information that it still deemed sensitive. The trial judge, Richard Bennett, made a series of evidentiary rulings that went against the government.

When the Justice Department added up what would have to be disclosed in public for a trial, the NSA balked. At that point, the Justice Department could have appealed the judge's rulings, but the case was already falling apart in other ways, and they were getting torn up in the media. They felt boxed in.

On Thursday, June 9, 2011, Breuer and Holder talked it over at Main Justice. They decided to make one last move. Breuer called Drake's defense lawyer, Wyda, and offered a new deal: prosecutors would drop all ten felony charges if Drake would agree to plead guilty to a single misdemeanor count of exceeding his authorized use of a computer. He'd serve no prison time. Breuer said he was intervening because he thought it was a good resolution and a way to bring closure for Drake, though Wyda of course had to do what was best for his client.

Drake took the deal.

The near-total collapse of the case was portrayed as a black eye for the government and a victory for Drake — and it was. But there was a hidden, somewhat cruel twist; inside the Justice Department, Drake's decision to plead guilty to the misdemeanor was greeted with a secret sigh of relief. It has never been reported that Breuer's offer was a bluff — a last gambit to save face in some small measure for the government. Top officials had already decided that if Drake rejected Breuer's offer, they would instruct Welch to go into court the next morning and ask the judge simply to dismiss the charges.

"We had lost," a senior law enforcement official said. "We couldn't go forward. And the department completely blamed the NSA, felt sandbagged by the NSA, both because of the stuff that came out in discovery that Hayden had done, and because it was unwilling to cooperate on the CIPA stuff. And of course the Justice Department takes the heat if it goes south. The decision was 'We're going to make him this offer and we hope he takes it, because if not, there was no choice'" — no choice but to terminate the case with nothing to show for it at all.

In accepting Drake's guilty plea to the misdemeanor, Judge Bennett told him that "this whole matter is really a tragedy" but also "you definitely did exercise very poor judgment."[64]

The conviction raised the question of what the punishment should be. Sentencing guidelines also called for a fine of $500 to $5,000. Welch asked Bennett to instead impose a $50,000 fine to "send a message" to the thousands of intelligence agency employees, down to the janitors, that they should take their nondisclosure obligations more seriously than he said Drake, a senior executive at the NSA, had done.

Bennett blew up. While he sentenced Drake to serve one year of probation and 240 hours of community service, he refused to impose *any* fine on top of a mandatory twenty-five-dollar court fee. He noted that "there has been financial devastation wrought upon this defendant" because of the investigation and that Drake would not be able to collect a federal pension. And he tore into the government about what kind of message *its* conduct had sent. The Justice Department had searched Drake's home in 2007, waited three years to finally charge him, indicted none of the others who were involved with him and whose homes were also raided, and then, after threatening him with thirty-five years in prison, all but dropped the case. He noted that the Justice Department could have appealed his evidentiary ruling but had not. The government had put Drake through "four years of hell," he said, going on to use terms like *extraordinary, very, very troubling, unconscionable,* and *doesn't pass the smell test.*

"The American public deserves better than this," the judge said.

12. The Sixth Case: Kiriakou

Meanwhile, a sixth criminal leak case was developing — entirely by accident. It would result in leak charges against John Kiriakou, a former CIA official, for telling reporters information about the identities of colleagues involved in the agency's rendition, detention, and interrogation program. But the investigation did not begin with a media leak referral.

The case traced back to two events in early 2009 at Guantánamo.

Defense lawyers representing Khalid Sheikh Mohammed and the other 9/11 defendants made a classified filing in the military commissions system listing dozens of CIA personnel who had something to do with the black-site prisons operation. The defense lawyers wanted to depose the operatives. It was not clear to the government how the lawyers knew their names, including some of operatives who worked undercover. Soon after, guards searching the detainees' cells discovered photographic lineups that included pictures of current and former CIA personnel along with shots of random people — none with names. Of the CIA veterans, most pictures came from TV or public appearances and none were of covert officials, but a few appeared to be pictures of retired officers whom someone had clandestinely photographed in public.[65] The CIA was alarmed. John Rizzo, then the acting general counsel of the agency, made a criminal referral to the Justice Department to investigate whether the defense lawyers had broken any laws.

The National Security Division initially oversaw the investigation. But in November 2009, Holder announced his ill-fated plan to prosecute the 9/11 case in federal court rather than a military tribunal. That meant civilian prosecutors in the division would be going up against those same defense attorneys in court, so it was a conflict of interest for the division to be investigating them. On March 8, 2010, Holder appointed U.S. attorney Pat Fitzgerald, who had led the Bush-era inquiry into the Valerie Plame Wilson CIA leak and stayed on in the Obama administration, to take over the investigation into the defense lawyers.

Fitzgerald learned that the defense team had been trying to identify potential witnesses whose testimony they could use to show that the CIA had tortured their clients. They needed that evidence for any mitigation phase of the eventual 9/11 trial, in order to argue against potential death sentences. He concluded they were just doing their jobs and had broken no laws.[66] But his investigators also figured out how it was the defense had learned some of the most sensitive information.[67] The names of CIA officials had been conveyed to the lawyers by a human rights investigator, John Sifton. He had assembled them from many sources, but one — that of an undercover operative — he had learned from Matthew Cole, a freelance reporter who sometimes worked with ABC News. And Cole in turn had been e-mailed that name by Kiriakou.[68]

Back in December 2007, Kiriakou had given an interview on ABC News in which he became the first CIA official to openly discuss the fact that the agency used waterboarding as an interrogation technique. (Rizzo told me he had made a separate criminal leak referral about Kiriakou after the ABC interview, but "I honestly never expected Justice to do anything about it and of course they didn't."[69]) After the ABC interview, investigative reporters looking into the CIA interrogation program began contacting Kiriakou for suggestions about former officials involved in it whom they could reach out to. He helped the reporters. Among those reporters he spoke with was Cole, who was then considering writing a book about the CIA operation in which a Muslim cleric was snatched in Milan, Italy. Another was my colleague Scott Shane, as the FBI discovered when it obtained Kiriakou's e-mails.

Kiriakou was charged with violating the Intelligence Identities Protection Act and the Espionage Act. As the case advanced, the Justice Department was retreating from charging anyone over the CIA's actual abuse of detainees. In 2009, Holder had announced with fanfare that he was reopening investigations in the CIA program that had been closed without charges under the Bush-Cheney administration. But by August 2012, the prosecutor he assigned to review the matter had terminated all the cases without bringing any charges.*

In October 2012, Kiriakou pleaded guilty to having told a reporter the name of a covert operative, marking only the second successful prosecution under the Intelligence Identities Protection Act and the first since 1985.[70] As part of Kiriakou's plea deal, the other charges were dropped and he received a thirty-month sentence.

---

* See chapter 4, section 15; chapter 7, section 15; and chapter 10, section 6.

13. A War on Whistleblowers?

"This case is not a case about a whistle-blower," Judge Brinkema declared at Kiriakou's sentencing hearing.[71] But Kiriakou and some of his supporters maintained otherwise. The antiwar group Code Pink, which hosted a party for him before he went to prison and later raised money to help his family avoid losing their house, described him on its website as "the first U.S. government official to identify the use of waterboarding as an interrogation technique" and a man who was imprisoned "for exposing aspects of the CIA's use of torture against detained terrorists."[72] When he got out of prison, the liberal news program Democracy Now! interviewed Kiriakou in a segment that introduced him as "the retired CIA agent who blew the whistle on torture" and played a clip from his ABC News interview.[73] More broadly, many critics of the Obama-era leak crackdown portrayed the whole enterprise as a "war on whistleblowers" and routinely characterized leak defendants, generically, in those terms. Such claims were so much a part of the fabric of the Obama era that they merit closer scrutiny.

Kiriakou's most famous contribution to the torture debate, the one most frequently cited by his supporters, was his December 2007 interview on ABC News. In it, he said that the CIA had waterboarded Abu Zubaydah, whom he had helped to capture in Pakistan. He called waterboarding "torture" and said he now did not think the country should use it "because we're Americans, and we're better than that." And he said he was talking about it to foster debate.

But in the same interview, Kiriakou portrayed the CIA's use of waterboarding in the early years after 9/11 as worth it. He explained that while waterboarding was "not something that's pretty to watch," no water actually went into a prisoner's nose or mouth. And, crucially, he said that after being subjected to the treatment for "probably thirty, thirty-five seconds," Zubaydah had broken and "from that day on he answered every question just like I'm sitting here speaking to you... in a willing way."[74]

Certain things about this interview clash with how it was later mythologized.

First, the CIA had not waterboarded a prisoner since 2003,[75] so defending its early use while saying it should not be used now amounted to an endorsement of the agency's actual practices. Second, the fact that the CIA had used waterboarding had been widely discussed in news reports for more than three years — though, to be sure, based on anonymous sources.[76] Waterboarding, and whether it was torture, had been a major topic at Attorney General Michael Mukasey's confirmation hearing before the Senate Judiciary Committee several months earlier.

More importantly, at the time Kiriakou's "thirty-five seconds" claim provided ammunition to *supporters*, not critics, of the CIA's program.[77] The day after the ABC News broadcast, Rush Limbaugh said on his radio show: "Thirty-five seconds, and Abu Zubaydah caved, and the information worked, and the Democrats and the liberals tell us that torture is ineffective because people say anything to get out of it and to stop it from happening," adding with sarcasm: "And, of course, waterboarding is horrible, just absolutely terrible, terrible, terrible."[78]

But it later turned out that what Kiriakou said was inaccurate. Rather than waterboarding Zubaydah once for just thirty-five seconds, the CIA had actually subjected him to eighty-three applications of the treatment over more than half a dozen lengthy sessions in August 2002. Each application, according to an internal CIA record related to Abu Zubaydah, "consisted of four broad steps: 1) demands for information interspersed with the application of the water just short of blocking his airway 2) escalation of the amount of water applied until it blocked his airway and he started to have involuntary spasms 3) raising the water-board to clear subject's airway 4) lowering of the water-board and return to demands for information."[79] And rather than water never getting into prisoners' bodies, the technique in practice did involve fluid intake, followed by vomiting. One application, for example, left him "completely unresponsive, with bubbles rising through his open, full mouth," until medical personnel revived him and he "expelled copious amounts of liquid," according to a contemporaneous CIA cable from the black-site prison to headquarters.[80]

Those descriptions from the CIA's own documents were quoted in the Senate Intelligence Committee torture report, which only became public in December 2014. But the thirty-five-seconds-and-done version came into question in April 2009, when the Obama administration released a Bush-era interrogation memo disclosing that the CIA had waterboarded Zubaydah eighty-three times in a month.* In early 2013, Kiriakou explained that his former CIA colleagues had misled him. They "told me it worked," he told the *New Yorker*. "And that was a lie."[81]

All this complicates the notion that Kiriakou *blew the whistle* on torture. That said, Kiriakou was the first official to disclose that Abu Zubaydah had been one of the prisoners on whom waterboarding had been used. And, much more importantly, in less visible conversations with reporters after the problematic ABC News interview brought him to prominence, Kiriakou played an indirect role in bringing accurate information to light by helping journalists figure out whom to call for their own research into the program.[82] And this help to the reporters, not what he said about waterboarding being (highly effective, briefly used) torture, was what he was actually prosecuted for.

As a journalist, I — obviously — oppose the criminalization of unauthorized disclosures. I think this shift in how the government deters leaks and deals with suspected leakers endangers a free society and undermines self-government. But I am also a critic of framing the Obama-era crackdown in terms of a war on *whistleblowing*. That word sets a very high standard — leaks that expose waste, fraud, abuse of power, or illegality. The activists who choose to frame the policy debate in terms of whistleblowing are well intentioned, but they make it too easy for crackdown defenders to discredit the entire line of criticism by pointing to some leak defendants whose disclosures do not seem to meet that standard.[83]

---

* See chapter 9, section 4.

The "war on whistleblowers" strategy also misses some of what is at stake. Providers of unauthorized disclosures to the news media can play a valuable social role even when they are not whistleblowers. They are a counterforce against overclassification, the widely acknowledged bureaucratic instinct to mark things secret that are harmless to disclose and should be made public. And they can enrich public understanding of how the world really works even if the topic is not waste, fraud, abuse, or illegality.

The problem with the leak crackdown is not just that it deters and punishes actual whistleblowers. The problem is that it inhibits the free flow of information *of all types* to the public by scaring a much larger number of current and former officials with socially valuable information into not speaking to reporters about it. I will concede, against interest, that there can be "bad leaks," the disclosure of information whose publication may impose social costs that outweigh its social benefits. But most leaks are not like that. And even if one stipulates that one leak or another falls into this category, dealing with that leak through *criminal charges* — as opposed to other types of formal or informal administrative reprisals — will have spillover effects by chilling unrelated "good leaks."

The question is which risk will the United States run: the risk that journalists will occasionally get it wrong and publish a bad leak, or the risk that voters will stay in the dark about a government secret that they really needed to know. Neither system is ideal, but I think it is obvious which type of society the Founders wanted America to be. Either way, any honest assessment of the new trend of criminalizing unauthorized disclosures to the public must grapple with both trade-offs.

14. "Aiding the Enemy"

The WikiLeaks-Manning investigation evolved in two ways that endangered national security–related investigative journalism.

The first focused on WikiLeaks. By December 2010, major credit card companies and banks started refusing to process donations to the organization, and members of Congress and national security agencies were putting enormous pressure on the Justice Department to go after WikiLeaks and Assange, in part as a deterrent to keep others from emulating the bulk leak model. In late November, amid the cable publications, Holder said there was "an active, ongoing criminal investigation" into the WikiLeaks affair, and at a news conference in early December he confirmed that prosecutors were examining whether Assange and WikiLeaks could be charged under the Espionage Act or some other statute. He also said he had authorized prosecutors to take "significant steps" in the probe.[84]

On December 14, the Justice Department obtained a subpoena from a grand jury in Alexandria, Virginia, requiring Twitter to turn over information for accounts associated with WikiLeaks activists. Twitter fought for permission to notify its users, bringing the existence of the rumored grand jury investigation into the sunlight. Meanwhile, Justice Department prosecutors were brainstorming about ways to build a case against Assange. Officials studied charges like trafficking in stolen government property, but since WikiLeaks wasn't selling the documents, that didn't seem like a good fit. The text of the Espionage Act seemed to allow prosecuting WikiLeaks for re-disseminating restricted information to people not authorized to receive it, but using that law against people other than government officials who had accepted obligations not to disclose classified information raised the same sensitive First Amendment issues the Bush-Cheney administration had blundered into with the AIPAC case.

Despite the leak crackdown, the Justice Department was reluctant to set a precedent that could be used to prosecute traditional news outlets like the *New York Times,* officials told me. Seeking another route, prosecutors focused on trying to assemble evidence that Assange colluded with Manning and aided in extracting the information. The idea was that if he had done so, then perhaps they could charge Assange as a conspirator in *Manning's* offense of unauthorized disclosures rather than portraying WikiLeaks' *publication* of those documents as a separate crime.[85]

It was not clear that this was a valid distinction. WikiLeaks might not appear to be a traditional news outlet like the *New York Times*. But for legal purposes, they did similar things. Investigative reporters are rarely passive recipients of secret documents that just show up in their mailboxes one day; rather, they cultivate confidential sources and actively pursue newsworthy information for the public. The *Times* has a website too, and it routinely posts leaked material accompanying its articles online.

For his part, Assange was reshaping WikiLeaks to emphasize its claim to the mantle of journalism and any First Amendment protections that might entail. It changed its characterization of itself on its website, dropping the word *classified* from a description of what kinds of documents it published and saying "WikiLeaks accepts a range of material, but we do not solicit it." Its revamped submissions page used words like *journalist* and *news* some twenty times. And it began putting up more original analysis to accompany the documents it was posting, saying its "journalists write news stories based on the material, and then provide a link to the supporting documentation to prove our stories are true."[86] (Perhaps more helpfully, in a later confession, Manning described the sequence of events in detail, insisting that Assange had not directed the leak.)

After a time there was little sign of active detective work anymore, but the Justice Department still had an open investigation into WikiLeaks as late as 2014, court records showed.[87]

The other development in the case that had serious implications for national-security investigative journalism came on March 2, 2011. In the midst of the mounting furor over Manning's treatment in the brig at Quantico, the military released a revised charge sheet against Manning. It contained twenty-two new offenses, adding to the two it had initially charged the previous July, shortly after arresting the soldier. One of the new charges in particular was explosive. Manning was accused of violating Article 104 of the Uniform Code of Military

Justice—"aiding the enemy"—by causing sensitive national security information to be published on the Internet, where enemies like al-Qaeda could access it.[88] The case was bolstered several months later when the commandos who raided Osama bin Laden's compound in Pakistan brought back a hard drive that had, among other things, some of the documents WikiLeaks had published.

Aiding the enemy is the military court-martial system's version of *treason*. While a conviction for violating the Espionage Act can yield a ten-year prison sentence, aiding the enemy is a capital offense. Prosecutors were not seeking Manning's execution, but a conviction on that charge would establish a precedent that leaking was treason-like, sending a new arctic blast through both the military and civilian ranks of national security officials.

"If Bradley Manning is convicted of aiding the enemy, the introduction of a capital offense into the mix would dramatically elevate the threat to whistleblowers," wrote Yochai Benkler, a Harvard Law School professor and Internet expert who later testified as a defense witness at the trial. "The consequences for the ability of the press to perform its critical watchdog function in the national security arena will be dire."[89]

Manning eventually stood up in court, confessed in full, and offered to plead guilty to a lesser version of the charges. But military prosecutors proceeded to a full court-martial trial in an effort to win convictions on the more serious charges they had brought.

In an important ruling that unfortunately was not accompanied by any written opinion explaining her reasoning, the military judge acquitted Manning of "aiding the enemy." But she found the soldier guilty of most of the remaining charges, including multiple Espionage Act counts. She imposed a thirty-five-year sentence, by far the longest for leaking in American history.[90]

While the effort to convict Manning of "aiding the enemy" failed, the mind-set behind it had lingering impacts. Together, the 2009 Fort Hood shootings and the 2010 WikiLeaks disclosures prompted the Obama administration to develop a "National Insider Threat Policy." It requires executive-branch agencies to place greater scrutiny on employees and contractors "to deter, detect and mitigate actions by employees who may represent a threat to national security." These include "potential espionage, violent acts against the government or the nation, and unauthorized disclosure of classified information, including the vast amounts of classified data available on interconnected United States government computer networks."[91]

This framing suggests an equivalence of sorts between a soldier who commits mass murder of his brothers and sisters in arms, and an official who discloses information about national-security matters to the press without authorization. A June 2012 strategic plan developed by a Defense Department working group on unauthorized disclosures, obtained by McClatchy, showed how the new training was institutionalizing the mind-set that, in the Internet age, an American official who provides classified information to the public without authorization is as harmful as a spy.

"Hammer this fact home," it said. "Leaking is tantamount to aiding the enemies of the United States."[92]

15. Pendulum Swing

Heading into the 2012 campaign, Democrats were confident that Obama — who had presided over a ruthless drone program and ordered the operation that killed Osama bin Laden — could not be attacked as soft on national security. Then a flurry of new leaks offered Republicans an opportunity to flip the script; the reason voters knew so much about American military and intelligence operations, they contended, was that Obama's people were recklessly leaking classified information about successful counterterrorism operations and practices, endangering America just to make Obama look tough in an election year.

The storm began on May 7, 2012, when the Associated Press reported that the CIA had thwarted another plot by al-Qaeda in the Arabian Peninsula to destroy a U.S.-bound airliner using an underwear bomb. The FBI had obtained the device, which was more sophisticated than the one that had failed to explode on Christmas in 2009, and was examining it.[93] A White House briefing for former officials who were going to go on television to discuss the news provided additional dots that were quickly connected: there was never any danger because the intended suicide bomber was a double agent who had penetrated the terrorist network.[94]

The one-two disclosures resulted in a confusing conflation. British and Saudi intelligence agencies, which had played primary roles in the operation, were said to have been hoping to send the double agent back in until the revelation derived from the White House briefing. That struck many as implausible. ("Hi, guys. Oops, I seem to have misplaced that underwear bomb somewhere. Anyway, what's our next evil scheme?") But security agencies were also furious about the original leak. Even though the AP had held off on *publishing* the story at the government's request — and the CIA had gotten the double agent safely out and conducted a major drone strike in the interim — they believed it had been reckless of somebody to disclose the information many days earlier, when the operation was still live.

Two weeks later, the political furor over leaks escalated. Within days, a flurry of books and articles appeared assessing Obama's national security record in light of his bid for reelection. They recounted insider deliberations in the White House Situation Room and other classified details. Reporters at the *New York Times* and *Newsweek*[95] looked at the administration's decision-making about drone strikes. An article and book by my *Times* colleague David Sanger[96] revealed new information about the so-called Stuxnet computer virus, describing a joint U.S.-Israeli covert operation, Operation Olympic Games, to sabotage Iranian nuclear centrifuges.* The articles and books came out at the height of the 2012 election campaign. Some Democrats, including Senators Dianne Feinstein and John Kerry, complained that leaking was getting out of control. Republicans went further, alleging high-level betrayal of the country for partisan advantage. "It is difficult to escape the

---

* See chapter 12, section 2.

conclusion that these recent leaks of highly classified information, all of which have the effect of making the President look strong and decisive on national security in the middle of his reelection campaign, have a deeper political motivation," said Senator John McCain.[97]

Obama denied any official sanction for leaks, promising criminal investigations. "The notion that my White House would purposely release classified national security information is offensive," he said.[98] Holder appointed two United States attorneys, Rod Rosenstein and Ronald Machen, to personally lead leak investigations into the AP's Yemen story and Sanger's cyberwar story, a symbolic step that elevated their bureaucratic stature. Republicans were not satisfied. They wanted special prosecutors wielding independent powers to subpoena reporters' testimony or phone records, saying Holder could not be trusted to approve them.[99] The administration that by then had already brought six leak-related criminal cases, doubling the previous combined total in American history, stood accused of being soft on leaking.

In May 2013, the leak pendulum swung. At the time, congressional Republicans were accusing the administration of cover-ups regarding its initial talking points about the September 2012 attack on the Benghazi consulate and about the IRS's scrutiny of Tea Party groups that applied for a type of tax-exempt status reserved for charities that do not engage in political activity. Then, in May 2013, the AP announced that prosecutors had subpoenaed two months of phone records involving twenty lines used by journalists in three major bureaus in what was obviously part of the investigation into the Yemen bomb-plot leak. These included lines used by many AP reporters who had nothing to do with the Yemen story, like the shared phone on the AP's desk in the congressional press gallery. There had been no advance notice and so no opportunity to negotiate over its scope or ask a judge to quash it. AP president Gary Pruitt called the sweeping subpoena "a massive and unprecedented intrusion" into First Amendment activities.

Holder let it be known that he had recused himself from overseeing that case because he was one of the people who had known about the thwarted Yemen plot before the leak. His deputy, Jim Cole, had approved the subpoena. Officials at the U.S. attorney's office and the FBI had maintained in the internal deliberations that all those numbers had been vetted and the calling records for them were necessary. But it later became clear that the subpoena had been sloppy, scooping in phone numbers that were not even active anymore as well. One was for the phone at the old desk of one of the reporters of the story back when he had worked in the AP's Hartford bureau, years earlier.

Advocates of press freedoms once again protested. But for once they were not alone in criticizing a leak investigation. Conservatives seized on the revelation as a third Obama scandal. The new narrative was that Obama's aggressive tactics in pursuing leaks was part of the same Nixonian abuses of power they saw in the Benghazi and IRS controversies. "Whether it is secretly targeting patriotic Americans participating in the electoral progress or reporters exercising their First Amendment rights, these new revelations suggest a pattern of intimidation by the Obama administration," said a spokesman for Representative Eric Cantor, the Republican majority leader.

Days later, the *Washington Post* unearthed and published the 2010 search warrant application for Fox News reporter James Rosen's e-mails in the Kim leak investigation. It made an explosive claim: Rosen himself was a criminal "as an aider, abettor and/or co-conspirator" in Kim's alleged Espionage Act violation. It appeared the administration was toying with escalating its leak crackdown by prosecuting a journalist.

The heat intensified. Fox News graphics proclaimed themes like "Targeting the Press." Senator Charles Grassley of Iowa, the ranking Republican on the Judiciary Committee who had lambasted Holder a year earlier for not doing enough to prosecute leaks, now lamented that "subpoenas seeking reporters' e-mails and telephone calls" showed why no one could trust the Obama administration.[100] But the criticism was bipartisan. "I am very leery about any investigative tool that involves even the appearance of an investigation directed at journalists," said Senator Richard Blumenthal, Democrat from Connecticut.[101]

There was more. After the AP announcement, Holder had assured Congress he knew of no effort to prosecute reporters. Citing the affidavit about Rosen, Republicans now raised the specter of perjury.[102] The Justice Department offered an ugly defense: it had made the claim about Rosen being a criminal only to circumvent a 1980 law, the Privacy Protection Act, which bans search warrants for reporters' work materials unless the reporter is a criminal suspect. Its explanation was that it had been gaming the law to get Rosen's e-mails but really had no intention of prosecuting him.

Just a few months earlier, after Obama's reelection, Holder had considered stepping down in triumph, having completed the term despite Republican efforts to drive him from office. But Holder had told friends that he didn't enjoy the lifestyle of private law practice and hoped the catharsis of the election would clear the air. Tracy Schmaler, his communications director at the time, later told me Holder stayed on "to get some distance from the controversies of the first term, to continue to work on the issues that matter to him into a second administration, and still accomplish what he would like to do so that he could leave on his own terms."[103]

Now that looked like a miscalculation. Republicans were on the attack again and Democrats were quietly expressing Holder fatigue as well. Holder convened a war cabinet of his closest current and former aides to craft a survival strategy. The idea was to first acknowledge leak investigation overreach and then tighten the rules, cleaning up a mess whose creation he had overseen. For the first step, Holder gave an interview to the *Daily Beast*; the article, "Holder's Regrets and Repairs," quoted him as saying that prosecutors had obeyed the rules but that the controversies were "reminders of the unique role the news media plays in our democratic system, and signal that both our laws and guidelines need to be updated." It also paraphrased aides saying Holder had begun "to feel a creeping sense of personal remorse."[104]

But Reid Weingarten, a lawyer and longtime friend of Holder's, told me that Holder had said nothing to him about any feelings of *guilt*. "He's not immune from the criticism, but I think he sees [the] First Amendment–security conflict as almost impossibly difficult," Weingarten said, adding: "He hasn't confessed or cried to me, that's for sure.

What I sense in conversations with him is how horribly difficult the dilemma is when you have this situation: 'It's important to get it right, and if we didn't get it right—and that's a big *if*—let's button up the process now.'"

After the AP controversy, Obama already instructed Holder to review guidelines for criminal investigations that affect the news media. In late May, Holder convened meetings between senior Justice Department officials and senior journalists and media lawyers, listening to their concerns and exploring potential changes. Then he came up with a new set of Justice Department guidelines for leak investigations.[105] There would be a stronger preference for notifying news organizations in advance about planned subpoenas for their phone records. Law enforcement agents could not portray news reporters as criminal conspirators to get around the Privacy Protection Act unless they really intended to prosecute them. Higher-level reviews would be required before subpoenaing journalists for testimony or notes. A Holder aide told me how they saw it: short of promising never to investigate leaks, it was pretty much as far as the executive branch could go on its own without congressional action on a media-shield bill.

Then, in the midst of Holder's attempt to ratchet back the leak crackdown, the *Guardian* published a top secret order from the FISA Court, signaling the beginning of an extraordinary new bulk spillage of national security secrets.

16. The Seventh Case: Snowden

On the evening of June 5, 2013, the website of the *Guardian* published an article by Glenn Greenwald.* It reported that the Foreign Intelligence Surveillance Court had issued a secret order to Verizon requiring it to turn over the phone records of its millions of customers to the NSA. As noted, *USA Today* had reported in 2006 that the NSA had a

---

* See chapter 11, section 6.

database of phone records for tens of millions of Americans, but it was never clear what was real about that or what happened to it.* Greenwald had proof: a copy of a top secret FISA Court order to the phone company. The public had never seen such a document before. It was the beginning of an extraordinary cascade — and the seventh Obama-era criminal leak case.

About a month earlier, Greenwald and two other journalists, Laura Poitras, a documentary filmmaker, and Ewen MacAskill, a national security reporter for the *Guardian,* were standing in an empty room on the conference-center floor of a Hong Kong hotel. They had come there on instructions from a mysterious source with whom Poitras and Greenwald had been communicating in encrypted online chats. The source had told them that if all appeared safe, he would walk past them holding a Rubik's Cube. And so he did.[106]

It was Edward J. Snowden, a twenty-nine-year-old contractor for the NSA. He had downloaded hundreds of thousands of classified documents about American and British surveillance activities and brought the archives with him to Hong Kong. After leading them to his hotel room, Snowden sat as Poitras put up her filming equipment, and Greenwald, a former litigator, grilled him for hours about who he was — testing to see if it was a setup.

But Snowden was real. A brilliant computer enthusiast, he had grown up in North Carolina, dropped out of high school, and enlisted in the army in 2004, only to break his legs in a training accident. He was discharged but acquired a top secret security clearance, allowing him to work as a computer specialist for the intelligence community. Snowden grew disenchanted, however, as he learned how the NSA was coming to dominate the Internet. He believed the security state was transforming a liberating technological revolution into a potential tool of oppression. Snowden decided to reveal to the world what the NSA was doing, even though there was a high likelihood that he would spend the rest of his life in prison for doing so.

---

* See chapter 5, section 9.

Over several months and employers, Snowden had used his computer skills, some of which the NSA had taught him, to download batches of files without detection. Then, telling his supervisor at a NSA facility in Hawaii that he needed to take some time off for medical treatment, he boarded a flight to Hong Kong—selected, he said, because its foreign affairs were controlled by China, which would be less likely to swiftly turn him over to the United States.

After giving his archives of files to Poitras and Greenwald—and a different set about the British version of NSA, called GCHQ, to MacAskill—Snowden boarded a flight to Russia. According to Greenwald, Snowden was planning to go on from there to Ecuador, but the United States revoked his visa and pressured other countries not to take him, stranding him in the transit zone in the Moscow airport for several weeks. Finally, the government of Vladimir Putin—an autocrat with a formidable surveillance state of his own—granted him asylum, defying American demands for his extradition.

Snowden's revelations about the scope and technical capabilities of NSA spying both at home and abroad represented, by some measures, the most extraordinary breach of national security secrets in American history. They set off anger abroad and a national debate at home, prompting a bipartisan embrace of reforms.*

Rather than waiting to be caught, Snowden came forward preemptively and acknowledged, in a short video filmed by Poitras in Hong Kong and posted on the *Guardian* website a few days after it started publishing stories based on his documents, that he was the source. Noting the Obama administration's record of prosecuting leakers, he explained why he had sacrificed his well-paid, comfortable life in Hawaii. "I'm willing to sacrifice all of that because I can't in good conscience allow the US government to destroy privacy, internet freedom and basic liberties for people around the world with this massive surveillance machine they're secretly building," he said.[107]

Snowden's critics, like Representative Mike Rogers, the Republican

---

* See chapter 11, sections 6–16.

chairman of the House Intelligence Committee, would repeatedly insinuate that Snowden was a Russian agent. Rogers never presented any evidence for that claim, and executive-branch officials said they had found no signs he was working with or for anyone. Snowden claimed he had brought no documents with him to Moscow after handing them off to the trio of reporters who came to Hong Kong. (He had also sent a partial set to Barton Gellman, a former *Washington Post* reporter to whom Poitras had reached out earlier in 2013 for help in assessing the claims by the then-still mysterious source; Gellman did not go to Hong Kong.)

The *Guardian* and the *Post* shared a Pulitzer Prize for Public Service for their reports about the Snowden documents. Greenwald eventually left the *Guardian* to co-found a new publication, the *Intercept,* which continued to work on them. Over time, many other news outlets would write stories using the documents, including *Der Spiegel* and the *New York Times*. I was among the reporters with whom Poitras shared subsets of unpublished documents from the archive, and co-wrote several stories that drew on that material.

Snowden, meanwhile, was charged on June 14, 2013, with violating the Espionage Act. He became the seventh leak case under Obama, though as of 2015 he remained free, a fugitive granted asylum to live in Russia.

17. "No First Amendment Testimonial Privilege"

On July 19, 2013, a panel on the federal appeals court in Richmond — the Fourth Circuit — issued a critically important ruling about whether Risen could be compelled to testify against Sterling.

For generations, it had been unclear whether a "reporter's privilege" exists — that is, whether federal judges had the power, under the First Amendment or common law, to quash subpoenas to reporters if they decided that press freedoms outweighed the need for the information sought. The main Supreme Court precedent that scrutinized this question, a 1972 case called *Branzburg v. Hayes*,[108] was "clear as mud," as one of the appeals court judges remarked during arguments in the Risen-Sterling case.[109]

In *Branzburg*, a newspaper reporter had been subpoenaed to tell a federal grand jury about a crime he had witnessed — not a leak of government secrets, but a clandestine drug-manufacturing operation. The reporter asked the judiciary to quash the subpoena. By a five-to-four vote, the Supreme Court declined to do so. Writing for the majority, Justice Byron White said the plaintiff was asking the court "to grant newsmen a testimonial privilege that other citizens do not enjoy. This we decline to do."

That seemed to mean that the First Amendment created no reporter's privilege. But the four dissenting justices said there *was* a reporter's privilege that lets judges invoke a balancing test and quash subpoenas. And one of the five justices in the majority, Lewis F. Powell Jr., wrote an enigmatic concurring opinion. He suggested that courts *could* protect journalists from subpoenas "on a case-by-case basis" if a judge, after balancing free press interests against society's need to solve crimes, decided that the testimony sought by prosecutors "implicates confidential source relationships without a legitimate need of law enforcement." Press advocates have argued that this means there was actually a shadow, five-justice majority for the existence of a qualified privilege that protects reporters from being forced to testify in some circumstances. If so, then Powell had only joined White's opinion, making the dissent into a seeming majority, because he just didn't think the reporters in *the particular case before him* met the standards for being protected.

The Supreme Court has not addressed the issue again. Different appeals courts reached opposing conclusions about whether or not a reporter's privilege existed and, if so, what its scope and limits were.[110] This ambiguity became pivotal in the fight over the subpoena to Risen in the Sterling case.

Since the confusing *Branzburg* decision, the Fourth Circuit had issued several rulings that adopted the view that Justice Powell's concurrence meant there *was* some First Amendment protection for reporters — enough to empower a judge to quash subpoenas requiring disclosure of confidential reporter-source information after weighing several factors, including whether the information could be obtained in another way. Most of those cases were civil lawsuits, not criminal matters, and none involved the higher stakes of a national security matter.

Invoking those precedents, in July 2011, Brinkema, the trial judge in the Sterling case, largely quashed the subpoena seeking Risen's testimony in the trial. This was a landmark decision. It was apparently the first time a federal judge anywhere in America had asserted that the First Amendment gave her the power to protect a journalist from testifying about a source in a criminal trial, as opposed to a grand jury investigation or a civil trial.

"A criminal trial subpoena is not a free pass for the government to rifle through a reporter's notebook," Brinkema wrote.[111]

But the Obama administration appealed. It urged the Fourth Circuit to overturn her ruling and declare that the First Amendment provides to reporters "no shield to identifying the person" who had illegally leaked information to them. Such a declaration by that court would have broad implications for national security investigative reporting because the Fourth Circuit includes Maryland, which is home to the NSA, and Virginia, which is home to the CIA and the Pentagon.

The appeals court panel took more than a year to decide the case, and in the interim, Welch retired from the Justice Department and a different prosecutor took over.[112] Then, on July 19, 2013, the appeals court panel finally spoke. It held, two to one, that Brinkema was wrong, the Obama administration was right, and if prosecutors who are trying to imprison a reporter's alleged source issue a subpoena to the reporter, he must testify in the trial.

"There is no First Amendment testimonial privilege, absolute or qualified, that protects a reporter from being compelled to testify by the prosecution or the defense in criminal proceedings about criminal conduct that the reporter personally witnessed or participated in, absent a showing of bad faith, harassment, or other such non-legitimate motive, even though the reporter promised confidentiality to his source," wrote Judge William Traxler for the majority.[113]

In a dissent, Judge Roger Gregory portrayed his colleagues' decision as "sad" and a serious threat to investigative journalism. "The majority exalts the interests of the government while unduly trampling those of the press, and in doing so, severely impinges on the press and the free flow of information in our society," he wrote.

A Holder spokesman said the department agreed with the ruling. Risen appealed again. The Justice Department urged the Supreme Court not to take the case, saying the appeals court had correctly decided it. In May 2014, the justices declined to review it. Henceforth, any limits on forcing journalists to testify about their sources as part of a criminal leak investigation would be only discretionary acts of executive grace, not constitutional mandates.

18. The Eighth Case: Sachtleben

After the Justice Department's controversial move to obtain the AP's phone records, it found a culprit in the Yemen bomb-plot leak, producing the eighth leak case of the Obama era.

The personal cell phone records of one of the AP reporters on the story, Adam Goldman, showed that during the relevant time period, he had been in repeated contact with Donald Sachtleben, a fifty-five-year-old retired FBI bomb technician living in a suburb of Indianapolis. Sachtleben was still working for the FBI as a consultant, and he had visited the Quantico lab where the new underwear bomb was being examined on May 1, 2012, a few hours before Goldman and a colleague, Matt Apuzzo, first called government officials to say they knew the FBI had intercepted a new underwear bomb from Yemen.

In a twist, it turned out that Sachtleben was already separately under investigation for trading child pornography on the Internet. His computer and cell phone were already in the government's possession in connection with that other case. (Investigators sought permission to go back and search them for messages or files showing contact with Gold-man.) He pleaded guilty to both sets of charges, receiving forty-three months in prison for violating the Espionage Act and additional prison time for the porn offenses.

The resolution further confirmed the rising power of electronic trails in solving leak cases. The court papers also underscored why FBI agents and prosecutors loathed Justice Department guidelines for media leak investigations that require investigators to exhaust other avenues before resorting to scrutinizing journalists. The law enforcement officials had spent months looking at every official who, records showed, knew about the bomb plot. But Sachtleben wasn't listed in those records. He had not accessed any documents about the bomb on the FBI's classified computer system, and he had not put his name on the sign-in sheet for access to the "specific room within the examination space for the Explosives Unit designated for the examination of the bomb." So they were looking at all the wrong people. Then, when they got the AP's phone logs, they solved the case in a snap.

After the beating the Justice Department had taken over its sub-poena for the AP phone logs, prosecutors crowed in a news release about their subpoena's role in identifying Sachtleben. Their statements did not address the core of the controversy, however — that the sub-poena had been so broad, sweeping in the sources of many AP report-ers who had nothing to do with the story, and that they had given the organization no advance notice or opportunity to negotiate and con-test it.

19. Cases That Weren't

The leak cases charged under Obama as of 2015 were an historically unprecedented surge, but there could have been more. Over time, word emerged of other leaks that were the subject of criminal investigations but ultimately did not lead to charges. Assessing them is part of under-standing the Obama-Holder record.

Toward the end of his tenure, in an appearance at the National Press Club in 2015, for example, Holder was asked about the numerous leak cases charged on his watch. Defending himself, Holder argued that each was justified on the merits, and he described the policy changes he had created to add new restrictions on how prosecutors interact with members of the press. He also raised the value of discretion and restraint, suggesting that it cut both ways; reporters should not indiscriminately publish government secrets just because they could, he said, and the Justice Department chose not to bring some leak cases even though it could have.[114]

"We have tried to be appropriately sensitive in bringing those cases that warranted prosecution," Holder said, "We have turned away… substantially greater numbers of cases that were presented to us and where prosecution was sought."

We don't have a comprehensive understanding of cases that were viable to prosecute but nevertheless did not result in charges. But we do know about some of the other leak investigations or referrals that occurred during the Obama years.

The Holder Justice Department subpoenaed at least one other reporter for testimony about his sources. The subpoena was issued in January 2011 to Mike Levine, then of Fox News, over a July 2009 report he wrote about several terrorism-related indictments that were then still under seal. Matthew Miller, the department's public affairs chief, and Holder had reviewed and approved this subpoena.[115] Levine asked Judge Royce Lamberth to quash the subpoena, but Lamberth upheld it. (After Levine revealed in 2014 that this had happened, I asked Lamberth to unseal these court documents, and he did so over the Justice Department's objections.) Levine told prosecutors that he had talked to five law enforcement officials, but that he did not remember which two had provided the specific information. He refused to identify the five officials and he never testified. In April 2012, the prosecutor handling the case called Levine's lawyer and said the department was dropping the matter, without further explanation.

In addition, Welch decided to close out some of the investigations he inherited from Tyrrell's leak task force without charges. As noted, Welch charged only Drake, not the other Thinthread whistleblowers. Welch also charged nobody in connection with the task force's main purpose: finding the sources of the leak about the NSA warrantless surveillance program to Risen and Lichtblau. The suspects the task force had scrutinized who escaped charges included Tamm, the former Justice Department lawyer who confessed in *Newsweek* during Obama's transition that he had been a source for Lichtblau. Welch called Tamm's lawyer around August or September of 2010 and informed him that Tamm would not be charged.[116] Defenders of the Holder-era leak crackdown sometimes pointed to the decision not to indict Tamm as showing that the Justice Department had exercised discretion and restraint, since he had confessed to his guilt.[117] This account may not be the whole story. It is true that *Newsweek*'s editors put Tamm on its cover with a headline saying he was "the" whistleblower who exposed warrantless wiretaps.[118] But Risen and Lichtblau had many sources, and this description of Tamm's contribution was an overstatement. By Tamm's own account, he was never told the classified, operational details of the program. A law enforcement official familiar with the investigation told me that it would have been difficult for prosecutors to prove at trial that Tamm had disclosed any specific classified fact. If so, a prosecution of Tamm was never viable.

Other leaks that did not lead to charges involved more senior officials.

In 2011, the CIA and the Pentagon cooperated extensively with film-makers working on *Zero Dark Thirty*, the film about the hunt for Osama bin Laden and the operation that killed him. A Pentagon inspector general report later slammed unauthorized disclosures that resulted from this arrangement. Among other things, Mark Boal, the screenwriter, had been invited to attend a closed ceremony at the CIA celebrating the SEAL Team Six operators who carried out the raid. During a speech at the ceremony, Leon Panetta, then the CIA director, said the name of the chief planner and team leader for the operation, along with other top secret information. Boal had no security clearance. Neither

Panetta nor anyone else was charged. Panetta had strongly supported helping the filmmakers do research for their movie, but it is not clear whether there was a viable case against him; the report did not say whether he knew Boal was there, and Panetta said he had been "assured that everyone in the audience was cleared."[119] The CIA public affairs staff and Panetta's chief of staff, Jeremy Bash, disagreed about who was responsible for Boal's presence.[120]

In yet another leak investigation, the retired Marine general James "Hoss" Cartwright, who had been the vice chairman of the Joint Chiefs of Staff from 2007 to 2011, became a prime suspect as a source for Sanger's reporting about the cyberattack on Iranian nuclear equipment. Cartwright had overseen the operation.[121] He was stripped of his security clearance — a humiliation that meant he could no longer participate on an outside Pentagon advisory panel.[122] But he was not charged either. One problem, the *Washington Post* reported, was that the White House counsel's office, during the tenure of Kathryn Ruemmler, was unwilling to declassify information for use at trial; neither the United States nor Israel had confirmed the operation.[123] It was also hard to ignore the fact that Cartwright was known as one of Obama's favorite and most trusted generals.

On July 12, 2013, when Holder put out a report saying he was going to tighten rules for criminal leak investigations, a White House spokesman reached out to me without my asking and e-mailed me a prepared, on-the-record statement saying that Obama supported the Justice Department changes. Notably, Obama's statement singled out for agreement a call, at the end of Holder's report, to find ways other than criminal charges to deal with some leaks of classified information.

"There are circumstances in which leaks are better addressed through administrative means, such as withdrawal of security clearances or imposition of other sanctions," the White House statement said. "The president agrees with the Justice Department's recommendation, and has directed his team to explore how the administration could more effectively use alternatives in appropriate cases."

After the inspector general report about Panetta and *Zero Dark*

Thirty, Steve Aftergood of the Project on Government Secrecy told *Politico*'s Josh Gerstein that the incident would never be charged but ought to prompt reconsideration of the leak crackdown.

"It illustrates the different standards in effect for senior officials and low-level officials. That's just a fact of life," Aftergood said, adding, "This episode ought to imbue everyone with a degree of humility about the working of the classification system. If someone of undoubted patriotism can violate the Espionage Act, then the legal regime is clearly out of whack."[124]

20. The Ninth Case: Petraeus

The fact that only low-level people were being charged with leaking was a recurring and cynical theme in the Obama-era crackdown. By the end, however, a high-level official was caught in the crackdown's snare — gently. It was David Petraeus, the famous general who had become the director of the CIA in September 2011.

On October 23, 2012, on the day Kiriakou pleaded guilty to disclosing a covert operative's identity to a reporter, Petraeus sent a message to CIA employees in which he portrayed the conviction as "an important victory for our Agency, for our Intelligence Community, and for our country. Oaths do matter, and there are indeed consequences for those who believe they are above the laws that protect our fellow officers and enable American intelligence agencies to operate with the requisite degree of secrecy."[125]

Just three days later, FBI agents came to Petraeus's office at the CIA to interview him. Investigating a convoluted cyberstalking case, they had stumbled into evidence that Petraeus had had an affair with his biographer, Paula Broadwell, and that he might have leaked information to her for her 2012 book, *All In: The Education of General David Petraeus*. The agents asked him if he had ever provided classified information to her. He said he had not. This, as he later admitted, was a false statement — a felony unto itself. In fact, in August 2011, he had lent her eight black notebooks containing his schedule and notes of meetings from his time as the top military commander in Afghanistan. Among the highly classified information in them were the identities of multiple covert agents. (Broadwell had a security clearance but was still not authorized to see this information. She did not publish it.)

Less than a month later, Petraeus resigned from the CIA.[126] He eventually took up a career as a partner in a private-equity firm and became a paid speaker on national security issues.[127]

Meanwhile, the investigation dragged on for several years, putting pressure on Holder from multiple directions. For example, McCain wrote Holder in December 2014 to complain about how the case was being handled. While saying he was not asking for any particular outcome, McCain made it clear that he thought Petraeus was being mistreated.

"It goes without saying that I greatly respect General Petraeus' remarkable record of service to our country in Iraq, Afghanistan, and later as Director of the CIA," McCain wrote. "His unique expertise and insight on matters of defense and national security are of deep value to many Americans, as well as policymakers across the political spectrum. At this critical moment in our nation's security, Congress and the American people cannot afford to have this voice silenced or curtailed by the shadow of a long-running, unresolved investigation marked by leaks from anonymous sources."[128]

A month later, someone leaked to the *Times* that FBI agents and lower-level prosecutors wanted to charge Petraeus, but Holder was sitting on the recommendation.[129] The anonymous sources said some law enforcement officials thought Petraeus was receiving special treatment.

On February 22, 2015, Petraeus signed a plea deal. Court filings focused on the eight black notebooks. FBI agents had obtained an August 2011 audiotaped interview in which Broadwell asked Petraeus about gaining access to the notebooks and he had hesitated, noting that they contained "highly classified" information, including "code word stuff," the highest level of restrictions. But several weeks later, Petraeus had sent her an e-mail agreeing to give her the books, and the next day he brought them to a house where she was staying. Three days later, he retrieved them and stored them at his own house. In a search of his house in April 2013, the FBI had found the black notebooks in an "unlocked desk drawer in the first-floor study."[130] In addition to information regarding the identities of covert officers, the notebooks contained classified information about "war strategy, intelligence capabilities and mechanisms, diplomatic discussions, quotes and deliberative discussions from high-level National Security Council meetings," and Petraeus's "discussions with the President of the United States of America."

The government had indicted defendants like Kim and Kiriakou under the Espionage Act, then offered them plea deals for felony convictions and prison time. But prosecutors did not indict Petraeus under the Espionage Act. Instead, they offered him a plea deal to settle the entire matter for a misdemeanor conviction on a charge of unauthorized removal and retention of classified documents. They recommended that he serve two years of probation and pay a $40,000 fine, which a judge later raised to $100,000.[131]

Lawyers for other leak defendants accused the Justice Department of using an unfair double standard in which it treated powerful and well-connected leakers better than lower-level leakers. Abbe Lowell, Kim's lawyer, sent the government a letter asking that it let his client out of prison early as a matter of equitable treatment. Both, after all, had admitted to the same activities — disclosing classified information and lying to the FBI — but the government had rejected Kim's offer to plead guilty to a misdemeanor.

"The resolution the Department is recommending for General Petraeus is supported by his record of service and the facts in the plea," Lowell wrote. "So too would have been that result for Mr. Kim. We know that you can come up with any number of factors (as lawyers are trained to do) to distinguish the two cases. However, that is just an exercise in lawyering. At the bottom line, the activities are the same."[132]

21. "A Price to Be Paid"

Holder had already started to pull back on the leak crackdown with his new investigation guidelines eighteen months before Petraeus got the good deal. And on May 14, 2014, when Holder had convened a group of journalists to talk about press-freedom issues, he hinted that he would not permit Risen to be jailed for refusing to discuss his sources in the Sterling trial.

"As long as I'm attorney general, no reporter who is doing his job is going to go to jail," Holder said.[133]

But on January 5, 2015, as prosecutors prepared for the Sterling trial, they called Risen to the witness stand for a very unusual court hearing to explore what he was prepared to say in front of a jury if forced to testify. Risen declared again that he would not reveal his sources or offer any other help to prosecutors.

"I'm not willing to provide information in any way that will prove or disprove a mosaic the government is trying to make," Risen said.

Holder had tied the prosecutors' hands, and they did not press Risen, avoiding setting up any contempt citation. The following week, they filed a motion before Judge Brinkema saying they would not call him as a witness at Sterling's trial.

It was a complicated end to Holder's legacy in presiding over the greatest leak crackdown in American history. He had approved reissuing the subpoena to Risen, and he had approved battling to the Supreme Court to establish that the First Amendment does not protect the confidentiality of reporter-source relationships. But he also issued restrictive new leak investigation rules and, in the end, saved Risen from prison.

Risen's attorney, Kurtzberg, celebrated the outcome for his client. But the result also made everything that had come before look worse. The Justice Department had harassed Risen for years, caused his book publisher to run up costly legal bills, and made it harder for him to do his job as an investigative reporter because everyone knew he was under scrutiny. The department had used his legal challenge to the subpoena to establish a definitive court precedent that the First Amendment offers no protection to journalists from being forced to testify against their sources. Then it dropped the matter.

"The significance of this goes beyond Jim Risen. It affects journalists everywhere. Journalists need to be able to uphold that confidentiality in order to do their jobs," Kurtzberg said, adding, "I worry about future administrations. Now there's bad precedent, and not every executive branch in the future will exercise their discretion the way this one did. It didn't have to go this way."[134]

Indeed, any sense of celebration for investigative journalism would prove to be short-lived. Sterling's trial proceeded without Risen's testimony, and the jury convicted him.

Justice Department prosecutors asked for a "severe" sentence and endorsed a sentencing guidelines range of nineteen to twenty-four years.[135] Defense attorneys asked for leniency, citing Petraeus's treatment.[136] On May 11, 2015, Brinkema sentenced Sterling to three and a half years in prison. She said the sentencing guidelines range was inappropriate, but Sterling had to be punished for endangering the life of the Russian scientist by revealing to the Iranians that he had been working for the CIA.

"If you knowingly reveal these secrets, there's going to be a price to be paid," she said.[137]

Afterwards, Sterling's lawyer, Barry Pollack, said jurors had gotten the verdict wrong but "the judge today got it right."

Sterling would appeal his conviction. But it seemed likely that his conviction and sentencing effectively ended the saga that had begun nine years earlier, when the Bush-Cheney administration, enraged by the *Times* article revealing NSA warrantless wiretapping, directed Steven Tyrrell to launch a task force to investigate national security leaks. The Obama administration had finished the job, and it had forged new ground on its own — some by happenstance, and some deliberately.

9

Secrecy and Secret Law

1. The al-Awlaki Lawsuit (State Secrets I)

In 2010, as word seeped out that the Obama administration was considering killing Anwar al-Awlaki,[1] lawyers with the American Civil Liberties Union and the Center for Constitutional Rights grew alarmed by the extraordinary precedent that would establish. They decided to ask a court to scrutinize whether this was permissible. In an attempt to find a plaintiff with legal standing, they traveled to Yemen to meet with al-Awlaki's father, Nasser al-Awlaki. Nasser was a former high-ranking Yemeni government official who had been studying in New Mexico when his son Anwar was born, making Anwar an American citizen. Nasser signed the paperwork to retain them, without compensation, on July 7, 2010. The next month, they filed a lawsuit. It was assigned to Judge John Bates, who was also the presiding judge on the FISA Court. The lawsuit asked Bates to issue an immediate injunction blocking the government from attempting to kill al-Awlaki and to order the government to disclose the criteria it used for deciding whether to kill a citizen.

The Justice Department had to respond to this request for an injunction by September 24, and it raised a dilemma: whether to invoke the state secrets privilege. The doctrine is an extraordinary secrecy power that had become controversial during the Bush-Cheney years. It allows the executive branch to trump a person's right to a day in court by asserting that litigating about a matter would mean disclosing information that would damage national security. The Constitution does not mention the state secrets privilege as a power vested in the presidency; rather, it is a judicially created doctrine. The Supreme Court first recognized the privilege in 1953, during the "imperial presidency era" that arose in the early Cold War.[2] There are two forms—both controversial, but one more so than the other. The less disputed version allows the executive branch to suppress specific evidence but permits the overall lawsuit to proceed. The more disputed version allows the executive branch to kill an entire case by arguing that its very subject matter demands dismissal.

While there were occasional examples of this second, more aggressive use of the privilege before 9/11,[3] the Bush-Cheney administration frequently invoked the privilege to block lawsuits over surveillance and interrogation policies, and critics contended that Bush was using it to avoid judicial scrutiny of lawbreaking and to cover up abuses. Obama's campaign website, under the heading "A Plan to Change Washington," identified as a "problem" the fact that Bush "invoked a legal tool known as the 'state secrets' privilege more than any other previous administration to get cases thrown out of civil court."[4] Once in office, the Obama administration had decided to keep the Bush-era claims going in lawsuits that it inherited, as I will discuss in a moment, but it had yet to make a fresh assertion of the state secrets privilege in a lawsuit over an action undertaken on its watch.[5]

Justice Department litigators, seeking extra insurance, now wanted to assert it.[6] But invoking the privilege was politically toxic. Harold Koh, the State Department legal adviser, argued to Tony West, the head of the Justice Department's Civil Division, that invoking it would seem extreme and would play into the hands of the human rights groups bringing the case by permitting them to accuse Obama of taking positions that were indistinguishable from Bush. He also contended that doing so was unnecessary since they could ask Bates to dismiss the lawsuit for other reasons.

Indeed, even some of the strongest public advocates of presidential powers, including David Rivkin, a former White House lawyer in the Bush-Quayle administration, recoiled at the idea that the government might invoke the privilege in such a case. He told me the court should dismiss the lawsuit because targeting decisions in war were not fit for judicial review, but it shouldn't be buried under a state secrets claim.

"I'm a huge fan of executive power, but if someone came up to you and said the government wants to target you and you can't even talk about it in court to try to stop it, that's too harsh even for me," Rivkin said.[7]

But Koh didn't get a vote—his principal, Hillary Clinton, didn't have to sign anything because the State Department did not need to make any classified declaration of facts about al-Awlaki and operations in Yemen to the judge. It would require signed declarations from the leaders of the intelligence community, Jim Clapper and Leon Panetta, and their lawyers, Bob Litt and Stephen Preston, were firmly in favor of invoking the privilege. At the Pentagon, Bob Gates, who would also have to sign a declaration, waffled. Jeh Johnson took no position but gave Gates a memo listing pros and cons. The advantage, he wrote, was that the government could tell the judge classified facts that could be kept secret from the public and the plaintiffs. The disadvantage was the bad optics, including the likelihood of a rebuke by the *New York Times'* editorial board. After reading it, Gates backed invoking the privilege too. The litigators in the Justice Department's Civil Division, focused on winning the case, wanted to invoke it, too.

The decision fell to Eric Holder. He sympathized with what Koh was saying, and in a last-ditch effort to avoid invoking the privilege, Holder instructed the litigators to ask Bates for permission to make their arguments in sequence, so they could play the state secrets trump card only if necessary. But Bates said the government had to invoke all its arguments at once or lose them. Stuart Delery, a top aide to Holder, picked up his office phone and called the attorney general, who was traveling that day, to tell him Bates's decision. Holder told Delery to do it, and he relayed the instructions to West.

The Justice Department still tried to have it both ways: It invoked the privilege in its response to the Nasser al-Awlaki lawsuit, but asked Bates to rely on it only if he first rejected every other basis they asserted for dismissing the case. The next morning, Matt Miller, Holder's spokes-man, defended the move, saying it was not covering up wrongdoing. "It strains credulity to argue that our laws require the government to dis-close to an active, operational terrorist any information about how, when and where we fight terrorism," he said.

But Jameel Jaffer, an American Civil Liberties Union attorney, said the Obama administration's secrecy claims amounted to a blank check for executive power. "They want to set secret criteria under which Americans are added to government kill lists and to determine for themselves whether those criteria are satisfied in any particular instance. It's a truly remarkable proposition, and one that surely would surely have been greeted with alarm had it been made by the last administration."

In December 2010, Bates threw out the case.[8] His grounds for doing so were that Nasser al-Awlaki lacked standing. Since it was his son who was affected by the government's policy, it should have been his son who filed the case. Bates also ruled that targeting decisions in wartime were for the "political" branches — the executive and Congress — to evaluate, not the courts.

Because those reasons were sufficient, Bates said it was unnecessary to address whether the state secrets privilege was a separately valid rea-son to dismiss the lawsuit. But the fact that the Obama administration had invoked it helped normalize a secrecy power that Democrats had criticized as an abuse when Bush had asserted it.

2. The Most Transparent in History (State Secrets II)

Critics said that the Obama team's decision to invoke the state secrets privilege in the al-Awlaki case clashed with Obama's first promise as president: to hold himself and his administration to "an unprecedented level of openness in government" that would reverse the culture of executive-branch secrecy he had inherited from George W. Bush.[9] Obama had made that promise just after lunch on January 21, 2009, the day after his inauguration, when he welcomed his senior staff to the White House's Roosevelt Room to be sworn in. Before they took the oath, Obama talked to them — and to the assembled reporters — about the kind of government he intended to run. The "way to make government accountable is to make it transparent, so that the American people can know exactly what decisions are being made, how they're being made, and whether their interests are being well served," he said.

Obama then paused to sign his first executive orders and policy memorandums. One of the orders pertained to the Freedom of Information Act. Commonly called FOIA, the information act is the core antisecrecy law in American government. Congress enacted it, in the words of an appeals court, "to pierce the veil of administrative secrecy and to open agency action to the light of public scrutiny."[10] Created in 1966 and strengthened in 1974 as part of the post-Watergate reforms, the law gives Americans a right to compel an executive agency to make documents public and to enforce that right in court. But the law also carves out categories that are exempt, including classified national security secrets and privileged internal documents. Most secrecy fights with the government center on whether it is valid for an agency to invoke an exemption.

Presidents have long chafed under the information act as an encroachment on executive secrecy powers. The Bush-Cheney administration adopted a policy of denying information act requests whenever there was a plausible argument that a document fell under an exemption, even if there was no conceivable harm in its release. That policy became a symbol of Bush's penchant for secrecy, and during Obama's postelection transition, Greg Craig, who became Obama's first White House counsel, drafted the order Obama was now signing to reverse it. Under the new policy, the government would presumptively make requested information public, even if it were technically exempt, unless there was a good reason not to disclose it.

"For a long time now, there's been too much secrecy in this city," Obama said. "That era is now over."[11]

The first sign Obama might fall short of his promise to roll back executive-branch secrecy arose nineteen days later. A group of former CIA detainees had sued a CIA contractor that operated the planes the agency had used to fly them between overseas prisons, accusing the firm of complicity in torture. The Bush-Cheney administration had persuaded a trial judge to throw out the case by invoking the state secrets privilege. The detainees appealed, and by the time a federal appeals court panel convened in San Francisco to hear arguments, Obama had become president. And now, a career lawyer from the Justice Department's Civil Division who had stayed on after the change of administration, Douglas Letter, walked into the courtroom and reiterated that the case must be thrown out lest it reveal state secrets.

"The change in administration has no bearing?" asked a judge.

"No, Your Honor," Letter replied, adding that the decision had been "thoroughly vetted with the appropriate officials within the new administration" and "these are the authorized positions."[12]

The position, it turned out, had been vetted by Holder, but no one had told the White House. Obama was furious that he only learned by reading a *New York Times* article about the position that his new administration had decided to take. It was four days later that I sat down with Craig in his new office in the West Wing to ask him about what I saw as an emerging pattern in which Obama's national security policies had more continuity with the Bush-Cheney administration than the expectations created by Obama's campaign rhetoric.*

The state secrets privilege was among the things we discussed. Craig defended the decision to reiterate the secrecy claim in that case, saying that it had been vetted up through Holder. (While Holder knew about it, I was later told by another official that Neal Katyal, the new deputy solicitor general, and Tom Perrelli, the new associate attorney general who oversaw the Civil Division, were the primary politically appointed officials who reviewed the materials.) But Craig also hastened to tell me that the administration had decided that the Justice Department should launch a systematic review of every pending lawsuit where the state

---

* See chapter 1, section 2.

secrets privilege had been invoked and a review of the Justice Department's general policy about using the privilege, so observers ought not to read too much into this one instance of continuity.

"Every president in my lifetime has invoked the state secrets privilege," Craig said. "The notion that invoking it in that case somehow means we are signing onto the Bush approach to the world is just an erroneous assumption."[13]

In April, the three-judge panel on the appeals court in San Francisco ruled against the Obama administration. The judges reinstated the lawsuit, saying that only specific evidence should be suppressed.[14] But the administration appealed to the full appeals court. Its secret filings, I was told later, centered on claims that if the U.S. government let the litigation proceed at all, it would reveal secret deals between the CIA and the intelligence services of various countries that had facilitated the black-site prison program — in some cases without the full knowledge of their broader governments. Such a revelation might damage the relationship between the CIA and those agencies, making them less willing or able to help the United States government on future sensitive operations. In 2010, the Obama administration won a six-to-five ruling throwing out the case after all; one of the judges expressed anguish over the "painful conflict between human rights and national security" but deferred to the executive branch's assertion that absolute secrecy was necessary.[15]

Meanwhile, the review of other pending state secrets cases and policy fell to Donald Verrilli, who was then an aide to the deputy attorney general and would later rise to solicitor general. Verrilli convened a task force containing a mix of career lawyers and political appointees, including Lisa Monaco, who had taken a political role in the deputy attorney general's office after being chief of staff to the FBI director, Bob Mueller.

Meeting in secure rooms, they reviewed each of the classified filings in the roughly fifteen cases left over from the Bush era. They also received briefings from the affected agencies about why each of the assertions had been necessary — what the intelligence sources and methods information was that the litigation threatened to expose, and why it would harm national security. Most involved John Rizzo, a top career lawyer at the CIA throughout the Bush years who stayed on for the first year of Obama.

"We said, 'Here's why we thought it was important in this case, and here are the documents,' and basically let them do their thing," Rizzo told me.

The new Obama appointees told their colleagues they were surprised to see how thorough the Bush-era classified filings to the judges had been — not a few pages, as they had been expecting, but richly detailed, inches-thick binders. The Obama team had gone in, following years of Democrats' complaints about Bush's prolific use of the privilege, certain that they would find abuses in which Bush officials had invoked it to cover up embarrassments and without any legitimate justification. But they came to believe that the Bush Justice Department had been much more serious about its responsibilities than they had thought. They also thought that the binders undermined concerns about the privilege being a unilateral executive power because judges had seen large amounts of secret material before making the call. In each case, they decided that the matter was more complex than they had understood and that there had been sufficiently strong reasons to assert the privilege.

Verrilli's group ended up giving separate briefings to Holder and Craig explaining their findings. It ended up keeping the assertion going for all of the pending cases, with only a small downsizing in arguments for one of them.

From one angle, that result vindicated the Bush team and retroactively discredited the Democratic attacks. From another, it looked as though Obama and his team were going native in the executive branch, caving in to the pressures brought by the permanent security state bureaucracy and abandoning the principles on which he ran.

Either way, it was awkward. And in that atmosphere, Verrilli turned toward a new policy to govern future assertions of the state secrets privilege. He convened an interagency group that included his Justice

Department team along with lawyers from the National Security Council, the Pentagon, the CIA, the Office of the Director of National Intelligence, the State Department, and the Office of the Vice President. They met several times in the White House Situation Room to thrash out the arguments.

There were three options. First, change nothing, on the grounds that the Bush team hadn't abused its powers after all. Second, draft new executive-branch procedures designed to reassure the public that the rules had been tightened. Third, accept proposed legislation by Democrats in Congress, Senator Patrick Leahy and Representative Jerrold Nadler, that would regulate the privilege by statute. One thing the Leahy-Nadler bill would do is require the government to provide meaningful, nonclassified summaries and substitutions for the secret evidence, as it did in criminal prosecutions under the Classified Information Procedures Act. Notably, in the previous Congress, Joe Biden and Hillary Clinton had cosponsored an earlier version of the Leahy-Nadler bill.

Doing nothing, on top of having withdrawn nothing, was deemed to be a political nonstarter. But military and intelligence agencies pushed back hard against embracing a new law.[16] Rizzo, the CIA lawyer, and Jeh Johnson, the Pentagon lawyer, argued that it would be too difficult to come up with substitutions in some cases and that, unlike a prosecution, where the executive branch can always drop the case instead of revealing something if it comes to that, in civil lawsuits the government is not in control.

Ultimately, the administration decided to quietly oppose any new state secrets law but to write new internal rules they hoped would reduce public cynicism about the privilege. Verrilli modeled the policy, crystallized in a three-page internal proposal dated June 15, 2009, after the Justice Department procedures for seeking the death penalty. An internal review group would meet to examine requests to invoke the privilege and make a recommendation to the attorney general, who would have to personally sign a document approving it. Invoking it was permitted "only when genuine and significant harm to national defense or foreign relations is at stake and only to the extent necessary to safe-guard those interests."[17] That standard was higher than the one the Supreme Court had set, which was "reasonable danger" that the disclosure "will expose military matters which, in the interest of national security," should remain secret.

Announcing the new policy with fanfare on September 23, 2009, Holder touted it as a major reform. Contrary to Verrilli's findings, Holder again insinuated that Bush had abused the privilege, and he portrayed the Obama administration as changing the way government worked: "This policy is an important step toward rebuilding the public's trust in the government's use of this privilege while recognizing the imperative need to protect national security," Holder said.[18]

But Rizzo later told me it was just a "face-saving measure" in his view, because for all practical purposes, "the new policy was not one iota different from the policy we'd been following in the Bush administration."[19]

3. The US Attorney Firings Subpoena (Executive Privilege I)

In addition to ongoing litigation involving the state secrets privilege, the Obama administration also inherited from Bush a major secrecy power dispute with Congress. The Obama team's response to that dispute foreshadowed fights to come over the control of government information.

After Democrats regained control of the legislative branch in 2007, they began investigating the Bush-Cheney administration's forced resignations of nine United States attorneys. A House committee issued a subpoena to the White House for documents and testimony that would reveal its role in the policy. Bush invoked executive privilege to block his chief of staff and White House counsel, Joshua Bolten and Harriet Miers, from complying with the subpoena. The Democrats then cited them for contempt. The Bush Justice Department declined to prosecute them, but Congress sued, asking a judge to enforce its subpoena. The case was assigned to — of all people — Judge John Bates. In July 2008, Bates ruled that the privilege did not extend as broadly as the Bush-Cheney administration had claimed. The case was still pending before an appeals court when Obama assumed control of presidential secrecy powers.

Executive privilege is a presidential power to lawfully avoid turning over information to Congress when the disclosure would amount to an unconstitutional intrusion into the president's authority. Like the state secrets privilege, executive privilege is a presidential secrecy power that is not mentioned in the Constitution. It also dates back, in its modern form, to the post–World War II "imperial presidency" era. The Supreme Court first recognized executive privilege only in 1974. In that case, it rejected Richard Nixon's claim that he could keep the Watergate tapes secret from Congress, but the justices said executive privilege might be valid in other contexts.[20] There have been few precedents to flesh out its scope and limits because presidents and lawmakers generally reach compromises in oversight disputes, avoiding definitive showdowns in court.

Many Democrats in Congress had hoped and assumed that when Senator Obama became president, he would drop Bush's privilege claim and immediately turn over the records — and implicitly threaten the Bush veterans with prosecution if they stayed silent. But weeks passed, and Obama did not do so. When I met with Greg Craig in February 2009, I pressed him about that decision too, and the tone of his answer raised my eyebrows.

"The president is very sympathetic to those who want to find out what happened," Craig told me. "But he is also mindful as president of the United States not to do anything that would undermine or weaken the institution of the presidency. So for that reason, he is urging both sides of this to settle."[21]

The following month, the Justice Department was due to file a brief at the appeals court saying whether Obama was reiterating the executive-privilege claim. But that day, Congress and the White House reached a deal. Congress got almost everything it wanted, but the legal fight was mooted. There would be no appeals court precedent—but Obama's views on the scope of executive privilege, now that he was the president instead of a senator, would become an issue again.

4. The Dover Photos and the Torture Memos

But there were major, meaningful steps toward transparency, too.

On February 26, 2009, Gates, the defense secretary, announced that Obama had asked him to review a policy that banned journalists from taking photographs of the caskets of slain soldiers arriving at Dover Air Force Base. The ban dated back to the Bush-Quayle administration. Critics had alleged that this secrecy policy, justified as protecting the privacy of the families of the dead even though no names were visible on the coffins, served to prevent the public from seeing, in a vivid way, the true costs of the ongoing wars in Afghanistan and Iraq. Gates lifted the ban on a case-by-case basis, letting family members decide—the same policy already in place for funerals at Arlington National Cemetery.[22]

Obama also took a significant step in a long-running Freedom of Information Act case brought by the American Civil Liberties Union about detainee abuses. Among other things, it was seeking disclosure of memos blessing certain interrogation techniques as legal. The Justice Department Office of Legal Counsel had written these interrogation memos, mostly in Bush's second term to replace those Jack Goldsmith had retracted in 2004.* Shortly after the Obama team took over, it had to decide whether to keep fighting to keep these additional memos secret. Verrilli oversaw this review for the deputy attorney general's office, too.

The Justice Department had an institutional interest in keeping the memos secret. Career lawyers argued that the candor of future confidential legal advice would be chilled if its attorneys had to fear that

---

* See chapter 10, section 20.

anything they wrote today might be exposed tomorrow due to a court order or a change of administrations. But the new political appointees had a different view. David Barron and Marty Lederman, the new top lawyers in the Office of Legal Counsel, were strongly focused on trying to find ways to, in their view, reclaim the legitimacy and rebuild the stature of that office, which they believed had been badly damaged. And Lederman, in particular, had spent the Bush-Cheney years dissecting on a legal blog the torture memos from Bush's first term; now, it was his job to go into a secure information facility to read these additional memos that had not yet come out. They showed that the Office of Legal Counsel in Bush's second term had come to institutionalize the same techniques, albeit with more legally polished writing and greater reassurances about medical monitoring than the first term batch.

At early meetings, Barron and Lederman argued that releasing the Bush torture memos was essential to turning a corner for the Office of Legal Counsel. They proposed releasing them as a discretionary matter as part of the new administration's transparency moment. But the idea stalled because the CIA, which owned the classified information and had to sign off on declassifying them absent a decision by Obama, had no interest in doing that.

Now, the FOIA case was forcing the executive branch to make a decision. Verrilli convened another meeting. A Justice Department litigator warned that because Obama had ended the program, it would make it harder to persuade the courts that the memos had to stay classified. Lederman suggested that they ask Obama to read the memos himself and make the decision. The meetings included other key new officials, including Ruemmler and Monaco, both of whom worked with Verrilli in the deputy attorney general's office and would later rise to higher positions in the White House, and Amy Jeffress, a national security aide to Holder. They focused on developing arguments for why disclosing the torture memos would be an exception and not establish a precedent, centering on the fact that the CIA interrogation program was already shut down and there was an unusually strong public interest in seeing the documents. Verrilli briefed David Ogden, the newly appointed deputy attorney general, about their consensus that the administration should not fight the disclosure of the memos. Ogden asked Verrilli to write a memo to the White House arguing that the administration should disclose the documents. Barron and Lederman helped edit it. Holder and Craig wanted the memos out too, and a few days later, Daniel Meltzer, Craig's deputy, called Verrilli and said the administration had decided to adopt his recommendation and disclose them.

It looked like the debate was over, but it was just beginning. In early March, Craig called Rizzo and said they would announce in three days that they were releasing the interrogation memos.[23]

We've been looking at the ACLU case, and the view here is that the government is going to lose on the issue of protecting the OLC memos, Craig said, according to Rizzo's later recollection. *Therefore, I want to let you know that we are going to inform the judge that the government is going to declassify the memos in their entirety.*

Rizzo wrote in his memoir that he was "flabbergasted" by Craig's plan because career Justice Department litigators had told *him* they would likely succeed in keeping the details of the memos secret. He reached out to three former CIA directors who had overseen the Bush-era program, George Tenet, Porter Goss, and Michael Hayden. They called Brennan, a CIA veteran who had become Obama's top counterterrorism adviser, urging him to reverse the decision.

Meanwhile, clandestine services officials at the CIA were also lobbying the new agency director, Panetta, to push the White House to keep the memos secret. They argued that the documents revealed sources and methods — specific interrogation techniques, including limits hidden from the detainees, like the fact that approval for confining a detainee in a coffin-like box with a live insect crawling on his body stipulated that the insect must be nonstinging, although the detainee would be told the opposite. While Obama had forbidden the use of such "enhanced" techniques, he or some other president might need to use them again and if the hidden limits were revealed, the techniques would become useless. Worse, it could set off a cascade of other disclosures, revealing the identities of the countries and personnel involved in the black-site program. Panetta had no previous intelligence experience and had pronounced the CIA interrogation program "torture" during his confirmation hearing. But now he made a decision Rizzo said helped him win "the gratitude and respect of the C.I.A. workforce."

Fuck it, Panetta said at a CIA meeting. *I am going to fight at the White House against the release of the memos.*[24]

That fight played out in a series of White House Situation Room debates. Rahm Emanuel, Obama's chief of staff and a former protégé of Panetta, opposed releasing the memos too. Panetta came back from one meeting, Rizzo said, and recounted how Emanuel had stormed out early — Obama had told him he was planning to ask his opinion next, but Emanuel said on his way out the door that the president knew his position already. But Dennis Blair, the national intelligence director, backed disclosing them, asserting it would be a one-day story. But he also said the truth was that the CIA had learned important information from detainees who underwent enhanced interrogation, though it was impossible to know whether they would have provided the same information through humane methods.

The momentum went back and forth, and the Justice Department obtained several deadline extensions from the court. It came down to the final night. Obama convened an impromptu debate, directing Craig and Denis McDonough, his Senate-era foreign policy adviser who was now head of strategic communications for the National Security Council, to articulate the best arguments for and against disclosing the memos.

McDonough invoked unintended consequences and loyalty: Presidents ask spies to keep secrets and do risky things for them, and if Obama said, "I will tell the world what you have done," that would break faith with the CIA. It could, potentially, make people at the agency feel like the White House was going after them rather than all of them being on the same team. His implication was that if Langley did not feel like the new administration had its back, it might passive-aggressively refuse to do Obama's bidding or make private complaints to Congress, causing all sorts of problems.

Against that, Craig invoked idealism and principle: releasing the memos would be an important step in making real the new president's pledge to restore the rule of law and America's moral standing.[25]

On April 16, 2009, Obama made the memos public. As a result, the public learned facts allowing it to better evaluate the Bush-Cheney administration's claim that it had not approved torture, only enhanced interrogation. That included, for example, the revelation that CIA interrogators had inflicted the suffocation tactic called waterboarding far more intensely than the public previously had understood, including 183 applications on KSM and 83 applications on Abu Zubaydah in a single month.[26]

Not everyone was convinced. But the release allowed a better informed public debate. For example, after the former CIA operative John Kiriakou told ABC News in December 2007 that Abu Zubaydah had started fully cooperating with interrogators after being waterboarded for half a minute,* the conservative *National Review* writer Jonah Goldberg had written a column about the torture debate. He said such "facts" contradicted allegations that the American government under Bush had become a "torture state," and exposed complaints about waterboarding as anti-Bush partisanship.[27]

In April 2009, when the memos came out, Goldberg revisited the issue.

"Whether it was worth it still seems open to debate, depending on the facts," he wrote. "But I think waterboarding someone 183 times in a month does amount to torture no matter how you slice it."[28]

5. Retrenchment

With the release of the torture memos, the new administration had resisted fierce pushback from the national security bureaucracy and lived up to Obama's promised ideal. For a brief moment, it looked like

---

* See chapter 8, section 13.

the start of a new era of routine openness in government. But the release turned out instead to be a high-water mark.

A week later, the Justice Department told the judge in the same Freedom of Information Act case that the government would also make public forty-four photographs depicting the abuse of detainees in Iraq and Afghanistan by American troops. But political heat was increasing. Dick Cheney, a key architect of the CIA interrogation program, was denouncing Obama for releasing the memos. He made clear that if Americans died in any future terrorist attack, Republicans would blame Obama's repudiation of Bush's interrogation program.

Against that backdrop, military commanders in Iraq and Afghanistan reiterated fears that disclosing the pictures could spark attacks against American troops. A trial judge and an appeals court panel had already rejected that argument on legal grounds, holding that the "significant public interest in the disclosure of these photographs" by enabling democratic accountability for official misconduct "far outweighs" any speculative harms to national security.[29] But Gates asked Obama to personally view the photographs and reconsider.[30] Gates also said that if Obama released the photos, the Pentagon needed time to ramp up security at every American military installation in Iraq and Afghanistan to try to partially mitigate the increased risk to service members that would result. One participant in the deliberations told me Gates's tone was strongly emotional, a "really hard-core sell."

Obama changed his mind. He explained that the conduct documented in the photos was already being investigated, not covered up, and argued that "the most direct consequence of releasing them, I believe, would be to further inflame anti-American opinion and to put our troops in greater danger."[31]

While the Justice Department delayed in court, Congress passed, and Obama signed, a special law granting Gates the power to exempt Bush-era detainee-abuse photographs from disclosure under the information act.

It would not be the last time that Obama's stated ideals bent before the force brought to bear by military and intelligence agencies — or, from another point of view, that Obama showed that he was willing to weigh such matters on a case-by-case basis rather than being an ideologue. Either way, in retrospect, Obama's effort to make the government more transparent had already reached its apex, and started to fall back. The retrenchment had begun.

6. *Hair on Fire* (Executive Privilege II)

In August 2009, Holder's decision to open a criminal investigation into the CIA's treatment of detainees during the Bush-Cheney administration* triggered a significant fight inside the Obama administration about executive privilege.

Panetta decided that the simplest way to cooperate with the prosecutors was to give them access to the special computer network, called RDINet, that the CIA had set up for the Senate Intelligence Committee staffers to go through files about the defunct rendition, detention, and interrogation program.† (The Guantánamo-detainee task force, which also needed access to those files, worked out of the same Northern Virginia building, too.) This step apparently focused the White House's attention on the implications of the fact that Panetta had struck a deal with the panel chairwoman, Senator Dianne Feinstein, to give her oversight staffers access to those documents.

Panetta had not cleared this deal with the White House, and it raised a big problem: many of the documents in the CIA's possession, from copies of presidential daily briefings to meeting notes and discussion papers used in Situation Room meetings, recounted communications with Bush or his top aides. Typically documents containing high-level White House internal deliberations are subject to executive privilege and the executive branch does not show them to Congress. While the documents all involved the previous administration, the Obama White

---

* See chapter 4, section 15.
† See chapter 4, section 6.

House had an institutional interest in preserving that principle: it did not want to set a precedent that Congress could use against it in some other fight over privileged documents down the line. At the point the White House realized what was happening, the CIA had already made some available to the Senate staffers, but it had not yet put all the documents that fell into this category in the computer network.

In Panetta's memoir, he recalled the White House summoning him with Preston, the newly confirmed CIA general counsel, to the Situation Room to meet with Emanuel, Blair, Brennan, McDonough, and Tom Donilon, the deputy national security adviser. They wanted an explanation of the deal Panetta had cut without running it by the White House first.

It soon got ugly, Panetta wrote.

The president wants to know who the fuck authorized this release to the committee, said Rahm Emanuel, Obama's chief of staff, slamming his hand down on the table. *I have a president with his hair on fire, and I want to know what the fuck you did to fuck this up so bad!*

But before Panetta could respond, Blair retorted: *If the president's hair is on fire, I want to know who the fuck set his hair on fire!*

They went back and forth for about fifteen minutes. Panetta recalled: "Brennan and I even exchanged sharp words when I, unfairly, accused him of not sticking up for the agency in the debate over the interrogation memos. Finally, the White House team realized that whether they liked it or not, there was no way that we could go back on our deal with the committee."[32]

Panetta's account did not make clear that the problem was about executive privilege, and instead characterized the blowup vaguely as a manifestation of how the Obama White House liked to centralize decisions about interactions with Congress. His memoir also did not coherently explain its resolution. What really happened, officials told me, was that they agreed that potentially privileged documents that had already been made available to the committee would stay in the computer network, but going forward, the CIA would set aside any additional batches that showed interactions with the White House rather than adding them to RDINet, too. The plan was that the White House and the Senate would negotiate to see if they could reach some accommodation over those files, which eventually grew to more than ninety-four hundred pages.

This arrangement was the origin of a dispute that arose in May 2010, although the public did not learn about the deal until Feinstein disclosed it in a speech several years later.* Intelligence Committee oversight staffers noticed that certain documents that they had previously seen in the computer network were now missing from it. The CIA initially denied taking anything out, then blamed information technology contractors for removing them without authority, and then said the White House had ordered the removal. Feinstein complained to the White House, which denied that it had given such an order. It emerged that the CIA had removed two batches of documents — eight hundred and seventy in February 2010, and fifty more in mid-May 2010 — because it had added them to the computer network by mistake. The documents fell within the category of potentially privileged files that were supposed to have been set aside. Feinstein met with Bob Bauer, who by then had succeeded Craig as White House counsel. The CIA did not restore the missing files, but Bauer and Preston told Feinstein that it would not happen again, and the CIA's director of congressional affairs apologized on behalf of the agency.[33]

For the next two years, negotiations over access to the potentially privileged materials continued sporadically and without resolution. From the Senate's perspective, the White House legal team, eventually led by Ruemmler after she succeeded Bauer as White House counsel, was stonewalling them.[34] From the White House's perspective, the negotiations were still ongoing when, to its surprise, Feinstein abruptly voted a draft of the report — written without access to those ninety-four hundred pages — out of committee in December 2012 and sent copies to the White House to open the next phase: discussion over what could be declassified. White House officials came to believe that Fein-

---

* See chapter 10, section 13.

stein wanted a bipartisan vote at that stage and so needed to abruptly get it done because the one remaining Republican on the committee who supported the torture investigation, Maine senator Olympia Snowe, was about to retire.

Even though the report was now basically done, Feinstein wrote three more letters to Ruemmler in 2013 — on January 3, May 22, and December 19 — requesting access to the additional documents, but "the Committee received no response from the White House," according to a footnote in the final report. Feinstein could have issued a subpoena. But by 2014, the panel was fighting with the CIA over an incident in which the agency had searched on the Senate staff's work drive and e-mails, and the priority, a Senate staffer told me, was just getting the thing done.

In short, the Obama White House successfully ran out the clock without making an accommodation or having to assert executive privilege, leaving the final report incomplete as a historical accounting. Still, the final report was filled with extraordinary revelations, including discussions of Bush-era Situation Room deliberations apparently based on documents that the CIA had already put into the computer network before the White House called Panetta in and yelled at him.*

7. Secret Law: The Patriot Act Interpretation

In the spring of 2011, as another Patriot Act reauthorization cycle neared, the public became aware that the Obama administration was keeping secret some kind of mysterious understanding of what the statute meant. It would not be until the 2013 leaks by the intelligence contractor Edward J. Snowden that the public would learn what it was: the NSA was collecting records about Americans' domestic phone calls in bulk. It did so under section 215 of the Patriot Act, the provision that

---

* See chapter 10, section 20.

on its face seemed only to authorize the FBI to collect business records that were relevant to a national security investigation.

Back in 2011, as the vote on reauthorizing the law neared, Senators Ron Wyden and Mark Udall, two Democrats on the Intelligence Committee, began making enigmatic warnings in floor speeches that the government was secretly interpreting the law in an alarming and non-obvious way. That had created a gap, they said, between what most people — including many lawmakers — thought the law allowed the government to do and what government officials secretly believed it allowed them to do. They said it was unacceptable in a democracy for the official meaning of the law to be kept classified. They proposed an amendment to the Patriot Act that would require declassification of the legal interpretation, one "that does not describe specific intelligence collection programs or activities, but that fully describes the legal interpretations and analysis necessary to understand the United States Government's official interpretation" of FISA.[35] And a preamble to their amendment disclosed that the Intelligence Committees had received a classified report from Holder and Clapper in February 2011 that apparently described what was happening.

Ahead of the 2011 vote, Feinstein persuaded Wyden and Udall to withdraw their amendment with a promise of a hearing. But its preamble had introduced a clue.

I filed a Freedom of Information Act request for the report. As I expected, the Justice Department acknowledged that such a report existed but declined to disclose it, saying it was classified. The *New York Times* and I filed a lawsuit. A few weeks later, the American Civil Liberties Union filed a similar but broader lawsuit for all documents related to the Patriot Act interpretation. Because the lawsuits concerned the same topic, they were both assigned to the same judge, William H. Pauley III, a 1998 Clinton appointee.

The government rejected the information act requests on the ground that the entire report was properly marked as classified. But we argued that the report apparently contained some legal analysis of section 215 of the Patriot Act, and that it was improper for the government to classify its official understanding of what a statute meant: surely there could be no "secret law." Thus, we argued, even if the portions of the report describing a classified intelligence program *based* on that theory could be withheld, the public had a right to see those portions of the memo that contained only abstract legal discussion. The Obama administration argued that the government could lawfully keep the entire report secret as classified.

In the course of the litigation, Wyden and Udall wrote a letter to Holder criticizing the Justice Department for fighting us.

"Americans expect their government to operate within the boundaries of publicly-understood law, and as voters they have a need and a right to know how the law is being interpreted, so that they can ratify or reject decisions made on their behalf," they wrote.[36]

Judge Pauley read the secret report for himself, and then in May 2012, he dismissed our lawsuits. We were seeking to test a new issue, and that novelty had worked against us.

"To support their 'secret law' theory, the *New York Times* and the ACLU cite no case in which a court applied the 'secret law doctrine' to mandate the disclosure of classified national security information… and this Court has found none," Pauley wrote.[37]

The officially approved channels had failed. For the American people to find out what their government thought the law meant, they would have to wait for someone to commit a crime by leaking the information.

8. The al-Awlaki Memo and *Glomar*

Nasser al-Awlaki's lawsuit seeking to block the government from killing his son may have failed, but it prompted Congress to take a closer look at what was happening — and to demand answers about what the legal basis for the intended kill operation was.

When Judge Bates dismissed the lawsuit, he emphasized that the judiciary lacked the capacity to evaluate a wartime decision to target a specific citizen hiding overseas, and the political branches were better equipped to evaluate it.[38] Bates's ruling prompted the Senate Intelligence Committee — including Wyden and the committee's general counsel, Michael Davidson — to press the administration to explain its legal reasoning to Congress. In April 2011, Wyden called Holder about the topic,[39] and I was later told that he threatened put a "hold" on a confirmation vote for Virginia Seitz, whom Obama had nominated to lead the Office of Legal Counsel, if the committees did not get more information. Seitz, a prominent appellate lawyer at Sidley Austin, appeared likely to be confirmed after the first nominee, Dawn Johnsen, had faltered, leaving David Barron and then Jonathan Cedarbaum in charge in an acting capacity. The White House was eager to get a vote on Seitz.

Hoping to satisfy the Intelligence Committee, the White House commissioned the Office of Legal Counsel to draft a classified white paper — an unsigned memo — summarizing its al-Awlaki opinion. The idea was that the executive branch could share an approximation of its secret memos without waiving any privilege to keep the real documents secret. The department finished it on May 25.[40] Wyden placed no hold on Seitz, and in June 2011 she became the first Senate-confirmed head of the Office of Legal Counsel since Jack Goldsmith had stepped down in 2004. It was no coincidence that 2004 was the year that the leaking of the first torture memos had placed a spotlight on the extraordinary power of that once-obscure office.

On September 30, an American drone strike in Yemen killed Anwar al-Awlaki, along with Samir Khan, another American citizen who helped make al-Qaeda in the Arabian Peninsula's propaganda magazine, *Inspire*, but who was not the target of the strike.* Later that morning, Obama hailed the killing of al-Awlaki in a carefully crafted statement that left ambiguous whether the American or the Yemeni government had fired the missile.[41] But it was widely reported that it had been an American operation.

Immediately, calls arose from lawmakers of both parties and from newspaper editorial boards for the Obama administration to disclose

---

* See chapter 6, section 17.

its legal reasoning so people could assess the precedent that the United States government had just established. But to say more to the American people, the government would have to violate its deal with Yemen. The word went out across the executive branch: stay silent.

I believed that the secrecy surrounding the killing of al-Awlaki raised a challenge to democratic accountability and America's system of self-government. Even if one concludes that killing al-Awlaki was legally and morally justified under the circumstances, the event established a precedent that altered the balance between the power of the presidency and the rights of individual citizens. For this legal shift to be or become legitimate, the American public needed to be able to debate it and to develop with their government a shared understanding of its limits.

I was not the only person who had that view. I spoke confidentially with people who had read Barron's long Office of Legal Counsel memo. By the end of the week, I was able to write a lengthy article piecing together a first public account of its analysis — including the information that it had addressed the statute prohibiting the murder of Americans overseas and identifying several of the key Supreme Court rulings on which it relied. I also reported on its estimated length, the rough time it was completed, the fact that Barron had signed it, and that he and Lederman had worked on it together.

The article appeared on the *New York Times* website on Saturday, October 8, and led the Sunday paper. Meanwhile, as I was completing the draft, I filed an information act request with the Justice Department seeking "all Office of Legal Counsel memorandums analyzing the circumstances under which it would be lawful for United States armed forces or intelligence community assets to target for killing a United States citizen who is deemed to be a terrorist."

Two weeks later, an American drone strike killed al-Awlaki's son Abdulrahman. Soon after, the American Civil Liberties Union filed a similar but broader information act request for records about killing citizens, seeking also drafts of legal memos, documents showing the bureaucratic decision-making process, and the intelligence behind the two strikes. On October 27, the Justice Department sent a response to me. They also sent a similar letter that same day to my colleague Scott Shane; back in June 2010 he had filed an information act request for all Office of Legal Counsel opinions since 2001 that addressed targeted killings in general — a request the government had been ignoring for over a year. They denied us both. They told Scott that they could acknowledge only that a Defense Department memo existed that was responsive to his request for targeted killing memos in general, but it was exempt from disclosure. To me, they said that the department "neither confirms nor denies the existence of the documents described in your request" for memos about killing American citizens, specifically.[42]

This was a so-called *Glomar* response, named for the *Glomar Explorer,* a supposed deep-sea drilling vessel that was actually built for a 1974 CIA operation to recover a sunken Soviet submarine. A journalist sued the CIA under the information act for any documents about the *Glomar.* The agency persuaded a court that it could lawfully respond by neither confirming or denying that it had any such documents. This added a judicially created gloss on the plain text of the information act, which says agencies must produce a list of responsive records even if it wants to claim that they are exempt from disclosure.[43] The idea was that if the agency even acknowledged having records about the *Glomar,* that would implicitly reveal that it was indeed related to a secret CIA operation.

Now, the Obama administration was telling us it could not let the public know whether the Justice Department lawyers had even considered the question of killing citizens, let alone what their analysis was.

On November 14, it rejected the American Civil Liberties Union's request too.

9. Talking About Killing Citizens

Congress was ratcheting up pressure on the Obama team to be more forthcoming, too. On November 7, 2011, Senator Patrick Leahy, the

Judiciary Committee chairman, confronted Holder at an oversight hearing and demanded that he show lawmakers the al-Awlaki memo. Holder replied that he "cannot address whether or not there is an opinion on this area."

Inside the administration, a debate raged over how to say more, officials told me. Some senior lawyers — Koh at State and Johnson at the Pentagon — argued that the administration needed to be much more forthright and open. But Preston and Litt, the top lawyers for the CIA and the Office of the Director of National Intelligence — opposed explicitly acknowledging the al-Awlaki strike. Seitz, at the Office of Legal Counsel, did not want to share the actual al-Awlaki memos with Congress, lest that establish a precedent eroding the confidentiality of such documents. And Ruemmler, the White House counsel, worried that giving the public too much information could make it harder to defend against future lawsuits, including those being brought under the Freedom of Information Act.

At a principals committee meeting in November, cabinet and agency heads echoed those positions. Napolitano, the secretary of Homeland Security, argued that the calls for transparency were quieting and that releasing anything more would just rev up new controversy.[44] The choice about how much to reveal came down to what McDonough, who was now deputy national security adviser, dubbed the Full Monty or the Half Monty, after the British comedy about male strippers — *full* and *half* referring to how much they revealed. Here, the Full Monty meant openly acknowledging the killing and showing the long al-Awlaki memo to Congress and a redacted version to the public. (Koh pushed for this position so hard that McDonough rechristened it the Full Harold, according to a later account by Daniel Klaidman.) The Half Monty meant explaining the administration's legal thinking about targeting citizens but not putting out the memo.

One Half Monty option was to write a new white paper that could be made public. As early as October 8, according to later court filings, attorneys at the Office of Legal Counsel began e-mailing one another about drafting a new one summarizing its analysis on targeting citizens.

The new white paper, unlike the one produced for Wyden the previous May, was unclassified—stripped of any intelligence about al-Awlaki or references to Yemen. They finished the draft on November 8 and circulated it for discussion, but ultimately shelved it. The administration later shared it with Congress, and someone eventually slipped it to NBC News.

Another Half Monty option was to publish an op-ed column under Holder's name that would lay out, in even broader strokes, a basic defense of the policy. Stuart Delery, Holder's aide, began drafting such a column. But it got too long for that format, and evolved into a potential speech instead.

On December 20, the *New York Times* filed a lawsuit based on Shane's and my information act requests. The American Civil Liberties Union filed a similar but broader lawsuit the following February. They were both assigned to Judge Colleen McMahon, a 1998 Clinton appointee.

Meanwhile, interagency deliberations were delaying and watering down Holder's potential speech. Delery's original draft, for example, openly discussed the fact that the United States had killed al-Awlaki. But that part was stripped out. Months were passing, and the Justice Department had not scheduled a venue for Holder to deliver it. Lawmakers were growing restless at the administration's continued public silence.

"The federal government's official views about the President's authority to kill specific Americans who have not necessarily been convicted of a crime are not a matter to be settled in secret by a small number of government lawyers," Wyden wrote in a February 2012 public letter to Holder. "Instead, the government's interpretation of relevant statutory and constitutional protections should be public knowledge, so that they can be publicly debated and understood."[45]

As the Justice Department stalled, Johnson took matters into his own hands. He leapfrogged over Holder and gave a speech at Yale Law School on national security legal policy in which he became the first administration official to publicly address the issue in any detail. "Belligerents who also happen to be U.S. citizens do not enjoy immunity where noncitizen belligerents are valid military objectives," Johnson said, adding that the war against al-Qaeda was not limited to the "hot" battlefield zone of Afghanistan.[46]

Holder finally delivered his own speech the next month at Northwestern University, and went a little bit further in explaining the executive branch's thinking.

"Some have argued that the president is required to get permission from a federal court before taking action against a United States citizen who is a senior operational leader of al-Qaeda or associated forces," Holder said. "This is simply not accurate. 'Due process' and 'judicial process' are not one and the same, particularly when it comes to national security. The Constitution guarantees due process, not judicial process."[47]

The Obama administration celebrated Holder's speech as fulfilling its need to be transparent. But, as Judge McMahon later put it in her ruling in our information act case seeking the real memo, "no lawyer worth his salt would equate Mr. Holder's statements with the sort of robust analysis that one finds in a properly constructed legal opinion addressed to a client by a lawyer...when you really dissect the speech, all it does is recite general principles of law and the government's legal conclusions."[48]

10. Acknowledging Secret Wars

Members of Congress were not satisfied either, and the administration continued to debate saying more in the face of institutional resistance.

"There was continuous discussion of 'how can we be as transparent as possible' against bureaucratic and institutional pressure to say nothing more," one administration official told me. "The permanent bureaucracy gets nothing from transparency and sees it only in terms of risk—'This is FOIA, there is a one percent chance it could unravel everything.' The political appointees understand that you need public support for things, that public buy-in is valuable."

In theory, of course, the political appointees are in charge. But the Obama team hesitated.

In late April, John Brennan was scheduled to deliver a speech of his own at the Wilson Center, setting up another potential Monty moment. His aide, Nate Jones, wrote two versions of the speech — a top secret "code-word" draft few had clearance to see, and an unclassified version. But Brennan delivered the latter one. His speech made a case that broader transparency was in the national security interest — that silence creates a void that becomes "filled with myths and falsehoods," eroding support with the public and foreign partners. But its only notable disclosure was the first direct acknowledgment of the fact that the United States used drones to kill specific people away from hot battlefields.

"Yes, in full accordance with the law, and in order to prevent terrorist attacks on the United States and to save American lives, the United States government conducts targeted strikes against specific al-Qaeda terrorists, sometimes using remotely piloted aircraft, often referred to publicly as drones," he said. "And I'm here today because President Obama has instructed us to be more open with the American people about these efforts."[49]

From inside the government, it had been a major bureaucratic heave to declassify this fact. From the outside, it was like acknowledging, with great fanfare, that the Washington Monument is tall. Brennan did not say that the United States had killed al-Awlaki, his son, or Samir Khan. He did not say how many terrorists it believed it had intentionally killed, nor how many civilians it believed it had killed as collateral damage. He did not identify the countries in which the United States used armed drones. And in talking about strikes targeted at specific terrorists, he did not acknowledge that the CIA was also using signature strikes to kill groups of suspected militants in tribal Pakistan whose identities it did not specifically know.

Six weeks later, the internal Monty deliberations prompted the administration to give another inch. On June 15, Obama declassified the unofficially well-known fact that the U.S. military had taken "direct action" against al-Qaeda members in Somalia and Yemen. The disclosure, which made no mention of the CIA, was part of a semiannual War Powers Resolution letter to Congress describing military deployments.[50] The disclosure meant lawmakers could now openly discuss the basic fact that the United States military was engaged in wartime actions in those two countries.

On June 20, the Justice Department filed a motion to dismiss the al-Awlaki information act lawsuits. Two days later, it pulled out the unclassified white paper it had prepared the previous fall and shared it with the Judiciary Committees, hoping that would satisfy their demands to see the real legal memos.[51] Even though it was unclassified, the lawmakers were told they could not share it with the public.

11. Chilling the Candor

On January 4, 2012, during the Senate's month-long winter break, Obama made four recess appointments, opening a new front in the wars over executive power. The Constitution empowers presidents to appoint executive-branch officials without Senate confirmation if Congress is in recess. Obama's move was controversial because the Senate was sending a lawmaker into its empty chamber every third day to bang the gavel, technically turning its long vacation into a string of three-day vacations, each considered too brief for recess appointments. Obama said these "pro forma" sessions were a sham and the Senate was actually on a single lengthy vacation, so he could use his recess powers. The move led to a fight over executive-branch lawyering that illustrated why some in the government do not want to make their internal legal memos public.

To bolster support for Obama's move, the White House took the rare step of voluntarily making public an Office of Legal Counsel memo saying that he had the legal authority to make these appointments. Written by Seitz and addressed to Ruemmler, it concluded that it was within the president's lawful power to deem that the Senate was functionally not in session—even though the Senate formally maintained that it was meeting every third day—and then exercise his powers which exist only during a recess.[52]

Ruemmler had already publicly disclosed the outlines of the administration's legal reasoning in an interview with me.[53] But the political reaction to seeing the actual memo was explosive. Senator Chuck Grassley, the ranking Republican on the Judiciary Committee, went to the Senate floor to denounce Seitz by name, calling her opinion "preposterous" and "entirely unconvincing" and portraying her as "a lackey for the administration."

"I gave the president and Ms. Seitz the benefit of the doubt in voting to confirm her nomination," he said. "However, after reading this misguided and dangerous legal opinion, I'm sorry the Senate confirmed her. It's likely to be the last confirmation she ever experiences."[54]

Grassley's raw threat—essentially, *Forget about ever becoming a judge, Seitz*—vividly illustrated the fears of those who supported keeping Office of Legal Counsel memos secret, chief among them Ruemmler and Seitz herself. Without an expectation of secrecy, ambitious lawyers might refuse to work at the Office of Legal Counsel. Or they might pull their punches on questions about where congressional power stops and executive power begins, even when there was a plausible argument that would allow the president, their client, to do what he wanted to do. However, greater risk aversion might not be such a bad thing; in June 2014, all nine Supreme Court justices agreed that Obama's recess appointments had been unconstitutional.*

The recess-appointments memo was interesting for another reason. It cited two Bush-era Office of Legal Counsel memos analyzing recess appointments, neither of which the public had known existed. I filed a request to make them public, but the Justice Department rejected it. The administration was treating them as legal precedents, but the public could not read them.

---

* See chapter 12, section 8.

This denial alone was notable. Back on July 16, 2010, Barron's last day running the Office of Legal Counsel before his return to Harvard Law School (and the same day he signed the longer al-Awlaki memo), he had signed a memo called "Best Practices for OLC Legal Advice and Written Opinions."[55]

Among other things, Barron said there would be a "presumption that it should make its significant opinions fully and promptly available to the public." And, he said, when someone made an information act request for an unpublished memo, the office should seriously consider disclosing it even if it was technically covered by an exception to the information act. In particular, Barron wrote, the office should not withhold an opinion "because of speculative or abstract fears," quoting Obama's January 21, 2009, order on transparency.

Still, Barron's edict made exceptions for classified information and preserving internal deliberations and confidential attorney-client information. The question was how broadly his successors would interpret those exceptions.

Seeking to test "secret law" outside the context of a classified national security secret, David McCraw, the *Times'* lawyer who was handling all these information act lawsuits, and I filed another lawsuit for the old recess appointment memos. The case was assigned to Judge Jed Rakoff, a 1996 Clinton appointee and former Justice Department prosecutor. The Justice Department urged him to toss out our lawsuit, once again citing the potential for legal advice to be chilled if the attorneys had to be concerned about public disclosure.[56]

Rakoff dismissed our case.[57]

Indeed, it became increasingly clear that Barron's exception had swallowed the rule: the Obama administration evidently considered *every* Office of Legal Counsel memo to be exempt from compelled disclosure under the information act, as they were all, by definition, internal deliberative materials and covered by attorney-client privilege. It fought in court to embed that principle into law—and it largely succeeded.[58]

12. Fast and Furious (Executive Privilege III)

Obama's decision to disclose the Bush-era torture memos in April 2009 was becoming a distant memory. And the change in attitude about being more transparent regarding Office of Legal Counsel memos was not the only early Obama view on secrecy that was evolving. A politically charged dispute with House Republicans over an oversight probe into a botched gun-trafficking case led to Obama's first invocation of executive privilege. Obama did so in a way that seemed to exceed the limits of executive power that he had articulated back when he was still a senator and was seeking the presidency.

The dispute centered on Operation Fast and Furious, an investigation by the Bureau of Alcohol, Tobacco, Firearms and Explosives, or ATF, into a Mexican drug cartel's gun-smuggling network in Arizona. The network purchased weapons in American gun stores using "straw buyers" — people who could pass a background check and who were paid to make the transaction and pretend the guns were for their personal use — and then funneled them across the border to Mexico, which has much stricter gun restrictions. Hoping to build a bigger case, the ATF passively monitored the network, keeping track of serial numbers of weapons purchased by suspects to trace where they went. This tactic of "letting guns walk" contradicted ATF policy of interdicting illegal weapons at the earliest opportunity. As a result, several thousand guns crossed the border and began showing up at crime scenes; two were found after a shoot-out in which an American Border Patrol agent was killed. In a letter to Congress responding to an inquiry from Grassley soon after that killing, the Justice Department falsely stated, based on erroneous assurances from the field, that "A.T.F. makes every effort to interdict weapons that have been purchased illegally and prevent their transportation to Mexico."[59]

The House Oversight Committee, led by Representative Darrell Issa, Republican from California, launched an investigation into Fast and Furious. Republicans pursued a theory that Holder had sanctioned the

ATF's reckless tactics and was trying to cover it up. The Justice Department's false claim in its early letter to Grassley provided a hook for that theory. Many Republicans called for Holder's resignation. However, a 471-page report by the department's independent inspector general showed that poorly supervised Arizona-based ATF agents had been using such reckless tactics since 2006 without high-level sanction.[60] That did not end the controversy, however.

The dispute evolved into a fight over the right of congressional overseers to obtain information that the executive branch wanted to keep secret. The committee subpoenaed all internal Justice Department documents about Fast and Furious — not just about the now-shuttered ATF operation itself, but documents related to the committee's subsequent probe of it. James Cole, the deputy attorney general, decided to turn over troves of documents about the operation as well as internal e-mails showing how Justice Department officials had come to draft the erroneous line in the letter to Congress. But Cole refused to turn over internal e-mails dated after that letter. The Justice Department maintained that Congress had no right to see them and that it would cripple the institution's ability to use e-mail if officials knew that Congress might someday compel the government to turn over their internal messages.

Issa threatened to hold Holder in criminal contempt of Congress for not turning over the rest. Holder, telling Issa he wanted to "buy peace," offered to make what he called a "fair compilation" of the additional documents available if Issa would first permanently cancel a contempt vote. But Issa declined to give up his leverage for the documents "sight unseen," as he later explained in a letter to Obama.[61] Historically, such disputes have usually ended in a compromise. But Obama officials distrusted Issa just as much as Issa distrusted them. Ron Weich, the assistant attorney general for legislative affairs, who had signed but not written the faulty letter to Congress, told his colleagues that their hopes for finding an accommodation to defuse the crisis were naive, as he later recounted to me.

They want the contempt vote for their own purposes. If we give them 99.9 percent, they will hold a contempt vote over the 0.1 percent, Weich argued.

The two branches of government were on a collision course.

The executive branch has a trump card in secrecy disputes with Congress: it is a crime to refuse to comply with a valid congressional subpoena, but only the Justice Department can decide whether to prosecute a crime. Invoking executive privilege would provide a basis to refuse to refer any congressional criminal contempt citation to a grand jury for indictment. The department could say that the subpoena was invalid because Congress was trying to obtain information that it had no constitutional right to extract from the executive branch.

But it was far from clear that executive privilege extended to all the e-mails the Justice Department was withholding from Congress. Legal specialists widely agree that communications involving the president or his close White House aides are covered, but there is far less support for the idea that Congress has no right to subpoena the files of an executive-branch agency. In my 2007 executive power survey for the *Boston Globe,* Obama said he believed that "executive privilege generally depends on the involvement of the President and the White House."[62]

President Obama's legal team had a broader view of the privilege than Senator Obama had espoused. Seitz, the head of the Office of Legal Counsel, told her colleagues that she was confident that executive privilege covered deliberative materials in agency files, even though they did not involve the White House. Still, she cautioned that the case was not as strong for other internal agency communications, such as e-mails inviting people to meetings. Those files would show who had participated in deliberations, but not what they said.

The Office of Legal Counsel drafted a memo for Holder advising that an assertion of executive privilege was legally defensible. Ruemmler, Obama's White House counsel, and Bill Daley, his chief of staff, met with Obama in the Oval Office on the evening of June 19 to talk about it.

Obama asked Ruemmler what the documents were, what the principle was, and whether she had seen any support for the idea that the Justice Department was covering up wrongdoing. Ruemmler told him she had not seen any evidence of a cover-up in looking through the documents, and that they were mostly memos about other memos. She also told him that it would erode the separation of powers if Congress could get at internal executive-branch conversations responding to congressional investigations in real time.

Obama invoked the privilege. On party lines, Issa's committee voted to recommend citing Holder for criminal contempt of Congress, and a week later the full House of Representatives did so — even as most Democrats walked out in protest.[63] This was the first time in American history Congress so sanctioned a sitting member of a president's cabinet.

The House referred its contempt citation of Holder to a prosecutor. But Cole announced that the Justice Department would not indict its attorney general because it was not a crime to withhold subpoenaed documents over which the president had asserted executive privilege. This was the third time that the executive branch had refused to take a congressional contempt citation of an executive-branch official to a grand jury, joining a 1982 dispute involving a subpoena to an Environmental Protection Agency leader in the Reagan administration and a 2008 dispute related to the mass firing of United States attorneys in the Bush-Cheney administration. This emerging pattern, the constitutional scholar Lou Fisher later observed, is gradually eroding the power of a threatened contempt citation by Congress to persuade the executive branch to turn over documents.[64]

House Republicans filed a civil lawsuit asking a judge to enforce the subpoena. It was assigned to Judge Amy Berman Jackson, a 2011 Obama appointee. Justice Department lawyers asked her to throw it out. Congressional lawyers denied the existence of any *agency deliberations privilege* to block congressional subpoenas. The scant prospects of political compromise created the conditions for a rare judicial determination clarifying the scope and limits of executive privilege.

In August 2014, Jackson delivered the first major ruling in the case.[65]

It was a split decision. She rejected the congressional argument that *only* White House communications could be shielded. But she also rejected as "unsustainable" the executive branch's argument that it could withhold *all* internal agency files, whether deliberative or not. She required the Justice Department to produce a detailed log of all the communications it was withholding. Those that were not deliberative, she said, had to be turned over. In practical terms, this ruling, wrote Andy Wright — a former associate White House counsel in the Obama administration, now working as a law professor — "pierces the Executive Branch firewall" by revealing to Congress who was talking to whom about the topic.[66]

Rather than appealing, the Justice Department turned over sixty-four thousand such e-mails on November 3, 2014 — Election Day. By then, Holder had announced he would resign upon the confirmation of his successor. The documents did not contradict the inspector general's conclusion that there had been no high-level sanction for the Arizona agents' tactics. But they showed Holder making hotheaded remarks to his colleagues, such as "Issa and his idiot cronies never gave a damn about this when all that was happening was that thousands of Mexicans were being killed with guns from our country. All they want to do — in reality — is cripple the A.T.F. and suck up to the gun lobby. Politics at its worst — maybe the media will get it."[67] The public exposure of such undiplomatic private comments was potentially embarrassing, but, according to Jackson, Obama had had no legal right to keep them secret from Congress.

13. "Alice in Wonderland"

On January 2, 2013, McMahon ruled that the Obama administration could keep its al-Awlaki–related memos secret. But her opinion — rejecting the Freedom of Information Act lawsuit the *New York Times* had brought on behalf of Shane and myself, as well as the parallel case brought by the American Civil Liberties Union — also signaled that she was deeply uncomfortable with ruling against us.[68]

"The Alice-in-Wonderland nature of this pronouncement is not lost on me," the judge wrote. But, she said, "I can find no way around the thicket of laws and precedents that effectively allow the executive branch of our government to proclaim as perfectly lawful certain actions that seem on their face incompatible with our Constitution and laws while keeping the reasons for their conclusion a secret."

McMahon did not read the memos before rendering her judgment, saying their contents were irrelevant to the question of whether the government had to disclose them. But in dicta — side commentary that went beyond the core legal holding — she made clear that she believed that the public *should* be allowed to assess the administration's legal reasoning. Making Obama officials wince, her ruling raised the foreign-killings statute and suggested that Obama might have authorized a murder. Barron's longer memo had mustered lengthy arguments about why that statute did not apply, but the administration was keeping that legal reasoning secret.

On February 1, the *Times* filed notice that it would appeal her ruling. Three days later, the reporter Michael Isikoff, then working for NBC News, published the second Obama administration white paper about the targeted killing of citizens — the unclassified one, which the administration had shared with the Judiciary Committees.[69] Someone had leaked it on the eve of a Senate debate about whether to confirm Obama's counterterrorism adviser, Brennan, to be the next director of the CIA.

Back in 2012, after a congressional letter had mentioned the existence of the second white paper (though it was not yet known that there was also an earlier, classified one), both Shane and the independent journalist Jason Leopold had requested a copy of it under the Freedom of Information Act. On January 23, 2013, the Justice Department sent Shane a letter rejecting his request. After NBC News published the leaked version of it, Shane complained to the Justice Department and the White House that the administration was violating Obama's 2009 anti-secrecy directive. Two days later, Melanie Pustay, the director of the Justice Department's Office of Information Policy, wrote back to Shane and said that in light of the leak, the Justice Department "is making a discretionary release of the record." A copy of the white paper was included.

Leopold received a similar letter and immediately uploaded the paper, allowing the public to read a clean version. NBC News, apparently to ensure that other news organizations would have to credit it for Isikoff's scoop, had unfortunately stamped its logo all over Isikoff's version, making it hard to read certain words. At first, that small victory for literal transparency seemed to be the only consequence, since the paper was already unofficially public in defaced form. But the fact that it had now been *officially* disclosed would turn out to have a dramatic legal impact.

14. #standwithrand

The sight of the unclassified white paper renewed bipartisan cries in Congress for the Obama administration to let lawmakers read the real Justice Department legal analysis about killing al-Awlaki. Because Brennan's nomination was pending, the Senate had leverage: lawmakers could hold up a confirmation vote if they did not get the memos. On February 6, the administration finally admitted that it had written an Office of Legal Counsel memo about the targeting of citizens — two of them, in fact — and directed the Justice Department to show them to the House and Senate Intelligence Committees, but not the rest of Congress. It also became clear that there were seven other memos about targeted killings. Feinstein said they would keep pressing for access to the rest but supported moving forward on Brennan.[70]

Some lawmakers who were not members of the Intelligence Committee were not satisfied. On February 20, Senator Rand Paul, the libertarian-leaning Republican from Kentucky, sent Brennan a letter asking whether Brennan believed that "the president has the power to authorize lethal force, such as a drone strike, against a U.S. citizen *on U.S. soil*, and without trial?"[71] (Emphasis added.) On March 4, Holder wrote back to Paul. The attorney general pointed out that such a thing had never happened and said that the Obama administration strongly believed it was better to incapacitate terrorists on domestic soil using law enforcement authorities, not military force. But Holder did not categorically rule it out, saying it was possible to imagine extraordinary circumstances in which the president would have the lawful power to authorize military force inside the United States. He cited emergencies like the Pearl Harbor attack of December 7, 1941, and 9/11.[72]

On the morning of March 6, Holder came before the Senate Judiciary Committee for an oversight hearing. Lawmakers of both parties criticized him for refusing to share the Office of Legal Counsel memos with them. Leahy, the chairman, said he was considering subpoenaing the executive branch to compel it to turn over the documents, which he had been seeking for more than a year.[73]

"I am not alone in my frustration or in my waning patience," Leahy said.

Picking up on Paul's theme, Senator Ted Cruz, Republican from Texas, pressed Holder to say more about when the administration believed it could use military force on domestic soil. Cruz raised a hypothetical situation in which a terrorism suspect presented no immediate threat — someone who was "sitting in a café" rather than "pointing a bazooka at the Pentagon" — and asked whether it would be unconstitutional for the military to simply kill that citizen. Holder repeatedly said that it would not be "appropriate" for the government to do that. He went back and forth with Cruz, who pressed him to say whether it would be *legal* for the government to do that and, with exasperation, said it was "remarkable" that Holder would not give a simple answer.

"You keep saying 'appropriate,' " Cruz said. "My question isn't about propriety. My question is about whether something is constitutional or not."

Finally, Holder said: "Let me be clear: Translate my 'appropriate' to 'no.' I thought I was saying 'no,' all right? No."

Cruz said that he was glad that "after much gymnastics," he had obtained a clear answer. He said he would introduce a bill barring the use of drones to kill Americans on domestic soil, although Holder later said that might be an unconstitutional intrusion on presidential power. Underscoring the scrambled partisan lines on such issues, Senator Lindsey Graham later said that in an extreme situation like 9/11, it would be legal to use military force on domestic soil — for example, to shoot down a hijacked plane — notwithstanding the concerns of his "well-meaning" colleagues.

Cruz got his clear answer from Holder at 10:38 a.m. An hour and nine minutes later, at 11:47 a.m., Paul, who was not on the Judiciary Committee, began speaking on the Senate floor in opposition to Brennan's confirmation. He would not relinquish control of the floor for nearly thirteen hours, leading a rare "talking" filibuster. Paul's central complaint was that the administration was too secretive about when it could use drones to kill Americans and refused to lay out clearly what it believed the legal limits were.

"It is like pulling teeth to get any answer from the president," Paul said. "Why is that? Because he doesn't want to answer the question the way he should as a good and moral and upstanding person — someone who believes in the Constitution should — that absolutely no American should ever be killed in America who is sitting in a cafe. No American should ever be killed in their house without a warrant and some kind of aggressive behavior by them. There is nothing American about being bombed in one's sleep. There is nothing constitutional about that. The President says to trust him. He says he hasn't done it yet. He says he doesn't intend to do so but he might. That is just not good enough."[74]

As the hours passed, Paul denounced the Obama administration for its secrecy about its legal memos, its refusal to explain what happened with the killing of the sixteen-year-old American citizen Abdulrahman al-Awlaki, and the vague standards of its signature strikes. He also said things like declaring it an intolerable abomination that the United States government might use its drones to kill Americans "in a café in San Francisco or in a restaurant in Houston or at their home in Bowling Green, Kentucky." It was an unexpected, messy, galvanizing spectacle. No member of Congress talked so openly about these things, and certainly not a Republican. Paul finally yielded the floor after midnight, at 12:39 p.m. on March 7.

The performance captivated civil libertarians on the left and the right while scrambling the usual partisan allegiances. Twitter lit up with posts by people watching him on C-SPAN, many using the hashtag #standwithrand. (On March 8, Paul registered to trademark that phrase for bumper stickers, T-shirts, posters, and campaign-fund-raising purposes.[75]) Illustrating the factional confusion, during his filibuster, the official Twitter account for the conservative Heritage Foundation posted a tweet consisting of the #standwithrand hashtag and a picture of Paul talking; superimposed on it was a quote from his speech, "I will not sit quietly and let [Obama] shred the Constitution," and the Heritage Foundation logo.[76] It was retweeted by other users more than twelve hundred times. Yet Heritage's vice president and head of policy research was none other than David Addington, former Vice President Cheney's top counsel and chief of staff and, essentially, the personification of everything Paul opposed in matters of security state powers.

Similarly, while fellow Tea Party Republican senators like Cruz and Mike Lee, Republican from Utah, had joined with Paul, giving him respites during his filibuster by making extended remarks under the banner of asking him a question, national security hawk Republicans, like McCain and Graham, defended the drone program and criticized Paul's filibuster as scaremongering.

"We've done, I think, a disservice to a lot of Americans by making them think that somehow they're in danger from their government," McCain said in a March 7 floor speech. "They're not. But we are in danger from a dedicated, long-standing, easily replaceable-leadership enemy that is hellbent on our destruction."[77]

That same day, the Obama administration responded to Paul's thirteen-hour speech with a two-sentence letter to him, written by Holder, that echoed what Cruz had forced Holder to say an hour before the filibuster began. "It has come to my attention that you have now asked an additional question: 'Does the President have the authority to use a weaponized drone to kill an American not engaged in combat on American soil?'" he wrote. "The answer to that question is no."[78]

Paul declared the Obama administration's unequivocal acknowledgment of a limit on the president's power as "a major victory for American civil liberties and ensures the protection of our basic Constitutional rights."[79]

15. Voluntary Transparency

Back in February 2013, Obama participated in an online, Google-sponsored "fireside chat." One questioner noted he had campaigned on a promise to have the most transparent administration in history, but his record "just feels a lot less transparent than I think we had all hoped it would be." She asked, "How has the reality of the presidency changed that promise?"[80] The moment provided an opportunity for Obama to explain how he saw what he was doing and to evaluate it.

"Well, actually, on a whole bunch of fronts we've kept that promise," Obama replied. "This is the most transparent administration in history and I can document how that is the case. Everything from — every visitor that comes into the White House is now part of the public record — that's something that we changed.... There are a handful of issues, mostly around national security, where people have legitimate questions ... but some of these programs are still classified which mean that we might have shared them, for example, with the congressional intelligence office [*sic*] but they're not on the front pages."

It was true that the administration was periodically posting most

White House visitor logs. And it took other meaningful steps to improve transparency which must be taken into account when assessing his record on secrecy.

For example, in May 2010, the Department of Defense, for the first time ever, disclosed the size of the United States' nuclear arsenal — 5,119 warheads.[81] The Obama administration also released the first unclassified Nuclear Posture Review, which explains American policy on strategy and force structure.

Obama signed a law and issued a presidential policy directive increasing protections for government employees who went to Congress or inspectors general — though not to news reporters — with whistleblower concerns. [82]

While critics said overclassification remained a problem, the total number of newly created classified secrets dropped rapidly, from about 200,000 a year under Bush and in Obama's first years to just 46,800 in 2014.[83]

The administration sometimes disclosed internal e-mails in situations when it had made a false statement. (Doing so was in its interest because it enabled the Obama team to argue that they had not intentionally lied.) In December 2011, as mentioned, it turned over e-mails showing how it had drafted the incorrect letter about Fast and Furious to Congress. In the spring of 2013, it made public e-mails showing how early talking points about the September 11, 2012, attack in Benghazi were drafted before being given to Susan Rice, then the UN ambassador, to recite on television. Rice falsely portrayed the attack as a spontaneous mob protest about an anti-Islam video rather than a planned assault by Islamist militants.[84]

And even as the administration resisted efforts to compel it to turn over internal legal memos, it did seek other ways, such as white papers and speeches, to explain the broad outlines of some of its legal thinking.

The administration's resistance to disclosing Office of Legal Counsel memos also had exceptions. It published several high-profile memos shortly after they were signed, including memos about Obama's decision to participate in the Libya air war without congressional authorization in 2011, about his disputed recess appointments in 2012, and about sweeping executive actions he took in 2014 to shield certain categories of immigrants who were in the country illegally from deportation. Each was a politically controversial step, and the purpose of making the memos public was to help confer legal legitimacy on the policies.[85]

Still, a power principle complicated these moments of transparency. To the administration, they were voluntary acts of executive grace, not rules that the executive branch was bound to obey because the public or Congress had a *right* to know the information. When outside parties sought to *compel* the executive branch to disclose information, Obama fought to keep it secret and avoid creating a precedent that the presidency could be forced to turn over such records.

In that light, the administration's decision to post White House visitor logs, and Obama's later citation of that policy to rebut criticism that he was too secretive, merits closer scrutiny.

The issue traced back to information act lawsuits challenging the Bush-Cheney administration's policy of keeping certain White House visitor logs secret. A similar dispute arose midway through Obama's first year regarding visits by coal-industry and health-care executives, leading to another lawsuit by the government watchdog group called Citizens for Responsibility and Ethics in Washington. In September 2009, the administration announced that it would disclose those specific records and voluntarily start posting nearly all its logs going forward. The watchdog group dropped the case and praised Obama for bringing "a historic level of transparency to the White House."[86]

But another government watchdog group, Judicial Watch, filed an information act lawsuit to compel the White House to disclose all its other visitor logs from before September. The administration won an appeals court ruling stating that the White House could keep secret records of Oval Office visitors. Thus, even as Obama lauded his visitor-log policy, he also established in law that it is within a president's discretionary power to control whether such information is disclosed.

This meant, among other things, that he or a successor could selectively disobey the policy to keep some visitors a secret from the public, or revoke it and start keeping them all secret again at any time.

"This legal fight, in which President Obama is fighting tooth and nail against full disclosure under law of his White House visitors, further exposes his big lie that his administration is the most transparent in history," said Tom Fitton, the Judicial Watch president.[87]

The statements by Citizens for Responsibility and Ethics in Washington and Judicial Watch seemed like incompatible takes on Obama and the White House visitor logs. But they were both true. In another example of the complexities of Obama's approach, one has to disaggregate his aggressive push to establish that strong executive powers existed to control the disclosure of White House visitor logs from the fact that he chose to exercise that power in a transparent manner.

There was a major exception to this pattern. In response to the leaking of NSA documents by the former intelligence contractor Edward Snowden in 2013, many Freedom of Information Act lawsuits were filed against the government, including my cases with the *New York Times* seeking FISA Court rulings and surveillance-related inspector general reports. The administration decided to make a concerted effort to declassify intelligence documents about surveillance, including to show that there was significant oversight of the NSA. As a result it often did not fight those information act lawsuits. The resulting outflow of documents revealed many problems the NSA had experienced following the rules, and significant portions of Chapter 5 and Chapter 11 of this book are based on disclosures in those now-declassified files. Still, even though those disclosures *followed* FOIA lawsuits, the administration agreed to produce these files, thereby settling or mooting the lawsuits without reaching a point where a judge issued any order forcing it to do anything. In that sense, it was still voluntary.

This insight helps explain a certain perverse logic or irony of the Obama years. Several administration officials told me that one of the reasons it was being so secretive about its drone policies and the strike that killed al-Awlaki was that disclosing anything could undermine its defense against the information act lawsuits brought by the *Times* and the American Civil Liberties Union. In general, because litigation seeking the revelation of secrets is adversarial and precedent-driven, and because there has to be a winner and a loser, the government is usually going to try hard to win such cases in part to preserve its discretion over the next dispute.

Jameel Jaffer of the ACLU said he had heard the same explanation and found it "ridiculous."

"They would have been more transparent if only we hadn't asked them for information?" Jaffer said. "We shouldn't file FOIA requests because it may dissuade them from releasing information they'd otherwise release? Give me a break."

16. Lifting the Veil

Obama was constantly reaffirming his supposed aversion to secrecy. But even some of his closest allies and advisers were increasingly frustrated that Obama often did not back up his words with deeds.

On March 13, 2013, John Podesta, the chairman of the Center for American Progress and the head of Obama's 2008 transition team, blasted the White House for being too secretive about the targeted-killing memos. He accused the president of undermining checks and balances and "acting in opposition to the democratic principles we hold most important," adding that "protecting technical means, human sources, operational details and intelligence methods cannot be an excuse for creating secret law to guide our institutions."[88]

Soon after, Johnson — during a brief period as a private citizen between serving as Pentagon general counsel and Homeland Security secretary — delivered a speech criticizing the administration for being too opaque on matters like targeted killings using drone strikes.[89] The perverse results, he lamented, included the fact that Rand Paul could filibuster against the government's secrecy and be "compared in iconic terms to Jimmy Stewart." Holder's statement, Johnson added, "that the executive branch does not claim the authority to kill an American non-combatant—something that was not, is not, and should never be an issue—is big news and trumpeted as a major victory for congressional oversight." Meanwhile, leaks made the government look "undisciplined and hypocritical," leading to criticism like Judge McMahon's "Alice-in-Wonderland" quip.'

"The problem is that the American public is suspicious of executive power shrouded in secrecy," he said. "In the absence of an official picture of what our government is doing, and by what authority, many in the public fill the void by imagining the worst."

Two months later, ahead of his May 2013 speech on counterterrorism policy at National Defense University, Obama finally declassified the fact that the government had killed Anwar al-Awlaki, along with three other Americans who had not been "specifically targeted," in late-2011 drone strikes.*

In his speech, Obama explained that he had declassified the information "to facilitate transparency and debate on this issue and to dismiss some of the more outlandish claims that have been made. For the record, I do not believe it would be constitutional for the government to target and kill any U.S. citizen—with a drone, or with a shotgun—without due process, nor should any president deploy armed drones over U.S. soil. But when a U.S. citizen goes abroad to wage war against America and is actively plotting to kill U.S. citizens, and when neither the United States, nor our partners are in a position to capture him before he carries out a plot, his citizenship should no more serve as a shield than a sniper shooting down on an innocent crowd should be protected from a SWAT team."[90]

Obama also issued a classified policy memo calling for the eventual transfer of the CIA's drones to the military; the agency's drone program was still officially covert, so the policy was explained to reporters on background in the sort of briefing that critics of the criminal-leak crackdown considered hypocrisy. The policy also was said to create a

---

* See chapter 6, section 17.

presumption that if a citizen was targeted in the future, the military should handle it if possible. The aspiration behind both was transparency; it's easier to talk about military operations than covert actions.[91]

But in the months and years that followed, the transfer did not happen, and no explanation was given. And the government remained as opaque as ever about drone strikes, refusing to explain the basis of a strike, who the target had been, and whether there had been any civilian casualties in its view.

17. Safety in Silence

Meanwhile, the Obama administration continued to find new ways to tighten executive-branch control over information.

In June 2012, Clapper issued a new directive targeting leaks. It added a question to a lie-detector test that officials with security clearances must periodically undergo. Now they would be asked whether they had ever made an unauthorized disclosure to the news media. He also empowered the intelligence community's inspector general to continue investigating leaks even if the Justice Department said it was declining to bring charges.[92]

In March 2014, Clapper issued another new directive. It aimed at limiting contact between reporters and government officials who deal with matters of national security and foreign affairs.[93] The rules already barred officials from discussing classified information with reporters. But Clapper now barred employees of all seventeen intelligence agencies from speaking with journalists about *unclassified* intelligence-related information without advance permission. Employees of the agencies were also required to file a report every time they had an unplanned contact with a journalist.

And in April 2014, Clapper's office issued a new prepublication review policy for its current and former employees, revising the rules for books, opinion columns, speeches, term papers, and other unofficial writings. As a condition of receiving access to classified information, officials agree to follow certain rules for the rest of their lives to prevent them from disclosing secrets. But there had been a traditional work-around that allowed former employees to participate in public discussions about widely known but technically still-classified information: citing published news reports, including those that were based on leaks.

The new policy seemed to close that loophole, saying current and former employees "must not use sourcing that comes from known leaks, or unauthorized disclosures of sensitive information," lest their use of such information "confirm the validity of an unauthorized disclosure and cause further harm to national security." A violation of the new policy could lead to the loss of a security clearance, on which many former intelligence officials who were now contractors depended for their livelihood.[94] It caused an uproar among former officials, and Clapper's office slightly walked it back, saying in a new memo that employees might still "cite more generally to the media as long as by doing so they do not confirm classified information."[95]

But former officials were on notice. The ambiguous new policy, combined with the criminal-leak crackdown, made clear that the safest course was silence.

18. "A Welcome Development"

Our long fight to make the government disclose its legal analysis about killing an American citizen began to reach its climax on February 10, 2014, although we plaintiffs did not know it. On that date, the three-judge panel on the federal appeals court in New York that was hearing our appeal in the information act lawsuit — Jon Newman, José Cabranes, and Rosemary Pooler — quietly reached out to the Obama administration. The judges said they were going to rule that the government must make public the legal analysis portions of the main al-Awlaki memo.

Moreover, the judges said, the government could not continue to pretend that the facts that al-Awlaki had been killed in Yemen and that the CIA had played an operational role were secret.[96]

Over the next few months, the Justice Department and the court negotiated over which portions of the ruling and the al-Awlaki memo should be redacted in the publicly released versions, as well as what additional portions should be disclosed if the department ultimately did not appeal the panel's coming ruling. Finally, on April 21, 2014, the panel publicly filed its judgment. As it had promised the Justice Department it would do, many key portions of its opinion were redacted, and the memo itself stayed secret as well while the Obama administration decided whether to appeal. This ruling was greeted as an extraordinarily rare plaintiff victory in an information act lawsuit, especially one involving legal advice and a national security matter.

In a coincidence, the release of the opinion—and the starting of a clock for Verrilli, now the solicitor general, to decide whether to accept the judgment or appeal it—came just as the Senate was considering whether to confirm Barron, the memo's principal author, to be a judge on the federal appeals court in Boston.

Several libertarian-leaning senators of both parties, including Paul and Udall, threatened to obstruct Barron's confirmation if the administration did not release more of the memos for the Senate and the public. Other Republicans, like Cruz, said Barron was too liberal on other issues. It became clear Barron would need nearly every Democrat to vote yes to be confirmed.[97]

But the CIA, whose general counsel was now Caroline Krass, the former National Security Council and Office of Legal Counsel lawyer, pressured Verrilli to appeal and keep fighting to keep the al-Awlaki memo secret. But Verrilli argued that the intelligence community's continued resistance had become short-sighted. At this point, he argued, everyone on earth knew a CIA drone had killed al-Awlaki. If the executive branch insisted on taking it up to the Supreme Court, it could potentially be like the Pentagon Papers case, in which the Nixon administration had argued, implausibly, that it would damage national security to publish historical information about the Vietnam War. It was important, he said, for the executive branch to exercise a self-policing function, because if it presented a national security claim and lost, it would be harder to win the next time.

On May 20, Verrilli told the White House that the Justice Department would not appeal, but instead would comply with the ruling and put out the redacted memo. "This is a welcome development for government transparency and affirms that although the government does have the right to keep national security secrets, it does not get to have secret law," Udall said, adding the words the administration had hoped to hear: "With this decision, I am now able to support the nomination of David Barron to the federal bench."[98]

On May 22, the Senate voted fifty-three to forty-five to confirm Barron to be a federal appeals court judge.[99]

19. "A Significant and Disturbing Shift"

Three days later, on May 30, 2014, John P. Fitzpatrick, the top official in charge of the classified-information system, issued an important ruling in a dispute over war-zone photographs showing abuses by American forces. It completed a slide that had begun five years earlier, when Obama changed his mind about putting out the detainee-abuse pictures in the American Civil Liberties Union's information act lawsuit left over from the Bush administration.

The controversy over the new set of disputed photographs began in January 2012, when someone posted on YouTube a video showing some low-level Marines urinating on corpses of Taliban fighters in Afghanistan. A military investigator, looking into the video, had gathered a number of additional images taken by the Marines on their personal cameras. They showed troops posing with Taliban corpses. A general deemed the additional images "classified" out of fear that their publication could inflame attacks on American troops.[100]

A Marine lawyer, Major James Weirick, filed a whistleblower

complaint, saying that this use of the classified-information system was illegal under Obama's executive order governing secrecy. The order explicitly barred marking something classified to keep illegal or embarrassing official conduct secret from the public. But Fitzpatrick, the classified-information official (and a former Clapper aide), ruled that Weirick was wrong and that photos of war-zone abuses could be stamped *classified*. His reasoning was that there was a line in the order that said "force protection" is a valid basis for secrecy. That has been traditionally understood to mean things like security arrangements at bases or the scheduled times and locations of patrols. But he argued that photos of misbehavior by American troops counted as a force protection issue, too, because their disclosure might prompt reprisal attacks against other American troops.

I later spoke to a senior White House official about whether Fitzgerald's interpretation was, in fact, what Obama intended his executive order to mean. The official told me that there was no satisfying answer to that question. The ban on using the classified system to cover up embarrassing or illegal government acts was a holdover from previous iterations of the executive order establishing a classified information system. It had been written with the premise that the consequences of disclosing such things would be political criticism, oversight hearings, or maybe even prosecutions. Nobody was thinking about riots across the Muslim world. It was another example of a mismatch between the premises on which the rules were written and the realities of twenty-first-century problems.

J. William Leonard, who had directed the information office now run by Fitzgerald from 2002 to 2007, called the move "a significant and disturbing shift" in the government's secrecy policy. He noted that the new interpretation meant the special legislation Obama had obtained from Congress to block the release of the Bush-era detainee-abuse photographs back in 2009 had been unnecessary — the military could have just stamped them *classified* instead.

Weirick, too, expressed disappointment, telling me that the military now had justification to use the secrecy system to suppress information about any war-zone abuses by American forces in the future.

20. Disclosing the al-Awlaki Memo

On June 23, the appeals court panel in the information act lawsuit finally made the al-Awlaki memo public.

There were limits to the disclosure. All eleven pages laying out the intelligence about al-Awlaki remained secret. Large portions of the memo about the complexities raised by the possibility that the CIA, a civilian agency, might carry out the strike, rather than the military, also stayed redacted. Nonetheless, at long last, the American public saw the actual words that had opened the door to killing a citizen, from the analysis of the Bill of Rights to the worries about the statute barring the murder of an American on foreign soil. The memo also showed that the Justice Department had also been worried about another statute that prohibits people from conspiring on American soil to kill *anyone* overseas, which was not mentioned in my October 2011 article nor in the white paper.

The public could also see that Barron had addressed the objection that Yemen was not an armed-conflict zone, citing the work of Notre Dame law professor Mary Ellen O'Connell, a trenchant critic of the Obama administration's drone strikes, and disagreed with her views in light of al-Qaeda's activities there. When she read the memo, O'Connell criticized the brevity with which Barron had addressed her argument as "astonishing," given the issue's importance as a "linchpin" of his legal rationale.

However, other critics of the administration's secrecy, after reading the memo, pronounced themselves satisfied. These included Wyden and Udall. The executive branch had permitted the Intelligence Committee to read an unredacted version of the memo earlier, as part of the 2013 fight over confirming Brennan to be CIA director, and the two senators had sent a letter to Holder afterward. To them, the Obama administration's secrecy was the objectionable thing, not the legal analysis about killing al-Awlaki, given the circumstances.

"Having carefully reviewed the matter, we believe that the decision to use lethal force against Anwar al-Awlaki was a legitimate use of the authority granted to the President," they wrote, saying al-Awlaki had "made himself a legitimate target for military action" and that the strike was "consistent with applicable international law."[101]

Later, the court case resulted in the release to the public of a heavily redacted version of Barron and Lederman's original memo about al-Awlaki—the short one that overlooked the foreign-murder statute. As with the torture debate after the April 2009 release of the Office of Legal Counsel memos, the controversy over the al-Awlaki killing would continue. But at least now the public would be better informed about it, enabling more meaningful conversation, understanding, and self-government.[102]

21. Victory or Defeat?

The basis for the appeals court decision that forced the Obama administration to disclose the al-Awlaki memo was that the administration had made so much of its legal analysis public in other forms that it could no longer pretend that similar information in the memo was still classified. That reasoning may have resulted in a victory for public disclosure in this case, but it also created an unfortunate incentive for future government secrecy.

The most notable revelation cited by the court was that the executive branch had officially released the second white paper on killing citizens to Leopold and Shane in February 2013, after someone had leaked a copy to Isikoff. As a result, the judges said, "The government may no longer validly claim that the legal analysis in the memorandum is a secret." The court also found that so many officials had acknowledged in various forums that the CIA had played a role in killing al-Awlaki, and that his death took place in Yemen, that those facts "no longer merit secrecy" either.

Some commentators celebrated this outcome as a rebuke to selective disclosure, the flipside of secrecy in the executive branch's power to control information. By keeping the full accounting of an event or document secret but releasing tidbits, government officials are able to put their policies in the most favorable light. Jaffer, the lawyer for the American Civil Liberties Union, which filed the parallel information act lawsuit for the al-Awlaki-related memos and shared equal credit for the outcome, focused on this upbeat interpretation.

"This is a resounding rejection of the government's effort to use secrecy, and selective disclosure, as a means of manipulating public opinion about the targeted killing program," he said.[103]

But skeptics said that even though it looked like a victory for transparency, the ruling also contained seeds of its long-term defeat. The few scraps of information the Obama administration had allowed Congress and the public to receive during its long, hard secrecy fight were the keys to its ultimate loss in court. Had Holder and the other officials not made those speeches, had the Justice Department not officially released the white paper, the appeals court ruling would have gone the other way. The lesson for the future was clear: be even more secretive, and use only unofficial, anonymous leaks when communicating anything to the public.

"In the long term, [the al-Awlaki memo ruling] will dis-incentivize *any* disclosure of secret legal rationales, lest even fairly limited disclosures empower FOIA-based arguments such as those upon which the Court of Appeals seized," wrote Steve Vladeck, an American University law professor.[104]

Indeed, Neil Eggleston, who succeeded Ruemmler as White House counsel midway through May 2014, swiftly issued instructions to the Obama legal team: throttle back the legal policy speeches, and no more white papers. Our Freedom of Information Act victory may have ended up making the "most transparent administration in history" more opaque.

PART IV

AMERICAN-STYLE DEMOCRACY

10

Wounds That Won't Heal (Captives 2011–2015)

1. The Romney Interrogation Memo

As Obama's first term wound down, torture seemed to be a dead issue. While people were still fighting over what history should say about the Bush-era past, the live debate centered on whether or when government interrogators should read Miranda warnings to newly captured terrorism suspects — not whether the government should torture them. But behind the scenes, influential voices were quietly planning to revive an enhanced-interrogation technique program. In assessing the legal-policy struggles and compromises of the Obama era, a parallel moment from Mitt Romney's presidential campaign offers a point of comparison.

By the fall of 2011, the Republican establishment was coalescing around Romney. Romney's primary campaign had organized a "national security law subcommittee" to provide legal-policy advice to him. It included fourteen Bush-Cheney administration veterans, including Michael Chertoff, Bush's Homeland Security secretary, Charles Stimson, Bush's top Pentagon detainee-policy official, and Steven Bradbury, who had led Bush's second-term Office of Legal Counsel. It also included several other notable hawkish conservative lawyers, including David Rivkin, an outspoken defender of executive power in national security matters who had served in the Bush-Quayle White House. The subcommittee developed several unsigned policy memos to shape

Romney's views and provide a blueprint of what he should do if he defeated Obama and became the forty-fifth president.

One Romney campaign memo, completed by the national security law subcommittee in September 2011, was called "Interrogation Techniques."[1] The campaign did not intend for the public to see it, but someone later gave me a copy. Romney's legal team urged him to pledge that, if elected, he would "rescind and replace President Obama's executive order" limiting all interrogators to techniques found in the army field manual and once again authorize secret "enhanced interrogation techniques against high-value detainees that are safe, legal and effective in generating intelligence to save American lives." The memo argued that Obama's approach had "hampered (or will hamper) the fight against terrorism" by forbidding techniques "that we should feel, as a nation, that we have a right to use against our enemies." If Romney did not promise to bring an enhanced-interrogation program back, they wrote, he would show "insufficient zeal for doing whatever it takes to protect America."

The memo writers also telegraphed that they anticipated, and were preparing to wage, a bureaucratic struggle over reviving the program once they were in power as part of a Romney administration legal team. They warned that any "reluctance by the Governor to expressly endorse such an outcome during the campaign could become a self-fulfilling prophecy once he takes office by signaling to the bureaucracy that this is not a deeply-felt priority."

The memo underscored something about how the American government really works that I did not understand until I came to Washington. For all the focus the media and historians tend to put on presidents as individuals — Bush did this, Obama did that — the world and the government are so complicated that a single person cannot pay attention to all of it. Presidents set the tone and the priorities, and they usually are the ones who make the very biggest decisions. But the overwhelming majority of what an administration does takes place in the trenches of the executive-branch bureaucracy. Dozens or hundreds of officials whose names are unknown to the public and who rarely show up in history books make decisions every day about matters that most likely will never be brought to the president's personal attention or that may be discussed only briefly in the Oval Office at a ten-thousand-foot level. Moreover, while presidents tend to surround themselves with personal loyalists at the very top, just below that level the same basic two pools of political appointees run the show; control of the executive branch is traded between Team Republican and Team Democrat. Many members of Obama's administration had previously served in the Clinton administration, and many Bush-Cheney veterans will work for the next Republican president.

Romney had not been part of the Bush-Cheney administration and he had no personal reason to make it a priority to vindicate its interrogation practices — to show that the United States should "feel" that it has a right, and therefore implicitly had one back then, too, to use those techniques against enemy prisoners. His legal-policy advisers privately conceded that "it is difficult to point to *concrete* ways in which the Obama administration's renunciation of enhanced interrogation techniques has undermined America's efforts in the fight against terrorism." They also acknowledged that Romney could instead say only that, if elected, he would review interrogation policy under Bush and Obama to see if there were additional techniques that would be both legal and effective, an alternative option that would present the candidate as "open-minded and empirically driven."

Nevertheless, Romney's expert advisers were telling him in the strongest terms that it would be better for him to promise right away to revive the program. On December 17, 2011, Romney embraced their thinking as his own. The occasion was a town-hall-style campaign event in Charleston, South Carolina. Asked about his views on waterboarding, Romney replied that he would "do what is essential to protect the lives of the American people," although he would "not authorize torture." Since many Bush-Cheney officials made the semantic argument that the suffering they had approved inflicting on captives to force them to talk was not "torture," a reporter afterward pressed Romney to clarify whether he thought waterboarding was torture.

"I don't," Romney said. He added: "We'll have a policy of doing what we think is in our best interest. We'll use enhanced interrogation techniques which go beyond those that are in the military handbook right now."[2]

2. Mandatory Military Detention

Ever since the Christmas underwear-bomb attack, legal policy about terrorism captives had taken on a partisan sheen. Congressional Republicans had coalesced around the view that military detention, interrogation, and prosecution should be the exclusive method of handling captured terrorists — not FBI interrogations and the civilian criminal justice system. In late 2011, this recurring debate led to a milestone in Obama's growing willingness to make aggressive use of executive powers to circumvent Congress on what the rules should be for handling terrorism captives.

As Congress prepared to pass the annual National Defense Authorization Act, the top Democrat and Republican on the Senate Armed Services Committee, Carl Levin and John McCain, struck a deal. Cutting out the Obama administration from their negotiations, Levin agreed to a provision requiring the government to place *all* newly captured noncitizen al-Qaeda suspects in military custody. Because Republicans controlled the House, if the Democratic-controlled Senate could agree on such a provision, it would certainly be included in the final bill. And if it became law, the provision could completely upend Obama's policy of handling terrorism investigations that arise on domestic soil exclusively with civilian law enforcement procedures, one of his key national security principles.

The original version of the provision, approved by the Senate Armed Services Committee in June 2011, said simply that any noncitizen al-Qaeda suspect shall be held in military custody, period.[3] The administration opposed this provision, but for several months the bill stalled out in Congress. In October, Jeh Johnson, the Pentagon lawyer, delivered a speech before the conservative Heritage Foundation in which he warned against "the danger of over-militarizing our approach to al-Qaeda." The speech singled out the mandatory military detention provision. While "some of my friends" in Congress believed it was meant to apply only to terrorists "captured in the course of hostilities," Johnson said, "read literally" it could apply even to people arrested by the FBI inside the United States.

"Must the agent stop a very revealing and productive interrogation and go call the army to take the suspect away?" Johnson asked.[4]

In mid November, Levin and McCain announced a revised bill. It altered the provision's language.[5] Now the mandatory military custody requirement explicitly said it applied only to those al-Qaeda terrorists who were "captured in the course of hostilities." But even after the change, Lisa Monaco, the head of the Justice Department's National Security Division, remained alarmed that it would disrupt the work of FBI agents and national security prosecutors.

The interagency legal team gathered in the Situation Room to talk about it in what became an unusually contentious meeting. This played out against a backdrop of repeated clashes in the Obama years between Pentagon and White House officials over whether Obama should sign or veto the annual defense bills. The bills often contained many things the Defense Department needed, but also other things the White Housed opposed, raising a dilemma.

Now, Johnson, reflecting the Pentagon's strong opposition to vetoing the overall bill, told Monaco she was exaggerating. He said the Justice Department's problem had been solved because the executive branch could interpret the provision narrowly. They could say it simply never applied to domestic-soil prisoners and investigations conducted by the FBI. His reasoning was that the military *captures* people, but the FBI instead *arrests* people. Moreover, if they loudly protested to Congress that the rewritten provision still *would* mess up domestic investigations, then they would be stuck saying it meant more than it had to, creating a problem. Therefore, the provision was not worth going to war with Levin and McCain over, he argued.

Johnson's forceful defense of the bill raised eyebrows among his colleagues at the Justice Department and the White House. In theory, executive-branch officials are not supposed to take positions in interactions with Congress that had not been approved by the White House's Office of Management and Budget as official administration policy. In practice, interactions between top officials in any given department and top lawmakers and staff on that department's oversight committees necessarily involve a lot of in-the-weeds dialogue. The Pentagon had a direct line to the two armed-services oversight committees, and Johnson talked often to Levin's top lawyer, Peter Levine. Several officials independently told me of widespread suspicions inside the administration that Johnson had signaled to Levine, without OMB clearance to do so, that the administration would back down if the committee revised it to add the part about "captured in the course of hostilities."

In any case, Virginia Seitz, the head of the Office of Legal Counsel, turned to Johnson and told him that his interpretation was wrong; the provision still contained no exception for al-Qaeda suspects taken into custody on domestic soil.

That's all fine that you don't think that's what it means, but the plain language clearly says that, Seitz told him.

The administration legal team decided it could not live with the mandate even as revised and would fight it. This raised a tactical problem: the most natural official to lobby lawmakers about dropping it was the attorney general, but Eric Holder had very little clout with Congress, especially among hawkish conservatives.

Monaco turned to a top law enforcement official who did command bipartisan respect, Robert Mueller, the FBI director. But, via the FBI's new top counsel, Andrew Weissmann, Mueller initially resisted; one reason he had support on both sides of the aisle was that he generally tried to stay above the fray in politically charged fights. Finally, three top White House officials — William Daley, the chief of staff; Kathryn Ruemmler, the White House counsel; and Tom Donilon, the national security adviser — agreed that Mueller was going to have to step in and told him so.

Mueller reluctantly sent a letter to Congress on November 28 raising concerns that the mandatory military custody provision would create operational problems for the FBI.[6] His intervention led to behind-the-scenes negotiations with the senators, producing a face-saving deal. The provision granted the president the power to waive the mandate, and the administration told the lawmakers that it would interpret that power extremely broadly — as giving Obama the ability to exempt from the mandate sweeping categories of suspects in the abstract and in advance, not just the ability to waive it for individual suspects on a case-by-case basis.

Ruemmler crafted a signing statement for Obama to issue indicating that he was approving the bill only because of that understanding, a statement that she, Daley, and Obama finalized in a conference call in late December while the president was in Hawaii and his two aides were vacationing separately in Mexico.

"Under no circumstances will my administration accept or adhere to a rigid across-the-board requirement for military detention," Obama's statement said.[7]

Monaco and Weissmann crafted the prospective categorical waivers, which Obama issued as a presidential policy directive, dubbed PPD-14, on February 28, 2012.[8] They were aggressive. The mandate would presumptively not cover any case in which officials decided that military custody might interfere with efforts to secure the prisoner's confession or cooperation with his home government. It would not cover anyone arrested by state or local police. It would not cover lawful permanent residents if they were arrested inside the United States or if they were arrested abroad for alleged actions on domestic soil. And so forth.

If a foreign terrorism suspect were arrested on domestic soil, there would still have to be an interagency discussion — *Is this a covered person? Is this a PPD-14 waiver case?* But as soon as the attorney general determined that a waiver applied, "no further action shall be required." And the waivers were so all-encompassing that Obama had effectively gutted the new law: no real mandate, as a practical matter, existed.

The Obama administration's legal-policy goals were an ambiguous mix of a civil liberties issue (preventing the militarization of counter-terrorism investigations on domestic soil) and a pragmatic issue (preserving flexibility for executive-branch national security officials). Whatever the merits of those goals, the way it went about achieving them was notable. It stood in contrast to Obama's vow, back in the spring of 2009, that as a matter of principle he would work with Congress on deciding what the rules would be for detaining Guantánamo prisoners, and his later acquiescence when lawmakers imposed the first restrictions on his ability to transfer those detainees. Since then, his attitude had evolved. His hands might remain tied on legacy captives, but he was determined to hold the line against any further intrusion from lawmakers on handling futures captives. Obama stopped short of making a Bush-like claim that the mandatory military custody provision was unconstitutional as encroachment on his executive powers. But interpreting his statutory waiver powers in a maximally aggressive way had the same result: stiff-arming Congress.

3. The Last Iraq War Detainee

Even as the administration and Congress argued over what the rules should be for newly captured terrorism suspects, a long-running dilemma over a man who had been in American military custody in Iraq since 2007 was coming to a climax.

In late 2011, the war in Iraq was officially ending and the United States was getting out of the wartime-detention business there. Under an agreement signed by the Bush-Cheney administration, the Iraqi government had final say over the disposition of any remaining wartime prisoners on its soil. By December, only one prisoner, Ali Musa Daqduq, a Lebanese man captured in 2007, remained in American control.

After initially pretending to be deaf and mute, Daqduq was said to have confessed to his captors, without any kind of abuse, that he was an Iranian-trained Hezbollah operative who had been working with Shiite militias taking part in the insurgency. He had helped to plan a January 2007 raid on an American outpost in Karbala in which militants wearing stolen American uniforms had killed a soldier, kidnapped four others, and then later shot them and dumped their bodies beside a road.[9]

As the December 31 deadline for ending detention operations neared, the Obama legal team aired several options for trying to keep Daqduq locked up. The issue consumed a series of deputies committee meetings chaired by Denis McDonough, now the deputy national security adviser. But there was no good answer; each option carried its own problems.[10]

One option was to turn Daqduq over to Iraq for prosecution. But his statements to American interrogators would probably not be accepted as evidence in an Iraqi court, and Prime Minister Nouri al-Maliki, a Shiite, might face pressure from Iran to let him go.

Another option was to take Daqduq out of Iraq for prosecution by the United States. His confession would likely not be admissible under civilian court standards, so only a military commission would work. The new commissions prosecutor, Mark Martins, had been the top military lawyer in Iraq at the time of the Karbala raid, and he pushed to prosecute Daqduq before a tribunal at the naval brig in Charleston. But even if the Iraqis would agree to let that happen, it was sure to create a domestic political backlash on both the civil liberties left and the national security right. South Carolina's senior senator, Lindsey Graham, told Eric Holder at a hearing in November that "all hell would break loose" if Obama brought Daqduq onto American soil.

Graham had a third idea: he urged the administration to send Daqduq to Guantánamo. But Obama did not want to add to the inmate population there, and al-Maliki was not about to consent to letting the United States take any Muslim to its notorious prison.

"To be blunt, a transfer to Gitmo was a nonstarter for the Iraqi government," Tommy Vietor, a spokesman for the National Security Council at the time, said.

To that objection, some conservatives scoffed that Obama should simply put Daqduq on a plane and fly him out anyway, without Iraqi permission. These included two of Romney's national security legal-policy advisers, Rivkin and Stimson. In a *Wall Street Journal* op-ed, they wrote that Obama's refusal to do so relied on "flawed, self-defeating legalistic arguments."[11] But the Obama team worried that violating Bush's agreement and taking Daqduq out unilaterally would violate Iraq's sovereignty at the very moment that the United States was trying to end the war and start a new era of being friends and allies with Iraq.

A few months earlier, in September 2011, in off-the-cuff remarks following a speech at Harvard Law School, John Brennan said that he had never found a case where legal interpretations by the lawyers group had prevented the administration from doing something that policymakers thought was in the United States' best interests.* But the Iraq War wind-down made Brennan's claim obsolete. When I asked Ben Rhodes in early 2014 if any examples came to mind of times when the Obama administration had not done something that it wanted to do because the lawyers said it would be illegal, Rhodes cited the Daqduq dilemma: they had wanted to keep him politically incapacitated. But in the end, the lawyers said it would be illegal to put him on a plane without Iraqi consent. While Obama was briefed on the case, he said, the question of doing that was never put to him because it was not seen as a legally viable option. Rhodes told me, "We [spent] dozens of hours in deputies committee meetings on this one case. From a policy perspective, we would have liked to exfiltrate him, but there was no legal way to do it. The same thing is happening with Afghanistan. At the end of war, detainees are released that you don't want to see released."

The military transferred Daqduq to Iraqi custody on December 16. Vietor announced that the United States had received assurances that Iraq would prosecute him. An official said that this was a reference to potential charges for entering Iraq illegally, which could carry a ten-year sentence.

On the day of the announcement, David Lucas, the brother of one of the four kidnapped and murdered soldiers, told me that he had hoped Daqduq would be prosecuted and imprisoned for life or executed;

---

* See chapter 6, section 16.

handing him to the Iraqis, he said, was "as good as letting him go free. It's just a matter of time before the guy is walking the streets there."[12]

On January 3, 2012, Martins swore out a charge sheet against Daqduq in the military commissions system anyway, accusing him of murder, perfidy, terrorism, and espionage, among other crimes. The government did not publicly announce the charges or post them on the commissions website docket, but I obtained a copy of the document a month later. It was the first time the system had been used against someone not connected to al-Qaeda.[13]

The Obama administration used the charges as a basis for an Interpol notice asking Iraq to extradite Daqduq. But al-Maliki refused. An Iraqi court ruled that the evidence against Daqduq was insufficient to charge him. In November 2012, Daqduq walked free.[14]

4. Holding Americans as Enemy Combatants

A remarkable fact about post-9/11 America was that even a decade after the attacks, one of the most fundamental questions raised by the Bush-Cheney administration's response remained unanswered: whether presidents have the power to hold American citizens, arrested on American soil and accused of being terrorists, in indefinite military custody without trial.* In late 2011, Congress finally took up this issue.

Lawmakers were forced to confront the question of holding citizens as enemy combatants because of another provision in the annual National Defense Authorization Act, the bill that also had the mandatory military detention requirement. This provision would spell out, in a federal statute, who could be placed in indefinite law-of-war detention under the 2001 Authorization for Use of Military Force against the perpetrators of 9/11. The provision basically codified the March 13 Standard, which the Obama administration had developed for the habeas corpus lawsuits by Guantánamo detainees.

---

* See chapter 4, section 4.

The new provision, however, would apply in general, not just to the Guantánamo detainees Obama had inherited. In light of that, Senator Dianne Feinstein, Democrat of California, proposed an amendment clarifying that Americans arrested on American soil could not be placed in military detention. The resulting debate made clear that nobody could agree even on what current law was. Some lawmakers thought the president *already* had the power to hold citizens that way — as Bush had done — so her proposal would subtract power from the executive branch, while others thought what Bush had done was illegal, so her proposal would merely prevent the legislation from adding to the executive branch's power.

Lawmakers also could not agree on what the law should be. For example, Graham argued that it would be "crazy" to exempt al-Qaeda suspects from battlefield-style detention and interrogation just because they were Americans arrested on American soil.

"When they say, 'I want my lawyer,' you tell them: 'Shut up. You don't get a lawyer,'" Graham said.

But Mike Lee, Graham's fellow Republican senator from Utah, said American citizens, even those suspected of being terrorists, should retain their "fundamental civil liberties."

"I think at a bare minimum, that means we will not allow U.S. military personnel to arrest and indefinitely detain U.S. citizens, regardless of what label we happen to apply to them," Lee said.

It was an opportunity for elected lawmakers to weigh in, finally, on this momentous question. But instead of holding a vote to see which of those two points of view commanded a majority, Congress punted. By a ninety-nine-to-one vote, the Senate approved a compromise amendment stating that the provision did not change "existing law" — whatever that was — about people arrested inside the United States. This was a disheartening moment for American-style democracy; the current officeholders in Congress had abdicated their institution's core constitutional role: to make the law. (Of course, Congress decides only what statutes say; there would still be a constitutional issue if a president threw an American citizen arrested on domestic soil into military detention.)

The detention provision had a notable coda. A group of journalists who said their reporting brought them into contact with terrorists, along with some WikiLeaks supporters and various activists, filed a lawsuit challenging the provision's constitutionality. They asked Judge Katherine Forrest, a former Justice Department antitrust official whom Obama had recently appointed to the bench in the Southern District of New York, to issue an injunction blocking the government from enforcing the statute. Their argument was that the law was too vague about what it meant to be a "supporter" of al-Qaeda and the Taliban or an "associated force" of them. This vagueness, they said, made them afraid that they might be detained without trial because the government might view them as supporting terrorists, so it chilled the exercise of their rights.

The Justice Department asked Forrest to dismiss the case, saying the group's concerns were too insubstantial to give its members the legal standing to bring the challenge. It also pointed out an oddity of the lawsuit: on its face, the statute did not create any new power. Instead, it merely expressed Congress's interpretation of the power it had previously created in the 2001 Authorization for Use of Military Force, and the lawsuit did not challenge that underlying statute.

But in a surprise ruling, Forrest sided with the plaintiffs. She ruled that the statute *did* create new detention powers because the 2001 authorization did not mention supporters or even associated forces of the main enemy. Her ruling seemed to reject the body of case law developed in the District of Columbia Guantánamo cases, even though she made no reference to the existence of that litigation. Forrest ordered the government not to detain anyone under the formulation expressed in the new statute, threatening contempt sanctions if it defied her.

At the Pentagon, Johnson was alarmed. A case that had seemed idiosyncratic suddenly had operational consequences. The United States was detaining hundreds of people in Afghanistan under the March 13 Standard, some of whom might best be characterized as supporters or associated forces of al-Qaeda or the Taliban, and Forrest was effectively now ordering the government to stop doing that.

The Justice Department filed an emergency appeal with the federal appeals court in New York. Johnson personally drafted parts of the brief. It complained that Forrest's "deeply flawed understanding" of the 2001 authorization clashed "with an interpretation of the military's detention authority that had previously been endorsed by all three branches of government" and injected "dangerous confusion into the conduct of military operations abroad during an active armed conflict."[15]

Johnson prevailed. The appeals court swiftly blocked Forrest's injunction, then dismissed the lawsuit.

5. The 9/11 Military Commission Begins

As Forrest was weighing the detention policy case from her federal courthouse in Manhattan, a very different kind of judicial proceeding was getting under way fourteen hundred miles to the south, at Guantánamo. It was May 5, 2012, and after years of delay stemming from Holder's failed attempt to prosecute the 9/11 case in civilian court, military prosecutors were re-arraigning Khalid Sheikh Mohammed (KSM) and his four codefendants before a military commission. In the final weeks of the Bush-Cheney administration, the five had claimed they were ready to plead guilty and forgo a trial, but then Obama had halted those proceedings. Now the five seemed determined to string out tribunal proceedings to the maximum extent possible — perhaps relishing their return to the spotlight or maybe simply enjoying the novelty after having sat for three and a half more years in their cells.

KSM, sporting an ad hoc turban he had fashioned out of a cloth after guards brought him into the high-security courtroom, sat with contemptuous defiance. He fingered his long, orange-dyed beard and refused to cooperate as the military judge, Colonel James Pohl, tried to get him to acknowledge that he understood the charges against him and accepted his lawyers as representing him. One of those lawyers, David Nevin, told Pohl that KSM's silence was a protest against what he saw as an unfair process. Pohl plowed ahead, saying he would assume there were no objections, then.

"He has that choice," Pohl said. "But he does not have a choice that would frustrate this commission going forward."[16]

Martins, the chief prosecutor, and his team sat across from the five defendants and their five sets of defense lawyers. Before the arraignment, the general had been on a public relations campaign, delivering speeches and giving interviews in which he touted the virtues of the reforms to the tribunals system and asked people to give it a chance to work. After all, he pointed out, Congresses and presidents of both parties had agreed that it was a valid option for terrorism trials.

Jeh Johnson had arranged for pretrial hearings before the commissions to be simulcast to viewing rooms inside the United States, including at Fort Meade. This was a significant improvement in their transparency from the previous cycle, under Bush, making it far easier for reporters to cover routine hearings. But a small horde of reporters from around the world had come to Guantánamo to watch in person as the 9/11 case was rebooted.

It turned out we could watch from two locations. One was a filing center in an old hangar near the secure courtroom, where we could take notes on our laptops and use e-mail while watching the same video feed shown at Fort Meade. The other was from behind soundproof glass at the back of the courtroom, separated from a small group of victims' family members by a black curtain.

As a protection against any release of information deemed classified — such as if a defendant started shouting something about his treatment at a CIA black-site prison — the video feed was on a forty-second delay. A security officer near Pohl could, at his direction, "close the court" by pushing a button that would make a red light go off and sever the feed from forty seconds earlier. Those watching from the soundproof room at the back of the court listened to the audio of the same delayed feed, creating a disorienting gap between what we were seeing and hearing.

Like Martins, Pohl seemed acutely aware that the legitimacy of the military commissions system itself was as much on trial as the defendants. Apparently because he was trying hard to be seen as fair, he put up with disruptions that no federal civilian judge would have tolerated.

Lawyers for each of the five defendants independently made the same objections over and over to procedures and rules, ignoring Pohl as he told them again and again that he would address such concerns later. At one point, one of the defendants, Ramzi bin al-Shibh, abruptly stood up, knelt, and started praying; at another, he shouted at the judge — causing the censor to cut off the audio briefly. When it cut back in, he was saying something about prison conditions and suggesting "maybe they are going to kill us and say that we have committed suicide."

Another defendant, Walid bin Attash, who was brought into the court in a wheeled restraint chair and later took off his shirt to show scars, insisted that prosecutors read the full charge sheet, including a list of the names of the nearly three thousand victims. That step alone added hours to the proceedings. Pohl did not order guards to intervene when bin al-Shibh began praying, nor did he do so later when all five detainees began a twenty-minute prayer session together just as the court was about to reconvene after an hour-long break.

"I fully respect the accused's request for prayer," Pohl said afterward to the lawyers. "It's a right for them to have it. But a right can still be abused, if you understand me."

Late that night, the arraignment hearing concluded. The five defendants each deferred entering pleas. Pohl set a date for the first pretrial motions hearing. There was no date for an actual trial, and we were told it was likely at least a year off.

At that point, the projected timeline sounded inefficient. But the chaotic arraignment was a foreshadowing of dysfunction to come. The notion that the case would get to trial by late 2013 would prove to be wildly optimistic.

6. Two Torture Investigations End

While military prosecutors' effort to hold KSM accountable for 9/11 finally began to inch forward, civilian prosecutors' consideration of holding American officials accountable for torture sputtered to an end.

In August 2012, the Justice Department announced that John Durham, the prosecutor leading the criminal investigation into the CIA program, had recommended closing out the two remaining CIA black-site cases — the ones that involved prisoners who had died in CIA custody — without charges. Durham's three-year criminal investigation had yielded zero prosecutions. The Obama administration refused to make public his reports to Holder explaining what he had learned and why he had decided that no charges were warranted.[17]

The end of the criminal investigation freed the Senate Intelligence Committee to interview CIA officials for its massive oversight investigation into the same program. But the committee staff's work based on its review of six million pages of contemporaneous CIA cables and e-mails, as well as records of what witnesses had told the CIA inspector general and had testified in oversight hearings, was already well along. A Senate staffer told me that they had begun producing and distributing draft versions of sections of the report in November 2011, and were more than three-quarters done with the nearly seven-thousand-page project when Durham ended his probe. Under tremendous pressure to get the report done, the committee was unwilling to stop and start over with new interviews. But the omission of interviews would provide ammunition for the CIA and its defenders, including Republicans on the committee, to reject the Senate report as a definitive historical account.

The draft report attacked the program on both moral and pragmatic grounds. It concluded that what the CIA had actually done to prisoners was much worse than what agency officials had told the public, Congress, or Bush-Cheney policymakers. It also accused the CIA of systematically misleading its overseers about the value of the information gleaned from the program. The report's bottom line was that torture had not produced unique intelligence that led plots to be disrupted, terrorists to be captured, or lives to be saved.

The Senate staff had reason to believe that the CIA leadership would largely agree with that conclusion. While searching CIA documents on the special computer network the agency had set up for them, the investigators had stumbled into the trove of internal agency reports from 2009 and early 2010 cataloging the historical documents it was putting into the network each week and summarizing the most damaging elements of them.* These reports, which Senator Mark Udall later dubbed the Panetta Review, apparently dovetailed with the Senate staffers' own findings.

It would take eight months for the CIA to respond to the findings in the draft report. When it did, the Senate staff was shocked.

7. Code Yellow

Soon after the Justice Department closed out its torture investigation, a code-yellow alarm echoed through alpha wing of Guantánamo's Camp 5, one of the three operating prison facilities. It was 2:05 p.m. on Saturday, September 8, 2012.[18] Obama's vow to close the prison was all but forgotten; it had been more than twenty months since any lower-level detainee had been transferred. Now, a color-coded signal — *yellow* meant a detainee had collapsed or was not responsive — sounded for one of the eighty-seven prisoners languishing on the list of men Matt Olsen's task force in 2009 had recommended letting go if security conditions could be met.

It was Adnan Latif, the brain-damaged Yemeni man who executive branch officials had been repeatedly recommended for transfer and who a district court judge had ordered released in 2010, only to have the Justice Department appeal that ruling and win its reversal.† Around dawn, fellow inmates on the cell block had started to raise alarms that Latif had not awoken to join them in morning prayers. But the guards said they had seen him sleeping and heard him snoring and so let him slumber on. Hours later, a guard's tap on his cell window produced no movement. An emergency team of guards and medical personnel converged and donned protective gear, preparing to enter his cell.

---

* See chapter 4, sections 6 and 15.
† See chapter 7, section 10.

They were surely apprehensive. A number of detainees, Latif among them, caused difficulties to protest their indefinite detention, both passively, by hunger-striking, and actively, by splashing cocktails of their own urine and feces at guards. But Latif was a special problem. Doctors at the base had diagnosed him with bipolar disorder and borderline personality disorder with antisocial traits. He was known for outbursts of erratic behavior, like banging his head against the wall and swallowing inedible objects. Doctors had prescribed Latif heavy dosages of psychotropic medications, and guards gave him special privileges — like unlimited TV time — to try to keep him calm. Medical corpsmen were supposed to watch him take his medication. But sometimes they did not, an investigative report later found.

Latif's behavior had grown worse since June 2012, when the Supreme Court declined to hear his appeal.[19] Since then, he had gone from the psych ward to a communal cell block and, finally, to the disciplinary cell block, where guards had moved him the day before he was found unresponsive. Entering his cell, the guards found Latif lying in a pool of vomit. A doctor pronounced him dead at 2:48 p.m. A military autopsy uncovered twenty-five capsules of Invega, a powerful antipsychotic medication, in Latif's stomach. Investigators surmised that he had hoarded his medicine, probably hiding the pills next to his groin.

Latif's death underscored how the political impasse over the future of Guantánamo had created a senseless policy in practice. Republicans wanted the military to bring new prisoners, which Obama refused to do. Obama wanted to release the lower-level prisoners and close the prison, which Congress refused to permit. In the resulting standoff, nobody arrived and nobody left — an outcome no one, on any side, supported. Now, pressure cracks were forming.

But Guantánamo posed a real dilemma. Many of Guantánamo's critics who wanted to see the prison closed, it is worth emphasizing again, vehemently disagreed with Obama's plan to do so by moving dozens of indefinite detainees to domestic soil and continuing to imprison them without trial. In January 2013, Jennifer Daskal, a former Obama administration legal team member, wrote that she had changed her mind about closing the prison because what it would take to do that would do more harm than good. (Daskal had served as a counsel to David Kris at the National Security Division from 2009 to 2011 and worked on the Wiegmann-Martins detention-policy task force.)

"The hard-won improvements in conditions would be ratcheted back half a decade to their previous level of harshness" in a supermax-style prison, she wrote in a *New York Times* opinion piece. "And Guantánamo would no longer be that failed experiment on an island many miles away. The Obama administration would be affirmatively creating a new system of detention without charge for terrorism suspects on American soil, setting a precedent and creating a facility readily available to future presidents wanting to rid themselves of a range of potentially dangerous actors."[20]

The atmosphere of surrender thickened in January 2013 — the two-year anniversary of the last time the administration transferred a lower-level detainee. In his second inaugural address, Obama said nothing about closing Guantánamo. But as Hillary Clinton prepared to step down as secretary of state, she sent a memo to the White House arguing that Obama needed to revive the effort to transfer the remaining lower-level detainees.[21] She also personally told Obama in the Oval Office that he needed to do more. In December 2011, Congress had added a case-by-case waiver power to the transfer restrictions if the secretary of defense certified that a release was in the national interest, but a year had passed and Leon Panetta had not invoked it; Clinton urged Obama to use it. She also recommended creating a high-level czar in the National Security Council staff to drive the interagency process — someone who saw it as his job to get the prison closed. The White House had had no one in that role since Greg Craig left.

But Clinton was not satisfied with the response she got from Obama and the White House to her request that the chief executive manage the situation more actively. So she decided, on her way out the door, to rescue Dan Fried, the State Department envoy charged with negotiating Guantánamo transfers. Even after Congress imposed the strict transfer restrictions, Fried had continued to develop deals, like a plan in early

2011 to resettle two detainees in Ukraine. But the defense secretaries —
first Robert Gates and then Panetta — had not approved any such deals,
so for two years Fried had been stuck in a frustrating predicament;
there was no point in negotiating deals to resettle detainees because the
Pentagon was not permitting any of them to go forward. Now Clinton
reassigned Fried to coordinate sanctions on Iran and Syria. The move
extricated him from the bureaucratic oblivion of trying to carry out
the administration's stated policy without any real backing from the
White House. And then, instead of replacing Fried, she ordered his
office closed and his staff and responsibilities transferred to the office of
the State Department legal adviser, signaling to the world that she
thought the closure effort was dead even though the White House was
still pretending otherwise.

I found out about Fried's transfer and wrote up a quick web story on
the morning of January 28.[22] It was an embarrassment to the administration. The White House learned what Clinton had done by reading
my article; in an implicit rebuke, she hadn't told them what she was
planning to do.

Fried ran into Clinton in the hallway shortly before she stepped
down.

Thank you for springing me from Gitmo, even if no one else can leave,
he told her.

I regret this so much, Clinton replied. *I'm still steamed at how all this
has unfolded.*

8. War Crimes, Real and Imagined

The political debate over whether the United States should prosecute
terrorists in civilian courts or before a military commission often centered on values, pitting concerns about protecting individual rights
against concerns about being resolute and tough in the war on terrorism. Occasionally pragmatic factors got aired, too. Proponents of tribunals, for example, noted that the military could stage a commission

trial on any of its bases anywhere in the world, while civilian trials took place in courthouses in the middle of domestic cities, and so entailed security risks and headaches. But there was also a pragmatic problem with tribunals that rarely got discussed: Civilian courts handle allegations that someone violated a domestic civilian law. Military commissions generally handle allegations that someone committed a war crime. Civilian law criminalizes many acts that are not recognized as offenses in the international laws of war.

The gap between civilian crimes and war crimes became important on October 16, 2012, when a federal appeals court issued a ruling that set off a major convulsion in the Obama legal team. The court threw out a military commissions's 2008 conviction of a onetime Guantánamo detainee, Salim Hamdan, a Yemeni man who had served as a driver and bodyguard to Osama bin Laden.[23] The tribunal found Hamdan guilty of "providing material support" to terrorists, a catchall crime for people who helped terrorists but were not involved in any specific plot.

The problem was that material support is an offense in domestic law, but it is not an internationally recognized war crime. A Republican Congress had nevertheless listed material support as an offense that prosecutors could charge when they wrote the 2006 Military Commissions Act. And in 2009, a Democratic Congress had kept that offense in the list when it revised that law. But the Constitution does not permit Congress to create new crimes retroactively, and almost all of the Guantánamo detainees, including Hamdan, had been captured years before 2006.

The Obama legal team had fought over this issue before. According to people who have read it, in his May 4, 2009, Office of Legal Counsel opinion about commissions,* David Barron predicted that the chances were high that courts would overturn material-support convictions in a commission. That opinion prompted Kris, the head of the Justice Department's National Security Division at the time, and Johnson to

---

* See chapter 4, section 11.

warn Congress not to keep the charge when it revised the commissions law. But the Senate Armed Services Committee had ignored them. Then, in the fall of 2009, Harold Koh, the State Department lawyer, argued with Johnson about the two detainees convicted of material support by a commission at the end of the Bush years: Hamdan, and another detainee named Ali al-Bahlul.

Lawyers for the two detainees had appealed their convictions to a military panel that reviewed tribunal matters before they reached the regular federal appeals court. And in this dispute, which has never been reported, Koh expressed fury that uniformed military prosecutors were filing a brief arguing that material support *was* a traditional war crime that *could* legitimately be brought before a commission,[24] something the administration had just told Congress it did not believe was true. According to people who read their widely cc'd e-mail exchanges, Koh demanded that the administration rein in the military prosecutors.

Johnson had pushed back, arguing that the Obama team had made its case but Congress had decided to keep the charge, so it was a tool they should use. Now, three years later, a federal appeals court panel in the District of Columbia, in an opinion by one of that court's most conservative judges, Brett Kavanaugh, threw out Hamdan's conviction, essentially validating Koh's position.

The October 2012 ruling meant relatively little for Hamdan; he had received a brief sentence and was already back in Yemen anyway.* But it devastated the chances of giving a commissions trial to most of the two dozen or so Guantánamo detainees who had been recommended for prosecution by Olsen's task force but not yet charged. Few of them were linked to any specific plot either.

The ruling also raised a new question about the other Bush-era case, the one involving al-Bahlul. His appeal was pending before a different panel on the same court. Al-Bahlul had admitted to, among other things, making a propaganda video for al-Qaeda about the 2000 bombing of the *Cole* and drawing up martyrdom wills for several of the 9/11

---

* See chapter 4, section 19.

hijackers. But he boycotted his trial and would not let his defense team make arguments on his behalf. The commission had sentenced al-Bahlul to life in prison after convicting him of material support, solicitation, and conspiracy. None of those three charges were internationally recognized war crimes, so it appeared that they would all have to be vacated by the same logic as the Hamdan case.

In January 2013, Mark Martins pushed to abandon al-Bahlul's convictions and move him back to law-of-war detention.[25] Rather than fighting a losing battle that would put a cloud over the tribunals system, he argued, it would be better to accept a narrower role for tribunals and focus on winning convictions in the 9/11 and *Cole* trials. Koh and Bob Taylor — who was serving as acting Defense Department general counsel after Johnson stepped down — backed Martins.

But the Justice Department wanted to keep fighting to preserve Bahlul's convictions. John DePue, a career appellate lawyer for national security issues, led this faction, and he had the backing of Monaco, the head of the National Security Division. They especially wanted to salvage the viability of "conspiracy" as a triable offense before a commission.

Conspiracy is powerful tool for prosecutors. It makes the mere agreement to commit a crime a separate and already completed offense, even if the conspirators never carried out their plans. It also permits prosecutors to introduce, as evidence against a defendant, what his coconspirators said and did. Like material support, it was a domestic-law crime, not a recognized international war crime, but Congress nevertheless listed it as a triable offense in the Military Commissions Act.

DePue and Monaco argued that the government had a duty to defend statutes and let the courts decide if Congress got it wrong on conspiracy. They also maintained that the chances of winning were better than Martins thought. The American military had charged people with conspiracy in commissions during the Civil War and World War II, so the Justice Department could argue that conspiracy was traditionally a *domestic* war crime under an American "common law of war," and therefore Congress had not retroactively created a new crime.

Under normal circumstances, the solicitor general, who was then

Donald Verrilli, decides whether the Justice Department will file an appeal and what it will say in such litigation. Verrilli convened a meeting in his conference room attended by DePue, Koh, Martins, and Monaco, as well as Verrilli's deputy, Sri Srinivasan, and Monaco's chief of staff, John Carlin. The two factions reprised their arguments. Koh also stressed the principle of *reciprocity* underlying the international law of armed conflict. If it was legitimate for the United States to charge al-Bahlul under military court rules for a domestic war crime, then it would be just as legitimate for the Iranian military to invent its own war crimes that no one else believed existed and prosecute a hypothetical captured American pilot for them.

After the meeting, officials said, Verrilli decided to back Martins. But first, he requested a meeting with Eric Holder, saying that the choice was consequential enough that he should let the attorney general know about it — a decision he made only about two or three times a year. Verrilli and Holder gathered with several other Justice Department officials in the large conference room adjacent to the attorney general's office. Verrilli explained the issue and his thinking.

Look, this is close, Verrilli said. *I've made the judgment we shouldn't pursue the appeal. We ought to defer to Mark Martins on this. He has very strong equities here and we ought to respect them. But there is a strong case to be made either way. There is also a reason to go the other way, and that reason is we wouldn't be defending the statute, or this application of the statute, if we abandon the convictions. But I believe not pursuing the case is the right call, unless you tell me otherwise.*

Holder and Verrilli kicked around the issue. There was another factor in play: The Obama administration had taken a lot of heat from congressional Republicans when it refused to defend the constitutionality of the Defense of Marriage Act in court.* It did not want to look like it was cavalier about not defending statutes.

We should keep fighting, Holder decided.

This was extraordinary; an attorney general almost never overrules

---

* See chapter 12, section 7.

the solicitor general on whether to appeal a case. But Verrilli had taken it to Holder and acknowledged that he could go either way about it.

Martins was furious. On January 9, 2013, the Justice Department filed a brief saying it would ask the full appeals court to bless the al-Bahlul convictions on material support, solicitation, and conspiracy. Martins pointedly did not sign it. [26] He also announced that he was asking Bruce MacDonald, the Pentagon official in charge of the military commissions system, to drop a similar conspiracy charge against KSM and the other 9/11 defendants.

"There is a clear path forward for legally sustainable charges," Martins said.

Things got uglier. MacDonald declined to drop the charge pending the outcome of the litigation. Martins then made a commissions filing saying that if defense lawyers in the 9/11 case eventually made a motion to strike the charge, he would not permit his prosecutors to defend against it. [27]

The al-Bahlul litigation would grind on for years, taking several trips between a three-judge panel and the full appeals court. [28] But the bottom line was that the court threw out all three charges against al-Bahlul on the grounds that they were not war crimes, not even conspiracy. Indeed, in June 2015, an appeals court panel declared that domestic-law offenses that are not recognized international war crimes can *never* be brought in a military commission — even for acts that take place *after* Congress has passed a statute that says the tribunals can be used to prosecute them. It was unconstitutional for Congress to steer such cases into anything other than a traditional civilian court.

"The government can always fall back on the apparatus it has used to try federal crimes for more than two centuries: the federal courts," Judge David S. Tatel wrote in an opinion concurring with the result. "Federal courts hand down thousands of conspiracy convictions each year, on everything from gunrunning to financial fraud to, most important here, terrorism." [29]

The following month, the administration appealed again, taking the long-running case back to the full Court of Appeals. The shadow Martins had feared pursuing the al-Bahlul case would cast over the military commission system was lingering on and on.

9. Red Light at the Military Commissions

Back on the afternoon of January 28, 2013 — the same day it became public that Clinton had shuttered the Guantánamo closure office — Nevin, the defense lawyer for KSM, brought up a motion in a pretrial hearing of the 9/11 military commission. The defense strategy in the 9/11 and *Cole* cases was to prevent the government from executing their clients, arguing that it had given up any right to do so because the CIA had tortured them. Nevin's motion sought an order from the judge to preserve any still-existing evidence "at a detention facility." As Nevin began to talk, a red light in the courtroom began flashing. For the reporters and family members in the sealed observation room at the back, the audio — which had been broadcasting what was said forty seconds earlier — abruptly cut off.

The abrupt triggering of the censorship system confused everyone in the courtroom. Nevin had mentioned nothing classified, as a transcript of what he had said just before the light went off made clear. The courtroom security officer working for the military judge, Colonel Pohl, had not touched the button to close the courtroom.[30]

"Trial counsel, note for the record that the 40-second delay was initiated, not by me," Pohl said, adding: "If some external body is turning the commission off under their own view of what things ought to be… then we are going to have a little meeting about who turns that light on or off."

Several days later, Pohl announced that he had been told that, unbeknownst to him, an "original classification authority" — which was widely understood to mean the CIA, since that was the agency that classified information about its former torture program — was secretly monitoring the proceedings through the closed-circuit feed, without the delay, and had its own button. Pohl angrily ordered it unhooked, saying it was "the last time" an outsider "will be permitted to unilaterally decide that the broadcast should be suspended."[31]

The red-light incident led to hearings and briefs about what had happened and what it all meant, delaying progress on getting to an actual trial. It was only the first of many tribunal sideshows that pushed their way onto center stage, muscling aside questions of guilt and punishment for 9/11.

10. The Guantánamo Hunger Strike

When Congress shut down the transfers of lower-level detainees in 2011, the guard force at Guantánamo gradually relaxed the rules into a live-and-let-live atmosphere. Guards did not search detainees' cells and bodies for contraband as stringently as the written procedures called for. But Latif's suicide prompted the warden, Colonel John Bogdan, who had taken over in mid-2012, to phase back in a stricter enforcement of the rules.[32] Guards began to shake down cells for contraband more often and, later, started physically searching the groins of detainees every time they were moved out of their cells.

In early February, rumors circulated among the cell blocks that a non-Muslim guard had touched a Koran during a search; the military denied it. Word began to filter out, via lawyers for the detainees, that a crackdown on prison conditions was under way — as was a growing hunger-strike protest.

The military responded to the hunger strike by force-feeding those detainees who had lost too much weight. The procedure involved strapping them into a restraint chair, inserting a feeding tube through their nose and into their stomach, and pouring liquid nutritional supplement through the tube. Groups like the American Medical Association criticized doctors and nurses for participating in this procedure, calling it unethical.[33] The military insisted it was legal.[34] Ethics and law, of course, are two different systems.

On March 20, in remarkably candid congressional testimony, General John Kelly, the leader of the United States Southern Command in Miami, which oversees Guantánamo, assessed the root cause of the growing unrest: after two years in which no lower-level detainee had left, the prisoners were in despair.

"In talking to the hunger strikers, so-called, they had great optimism that Guantánamo would be closed," Kelly said. "They were devastated when the president, you know, backed off — at least their perception — of closing the facility."

Kelly also asked for two hundred million dollars to rebuild crumbling infrastructure at Guantánamo. Investing all that taxpayer money to build up a prison Obama was trying to close was awkward, especially amid budget cuts. But it was necessary, he said.

"These are things that we have to do right now," he explained to Congress. "I'm assuming Guantánamo will be closed someday, but if we look into the past 11 years, it was supposed to be temporary. Who knows where it's going?"

In April, the guard force conducted a predawn raid on the communal cell blocks and forced each prisoner into individual lockdown. The military had been refusing requests by me and several other reporters to visit during the hunger strike, but immediately after the raid it told five of us — me, Carol Rosenberg of the *Miami Herald,* Ryan Reilly of the *Huffington Post,* and Ben Fox and Suzette Laboy of the Associated Press — to get on a plane. We were permitted to walk through the seemingly calm cell blocks — though the official hunger-strike count had doubled after the raid, peaking at 106 of the 166 prisoners then at the base — and to talk with Bogdan and the other officers, though not the prisoners.[35]

The military officials described an increasingly chaotic deterioration before the raid. Prisoners in the communal cell blocks, they said, had begun refusing to go into their cells for the nightly lockdown, so guards were unable to go into the common spaces to look around, as prison rules called for them to do. The detainees were also covering up windows and surveillance cameras.[36] Bogdan told us he had spoken to detainee leaders about the need to uncover the cameras and windows and expressed a willingness to negotiate if they first began complying with the rules, but he had been unable to deliver what they wanted.

"They were asking to be released from Gitmo," he told us. "I can't do that."

We also spoke with "Zak," a Muslim cultural adviser to the military who had lived since 2005 at the base as a contractor and who served as a liaison between the guard force and the detainees. He said the level of unrest was qualitatively different than anything he'd seen before.

"They are not done yet, and there will be more than one death," Zak warned us. "The detainees have lost hope. If there is one [departure], one detainee, that will change everything. At least they will know they have accomplished their goal and made the world listen to them.... What's going on right now is that they are worried about nothing but leaving Guantánamo alive."

I came back from Guantánamo and wrote a lengthy piece about the events, which the *Times* published on April 24. It cited Kelly's testimony and quoted Kenneth Wainstein, the former head of the Justice Department's National Security Division and then White House counterterrorism adviser in the second term of the Bush-Cheney administration. He said that despite the standoff between Obama and Congress, the government could not simply ignore Guantánamo for much longer.

"The situation is not sustainable," Wainstein said. "There are strong, principled arguments on both sides, but all of us across the spectrum have to acknowledge that this is far from an ideal situation and we need an exit strategy."

The mass protest worked. For two years, Obama and the people around him had essentially thrown up their hands about Guantánamo and focused on other things. It was that attitude of managerial neglect — the issue was too hard and the politics too ugly, so leave it on the back burner for now — that had driven Clinton to shutter Fried's office in disgust just three months before. Now, Obama refocused on the issue. One of his aides told me that amid the hunger strike, and its obvious connection to the fact that it had been more than two years since any lower-level detainee had been transferred out of the prison, "Obama got frustrated and reached a boiling point" and privately "started driving people to be more aggressive" in moving out lower-level prisoners.

Speaking in public at an April 30 press conference, Obama also expressed frustration that his policy of closing the prison had failed, but he vowed to recommit his administration to achieving it. In doing so, he offered an emotional critique that echoed Wainstein's lament. It also clashed with his own administration's exit strategy: to close the Guantánamo prison by transferring dozens of the prisoners to some other prison and continue to hold them in indefinite detention there.

"It's not sustainable," Obama said. "The notion that we're going to keep 100 individuals in no man's land in perpetuity," he added, made no sense. "All of us should reflect on why exactly are we doing this? Why are we doing this?"[37]

11. Handling the Boston Marathon Bomber

On April 15, 2013, while I was at Guantánamo, two homemade bombs exploded at the Boston Marathon, killing three people and injuring 264 others, some of whom lost their legs. The culprits were soon identified as two Chechen brothers, Dzhokhar and Tamerlan Tsarnaev, who had been living in the United States for a decade. Dzhokhar, the younger brother, was a naturalized American citizen. His capture would raise critical questions about the handling of terrorism suspects who are U.S. citizens and Islamist terrorists who are not part of al-Qaeda.

During a massive manhunt for the terrorists that shut down Boston, Tamerlan was killed. His younger brother, Dzhokhar, was shot and taken into custody on Friday, April 19. The nineteen-year-old was questioned without any Miranda warning, until a magistrate judge delivered it in his hospital room the following Monday morning. Tsarnaev had been shot in the head and could not talk, but had been answering interrogators' questions by writing in a notebook. The notebook scribblings showed that he had repeatedly asked for a lawyer, according to a defense court filing.[38]

The Russian government had tipped off the FBI in 2011 that Tamerlan might be becoming an Islamist terrorist but had provided no evidence. Agents had opened the lowest level of an investigation, an "assessment," which requires no factual predicate but comes with a limited number of permissible techniques. They found no evidence and closed it. After the bombing, the FBI searched a computer belonging to one of the brothers — a technique that is permissible only at a higher level of investigation with greater basis to suspect wrongdoing. It contained videos downloaded from the Internet of al-Awlaki's sermons and copies of al-Qaeda in the Arabian Peninsula's *Inspire* magazine, including the issue with the article about how to build a bomb using a pressure cooker — the device the Tsarnaev brothers had used.[39] After the attacks, the National Security Agency searched its vast storehouse of intercepted communications for information about the brothers and found something relevant that no one had reviewed before the bombings, a redacted inspector general report later disclosed.[40] But at no point did any evidence or allegation emerge that they were linked to al-Qaeda; they were instead self-radicalized "lone wolf" terrorists.

Nevertheless, shortly after police arrested Dzhokhar Tsarnaev, Lindsey Graham and John McCain put out a joint statement urging Obama to place him in military custody.

"Under the Law of War we can hold this suspect as a potential enemy combatant not entitled to Miranda warnings or the appointment of counsel," the senators said.[41]

This call to place Tsarnaev in military detention, which several other Republican lawmakers echoed, was a new twist in the recurring debate over how to handle terrorism captives. The issue was not just that Tsarnaev was an American citizen arrested on American soil. It was also unclear what legal authority would permit the government to hold him in law-of-war detention. The United States was at war with al-Qaeda and its allies — those responsible for 9/11, against whom Congress had authorized the use of military force. It was not at war with every single Islamist-minded terrorist in the world. As Senator Carl Levin pointed out in a statement of his own, there was simply no evidence Tsarnaev was "part of any organized group, let alone al-Qaeda, the Taliban or one of their affiliates — the only organizations whose members are subject" to law-of-war detention.

"In the absence of such evidence, I know of no legal basis for his detention as an enemy combatant," Levin added. "To hold the suspect as an enemy combatant under these circumstances would be contrary to our laws and may even jeopardize our efforts to prosecute him for his crimes."

That weekend, I reached out to Graham and asked him to explain his thinking. His views were more nuanced than the press release or Twitter versions indicated. Graham told me that if no evidence ever emerged linking Tsarnaev to al-Qaeda, then he agreed that the government should not *continue* to hold him as an enemy combatant. But he argued that it was reasonable to do so at the onset of the investigation while hunting for evidence of such a link. Graham said that he thought thirty days of military confinement and interrogation without a Miranda warning or a defense lawyer would be appropriate and that he believed judges would not object under the circumstances.

"You can't hold every person who commits a terrorist attack as an enemy combatant, I agree with that," Graham said. "But you have a right, with his radical Islamist ties and the fact that Chechens are all over the world fighting with al-Qaeda — I think you have a reasonable belief to go down that road, and it would be a big mistake not to go down that road. If we didn't hold him for intelligence-gathering purposes, that would be unconscionable."[42]

But Obama and his legal team were determined not to go down that road. Exclusively using civilian law enforcement procedures rather than military force on American soil — meaning not holding Americans accused of terrorism as enemy combatants — was a core legal and civil liberties principle the administration did not back away from.

12. Reviving the Guantánamo Closure Effort

On May 23, 2013, three weeks after his press conference in which he vowed to revive the effort to close Guantánamo, Obama delivered a major speech on counterterrorism legal policy at National Defense University. It contained public arguments for a new push to close the Guantánamo prison. Inside the halls of government, he was also starting to drive his legal team to remove bureaucratic hurdles to achieving that goal, including resolving a long-simmering dispute over evidence about detainees that was derived from torture and installing new officials in the bureaucracy with a mandate to get the transfer process moving.

In his speech, Obama focused on only the second of those steps. He announced that the administration would fill the vacancy left by Fried at the State Department and create a new, parallel envoy at the Pentagon to help in arranging to repatriate or resettle the remaining lower-level detainees. Still, he acknowledged, even if all of them were gone someday, there would still remain dozens of prisoners who were not approved for transfer and who could not be prosecuted, either.

"Once we commit to a process of closing Gitmo, I am confident that this legacy problem can be resolved, consistent with our commitment to the rule of law," Obama said. "I know the politics are hard. But history will cast a harsh judgment on this aspect of our fight against terrorism and those of us who fail to end it."[43]

Obama did not spell out how the legacy problem could be resolved. But there was kind of an answer: parole-like periodic review boards to reexamine whether it remained necessary to keep holding those detainees. The idea was that over time, as they grew older or other circumstances changed making their release less risky, the boards would gradually move them into the transfer bucket, winnowing their numbers. Obama had directed his administration to establish those boards in his 2011 executive order on detention, but two years had passed and they remained on the drawing board.

Torture was the holdup. Back when the Obama team had been crafting the executive order, the periodic review boards had been another topic at the January 7, 2011, principals committee meeting on Guantá-namo.* Hillary Clinton had said that the International Committee for the Red Cross felt very strongly about the reviews, and they needed to have international legitimacy and be improved over the review process Bush had used.[44]

But the creation of the review boards raised a new problem: in evalu-ating whether a detainee was still too dangerous to release, would the boards be shown evidence that was derived from torture or cruel treatment—the sort of thing that would be suppressed in court? Donilon, Obama's national security adviser, said they needed to reach a clear decision about whether the boards would use such evidence. Clin-ton said the periodic review boards were very unlikely to release any-one anyway, and they needed to show a commitment to the rule of law—meaning not using torture-tainted evidence. Susan Rice, the UN ambassador, agreed.

We need to agree in principle not to use it and work out the details, or we'll face a shitstorm, Rice said.

Brennan agreed.

The impact on detention is negligible, he said. *What matters is the optics.*

Two months later, after Obama issued the March 2011 executive order, Ryan Vogel, a lawyer in Bill Lietzau's detention policy office at the Pentagon, drew up a proposed set of procedures for the boards. Each of the six agencies that had participated in Olsen's detainee review task force would contribute a member. The board would question the detainee, who would be represented by a lawyer for the review, and it would examine a dossier of classified intelligence about him.

Back in 2009, Olsen's task force had looked at everything the govern-ment had about each detainee, including CIA files. But for a board sys-tem, there had to be formal, written procedures, and the question of how they would address tortured evidence set off a complex debate. At

---

* See chapter 7, section 12.

the Pentagon, Lietzau thought the boards should be told everything, but that information tainted by torture should be flagged as potentially unreliable. At the State Department, Koh argued that torture-tainted information should be withheld from the board. But the CIA opposed *both* proposals, as they each required the government to formally characterize information from its defunct interrogation program in a damning way. Stephen Preston, the top CIA lawyer, expressed concern that an official acknowledgment that certain interrogation sessions had crossed the line into cruelty or torture could expose lower-level personnel who had participated in the interrogation program to greater legal risk.

The dilemma was still unresolved at the time of Obama's 2013 National Defense University speech vowing to restart the closure effort. Now it had to be dealt with.

The administration came up with a new process, whose rules have never been reported. The National Counterterrorism Center — now led by Olsen, the former Guantánamo review task force leader, by coincidence — would draft the initial dossiers, which would contain all the relevant information. But the Justice Department would screen torture-tainted information out of the dossiers before they went to the board. Still, Robin Jacobsohn, who had worked on detainee issues as a Pentagon lawyer in Obama's first term and was now a top national security official in the office of the deputy attorney general, argued that if tainted evidence would *help* a detainee, it should remain in the dossier, participants said. That exception became part of the rules too.

The first board hearings began in the fall of 2013. The early numbers suggested that Clinton and Brennan may have been wrong about whether they would have a substantial impact on detention: of the first fifteen detainees to receive hearings, the boards unanimously moved ten to the transferrable list. I asked officials familiar with the process whether the explanation for the relatively high rate was that there was torture-tainted evidence of dangerousness the boards had not seen. But they maintained that the explanation was instead that the simplest cases were going first.

Meanwhile, over the summer of 2013, Obama urged Lisa Monaco, who had now succeeded Brennan as White House counterterrorism adviser, to push the bureaucracy to try harder to close Guantánamo. In June, the new secretary of state, John Kerry, named a longtime confidant, Cliff Sloan, a high-powered Washington lawyer who had held several government jobs, to be the new envoy for negotiating Guantánamo detainee transfers. Fried's old office was reopened, and his former staffers, including Ian Moss, returned from exile to their previous desks. Energetic to the point of restlessness, Sloan began traveling the world and striking transfer deals.

At the Pentagon, Obama's announcement that there would be a Guantánamo closure defense envoy blindsided Lietzau. The only purpose of creating the new role seemed to be to remove that policy authority from his office. He stepped down in July for a job in the private sector, leaving his office in the hands of his deputy, Alan Liotta.[45] In November, Paul Lewis, the former top Democratic staff lawyer on the House Armed Services Committee, took the Pentagon Gitmo closure envoy position.

Where Gates and Panetta had been unwilling to issue waivers and approve deals, the new defense secretary, Chuck Hagel, approved a dozen transfers Sloan negotiated in late 2013. One of those transfers demonstrated the White House's renewed determination in the post-hunger strike atmosphere. It involved a Sudanese man recommended for transfer by the 2009 detainee review task force. The restrictions imposed by Congress said no detainee could be sent to a country deemed to be a state sponsor of terrorism, such as Sudan. But the restrictions did not apply to detainees ordered freed by a judge. The Sudanese man's lawyers filed a novel habeas petition arguing that their client was too sickly to engage in terrorism. Pentagon officials wanted to contest the lawsuit. At the Justice Department, Stuart Delery, now the head of the Civil Division, took no position. Monaco overrode the Pentagon and told Delery not to oppose the lawsuit, and the judge ordered the man freed — thereby permitting the executive branch to repatriate him despite the statute.

Obama met with Sloan and Lewis in the Oval Office at 3:00 p.m. on November 4, 2013. The meeting lasted just ten minutes, and Obama got right to the point. He promised to help them wage their bureaucratic fights as they tried to get his administration's fitful effort to move out lower-level detainees going again. It was football season, and he used a sports metaphor.

I'll be your blocking back, Obama told them.

13. The CIA versus the Intelligence Committee

The Senate Intelligence Committee's effort to investigate CIA torture led to one of the most striking legal, political, and national security fights of the Obama era—a near constitutional crisis between an executive-branch agency and its congressional overseers.

It began, in a sense, in June 2013, when the CIA presented the Senate Select Committee on Intelligence with a 136-page rebuttal to its torture report. The agency denied that it had systematically misled overseers and policymakers. And it insisted that intelligence from its enhanced-interrogation program had disrupted terrorist plots and saved lives.[46] It was total resistance to the Senate's findings. What the CIA did not know was that the Senate staffers had seen the CIA's own weekly reports that agency officials had written in 2009 and 2010, assessing what was in the historical documents — and which apparently said the opposite of what the agency was now insisting was true. Udall, who had dubbed these the Panetta Review, would call the review a "smoking gun" that showed the CIA was simply "lying."[47]

The CIA had previously removed several hundred pages of files from RDINet, the computer network it created for the Intelligence Committee staff to view its Top Secret files, after deciding it had made the pages available to the Intelligence Committee by mistake.* A committee staffer — reportedly Dan Jones, the team leader[48] — printed out por-

---

* See chapter 9, section 6.

tions of the Panetta Review files, took them out of the CIA's secure facility, and brought them to the Intelligence Committee's safe on Capitol Hill. Feinstein later said this extraordinary step was to "preserve and protect it" in light of the CIA's history. When CIA officials found out, they considered it theft.

The jaw-dropping fight began when Udall revealed the existence of the Panetta Review in December 2013 at a Senate Intelligence Committee confirmation hearing for Caroline Krass to be the CIA's top lawyer.[49] The CIA, which had never meant for the Senate to know about those files, concluded that it had a security breach.[50] Trying to find out where the Senate had learned about internal CIA files, a group of CIA officials searched the Senate work side of the special computer network it had built for the staffers to look at its Top Secret interrogation documents. The Senate thought the CIA had agreed to wall off its work drive from being accessed by agency officials. The CIA thought that rule did not apply to security-breach situations.

The searches revealed that no one had deliberately made the Panetta Review files accessible to the Senate staffers. Nevertheless, a copy of them was somehow saved in one staffer's work files. Audit logs further showed that the staffer had somehow managed to access 166 of the Panetta Review files as far back as November 2010. It turned out that the CIA had misconfigured a search program it provided to the Senate staffers to help them work with the documents. The program had indexed the entire server, including files on the CIA side that the staffers were not supposed to know about or be able to access. That enabled the staffers to download them. (The CIA permitted Justice Department investigators working for Durham to see these files on RDINet because the executive branch did not consider anything to be privileged from itself.)

Things were starting to spin out of control. Brennan had sanctioned the earlier searches of the work drive, but he had ordered the agency to stop the forensic audits. But the order did not reach a counterespionage security team at the CIA, which proceeded to keyword-search for references to the disputed documents in the staffers' e-mails on the work drive, reading five of them.

Brennan told Feinstein what was happening on January 15 and proposed a joint probe. She strongly objected, telling him the CIA's investigation of her staffers "undermined the constitutional framework essential to effective congressional oversight of intelligence activities or any other government function."

Matters soon deteriorated further. Brennan asked the CIA inspector general, David Buckley, to investigate. After a preliminary review, Buckley asked the Justice Department to open a criminal investigation into the officials who had searched the Senate server. Four days later, the CIA bureaucracy fired back: Robert Eatinger, a career agency lawyer, asked the Justice Department to launch a criminal investigation into the Senate staffers. Eatinger had been serving as the acting CIA general counsel since 2013, when Preston left the agency to succeed Johnson as the Pentagon's top lawyer.

The extraordinary dispute spilled into the open the following month when Feinstein revealed what had been going on in a forty-five-minute Senate floor speech. She portrayed the CIA as taking unconstitutional and illegal steps to thwart the torture investigation. Brennan insisted that the CIA had not spied on the Senate.

Feinstein also attacked Eatinger's decision to make a criminal referral, saying he was trying to intimidate oversight staff and that his own name appeared more than sixteen hundred times in the committee's torture report; Eatinger had previously worked for the section of the agency that ran the interrogation program. His defenders maintained that he had been obliged to make the referral under executive-branch rules. The Senate swiftly confirmed Caroline Krass to be the top lawyer at the CIA, displacing Eatinger from that role.

Holder wanted nothing to do with the dispute; in July 2014, the Justice Department announced that it would bring no charges against either the CIA officials or the Senate staffers.[51]

After the Justice Department announcement, Buckley finalized his inspector general report. It concluded that the CIA had indeed penetrated the Senate side of the network and read their e-mails. The Senate reacted with fury across party lines. Senator Saxby Chambliss, the

Republican vice chair of the Intelligence Committee, called for the five CIA employees criticized in Buckley's report to be "dealt with very harshly."[52] Udall called for Brennan to resign.

Brennan apologized to Feinstein and Chambliss and said he would appoint an accountability board to recommend what to do. The board consisted of three CIA officials who were not publicly identified as well as former senator Evan Bayh, a Democrat, and Bob Bauer, Obama's second White House counsel, who was now in private practice. Brennan recused himself from the matter, leaving his deputy director, Avril Haines, the former National Security Council legal adviser, in charge. In December 2014, the board met with her.

The board sharply disagreed with Buckley's report, saying the rules had been murky, the CIA officials had faced a dilemma with no good options, and their actions had not been unreasonable. In January 2015, just before leaving the CIA to become Obama's deputy national security adviser, Haines accepted the accountability board's recommendation not to hold anyone at the CIA accountable for what had happened.

Buckley resigned that same month. The CIA press office said the timing was a coincidence.[53]

14. Risk Aversion

By the end of 2013, it looked like Obama's effort to wind down Guantánamo was back on track. But in 2014, a confluence of events at Guantánamo combined to drastically aggravate the Obama administration's legal and political turmoil over the prison.

It began with aftermath from the hunger strike. During the 2013 unrest, four detainees had asked Judge Gladys Kessler to stop the military from force-feeding them. Kessler had made clear that she abhorred the practice, calling it "a painful, humiliating and degrading process," but ruled that she had no jurisdiction over conditions of confinement at Guantánamo.[54] The detainees appealed, and in February 2014, in a surprise ruling, a panel on the federal appeals court for the District of

Columbia sided against the government. It ruled courts *did* have the power to intervene in prison camp practices.[55]

Preston, now the Pentagon's top lawyer, urged Verrilli to appeal the ruling to the full appeals court. He argued that the government would be besieged by new lawsuits claiming abuses and that while most of the allegations would be baseless, the public and the press would accept them as true. This in turn would cause the military officials running Guantánamo to pull their punches, disrupting their ability to run the operation.

But Verrilli told Preston that there was a significant chance that the executive branch might lose such an appeal. He also noted that the ruling, for now, did not order the government to do anything, so they could still raise the jurisdictional issue at a later stage or in a different case. He let the ruling stand, and the force-feeding case came back to Kessler.

Meanwhile, Sloan and Lewis traveled to Uruguay in January 2014 and struck a deal with its president, José Mujica, to resettle six low-level detainees from home countries with troubled security situations, like Syria. Mujica was a former urban guerrilla who had spent fourteen years in prison, including over a decade in solitary confinement. No South American country had resettled a detainee, and the news prompted similar talks with Brazil, Chile, and Colombia, raising the prospect of creating momentum to find homes far from the Middle East for many of the remaining low-level prisoners. By early March, interagency officials agreed on the details and the proposal went to Hagel's desk for approval. One of the six men in the Uruguay deal was Jihad Ahmed Diyab, the main plaintiff in the force-feeding case. His transfer would have the side benefit, from the government's perspective, of mooting the matter.

Under the transfer restrictions, the secretary of defense had to give thirty days' notice to Congress that he had determined that releasing a detainee was a good idea, effectively giving final say to Hagel. He abruptly shut down. The deal sat on his desk that spring without action. So did several other deals that were also submitted to Hagel around that time or were nearly done, including a proposal to repatriate the last four Afghans on the transfer list. One factor, I was told, was that Hagel's military advisers, including General Martin Dempsey, the chairman of the Joint Chiefs, took a cautious approach to evaluating the risk of re-engagement; Uruguay, for example, had a large and porous border, and American forces were still on the ground in Afghanistan. At a principals committee meeting in April 2014 about Guantánamo, Hagel refused to commit to signing off on the deals.

I'll keep looking at it, he said.

Diyab had started eating when he was told Uruguay had offered to resettle him, but as time passed and nothing happened, he resumed his hunger strike. On May 13, Kessler ordered the military to stop force-feeding him.[56] But his health rapidly declined, and a week later she permitted the military to resume, describing the dilemma as "an anguishing Hobson's choice" and blasting the military for refusing to agree to change certain procedures she said caused unnecessary "agony."

The case put Obama's Guantánamo policy back on the front page. Jon Eisenberg, one of Diyab's attorneys, told me: "The real responsibility lies at the door of President Obama, who utters lofty words but fails to stop the terrible things that are happening at Guantánamo Bay on his watch."[57]

Had Hagel approved the Uruguay deal when it was ready to go, the court would have dismissed Diyab's case. And the delay came just as the White House had thought that Obama's policy was taking on momentum. The transfer deals had been moving, and on May 14, 2014, his legal team had completed a report to Congress analyzing the legal rights Guantánamo detainees would have if they were moved to domestic soil.[58] Despite Obama's National Archives speech framework and proposal to move the remaining detainees to the prison in Thomson, Illinois, Obama's critics had repeatedly contended that he had no real plan to close Guantánamo. One part of that critique was that if the prison was on domestic soil and a court ordered a detainee released but there was no good place to send him—like the Chinese Uighurs situation—judges might order the government to release the man into

American society. The report analyzed that issue and concluded that this risk was low and that Congress could enact a statute to further reduce it. But if they couldn't get rid of the many dozens of lower-level detainees first, bringing the rest to domestic soil would be much harder.

Now, seeking to break the logjam, Monaco drafted a three-page memo to Hagel. Rice, who had succeeded Donilon as Obama's national security adviser, signed it on May 24. The Rice memo, copied to Dempsey and Kerry, said it contained Obama's instructions for how to interpret the legal standards Congress had set for transfers. It said Hagel should *presume* that the transfer of any detainee on the recommended list was in America's national security interest. And, it said, he should use a flexible view of the requirement that risks had been substantially mitigated.

"As is the case with all decisions to return persons detained in an armed conflict, this is not a 'zero risk' standard, and this standard reflects in part the increased harm to the national security caused by continued operation of the facility," the Rice memo said.[59]

Although I obtained a copy of this memo only when researching this book, I first learned about it four days after Rice signed it — just as my colleague Helene Cooper, who covered the Pentagon, was about to fly with Hagel on a trip to Asia. I gave Helene some questions about the Uruguay deal to ask Hagel if she had an opportunity. She got Hagel to open up, speaking more expansively about Guantánamo issues than he did before or after. Hagel told Helene he'd make a decision about Uruguay soon, but he also reflected on the burden of being the one official who had to personally determine that it was a good idea to release any particular detainee.

"My name is going on that document. That's a big responsibility," Hagel said, adding, "What I'm doing is, I am taking my time. I owe that to the American people, to ensure that any decision I make is, in my mind, responsible. . . . I have a system that I have developed, put in place, to look at every element, first of all complying with the law, risks, mitigation of risk. Does it hit the thresholds of the legalities required? Can I ensure compliance with all those requirements? There is a risk in everything."[60]

Hagel's reluctance to move forward swiftly frustrated officials at the White House and the State Department. But his risk-aversion and careful deliberation, stemming from the fact that he could be seen as personally accountable if any released detainee killed someone, was precisely what the drafters of the transfer-restrictions law had hoped to achieve.

15. Violating the Transfer Restrictions to Save Bergdahl

Hagel's emerging reluctance to approve the transfer of lower-level Guantánamo detainees took a twist on May 31, 2014, with the surprise announcement that five *higher-level* Taliban detainees from Guantánamo had been transferred to Qatar in exchange for the release of Sergeant Bowe Bergdahl, America's only prisoner of war in the Afghanistan conflict. The military transferred the five Taliban detainees without obeying the law requiring Hagel to tell notify Congress thirty days in advance of any transfer from the prison.

Obama's justification was that he was trying to save Bergdahl. The soldier had been captured in 2009, taken across the border to tribal Pakistan, and held, under horrific conditions,[61] by a Taliban-linked militant group for five years. The possibility of such a swap had been floated several times in previous years as a potential "confidence building" gesture ahead of peace talks, and members of Congress of both parties had expressed skepticism that it was a good idea. Now, abruptly, it had happened — not as a part of peace talks, but as an end in itself. It turned out that Preston had been in Doha for several weeks, secretly negotiating with the government of Qatar over security conditions like surveillance and travel restrictions for the ex-prisoners. The Qataris in turn negotiated with the Taliban to secure Bergdahl's release.

Some critics said it was a bad deal and that it created an incentive for more kidnappings of soldiers. The five Taliban detainees were not lower-level nobodies recommended for transfer. Rather, they were high-level leaders in the pre-9/11 Taliban government, and two were accused of complicity in the murder of thousands of Shiites in Afghanistan.[62] Worse, the White House seemed initially clueless about the real circumstances of Bergdahl's capture; Obama appeared in the Rose Garden with Bergdahl's parents to celebrate his return, and Rice declared that he had "served the United States with honor and distinction."[63] But it turned out that Bergdahl had left his firebase without permission and got himself captured; the military charged him with desertion in 2015.

Almost lost in the debate was a deadline: on December 31, 2014, the thirteen-year-old war in Afghanistan was set to come to an official end. Under the laws of war, when hostilities end, wartime prisoners must be prosecuted or released. The Obama legal team, officials told me around that time, intended to argue after 2014 that the war against *al-Qaeda* continued, so its legal right to keep holding most Guantánamo detainees also continued. But there was a risk courts might order purely *Taliban* detainees released as soon as 2015.* By moving the pure Taliban prisoners out before any such legal confrontation, the United States had both secured Bergdahl's release and put them in a place away from Afghanistan where they were subject to monitoring.

Obama said, "By definition, you don't do prisoner exchanges with your friends, you do 'em with your enemies. And as we wind down this war in Afghanistan — it is important not only that we got back an individual who had worn this nation's uniform. But it's also important for us to recognize that the transition process of ending a war is going to involve, on occasion, releasing folks who we may not trust but we can't convict."[64]

Whatever the policy merits, from a legal perspective, the most disputed aspect of the deal was that Hagel did not give Congress the thirty days' advance warning as the transfer restrictions statute seemed to

---

* But see chapter 12, section 15.

plainly require. The top Republicans on the House and Senate Armed Services Committees, Representative Buck McKeon of California and Senator James Inhofe of Oklahoma, maintained that the Obama administration had broken the law.

In its defense, the Obama administration made a Bush-like claim: his constitutional powers as commander-in-chief trumped the notice law. In preceding years, the Obama administration had sometimes come up with aggressively narrow interpretations of what a statute meant, in order to maintain flexibility in a national-security situation. But Obama had resisted claiming that he could invoke wartime powers to simply override a statutory constraint. Now, his administration went there.

"We believe that the president of the United States is commander in chief, has the power and authority to make the decision that he did under Article II of the Constitution," Hagel said.[65]

The administration also said that any delay after striking the deal would have endangered Bergdahl's life. It also pointed to Obama's signing statement in December 2013, when Congress had enacted the most recent version of the restrictions.* Obama had said back then that he might need "to act swiftly in conducting negotiations with foreign countries regarding the circumstances of detainee transfers," and in the event that the transfer restrictions "operate in a manner that violates constitutional separation of powers principles, my Administration will implement them in a manner that avoids the constitutional conflict."[66]

The Government Accountability Office, an independent watchdog agency overseen by Congress, concluded that the Obama administration had violated three laws: the notice provision, a budget bill that said the Pentagon could not spend money to move Guantánamo detainees without obeying the transfer restrictions, and the Anti-Deficiency Act, which generally prohibits spending money not appropriated by Congress.[67]

The Pentagon said the accountability office was wrong.[68] It offered three arguments, saying the Justice Department concurred with all

---

* For an additional discussion of Obama's evolution on signing statements, see chapter 12, section 10.

three. (This meant the Office of Legal Counsel was on board. Obama had installed Karl Thompson as its acting head after Krass became CIA general counsel in March 2014. Notably, as Obama entered the home stretch of his presidency with executive-power battles looming on topics ranging from immigration to the Guantánamo restrictions, he did not nominate Thompson or anyone else to be permanent head of the Office of Legal Counsel — bypassing the Senate confirmation process for that powerful position.[69])

In more detailed, written legal analysis put forward by the Obama administration, its first two arguments for why the transfers had been legal were matters of statutory interpretation. Maybe the limits on using funds applied only to the *substantive* restriction that Hagel must determine the transfer was in the national interest, not the thirty-days-notice part. Or maybe Congress did not intend the limits to apply to the specific circumstance of securing the release of a captive soldier whose life might be endangered by a delay. The third was the constitutional trump card: if the legal limits *did* apply to this kind of transfer, then they were unconstitutional, because Obama's commander-in-chief role empowered him to protect the lives of service members and Americans abroad.

The Government Accountability Office rejected the administration's interpretation of the statute, saying it "would render the notification requirement meaningless." But the office did not address the commander-in-chief argument, saying its role was not to pronounce duly enacted statutes unconstitutional. The Pentagon, in its rejoinder, dismissed the Government Accountability Office's analysis since it did not engage with this core issue: "the legal analysis in the opinion is incomplete, and the stated conclusion is unfounded."

This was an important moment. The administration's constitutional argument claimed the same commander-in-chief powers to override a statute that Obama and many members of his legal team had once criticized Bush for exercising. It was a callback to the January 2010 complaints by Harold Koh — now long gone from the administration legal team — that *Democrats get to be president, too,* and that Thompson's predecessor, David Barron, was being too timid about invoking commander-in-chief powers to resist congressional efforts to stop Obama from winding down Guantánamo.* The Bergdahl transfer deal was a milestone in Obama becoming less deferential to Congress and more willing to act unilaterally.

16. A Visit to Guantánamo

By the summer of 2014, it was clear that the Obama administration's Guantánamo closure effort was once again jammed.

In early July, Hagel finally notified Congress that he had approved the transfer of the six detainees to Uruguay, stressing that he would comply with the thirty-day waiting requirement in a return to normal order.[70] A month later, on the afternoon of August 11, 2014, an air force C-17 landed on Guantánamo's airstrip to take the detainees to a new life in South America. But Hagel had waited too long. Uruguay's presidential election had gotten near, and Mujica wanted to avoid the media spectacle of six Guantánamo detainees arriving in its midst. Vice President Biden personally called Mujica and pressed him to move forward, but Mujica said it would have to wait. On August 14, the C-17 flew away, empty.[71]

That same month, terrorists with the Islamic State — the descendant of al-Qaeda's affiliate among the insurgents in the Iraq War, which had been pushed into Syria and was now taking back swaths of Sunni territory in Iraq[†] — released videos showing the beheadings of kidnapped American journalists. It had dressed its victims in Guantánamo-style orange prison garb.

Later that month, I visited Guantánamo again, this time with *Times* photographer Damon Winter. We walked through the cell blocks, spoke to the new warden and the new task force commander, and

---

* See chapter 7, section 2.
† See chapter 12, section 15.

climbed to the roof of one prison building to look down on a dusty soccer field and some pots in which detainees were trying to grow beans
and mint. An instructor stood on the other side of the fence with his
own pot and trowel during their gardening classes, a guard told us.

The prison had changed much since I had first come there, back in
2003. At that time, the military was housing most of the 662 men then
detained there in the mesh-sided individual cell blocks of Camp Delta,
sweltering amid the din of motorized fans and the shouts of prisoners
in adjacent cell blocks.

Delta now stood quiet and largely empty except for a medical clinic and
trailer where the military kept a small library for the detainees. It had
about 18,000 books and DVDs. The most popular, a military librarian
said, were religious books in Arabic and Pashto. But it also had in translation and in English well-thumbed copies of familiar titles, from the
Harry Potter and Lord of the Rings series to *The Odyssey* and *The Girl
with the Dragon Tattoo*. Detainees who obeyed the rules were permitted to
keep two books at a time, picking out of a bin that guards brought around
the cellblocks or making specific requests. Donations to specific detainees
went through the library. David Remes, a lawyer for Adnan Latif and several other Guantánamo detainees, told me that one of his clients had
requested romance novels, and others had asked for mountain-climbing
and surfing magazines "because they never see nature."[72]

The original crude concrete-and-wire prison, Camp X-Ray, which
remained stuck in popular consciousness even though it had been used
only for four months in 2002 while Delta was being built, was now a
ghost prison, overrun by vines, snakes, and marmot-like banana rats.[73]
Most of the remaining 149 detainees were now living in the concrete-
walled, air-conditioned Camp 5 and Camp 6 buildings. KSM and the
other former CIA black-site prisoners lived separately in Camp 7,
labeled the "Intelligence Operations Center" on an official-use-only
military map of the base. The military did not permit journalists to
visit Camp 7, and it was subject to security-theater treatment. When
James Connell, a lawyer for the 9/11 case defendant Ammar al-Baluchi,
went to inspect his client's cell, the military drove him in circles first to

hide its location,[74] despite the fact that it is clearly visible in Google Earth satellite photographs as the only other prison building in the barren landscape.[75]

We also spent some time in the detainee health clinic talking to the top military doctor. We talked about the ethical dilemmas raised by force-feeding hunger strikers to keep them alive, a practice the American Medical Association opposes but the Bureau of Prisons permits. He also showed me a new "Detainee Acute Care Unit" whose construction he had overseen. It had several beds, cardiac monitors, oxygen tanks, ventilators, and other equipment. Health care was mounting as a concern for the military. Medical facilities at the base were too basic — equivalent to a small-town hospital — to serve an aging population that would inevitably start to have problems like heart disease and cancer. American troops deployed to Guantánamo who experience serious health problems are brought back to the United States for access to more advanced equipment and specialists. But the congressional ban on bringing any Guantánamo detainee onto domestic soil made no exception for a medical crisis.

Around this time, I obtained, via a Freedom of Information Act lawsuit, a February 2013 e-mail from a Pentagon policy official, Kathleen Hicks, to General Kelly. Kelly had raised the question of whether it would be a war crime not to airlift a detainee in a health crisis to Miami. Hicks told him that a Pentagon lawyer had opined that the Geneva Conventions required giving wartime detainees the same care that American troops could get *at the same base*. But the law of war did not require medevacing wartime detainees to the United States for medical care "even if we would do so for our own personnel." (She copied her e-mail to Bob Taylor, the acting Pentagon general counsel between Jeh Johnson and Stephen Preston.)[76]

A few years earlier, Hicks added, Lietzau's detention-policy office and the State Department reached out to Latin American countries to see if they would be willing to let the United States bring an ailing detainee to one of their hospitals. But none offered to help. Instead, Lietzau's office worked up plans to fly specialists and equipment to Guantánamo quickly if a need arose.

This was the best they could do. It was just not cost effective to replicate modern medical facilities at the remote base to serve an inmate population of a hundred and fifty or so. Officials at the base told me the military once spent one million dollars on a mobile cardiac lab for a single detainee who needed a stent in his coronary artery, only to have the detainee refuse the procedure; the unused equipment, stored in the tropical weather, deteriorated. Shortly before my visit, a detainee had needed a kidney stone removed. That's a routine outpatient procedure in the United States, but the military had had to fly in a laser lithotripsy machine and a specialist to operate it. The senior medical officer was not sure what that had cost taxpayers.

Beyond health care, the infrastructure needs for which Kelly had requested two hundred million dollars in 2013, most of which he had not received, were visibly evident. There were, for example, pervasive rust holes in the walls and ceiling of the ragingly hot kitchen building where meals for both detainees and guards were prepared, through which sunlight shone; during storms, the head cook said, they covered the stores with plastic because the rainwater poured in. Rear Admiral Kyle Cozad, who had just taken command of the prison task force, said the military was working on a plan to build all the requested items more gradually. By tapping general military construction funds, they would not need to seek line-item approval from Congress in spending bills.

"We are forced to at least forecast so that we're prepared if this detention facility is open two years from now, twelve years from now, twenty-two years from now, so that we're prepared to be able to continue to do the mission," Cozad told me.

17. Pressuring Hagel to Make Decisions

By late August 2014, Sloan, the State Department Guantánamo envoy, was frustrated and fed up. Notwithstanding the departure of the five higher-level Taliban detainees in the Bergdahl deal, just one lower-level detainee had departed Guantánamo in all of 2014. Deals to move thirty more were rotting on the vine, punctuated by the Uruguay debacle. Because of Hagel's reluctance to act, the year was being wasted. It was time to take Obama up on his offer to be a blocking back.

Sloan reached out to Kerry and proposed writing a memo to Obama telling him bluntly his Guantánamo policy was failing again. Kerry agreed and Sloan and his staff drafted the memo. It told Obama that they were at a crossroads and proposed setting a goal of moving many detainees by the end of the year.

"Every month counts," Sloan told me around that same time. "The period between now and the end of the year is critical because the path to closure demands substantial progress in moving people from Guantánamo."[77]

In the roughly three-page memo to Obama, the State Department also proposed a specific way to drive the bureaucracy harder. The idea was to schedule both a principals committee meeting, chaired by Rice, and a follow-up National Security Council meeting, chaired by Obama, devoted to the issue. The meetings would focus everyone's mind on making progress. Kerry hand-delivered the memo to Obama at his next weekly meeting with him, and Obama ordered it done.

At the October 3 principals meeting, a participant said, Kerry opened with a forceful presentation reaching out to Hagel.

We've had these decisions for almost five years, approving these people for transfer. It's important to move forward and get these done by the end of the year, Kerry said.

Many other officials at the meeting—including Brennan, Holder, Samantha Power, the UN ambassador, and Johnson, who was now back as the Homeland Security secretary—weighed in, supporting what Kerry had said. Hagel was defensive and somewhat prickly. He noted that he had supported closing Guantánamo even when he was a Republican senator and insisted that he was on the same page as the president. He said he was just taking his time to look at the deals; he did not oppose them. But Hagel also reiterated that it was his name alone on the notice to Congress endorsing a given transfer.

That gave Holder an idea: *Let's put all of our names on it. We'll all sign it.*

Kerry agreed with that proposal, though it would prove to be unnecessary. After marching through the various deals awaiting Hagel's decision, the meeting ended with consensus that he would soon move on several. For example, as soon as the newly elected Afghan president, Ashraf Ghani, agreed to a certain security condition, Hagel was to give the thirty-day notice to Congress about repatriating the four remaining lower-level Afghans.

Meanwhile, the force-feeding case, which the government could have avoided had Hagel approved sending Diyab to Uruguay in March, was causing turbulence. A few days later, Kessler held a miniature trial about the military's force-feeding procedures, pushing Pentagon officials to testify and justify them.[78]

The evidence included military videotapes, filed under seal, showing Diyab being forcibly extracted from his cell and force-fed. (A group of news organizations, including my own, asked Kessler to make them public, setting off a protracted legal battle.[79]) Against that backdrop, Hagel signed off on several transfers, which took place in November. They included two significant milestones. One was a Kuwaiti whose repatriation marked the first release resulting from a decision by the new periodic review board to downgrade his status from recommended-for-continued-detention to recommended-for-transfer. The other was a group of lower-level Yemenis whose resettlement in Eastern Europe inaugurated a new policy of not waiting for security conditions to get better in Yemen before letting some of them go.[80]

But even though the Afghan government in mid-October agreed to the security condition for monitoring the four lower-level Afghan detainees, Hagel did not notify Congress that the military would move them out in 30 days. By early November, it was clear that Hagel was unilaterally reconsidering the timing of those transfers — notwithstanding the agreement in the October cabinet-level meeting. The cause of this reversal was that General John F. Campbell, the top military leader in Afghanistan, had sent Hagel a memo expressing concerns that the detainees might attack American or Afghan troops.

At 3:10 p.m. on November 17, Obama walked into the Situation

Room for the planned National Security Council meeting. He opened the fifty-eight-minute meeting with a monologue. For some ten minutes, he made clear how determined he was to close Guantánamo before leaving the White House.

This is really important to me and to the country, he said.

In the ensuing discussion, no one disagreed with Obama. The focus was on how to move forward and on the various actions that could be taken to drive down the numbers by getting the rest of the 83 lower-level ones out. The smaller the inmate population, the more manageable it would be, on both a political and a logistical level, to move them. One option was to clear out a few wings of an existing military prison, like the Charleston naval brig — which could hold 382 general inmate population prisoners and had eighteen cells for segregating detainees — and stick the Guantánamo detainees there while a longer-term solution, like converting a wing of the prison at Thomson, Illinois, was made ready.

It was now costing taxpayers some three million dollars *per prisoner* each year to house the remaining detainees at Guantánamo. By comparison, it costs about thirty thousand dollars a year to house an inmate in a domestic maximum-security prison.[81] Because many of the costs were fixed, if the rest of the lower-level detainees departed, the per capita cost of keeping the final sixty-four at the remote naval base would approach six million dollars a year, or some two hundred times as much as a domestic inmate. The Obama team's optimistic scenario was that the spectacle of such astronomical waste, along with the smaller psychological burden of dealing with a merely a two-digit inmate population, would persuade Congress to relent and lift the ban on bringing the remaining detainees to a domestic-soil prison. Floating in the background was a less optimistic scenario, in which Congress, or at least the House of Representatives, was not persuadable, and so closing the prison before Obama left office in 2017 would require some kind of unorthodox move — more on this later.

On November 24, 2014, Hagel resigned under pressure amid a variety of tensions with the White House. But he stayed on until his successor,

Ashton Carter, was confirmed in February 2015. In his final months, Hagel signed off on most of the remaining deals waiting on his desk, clearing out the backlog. Between November 2014 and January 2015, there was a flurry of twenty-seven transfers; among them were the four Afghans and the six who were finally resettled in Uruguay after its presidential election was over.[82] Meanwhile, at the end of 2014, Sloan abruptly stepped down as the State Department envoy for closing the prison and rejoined his former law firm. While his departure coincided with a high point in Guantánamo issues, he had quietly started planning his exit months earlier, when everything seemed stuck.

Despite the coincidence in timing, several officials, including Ben Rhodes, maintained that the Guantánamo frictions were not the precipitating factor in Obama's decision to replace Hagel; the logjam was already clearing. In the end, for all his delays, Hagel approved releasing thirty-five lower-level detainees, whereas his predecessor, Panetta, had moved none.

18. Unwinding the Parwan Prison at Bagram

Late in 2014, the Obama team confronted a situation in Afghanistan that was similar to the one it had faced in Iraq: combat operations were due to formally end, and the United States had agreed to turn over its remaining military detention operations at Parwan, the prison it had built on the edge of Bagram Airfield, to the Afghan government. The wind-down of Afghan detention operations would raise a policy dilemma that echoed the late 2011 question of what to do about Daqduq. But the outcome was very different.

The American military had already transferred some thirty-two hundred Afghan nationals to the Afghan government. This process, which began in late 2011, had been bumpy. As part of the deal, the Karzai administration had agreed to create a system of preventive detention for detainees deemed untriable but too dangerous to release, but Afghan lawmakers had refused to ratify the agreement and many of the men ended up being freed. Because the United States still had forces on the ground, this led to frictions. Still, the United States did not have the authority to dictate its own terms, and many other Afghan detainees were prosecuted in Afghan courts.

"The bottom line is, we're not in a war by ourselves against an enemy that is just our enemy," Lietzau had told me in the fall of 2012, in an interview about the handover of detainees in Afghanistan. "We're in a war where the only way to win is with our alliance."[83]

In early 2013, while Obama and his aides were developing the section of his National Defense University speech that reiterated the call to close Guantánamo, Obama pointed out an irony about the politics of detainees, Rhodes later told me. The dozens of lower-level detainees stuck at Guantánamo were essentially identical to the hundreds of such detainees the United States was handing over to the Afghan government. These Bagram transfers took place virtually without political controversy, but each transfer out of Guantánamo was put under a political microscope.

Karzai had never demanded custody of non-Afghan detainees, so the American military retained control of a wing of the Parwan prison where it was holding on to about fifty non-Afghans. Each had been deemed to pose an "enduring security threat." Some were accused foreign fighters from the Middle East; the bulk were from neighboring Pakistan.

Over the course of 2014, Liotta had worked to wind down this final phase of the Afghanistan War detention operations.[84] That August, the United States repatriated two Yemenis, one of whom was the plaintiff in the ill-fated lawsuit that had unsuccessfully sought to win Guantánamo-style habeas corpus rights for Bagram detainees.[85] That transfer underscored another irony flowing from an arbitrary factor in the rules imposed by Congress. Its restrictions against transferring a detainee to a country with troubled security applied only to Guantánamo. As a result, Yemenis captured in Afghanistan and held at Bagram could be sent home — despite having no habeas rights. Yemenis captured in Afghanistan and held in Guantánamo got habeas rights but remained stuck — even those who had been deemed to pose a lower risk than the ones at Bagram.

But several Bagram prisoners could not easily be repatriated. One of them was Irek Hamidullin. He was a former Russian army tank commander who had deserted during the Soviet-Afghan war in the 1980s, converted to Islam, and eventually joined the Taliban and the Haqqani Network, a Taliban ally that operated out of the tribal areas of Pakistan. The United States had captured Hamidullin in November 2009. It accused him of having led an attack on an Afghan border patrol outpost with the intent of shooting down American helicopters when they swooped in to help. The ambush did not go as he had planned. The anti-aircraft weapons did not work, and no American or Afghan troops were killed, but about 30 insurgents died. The next day, as American and Afghan troops were assessing the area, they found him hiding on the battlefield. Seriously wounded, he was nevertheless captured alive and had been held at Bagram ever since.

The end-of-war agreement with the Afghan government, unlike the one with Iraq, did not clearly give it veto power over the fate of non-Afghan detainees, so the United States had more flexibility in deciding what to do with Hamidullin than it had had with Daqduq. Martins was again at the center of the deliberations. Back in 2009, when Hamidullin was captured, Martins had been leading detention operations in Afghanistan and was fresh off the detention-policy task force. One of its big takeaway insights was that when a terrorism suspect was captured, officials should start thinking early about securing a long-term disposition to keep him locked up in a stable way. From the other side of the world, Martins had lobbied the Justice Department and U.S. Central Command to bring FBI agents to Afghanistan to take witness interviews of the soldiers who had captured Hamidullin while they were still deployed with fresh memories, and otherwise to gather evidence about the Russian that could meet civilian court standards. That had taken some doing. Sending law enforcement agents to Mirandize a war-zone detainee was a politically risky proposition in the immediate aftermath of the Christmas underwear-bombing attempt. But there was no operating military commission system at the time, and Martins eventually prevailed in getting an FBI team flown in.

Now there *was* a commissions system — and Martins was its chief prosecutor. Starting around October 2013, Martins began pushing to try Hamidullin before a military tribunal — not at Guantánamo, but at Charleston. He argued that Hamidullin was accused of combat-related offenses, making him a classic military commissions defendant. The National Security Council considered Martins's arguments. But despite his enthusiasm for expanding the tribunals, in practice, the commissions system was bogged down with many problems. And holding a tribunal in Charleston would mean entrenching and expanding the commissions system.

This time, Martins lost the policy debate. On October 8, 2014, the Justice Department obtained a grand jury indictment of Hamidullin in the Eastern District of Virginia on a dozen counts, including providing material support for terrorism, conspiracy, and attempting to kill Americans and destroy American aircraft. The government flew Hamidullin to the United States that November to face prosecution.[86] And in August 2015, following a five-day trial, a jury convicted him. The judge scheduled him to be sentenced in November, and he faced a potential life term.[87] Once again, using the civilian criminal justice system to resolve a terrorism case had worked smoothly. But a big factor in its success was Martins's intervention, years earlier, to ensure that the government gathered evidence against Hamidullin in a way that met civilian court standards even though it came from the battlefield.

Back on December 9, 2014, the United States military transferred to Afghan custody the last six remaining non-Afghan detainees whom it could not repatriate or find another suitable country to take: two Tunisians, two Tajiks, an Uzbek, and an Egyptian. All were accused of being linked to al-Qaeda, and one of the Tunisians had been tortured in a CIA black-site prison known as Cobalt or the Salt Pit.[88] By putting the six in the Afghan government's hands, Obama had transferred the dilemma and responsibility of what to do with them to someone else, and it was not clear what their fate would be.

It was a messy ending, but for the first time in twelve years, the United States military was no longer running long-term detention operations in Afghanistan. From a separation-of-powers perspective, it was no coincidence that the executive branch succeeded in its policy goal of closing the wartime prison at Bagram, which remained relatively free of interference from Congress and the courts, while it had far more trouble with closing the wartime prison at Guantánamo, where the other two branches placed limits on what it could do.

19. A Legal Obligation to Refrain from Cruelty

As Obama's second term approached its midpoint, it was clearer than ever that on many issues — surveillance, drone strikes, the continued use of indefinite detention at Guantánamo, military commissions, and his revival of combat operations in Iraq by ordering air strikes targeting the Islamic State* — his tenure had lines of continuity with that of George W. Bush. By contrast, on forbidding torture, Obama seemed to have made a clean break with the Bush-Cheney era. But in the fall of 2014, it looked like he was about to compromise, just a bit, on that stance too.

The administration was preparing to send a delegation to a United Nations committee in Geneva that monitored compliance with the Convention Against Torture. This was America's first such presentation before that panel since the Bush-Cheney administration had advanced a controversially narrow interpretation of where the treaty applied, raising the question of whether Obama would reaffirm or reverse that stance.

Most of the treaty has no jurisdictional limits. But article 16, which bars cruel, inhuman, and degrading treatment that falls short of torture, contained an ambiguous phrase. It says the obligations apply to a

---

* See chapter 12, section 15.

state's conduct only "in any territory under its jurisdiction." People disagree about whether this applies to American wartime prisons located on foreign soil.

In 2005, the Bush-Cheney administration revealed that its lawyers had interpreted the cruelty ban as applying only on domestic soil. If so, the treaty imposed no obligations on the United States not to use cruelty when interrogating detainees in its overseas prisons. This revelation helped prompt McCain to push his legislation making clear that the law barred American interrogators from using cruelty everywhere. At the time, Senator Obama said McCain's bill merely "acknowledges and confirms existing obligations" under the treaty, meaning Obama interpreted the treaty ban as applying to American prisons abroad.

As noted, after Congress passed McCain's torture ban, Bush issued a signing statement reserving a right to override the new statute. This left a cloud over it until Obama's January 2009 executive order that required strict adherence to the anti-cruelty standard. But the question of where the executive branch thought the treaty applied *as a matter of binding international law* remained open.

From one vantage point, this did not make any difference: in practice, under current domestic law and policy, the United States was no longer abusing its wartime prisoners anyway. From another vantage point, it made a significant difference. If the United States accepted itself as legally bound by the global treaty not to abuse prisoners, its stance would help spread acceptance of that rule elsewhere in the world. Moreover, it would be harder for the American government, under some future president, to return to using abusive interrogation practices. In Obama's first term, Koh, along with Michael Posner, the State Department's top official for human rights, pushed to change the interpretation of the treaty's reach, but no final decisions were made. In January 2013, on his last day at the State Department, Koh signed a ninety-page internal memo, which I later obtained and published. It concluded, "In my legal opinion, it is not legally available to policy makers to claim" that the the treaty had no application abroad.[89]

Koh's acting replacement, Mary McLeod, a career State Department lawyer, carried on his push; in early October 2014, her office circulated a roughly seventy-page memo making the case to change the interpretation. But now, as the Geneva presentation neared, I learned that Obama's second-term legal team was engaged in a high-level debate over whether to accept and keep the Bush interpretation after all. Military and intelligence lawyers were resisting McLeod's proposal. They insisted that they were not in favor of inflicting cruelty on prisoners, which Obama's order forbade in practice anyway. But they worried that accepting legal obligations under the treaty could have unpredictable operational impacts, including spillover effects to unrelated treaties that had similar jurisdictional language.[90] On October 15, Brian Egan, the top National Security Council lawyer, convened an interagency meeting of the lawyers group at the White House to work through the question of what to tell the UN, but it ended without consensus.

After I wrote about this internal debate, a dozen of Obama's fellow Nobel Peace Prize laureates sent him a joint letter urging him to adopt "firm policy and oversight restating and upholding international law related to conflict, including the Geneva Convention and the U.N. Convention Against Torture." Their letter said the United States was at a "crossroads" and linked the treaty issue to the question of whether Obama would declassify the Senate Intelligence Committee torture report.[91] Archbishop Desmond Tutu of South Africa and former president José Ramos-Horta of East Timor had organized the letter.

I spoke by phone with Tutu about it. He told me it was "disturbing" that Obama's legal team was even considering embracing the "foul thinking" that the American government was legally permitted to do "ghastly things" abroad that the law would bar it from doing on domestic soil. That dovetailed with other matters, he said, like the continued use of indefinite detention without trial at Guantánamo, which contributed to "a grave sense of sadness and of being let down" by Obama. Other liberals, rights advocates, and some Democratic lawmakers shared this critique of the treaty interpretation dispute.

The critics' argument was significantly overstated, since opponents of accepting the treaty as applying outside the United States thought that cruel interrogations were legally forbidden by other authorities. But symbolism was drowning out nuance. Against the backdrop of such pressure, the Obama legal team decided to change the government's view.

The interagency lawyers group cleared the delegation — led by McLeod, Tom Malinowski, who had succeeded Posner as the State Department's top human rights official, and Brigadier General Rich Gross, the top legal adviser to the Joint Chiefs of Staff — to say that the treaty's cruelty ban applied *wherever the United States exercised governmental authority*. This explicitly included the Guantánamo Bay naval base, given the unusual circumstances surrounding American control of it, as well as American-flagged ships and aircraft in international waters and airspace. But it left ambiguous whether the treaty imposed obligations in American-run prisons on the sovereign soil of another government, like the one the United States was pulling out of at Bagram Airfield, or in the former CIA black-site prisons.

The Obama team took a similarly subtle approach to a related issue: whether, in war, the standards of the Geneva Conventions *displaced* the Convention Against Torture or both applied simultaneously. The Obama team said they both applied, but if the two bodies of law came into conflict, the law of war trumped the torture treaty. It was not clear at the time what the significance of this was, since the law of war as described in the Geneva Conventions required humane treatment of prisoners, too. But an official later told me that the Obama team had identified one such conflict, and they just hadn't wanted to draw public attention to it. The anti-torture treaty has a rule, not found in the Geneva Conventions, that requires ensuring that victims of torture are compensated. There was no way, as a political matter, that the United States government was going to give money to KSM and the other former CIA black-site prisoners it had tortured, so this was their workaround. Notably, in July 2014, the European Court of Human Rights in France had ordered Poland to pay $262,000 in compensation to two Guantánamo detainees for its complicity in the CIA's torture of them at a black site in that country, due to a similar provision in a European human rights treaty.[92]

Despite such hedges, the change was significant. It was only the second new legal obligation the United States accepted regarding the treatment of prisoners abroad on Obama's watch,[93] and in one way it made a practical difference. The United States now had to answer questions from the United Nations Committee Against Torture about its conduct at Guantánamo and its interrogation practices, including the seemingly open-to-abuse four-hour-sleep rule in appendix M of the army field manual on interrogation.* It could no longer dismiss such questions by saying the panel had no jurisdiction to ask them, meaning high-level officials had think about and justify the country's practices.

20. The Senate Torture Report and Bush-Cheney Lawyering

On December 9, after months of fighting between the Senate and the CIA over redactions, the Intelligence Committee made public the five-hundred-page summary of its torture report. The report's conclusions that the CIA had exaggerated the value of the information and understated the severity of the techniques had long since been leaked. But the report provided exhaustive details to back those conclusions, along with lurid revelations about previously unknown practices like the "rectal rehydration" and "rectal feeding" water and pureed food into uncooperative prisoners to demonstrate "total control over the detainee," in a chief interrogator's words.[94] The sheer scale of densely footnoted information in the summary alone — it remained unclear whether the full, six-thousand-page version would ever see public light — provided the historical accountability that Obama, by rejecting the idea of a truth commission or after-action review back in 2009, had forgone. It was arguably Congress's most searching and adversarial act of watchdog oversight of the national security bureaucracy in decades. It provided a major counterexample to the same committee's passive cheerleading for post-9/11 expansions of government surveillance.

---

* See chapter 4, section 14.

Former CIA officials led a media campaign to push back. They insisted that the program had been effective in generating information that resulted in the killing or capture of high-level al-Qaeda terrorists, thereby saving lives. They dismissed the Senate report as biased, saying that, "astonishingly, the staff avoided interviewing any of us who had been involved in establishing or running the program."[95]

The report's demonstration that the CIA gave misinformation to policymakers offered Bush-era officials responsible for authorizing the program an opportunity to distance themselves, but they largely closed ranks.[96]

"I'd do it again in a minute," Cheney said five days after the report came out. "I have no problem as long as we achieve our objective. And our objective is to get the guys who did 9/11 and it is to avoid another attack against the United States."[97]

Another set of newly available facts disclosed in the report shed light on how executive-branch lawyering had sometimes worked in practice in the Bush-Cheney administration, offering a point of comparison to the Obama administration's national security legal policymaking. If the Obama team was vulnerable to criticism that it tended to *overlawyer* national security policy questions, the Bush-Cheney administration exemplified the opposite. This was vividly illustrated at a key moment of transition in 2004, when the CIA briefly shut down its interrogation program because a new head of the Office of Legal Counsel, Jack Goldsmith, had raised legal doubts about it. But the Justice Department reapproved the program, after which it continued to operate for several more years. Some puzzle pieces from this moment in post-9/11 history were previously available, but the Senate report provided crucial information that showed how it all fit together.[98]

In May 2004, amid a public uproar over the torture photos from the military's Abu Ghraib prison in Iraq, there was an internal convulsion. The CIA's inspector general produced an entirely classified report concluding that the techniques agency interrogators were using in practice went beyond what the broader executive branch had approved. For example, interrogators were waterboarding prisoners more frequently and ferociously than understood. As noted, when the program began in 2002, the CIA had obtained memos from the Justice Department's Office of Legal Counsel, written by John Yoo and signed by Jay Bybee, that said its "enhanced interrogation" techniques were legally authorized. But those memos were premised on more limited descriptions of what interrogators would do to prisoners. The CIA saw those memos as shielding its people from prosecution, but now their applicability was in doubt.

By then, Bybee was a federal appeals court judge and Yoo was back teaching at the University of California at Berkeley law school. Goldsmith was in charge of the Office of Legal Counsel. The CIA asked Goldsmith to affirm that its interrogation program was legal. The agency was especially insistent on his saying that the program did not violate the treaty ban on cruel, inhuman, or degrading treatment that falls short of torture, and that it did not violate the Constitution's ban on cruel and unusual treatment and government behavior that shocks the conscience. It turned out that the Office of Legal Counsel had never addressed those issues beyond an unsigned, undated three-page list of bullet points by Yoo that summarily stated that they did not apply to the CIA program.[99]

Goldsmith declined to immediately tell the CIA that it was all legal, insisting that he needed to do real legal research and analysis first. Recognizing this as a huge vulnerability, the CIA director, George Tenet, suspended the interrogation program.

Goldsmith had already roiled the Bush-Cheney national security legal team by raising questions about the legality of aspects of the Stellarwind surveillance program that Yoo had approved, concluding that the legal analysis was deeply flawed.* Now he was dismantling another golden shield. Matters quickly escalated when someone leaked to the press a Yoo memo analyzing the anti-torture statute in a way that gutted it. The memo was instantly notorious, and Goldsmith decided to withdraw it. In early June, he told Attorney General John Ashcroft that

---

* See chapter 5, section 8.

he intended to redo the government's entire legal analysis of torture issues, including the issues that the Office of Legal Counsel had never really opined about, after which he would resign at the end of July.[100] Goldsmith had also told the CIA that it could not use waterboarding in the interim because the facts of the program did not comport with his predecessors' assumptions. But the Office of Legal Counsel's prior advice that nine other specific techniques did not violate the anti-torture statute, at least, would stay in place until Goldsmith could complete the research about where to redraw the line.

This was a moment of maximum legal peril for the Bush-Cheney officials who had pushed the program and the CIA officials who had carried it out: What if Goldsmith decided it had been illegal all along?

Then, in late June, as Goldsmith was working away, something happened that shifted the balance. A foreign government captured a terrorism suspect named Janat Gul, and the CIA prepared to take custody of him. Tenet asked Bush's national security adviser, Condoleezza Rice, for a principals committee meeting to discuss using enhanced-interrogation techniques on Gul. Tenet said they had a terrorist informant who had told them that Gul had "almost certain knowledge" of a pre-election plot to attack the United States, and the techniques were necessary to "obtain from Gul critical intelligence necessary to save American lives." Rice convened the meeting in the Situation Room on Friday, July 2. Ashcroft brought his deputy, James Comey — not Goldsmith.

There was a problem with just turning the program back on. Goldsmith was not done analyzing whether those techniques were lawful. But the attorney general has the power to overrule the Office of Legal Counsel. After Tenet explained his proposal, Ashcroft simply declared that nine of ten previously approved enhanced techniques were clearly lawful under both U.S. law and its treaty obligations too; he reserved judgment about the tenth, waterboarding, due to the inspector general's findings.[101] By making this pronouncement, Ashcroft short-circuited Goldsmith's legal analysis, including on the constitutional issues the Justice Department had never actually examined. Goldsmith got the message and moved up his planned departure without completing the new analysis of torture issues. His last day at the Justice Department was Friday, July 16.[102] With Goldsmith out of the way, on Tuesday, July 20, the national security principals committee convened again, this time with Cheney.[103]

At the meeting, Ashcroft was "directed" to send a written memo to the CIA addressing the use of the nine techniques, which he did on July 22. It stated that using them on Gul would not violate the Constitution, any federal statute, or any treaty obligation.[104] This document was the world's shortest torture memo: it consisted of one conclusory sentence and contained no supporting legal analysis.

Gul was rendered to a CIA black-site prison in late July, and Ashcroft appointed a counselor from his office, Daniel Levin, to be temporary head of the Office of Legal Counsel. In response to a CIA request, in early August Levin sent another short memo to the agency stating that waterboarding Gul would be legal too.[105]

The agency did not waterboard Gul. But it tortured him in other ways. For example, it shackled him in painful stress positions and deprived him of sleep for so long that he began to hallucinate, saying he "saw his wife and children in the mirror and had heard their voices in the white noise" that interrogators were also blasting him with. Eventually he "asked to die, or just be killed," CIA cables reported to headquarters.

But Gul did not provide any information. Tenet's justification, that Gul had "almost certain knowledge" of a pre-election plot, was not being borne out. An August 19 internal CIA memo said the interrogation team did *not* believe Gul had any imminent threat information. On August 25, the interrogation team sent a cable to CIA headquarters reiterating these doubts. But that same day, August 25, a CIA lawyer instead wrote to Levin that the agency believed Gul was withholding imminent threat information and requested legal approval to use four additional techniques — methods, including forced nudity and water dousing, that it had previously used on other prisoners even though they had not been blessed in the Justice Department's memos. That same day, Levin provided another conclusory memo saying using those four on Gul would also be lawful.[106]

Now, the post-Goldsmith Justice Department had said that fourteen enhanced techniques were lawful in every respect, locking it into those conclusions, with legal analysis to be developed later. But it appears there was no genuine interest in using these four additional techniques on Gul. As soon as the CIA had the second Levin memo in hand, on August 26, "after a forty-seven-hour session of standing sleep deprivation, Janat Gul was returned to his cell, allowed to remove his diaper, given a towel and a meal, and permitted to sleep," the Senate report said.

Gul never provided any intelligence because he had none to provide. That October, after being polygraphed, the CIA's informant who had fingered Gul admitted that he, the informant, had fabricated the information about Gul and a pre-election plot. The agency eventually let Gul go free. But the CIA never told the Justice Department any of this, and when Stephen Bradbury, who succeeded Levin as acting head of the Office of Legal Counsel, wrote full-length replacement torture memos in 2005, he cited Gul as exactly the kind of high-value terrorist leader for whom enhanced-interrogation techniques were justified. Based on those memos, the program went on.

It was convenient for proponents of the CIA torture program that in the summer of 2004, an urgent, life-or-death interrogation need arose that pressured the Justice Department into rushing to state anew that what the agency had done before was still not a crime, with the legal rationale justifying that conclusion to be filled in later. While there was legitimate reason to take seriously the idea that al-Qaeda might want to attack an event during the American election,[107] there is also reason to be suspicious about this coincidence regarding Gul and the urgent need to torture him, specifically. Senate staffers found internal agency memos from March 2004 showing that from the beginning, the CIA's top al-Qaeda analysts had privately expressed doubts about the credibility of that informant.[108]

21. Tribunals Quagmire

The partial declassification of the Senate Intelligence Committee torture report led to a bright spot for the military commissions system because it permitted the defense lawyers and their clients to talk openly about what the CIA had done to them at the black-site prisons.

The official secrecy surrounding CIA torture had plagued the system's perceived legitimacy from the beginning. The tribunal rules prevented the defendants or their lawyers from speaking in public, including open court, about classified information. As noted, the core strategy of the defense was to try to prevent a death sentence by arguing that the United States government had forfeited the right to do that when it tortured them. As a result, this gag rule functioned for years as "an unnecessary and counterproductive (and legally problematic) blight on the commissions," in the words of Marty Lederman after he left the government.[109]

Behind the scenes, Martins—acutely aware of this problem—had been pushing since 2013 for the CIA to declassify the details of the interrogation techniques used on the defendants and about conditions in the black-site prisons. His requests got swept into the parallel fight between the CIA and the Senate Intelligence Committee, which had its own lengthy delays.[110] In one of his court filings, he took the unusual step of appending a private letter sent in February 2014 from Kathy Ruemmler, the White House counsel, to Senators Dianne Feinstein and Carl Levin; Ruemmler wrote that Brennan was taking steps to "declassify certain information relating to the former program in support of the current military commissions proceedings."[111] Finally, after the executive summary of the Senate report was made public in December 2014, Martins asked the judges to ungag the defense lawyers and the defendants, allowing them to speak openly about their treatment.

The fight wasn't entirely over; defense lawyers still wanted the names of former black-site personnel, whom they hoped to depose as witnesses, and the CIA did not want to provide them. But Martins also pushed for access to review the full, almost-seven-thousand-page report so that prosecutors could make available to the defense anything additional in it about now-declassified categories of information. When he obtained it, he hailed the "milestone" and promised to "continue to work diligently — seven days a week — to fully comply" with an order to give relevant information to the defense.[112]

But that was a rare moment of progress for the troubled commissions system. Years had passed, and still no trial was in sight for the *Cole* and 9/11 cases. Instead, they had careened from one dysfunction to the next, running aground again each time they appeared to be on the cusp of getting somewhere. Defense lawyers discovered that what appeared to be a smoke detector on the ceiling of a room where they met with their clients was in fact a microphone, though prosecutors said it was there because those rooms were used for other purposes and insisted that the government had not used it to spy on their privileged attorney-client communications. Then Pentagon technicians, trying to sync computer files between legal offices in the United States and Guantánamo, made a mistake that caused confidential defense work products to show up on prosecutors' computers. Next, the FBI asked a member of a defense team to become a confidential informant for a criminal investigation into whether another member — neither were attorneys — had illegally facilitated communication between the detainee and people overseas. That investigation was closed without charges.

The hurdles continued. Martins himself asked for psychiatric evaluations of both al-Nashiri, the *Cole* defendant, and Ramzi bin al-Shibh, one of the 9/11 defendants, to make sure they were mentally competent to assist in their own defense. When bin al-Shibh refused for months to cooperate, the judge severed him from the case — meaning there would have to be *two* 9/11 trials — until Martins persuaded him to rescind the order. Then a newly hired translator for the defense was recognized in court by several detainees as being the same person who had worked for the CIA at one of its black-site prisons.

These and other bizarre episodes compounded problems raised by prosecuting the cases in a brand-new, legally untested judicial system. In contrast to federal court, where virtually every permutation of every procedure has long since been settled, the defense lawyers were able to challenge every rule and procedural step in a blizzard of pretrial motions, demanding arguments about each one. Because of the difficulties of holding the court in such a remote location where everyone — judge, prosecutors, defense lawyers, victims' relatives, and reporters — flew in and out together from Andrews Air Force Base, there were only pretrial hearing weeks every two months. Every time one of these additional problems cropped up, planned arguments were postponed and new hearings and briefs scrutinizing the latest mishap took their place.

Martins occasionally made progress with minor issues. He struck plea deals in 2012 and 2014 with two detainees who agreed to testify in the *Cole* and 9/11 cases in exchange for receiving defined prison sentences and exit dates without a trial. He also charged one of the only detainees captured after the Military Commissions Act of 2006 with "material support for terrorism," setting up a test of whether Congress has the power to make that an offense triable in a war court even though it is not a war crime. But on the main two cases, 2012 went by, then 2013, then 2014, then 2015, and still the prospect of an actual trial remained beyond the horizon. The commissions saga was becoming more and more detached from the only real question: whether the 9/11 defendants will be executed or die in prison from old age.

In the fall of 2014, a newly appointed civilian overseer for the commissions, a retired Marine major general named Vaughn Ary, came up with some stark figures. In fiscal year 2014, the government had spent $78 million, not counting the personnel costs for 153 uniformed officials working on commissions, to achieve just thirty-three days of hearings — 107 hours and 50 minutes of court time. The three cases that did not involve a guilty plea were "still in the beginning stages" of the process.

"The status quo," he wrote, "does not support the pace of litigation necessary to bring these cases to their just conclusion."

Ary persuaded the deputy defense secretary of defense, Robert Work, to change the rules in January 2015 so that military commission judges would have to move to Guantánamo and work exclusively on the cases. But instead of speeding things up, the January 2015 move made things even worse. Defense lawyers cried foul, saying it was unlawful influence to pressure judges to rush the cases. In February 2015, the 9/11 case judge, James Pohl, agreed. He froze any further pretrial hearings, forcing Work to rescind the order.[113] The judge in the *Cole* case, air force colonel Vance Spath, went further, ordering Ary and his legal team removed from overseeing the case and canceling a week of planned pretrial hearings that April just to demonstrate that he felt no pressure to accelerate the pace.[114] Ary stepped down.

As the 9/11 and *Cole* cases stayed bogged down and several of the convictions the system had achieved, like in the Hamdan and Bahlul cases, came under a cloud, Holder repeatedly claimed bitter vindication. As early as December 2011, Holder told me that had his original plan to try the case in the Southern District of New York not been scuttled, "we would not have closed down Lower Manhattan. We'd be finished with that trial by now. And it could be something we could point to and show that we can be fair even to those we despise."

The political conversation about military commissions has been largely dominated by ideology viewed through the lens of human rights and state power. The Obama team's decision to reform but keep tribunals as an available option for a narrow band of cases looked pragmatic to them in 2009. This step was criticized by civil liberties–minded liberals who insisted that tribunals were inherently kangaroo courts, even after the reforms. Meanwhile, Republicans denounced any use of civilian courts for terrorism cases as weakness because this was war. These party lines remained entrenched even as commissions floundered in practice in terms of basic functionality. There was no space for the conservative insight — conservative in the sense of the eighteenth-century British parliamentarian and political philosopher Edmund Burke — that traditional institutions and practices that evolved over time should not be lightly tossed aside for untested replacements because it's hard to make a complex new system work.

The civilian court system offered a contrast. On March 4, 2015, the

death-penalty trial of Tsarnaev, the surviving terrorist in the Boston
Marathon attacks, began in the federal courthouse in Boston. One of
the first witnesses after opening statements, Rebekah Gregory, twenty-
seven, walked to the stand with a prosthetic left leg. After she had
endured seventeen different operations and two months in hospitals,
doctors had given up and amputated the lower part of her leg the previous November. At the time of the blast, her five-year-old son, Noah,
had been sitting on her feet, and shrapnel had penetrated his leg to the
bone. As she lay on the ground, Gregory recalled, she had looked for
her son, saw a dead woman to her right, then heard Noah screaming
"Mommy" over and over again behind her. She tried to reach out for
him but found she could not.

"My bones were literally lying next to me on the sidewalk....I
thought that was the day I would die," she said.[115]

After her testimony, Gregory went home and wrote a Facebook post
styled as an open letter to Tsarnaev, mocking him as "a coward. A little
boy who wouldn't even look me in the eyes," and saying the experience
of testifying had been emotionally liberating.

"Up until now, I have been truly scared of you and because of this,
fearful of everything else people might be capable of," she wrote, but
"TODAY...I looked at you right in the face...and realized I wasn't
afraid anymore. And today I realized that sitting across from you was
somehow the crazy kind of step forward that I needed all along."[116]

In May 2015, just over two years after the bombings, a civilian jury
decided that Tsarnaev should be sentenced to death.

The Boston Marathon bombing was the worst terrorist attack inside
the United States since 9/11. The government prosecuted the case in the
Article III civilian criminal justice system, inside a courthouse in a
crowded city and that stood less than two miles from where the bombs
had gone off. Boston did not shut down for the kind of heavy-handed
security plan that helped derail the KSM trial in New York. The case got
to trial in less than two years. The focus stayed on the terrorist's deeds,
not the system's rules and legitimacy. A civilian jury convicted the
defendant and imposed the harshest sentence.

In short, because the civilian court system works, the surviving victims and relatives of those killed in the Boston Marathon attack experienced a measure of catharsis. Because the military commissions system has failed to work, despite the best efforts of committed public servants like Martins, the victims of the *Cole* and 9/11 attacks were still waiting.

22. Obama's Guantánamo Endgame Begins

Back in January 2014, Obama declared in his State of the Union speech that "with the Afghan war ending, this needs to be the year Congress lifts the remaining restrictions on detainee transfers and we close the prison at Guantánamo Bay."[117] But when Congress passed the annual National Defense Authorization Act in December 2014, lawmakers left the restrictions in place, including the ban on bringing any detainees to a prison on domestic soil. Obama issued a five-hundred-word signing statement, drafted by his new White House counsel, Neil Eggleston, denouncing the restrictions in his most aggressive language yet. He portrayed the prison closure as "a national imperative," invoked the prospect that the restrictions might be unconstitutional, and called on "members from both sides of the aisle to work with us to bring this chapter of American history to a close."[118]

The following month, the final Congress of Obama's presidency took office. Republicans strengthened their majority in the House and took control of the Senate. Newly empowered Republican senators rallied around a bill filed by Kelly Ayotte that would block the transfer, to anywhere, of any detainee still left at Guantánamo, regardless of individual circumstances. It was cosponsored by Lindsey Graham; Richard Burr, now the chairman of the Intelligence Committee; and John McCain, now the chairman of the Armed Services Committee.

McCain's support for the bill was surprising. As recently as November 2013, he had cosponsored an amendment to make it easier to transfer the remaining detainees to a prison on American soil, portraying the Guantánamo prison as a waste of money and a symbol of torture that terrorists used for recruiting new members.[119] Now McCain portrayed Obama's recent flurry of transfers — the cluster of departures as Hagel, preparing to step down, cleared out the backlog that had built up on his watch — as reckless, claiming that one in three of them would likely re-engage in jihadism.[120] But McCain also maintained he might still support closing the prison if Obama ever came up with a plan for doing so.

While critics of Obama's Guantánamo did not like his plan, Obama had been putting one forward for years: transfer lower-level detainees out, and bring the rump group of those deemed too-dangerous-to-release to a prison in the United States for prosecution or for continued wartime detention subject to periodic review.

In February 2015, McCain dedicated one of the first Senate Armed Services Committee hearings under his chairmanship to Guantánamo.[121] The topic of the hearing also roamed into Obama's policy for newly captured terrorism suspects, whom many Republicans believed should be brought to Guantánamo. Ayotte declared that the administration's model of interrogating newly captured prisoners aboard a ship for intelligence purposes and then transferring them to the criminal justice system did not work, asserting that Ahmed Warsame had been interrogated for a "far too insufficient amount of time" to get good intelligence from him. Senator Jeff Sessions said prosecuting terrorists before military commissions made more sense than civilian court, and he predicted that another detainee who had been interrogated aboard a ship in 2013 before his transfer to the regular court system, Abu Anas al-Libi, would use civilian trial rights to demand access to classified information the government did not want to reveal.

Much of the hearing was filled up by tussling over what the facts were, leaving little space for any real attempt to think about what the best policy arising from those facts would be. In testimony, Brian McKeon, the principal undersecretary of defense for policy, questioned the one-in-three "recidivism" rate for ex-Guantánamo detainees that critics frequently cited as predictive of the Obama-era transfers. In fact, he noted, that number corresponded to the rate of suspected or confirmed problems among the detainees who had been transferred during the latter Bush-Cheney era, when Bush had started trying to close Guantánamo via bulk repatriations of prisoners to favored countries like Saudi Arabia. There were still some problems arising from the Obama-era individualized review process, but the rate was 6 percent.[122]

McKeon also replied to Ayotte that Warsame had provided a tremendous amount of intelligence and, indeed, had continued to cooperate freely with interrogators "even after he went into the federal court system."*

And he pointed out to Sessions that al-Libi was dead, so there would be no trial. (He had liver disease and had died in custody a month earlier, while awaiting trial.) A more substantive point in response to Sessions's concerns would have been to note that the rules for the defense to obtain classified evidence, at least on paper, were basically the same in the civilian and military trial systems.

But McKeon had no answer for Tom Cotton, a newly elected thirty-seven-year-old Republican senator from Arkansas and rising neoconservative whose résumé included two Harvard degrees and combat stints in Afghanistan and Iraq. Noting that Islamist terrorists had repeatedly attacked the United States long before Bush opened the Guantánamo prison in 2002, Cotton rejected the Obama argument that closing it would improve national security by removing a symbol that fueled anti-American sentiment abroad. Cotton maintained that the administration's argument was a pretext and Obama's real motive was political: to fulfill a campaign promise. His comment seemed to capture what was really going on.

"In my opinion, the only problem of Guantánamo Bay is there are too many empty beds and cells there right now," Cotton said, his voice rising. "We should be sending more terrorists there for further interrogation to keep this country safe. As far as I'm concerned, every last one of them can rot in hell, but as long as they don't do that, then they can rot in Guantánamo Bay."

---

* See chapter 7, sections 16 through 18.

Cotton turned off his microphone and a fifteen-second silence filled the hearing room. But earlier, in a more temperate phase of his questioning of McKeon, Cotton had asked about something that was close to a question on my mind as well. Obama was displaying increasing willingness to take "executive actions" in the face of congressional opposition, and he was voicing escalating rhetoric about the imperative of closing the Guantánamo prison. It seemed conceivable that Obama might eventually — say, sometime after the November 2016 election and before the January 2017 inauguration of his successor — command the Pentagon to bring all the remaining detainees to a military prison inside the United States *despite the ban*. That would require a Bush-like claim by Obama that his commander-in-chief powers overrode a statute purporting to restrict his ability to move or prosecute wartime prisoners.[123] But Obama had already done that, albeit in a far more limited way, for the Bergdahl-Taliban deal.

"This administration has a habit of surprising the American people on national security matters," Cotton said. "What assurance can we receive that there will not be a Guantánamo detainee on our shores tomorrow morning?"

McKeon testified that he was not aware of any conversations about moving detainees to American soil despite the statutory ban.

Just a day earlier, the same committee had held the confirmation hearing for Hagel's successor as secretary of defense, Ash Carter. Ayotte and Cotton both brought up reports that Hagel had been pressured by the White House to sign off on transfers from Guantánamo. Ayotte asked Carter not to "succumb to any pressure by this administration to increase the pace of transfers from Guantánamo. Will you commit to that?"

"Absolutely, senator," Carter replied. "I understand my responsibilities under that statute, and I'll, as in everything else I do, I'll play it absolutely straight."[124]

For his part, Obama remained determined. On May 14, 2015, he met at Camp David with leaders from the six Gulf Cooperation Council countries — including the emirs of Qatar and Kuwait, and senior representatives of Saudi Arabia, United Arab Emirates, Oman, and Bahrain — to reassure them that a nuclear deal with Iran, then in its end stages of negotiations, would not put them at risk. That part of the meeting was reported; what wasn't reported was that after those discussions, Obama asked them to consider resettling groups of Guantánamo detainees on the transfer list, apparently receiving tentative commitments from several.

Meanwhile, McCain seemed to be edging back toward being willing to help close Guantánamo. He included, in the Senate's version of the annual National Defense Authorization Act, a provision that would require the administration to submit a plan for closing Guantánamo to Congress. If both chambers voted to approve it, the ban on bringing detainees into the United States would be lifted. McCain met with Obama in mid-May at the White House to discuss this idea, and three days later Carter and Monaco visited McCain in his suite at the Russell Senate Office Building and promised to give him a plan.[125] It wasn't clear how anything would get through the House regardless, but it still seemed prudent to White House aides to work with him. Still, Obama was threatening to veto either version of the bill.

At the end of June, Kerry appointed a new State Department envoy, Lee Wolosky, to succeed Sloan following a six-month gap. Yet another lawyer selected for a policy role, Wolosky had worked on terrorism financing issues at the National Security Council in both the late Clinton and early Bush-Cheney administrations before leaving government for private practice. With a family and a law firm partnership in New York to return to, Wolosky had the profile of someone who would not fear making bureaucratic enemies.

"The harder the mission, the more I'm interested in trying to tackle it," Wolosky told me on the day Kerry announced his appointment.

But by the summer of 2015, the familiar pattern of delay began to reassert itself. In his first six months as secretary of defense, Carter had permitted just one deal to go through — a group of six Yemenis who were resettled in Oman in June 2015, completing a ten-detainee resettlement deal that Hagel had previously signed off on.[126] Other than that, Carter had approved no transfer packages sitting on his desk, including the repatriation of a Mauritanian and a Moroccan. Advised by Dempsey to be cautious, he also voiced skepticism in internal deliberations about sending Shaker Aamer, a high-profile Saudi citizen and British resident, to Britain, even though that close ally had been requesting his transfer.

Going back to the Hagel playbook, in June, Rice and Monaco proposed holding a principals committee meeting devoted solely to the topic of Guantánamo. The meeting finally convened on the afternoon of Monday, July 13. The Cabinet officials spent some of the time talking about the plan for McCain. But much of the ninety-minute meeting involved these high-level officials diving deep into the weeds of proposed transfers — the sort of policy conversation that usually would take place at a much lower level of government.

To his surprise, Carter was also presented with an unsigned National Security Council memo declaring that he must make decisions within thirty days about whether to notify Congress that he had approved a proposed transfer or to reject it. In other words, he would face deadlines to move and could no longer let matters drift indefinitely without resolution, as Hagel also had done. It was not clear what this memo was — a rule? a proposal? — making it the latest unorthodox move in a bureaucratic decision-making process that was warped by the notice statute.

Carter said he would think about the transfers some more, but the results of the meeting were ambiguous. He made no commitments to move on the existing proposals, and it was unclear whether he accepted the thirty-day deadline as a binding rule for new ones.

At that point, with slightly less than a year and a half left in Obama's presidency, there were 116 detainees remaining, of whom 52 were on the transfer list. Even if homes could be found for each and Carter approved the transfers, that would leave 64 who had to be taken somewhere else if Obama's policy was not to end in failure. Inside the White House, Obama pressed his team to try harder. He said he did not want to leave Guantánamo as a mess for his successor to deal with.

11

Institutionalized
(Surveillance 2009–2015)

1. Defending and Entrenching Warrantless Surveillance

On October 29, 2012, as Hurricane Sandy drenched Washington and American voters mulled the imminent presidential election between Barack Obama and Mitt Romney, two elite lawyers drove through the rain to the Supreme Court to argue about surveillance.[1] They were Donald Verrilli, the solicitor general of the United States, and Jameel Jaffer, who oversaw the American Civil Liberties Union's Center for Democracy, which performs the organization's work on human rights, national security, free speech, privacy, and technology. The focus of their dispute that day was the 2008 law that legalized the NSA's post-9/11 warrantless surveillance program. By the end of the arguments, Verrilli would make a claim that came back to haunt the Obama administration.

After the *New York Times* had revealed the original warrantless-wiretapping program in 2005, the American Civil Liberties Union was one of the groups that filed lawsuits challenging it. But the FISA Amendments Act in 2008, enacted with the vote of then-Senator Barack Obama,* had killed that litigation. It granted retroactive legal immunity to the phone and network companies that had turned over

---

* See chapter 2, section 7.

their customers' communications to the NSA without warrants. The 2008 law also legalized surveillance without warrants on domestic soil going forward, so long as the target was a foreigner abroad. That took care of the statutory problem with Stellarwind's content component — that it violated the Foreign Intelligence Surveillance Act. But a question remained: did warrantless surveillance on domestic soil violate the Constitution? Hours after President George W. Bush signed the FISA Amendments Act, the ACLU filed a new case challenging the new law as unconstitutional. The civil liberties group had enlisted a group of plaintiffs, led by Amnesty International, who frequently communicated with people overseas. The plaintiffs contended that this arrangement would end up collecting their messages, too, in violation of their Fourth Amendment rights. They also argued that even the risk of that happening would make them less likely to call people overseas, chilling their exercise of their first Amendment rights.

Judge John Koeltl, a district court judge in New York, heard the first arguments in the case on July 22, 2009. Jaffer had been in that courtroom as well. He maintained that the program would suck in so many international messages to and from Americans that it effectively "allows the government to engage in dragnet, suspicionless surveillance of Americans' calls and e-mails."[2]

The government dismissed such claims as hyperbole: among other things, while it was common for privacy advocates to label the FISA Amendments Act program "dragnet," that term implied the indiscriminate collection of *everything,* not surveillance that targeted specific individuals. In the courtroom, Justice Department lawyers told Koeltl that Jaffer was wrong, but also that the judge should not even think about what Jaffer was saying. Instead, they urged Koeltl to simply dismiss the case because the plaintiffs' fears that their communications would be intercepted under the 2008 law were too speculative to give them standing to challenge the statute. They also urged him to defer to the FISA Court in making sure that the surveillance program complied with the Constitution.

Koeltl sided with the government. He dismissed the case, agreeing that the plaintiffs lacked standing to bring it.[3] The plaintiffs appealed, now just trying to win the right to have a day in court. The case began its slow march toward the Supreme Court.

Even as the Obama administration was fighting in open court to prevent judges in the regular judicial system from scrutinizing the FISA Amendments Act, it was taking steps behind the scenes to significantly expand warrantless surveillance under that law. For example, the Obama team inherited from the Bush-Cheney administration a system that used the law to hunt for two types of messages: those linked to terrorists and those linked to foreign governments. In March 2009, the Obama Justice Department gained the FISA Court's approval to expand it for a third purpose: tracking people suspected of trafficking in biological, chemical, or nuclear weapons.[4]

Other types of expansion followed. Initially, only the NSA stored a copy of raw Internet communications gathered under the 2008 law, and it processed the data to remove innocent Americans' names and private information before sharing anything with other agencies. But in October 2009, the Obama administration won the FISA Court's approval for the FBI to keep and use its own copy of certain raw messages collected under the FISA Amendments Act. The FBI was helping to administer the Prism system, which the NSA used to gather foreigners' messages from e-mail providers like Yahoo, Google, and Microsoft, and the FBI began keeping a copy of communications gathered through Prism.[5] FBI agents gained the power to search the database using the names of Americans whom they were scrutinizing, including for unrelated criminal investigations, and read any messages by those Americans that were swept up incidentally and without a warrant. Two years later, the Obama administration won a further loosening of the rules. In October 2011, the FISA Court granted its request to let NSA and CIA analysts search for incidentally collected Americans' messages in the raw storehouse, too. Those analysts had to have a "foreign intelligence" purpose when conducting that search."[6] (I will return to this so-called "backdoor search" issue later.)

Yet another expansion came in April 2012. The FBI gained the power for agents to make their own nominations for which foreigners to target for surveillance without warrants using the Prism system.[7]

And in May and July 2012, Eric Holder's Justice Department — with informal guidance from the surveillance court — wrote two secret memos expanding the NSA's use of the other system by which it conducted Internet surveillance under the FISA Amendments Act: its "upstream" collection of data crossing network switches. Previously, the NSA used only phone numbers and e-mail addresses as "selectors" for targeting and collecting messages. But the memos cleared the way for it to begin using as selectors the Internet addresses and cyber patterns of hackers who appeared to be linked to foreign governments, even if their personal identities were not known.

This "cyber targeting" was particularly significant because the government makes its own copy of the data that foreign hackers are downloading from American computers. It considers American hacker-victim data to be incidental collection, a by-product of targeting the foreigner just like an e-mail an American sent to a foreign target — and thus, apparently, fair game for searching by intelligence analysts. But for hacker victims, the volume of incidental collection could be gigabytes of private computer files at a shot, not just singular messages, and these victims had no connection to the foreign target.[8]

Although these changes to the rules significantly expanded government surveillance powers and activities under the FISA Amendments Act, the Obama administration did not disclose any of them to the public for scrutiny and debate.

Meanwhile, the lawsuit the American Civil Liberties Union and Amnesty International had brought seeking judicial review of the FISA Amendments Act had slowly worked its way up through the court system. In March 2011, a federal appeals court panel in New York reversed the trial judge's decision, holding that the plaintiffs *did* have standing to bring the lawsuit.[9] Now it was the Justice Department's turn to appeal. And so it was, on that rainy day just before the presidential election, that the lawsuit seeking the right to challenge the 2008 act came before the Supreme Court.

Standing before the nine justices in their black robes, Verrilli argued that Amnesty International and the other clients of the American Civil Liberties Union had no idea whether any of their conversations had been intercepted. The Justice Department had made that point at earlier stages in the litigation. But Verrilli also assured the justices that if they threw out this lawsuit for standing reasons, the regular judiciary would still get a chance to scrutinize the constitutionality of the FISA Amendments Act. If the government intended to use information from the warrantless surveillance program against someone in a criminal trial, Verrilli said, the government must inform that defendant that he faced evidence obtained or derived from wiretapping under the FISA Amendments Act. Such a criminal defendant *would* have proper legal standing to challenge the underlying law because he had a right to ask a court to suppress the evidence if it had come from an illegal search, queuing up the question of whether the surveillance had been constitutional.

There was, in hindsight, something very odd about Verrilli's assertion. By then, the warrantless surveillance program had been operating under FISA for nearly six years. And yet, in all that time, federal prosecutors had *never given such a notice to any criminal defendant.* But Verrilli had referenced the same requirement in his briefs, and the Supreme Court accepted what he was saying about government practices as true.

On February 26, 2013, Verrilli won his case — barely. The Supreme Court ruled, five to four, that the plaintiffs lacked standing and so could not bring the case. There would be no constitutional review of the law for now. In the majority opinion, Justice Samuel Alito Jr. echoed Verrilli's assertion that prosecutors would tell criminal defendants if they faced evidence derived from the program, and so those defendants would have standing to challenge the wiretapping law.[10]

Meanwhile, in December 2012, between the oral arguments and the court's decision, Dianne Feinstein, the chairwoman of the Senate Intelligence Committee, seemed to reveal several criminal cases that had involved such surveillance. She did so in a Senate floor speech in favor of extending the FISA Amendments Act, which was set to expire at the end of the year if Congress did not pass a bill pushing back its so-called "sunset" date.

Congress was clearly going to extend the warrantless surveillance program without changes regardless of what Feinstein said; the final vote was a lopsided seventy-three to twenty-three.[11] But Feinstein, leaving nothing to chance, delivered a strong speech urging her colleagues to pass a bill pushing back the sunset to the end of 2017. In that speech, she noted that there had been one hundred arrests in terrorism-related cases since 2009; for "some of them," she said, "the information came right from this program." She then described eight cases, adding, "So this has worked."[12]

As it happened, two of those eight cases — one in South Florida and one in Chicago — were still in pretrial stages. In the spring of 2013, citing Feinstein's speech, defense lawyers in both cases asked magistrate judges to compel the Justice Department to tell them what evidence their clients faced that was derived from warrantless surveillance under the FISA Amendments Act. But prosecutors replied that the Justice Department was under no obligation to disclose whether there was *any* such evidence — the exact opposite of what Verrilli had assured the Supreme Court the government would do.[13]

The administration's double talk at first got little attention. But after the leaks by the former intelligence contractor Edward Snowden in June, a scorching spotlight descended upon everything related to surveillance legal policy. The disconnect between what Verrilli had told the Supreme Court and what national-security prosecutors were telling magistrate judges stood exposed in that glare, leading to an extraordinary fight inside the Obama administration.

2. Hidden Headaches with Bulk Collection

Obama's approach to surveillance was different from his position on many other post-9/11 national security legal-policy matters. From the start, Obama saw no need to scale back the spying programs he had inherited from Bush, beyond adding some extra layers of internal oversight. Obama and his advisers believed that the programs provided valuable intelligence that was truly necessary for protecting national security, and they were satisfied that the problem *they* had seen with Bush's Stellarwind program — that it violated FISA — had been solved by 2009. Surveillance and bulk data collection, as well, were invisible tools for protecting against terrorism and achieving other foreign-policy aims. There were no troops dying on the ground, no drones killing civilian bystanders, and no spectacle of prisoners being held without trial. Where Obama battled conservatives over policy goals like closing the prison at Guantánamo, he battled liberals by defending the surveillance programs from legal scrutiny.

As we have seen, Obama decided early on to keep the classified programs that were systematically harvesting bulk records of Americans' phone and e-mail communications.* Still, throughout his first term, the administration struggled behind closed doors with internal legal and policy controversies about these still-secret dragnet metadata programs — fights that became public knowledge only years later.

In July 2009, for example, the FISA Court approved an order to Sprint requiring it to turn over all of its customers' calling logs to the NSA on a daily basis. The order, like those issued to other phone companies, was terse and simply stated that it was being issued under section 215 of the Patriot Act; there was no explanation of how that law, which said the FBI could get records that were "relevant" to an investigation, could possibly justify such a sweeping demand.

Remarkably, the government was keeping its legal theory secret even from the phone companies participating in the bulk phone records program. Equally remarkably, up until July 2009, all the companies that had received such orders simply complied with them without bothering to find out if they made any sense. But that month, Sprint and its outside lawyer, Michael Sussmann, began pushing the Justice Department to divulge the legal theory to the company.† This fight became public in 2014, when the government declassified and released FISA

---

* See chapter 5, section 1.
† See also chapter 8, section 2.

Court documents from it. Those documents redacted the name of the company and its lawyer, but the *Washington Post* first reported that it was Sprint and Sussmann, and numerous officials familiar with the episode confirmed to me that this was correct.[14]

From the Justice Department's perspective, Sprint's demand to see the legal interpretation behind the orders put the government in a bind. The underlying briefs and opinions were classified by the NSA and sealed by the FISA Court, so it was not their information to provide. Moreover, the key FISA Court precedent for making sense of the secret bulk phone records program was Judge Colleen Kollar-Kotelly's 2004 opinion that laid out a legal rationale for the other bulk program, the one for harvesting e-mail records using "pen register/trap and trace" devices installed on Internet routers.* Sprint did not participate in that program. So to show the Sprint lawyers the key legal ruling, the Justice Department would have to reveal *another* classified program to them. It was a mess.

The department tried to dissuade Sprint from pressing further to see the secret legal theory, maintaining that the fact that the firm had received an order signed by a judge should be enough to satisfy it that everything was lawful. But the firm's lawyers were not satisfied, saying they had an obligation to make sure the company was complying with the law.

Officials confirmed to me that Sussmann had drafted an extensive motion challenging the order as unlawful, and Sprint threatened to file the challenge with the FISA Court. It took a pre-Christmas intervention by Bob Litt, the top lawyer for the Office of the Director of National Intelligence, to force the Justice Department to ask the FISA Court to let Sprint read the documents. But after reading them in January 2010 — just after the Christmas airline-bombing attempt — Sprint's general counsel, Charles Wunsch, decided not to file the challenge after all.

As Sprint was weighing its challenge, the program also came under fire from the inside. A senior technical official at the NSA began raising

---

* See chapter 5, section 9.

concerns about the phone records program.[15] This official approached the NSA director, Keith Alexander, and later Matt Olsen, who became the NSA general counsel in August 2010.

I don't think we should be doing this, he said.

The official listed various arguments. Collecting domestic records about Americans went against the agency's post–Church Committee culture and values. The program was not producing enough real information to be worth its time and cost. And the NSA systems were having trouble keeping up with the massive data flow.[16]

The technical official proposed an alternative model: keep the bulk records in the hands of the phone companies and just gather those records linked to a suspect. But NSA and Justice Department officials decided it would be too hard to maintain the program's ability to swiftly analyze links to callers one or two layers removed from an initial suspect because some of those callers would be customers of different phone companies. The technical official's idea lapsed.

Others in the executive branch were taking steps to entrench the program. In late 2009 and early 2010, the NSA built a new system with more rigorous controls to make sure it stayed within the rules the FISA Court had imposed, and the Obama administration persuaded Congress to reauthorize the Patriot Act without changes.*

Later in 2010 and 2011, the NSA flirted with expanding the program so that it would also track the physical movements of every American with a cell phone. It would do this by triangulating their locations from records of which cell towers were in closest contact with the devices at any given time. The agency used Patriot Act orders to get real data about Americans' locations to test whether its systems could handle the massive volume of data this would entail, but did not use it for operational purposes. It eventually shelved the project without moving forward.[17] At the time, it also promised the congressional oversight committees that if it changed its mind and decided to collect domestic cell phone locational records in bulk in the future, it would notify them

---

* See chapter 5, sections 1 and 17.

first and seek specific permission from the FISA Court. In August 2011, AT&T began supplying 1.1 billion cell phone calling records a day to the program, on top of the 700 million landline calling records it was already providing.[18] But at the NSA's request, it stripped out the locational data from its records before turning them over.[19]

The *other* bulk metadata program, the one collecting records of e-mails, caused even greater legal problems for the Obama administration in its first term. Sometime in mid-2009,[20] the Justice Department confessed to the FISA Court that the NSA had discovered yet another compliance problem with the program: the agency had been systematically collecting more categories of metadata about e-mails than the court orders had authorized it to gather. The gathering of these extra categories without judicial sanction amounted to illegal "electronic surveillance" under FISA. This problem infected almost every record the NSA had collected since the court had first approved the program in 2004.[21]

Judge Reggie Walton expressed concerns about keeping the program going knowing that was happening, and the National Security Division did not apply for an order reauthorizing the Internet program when it expired that fall.

But in mid-2010, the Justice Department declared that the NSA had fixed the problems and asked the FISA Court for permission to turn the program back on. In fact, the administration wanted to do something additional that would increase the data it was permitted to collect by eleven- to twenty-four-fold. It also wanted permission to use the extra categories of data it had unlawfully collected before the fix.

By now, Judge John Bates had succeeded Kollar-Kotelly as the FISA Court's presiding judge, and he took over oversight of the NSA's problems complying with the rules. In July 2010,[22] in a lengthy opinion about the Obama administration's request to turn back on — and expand — the bulk Internet records program, Bates excoriated the executive branch for its pattern of "continuously" violating court-imposed rules and misleading the court about how NSA programs worked. He marveled that despite all that, it wanted to "expand authorization in ways that test the limits of what the applicable FISA provisions will bear." He would not let the NSA use the older Internet data it had illegally collected beyond the scope of the court's orders at the time. Nevertheless, he granted the NSA's request to turn the program back on and to collect and use the wider swath of information going forward.[23]

The program was back and bigger than ever — but only for about a year. In late 2011, the NSA shut down the bulk e-mail records program for good. When the former existence of the program came to light in 2013, intelligence officials were vague in explaining why they had changed their minds about the need for a program that the government had repeatedly told Congress and the FISA Court was vital for national security. Now, they said only that its operational value as a "unique source of foreign intelligence information" had dropped.[24]

It remains unclear what the real story was, and there are different theories.

One set of explanations is premised on the idea that the program really did end. Ron Wyden and Mark Udall would take political credit for ending the program, claiming that their hard questions pressing officials to "provide evidence of its effectiveness" had led to the decision.[25]

A variant is that the program had once been useful but that its utility was going down because around this time, e-mail providers like Google started automatically encrypting the flow of data between their servers and users' computers, making it harder to collect bulk e-mail metadata from network switches.[26]

Yet another theory, first put forward by the national security analyst Marcy Wheeler of the *Emptywheel* blog, was that the program might not have stopped so much as *migrated.*[27] In November 2010, the NSA — finishing what the Bush-Cheney administration had started in 2008* — changed internal rules in order to permit analysts to use bulk data about Americans' communications that the NSA had gathered abroad under Executive Order 12333 rules.[28] Previously, when analyzing links between people using bulk data gathered abroad, the NSA had to stop a chain if it hit an American's data. Now they could keep going to see the

---

* See chapter 5, section 15.

American's contacts. Wheeler argued that the NSA might have given up on trying to comply with the FISA Court's limits and moved the same activity offshore, where it had greater flexibility and fewer oversight restrictions.

Several officials later told me that Wyden and Udall were overstating their influence, but there were elements of truth to the latter two explanations. In particular, they said, the FISA Court's bulk e-mail records program was providing less of a unique source of information because the NSA was getting more Internet-communications logs from other sources. One source was from Executive Order 12333 collection abroad, and another was the FISA Amendments Act. When the government used the Prism system to target non-citizens abroad under that law, it was now able to assemble a vast pool of metadata by sucking in its targets' entire e-mail accounts from companies like Yahoo or Microsoft and harvesting the headers from years of old messages.[29] But the officials cautioned that this was not a one-for-one switch. While these other sources had made the bulk e-mail records program relatively less important, it had still been more comprehensive when it came to records of Americans' e-mails.

Whatever the explanation, the bottom line was that the story of one of the three major parts of Stellarwind, one that played a major role in the famous March 2004 John Ashcroft hospital-room incident, had come to an end. The Obama-era NSA had ended one of the most sweeping secret surveillance programs that came out of the Bush-Cheney era — but for technical reasons, not civil liberties ones.

3. Going Dark

In September 2010, when all of those Obama administration maneuvers at the NSA and before the FISA Court were still secret, I heard that the FBI was developing a proposal to make it easier for the government, armed with court orders, to wiretap Internet companies. That seemed like something worth digging into.

The project began with a premise. The government had long been able to wiretap ordinary phone calls — a basic technology operated by only a few companies that were used to receiving, and cooperating with, court orders. But increasingly, people were communicating online instead of by traditional phone, and the number of companies that operated services that permitted messaging — not just web-based e-mail, but chat rooms, interactive games that let players talk to each other, and so forth — was exploding. Many were start-ups that had never interacted with the government or thought about building an interception capability into their systems. Some of the services also encrypted communications between end users, meaning even those firms could not tell what their customers were saying to each other. Even before Snowden, we knew that the NSA had developed extraordinary ways to break encryption and spy on Internet communications. But it turned out that the agency was reluctant to share those secret intelligence capabilities with the FBI — let alone state and local police — for ordinary criminal investigations, because that would risk exposing those capabilities and ruining them for intelligence purposes. The FBI's nightmare scenario: law enforcement officials would get a court order to wiretap a suspected criminal, but the company whose service their suspect is using to communicate has no immediate technical ability to comply with the order. FBI engineers could help such firms retrofit their systems to permit wiretapping, but that could take weeks, losing valuable time — and in some cases it was impossible to make it work. The FBI called this problem Going Dark, and its proposal was designed to keep the lights on.

I was able to piece together enough about the developing Going Dark proposal that Valerie Caproni, the FBI lawyer, agreed to talk with me about the rest. I went to her office at the FBI's J. Edgar Hoover Building, a Brutalist concrete high-rise across Pennsylvania Avenue from the Justice Department's headquarters. Caproni was a plain-talking and candid person with a hint of twang from her Georgia childhood, and Obama later made her a federal district court judge in New York. She and an aide filled in the gaps in my reporting.

Although I was the first to write about it, it turned out the bureau had been quietly developing the proposal since the late Bush years, and it was now preparing to ask the Obama White House for permission to make it an official executive-branch request to Congress. The bureau wanted to expand a 1994 law — the Communications Assistance for Law Enforcement Act, or CALEA — that requires phone companies to build into their networks, from the moment they become commercially operational, a technical ability to intercept a particular customer's phone calls. The 1994 law applies only to network firms that are regulated by the Federal Communications Commission, like AT&T and Verizon. It does not apply to Internet companies that *use* the network but do not *operate* it, like Google and Yahoo. The FBI wanted to expand the law to cover all companies that enable people to communicate.

The FBI also wanted to bar services like BlackBerry's corporate enterprise system, which encrypted communications from one end to the other in a way that even BlackBerry could not unscramble. Any communications-enabling firm would have to have a way to intercept and unscramble a customer's messages if ordered to do so by a court. Finally, the FBI wanted foreign-based Internet companies that do business in the United States to route communications through a hub on American soil where wiretap orders could be served.

"We're talking about lawfully authorized intercepts," Caproni said. "We're not talking expanding authority. We're talking about preserving our ability to execute our existing authority in order to protect the public safety and national security.... No one should be promising their customers that they will thumb their nose at a U.S. court order. They can promise strong encryption. They just need to figure out how they can provide us plain text."[30]

Privacy and technology groups did not see it that way. They said banning strong end-to-end encryption would make everyone's communications vulnerable to malicious hackers, damaging privacy. They worried that requiring start-ups to build in interception capabilities from the beginning would increase costs and complexity, quashing innovation. And they warned that requiring overseas firms to route their data through a hub on American soil would prompt foreign countries — including unsavory regimes hoping to spy on political dissidents — to do likewise to American firms.

Soon after my article ran, Obama met with senior law enforcement and national security officials in the Oval Office. At that gathering, Obama pressed Bob Mueller, the FBI director, to tell him what, if anything, he needed or what was important to him. Mueller used the opportunity to bring up the Going Dark initiative, now that it was out there.

Obama's counterterrorism adviser, John Brennan, convened a deputies committee meeting in the Situation Room so the White House could get a handle on the proposal. Caproni brought an operational official from the FBI to present slides about the problem. A range of intelligence and Justice Department officials attended, as well as Cameron Kerry, the general counsel of the Commerce Department, and Jim Kohlenberger, the chief of staff for the White House Office of Science and Technology Policy.

The presence of economic and science experts brought a different tenor to the national security policy meeting. Kohlenberger grilled the FBI briefer, trying to figure out how real the problem was. The FBI's list of real-world examples struck some observers as unimpressive. Several of the services that had interception problems had since ceased operating anyway.

Caproni did not yield. From the FBI's perspective, the issue was less what had happened already and more what it foretold about the future.

At the end of the meeting, Brennan said the policy development could go forward but warned that he did not want to read anything more about their deliberations in the newspaper. Brennan assigned his aide Nate Jones to lead the process from the White House. Jones convened meetings and circulated drafts of potential policy language. In November 2010, Mueller and Caproni went on a tour of Silicon Valley, urging executives at firms like Google and Facebook not to lobby against their proposal.[31]

The FBI's Going Dark push proceeded in fits and starts over the next two years. It went quiet for a while after Caproni left the FBI. But Mueller made it a last policy wish-list item as his term wound down, and in 2012, Caproni's successor as the FBI's top lawyer, Andrew Weissmann, revived the effort. By the end of that year, the bureau switched to a different approach. It dropped its demand to ban end-to-end encryption services and regulate Internet companies under the 1994 phone law. Instead, it proposed legislation that would impose steep and automatic fines on large companies that failed to swiftly comply with wiretap orders for reasons other than that their services used encryption.[32] Smaller firms would be exempt until they had received their first wiretap order or until the attorney general notified them that they might receive one, after which they would get a waiting period to engineer an interception capability.

In May 2013, the White House was poised to take up this scaled-back idea and make it an official administration-endorsed proposal to Congress, fulfilling Mueller's last goal.[33] But a month later came the Snowden leaks. The backlash against government surveillance seemed to kill any chances for the idea.

The Snowden leaks changed the behavior of communications companies. Firms began to compete, in part as a marketing move, to be seen as protecting the security of users' private messages. In September 2014, Apple announced that its new iPhone operating system would be encrypted by default in such a way that the company itself could not break into a phone — even if presented with a court order to unlock it. Mueller's successor as FBI director, Jim Comey, denounced the plan and the larger trend it exemplified. He said the government should have to get a warrant to search a phone, but he could not understand why companies would "market something expressly to allow people to place themselves beyond the law."

"I get that the post-Snowden world has started an understandable pendulum swing," Comey said. "Maybe that pendulum swung too far."[34]

Comey would expand on that idea in a speech entitled "Going Dark" the following month at the Brookings Institution.[35] He did not get clearance from the Justice Department or the White House to make the public policy push. But, sick of waiting for broader administration approval, the FBI was taking its case to the public on its own. Still, Jeh Johnson, in his role as Homeland Security secretary,[36] later echoed Comey's warnings about the downside of strong encryption, if not his preferred policy prescriptions — as did Obama himself — when asked about the topic.

"I'm as strong [on civil liberties] as I have been," Obama insisted in early 2015. "I think the only concern is our law enforcement is expected to stop every plot. Every attack. Any bomb on a plane. The first time that attack takes place in which it turns out that we had a lead and we couldn't follow up on it, the public's going to demand answers.... There are times where folks who see this through a civil-liberties or privacy lens reject that there's any trade-offs involved, and in fact there are. And you've got to own the fact that it may be we want to value privacy and civil liberty far more than we do the safety issues. But we can't pretend that there are no trade-offs whatsoever."[37]

4. Violating the Fourth Amendment

The Snowden leaks would also make clear what several half-glimpsed mysteries during Obama's first term had been about. Back in July 2012, for example, Wyden made a startling statement. He announced that he had been negotiating with the government and obtained its permission to say that "on at least one occasion the Foreign Intelligence Surveillance Court held that some collection carried out" pursuant to the FISA Amendments Act "was unreasonable under the Fourth Amendment." The government asked him to add that the problem had been fixed.[38] But that was all the executive branch permitted him to say. Nobody knew what he was talking about.

A year after Wyden's cryptic disclosure, as part of the fallout from the Snowden leaks, the Obama administration unsealed and declassified FISA Court records revealing what had happened. The story had begun in May 2011, when the Justice Department brought to the FISA Court's attention a problem with the warrantless surveillance program authorized by the FISA Amendments Act. As noted, the law permitted the NSA to collect the Internet messages of foreigners abroad from network switches inside the United States — including messages to or about a foreign target from people on American soil. *But at least one end of such a message had to be foreign.* And it turned out that for technical reasons,[39] the agency's system had also been sucking in at least 56,000 *wholly domestic* communications each year.[40]

The NSA had been putting these wholly domestic messages of Americans, collected without a warrant, into its general storehouse of intercepted e-mails, and its analysts had been searching them. Collecting the occasional wholly domestic message was an unavoidable by-product of doing "upstream" collection off network switches for technical reasons, the government now explained to the FISA Court. But it had been happening from the start, and the government had only just gotten around to telling the FISA Court about it.

Bates, the presiding judge on the FISA Court, again dealt with the problem. In October 2011, he scolded the NSA and the Justice Department for again misleading the court about how the technology of a surveillance program worked. He ruled that the NSA's collection, retention, and use of those messages violated the Fourth Amendment.[41] The Senate Intelligence Committee was briefed about this ruling, and this was what Wyden later obtained permission to hint about.

The NSA's interim general counsel, Patrick Reynolds, let it be known within the agency that he was considering appealing the ruling that this collection was unreasonable.[42] But the next month, the NSA and the Justice Department's National Security Division, now led by Lisa Monaco, offered a new plan. The government would continue to collect some wholly domestic messages without a warrant, but in the future, the NSA would segregate those message streams that might have some purely domestic messages intermingled. It would put those into a special archive for extra scrutiny and more limited access.

Bates agreed to the change. He ruled that these additional back-end safeguards made everything reasonable and so resolved the Fourth Amendment violation.

But there remained the problem of what to do about the previously collected messages. The NSA said it could not go back and systematically identify those in its storehouse that might be wholly domestic. Ultimately, in 2012, the Obama administration came up with a sweeping solution. The NSA purged *all* of the raw data that had been collected from switches as part of the program before the new restrictions went into effect. Bates said he was satisfied with that.

The history of the FISA Court revealed after the Snowden leaks showed that it often seemed to rubber-stamp what the NSA wanted to do, especially in repeatedly adopting stretched legal theories in order to keep Stellarwind operating. But the judges could become furious when it came to light that the NSA did not adhere to the rules the court had imposed when granting that permission. The purging of the older upstream storehouse in response to Bates's Fourth Amendment ruling is arguably the most significant example of an instance in which the FISA Court had genuine oversight teeth.

5. Databases about Americans

There was one other major surveillance-related policy dispute in Obama's first term. The National Counterterrorism Center sought access to vast databases of information about Americans that the other parts of the government had collected. The center wanted to root through that information in its hunt for terrorists. This push began under Michael Leiter, Obama's first director of the center, and culminated under Matt Olsen, Leiter's successor. The Department of Homeland Security strongly opposed this proposal.

The National Counterterrorism Center was founded after 9/11 to be a clearinghouse of threat information from across the government. But for the most part, its analysts did not have direct access to other agencies' databases. Instead, the center submitted requests to other agencies for specific data about specific people it was already looking at, and if the center obtained information about Americans for whom there was no known link to terrorism, it had to purge that data after 180 days. Leiter wanted the center to be empowered to make its own copy of other agencies' databases so its analysts could directly access the information. He also wanted it to be able to retain seemingly irrelevant data about Americans for up to five years.

Some of the information to which the center wanted access, like raw or unprocessed communications the FBI had gathered with FISA wiretaps, had some connection to hunting for wrongdoers. But other databases to which it wanted less fettered access mostly contained information about people for whom there was no suspicion of any wrongdoing — like a Department of Homeland Security system which scooped up flight manifests with information about all passengers flying into the United States.

The center's first success was gaining official access to FISA information. As of 2009, the only people working at the center who had access to that database were FBI agents on temporary assignment. The agents were supposed to have had their FISA access stripped when they were assigned to work for the center, but because of a bureaucratic mistake, that hadn't happened, and they could still log in, officials told me. After the November 2009 Fort Hood shooting, the bureaucratic barriers melted away. By 2010, the center was permitted to directly access "minimized" reports of information derived from FISA wiretaps, which had irrelevant private information about Americans masked. But it wanted raw, unprocessed intercepts, including data from the warrantless-wiretapping program, as well as access to many other agencies' databases.

The proposal to take in databases held by other parts of the government ran into resistance from Jane Lute, the deputy secretary of the Department of Homeland Security, and Mary Ellen Callahan, that department's chief privacy officer. Callahan had no problem giving the center bulk data the department had collected about foreigners. But she opposed taking every interaction hundreds of millions of ordinary Americans had had with their government, down to records generated when American families adopted foreign-born children, and making it fair game to scrutinize for terrorism suspicions.

After a two-year bureaucratic struggle over this proposal,[43] Lute and Callahan pushed for a deputies committee meeting to air their broader philosophical concerns about privacy. On March 9, 2012, at eleven thirty a.m., Lute came to the White House Situation Room to discuss the issue, bringing Callahan.[44] Brennan chaired the meeting, which included Olsen and the number-two officials from the FBI, the Justice Department, and the Office of the Director of National Intelligence, along with the agencies' lawyers. Non-intelligence-community agencies — including those who would be giving up their data — were not invited.

Callahan told the group that acceding to the counterterrorism center's request would be a "sea change," essentially making everyone a terrorism suspect. She also complained that the idea hadn't been briefed to Congress or aired with other agencies that would be giving up their data.

But Bob Litt, sitting next to Callahan, responded that what the National Counterterrorism Center was proposing was not a big deal, she recalled. (Only after the Snowden leaks, Callahan said, did she understand why colleagues familiar with the NSA thought that what the center had wanted to do seemed routine.)

At the end of the meeting, Brennan directed them to do more briefings and research with lawmakers, outside privacy advocates, and other agencies about what the impact and response to the change would be.

A week and a half later, on Monday, March 20, I got a tip that Holder and James Clapper, the director of national intelligence, were about to sign new rules for sharing large government databases with the counterterrorism center. Late that afternoon, I e-mailed several press offices about what I was working on. The next day, they told me that if I could wait one more day before publishing anything, they'd invite me out to Liberty Crossing, where the Office of the Director of National Intelligence and the center shared the same campus, and they would give me a detailed briefing. I agreed to wait.

Callahan and Lute were out in California for a cybersecurity event when Lute got an e-mail on her BlackBerry. The message said that Charlie Savage of the *Times* had asked questions about the proposal, and so they were just going to go ahead and sign the new procedures without the extra briefings and research. That way they could have me out for a briefing with the paperwork already signed.

We just got rolled, Lute said to Callahan.

They were convinced someone who supported the changes had leaked it to me to produce that outcome, Callahan later told me. I told her that my source had opposed the changes, so I did not think it was a conspiracy.

I did not know about any of this at the time, however. Clapper and Olsen signed the guidelines on Tuesday, and Holder signed them on Wednesday. That same day I drove out to Liberty Crossing and met with a handful of officials, including Litt and Alex Joel, the Office of the Director of National Intelligence's privacy officer. Olsen was out of the country.

They explained that the change traced back to the aftermath of the Christmas underwear-bombing attempt and the discovery that different agencies had had information about the terrorist ahead of time, but no one had connected the dots. This new policy was the latest iteration of the long-term trend toward greater information sharing within the government for counterterrorism purposes. They also stressed that there would be audits to make sure the center's analysts did not abuse their access to the records.[45]

"There is a genuine operational need to try to get us into a position where we can make the maximum use of the information the government already has to protect people," Litt said. "We have to manage to do that in a way that provides protection to people's civil liberties and privacy. And I really think this has been a good-faith and reasonably successful effort to do that."

Litt gave me an example of what the center could do if it had the complete data sets: Person A applies for a visa to the United States and lists a certain address. Two years later, Person B applies for a visa and lists the same address. Person B is a known terrorism suspect. If the center has a copy of the entire database of visa applicants, it could design a system that would automatically alert analysts that there was now a reason to go back and scrutinize Person A.

That made sense, but the center had already absorbed copies of databases about refugees, foreign students, and international travelers — though this would let it keep the data longer. What was odd was that they would not tell me which *additional* databases they were specifically preparing to gain access to. The answer to that, they said, was classified.

Although the Department of Homeland Security had put up the fight, its data was not the most coveted prize the center was seeking. I later learned that one of its biggest acquisitions — one of the data sets the officials did not want to tell me about — was the storehouse of raw FISA information that did not yet have the names and nonpublic information about (seemingly) innocent Americans removed. The FBI, CIA, and NSA had been sharing raw information gathered with a traditional FISA warrant since 2002, and the court had approved letting them share some of the type gathered through the new, warrantless variety of FISA surveillance under the 2008 law.* The center wanted it too — and now got it.[46]

On March 21, 2012 — the day after I had reached out — the center signed off on a set of procedures for how it would use raw FISA information, according to a set of FISA Court documents the government declassified three years later in response to one of my Freedom of Information Act lawsuits.[47] It would take another month for Holder to approve the procedures and for Lisa Monaco's National Security Division to submit the proposed procedures to the FISA Court. But on May 18, 2012, a FISA Court judge, Mary McLaughlin, approved giving the center access to the raw FISA information database.

I also later learned that another set of data the center acquired as part of this push — another one of the things they did not want to tell me — was "native" access to the FBI's Automated Case Support System, the computer network where the bureau saves and shares investigative files. This access, which has never been reported, was the crown jewel of the change and had led to its own internal fight. The operational side of the bureau did not want to give the National Counterterrorism Center unfettered access to their information because it did not want the center to generate its own analysis of its case

---

* See chapter 5, section 7.

files. The fear was that if an analyst at the center wrote a report indicating that a certain cooperating FBI witness did not seem credible, prosecutors could end up having to turn that report over to defense lawyers and it could mess up a trial. Olsen negotiated an agreement with the FBI deputy director, Sean Joyce, in which the center promised that its analysts, when writing a report using FBI files, would coordinate what they said with FBI agents who had generated the information in question.

But the public was not let in on the existence of this deal.

6. The "Least Untruthful" Answer

For years, as we have seen, the Bush-Cheney and Obama administrations, working with the FISA Court, had harbored a secret understanding of what the law meant. The government believed that provisions of FISA which permit the FBI to get court orders for records that are "relevant" to a national-security investigation — including the provision added to FISA by section 215 of the Patriot Act — meant that the NSA could engage in untargeted, bulk collection of records about Americans. The government did not just hide the existence of operations that relied upon this interpretation — like the bulk e-mail and phone records programs that grew out of Stellarwind. It kept classified the abstract interpretation of the law itself. This secrecy thwarted meaningful congressional, presidential-election-campaign, and public debate throughout Obama's first term.

Back in 2009, when section 215 and several other parts of the Patriot Act came up for renewal, Senator Patrick Leahy, Democrat of Vermont and chairman of the Judiciary Committee, had introduced a bill that would tighten its standards. His bill would require the government to show that the person whose records it acquired had some personal connection to terrorism. But a majority of the lawmakers on the panel — who had been briefed on how the law was secretly being used — voted against that provision. That prompted Senator Dick Durbin, Democrat from Illinois and a supporter of Leahy's idea, to make an inscrutable lament.

"Now, there are many reasons given for taking out this constitutional protection," Durbin said at a Judiciary Committee meeting on October 1, 2009. "But the real reason for resisting this obvious, common-sense modification of section 215 is unfortunately cloaked in secrecy. Some day that cloak will be lifted, and future generations will ask whether our actions today meet the test of a democratic society: transparency, accountability, and fidelity to the rule of law and our Constitution."[48]

Soon after, Durbin, Wyden, and Senator Russ Feingold asked Holder to declassify the legal theory ahead of the floor debate over whether to reauthorize the Patriot Act. But after the Christmas underwear bombing, Holder rejected the idea.* In 2011, as section 215 again came up for renewal, Wyden and the newly elected Senator Mark Udall, Democrat of Colorado, began issuing loud but mysterious warnings about "secret law." Udall, who had been assigned to the Intelligence Committee and learned how the Patriot Act was being interpreted, said the public would be "alarmed" if they knew how the government was carrying out the law. Wyden said there is a "growing gap…between what the public believes that [the] law says and the secret interpretation of the Justice Department."[49]

But their warnings were too vague to shake loose the secret, despite the best efforts of reporters like me to figure out what they were talking about by filing a Freedom of Information Act lawsuit and by talking to potential sources.† Moreover, once again in 2011, as had happened during the previous cycle, many lawmakers never went to a classified briefing to learn what they were really voting for. Indeed, this time the House Intelligence Committee chairman, Representative Mike Rogers, Republican of Michigan, did not even inform his House colleagues who were not on that panel that there was something they might want to get briefed about before casting their votes.

The same secrecy also interfered with public policy debates during the presidential campaign. In September 2011, the Mitt Romney campaign national security law subcommittee‡ produced an internal policy

---

* See chapter 5, section 17.
† See chapter 8, section 2, and chapter 9, section 7.
‡ See chapter 10, section 1.

paper on the Patriot Act for the future GOP presidential nominee to read. I obtained a copy of this five-page memo, the existence of which has never been reported. Its discussion of section 215 explained to Romney that the provision functioned just like a grand jury subpoena for a regular criminal investigation, except that it came with an automatic gag order to its recipient. It recommended that the would-be president take the position that the law should be made permanent.

"There is significant evidence that law enforcement has been quite measured in its use of the FISA business records provision," the internal memo told Romney. "It is difficult to accuse law enforcement of using Section 215 with undue frequency: the Justice Department seeks and obtains fewer than 40 Section 215 orders per year."

What Romney was not told, of course, was that four of those orders each year were nothing at all like grand jury subpoenas. Instead, each empowered the NSA to collect every American's domestic phone records in bulk for the next three months. To be sure, Romney probably would have supported that program had he known about it, given his generally hawkish views on national security legal-policy issues. But it is still remarkable that the presidential nominee for one of the two major parties had no opportunity even to consider the issue.[50]

Then, on March 12, 2013, the Senate Intelligence Committee held a rare public oversight hearing that would later become notorious. Its topic was national security threats to the United States, and the witnesses included Clapper, the director of national intelligence; Brennan, now the newly appointed CIA director; Mueller, in his waning days as the FBI director; and Olsen, the National Counterterrorism Center director. They all knew about the bulk call records program. When it was his turn to speak, Wyden asked Clapper for a yes-or-no response to this question: "Does the NSA collect *any type of data at all* on millions or hundreds of millions of Americans?"

Days before the hearing, Wyden's intelligence staffer, John Dickas, had alerted Clapper's office that Wyden was planning to ask that question. The truthful answer to it was yes. Clapper could have said yes, or — more realistically — he could have sidestepped the question saying he was not comfortable discussing the NSA in public but would be happy to engage with Wyden in closed session. He did something else.

"No, sir," Clapper said.

"It does not?" Wyden asked.

"Not wittingly," Clapper said. "There are cases where they could inadvertently, perhaps, collect, but not wittingly."[51]

Two months later, on June 5, 2013, at the White House, Caitlin Hayden, the National Security Council spokeswoman, received an e-mail from Spencer Ackerman, a national security reporter whom the British newspaper the *Guardian* had just hired away from *Wired* to help build out its new online operation in the United States. Ackerman told her the *Guardian* had obtained a document he needed to discuss with her. Things were busy with the National Security Council staff at that moment: in a ceremony in the Rose Garden, Obama was about to swear in Susan Rice as his new national security adviser, succeeding Tom Donilon, and Samantha Power as the new ambassador to the United Nations, succeeding Rice. It took a couple of hours for Hayden to get back to him.

When she did, Ackerman said the *Guardian* had obtained a top secret FISA Court order to Verizon requiring it to give the NSA the domestic and international calling records for all of its customers. Hayden had no idea what he was talking about but began to raise alarms internally. Soon, Ackerman was also on the line with Shawn Turner, Clapper's spokesman at the Office of the Director of National Intelligence. Turner later told me he usually prided himself on knowing what reporters who obtained classified information were talking about when they called, but this time he had no idea. He took notes and called up Bob Litt to tell him what Ackerman had said.

You need to come down here, Litt said.

Litt gathered several other top officials in his office and said *we've got a problem.* Lawyers and operational officials at the White House, the Justice Department, and the NSA were similarly scrambling. They convened a conference call to try to persuade the top editor for the *Guardian*'s American operations, Janine Gibson, not to publish the story — or at least to give them another day. She declined to hold it back. That evening, a story by Glenn Greenwald, headlined "NSA collecting phone records of millions of Verizon customers daily," appeared on the *Guardian* website along with the court order.*

The next morning, Dianne Feinstein and Saxby Chambliss, the top Democrat and Republican on the Senate Intelligence Committee, hastily convened a press conference. They explained that the Verizon order was part of a broader counterterrorism program that the FISA Court had been authorizing for seven years under section 215 of the Patriot Act, and that the oversight committees knew all about it.[52] The Office of the Director of National Intelligence had "coordinated" with the senators about their intent to disclose details of the program, Turner told me.

That afternoon, the *Washington Post* and Bart Gellman published the first story about the Prism system — beating a version by the *Guardian* by a few minutes.† Gellman had previously made some calls to people in the government, but he had been cagey about what he had. Now, it was becoming clear that multiple highly classified surveillance documents were suddenly in the hands of reporters at multiple outlets.

And across the United States and the world, a public uproar about NSA surveillance was beginning. Clapper's "no, sir" answer to Wyden faced sharp scrutiny. The following Saturday, NBC News' Andrea Mitchell came to Liberty Crossing to interview Clapper. He explained to her that Wyden had put him in an impossible situation, "so I responded in what I thought was the most truthful, or least untruthful manner, by saying 'no.'"[53] A few weeks later, in a letter apologizing to Feinstein for his "clearly erroneous answer," Clapper would say instead that he had misunderstood which program Wyden was referring to and had not deliberately provided misleading testimony.[54]

After the interview, as Clapper and Mitchell were chatting, a member of Clapper's security detail came over and said the director had an urgent phone call. Clapper thanked Mitchell and left to get the call.

---

* See chapter 8, section 16.
† See chapter 5, section 14.

That was the moment, Turner later told me, that the intelligence community found out definitely that the leaker was an employee of the defense contractor Booz Allen Hamilton who had helped run the computer system for an NSA outpost in Hawaii. His name was Edward Snowden. And he was in Hong Kong.

The NSA station in Hawaii had noticed some aberrations in its system — programs running continuously overnight that it did not understand, and which turned out to have been systematically accessing and downloading large volumes of documents under different users' log-in names. And Snowden had stopped showing up for work. Now, by tracing his travel, they had figured out where he had gone. Their first suspicion was that he was a spy for China. But no evidence ever emerged to support this theory. The rest of the world would learn his identity three days later, when the *Guardian* posted a short interview of him by Greenwald. It was filmed by Laura Poitras, a documentary filmmaker to whom he had reached out, and who would later win an Academy Award for her movie about him, *Citizenfour*.

"My sole motive is to inform the public as to that which is done in their name and that which is done against them," Snowden said.[55]

7. Uproar

The revelation of the bulk phone records program angered both the civil liberties left and the libertarian right, scrambling the usual party lines. Among the lawmakers opposed to the program was Representative James Sensenbrenner, Republican from Wisconsin and chief sponsor of the original USA PATRIOT Act in 2001. He said lawmakers never intended the government to be able to use the business-records provision that way and called the program an abuse. (Sensenbrenner had voted to extend section 215 without changes in 2010 and 2011. He was one of many lawmakers who had not attended the classified briefings about the law before casting those votes.)

In July, the House of Representatives nearly voted to defund the program. The proposal, sponsored by Representative Justin Amash, a Tea Party Republican, and Representative John Conyers, a liberal Democrat, was defeated in a squeaker vote of 205 to 217 after leaders of both parties whipped votes against it.[56]

Three days later, Monaco — who had now become Obama's counter-terrorism adviser, replacing Brennan after he became CIA director — asked top staff from the Intelligence and Judiciary committees, along with staffers from congressional leadership, to come to the White House Situation Room to assess how big a problem this had become. Monaco opened the meeting by thanking staffers for the leaders for beating back the Amash-Conyers amendment. Aaron Hiller, a lawyer for Conyers, fumed silently as Heather Sawyer, a lawyer for Representative Jerrold Nadler, a liberal Democrat from New York, nudged Hiller under the table to warn him to keep his cool. But with section 215 set to expire automatically if Congress did not renew it by June 1, 2015, a White House legislative affairs staffer raised the possibility that it could be "cleanly" extended again without changes, as it had been in 2010 and again in 2011.

Hiller went off.

There is no way the House Judiciary Committee will pass a clean reauthorization of 215, he snapped. *You won't get it to the House floor. We have Sensenbrenner in our corner. He wrote the thing and he said this doesn't work. I don't think you have a trump card that beats that.*

Finally in the light, the program was coming under belated debate. One focus was how valuable the program had proven to be in practice over twelve years — the seven years it had operated based on FISA Court orders, plus the original five years when it had operated based on Bush's say-so alone. Intelligence officials, like Alexander, the NSA head, said in speeches that the agency's programs — plural — had disrupted terrorist activity fifty-four times. Outspoken NSA supporters, like Rogers, the chairman of the House Intelligence Committee, turned this into a claim that the bulk phone records program, singular, had itself thwarted "54 terrorist attacks" and "saved real American lives and our allies as well."[57]

This oversold claim, and many like it, collapsed under scrutiny. It turned out that the list conflated "thwarting attacks" with just being useful in some way in a terrorism-related investigation, and it conflated the Patriot Act section 215 bulk phone records program with the FISA Amendments Act warrantless surveillance program. In fact, for all the intelligence community's assertions to judges, lawmakers, and policymakers over the years that the phone records program was crucial, it had *never thwarted any terrorist attack.* The best example of a concrete counterterrorism victory that would not have happened but for the program turned out to be the discovery that several Somali immigrants in San Diego had donated a few thousand dollars to al-Shabaab in Somalia.[58] There was no accusation that the men were planning a terrorist attack.

Supporters of the program fell back on a different claim: a lack of thwarted attacks was the wrong measuring stick of its value. It was a helpful investigative tool, and part of its utility was the ability to triage when investigators discovered new terrorist-linked phone numbers — at least providing peace of mind that no one on domestic soil had been in contact with those numbers. Moreover, they argued, just because this tool had not thwarted an attack since 2001 did not mean it would never do so in the future.

A second focus was whether the program filled a demonstrated gap in counterterrorism intelligence. Its proponents noted that back in 2001, one of the future 9/11 hijackers had called an al-Qaeda safe house in Yemen that the NSA was monitoring. But the agency couldn't see where the call was coming from and did not know the caller was inside the United States. Had the program existed then, they said, the NSA would have immediately known that someone inside the United States was the caller, and the government might have foiled the plot. Still, skeptics of the utility of the program noted that the government would have discovered the future hijacker anyway if only the CIA had shared what it knew about him with the FBI rather than hoarding the information. They also pointed out that the government could use conventional subpoenas to get records from phone companies of customers who have placed or received calls to a suspicious foreign number.

At a Senate Judiciary Committee hearing on the last day of July, senators from both parties sharply challenged intelligence officials' claims about the value of the program. While Feinstein, the Intelligence Committee chairwoman, defended the phone program, saying it helped prevent terrorist attacks, Leahy, the Judiciary Committee chairman, growled, "If this program is not effective it has to end. So far, I'm not convinced by what I've seen."[59]

Some administration officials were also unconvinced. In August 2013, during a principals committee meeting, Holder spoke up with a note of skepticism. He and his deputy, James Cole, were both vacationing on Martha's Vineyard, and they crammed into a trailer where the Justice Department had set up a mobile command center with a secure communications link. There was only one camera, so they had to sit awkwardly close to each other staring into it, both of them shivering in short sleeves in the overly air-conditioned room for the hours-long meeting — an odd scene for those in the Situation Room watching them on the screen. Holder said that while he understood the theory of why the program might be useful, when you looked at what it had done in practice, there did not seem to be much there.

Is the section 215 program really something the administration should be defending? Holder asked. *Is this really worth it?*

But Denis McDonough, Obama's White House chief of staff, rebuked him with a clipped, excessively formal inquiry.

Is the attorney general of the United States saying 215 is not worth defending?

Holder immediately backed off.

I'm not going that far, he said. *Just raising the question.*

8. Evidence Derived from Warrantless Surveillance

The attention to surveillance issues that followed the Snowden leaks also led to a major internal Justice Department fight. It traced back to 2012, when Verrilli had made his assurances to the Supreme Court in the case challenging the FISA Amendments Act and Dianne Feinstein had delivered her Senate floor speech urging her colleagues to reauthorize that law.

On June 7, 2013, two days into the tumult caused by the Snowden leaks, two colleagues and I cowrote a front-page story for the *Times* about how surveillance had been used. My contribution was a section about the terrorism cases Feinstein had cited in her speech. The section also pointed out that Verrilli had promised the Supreme Court that criminal defendants would be notified if evidence derived from warrantless surveillance under that law was used against them, but prosecutors in the South Florida and Chicago cases mentioned by Feinstein were refusing to do that. I quoted Alexander Abdo of the American Civil Liberties Union accusing the government of playing a shell game. "It's a strategy meant to insulate the 2008 law from judicial review, and thus far the strategy that has succeeded," he said.[60]

Among that article's readers was Verrilli.[61] He called up the National Security Division lawyers who had vetted his briefs and helped him practice his oral arguments. They had known that he intended to tell the court the Justice Department would provide notice of warrantless surveillance to defendants, and they had raised no objections. Verrilli convened a meeting with those lawyers and Brad Wiegmann, the number-two official in the division, and asked what was going on.

The national security prosecutors explained that their division had long used a narrower definition of what *derived from* means for FISA wiretaps than for ordinary criminal-law wiretaps. In ordinary criminal cases, defendants eventually see almost everything, including the original application to a magistrate for the wiretap, which contains the evidence that justified the privacy intrusion. By contrast, in national security cases, prosecutors will tell defendants if there is evidence from a FISA order, but they say nothing about what information went into the application for it — or even if there was more than one such order. That permits defendants to challenge the constitutionality of FISA procedures in the abstract without the government having to risk their revealing sensitive intelligence — like the identity of someone else who

is under surveillance as a spy or terrorist. (No challenge to the traditional FISA procedures had succeeded, although the Supreme Court
has never reviewed the statute.)

The Justice Department, however, had developed that policy when
there was only one kind of FISA wiretap. Starting in 2007, there were
two kinds — one with warrants, and one without them. But, without
telling anyone what its system was, the division had not changed its
practice or made it clear to outsiders. This had the effect of concealing
something very important. Sometimes, the warrantless surveillance
program, while targeting a foreigner, intercepted communications from
an American writing to or about that target. The Justice Department
then submitted those intercepts to the FISA Court as evidence to justify
a traditional wiretap order against the American. Then it prosecuted
that American on the basis of evidence gathered with the traditional
wiretap order. Such a criminal defendant might want to ask a judge to
suppress that evidence, and because the investigative chain traced back
to the FISA Amendments Act warrantless program, that gave him legal
standing to challenge its constitutionality. But nobody had filed such a
challenge because *nobody knew he was in a position to do so.* The Justice
Department's practice hid that fact from such criminal defendants,
effectively shielding the 2008 law from judicial review.

The division lawyers argued to Verrilli that it was just a good-faith
misunderstanding about what *derived from* meant. But their narrow
interpretation clashed with what *derived from* means in ordinary criminal wiretap case law, and it raised a question of whether prosecutors
had violated defendants' rights to due process and its obligation to provide helpful information to the defense. Verrilli's concerns now grew
beyond whether the division had induced him to mislead the Supreme
Court. He told colleagues that the division's practice looked illegal. He
sought a meeting with John Carlin, the acting head of the division, who
Obama later appointed as its permanent chief.

Carlin had not been involved in preparing Verrilli and was not previously acquainted with the issue. But he raised operational concerns
about changing the practice: if the Justice Department told defendants

they had been overheard due to the 2008 law, that might tip off their contacts abroad, who were presumably still at large, that their communications were being targeted for surveillance. As a result, the NSA might become reluctant to share information with law enforcement officials, rebuilding a form of the "Wall" between intelligence investigators and criminal investigators, which the government had torn down after 9/11.*

The National Security Division retreated to study the issue. Carlin called his predecessors, including Lisa Monaco, Todd Hinnen, and David Kris, along with previous intelligence oversight lawyers who had dealt with the FISA Court, like John Demers and Matt Olsen. He asked if they had addressed the issue and if there was any thought-out reason for the division's notification practice. They came up with nothing substantial.

Meanwhile, around July 8, Carlin's staff developed and circulated an initial memo analyzing the issue of what *derived from* might mean and setting out various courses of action. It has not been made public, and the Justice Department, citing attorney-client privilege, refused to turn it over in response to a Freedom of Information Act lawsuit filed by the American Civil Liberties Union.[62] I was told it broke down four options: (1) sticking with the status quo policy; (2) changing to a generic notice that would say there was FISA information in the case without saying which of the two types it was; (3) changing to a notice that would specifically say if there was either kind; and (4) asking Congress to change the notice law.

Inside the National Security Division, there were different factions supporting different options. The main focus was on consequences. What other cases would be affected if they changed their practices? Would they have to brief Congress about it? As the days passed and Carlin produced no answer, Verrilli asked Cole, the deputy attorney general, to resolve the dispute. Cole scheduled an interagency meeting for July 17.

About a week before the meeting, Verrilli's staff produced an internal

---

* See chapter 5, section 7.

paper arguing that the Justice Department *must* change to the third option: providing specific notice about either and both types of surveillance. Meanwhile, Adam Liptak, my colleague at the *Times* who covers the Supreme Court, began calling the Justice Department. He wrote a legal affairs column every two weeks, and he had decided to devote the next one to the disconnect between what Verrilli had told the justices and what the Justice Department was actually doing. The *Times* would publish the column by the time of Cole's meeting.[63] Margaret Richardson, Holder's chief of staff, proposed making the change Verrilli was seeking without waiting for the meeting so they could tell Liptak that the problem was resolved. But Carlin's staff now circulated a paper arguing for keeping the status quo position — refusing to tell a defendant if warrantless surveillance lurked somewhere up the chain of evidence. That meant there was no consensus, and so the process would have to play out with full deliberations.

Over the final weekend, there were multiple conference calls and back-channel conversations. National Security Division lawyers reached out to the top lawyers at related agencies, like Andrew Weissmann at the FBI, Rajesh De at the NSA, and Bob Litt at the Office of the Director of National Intelligence, lobbying them to take their side. They also reached out to several important United States attorneys. One was Loretta Lynch, the top prosecutor in the Eastern District of New York, who was chairwoman of a committee of federal prosecutors that advised Holder. (She would succeed him as attorney general.) Another was Neil MacBride of the Eastern District of Virginia, who chaired the terrorism and national security subcommittee of the advisory committee. Others included Steven Dettelbach of the Northern District of Ohio and Barbara McQuade of the Eastern District of Michigan, who oversaw the prosecution of the Christmas 2009 underwear bomber. In these calls, the division lawyers argued that it was a policy call, not a legal call like the solicitor general's office was saying. The Justice Department as an institution, they claimed, thought the existing practice was best.

Some of the recipients of that message were more open to it than others. In particular, the U.S. attorneys were persuaded that there was no need to change the notification policy, and there were real operational downsides to that idea. But the Washington-based security agency lawyers saw things differently. They thought that the arguments for the status quo policy were thin and unpersuasive as a legal matter.

Early the next week, Carlin changed his position. He produced a memo saying that the division no longer supported the status quo notice policy. The division now supported shifting to a generic notice in which prosecutors would tell defendants that evidence in their case came from FISA surveillance but without saying which type. However, his e-mail may not have been copied to the U.S. attorneys, who apparently remained unaware of it. Shortly before the meeting, the U.S. attorneys produced a memo of their own, in the name of MacBride's subcommittee but not signed by anyone. Awkwardly, it endorsed the status quo position that the National Security Division had just abandoned.

The meeting convened in the conference room adjacent to Cole's office, with the U.S. attorneys participating by speakerphone. The first question Cole asked, I was told by multiple participants, was addressed to Carlin:

Isn't it true that the division knew what Don was going to tell the Supreme Court?

One of the arguments some National Security Division lawyers had apparently been making in the weekend lobbying campaign was that Verrilli had blurted out the wrong thing to the Supreme Court on his own and without clearance, and was now trying to make his own problem into a problem for the department. But Carlin acknowledged that division staffers had known what Verrilli was going to say in arguments and had reviewed his written brief saying the same thing.

Cole then went around the room soliciting everyone's view. McQuade took the lead for the U.S. attorneys. She spoke forcefully about the worry that the NSA would not share important intelligence with criminal investigators and prosecutors if it had to provide more fulsome notice to defendants. And she said the U.S. attorneys were backing the National Security Division's position that the status quo was fine, which led to confusion since Carlin had abandoned that position.

Everyone else agreed there were operational downsides to changing the practice too. But that wasn't the primary question.

Do any of you think this is lawful? Verrilli asked.

There was silence. With no legal argument offered by the other side, the three lawyers representing the intelligence community — Weissmann, Litt, and a senior NSA lawyer Raj De had sent in his place because he was out of town — all backed Verrilli's view, and Carlin acquiesced to providing notice about both kinds of FISA surveillance.

We're going to make the disclosure, Cole said.

That left the problem of what to do about existing cases. Cole directed the National Security Division to go through its files, starting with still pending cases. That fall, the department belatedly notified two defendants that they faced evidence derived from FISA Amendments Act surveillance: a Colorado man charged with planning to travel to Uzbekistan to join an Islamist group[64] and an Oregon man caught in an FBI sting operation who had been convicted, but not yet sentenced, for trying to bomb a Christmas tree–lighting ceremony in Portland.[65]

There were surprisingly few other notifications, and the department was evasive about how it was interpreting its obligations under the new policy. Cole's policy decision — which apparently nobody ever wrote down, foiling the later attempt by the American Civil Liberties Union to make it public with a Freedom of Information Act lawsuit — was that not every case that involved warrantless surveillance information would qualify for disclosure. The use of that information, in an indictment or as evidence, had to have been *material* or a *critical element* in the eyes of the National Security Division prosecutors.

But it would take just one case for the Supreme Court to have a chance to review the law on the merits, which was the real point.

The defendants who did receive notice filed challenges, finally beginning judicial review of the FISA Amendments Act before the regular court system. The district court judge who had presided over the Oregon man's trial swiftly upheld the law and sentenced him to serve thirty years in prison, but it seemed likely that the Supreme Court would have the final say.[66]

In a twist, even after the policy shift, prosecutors in the Chicago and South Florida cases Feinstein mentioned in her Senate speech said those defendants were *still* owed no notification that they faced evidence derived from warrantless surveillance. A Senate lawyer sent a letter saying Feinstein's remarks had been misinterpreted.[67] She had just been reading down a *generic* list of terrorism cases, he said. The best spin on this was Feinstein had meant only to make the argument that terrorism remained a big problem, but inarticulately created a false impression that the FISA Amendments Act, specifically, had uncovered those terrorism suspects. If true, then in trying to bolster that law, she unwittingly set in motion events that finally allowed its constitutionality to be challenged.

9. Roberts's Court

The furor surrounding the Snowden leaks also caused people to take a closer look at the FISA Court and its role in blessing the bulk phone records program under a secret and counterintuitive interpretation of the law. The events raised the question of whether the FISA Court remained a credible institution now that it had taken on a role for which it was not designed: engaging in complex legal analysis, developing a secret body of law, and regulating and overseeing NSA surveillance activities at a programmatic level.

Normal courts, when interpreting what the law means or reviewing an agency's actions, rely on an adversarial process. There are lawyers on both sides who critique each other's arguments, and the losing side can file an appeal. But the FISA Court, because Congress designed it only to review routine wiretap applications, does not have the benefit of this clash of ideas. It hears secret arguments only from the Justice Department, and when it issues secret rulings giving the government what it wants, there is usually no one to file an appeal.

Normal courts, moreover, are made up of an ideologically diverse array of judges. Republican presidents nominated some of them, and

Democratic presidents nominated others. But the FISA Court is assembled differently. The chief justice of the Supreme Court, in his role as the chief administrator of the federal judiciary, unilaterally selects which judges will serve seven-year terms on the FISA Court. When Congress designed this process in 1978, it did not matter that one single person would wield unchecked power to compose the court because its role was so limited. But reviewing ordinary wiretap applications for national security investigations is no longer the FISA Court's most important job description.

Before the Snowden leaks, the FISA Court was obscure and no one was paying attention to what Chief Justice John G. Roberts Jr. was doing with it. After the leaks, I took a hard look at it. Ten of the eleven judges then serving on the court — each selected by Roberts from the ranks of sitting federal judges — were Republican appointees. The eleventh, Judge Mary McLaughlin, had been appointed by Bill Clinton in 2000, but nominating her for the federal bench had not been the Clinton White House's idea.[68] Rather, she had been part of a political deal between the Clinton administration and Pennsylvania's two Republican senators — Rick Santorum and Arlen Specter — late in Clinton's tenure, when Republicans controlled the Senate and were moving very few of his nominees. Clinton permitted them to pick a few Pennsylvania judicial nominees in exchange for letting a few others picked by him get through.[69] Remarkably, Roberts had quietly used his unfettered authority to construct a FISA Court consisting of *eleven out of eleven Republican selectees,* giving a partisan sheen to what was supposed to be a neutral and independent body.

While the identities of the FISA Court judges were not classified, there was no formal mechanism for announcing new selections. So little attention had been paid to the court, especially before 9/11, that a complete list of the court's members dating back to 1978 had never been public. But in the summer of 2013 I obtained a comprehensive list of the historical lineup of judges and analyzed it. The results showed that the court was taking on an increasingly partisan and executive-branch-friendly tilt. All three chief justices since 1978 — Warren Burger,

William Rehnquist, and Roberts—were conservative, Republican-appointed judges. But Roberts, more than his predecessors, had been disproportionately selecting Republican-appointed judges who had formerly served as executive-branch officials, just as Roberts had served as a White House and Justice Department lawyer in the Reagan and Bush-Quayle administrations. Specifically, since Roberts had become chief justice in 2005, 86 percent of FISA Court selections had been GOP appointees, and 50 percent were executive-branch veterans. Under his two predecessors, 66 percent had been GOP appointees, and 39 percent had been executive-branch veterans.[70]

I e-mailed my data to Roberts via a Supreme Court spokeswoman and asked for comment, but he declined. A month later, at the next judicial opening—for a slot on the three-judge FISA Court of Review, which rarely met—Roberts selected Judge José Cabranes of the appeals court in New York. Cabranes was a Clinton appointee who had never served in the executive branch. But he was also arguably the most conservative Democratic appointee on the appellate bench, and he had ruled for the government in several high-profile surveillance-related cases.[71] In the spring of 2014, when another vacancy opened up on the FISA Court of Review, Roberts named another Clinton appointee, Judge Richard Tallman of the federal appeals court in San Francisco, to it, giving the review panel a superficial two-to-one Democratic-appointed majority. Except Tallman, a former federal prosecutor and a conservative, was like McLaughlin: he had been part of a political deal over nominations in which Clinton appointed someone acceptable to a Republican senator, Slade Gorton of Washington State.[72]

But Roberts did eventually start to diversify the main FISA Court. In the spring of 2014, he designated Judge Jeb Boasberg, an Obama appointee on the Federal District Court for the District of Columbia and a former federal prosecutor, for the main FISA Court.[73] Boasberg's arrival brought the main FISA Court down to merely ten out of eleven Republican-selected judges.[74] In the spring of 2015, Roberts designated Judge Thomas B. Russell of the Western District of Kentucky and Judge James Jones of the Western District of Virginia for the FISA Court;

both were also true Clinton selectees. Their arrival brought the court to eight out of eleven Republican-selected judges.

To be clear, the FISA Court's record of secretly accepting stretched legal theories between 2004 and 2007 to keep Stellarwind going, as recounted in Chapter 5, cannot be attributed to Roberts's stacking the deck. He became chief justice only in 2005, so judges selected by Rehnquist were primarily responsible for those rulings. Rehnquist, too, had put his thumb on the scale — 69 percent of his overall selections to the FISA Court were Republican-appointed judges, and the 2005 iteration of the FISA Court assembled by Rehnquist at the time of his death had consisted of seven Republican-appointed judges and four Democratic-appointed ones. So Roberts was taking a preexisting tilt and just making it more extreme.

It is also important to acknowledge that individual judges cannot be reduced to the party of the president who appointed them. For example, after the revelation of the bulk phone records program in 2013 sparked parallel lawsuits before regular courts, the program was ruled unconstitutional by Richard Leon, a Bush-appointed judge, but upheld by William Pauley, a Clinton-appointed judge. Colleen Kollar-Kotelly, the FISA Court judge who originally approved the stretched "relevance" theory to revive the bulk e-mail record program back in 2004, was also a Clinton appointee. Still, academic studies have shown that in the aggregate, judges appointed by Republicans since Reagan and the rise of the conservative legal movement are more likely than their colleagues to rule in favor of government power over people claiming civil liberties violations.[75]

I could not find data analyzing whether having a background as an executive-branch official made a difference in outcomes. Senator Richard Blumenthal, citing his own experiences as a former United States attorney and state prosecutor, told me that judges who used to be executive-branch lawyers generally shared a "get the bad guys" mindset and were more likely to be deferential when the Justice Department argued that additional government surveillance powers were justified. On the other hand, a federal judge who used to be an executive-branch law enforcement official made the opposite argument to me: such judges know all the tricks and so are more likely to be skeptical of government claims, this judge maintained.

Blumenthal proposed legislation to change how FISA Court judges are selected, aimed at ensuring greater ideological diversity. Another court reform proposal after Snowden, as we will see, included requiring the court to disclose redacted versions of any significant interpretations of the law. Yet another was to create a "public advocate" with a top secret security clearance and independent authority to intervene when the Justice Department asked the FISA Court to grant new surveillance powers, offering adversarial counterarguments to whatever the government was saying and filing an appeal.

Judge Bates wrote to Congress to argue against such ideas, saying that Roberts "has requested that I act as a liaison for the Judiciary on matters concerning the Foreign Intelligence Surveillance Act." Creating a public advocate with independent power to intervene, regardless of whether the FISA Court judge wanted to hear opposing views, would be "counterproductive," he wrote, because it might make the government less candid in its own representatives to the court. Requiring the court to release redacted summaries of its opinions would only "promote confusion and misunderstanding." And the chief justice was "uniquely positioned to select qualified judges" to serve on the court.[76]

As Congress debated surveillance-reform bills, Obama weighed in on various ideas. But Obama said nothing about the proposal to change how the FISA Court members were selected. The idea gradually faded away in Congress, too.

10. Outside the Oval Office (Freedom Act I)

On August 1, 2013, Obama, trying to get a handle on the growing congressional unrest from the Snowden revelations, invited key committee chairs and lawmakers of both parties who were outspoken about NSA issues to come meet with him in the Oval Office. He also invited Vice

President Biden; Kathy Ruemmler, the White House counsel; and Susan Rice, the new national security adviser. The meeting consisted mainly of the lawmakers reiterating the same talking points they were saying elsewhere, in criticism or defense of the phone records program and NSA surveillance more broadly. Afterward, Wyden told me that Obama "was open and fair to everyone, wanted to hear all sides — everybody got a chance to talk — and he was interested in suggestions."[77]

Wyden had brought his Intelligence Committee staffer, John Dickas, with him to the meeting. But Dickas, a thirty-four-year-old native of Beaverton, Oregon, who had worked for years with Wyden on surveillance reform efforts, was not allowed inside. Three other lawmakers had also brought aides, including Barton Forsyth, a thirty-five-year-old lawyer from Connecticut who had worked as a Republican staffer on several committees and had recently become Sensenbrenner's chief of staff. While their bosses went inside to the Oval Office, the aides stayed on a couch and chairs across from one of the president's secretaries. Dickas and Forsyth started kicking around ideas for a bipartisan collaboration their bosses might work on together. Everyone ignored them, except when a White House staffer told them to stand up because Abdo Rabu Mansour Hadi, the president of Yemen, was about to walk through the room. At another point, Denis McDonough, the White House chief of staff, bustled past without a glance in their direction. Journalists like me reported that day about the meeting of the prominent and veteran elected officials inside the Oval Office, but the origin story of the most significant new restrictions imposed by Congress on surveillance since 1978 was the spontaneous conversation among their unheralded young aides outside its door.

During Congress's annual August recess, Forsyth, Dickas, and several other legislative aides — Chan Park and Lara Flint, two Senate Judiciary Committee aides to Leahy, and Jennifer Barrett, Udall's staffer on the Senate Intelligence Committee, who had also been waiting outside the Oval Office — worked on a reform bill. By September, they had finished a rough draft. It amounted to a wish list for surveillance reformers. It would ban bulk collection. It would force the FISA Court to declassify significant rulings. It would create a "constitutional advocate" with a security clearance who could intervene before the FISA Court to argue against the Justice Department and file appeals. And it would require the government to get a warrant before searching for an American's incidentally intercepted e-mails that were swept up without a warrant under the FISA Amendments Act. The moment was heady.

But midway through September, a schism emerged between Wyden and Leahy. Wyden wanted to introduce their bill quickly, before the Intelligence Committee — led by Feinstein and Chambliss, both outspoken supporters of NSA surveillance — could pass its own surveillance bill. Wyden argued that if the Intelligence Committee bill became the vehicle for Congress to respond to Snowden, it was unlikely to result in substantive change. But Leahy thought it was more important to refine their legislation. The strategic dispute in turn brought an ego issue to the fore: who was going to be the Senate lead on this bill, Wyden or Leahy? On the one hand, Wyden had been leading the charge against the Patriot Act program for years. On the other hand, Leahy was arguably better positioned to be the face of the bill as the chairman of the Senate Judiciary Committee and the most senior Democratic member in the chamber.

The dispute came to a head in late September, when Wyden scheduled a press conference, invited the others to join him, and insisted that they had to introduce the bill immediately. Udall joined him, but Leahy and Sensenbrenner did not. So on September 25, Wyden introduced a bill derived from their collective draft as his own.[78]

In late October, the Intelligence Committee met behind closed doors to consider Feinstein's bill.[79] As Wyden had feared, Feinstein wanted to provide explicit legal authority for the NSA to continue collecting domestic calling records in bulk. This approach echoed how the FISA Amendments Act had tackled the *rule-of-law* problem with Stellarwind's warrantless wiretapping component without satisfying what privacy advocates saw as a *civil-liberties* problem with it. During the committee debate, Wyden proposed deleting Feinstein's text entirely and substituting the text from his own bill in its place. The panel rejected his idea, three to twelve.[80]

Meanwhile, Forsyth, Park, and Flint had continued to refine their draft. On October 29, Sensenbrenner and Leahy introduced a House and Senate version of their bill together, as planned.[81] Back in 2001, Sensenbrenner had named the original law the USA PATRIOT Act, which was based on an acronym his staff back then had invented: *Uniting and Strengthening America by Providing Appropriate Tools Required to Intercept and Obstruct Terrorism.* They called the new bill the USA FREEDOM Act, based on a new acronym that Forsyth and two high school friends had come up with: *Uniting and Strengthening America by Fulfilling Rights and Ending Eavesdropping, Dragnet-collection, and Online Monitoring.*

On Halloween, the Senate Intelligence Committee approved and publicly unveiled the Feinstein bill. She proclaimed, "The NSA call-records program is legal and subject to extensive congressional and judicial oversight, and I believe it contributes to our national security. But more can and should be done to increase transparency and build public support for privacy protections in place."[82] Sensenbrenner later dismissed her bill as "a joke."[83]

Leahy and Wyden publicly reconciled on November 5. They signed on as cosponsors to each other's bills, and Wyden put out a statement saying that Leahy's version should be the vehicle for reform going forward.[84] But Wyden and Dickas never participated in the Freedom Act negotiations after that split.

11. Ending the DEA's Bulk Phone Records Program

Meanwhile, inside the Obama administration, the attention to the NSA's bulk metadata program was flushing out an awkward fact. It turned out that many security and law enforcement agencies had their own versions of metadata programs. The CIA, the DEA, the FBI, and the NSA were redundantly paying companies like AT&T for access to *the same data,* over and over again, under a patchwork of rules and procedures.[85] Each had been so closely guarding the fact of those programs that no one in the government had been fully aware of them all.

Most of those programs involved a phone company giving the government particular records — sometimes in response to legal orders, sometimes voluntarily, depending on the details. A secret program at the Drug Enforcement Administration, however, involved bulk collection by the government, just like the now-exposed NSA program. It turned out that ever since the Bush-Quayle administration, the DEA had been using administrative subpoenas to phone companies to secretly gather bulk records about outgoing international calls from the United States to certain countries linked to drug trafficking.[86]

The existence of the DEA program called into question one of the core arguments being made by Justice Department litigators as they defended the NSA program against a sprouting array of lawsuits. The Justice Department was telling courts that the NSA's extraordinary bulk collection was reasonable because it "serves special governmental needs above and beyond normal law enforcement."[87] But the DEA program did much the same thing — although only with one-end domestic calling data, not purely domestic records — and it served a normal law enforcement purpose.

It is not clear whether politically appointed leaders at Justice Department headquarters, like Holder or Cole, had been told — or, at least, understood — what the DEA program was doing until after the Snowden leaks. Like every other law enforcement agency, the DEA had briefed incoming Obama Justice Department political appointees at a high level in 2009, listing a blizzard of code-names for a long list of secret programs and operations, often without getting into the details. (And Cole had not joined the administration until December 2010.) Either way, it now had their full attention.

Michele Leonhart, the DEA administrator, and James Capra, the agency's chief of operations, gave them a briefing. The top two Justice Department officials displayed incredulity. As with the NSA's program, the DEA was unable, when pressed, to point to much in the way of concrete accomplishment by its own bulk phone records program. Moreover, the DEA didn't have limits on accessing its database like anything approaching the FISA Court–imposed rules limiting access to the NSA's database. The NSA program, sometimes called "215" as shorthand after the Patriot Act section about business records, had had trouble obeying those rules, but at least the rules existed.

215 has a shitload of controls on it, Cole said. *What are your controls? Where is the rigor?*

Holder called Rice and told her that the DEA had a program similar to the NSA's Patriot Act program and the White House needed to know about it. The DEA sent several operational officials to the White House. They briefed Rice, Ruemmler, Monaco, and Brian Egan, the new legal adviser to the National Security Council. After their rough handling at the Justice Department, the DEA briefers displayed trepidation. But as they described the program, Ruemmler — who had started at the Obama administration as the top assistant to the deputy attorney general — suddenly spoke up.

I was read into this, wasn't I? she said.

A Justice Department official in the briefing confirmed that she had been told about it. The DEA officials relaxed: Ruemmler's acknowledgment of that fact meant that it was unlikely that the White House would portray the agency as rogue. But Holder ordered the DEA to shut down the program and purge the data in September 2013. The Justice Department waited until 2015 to declassify its former existence. No one on the outside knew it yet, but the Snowden leaks had already killed a major, long-running program that was collecting data about Americans' communications in bulk.

Around that time, Holder came to the White House Situation Room for a principals committee meeting. He sat next to Rick Ledgett, the NSA deputy director, who was attending because Keith Alexander was out of town. Staring straight ahead, Holder suggested that he didn't trust the intelligence community on surveillance issues anymore.*

I don't understand what they are doing, Holder said. *I can't get a straight answer out of these guys.*

---

* A participant told me about this exchange and another participant recalled it after I asked about it. Through an intermediary, Holder told me that he did not recall it.

Several key lawyers in the room exchanged "whoa" looks. Rice, who chaired the meeting, leaned in. *What do you mean?* she asked. *I can't even understand what the DEA is doing,* Holder replied.

12. Obama Under Pressure (Freedom Act II)

Feinstein's position on the NSA's bulk phone records program — that there was nothing wrong with it, and there just needed to be enhanced oversight to make Americans more comfortable that it would not be abused — is where Obama appeared to be in the first months after the Snowden leaks, too. But on August 13, Obama had appointed a group of five former high-level national security officials and law professors he knew to review surveillance policy issues, instructing them to make recommendations by the end of the year about any needed changes.[88] Few expected that a hand-picked group of insiders would say much that was critical.

But when the review group completed its work in December 2013, it delivered surprisingly tough findings. Among other things, it told Obama that the government should stop collecting Americans' phone records in bulk because the risk of abuse was too high and the program had not been important in thwarting any attacks. Still, the group considered the program's operational capabilities to be like an insurance policy that had never been used but might someday prove to be crucial. So it argued that the government should find a way to maintain those capabilities without itself holding the bulk data. As an added safeguard, they recommended that the government get the FISA Court's permission each time it wanted to analyze calling links associated with a newly suspicious phone number.[89]

While the White House was absorbing those recommendations, two federal judges in different districts handed down conflicting rulings about the program within a week — one concluding that it was likely unconstitutional,[90] and the other ruling that the program was legal.[91]

And as the losing sides in each of those cases appealed, the Privacy and Civil Liberties Oversight Board[92] came to the White House on January 8, 2014, to preview its own forthcoming report on the bulk phone records program. It was a five-member bipartisan watchdog board established by Congress on the recommendation of the commission that had studied the 9/11 attacks, although the board had only recently become operational. All five members of the board believed Obama should shut down the program; like the presidential review group, they had concluded, after receiving classified briefings, that the program had done little. Its three Democratic-selected members also went further, saying that the program was illegal, while its two Republican-selected members rejected that conclusion. The board's final report argued, in dozens of pages of legal analysis, that stretching the Patriot Act's word "relevant" to permit bulk collection was an untenable subversion of the statute's text and intent.

"It may have been a laudable goal for the executive branch to bring this program under the supervision of the FISA Court" back in 2006, the report said. "Ultimately, however, that effort represents an unsustainable attempt to shoehorn a preexisting surveillance program into the text of a statute with which it is not compatible."[93]

The privacy board's preview of its legal analysis — or at least that embraced by its three Democratic members — made a big impact inside the White House. Until then, the Obama team had not seriously considered the possibility that section 215 of the Patriot Act might not legitimately authorize the program. After all, numerous FISA Court judges had approved it. The Obama administration officially stuck to the position that the program was legal, but the privacy board's arguments added to its growing unease and internal pressures to wind down the program.

Ruemmler and Monaco were leading an effort to come up with a policy response to the surveillance problem unleashed by the Snowden leaks. The plan was for Obama to deliver a high-profile speech in mid January announcing an initial series of reforms that he could make on his own, including with a new presidential policy directive — a kind of executive order. He would also embrace other changes that would require action from Congress. The reforms and speech needed to address two different

audiences: foreigners subject to Executive Order 12333–regulated surveillance and Americans subject to FISA-regulated surveillance.

For the foreign audience, the administration came up with a series of
reforms that were at once revolutionary and trivial. For example,
Obama announced plans to treat data gathered about foreigners with
protections similar to those for data about Americans, like only permitting private information to be shared for certain purposes and generally requiring it to be purged after five years. Because no country in
the world that had significant surveillance capabilities had extended
privacy protections, as a binding concept, to noncitizens abroad, this
was an important moment. Still, upon close inspection, this change
largely meant codifying already existing practices.

Similarly, Obama imposed a new requirement for a high-level review
of any decision to place a foreign leader under surveillance, a reaction
to outrage in Germany when it emerged that the cell phone of German
chancellor Angela Merkel had been targeted. (The Obama administration had told the United Nations in October 2013 that it would not
monitor communications at its headquarters in New York; Snowden
documents showed that there had been a FISA Court order permitting
"full take" collection from its Internet the year before.[94]) On the other
hand, no such review was necessary to target the cell phones and e-mail
accounts of all of a foreign leader's closest aides and associates.

And Obama decreed that when the NSA collected content in bulk
without targeting anyone — as it was only permitted to do abroad or with
transiting foreign-to-foreign communications — it could search that data
for only six security-related topics: espionage, terrorism, the proliferation of banned weapons, cyberwar, threats to American or allied
troops, and transnational crime. That cut off a few topics that counted
as "foreign intelligence" but not a threat, like spying on trade talks, but
it was not a huge contraction.[95]

The reforms aimed at the American audience focused on the bulk
phone records program, and led to a last-minute internal flurry. Obama
was preparing to make one immediate change to the phone records
program and to call for another that would require legislation. The

immediate change was that he lowered, from three to two, the number of links out from a suspicious phone number that analysts could go in examining people's calling data. This meant NSA analysts would scrutinize exponentially fewer people's calling patterns. When Ruemmler and Monaco had canvassed intelligence community operators, some had told them that in practice, little valuable information was found at the third level anyway.

The change that Obama embraced in theory, if Congress could pass legislation to make it work, was to get the NSA out of the business of holding the bulk records — but in a way that would preserve the program's operational ability, as the presidential review group had recommended. There were several ideas for how that might work, including having the phone companies create and run a consortium where they would pool their customers' data for the NSA to dip into, or keeping each firm's records at that firm but creating a way for the government to access them systematically. Both had drawbacks.

On January 15, two days before Obama was set to deliver his speech announcing these reforms, Ruemmler and Monaco met with the review group to outline what he would say. But one of the group's ideas — requiring the government to get a judge's permission before querying the bulk phone data — wasn't on the list of proposals they said he was preparing to endorse.

That's half, a member of the review group said, according to an account in the *Wall Street Journal.*[96] The review group warned that if the White House reforms did not go far enough, people would be disappointed that Obama had missed the moment.

The next day, Monaco and Ruemmler reopened the question of requiring judicial review for each query. Monaco convened a secure video teleconference with the different agency leaders. At the National Counterterrorism Center, Olsen looked up at the camera and objected, arguing that it was legally unnecessary.

Legally, sure, Ruemmler responded. *But is it worth fighting about?*

Olsen backed down. Late that night, an official with the Justice Department's National Security Division called up a FISA Court judge to explore whether there was legal authority for the court to assume that role. The judge agreed to accept the role.[97] Ruemmler recommended that Obama add the court-permission step to the list of reforms.

The last-minute decision to add this step appalled some intelligence officials, not so much because of the impact — by then, only about three hundred new numbers were being queried each year — but because they saw the policymaking process as slapdash or politicized. Still, from another perspective, the reform meant that Obama was going pretty much as far as he could go on his own, short of simply ending the program.[98]

In his January 17 speech, Obama announced these changes and his proposal to find a new approach that would "end the Section 215 bulk metadata program as it currently exists, and establish a mechanism that preserves the capabilities we need without the government holding this bulk metadata." He also said he said he would direct his administration to look for further changes to make.[99] But he defended his decision not to roll back the post-9/11 surveillance state he had inherited, offering a window into his thinking.

"I maintained a healthy skepticism toward our surveillance programs after I became president," Obama said. "I ordered that our programs be reviewed by my national security team and our lawyers, and in some cases I ordered changes in how we did business. We increased oversight and auditing, including new structures aimed at compliance.... What I did not do is stop these programs wholesale — not only because I felt that they made us more secure, but also because nothing in that initial review, and nothing that I have learned since, indicated that our intelligence community has sought to violate the law or is cavalier about the civil liberties of their fellow citizens."[100]

After Obama's speech, his national-security team needed to work out the details of what kind of bill the intelligence community and White House could live with. Monaco assigned an aide, Stuart Evans, a longtime Justice Department intelligence official who was temporarily working at the White House, to come up with a first cut by convening lower-level lawyers and operators at the NSA, the FBI, the Justice Department, and the Office of the Director of National Intelligence. Their work went to Monaco, who dug into them at about five deputies committee meetings in the Situation Room. On March 4, Rice convened a cabinet-level principals committee meeting to finalize the recommendations. Obama also met separately in the Situation Room on March 19 with Holder and intelligence agency leaders to hear their views directly.[101]

Obama's advisers decided to scrap the idea of having the phone companies set up a consortium to pool and hold a copy of Americans' call records for the NSA to access because there did not seem to be enough difference between that and the NSA just keeping the data on its own servers. Instead, they recommended building a system in which the government, after getting a court order, could make a single query that would check all of the firms' databases at once and return the records of callers up to two links away from a suspect. They initially hoped this change would only apply to phone records, so the government's power to collect other types of records in bulk under section 215 might go on.

In one way, this plan would make the NSA more powerful: the new orders would make the program more exhaustive by permitting the government to include every phone company in the revamped program. As of 2010, at least, only AT&T, Verizon, and Sprint were participating, because the intelligence community had not trusted smaller and newer companies to keep the classified program secret.[102]

In another way, the plan would make the NSA less powerful. The existing NSA program held on to the bulk phone records for five years before deleting them. But regulations permitted phone companies to purge customers' landline-phone records after eighteen months and imposed no retention requirement on cell-phone records. The administration decided not to seek any new data retention mandate, calculating that pushback to such a bill from the industry and civil libertarians would outweigh any marginal advantage of ensuring that older data remained available.

The Obama administration did not announce what it had decided to seek in negotiations from Congress, but I found out and wrote an article about it.[103] The next day, Obama acknowledged, in a press conference in the Netherlands, that his national security advisers had come up with a plan.

"They have presented me now with an option that I think is workable," Obama said. "I'm confident that it allows us to do what is necessary in order to deal with the dangers of a terrorist attack, but does so in a way that addresses some of the concerns that people had raised."[104]

13. Asking to be Forced

The Snowden earthquake shifted the relationship between the government and communications companies. Silicon Valley firms became openly hostile to the NSA, challenging the government in court to be allowed to say more about its national-security demands for information about their users[105] and rushing to encrypt their products, which accelerated the FBI's fears about "Going Dark." Less visibly, the telecommunications industry—those that operated the network—were changing, too.

As noted, the telecoms had long quietly cooperated with the government on certain surveillance matters—and not just in response to court orders and subpoenas. Several of them—particularly AT&T and Verizon, which included the old MCI—had collaborated with the NSA. They had voluntarily provided the government with access to massive volumes of foreign-to-foreign communications transiting across their cables on American soil.[106] But now the firms were facing market pressures. They had to worry about suspicion by regulators abroad[107] and potential consumer backlash at home in a pitched anti-surveillance atmosphere. They did not want to be *partners* who did things voluntarily for the NSA anymore—just normal companies who do what the law required them to do when presented with court orders or subpoenas.

For twenty-five years, the vacuum of law surrounding transiting foreign communications had worked to the government's advantage. But now it was a problem. As I have explained, just as no law *barred* the companies from handing the NSA purely foreign messages, no law *empowered* the government to force the firms to do so, either.* If FISA

---

* See chapter 5, section 4.

did not cover those messages, the FISA Court had no jurisdiction to issue the orders the companies now craved.

The anxiety reached a crescendo in December 2013. A major telecommunications company privately threatened to shut down all its voluntary help — meaning no more provision of transiting foreign-to-foreign e-mails in bulk. The intelligence community, in desperation, asked Obama to call its CEO and play for more time to find a solution. He did so, but it was only a temporary reprieve.

Negotiations over what would change spilled into 2014. By the middle of that year, as the national mood about individual rights and collective security started to shift again with the rise of the Islamic State, the companies got to a place where they felt comfortable. In August 2015, I asked AT&T if it, as of then, provided surveillance help to the government voluntarily rather than in response to legal compulsion. A spokesman replied, "We do not voluntarily provide information to any investigating authorities other than if a person's life is in danger and time is of the essence," but declined to elaborate on what that meant.

As of this writing, I do not understand how these tensions were resolved. I spoke with many people. But they were cagey about it, and several offered me seemingly conflicting suggestions. Some pointed me to a scenario in which the firms eventually turned off their voluntary provision of transiting foreign data, but in the meantime the NSA had figured out how to get access to much of the same traffic another way. Others pointed me toward a scenario in which the lawyers had figured out a way to do that which previously no one had thought could be done — analogous to the creative re-imaginings of the meaning of words in FISA that had permitted the FISA Court to start issuing orders authorizing each component of Stellarwind between 2004 and 2007. Under this version, the firms were still providing much of the same foreign data, but now somehow felt compelled, or compelled *enough*, to be at ease again.[108] It was all a muddle and speculation, and perhaps there were elements of truth to both scenarios, depending on the firm or the type of data. Someday we will learn more about this moment.

But the broader theme from this moment is clear. Just because some surveillance power was *legal* was no longer necessarily good enough. For the lawyerly Obama administration, this was a counterintuitive idea, but one they were starting to absorb — to some criticism from current and former career intelligence officials.

Around April 2014, a group of about two dozen retired senior intelligence officials and defense industry executives came to Liberty Crossing. They were members of the "Intelligence Community's Strategic Studies Group," and served as consultants to the current leaders of the security state. The group gathered in a secure conference room for a day of give-and-take. Clapper's director of public affairs, Shawn Turner, told me he gave a briefing about what the intelligence community was doing with communications outreach in the Snowden upheaval. The group was clearly upset about what was happening, and several members of the group suggested to him that the problem was messaging. Why weren't they out there pushing the narrative that Congress and the FISA Court had granted the NSA the power to conduct surveillance because it was necessary in a dangerous world, and that the press was irresponsible and hurting national security by publishing these secrets?

What you have to understand is that this is not just a communications issue, Turner replied. *We've learned, in telling that story, that people really don't care that the intelligence community is operating within the constraints of the law. The problem is that people really don't like that we've been given these authorities. They don't like that the oversight is something they can't see and validate. We've lost their trust. We're going to have to change. We're going to have to become more transparent.*

That was not a message the group of old-school spy hands wanted to hear. They had been fidgeting in their seats in irritation. Now they started talking over each other and venting with increasing belligerence. They thought the only problem was that the Obama national security communications team was incompetent. After taking his beating, Turner gave way to Clapper, who knew what had just happened. As he took the podium, Clapper remarked that he understood the group had just heard from his director of public affairs.

Yeah, what's left of him, one retired official said.

14. A Bill That Can Pass (Freedom Act III)

Meanwhile, the center of activity in the dispute over the bulk phone records program was moving to the House of Representatives. In late March 2014, Rogers, the House Intelligence Committee chairman, introduced his own bill, cosponsored by Representative Dutch Ruppersberger, the panel's ranking Democrat.[109] If the fall 2013 version of the Freedom Act was a pie-in-the-sky ideal from a reformer perspective, Rogers's bill was the intelligence community's equivalent.

Rogers's bill would end the bulk collection of phone records as Obama wanted, instead keeping them in phone company hands but accessible to the NSA. But the executive branch could order the phone companies to turn over calling records of people up to several links away from a suspect without prior permission from the FISA Court. E-mail providers would be subject to the same kind of order, resurrecting a new form of the now-defunct bulk Internet records program. And the government would be able to use this power for *any* foreign intelligence purpose, not just counterterrorism — just like the legalization of the warrantless wiretapping part of Stellarwind had permitted it to be used in a much broader way. While the Rogers bill banned bulk collection of a certain list of records the government wasn't systematically collecting anyway, like library circulation and firearm purchase records, he left *financial* records off the list. This would protect another bulk records collection program based on the same provision of the Patriot Act, which (as we at the *Times* and the *Wall Street Journal* both reported existed, even though the government never acknowledged it) was sucking in records of international money transfers from companies like Western Union.[110]

On April 4, 2014, the Judiciary Committee chairman, Bob Goodlatte, Republican of Virginia, convened a meeting in his personal office with Sensenbrenner, Conyers, and Nadler. Goodlatte had not taken a clear position on the issue, but now he was irritated: House GOP leaders had told him they were going to bring a surveillance bill to the floor, and Rogers was encroaching on Goodlatte's turf.

They are going to try to steal our jurisdiction, Goodlatte said of the Intelligence Committee.

Goodlatte was now off the fence. He wanted to move Sensenbrenner's Freedom Act through the committee and get it to the House floor fast. But Goodlatte also wanted a far narrower bill. He assigned his top national security staff lawyer, Caroline Lynch, to negotiate a stripped-down version of the bill with staffers for the bill's proponents. Over the next month, Forsyth and Lynch, along with Hiller and Sawyer, the lawyers for Conyers and Nadler, worked through marathon meetings.

Lynch was more of a national security hawk than the other aides, and was often at odds with them at first. In response to her objections, they dropped the FISA Amendments Act reforms and the special powers for a public advocate at the FISA Court — fights for another day. And they changed the way the bill ended bulk collection: now, records requests had to be based on a "specific selection term" associated with a terrorist, a technique she said the FBI liked better. Once Lynch had agreed on the revised draft, she became a strong advocate for it with her fellow Republicans and with intelligence agency lawyers who remained skeptical.

In the first week of May 2014, both the Judiciary and the Intelligence committees were preparing to "mark up," meaning amend and pass, their rival bills.[111] Seeking to head off an open conflict, the House Majority Leader, Representative Eric Cantor, Republican of Virginia, ordered them to compromise on one bill. Rogers's staff pushed to limit the ban on bulk collection just to phone records, but the Judiciary Committee staff insisted on keeping a ban on all types of bulk collection. The Intelligence Committee won on other demands, including further watering down the FISA Court changes and dropping the acronym behind USA FREEDOM, which they said was pejorative. On May 8 and May 9, the two committees passed the compromise bill.[112]

Now it was the Obama administration's turn to demand more adjustments. Bob Litt led the executive-branch negotiating team that trundled over to the halls of Congress. But it was a huge group, including Jim Baker, who had just returned to government as the new general counsel to the FBI; Raj De from the NSA; and Brad Weigmann from the Justice Department's National Security Division.

The biggest change the Obama team wanted was to relax the definition of what could count as a "specific selection term" so that it could mean an entire location or facility. They argued that it was legitimate and not controversial for the FBI to use a section 215 order to obtain records from a particular hotel of everyone who had stayed there some night, or from a particular car rental facility of everyone who had obtained a vehicle over a certain date range. The House negotiators agreed to that and other changes in exchange for a promise that Obama would sign the bill.

These stages gradually eliminated or diluted the sweeping changes envisioned in the original October 2013 Freedom Act. Privacy groups and Internet firms that had endorsed the original version of the bill began withdrawing their support for it. By the time it reached the House floor, critics argued that it contained big loopholes that would permit the government to still collect vast amounts of records about Americans — like, say, using an entire zip code as the selection term.[113] Nevertheless, the House passed the bill on May 22 by a vote of 303 to 121, with majorities from both parties in favor.[114]

Privately, the staffers for the reform-minded lawmakers urged their counterparts in the Senate to fix it.

15. "NSA Reform That Only ISIS Could Love" (Freedom Act IV)

Time seemed short as Leahy and Senate staffers took over the lead. The midterm election was getting closer, and polls showed that it was likely that Republicans would retake the Senate. Udall, one of the biggest supporters of surveillance reform, was among those whose reelection was in doubt. On June 19, at 3:45 p.m., Leahy met with Obama in the Oval Office. Leahy told Obama that he was concerned about how the weakened bill that had come out of the House had lost the support of privacy groups and the technology industry. He said he intended to tighten the bill back up. And he urged Obama to lean on his executive-branch negotiators to agree to a new compromise quickly so they could get it done before conservative hawks opposed to the changes Obama had endorsed gained greater sway in the Senate.

Over June and July, Leahy's aides, Park and Flint, formed a new negotiating bloc with staffers from several other senators.[115] Working with Litt's team, they came up with a new version of the Freedom Act that strengthened its reforms.[116] For example, they added language saying a "specific selection term" could not be a "broad geographic region" like a city, and if the government used a term that did not identify a specific individual, like a hotel ledger, it had to destroy irrelevant data after a reasonable period. Another tweak said that if the FISA Court chose to appoint a special advocate for a surveillance case, he or she would have the specific mandate of arguing from an individual privacy rights perspective. Leahy's staff also came up with a different acronym for USA FREEDOM — changing "Ending Eavesdropping, Dragnet-collection, and Online Monitoring" to the milder "Ensuring Effective Discipline Over Monitoring" — and stuck it back in the text, so the bill's name stood for something again.

The new Senate version of the Freedom Act succeeded in regaining the support of most civil liberties groups and a coalition of technology companies. Clapper and Holder endorsed that version, too.[117] It looked like there was a deal.

In November, Republicans prevailed in the midterm election. Udall was indeed among the Democratic casualties. Although time was short for the Senate, under lame-duck Democratic control, to confirm a few more of Obama's judicial and executive-branch nominees, Leahy persuaded the Senate Majority Leader, Harry Reid, to bring the revised Freedom Act to the floor. But national security conservatives now closed ranks against it. Two former Bush-Cheney administration officials — Mike Hayden, the former NSA and CIA director, and Michael Mukasey, the former attorney general — called Leahy's bill a gift to Islamic State terrorists in a jointly penned op-ed in the *Wall Street Journal* headlined "NSA Reform That Only ISIS Could Love."[118]

Mitch McConnell, the Republican minority leader, argued that "this is the worst possible time to be tying our hands behind our backs."

The Obama administration and even Feinstein, who had strongly supported the original program, now warned that failing to pass the Freedom Act was putting at risk the NSA's ability to contact-chain through call records to hunt for terrorism suspects. If nothing passed, section 215 would automatically expire just after midnight on June 1, 2015, likely taking the NSA program with it and without any replacement capability.[119] But with McConnell telling Republican senators to block it, the Freedom Act fell two votes short of the sixty votes needed to break a Republican filibuster and receive an up-or-down vote.[120] The gridlock meant the next Congress — with McConnell as Senate majority leader, wielding the power to decide what bills came to the floor — would have to figure out what to do about the law.

16. Reform (Freedom Act V)

When Congress convened in 2015, with the Senate now under Republican control, staffers for lawmakers in both chambers who supported the Freedom Act met quietly to figure out how to proceed.[121] They assumed that McConnell wanted to wait until the last minute, pass a "clean" extension of the Patriot Act without changes in the Senate, and jam the House into passing it, too. Their strategy was to negotiate a compromise Freedom Act, roughly halfway between the version the House had passed and the filibustered Leahy bill, and then present McConnell with a choice: pass their bill or let section 215 expire, taking the bulk phone records program with it.

There were immediately complications. Goodlatte insisted that they include the new Senate Judiciary Committee chairman, Senator Charles Grassley, Republican of Iowa, in the negotiations over merging the two bills. But Grassley had previously shown little interest in the effort. He sent two staffers to the meetings who proposed adding provisions to increase penalties on leakers of classified information about surveillance, like Snowden, and to expand the FBI's power to collect records of suspects' Internet activity without court orders.[122] The Freedom Act supporters declined. Grassley's staffers eventually drifted away, saying their boss did not support the bill. That simplified matters, and they filed the new bill, with Sensenbrenner again sponsoring the House version but Leahy giving way to a Republican, Senator Mike Lee of Utah, as its primary Senate sponsor.[123] Once again the House went first, and the full House passed it, 338 to 88, on May 13, with just over two weeks to go before the deadline. That step just repeated what had happened the year before, but no one knew what to expect in the Senate.

As June 1 grew nearer — and with the Senate scheduled to take the last week of May off — McConnell appeared to be in no hurry, devoting floor time to unrelated matters. Finally, he turned to the Patriot Act. He and Senator Richard Burr of North Carolina, the new chairman of the Senate Intelligence Committee, argued that the existing program worked and it was risky to scrap it for something new and untested.

As that debate was starting to unfold, a federal appeals court in New York suddenly ruled that the bulk phone records program was illegal. The American Civil Liberties Union had brought the case in its own name. Judge Pauley had ruled against it at the district court level. But a three-judge panel declared that section 215 of the Patriot Act — and its "relevant" standard — could not legitimately be interpreted to authorize the bulk collection of Americans' phone records, echoing the Privacy and Civil Liberties Oversight Board's analysis.

"Such expansive development of government repositories of formerly private records would be an unprecedented contraction of the privacy expectations of all Americans," Judge Gerard Lynch wrote. "Perhaps such a contraction is required by national security needs in the face of the dangers of contemporary domestic and international terrorism. But we would expect such a momentous decision to be preceded by substantial debate, and expressed in unmistakable language."[124]

The ruling had surprisingly little impact on the debate. McConnell pressed forward with a proposal to simply extend section 215 as written so the bulk phone records program could go on, without explaining how that would work given the appeals court's ruling that the current text of the statute did not authorize the program.

As the deadline neared, the political rhetoric grew increasingly alarmist. Each side suggested that if continued gridlock permitted section 215 (and two other expiring counterterrorism statutes that were much less important) to lapse, the blood of any subsequent terrorist attack would be on the other side's hands. McConnell eventually floated the idea of just extending the status quo for a few weeks so they could take more time to debate. But zealous surveillance critics like Ron Wyden and Rand Paul vowed to filibuster any such attempt.

It was the Freedom Act or nothing. McConnell bowed. He brought back the Senate from vacation a day early for a rare Sunday session on May 31 and tried to swiftly pass the bill. But Paul used Senate rules to block anything from moving forward faster than normal, so the bill could not be passed until after thirty more hours of debate.

Thus it was, at 12:01 a.m. on Monday, June 1, that the three provisions lapsed, including section 215. On that day, for the first time since the aftermath of 9/11, Americans were free again to place phone calls without having logs of their communications vacuumed up in bulk by the NSA. And if national-security investigators identified a new phone number that appeared to be linked to a new terrorism investigation, they had to go to the phone companies to get any recent records of Americans who had dialed or received calls from that number. The officials could not simply search the NSA's database.

The moment did not last long. On Tuesday, June 2, as soon as the thirty hours elapsed, the Senate took up the House-passed version of the bill and passed it. Obama swiftly signed it. The Freedom Act was law. After so much drama, it came as something of a shock that it was suddenly over. Several of the legislative aides who had worked on it — Dickas, Flint, Forsyth, Hiller, Lynch, Park, and others — convened that evening for an impromptu happy hour at Bar 201, a lounge a few blocks from the Senate side of the Capitol.

The chaos surrounding its enactment left certain things about the Freedom Act a muddle. Its ban on bulk collection did not kick in for 180 days, permitting a transition to the new system. But the new law contained no language either repudiating or embracing the appeals court's interpretation of section 215 as a statute that did not authorize bulk collection. That left ambiguous whether the program could resume in the interim. The administration said it could, and won a FISA Court order that expressly disagreed with the appeals court's legal analysis and permitted the NSA to turn the program back on.[125] The ACLU then asked the appeals court to issue an injunction partially blocking the program.[126] As of this writing, it was not clear how that litigation would play out.

But while the continuing dustups were interesting, it was an important moment to pause and reflect on what had happened. The Freedom Act had been beaten and battered and stripped down from the original vision that the aides to Leahy, Sensenbrenner, Udall, and Wyden had brainstormed up in the fall of 2013. But its core reform — ending bulk collection of Americans' phone records — was law. From one perspective, this change was modest. Among those who said that was Mike Hayden, who had told the *Wall Street Journal*'s readers the previous November that the bill was a gift to the Islamic State. Now, he mocked it as trivial.

"If somebody would come up to me and say, 'Look, Hayden, here's the thing: This Snowden thing is going to be a nightmare for you guys for about two years. And when we get all done with it, what you're going to be required to do is that little 215 program about American telephony metadata — and by the way, you can still have access to it, but you got to go to the court and get access to it from the companies, rather than keep it to yourself' — I go: 'And this is it after two years? Cool!'"[127]

But from another perspective, the enactment of the Freedom Act was a hugely important step. The bill closed many doors to bulk collection of domestic data, existing or potential. It pressured the FISA Court to disclose more about its important rulings, and to consider appointing outside voices to make arguments against the government's position when dealing with novel and significant legal questions. And its enactment demonstrated that there was now bipartisan support in Congress — a rarity on nearly any issue in the Obama era — for imposing some limits on government spying powers. The post-9/11 era had reached a new phase.

It had been a long and difficult path since that early August day in 2013, when the aides had sat outside the Oval Office, waiting for their bosses to finish talking to the president, and started spitballing ideas for a surveillance reform bill that might actually pass. All the staffers who had eventually worked on the bill certainly felt like it was worth celebrating. Park and Flint organized an after-work event on June 11, on the rooftop deck of Pacifico, a restaurant and bar on Capitol Hill. I caught wind of it and stopped by to check it out. It was a scene of bipartisan rapport, rare in Washington these days. Dozens of staffers for lawmakers from both political parties gathered with privacy-group activists and Internet company lobbyists, the men gradually shedding their suit jackets and ties and rolling up their sleeves in the hot summer sun, as they all shared pitchers of frozen margaritas late into the evening.

17. Untargeted Collection (12333)

Even as Congress was struggling mightily to deal with the bulk phone records program, a sneaking suspicion arose that the fight might be the proverbial bright shiny object, distracting attention away from far more significant surveillance programs. One person voicing that warning was John Napier Tye, a former head of the State Department's Internet Freedom section. A tall, earnest former Rhodes Scholar, Tye had been a student of Harold Koh at Yale Law School during the Bush-Cheney years. He worked at Koh's civil liberties legal clinic on post-9/11 cases, helping to draft briefs seeking legal rights for Jose Padilla, the American citizen Bush held as an enemy combatant. After law school, Tye moved to post–Hurricane Katrina New Orleans and represented poor people in housing disputes. When he was ready for a change, a recommendation from Koh helped him get a job at the State Department. He received a top secret clearance, and shortly after the Snowden leaks, he attended a classified briefing on NSA surveillance activities.

Tye became intently focused on what he believed was a major issue being overlooked in the debate. Despite all the attention to the Patriot

Act and the FISA Amendments Act, most of the content and metadata the agency was sucking in took place under the looser rules of Executive Order 12333. That framework — in which the agency is relatively heavily regulated when operating on domestic soil but has a freer hand when operating abroad — was designed in and for an era when domestic communications stayed on the domestic network. That era is over. Among other things, Silicon Valley firms like Google and Yahoo now routinely store redundant backup copies of their customers' e-mail accounts in data centers abroad.

Even after he went public, Tye could not talk about what he learned in the classified NSA briefing. But in October 2013, the *Washington Post* reported, using Snowden documents, that the NSA's British partner agency, GCHQ, had penetrated Google's and Yahoo's private links connecting their overseas data centers. Invoking the looser restrictions of 12333 rules, the NSA had joined in the looting; one document showed that in a single month in 2012, 181 million content and metadata records were sent to Fort Meade. Another showed that at one point that same year, when Yahoo was transferring many archives of user accounts between its data centers, the system was choking at the volume and the NSA had to throttle back its intake.[128]

The important thing to remember is that the NSA *already* had legal, front-door access to foreigners' Yahoo and Google accounts without a warrant under the FISA Amendments Act and the court-approved rules of the Prism system. But FISA, even the warrantless variety, required *targeted* collection of specific users' data. The NSA's clandestine overseas ingestion of user data from the same companies, especially at the volumes the documents indicated, strongly suggested that it was exploiting the looser rules of Executive Order 12333 to use *bulk content collection* techniques FISA generally forbids on domestic soil. It's not clear how much of that involved the accounts of foreigners versus Americans; the NSA likely had no idea either.

Throughout the post-Snowden surveillance debate, the NSA had frequently noted that it complied with the law that forbids targeting any American, whether at home or abroad, for collection without a warrant.

The government acknowledged that the NSA sometimes collected Americans' content without a warrant *incidentally*. If analysts discovered information of foreign intelligence value in such content, they could keep and use it, and if they happened across evidence of a crime in such content, they were required to forward it to the Justice Department. But the discussion of that risk had focused on the relatively limited circumstances in which that might occur under the FISA Amendments Act: if the American happened to be sending a specific international message to or about a foreigner who was being scrutinized by the NSA.

That was controversial. But it was also true that most Americans were not likely to be talking to or about a foreigner the NSA was interested in. Under 12333 rules, however, incidental collection could occur in a far more sweeping way. After all, when the NSA vacuums up bulk content abroad, even from companies that have millions of American users, it is not targeting anyone. The loophole is like a passage in Joseph Heller's novel *Catch-22*:

"They're trying to kill me," Yossarian told him calmly.
"No one's trying to kill you," Clevinger cried.
"Then why are they shooting at me?" Yossarian asked.
"They're shooting at *everyone*," Clevinger answered. "They're trying to kill everyone."
"And what difference does that make?"[129]

Speaking at a legal conference the day the *Post* published the data-link article, Raj De, the NSA general counsel, dismissed the piece as overhyped and misleading. He noted that it announced in its second paragraph that the NSA had positioned itself to collect at will from American users' accounts but waited until the thirty-third paragraph to acknowledge that "it is not clear how much data from Americans is collected and how much of that is retained."

"The implication, the insinuation, suggestion or the outright statement that an agency like NSA would use authority under Executive Order 12333 to evade, skirt or go around FISA is simply inaccurate," De said, adding: "The suggestion of that requires some backing up."[130]

It is true that the public debate is missing crucial data about the scale of incidental collection of Americans' communications under 12333 rules. What is the absolute and relative volume of Americans' messages in the 12333 storehouse? For there to be meaningful self-government on this issue — to debate whether the rules for collecting, searching, and using those private messages are the right rules — one would have to know that answer. To date, the NSA has not provided it. One intelligence official told me that the types of data the NSA collects are so varied that is simply too hard to come up with a representative sampling and do a valid study.

Back in December 2013, Tye's role had given him a good view of internal Obama administration deliberations about surveillance issues, including 12333 rules. When the presidentially appointed review group delivered its report and recommendations, most of the attention it attracted centered on the report's discussion of the Patriot Act phone records program. But Tye noticed that recommendation number twelve called for increasing protections for Americans' private information that the NSA gathered incidentally as part of its warrantless surveillance programs targeting foreigners abroad — meaning collection under both the FISA Amendments Act and 12333. There is a risk, the group wrote, that the government can later search through its database of such communications "in a way that invades the legitimate privacy interests of United States persons."[131]

Inside the White House, Monaco and Ruemmler had developed an internal document called the Disclosures Action Tracker.[132] It was an eight-page chart listing every promise made by Obama and every reform recommendation made to him, with brief analysis and assignments of who was in charge of following up on each. Its entry for the review group's recommendation twelve noted that accepting it would require "significant changes" for information about Americans gathered incidentally under Executive Order 12333.

In January 2014, when Obama gave his surveillance speech describing which reform recommendations he was accepting, he said nothing about rules for handling Americans' information gathered under 12333. Tye was deeply disillusioned.

"The government ignored that recommendation and hoped nobody would notice it," Tye said.[133]

Tye decided to leave government. But before he resigned, he filed a whistleblower complaint alleging that the NSA's 12333 surveillance practices violated Americans' Fourth Amendment rights. The NSA inspector general and the Intelligence Committees blew him off. But Tye wrote an op-ed about his views, published by the *Washington Post*, raising awareness of the 12333 loophole.[134] It was maddeningly vague, not unlike the pre-Snowden warnings from Wyden and Udall. Tye spent thousands of dollars on legal fees during both the whistleblower complaint and public advocacy phases of what he did, seeking to avoid being prosecuted. But he succeeded in focusing attention on the fact that for all the discussion inside the United States about reforming the bulk phone records program, we knew very little about 12333 surveillance and Americans' privacy rights.

Indeed, the public did not even fully know the government's own rules for handling such information. After talking to Tye, I decided to go hunting for them, even those that were still classified. I discovered that limits on analyzing Americans' phone and e-mail records gathered under 12333 were weaker than the Patriot Act's section 215 bulk phone records program (which is, as noted, part of FISA).[135] However, limits on searching for Americans' content that the NSA incidentally collected under 12333 were *stronger* than FISA Amendments Act rules.[136] In other words, for 12333 content, at least, because there was a wider aperture at the front end, the government had imposed more robust protections for Americans' privacy at the back end.

But there was a catch. In 2008, Bush had amended Executive Order 12333 to permit the NSA to share raw signals intercepts with other agencies, if and when the Justice Department and Pentagon agreed on procedures.* I learned that the Obama legal team had been working on drafting procedures to do just that, and a proposal was sitting at the Justice Department. It was not clear how much leeway, if any, the draft sharing procedures would give officials at other agencies, like the FBI,

---

* See chapter 5, section 15.

to search for Americans' communications within data that the NSA had swept up in bulk under 12333 rules. In any case, the Snowden controversies had apparently derailed the effort to finish the sharing procedures. But if the Obama administration or its successor finalized them, the public might never know what the new rules were. After all, back in November 2010, when the NSA dropped its ban on using Americans' metadata gathered under 12333, it kept the change secret.

18. Backdoor Searches and Battles to Come

When Hayden mocked the Freedom Act—"And this is it after two years? Cool!"—part of his premise was that the difficult passage of that law had exhausted the reform energies unleashed by the Snowden leaks, leaving 99 percent of America's post-9/11 surveillance state untouched. But the surveillance critics in Congress vowed they would press on to add new curbs to the FISA Amendments Act.

Their focus was what critics call *backdoor searches*—the practice by government agents of searching for incidentally collected messages of Americans that it had gathered without a warrant in the course of foreign intelligence surveillance. Critics said the government should get a warrant to query for an American's messages in such a database. The intelligence community shot back that the government had always been allowed to use information it already possessed and had collected lawfully, and requiring it to get a warrant would inhibit its ability to stop terrorist attacks and solve crimes. According to a letter Clapper's office sent Wyden, in 2013, the NSA had searched for Americans' names in FISA Amendments Act–acquired content 198 times, and the CIA had done so about 1,900 times.[137] The FBI didn't track how often its agents conducted such a search, the letter said, but believed the numbers were "substantial."[138]

On June 11, a week after Obama signed the Freedom Act, the House voted 255 to 174 to attach an amendment to a military spending bill requiring warrants for such backdoor searches.[139] It was sponsored by Representatives Thomas Massie, Republican from Kentucky, and Zoe

Lofgren, Democrat from California. The House had approved the same amendment in 2014, but it died in negotiations with the Senate. But now, the Freedom Act fight had demonstrated that a bipartisan House majority, combined with a "sunset" deadline that risked letting the entire law expire if no bill at all passed, could overcome resistance. The FISA Amendments Act was set to expire on December 17, 2017.

Meanwhile, the hints about the potential volumes of incidental collection via 12333 surveillance suggested that for all Snowden's revelations, Americans still had more to learn. The public was only now starting to understand the full implications of the technological scrambling of the geographic distinction between domestic and foreign communications that existed in 1978, when Congress enacted the original FISA. The intelligence community, through transit authority, the temporary fix of Stellarwind, and the essentially permanent fix of the FISA Amendments Act, has solved its half of the problem. It has gained largely unfettered access to the foreign communications that are now routinely found on domestic networks.

But that still left the other half of the problem. For the same reason, Americans' domestic communications are now routinely found on networks abroad too. Congress took a first step in updating privacy rules for twenty-first-century facts in 2008 when, as part of the FISA Amendments Act, it required the NSA to obtain a warrant to *target* an American's e-mail or phone number for collection no matter where in the world the NSA was operating or where the American was located. But lawmakers have yet to demonstrate much awareness of or interest in the fact that the NSA has both the legal power and, now, the technical ability to vacuum up Americans' communications on a massive scale from fiber-optic lines overseas, justified under Executive Order 12333 as incidental and untargeted bulk collection.

Congress may yet impose further checks and balances on when government agents may search surveillance databases for incidentally collected private communications of Americans—regardless of which legal authority the government used to collect them. But as Obama's time in power neared its end, there was little sign that he would be the president who ushered in that change.

12

The Tug of War

War Powers

1. "A Red Line" in Syria

In the summer of 2012, an intelligence official told Obama that forces loyal to the government of President Bashar Assad appeared to be removing chemical weapons in Syria from the bunkers in which they were stored. The United States had stayed out of the civil war that had erupted in Syria in 2011 as Assad cracked down violently on antigovernment protests. The situation was horrific for civilians caught in the crossfire. Tens of thousands died. But other than sending humanitarian aid, it was not clear what could be done about it. The war pitted a brutal dictatorship with ties to Iran and Russia against rebel militias, many of whom appeared to be jihadists who shared al-Qaeda's ideology. The Obama team spent nearly two years debating whether to send covert shipments of weapons and provide limited training to a so-called moderate faction of the rebels. But the Obama team feared that injecting more firepower that could easily end up in the hands of hard-core Islamists could do more harm than good.[1] With no one, really, to root for, there was little appetite for a direct military intervention.

But now, the prospect that Assad's forces might use chemical weapons opened a new dimension. Poison gas is an inherently indiscriminate weapon, and one the civilized world had been trying to abolish since the horrors of World War I. The Obama administration decided to warn Assad not to use the banned weapons without committing the

United States to any specific response. But at an August 20 press conference, Obama, in what aides later said was an off-the-cuff phrase, made a more aggressive warning than planned. Obama said if Assad moved or used "a whole bunch of chemical weapons," it would be "a red line" that would change his calculations about not intervening in Syria with armed force.[2]

Obama's unplanned phrase put the administration in the position of having to create a real policy. In the months that followed, lawyers with the Departments of Defense, Justice, and State, along with the Joint Staff and the National Security Council — that is, Jeh Johnson, Virginia Seitz, Harold Koh, Rich Gross, Avril Haines, and their aides — gathered to analyze whether Obama had the authority to launch a punitive military strike if Assad crossed this red line. The lawyers group collectively produced a seventeen-page unsigned paper whose existence has never been reported. It assessed a legal case for the use of force in such a hypothetical situation.

As a matter of international law, this was a problematic case to make. Chemical weapons are banned under two treaties, but Syria had signed only one of them, and neither contained an enforcement mechanism that independently authorized other countries to attack a violator.

Moreover, each of the historically recognized ways to obtain authority to carry out an attack on the soil of another country looked unavailable. The first option was a United Nations Security Council authorization, but under the UN charter, Russia, an ally to Assad, could veto any such resolution and almost certainly would do so.

The second way was to obtain the consent of the host government. This was also a nonstarter; none of the rebel groups was in a position to be recognized as a legitimate alternative government to Assad, the lawyers wrote in their memo.

The third way was a claim of self-defense. The United States itself had no obvious individual self-defense claim to invoke. But *if* attacks ramped up along and across the Turkish border and it looked like chemical weapons might be used there, the lawyers mused, maybe the United States could invoke its right to protect American forces stationed in Turkey, or Turkey might ask the United States to help in its collective right to self-defense.

The lawyers also looked at a fourth, more disputed option. If the real point of all this was to impose consequences for the use of chemical weapons, then that had the air of a humanitarian intervention, or a military action to end human rights violations — albeit one aimed at punishing a past war crime and deterring any repetition of it, rather than preventing an imminent atrocity.

The problem was that without authorization by the United Nations, even a traditional humanitarian intervention was controversial as a legal basis for an attack under international law. Indeed, the United States had never said that an unauthorized humanitarian intervention could be legal. It feared that such a doctrine would be too easy for other countries to abuse — thereby weakening global constraints on war. For example, Russia might claim a need to protect ethnic Russians in the nations surrounding its borders as an excuse to invade them.

However, there was a precedent of sorts. Back in 1999, the United States had led the NATO air war in Kosovo, a humanitarian intervention in all but name and which did not have UN authorization; Russia was an ally to the Serbs and would not permit a UN Security Council resolution to stop their ethnic-cleansing campaign. The Clinton legal team had stopped short of articulating any clear legal rationale for that war. Instead, to justify the NATO operation, it had cited a vague collection of "factors" — like the threat to peace and stability, the danger of a humanitarian disaster, and the inability of the UN Security Council to make a clear decision — without ever saying how they added up to a theory by which the air war was lawful. The participants in the whole legal discussion, such as it was, had an air of embarrassment; they also asserted that the episode would not serve as a precedent.[3]

The Obama legal team decided Kosovo could nevertheless serve as a precedent. In their seventeen-page memo, they came up with a similar list of "factors" the United States could cite to justify an attack on Syria. These included an assessment that intervention would prevent further indiscriminate use of chemical weapons against civilians and avert a broader humanitarian disaster, and that not taking action would lead to "unconscionable follow-on consequences." Their memo also noted that a hypothetical intervention would be multilateral, like Kosovo was, if NATO or the Arab League would support it.

But their memo warned Obama that there were many reasons to be cautious. The Assad regime would likely deny that it used chemical weapons, so the facts would be hard to ascertain or discuss in public if they were based on secret intelligence sources. An intervention could broaden the conflict, create a negative precedent that Iran or Russia could use to intervene for its own purposes in Syria, or inadvertently increase the risk of chemical-weapons facilities falling into the hands of terrorists.

International law, moreover, was only half the problem. Questions like UN Security Council resolutions concern whether and when it is legal for any nation to use force on another's sovereign soil. But that is separate from the *domestic*-law question of who, under the Constitution, gets to decide whether the United States will participate in a military campaign — Congress or the president.

There would, of course, be no question that punitive strikes on Assad's forces would be legal, domestically, if Congress authorized Obama to carry them out. If there were no congressional authorization, however, Obama would have to rely on his commander-in-chief powers. The Constitution gives Congress the power to declare war, but the executive branch, over time, had developed the theory that a president could carry out military attacks on his own if the anticipated use of force was not big enough to count as a war and if he determined that the intervention would further an important national interest. In this hypothetical case, the memo said, Obama could cite national interests in preserving regional stability, trying to impede the use or proliferation of chemical weapons, or protecting allies like Israel and Turkey. But, citing an intervention in Libya earlier in Obama's presidency that had turned sour, legally and politically, Obama's lawyers urged him to consider going to Congress before striking Assad's forces, even though they did not say it would be required.

"If the Administration decides to pursue military action, the lawyers group believes it would be prudent to make an explicit request for congressional authorization at the outset, particularly in light of the Libya experience last year," the secret memo said.

2. Separation of Powers and the Initiation of War in the Twenty-First Century

Because the stakes are so high, the power to decide when the United States will commit an act of war is the most fraught of all the contested territory between the presidency and Congress. Back in 2007, when Obama was still a senator and a presidential candidate, he had embraced a far more limited view about a commander in chief's war power than his legal team later laid out in their Syria memo.

The backdrop to Obama's 2007 statement was the ceaseless violence in Iraq following Bush's 2003 invasion of that country, a dispiriting chaos that had helped Democrats take control of Congress. When the Bush-Cheney administration rattled its saber about possibly bombing suspected Iranian nuclear sites, opposition lawmakers like Senator Joe Biden threatened to impeach Bush if he did so without going to Congress for permission.[4] Meanwhile, as a *Boston Globe* reporter, I was preparing my executive-power survey of presidential candidates. I asked them each to say under what circumstances, if any, they believed that the Constitution permitted a president to attack another country absent an imminent threat or congressional authorization. Obama's answer was very clear.

"The President does not have power under the Constitution to unilaterally authorize a military attack in a situation that does not involve stopping an actual or imminent threat to the nation," Obama said.[5]

Other Democratic presidential candidates, including Biden and Senator Hillary Clinton, said similar things in their answers to the survey.[6] Those statements comported with how most scholars read the Constitution, and yet in a sense they were radical.

In the middle of the twentieth century, a profound disconnect emerged between the way the United States went to war in practice, and the way that most scholars believe the Founders originally wanted the United States to decide whether to use armed force abroad. As World War II blurred into the era of the Cold War, the United States kept a large standing army based around the world instead of demobilizing it. This removed a practical check on executive war-making power — the need for the president to ask Congress to raise an army for him to deploy. Starting with Truman in the Korean War, presidents of both parties had ordered American forces into combat without seeking legislative permission. Congress acquiesced rather than impeaching the presidents who did so, and the practice has become so accepted that it is difficult to say what the law is or requires in the modern era.

"There's no more dramatic example of the 'living Constitution' than in this area," said David Golove, a New York University law professor.[7]

In 1973, as the Vietnam War ended, Congress sought to restore its role in deciding whether the nation would go to war by enacting, over Nixon's veto, the War Powers Resolution. It declared that presidents should consult with Congress before introducing forces into actual or imminent hostilities. But it also implicitly recognized that in the modern world that might not always happen. So it required presidents to terminate any combat deployments after sixty days — with an additional thirty-day wind-down period, if necessary — if Congress had not voted to authorize the missions to continue.

But the War Powers Resolution failed to prevent presidents from unilaterally launching air strikes, invasions, and peacekeeping operations in troubled countries ranging from Grenada and Panama to Somalia and the Balkans. And the expansion of presidential war-making powers continued to be a bipartisan enterprise. In 1994, Walter Dellinger, a head of the Office of Legal Counsel in the Clinton administration, fleshed out a legal theory for why presidents had that power. Presidents could authorize military operations that fell short of war *in the constitutional sense,* based on their anticipated nature, scope, duration, and the likelihood that American forces would suffer or inflict significant casualties, he wrote.[8]

In making his answer to my survey, Senator Obama seemed to be saying that he intended to roll back this central feature of the bipartisan imperial presidency era. But the problems of the world and presidential war powers would look more complicated from the Oval Office than they had from the campaign trail.

For example, Obama inherited a Drug Enforcement Administration program that blurred the lines between the war on drugs and the war on terrorism. The program, called Foreign-Deployed Advisory Support Team, or FAST, consisted of squads of specially trained and equipped American agents who worked with vetted units of local police in countries beset by transnational drug cartels, like Honduras, Haiti, the Dominican Republic, and Belize. While officially law enforcement agents, the FAST units were effectively military; their members were generally former Special Operations troops, and their leader was a former Navy SEAL. The DEA developed the FAST program for going after Taliban-linked narcotics operations in the Afghanistan war zone. But in the final year of the Bush-Cheney administration, the DEA expanded its mission. It began deploying the squads to the Western Hemisphere, where there was no armed conflict. The Obama administration permitted the program to continue. In 2010 and 2011, American commando-agents, under the banner of trainers and advisers, began going into harm's way and taking part in firefights in the jungles of Honduras, killing people.[9] As members of Congress began to question whether the American agents were really taking the lead in paramilitary missions, the DEA in 2012 suspended and rethought the operation there.[10]

Cyberweapons were another complexity that confounded simple campaign rhetoric about war and peace. Soon after Obama took office, he was briefed about a highly classified, ongoing covert scheme to sabotage Iran's nuclear program using computer viruses.[11] Dubbed Operation Olympic Games, the cyberweapon, which the National Security Agency apparently developed with its Israeli counterpart, made centrifuges that enriched uranium suddenly spin out of control and destroy themselves. This damage was brought about by changing zeros and ones in software, but the end result was the same as dropping a bomb:

the United States had destroyed another nation's property on its sovereign soil. Nation-states by then had a long history of cyberespionage — hacking each other's computers to steal information — but this was the most sophisticated known incident of one state using a cyberweapon to attack another. Obama himself had just said that bombing Iranian nuclear facilities would require congressional authorization. Still, this operation was covert, and it was intended to delay or prevent a conventional war. The operation worked in phases, with different versions of the virus (one of which later escaped onto the global network and was dubbed Stuxnet) used in turn. Obama permitted the operation to continue.

Clearly, if the United States could do that to Iran, another country could do it to the United States, too. The military was developing an understanding, from a defensive perspective, that if a foreign adversary used computers to destroy infrastructure inside the United States, the president could consider it an act of war and respond with military force. But the Obama legal team struggled to map the twenty-first-century tool of cyberweapons onto twentieth-century rules for conventional war. Early in 2009, the National Security Council's top cyberspace policy official, Melissa Hathaway, led a sixty-day review of cyberpolicy issues for the new administration. She commissioned more than 100 papers from different experts that informed her report and recommendations. As part of that effort, the National Security Council legal adviser, Mary DeRosa, was assigned to write a memo fleshing out the general legal rules for the use of force in cyberspace. But DeRosa successfully resisted the task, arguing that there were too many problems in writing legal conclusions in the abstract and without a specific factual scenario in mind. When Hathaway turned in her report that May, a classified annex contained cursory discussion of legal issues that boiled down to saying that more study was required. [12]

By 2012, after three more years of wrangling, the interagency lawyers produced a speech for Koh to deliver at Fort Meade — home of Cyber Command and the NSA, the American surveillance and cyberwar powerhouses — in which he made the basic and yet groundbreaking assertion that international law does indeed apply in cyberspace. Koh said, "If the physical consequences of a cyber attack work the kind of physical damage that dropping a bomb or firing a missile would, that cyber attack should equally be considered a use of force."[13] The next month, Obama secretly signed a classified presidential policy directive that set rules for "Offensive Cyber Effects Operations." The same legal analysis undergirded it. The directive said cyberweapons could be used only "consistent with its obligations under international law, including with regard to matters of sovereignty and neutrality, and, as applicable, the law of armed conflict."[14] By those standards, Operation Olympic Games had apparently been violating international law for years. The directive discussed no role for Congress in deciding whether to deploy such a weapon.

Both the DEA's FAST program in the Western Hemisphere and Operation Olympic Games were security state initiatives that blurred the lines, that had begun late in the Bush-Cheney administration, and that continued or expanded in the Obama years. But midway through Obama's first term, he was confronted with a new situation in Libya that pitted his principles about conventional warfare against each other.

3. Initiating the Libya Air War

In early 2011, antigovernment protests erupted across the Arab world as people clamored for an end to the dictatorships under which they had long been suffering. Dubbed the Arab Spring, it was a moment of great optimism: perhaps democracy would sweep that long-troubled region, render al-Qaeda's ideology irrelevant, and make the world a better place for millions of ordinary people. But after the longtime strongman leaders of Egypt and Tunisia were ousted, Colonel Muammar Gadhafi, their counterpart in Libya, the country sandwiched between theirs, was determined not to go down the same way. He launched a violent crackdown on the protests, which evolved into an armed rebellion against Tripoli's rule, based out of the eastern Libyan city of Benghazi.

The question arose: Would the Western world intervene? On March 1, the United States Senate approved, by unanimous consent, a resolution asking the United Nations Security Council to impose a no-fly zone.[15] But it did not look like the UN Security Council would authorize a military intervention in Libya because Russia and China, which could veto such resolutions, generally opposed interference in other countries' internal affairs. Then, however, Arab League countries said they would support an intervention, and on Thursday, March 17, as Gadhafi's forces neared Benghazi, he vowed on the radio that they would "have no mercy and no pity" against foes who refused to surrender, and would "come house by house, room by room."[16]

The suggestion that a slaughter of civilians was imminent and the Arab League's support for an intervention changed the dynamic. Russia and China abruptly agreed to abstain rather than use their veto power, and later in the day on March 17, the UN Security Council passed a resolution authorizing a no-fly zone in Libya and "all necessary measures" to protect civilians, short of occupying ground forces.[17] NATO had plans for American aircraft to push back Gadhafi's forces from Benghazi and destroy Libya's air defenses, after which the United States would provide support but its European and Arab allies would police the no-fly zone.

The UN action made an intervention by the United States on Libyan soil legal as a matter of international law. But there remained the separate, domestic-law problem: whether Obama needed to ask Congress for authorization to participate in the NATO operation. As an informal matter, there appeared to be general political support in Congress for an intervention in Libya, as reflected in the March 1 Senate resolution. But the diplomatic roadblocks had abruptly cleared at the worst possible time for Congress to act. At that moment, Congress was distracted and exhausted by a bitter fight over spending. The House, newly under Republican control following the Tea Party election in November 2010, had just passed a short-term spending bill to avert a government shutdown for just three weeks. The Tea Party caucus had refused to support the bill even though the Republican Speaker of the House, John

Boehner, backed it. Boehner had been forced to rely on Democratic votes to pass it. Now, members were already heading to the airport for a scheduled recess.

The political reality was that Congress was not capable, at that moment, of swiftly taking up and passing an authorization to use military force in Libya before Gadhafi's troops entered Benghazi. Memories differ about the details of the conversations between the White House and congressional leaders that took place at this moment. Current and former executive-branch officials told me that the congressional leadership of both parties privately urged the White House to go ahead and launch the intervention without formal legislative permission. Current and former Republican congressional staffers had a different memory. They told me that the White House had done no advance work to let Congress know that it might move fast if diplomatic conditions changed, and that it merely notified the legislative leaders that it was now thinking of acting, without offering details. The Republican congressional leaders, they maintained, neither blessed any operation nor objected to one, but were, rather, in "receive mode" and said nothing more than "Keep us posted."

Not everyone was passive. At a Senate Foreign Relations Committee hearing, also on March 17, the ranking Republican, Senator Richard Lugar from Indiana, said, "If we are going to declare war against Libya, then we ought to have a congressional declaration of war." But the Democratic chairman, Senator John Kerry of Massachusetts, disagreed. He told Lugar that "life does not always present us with circumstances that afford us the opportunity to do that.... Republican and Democratic presidents alike have had to make tough choices, faced with the moment."[18]

On March 18, Caroline Krass, whom Obama had recently installed as the acting head of the Justice Department's Office of Legal Counsel, orally advised that it would be lawful for Obama to order the envisioned military operations without congressional permission. Obama directed the military to commence the air war the next afternoon.

Krass then wrote a fourteen-page memorandum memorializing her legal reasoning.[19] She signed it on April 1. Citing previous executive-branch memos and historical precedents, Krass wrote that the envisioned air strikes were of such limited nature, scope, and duration that they did not require authorization from Congress.[20] Obama, she also wrote, had inherent authority from the Constitution to order an intervention to advance American interests, which backing the credibility of the United Nations process and preventing a destabilizing flood of Libyan refugees into neighboring Tunisia and Egypt would do. She did not mention Obama's contrary view in my *Boston Globe* survey.

At first, only a few voices in Congress, mostly at the liberal and libertarian fringes, publicly objected. Representative Dennis Kucinich, Democrat from Ohio, said Obama's decision was a "serious" constitutional abuse.[21] Soon after, Senator Rand Paul, Republican from Kentucky, went to the Senate floor with a poster of Obama's *Boston Globe* quote. He proposed having the Senate endorse, verbatim, what Obama had said then. But the Senate voted him down, ninety to ten.[22]

Obama's initiation of war in Libya was a milestone. Despite the fact that he had previously stated that such a decision was for Congress to make, from Obama's vantage point, he was confronted with a choice between two evils. One was to stick to his prior constitutional principles and do nothing because Congress had not acted, in which case many people in Benghazi would probably die. The other was to violate those principles and intervene without congressional authorization, in which case the United States might save those people's lives.

Obama chose the latter option. His unilateral initiation of the air strikes dovetailed with what other presidents had done since World War II. But it was a dramatic break from the expectations created by his own campaign rhetoric. It was also his first taste of solving a problem through executive action, justifying it to himself on the basis that Congress could not act. It would not be his last.

4. The War Powers Resolution

When Congress returned from its recess in April 2011, the administration held classified briefings for the full House and Senate in a congressional auditorium. Several executive-branch officials, including Secretary of State Hillary Clinton and Defense Secretary Bob Gates, described the early bombardment and then took questions. The meeting left a sour taste in the mouths of lawmakers of both parties. At one point, Representative Jerrold Nadler, a liberal Democrat from New York, stepped to the microphone and asked "Hillary," as he addressed his former New York delegation colleague, whether the administration thought it needed congressional authorization, as he, Nadler, believed it did.

Jerry, Clinton responded, according to a participant, *we don't need congressional authorization. But if Congress wants to help by passing a resolution to support it, we'd welcome it.*

Nadler told me that he did not remember the briefing specifically but that it was consistent with his broader view that Obama, like many post–World War II presidents before him, had violated the Constitution by initiating a war without congressional authorization. He said he rejected the idea that the situation required the government to move without Congress, noting that it had had time to consult the Arab League and NATO.

But as House Republicans and the White House girded for yet another budget battle to avert yet another imminent government shutdown, Obama did not ask Congress to retroactively authorize the Libya operation. At the time, his team thought that the American contribution to the NATO effort would soon no longer involve direct strikes and that the Libyan rebels would overthrow Gadhafi in short order anyway.[23] If so, they would have essentially bluffed their way through the potential problem. But their assumptions were wrong, leading to a crisis and one of the most disputed legal-policy moves of Obama's presidency.

The rebels proved disorganized, and the civil war in Libya continued for eight months before Gadhafi finally fell. In the meantime, pro-Gadhafi forces kept turning on or rebuilding air-defense installations, and only American jets carried the special radar-seeking missiles that were best for destroying them, so Americans kept firing missiles. Moreover, only the United States had armed Predator drones. Gates, who had opposed the intervention as not in the direct national security interest of the United States, initially told NATO it could use the drones only for surveillance. But General Ralph Jodice, the air-component commander for the NATO operation in Libya, told me after his retirement that there were several frustrating incidents in which NATO commanders watched from Predator cameras as pro-Gadhafi forces fired randomly into towns without a fighter jet nearby. NATO lobbied Gates to relax the rules, and after April 21, Gates permitted it to use the Predators to fire missiles to stop such incidents. Between April and mid-June, the United States carried out about sixty air strikes from piloted aircraft and thirty from drones, my colleague Thom Shanker and I later reported; this averaged about one a day.[24] As the weeks passed and it became clear that American forces were continuing to blow things up and kill pro-Gadhafi fighters, the Obama lawyers began asking a question with increasing urgency: What about the War Powers Resolution's sixty-day limit for unauthorized wars?

There is an oddly widespread myth that every president since Nixon has declared this limit to be unconstitutional.[25] This is simply false. Subsequent presidents have challenged *other* provisions of the War Powers Resolution, but not the sixty-day provision. Indeed, the Carter administration's Office of Legal Counsel in 1980 concluded that the clock was a constitutional limit on presidential power, and no subsequent administration has revoked that memorandum opinion.[26] For the most part, the issue has not arisen. Presidents generally continued to get congressional authorization for bigger military operations, like the First Gulf War, the Afghanistan War, and the Iraq War. Most smaller operations were either too short-lived to raise questions, like Grenada and Panama, or the fighting was so intermittent, such as on peacekeeping missions, that the executive branch claimed that the sixty-day law did not apply. The greatest challenge to the sixty-day law came in 1999, when Clinton unilaterally ordered the United States military to participate in the NATO air war in Kosovo, which lasted for seventy-eight days. Congress did not authorize it, but it *did* specifically appropriate funds for that mission just before day sixty, and Clinton's

Office of Legal Counsel, then led by Randolph Moss (whom Obama would appoint as a federal district court judge), said this counted as implicit authorization.[27]

Moss's legal theory for Kosovo had been controversial, but the Obama legal team did not even have a specific appropriation to work with for Libya. As day sixty — May 20 — grew closer, Obama's lawyers struggled to get data from the field about what was happening and talked about whether the pace of strikes fell below the threshold that would count as the sort of hostilities that the sixty-day law covered. But given the number of American bombs that were still falling, Krass said the Office of Legal Counsel had never interpreted the War Powers Resolution that way.

The lawyers group wondered whether they could get some kind of quick authorization from Congress, where Senators John McCain and Kerry — both major supporters of the Libya intervention — had talked about pushing a resolution but had yet to come up with one. And in mid-May, around day fifty, at a National Security Council meeting on Libya, Bob Bauer, Obama's White House counsel, told the president about the looming problem. Obama said that he wanted to explore getting congressional authorization. The lawyers were relieved.

But about a week later, the message came back that congressional leaders had advised the White House that there was no political appetite to enact an authorization. Republicans had rapidly shifted against any intervention in Libya once Obama embraced it and as Gadhafi lingered in power. For several weeks, conservatives had been criticizing Obama for not consulting with Congress more and for carrying out a vague and perhaps foolish strategy,[28] and after the bin Laden raid in early May, when Obama was riding high on national security issues, criticizing his Libya war became a way to push back. McCain and Kerry, seeing that there was no chance of getting a resolution through the House anyway, had shelved their plans to push one in the Senate.

Things looked different from Congress, where Obama's Libya policy put Boehner in a dilemma. Boehner had long believed that the War Powers Resolution was entirely unconstitutional, senior Republican staffers said, but he also had to represent the institutional interests of Congress and manage his unruly Republican caucus, which was in a populist mode and wanting to fight Obama on Libya just like on the budget. Boehner was at once irritated with the White House's imperious manner — informing rather than truly consulting about the operation — but also fearful that the House might vote for something that would undermine the troops in Libya and undercut NATO allies, who were also playing an important role in Afghanistan. That role isolated Boehner from his own caucus.

In March and April, Boehner followed that line by publicly saying skeptical things about the operation but focusing his questions on its strategy and tactics rather than its legality. But as the operation went on, and anger grew in the House, he began voicing more aggressive criticism, including hinting that the operation might not be legal. Republican aides told me that this was a strategy to serve as a pressure release valve for anti-Obama sentiment in his caucus while trying to prevent the House from taking any formal action, since anything that could pass would likely be damaging to the national interest as he saw it.

On May 17, three days before the deadline, the White House summoned senior national-security staffers for the House and Senate leaders of both parties to the Situation Room for a meeting with Denis McDonough, then the deputy national security adviser. In proposing this meeting, a senior White House official had supposedly told the chiefs of staff for the four leading lawmakers that the continued use of armed Predator drones had triggered a threshold, creating a "legal imperative" to get congressional authorization.

When the leadership staffers got to the meeting, McDonough asked them to consider pushing a joint resolution through Congress supporting the Libya operation. But McDonough framed the request as something that would be important merely for diplomatic reasons, not legal ones. Jen Stewart, the national security adviser to Boehner, asked McDonough to explain how the drones had triggered a "legal imperative" issue. Confusingly, McDonough denied that there was any legal imperative. In other words, the administration wanted Congress to pass an authorization without making any acknowledgment that it was, in fact, necessary. The Republican congressional staffers told him that there was no guarantee that an authorization Obama considered to be legally irrelevant could pass in either chamber, and Stewart told McDonough to consider the consequences if he asked for such a resolution but lawmakers voted it down. At the end of the meeting, McDonough said the White House had language they were thinking of sending to Congress to review, but none ever arrived.[29]

The Obama national security lawyers group did not attend that meeting, but there was a widespread understanding within the Obama administration that congressional leaders of *both* parties in each chamber had separately and privately told the president that they did not think authorization was legally necessary. (The truth of this is hard to pin down, but after the sixty-day deadline passed, all four of them — Boehner, Nancy Pelosi, Harry Reid, and Mitch McConnell — each made public comments that suggested they did not think the administration was violating the War Powers Resolution.[30])

With the deadline now days away, the lawyers scrambled to answer the question of what, if anything, had to change on day sixty. The Pentagon's Johnson circulated a discussion paper, which he personally signed, saying that the administration would have a stronger argument that it was complying with the statute if its military activity receded to a purely supporting role, like refueling allied warplanes and providing surveillance. That could mean no more American missile strikes at air defenses and returning to the rule that Predator drones were for surveillance only. Krass did not circulate a paper of her own, but she made some minor tweaks to Johnson's, which suggested that she agreed with its substance. A young State Department lawyer serving as an aide to Koh — David Pozen, later a Columbia law professor — had also produced a discussion paper that dovetailed with Johnson's approach; Pozen warned of potential legal problems if the operational tempo continued unchanged after the sixtieth day, although his memo was not put out in Koh's name. (The existence of these discussion papers has not previously been reported.) As the sixtieth day neared, it appeared to most participants that Johnson's paper represented the consensus view. Krass backed it. DeRosa backed it. And Koh had not clearly objected to it.

On an operational level, this was bad news. Without the availability of the United States' unique weapons systems, the risk would go up that pro-Gadhafi forces would shoot down a NATO aircraft. Moreover, NATO was also using the Predators to keep an eye on chemical-weapons depots, and it wanted to be able to use them to strike immediately if anyone tried to go into one. At another Situation Room meeting about Libya, Obama decided that he would not ratchet down the mission. The word came to the lawyers that the military would keep going without changes after May 20. The White House was adopting a different legal interpretation than the lawyers' apparent consensus of the best reading of the law: It now maintained that the constellation of American contributions to the mission fell short of the type of hostilities that was covered by the sixty-day law.

There were never interagency lawyers group meetings about this new theory. Instead, Bauer—who had not participated directly in the deliberations before that point—took control of them. He talked one-on-one about the legal options with the major participants. Among them was Koh. It turned out Koh was not as sure as the other members of the interagency team that the sixty-day law applied to this kind of narrow air campaign, as opposed to a major Vietnam-style ground war. Notably, Koh was a proponent of humanitarian interventions, like Clinton's air war to stop the Serbs' ethnic cleansing in Kosovo, when Koh had served as the top human rights official in the State Department. This alternative interpretation of the War Powers Resolution would liberate such limited air strikes from the sixty-day clock, making it easier for American presidents to conduct humanitarian interventions in the future.

As Obama weighed his decision, Bauer had told him that there was another interpretation of the War Powers Resolution. Embracing this theory of what the statute meant would permit Obama to keep the mission going without changes. Bauer warned that this approach was not the *favored* interpretation of the law among others on the administration legal team and predicted that Obama would be criticized for embracing it. But, he maintained, it was *legally available.*

Obama decided to go forward with the operation on that basis. And over the next few weeks, Bauer and Koh developed their initially bare-bones "non-hostilities" theory into a four-factor test. The sixty-day law did not apply to operations where there was no sustained fighting or *exchanges* of fire with hostile forces, no American ground troops, no serious threat of American casualties, and — because the mission was constrained by the terms of the UN Security Council resolution — no significant chance of an escalation.

This was a very aggressive interpretation of the statute. It wasn't "hostilities" for the United States to bomb another country's armed forces pretty much *every day,* so long as those forces could not shoot back at the Americans and it was a UN-authorized mission? There was a far less elaborate and direct solution — to simply say that the sixty-day law was an unconstitutional intrusion on a president's powers as commander in chief. But that was the kind of sweeping, Bush-like claim that Obama hated to make, and it would have set a precedent that future presidents could also cite to ignore the time limit even for major ground wars.

I later asked Tom Donilon, then Obama's national security adviser, whether the not-hostilities theory predated Obama's decision to keep going after day sixty without changes, or whether the lawyers had instead put forward the rationale later, as a milder way to justify the decision than relying on a commander-in-chief-override theory. Donilon said the not-hostilities theory "was on the table before the decision" and so was not an after-the-fact rationalization.

5. "We Are Acting Lawfully"

The not-hostilities rationale the administration put forward was controversial, even before the administration made it public. Other lawyers on Obama's team did not endorse Bauer's and Koh's interpretation of the War Powers Resolution. Johnson told Bauer he was sticking with what he said in his discussion paper. Krass made clear that if Bauer asked the Office of Legal Counsel to write a formal, authoritative memo analyzing the question, she was unlikely to give the White House the answer it wanted to hear. DeRosa, who was subordinate to Bauer, kept her head down; her position was also in a state of flux, as she was slated to step down and hand over the role of National Security Council legal adviser to her deputy, Avril Haines, in early June. Late in the process, Holder — who had the authority to override the Office of Legal Counsel and come up with the official Justice Department interpretation of the law himself — told the White House that he was backing Krass. But Obama had already made the decision by then, and Holder registered the point mildly. He could have jammed Obama by saying that the Justice Department believed going forward without changes in Libya was clearly illegal, but he instead apparently took a more nuanced approach. He indicated that the Bauer-Koh theory was not the best interpretation in the eyes of the department, but that was not the same thing as pronouncing the theory legally unavailable and out-of-bounds.

While its members argued internally, the Obama administration initially offered no public explanation for why day sixty had come and gone without any change in the American participation in the Libya air war.[31] The silence fueled bipartisan anger. At a May 25 House Foreign Affairs Committee meeting, Representative Dan Burton, Republican from Indiana, said Obama was acting "like a king," and Representative Brad Sherman, Democrat from California, lamented that Congress was being made irrelevant.

"It's time to stop shredding the U.S. Constitution in a presumed effort to bring democracy and constitutional rule of law to Libya," Sherman said.[32]

In early June, Kucinich proposed a House resolution directing Obama to remove forces from Libya immediately. But when it looked like it might pass, Boehner introduced a rival resolution that merely expressed opposition to using ground forces in Libya — which Obama did not want to do anyway — and directed the White House to provide a report to Congress explaining its Libya policy. Boehner's symbolic measure became the outlet for congressional rebuke and it passed, while Kucinich's failed.[33]

Boehner's requested report was due on Thursday, June 16, shortly before the operation would reach day ninety. Earlier that week, I got a phone call from a White House press official. I had been writing about the War Powers Resolution problem more than any other journalist, and Bauer wanted to talk about it. Bauer was leaving the government at the end of that week to take a role in Obama's reelection campaign, and the contents of his office were already half boxed up. When I walked inside, I was surprised to see Koh sitting on his sofa. The ground rules were that I could not publish what they told me until Congress got the report. Bauer then turned the meeting over to Koh to explain their theory.

"We are acting lawfully," Koh said. "We are not saying the president can take the country into war on his own. We are not saying the War Powers Resolution is unconstitutional or should be scrapped or that we can refuse to consult Congress. We are saying the limited nature of this particular mission is not the kind of 'hostilities' envisioned by the War Powers Resolution."[34]

When it became public, this interpretation of the War Powers Resolution was subjected to sharp scrutiny. Many critics found it unreasonable; the Pentagon was on track to spend over one billion dollars on the operation, and the United States was killing Libyan forces regularly. Jack Goldsmith, the former Office of Legal Counsel head and now a Harvard law professor, said Obama was setting a precedent expanding a president's unilateral powers to wage an open-ended war using drones and missiles from ships, since that carried no risk of American casualties.

Still, Rick Pildes, a New York University law professor, noted that the statute did not define *hostilities*. And the Supreme Court had never ruled on what level of fighting was sufficient to trigger it. The resolution to the dispute would depend on whether Congress acquiesced to Obama's move, he said.

That Friday morning, Koh gave a speech before a liberal legal group in which he acknowledged that some people thought he was a "hypocrite" because he had defended Obama's drone strikes and, now, the War Powers Resolution interpretation, among other policies. (Indeed, his critics pointed out that long before 9/11, Koh had been known for his outspoken skepticism about expansive theories of executive power.[35]) Koh said he did not think his positions were inconsistent with his previous academic writings, but if any were, it was because he had learned through experience. He also reflected on how the role of a government lawyer is different from that of a legal academic, who is freer because he speaks only for himself. As a member of the Obama legal team, Koh said, he argued "fiercely" inside the administration for his preferred legal policies. But once a decision was made, so long as he believed it was a "legally available option," he defended it "honestly."

"Sometimes people ask me, 'Isn't it hard as a government lawyer, having to say all those things you don't really believe?'" Koh said. "My answer is, I never say anything I don't believe.... If you hear me say something, you can be absolutely sure that I believe it."[36]

That Friday afternoon, I wrote an article disclosing the split in the administration's legal team.[37] The revelation that Obama had rejected what top Pentagon and Justice Department lawyers thought was the best reading of the War Powers Resolution provoked criticism. Bruce Ackerman, a Yale Law School professor, accused Obama of coming up with a new twist on gaming executive-branch lawyering: using the White House counsel — an office that does not require Senate confirmation and often goes to a president's personal friends — to transform law into "an infinitely malleable instrument of presidential power."

Ackerman wrote, "If the precedent Mr. Obama has created is allowed to stand, future presidents who do not like what the Justice Department is telling them could simply cite the example of Mr. Obama's war in Libya and instruct the White House counsel to organize a supportive 'coalition of the willing' made up of the administration's top lawyers."[38]

Koh, too, was criticized. On June 26, he testified before the Senate Foreign Relations Committee about Libya and war powers. Senator

Bob Corker, Republican from Tennessee, told Koh that the theory was "preposterous," that it "undermined the credibility of this administration," and that it set a precedent that expanded presidential power to wage war without congressional involvement.

But it turned out that despite all the rage of individual lawmakers, Congress as an institution was unable to come up with a coherent response. The House voted on three different potential reactions to Obama's move. On June 3, it voted on Kucinich's resolution to terminate the military operation. And on June 24, it voted on one resolution that would authorize the operation with continued air strikes by American aircraft, and on another resolution that would authorize an operation in which the United States would keep providing support to NATO allies but without any more direct strikes. The chamber split three ways between these options, so all three failed to pass.[39]

"We've been inept and irrelevant on the war actions," lamented Representative Jason Chaffetz, Republican from Utah. "We have not lived up to our constitutional duty."[40]

The Libya war-powers episode offered another taste of unilateralism to Obama — and a lesson in governing realpolitik in an era of congressional gridlock: if he asked for permission from Congress, its unwillingness or inability to act could limit his power. But if he claimed the authority to act on his own and Congress could not muster votes to object in any formal way, *that same paralysis enhanced his power* because it amounted to acquiescence.

The precedent Obama had carved out of the War Powers Resolution stood uncontested by Congress as an institution, and at a June 29 press conference, Obama took ownership of the theory that the sixty-day statute did not apply to what was happening in Libya, dismissing the legal controversy — and Congress too.

"A lot of this fuss is politics," Obama said, adding: "We have engaged in a limited operation to help a lot of people against one of the worst tyrants in the world...and this suddenly becomes the cause célèbre for some folks in Congress? Come on."[41]

6. Going to Congress for Syria in 2013

The NATO intervention achieved Obama's immediate goal of preventing Gadhafi from massacring civilians in Benghazi without any American loss of life. But after Gadhafi finally fell in October of 2011, Libya disintegrated into a slower-motion humanitarian disaster, spreading refugees and violence to its neighbors. Its descent into dangerous instability was underscored by an attack by Islamist militants on the American consulate in Benghazi and a nearby CIA station on September 11, 2012, in which Ambassador J. Christopher Stevens and three other Americans were killed.

The disillusioning experience led the Obama administration to greater caution as the Arab Spring protests turned into revolts and civil war elsewhere — especially in Syria. As noted, Obama spent nearly two years weighing whether sending covert arms to the rebels would make things better or just end up arming Islamist zealots, and he made it plain that he wanted to steer clear of any direct American intervention.[42] Then, however, he spoke of chemical weapons being a "red line."

Several subsequent incidents in Syria appeared to involve poisonous gas, but the circumstances were murky. It was undeniable, however, that there was a major chemical-weapons assault on August 21, 2013. Shells landed on Damascus suburbs that rebels either controlled or contested. As many as fifteen hundred people died — hundreds of them children. The report by the United States government cited "streams of human, signals and geospatial intelligence" as proving that Syrian government forces were behind the attack.[43]

Assad denied responsibility, but Obama himself said that his red line had been crossed. At a National Security Council meeting on Saturday, August 24, most of Obama's policy advisers told him the United States needed to do something about it because he had said it would be a "red line." The only note of policy disagreement came from Dennis McDonough, his chief of staff and longtime foreign-policy aide, who was not sure it was a good idea.

I don't think this is our fight, McDonough said.

As August drew to a close, the Obama administration made clear that it was about to attack Syrian forces for having used chemical weapons. As the lawyers had anticipated, there was no chance of a UN Security Council resolution — Russia and China, angry over how NATO had turned a limited mandate to protect civilians in Libya into a de facto regime-change mission, were unwilling to permit any resolution even asking Assad to step down, lest it become a pretext for a Western intervention.[44] Back in his 2009 Nobel Peace Prize acceptance speech, Obama had said that "those who claim to respect international law cannot avert their eyes when those laws are flouted" and that he believed "force can be justified on humanitarian grounds, as it was in the Balkans." In that speech, he had not made clear whether he meant the Bosnia intervention, which had some UN sanction, or the Kosovo one, which did not.[45] Now he showed that he was losing respect for a UN Security Council that was blocked by persistent Russian and Chinese obstructionism, saying that "Security Council paralysis" justified making the "hard" and "unappetizing" choice of acting unilaterally, outside of traditional institutional constraints, because inaction meant "allowing... terrible things to happen."[46]

"If we end up using the U.N. Security Council not as a means of enforcing international norms and international law, but rather as a barrier to acting on behalf of international norms and international law," Obama said, "then I think people, rightly, are going to be pretty skeptical about the system and whether it can work to protect those children that we saw in those videos" of victims of the chemical weapons.[47]

But there was widespread public resistance to getting involved in another Middle East war, even in a limited way. On August 29, the British Parliament rejected taking part in any military action, and Prime Minister David Cameron said he would respect that vote and stay out of it.[48] The already strained international-law justification the lawyers had envisioned was getting weaker. Obama was proposing something unprecedented — an attack on the sovereign soil of another country for the purpose of punishing an alleged war crime that had already taken place rather than to prevent an imminent atrocity; a strike without United Nations permission, without a self-defense claim, and without even the multilateral NATO alliance of democracies at the United States' side.

Obama deliberated in another National Security Council meeting on Wednesday, August 28, and the morning of Friday the 30th, after the surprise vote by the British Parliament to stay out of any strikes on Syria. Obama's White House counsel, Kathryn Ruemmler, speaking for the lawyers group on a Situation Room screen while attempting to vacation in Colorado for the latter two meetings, was a lone voice urging Obama to seriously consider going to Congress before launching an attack.

Soon after, she echoed her arguments in those meetings in an on-the-record interview with me. As a matter of international law, Obama's assertion that the United States would be justified in launching an attack on Assad's forces without UN Security Council permission was ambiguous. I pressed Ruemmler to explain whether the administration's position was that such an intervention would be technically illegal but *morally justified,* or whether it was saying that bombing Syria would actually be *lawful.* She said it would be "justified and legitimate under international law," given the novel factors and circumstances.

The international-law and domestic-law questions were feeding into each other, she went on to explain. Because it would be "more controversial for the president to act alone in these circumstances" as a matter of international law, it would be better to get Congress on board as a matter of domestic law "to enhance the legitimacy" of the action, she said. Legislative authorization would show "that there was a unified American response to the horrendous violation of the international norm against chemical weapons use."[49]

Most of Obama's policy aides dismissed the idea of seeking authorization from Congress, saying that the present Congress had demonstrated that it was too dysfunctional to act on even urgent matters. (The political atmosphere was particularly sour at that moment; just over a month later, in October 2013, the government would shut down for sixteen days because House Republicans refused to approve any budget that would not delay and defund the Affordable Care Act.)

But around six o'clock on Friday evening, Obama took a forty-five-minute walk around the White House grounds with McDonough. When they returned, Obama convened a two-hour meeting in the Oval Office with his top national security advisers.[50] He said he was now inclined to seek congressional authorization after all.

Many of his advisers were shocked and warned again that Congress might not vote for it, or even hold a vote *on* it. But Obama — in a reference to Libya — said he was sick of congressional Republicans attacking him for not acting, then attacking him when he did act. (Obama later explained in public that the United States needed to "get out of the habit" of having the president "stretch the boundaries of his authority as far as he can" while lawmakers "snipe" from the sidelines.[51]) He wanted to force them to go on the record about what they thought the United States should do. He was also thinking about his legacy as commander in chief. Ben Rhodes, one of Obama's national security advisers, participated in the meeting and later told me that Obama brought up his answer to my *Boston Globe* survey back in 2007. This time, unlike the Libya crisis of March 2011, there was no time crunch that made going to Congress impractical.

I believe that is true, Obama now told his aides about his *Boston Globe* answer. *I agree with the person who said that in 2007.*

Rhodes also said that it was still a choice, not a necessity, to go to Congress because "it's not like the lawyers couldn't have come up with a theory." Still, he said, "in Syria we did not have clear arguments from an international law perspective. It's easy to get lawyers to do clever wordings, and we could point to Kosovo" as a precedent, even though, he acknowledged, the Clinton legal team "had come up with a not-particularly-persuasive rationale" back then.

The Senate Foreign Relations Committee soon approved a resolution authorizing a strike. But it looked extremely doubtful that there was majority support in the House for giving Obama what he had asked for. Polls showed that most Americans opposed air strikes across ideological lines. Very few thought an attack would deter other world leaders from using chemical weapons, and a majority feared it risked leading to a long-term military commitment in Syria.[52] As the conventional wisdom shifted to consensus that Congress would vote down Obama's request for authorization, Russian president Vladimir Putin raised a potential face-saving way for Obama to climb down.[53] Putin proposed that Russia would secure and remove Assad's chemical weapons. Plans for a vote in Congress faded away as Obama accepted that alternative, dropping his threat.[54] There would be no American attack on Assad's forces to punish their alleged use of chemical weapons after all.

As the dust settled, Obama's decision to seek congressional authorization led to criticism from many, including allies like his first two defense secretaries, Gates and Leon Panetta. While Gates opposed an intervention in Syria and Panetta supported one, both said Obama had damaged the presidency as an institution by showing that an American president could warn that something was a "red line" but then defer to Congress about whether to approve consequences for crossing that line. Gates, for example, said that asking for authorization was a mistake because if Congress voted no, "it would weaken him. It would weaken our country. It would weaken us in the eyes of our allies, as well as our adversaries around the world."[55]

But David Cole, a Georgetown University law professor, said Obama had done the right thing. By seeking congressional authorization, he had bought time for a peaceful resolution to the dispute over chemical weapons, and the Founders intended the congressional authorization process to "clog" the path to war, he said.[56]

"What Obama did was adhere to the Constitution — and by doing so, he has now opened the way for a much better resolution of the issue," Cole wrote. "Avoiding immediate recourse to military action should be seen not as an embarrassment for the administration, but as a triumph for the Constitution — made possible by President Obama's brave decision to go to the people's representatives even when he could not be sure they would give him what he wanted."

Domestic Policy

7. Polarization and the Path to Unilateralism

Obama's evolving approach to his power to initiate war is inseparable from his larger relationship with Congress and his far more aggressive turn to unilateralism in domestic policy. After the Republican takeover of the House of Representatives starting with the Tea Party 2010 midterm election, Congress became far less cooperative with the White House. And Congress as an institution had difficulty passing bills of any type. Citing congressional paralysis and dysfunction as justification, Obama became increasingly willing to take assertive executive actions on his own, and Republicans accused him of becoming an imperial president.

William G. Howell, a University of Chicago political science professor, told me in 2012 that Obama's increasing use of executive powers to advance policies that he could not get through Congress fit into a well-established historical pattern seen in presidents of both parties. Still, he said, it was remarkable to see Obama take his place among his predecessors, since he had previously stressed a commitment to respect the role of Congress.

Obama "is coming around to responding to the incentives that are built into the institution of the presidency," Howell said. "Even someone who has studied the Constitution and holds it in high regard — he, too, is going to exercise these unilateral powers because his long-term legacy and his standing in the polls crucially depend upon action."[57]

During this era of stark partisan polarization, Republicans in Congress would give Obama plenty to complain about. But *he* made the first move following the Republican takeover of the House. It centered on the Defense of Marriage Act, a statute that barred the federal government from recognizing same-sex marriages that were legal under state law. During Obama's first two years in office, Justice Department lawyers had defended Congress's right to enact the statute even as Obama called on Congress to repeal it. But with Republicans in control of the House, there was no chance that Congress would repeal it. In February 2011, Obama instructed the Justice Department to abandon its defense of the marriage law and tell courts that the government agreed it was unconstitutional.[58] (House Republicans hired private-sector lawyers to defend the marriage law, but the Supreme Court in 2013 struck it down[59] and went on, in 2015, to proclaim that the Constitution gave same-sex couples the right to wed, both by five-to-four votes.[60]) Refusing to defend a congressional statute in court was an unusual move and it looked aggressive at the time. But relative to what came later, Obama acted with restraint because he had kept *enforcing* that law until the Supreme Court ruling.[61]

Obama still exhibited this modest philosophy about his duty to enforce the law a month later in the context of immigration. A journalist from the Spanish-language television network Univision asked him whether he could issue an executive order to shield from deportation hundreds of thousands of undocumented immigrants who had been brought illegally to the United States as children and grew up as Americans. In 2010, the Democratic House had passed a bill, the so-called Dream Act, to let them stay, but Senate Republicans had blocked an up-or-down vote on it.[62] Obama told the journalist that he lacked authority to help the young immigrants on his own.

"With respect to the notion that I can just suspend deportations through executive order, that's just not the case, because there are laws on the books that Congress has passed...that are very clear in terms of how we have to enforce our immigration system," Obama said. "For me to simply, through executive order, ignore those congressional mandates, would not conform with my appropriate role as president."[63]

But later, as Congress stayed gridlocked, Obama's attitude about not enforcing laws he disagreed with would change. He would end up doing what he had indicated he could not do — use an executive action to suspend deportations on a massive scale.

8. "We Can't Wait"

Obama's next step down the path to domestic unilateralism came in the summer of 2011, after the Libya intervention. Local school districts were groaning under federal testing standards established by the No Child Left Behind Act of 2002. The standards went up every year and had reached unrealistic levels; half the schools in America were deemed to be failing. Because Congress did not act to fix the law, Obama's Education Department began issuing broad waivers to states. It granted them relief from sanctions on the condition that they adopt a White House–preferred set of reforms. The statute explicitly granted the executive branch the power to issue such waivers but said nothing about conditioning it on particular policy reforms. The 2002 law essentially disappeared and a new federal education policy favored by Obama took its place — without Congress passing anything.[64]

Meanwhile that summer, Obama and John Boehner tried to negotiate a "grand bargain" to reduce the long-term deficit, but the talks failed. Then the Tea Party caucus almost refused to raise the federal borrowing limit, nearly causing the government to default on federal bonds and roiling economic markets. Obama proposed a set of measures to help the economy and went around the country delivering speeches in which he called upon Congress to pass the bill, knowing it would not. Then, one Saturday that fall, at a policy and campaign strategy meeting in the White House's Roosevelt Room, Obama declared that the administration needed to find ways to use executive power to govern despite congressional obstruction.

"We had been attempting to highlight the inability of Congress to do anything," William Daley, Obama's White House chief of staff at the time, said. "The president expressed frustration, saying we have got to scour everything and push the envelope in finding things we can do on our own."

This was the next major step in Obama's turn to unilateralism: affirmatively seeking out ways to use executive power rather than just turning to executive power to solve discrete policy problems. Obama himself, at that Saturday meeting, coined the political slogan they would use to highlight those steps: We Can't Wait. Most of the dozens of policies rolled out under that banner were clearly legal, such as raising fuel-efficiency standards for cars and encouraging drug companies to take steps to avoid shortages. But a few were edgier.

In January 2012, Obama announced that he was using his recess-appointment powers to install, without Senate confirmation, officials at two economic-related agencies that would be unable to function with their leadership posts vacant. One department resolved labor union disputes and the other was a newly created agency that protected consumers in financial matters; Republicans were filibustering Obama's nominee to the new consumer-protection agency because they opposed its powers and wanted changes to it.

"I refuse to take 'no' for an answer," Obama declared beneath a *We Can't Wait* banner. He added: "When Congress refuses to act and — as a result — hurts our economy and puts people at risk, I have an obligation as president to do what I can without them."[65]

The recess appointments were among Obama's most aggressive legal-policy moves because the Senate did not consider itself to be in recess. Although the Senate was on its lengthy annual winter break, a senator went into the empty chamber every three days to bang the gavel. Democrats had invented the pro forma session tactic to use against Bush in 2007, and now Republicans were using it against Obama.[66] This raised the prospect that Congress had found a way to permanently remove the president's power to bypass the Senate confirmation process.

Ruemmler advised Obama that if he challenged this new practice and lost, the institution of the presidency would be no worse off than if he acquiesced to it. Virginia Seitz, the Office of Legal Counsel head, concluded that there was a reasonable argument that Obama could declare the pro forma sessions a sham, proclaim that the Senate was really on a very lengthy break, and make recess appointments. Still, she warned, that there was a risk that courts would disagree.*

---

* See chapter 9, section 11.

Republicans in Congress pronounced the move an unconstitutional power grab. Some liberals, too, worried about the precedent Obama was setting; if it were up to the president and not the Senate to decide whether it was "really" in session, what was to stop some future president from systematically bypassing the confirmation process for his nominees? In June 2014, the Supreme Court voted unanimously to invalidate Obama's recess appointments.[67]

"The Senate is in session when it says it is," wrote Justice Stephen Breyer.

The nine-to-zero rebuke from a court that included two of Obama's own appointees meant it would be remembered as a clear overreach.[68]

9. Executive Actions and Self-Restraint

"We are not just going to be waiting for a legislation in order to make sure that we're providing Americans the kind of help that they need," Obama told reporters on January 14, 2014, ahead of a Cabinet meeting. "I've got a pen and I've got a phone. And I can use that pen to sign executive orders and take executive actions and administrative actions that move the ball forward."[69]

Obama's rhetoric was not the only thing becoming more aggressive. As he became increasingly frustrated by gridlock in Congress, his administration took many other executive actions to achieve his domestic-policy goals. Some were items that might have passed in a Congress that was less bogged down. For example, Holder instructed prosecutors not to list quantities of drugs in indictments of nonviolent offenders, a way to avoid triggering harsh minimum-sentencing laws that were contributing to prison overcrowding.[70] Those mandatory minimum laws — and the mass incarceration they had helped cause — had fallen out of favor with Republicans and conservatives, not just with the left.[71] But there was no sign that Congress would actually pass a bill to change the laws, so Holder's move bypassed them.

Republicans actively opposed other executive actions the

administration took. The Affordable Care Act turned out to have several glitches and problems that could easily have been fixed through technical amendments, but Republicans wanted to repeal the law, not enact legislation to make it work better. So the administration stretched its interpretation of the law, delaying enforcement of some provisions and applying others in nonobvious ways. Similarly, because Republicans opposed legislation to reduce the emission of greenhouse gases into the atmosphere, the administration used regulations by the Environmental Protection Agency under the Clean Air Act to clamp down on coal-fired power plants. Both policies led to accusations of overreach and lawsuits, although the executive branch largely prevailed in court.[72]

But Obama's most aggressive move came in immigration policy. With an estimated eleven million people living without legal status in the United States — many of them often too afraid to call the police, pay taxes, purchase insurance, or do anything else that would call attention to themselves — the system was viewed across party lines as broken. But Republicans and Democrats could not agree on how to fix it. In the summer of 2012, Obama moved on his own, announcing the Deferred Action for Childhood Arrivals program. This was a sweeping executive action to grant "temporary" relief to the hundreds of thousands of young people who would have been helped had Congress passed the Dream Act. The so-called "Dreamers" could apply to be shielded from deportation and to obtain work permits.

The administration's claimed legal basis for this act was Obama's power of prosecutorial discretion — a prosecutor can choose how to allocate resources, such as deciding what charges to bring, what plea deals to offer and accept, and when not to charge a case. The idea was that Congress had provided limited resources for deporting people, so the executive branch had to set priorities, and it was reasonable to concentrate on deporting violent criminals rather than people who had not willfully violated immigration laws. In a hardball twist, the administration set up the program so that it was self-funded through applicant fees to operate it. That meant Congress could not block it by refusing to appropriate taxpayer dollars for it.

Whether or not this was the right policy, Obama had done the very thing he had said back in March 2011 that he lacked executive authority to do: shield the "Dreamers" from deportation without a new statute from Congress. Senator Charles Grassley of Iowa, the ranking Republican on the Senate Judiciary Committee, said the move was outrageous.

"The president's action is an affront to the process of representative government by circumventing Congress and with a directive he may not have the authority to execute," Grassley said. "It seems the president has put election-year politics above responsible policies."[73]

Several conservative states filed a lawsuit to block it, but they faced steep hurdles to establishing their standing to sue — let alone showing that the action was not just a violation of norms but actually illegal.

After Obama won reelection, the Senate, in a rare bipartisan vote, passed a bill to comprehensively overhaul the immigration system. It provided a path to citizenship for the estimated eleven million unauthorized immigrants inside the United States while requiring tough new border-security enforcement.[74] With the votes of most Democrats and some Republicans, there was likely a majority in the House to pass the bill too. But Boehner — under pressure from the most conservative bloc in his caucus[75] — refused to bring it up for a vote.

By June 2014, it was clear that Congress would not enact any immigration reform legislation before Obama's presidency was over. Vowing to do as much as he could to fix the system without Congress, Obama asked for options. His policy-decision process, characteristically, was heavily legalized. In meetings with immigration advocacy groups, Obama would point to Neil Eggleston, his new White House counsel, and tell them, *I'm going to go as far as he says I can.* Eggleston, in turn, conferred with Karl Thompson, the new acting head of the Office of Legal Counsel.[76]

They also received advice from lawyers at the Department of Homeland Security, many of whom were former Democratic staffers in Congress.[77] In September, Lucas Guttentag, a professor at Stanford and Yale Law Schools and a former longtime immigrant rights advocate with the American Civil Liberties Union, joined the department too and began working with them on the actions. The Obama immigration legal-policy team came up with a plan to expand the number of young people eligible for the 2012 program while adding a second, even bigger program: Deferred Action for Parents of Americans. Some four million illegal immigrants were parents of children who had been born on domestic soil and so were citizens. Under existing immigration law, when those children turned twenty-one, they would be eligible to apply to have their close relatives stay in the country. So that group of parents would now be presumptively shielded from deportation.

The Obama team also looked at granting the same relief to several million additional parents of the noncitizen "Dreamers," the younger immigrants brought to American soil as children, and whom the executive branch had granted essentially indefinite protection from deportation under the 2012 program. But Thompson, the Office of Legal Counsel lawyer, argued that that would be a step too far. Existing immigration law did not make close relatives of noncitizens eligible to apply to stay in the United States, even if those noncitizens had been granted temporary relief from deportation. Thompson's idea was that drawing this line made Obama's plan for allocating prosecutorial resources dovetail with the structure of immigration law as Congress had enacted it. Thompson's objection to including parents of "Dreamers" raised the question of whether the Obama administration should record his legal analysis on that issue in an authoritative Office of Legal Counsel memo he was writing, or whether the memo should only address the steps the administration was going to actually take. Guttentag believed that Thompson had drawn the line too narrowly by focusing unduly on whether someone had a child who is an American citizen, to the exclusion of other grounds in the law that an immigrant could use to gain legal status. Guttentag argued against memorializing Thompson's advice in the memo, saying it would preclude the executive branch from having the option of choosing to help that group of people in the future. But Eggleston argued that showing that Thompson had said some steps they had considered would not be lawful would show that they had really thought about it and obeyed legal limits.

This is the high-water mark, Eggleston added. *There is never going to be anything more after this.*

Eggleston directed Thompson to include the negative analysis about parents of "Dreamers" in his formal written memo, which the administration made public. But Eggleston may have been wrong about the high-water mark, because executive power tends to act like a ratchet: a president does something unprecedented that seems like the new outer boundary, but then a successor treats that as a baseline and goes even further. In May 2015, Hillary Clinton, running for president, declared that she supported legislation to reform the immigration system comprehensively and would not just keep Obama's executive actions but do more.

"We can't wait any longer. We can't wait for a path to equal citizenship," she said, adding, "If Congress continues to refuse to act, as president I would do everything possible under the law to go even further. There are more people — like many parents of 'Dreamers,' and others with deep ties and contributions to our communities — who deserve a chance to stay, and I will fight for them."[78]

Critics of Obama's actions called both the 2012 and 2014 programs lawless executive amnesty and filed lawsuits against each. A federal judge in Texas threw out a challenge to the 2012 program for children,[79] but a different Texas judge issued an injunction against the bigger 2014 program for parents.[80] Both rulings cited technical grounds. The bigger program seemed destined to remain bogged down in litigation for much of the rest of Obama's term.[81]

As matters of legal substance, there were many previous examples of the executive branch using its broad discretion in how to enforce immigration law to do the same thing on a smaller scale. What really made Obama's actions new and extraordinary was the sheer *volume*. It was an erosion of constitutional norms of self-restraint to invoke prosecutorial discretion in such a sweeping way.

"Imagine a President Ted Cruz decides not to enforce environmental laws or imagine if a President Rand Paul decides not to enforce a corporate income tax," said Josh Blackman, a law professor at the South Texas

College of Law. "The president's ability to suspend the laws and not enforce them raises serious implications."[82]

Obama seemed to speak most candidly about what was going on here under the rules of humor. In December 2014, Obama went on *The Colbert Report,* the satirical news program. The host, Stephen Colbert, whose shtick was adopting the exaggerated persona of a Fox News host, asked him questions like "Why did you burn the Constitution and become an emperor?" and requested the nuclear launch codes. One question in particular prompted a revealing response:

> **Colbert:** Speaking of trusting people with extraordinary power, I want to go back for a second to 2008. Part of your campaign was believing that the president at the time had invested the executive with too much power. Then you became president and you seem to have a whole lot of power. Does that happen to every president, where you get into the office and you think, oh, you know what, I might be the only one I trust with this much power so I'll hold on to it?
>
> **Obama:** Well, for the first time you're asking a sensible question. [Laughter.] What is true — the structure of our democracy is checks and balances, and every president — even if on the outside, they were complaining — there's always the temptation to want to go ahead and get stuff done. And democracy is messy, and it's complicated. So the tendency is to say, well, let me see if I can get this done — just because things are so bottled up, especially at a moment when there's a lot of gridlock.
>
> What I've tried to do is to make sure that the Office of Legal Counsel, which weighs in on what we can and cannot do, is fiercely independent. They make decisions. We work well within the lines of that.
>
> But my preference would be to get a whole lot more done through Congress — which is why, for example, in the immigration legislation what I said to them is if you don't agree with how we're approaching this executive action, there's an easy solution:

Pass a bill. If you pass a bill, then we're going to be able to get things done. And too often what we have is a Congress that is stuck, and then the executive and/or the courts end up filling the gaps. And I think that the more we can get Congress to actually work the way it's supposed to, the less these problems come up.[83]

And in April 2015, in his humorous speech at the White House Correspondents' Dinner, Obama said:

After the midterm elections, my advisers asked me, "Mr. President, do you have a bucket list?" And I said, "Well, I have something that rhymes with bucket list." [Laughter and applause.] Take executive action on immigration? Bucket. [Laughter.] New climate regulations? Bucket. It's the right thing to do. [Laughter and applause.][84]

The liberal policy commentator Ezra Klein, citing this as well as Obama's zingers aimed at the press and his political critics ("A few weeks ago, Dick Cheney says he thinks I'm the worst president of his lifetime. Which is interesting, because I think Dick Cheney is the worst president of my lifetime. It's quite a coincidence"), argued that the joke was that Obama was saying what he really believed but was not usually allowed to say.

"The tip-off there is, 'It's the right thing to do,'" Klein wrote. "That's not a joke. That's Obama's actual justification for the aggressive executive actions of his second term —'fuck it, it's the right thing to do.' But the norms of politics are such that he typically has to frame his actions as routine, dull, even necessary. He has to search for precedent and downplay the consequences. It's only on the evening of the White House Correspondents' Dinner when he can say what everyone already knows: his actions are huge, they are controversial, they push the norms of American politics, but fuck it, at a moment when American politics seems increasingly broken, Obama has decided to just go ahead and do what he thinks is right."[85]

Surveying Obama's actions from another angle, the conservative political commentator George F. Will puzzled over what he called a "paradox" of Obama's presidency. Obama's "disdain for constitutional etiquette — his contempt for the institutional self-restraint that enables equilibrium under the separation of powers — has been primarily in domestic policy" rather than in "foreign policy, where constitutional logic and historical precedents are most supportive of presidential discretion," Will wrote.[86]

Over the course of my conversations with some of Obama's legal advisers, I became convinced that this seeming paradox made perfect sense to him. One factor, surely, was that he deeply believed in the virtues of the domestic-policy outcomes he was trying to achieve, whereas he was always conflicted about war. But Obama also felt far more comfortable about using assertive executive powers in the domestic arena precisely *because* the president's power there is far more constrained; Congress has greater powers to push back, and what the president is doing is out in the open, so critics can more easily challenge it through the political or legal process. By contrast, precisely *because* there are far fewer countervailing forces in matters of national security and foreign affairs, Obama seemed to feel that it was more important there to seek out and identify constraints to his own authority and that of future presidents. This instinct explains Obama's deep reluctance, relative to Bush, to claim that his commander-in-chief powers could override a statute, and Obama's insistence that the international law of war limited his detention powers.

Foreign Affairs

10. Signing Statements

That said, the Libya intervention was not the only time Obama took a unilateral executive power approach in the realm of foreign policy. Indeed, one of the first legal-policy controversies of his presidency —

long before Democrats lost control of Congress—came when he claimed that he could bypass a new statute that interfered with his ability to conduct foreign affairs. Obama made this claim by issuing a signing statement—an official document, filed in the *Federal Register* and used by presidents to reserve a constitutional right to override provisions in bills that they are signing into law.

The dispute began in June 2009, when Congress enacted a major spending bill. It included a provision authorizing the government to make a contribution to the International Monetary Fund for work shoring up smaller nations' economies in the global financial crisis. Lawmakers attached a condition to their approval for those funds: the executive branch must push the IMF to adopt certain policies. Obama flagged the provision in a signing statement, asserting that the Constitution did not let Congress tell him what positions to take while conducting foreign affairs. Essentially, he accepted the permission to spend the money but rejected the condition by which lawmakers had granted it.

"I will not treat these provisions as limiting my ability to engage in foreign diplomacy or negotiations," Obama said in the signing statement.[87]

Funding conditions are a routine way for Congress to try to shape all kinds of government policies, and many presidents had previously said similar things about such provisions when it came to foreign affairs. But this particular funding condition was very high profile; the condition had been politically necessary to get the new taxpayer spending on foreign aid through a reluctant Congress in the midst of a terrible recession. The House of Representatives erupted in anger, voting 429 to 2 to rebuke the administration.

The White House protested that it always intended to act consistently with the statute anyway and was just making the abstract point that Congress could not compel a president to take any particular negotiating position. But the two top Democrats, Representatives Barney Frank of Massachusetts and David Obey of Wisconsin, wrote a scathing letter to Obama accusing him of acting like Bush.

"During the previous administration, all of us were critical of the president's assertion that he could pick and choose which aspects of

Congressional statutes he was required to enforce," they wrote. "We were therefore chagrined to see you appear to express a similar attitude."[88]

The blowup revived a fracas over signing statements that had previously raged in 2006, just as Obama was starting to run for president. Signing statements used to be rare and obscure, but starting in Reagan's second term, the executive branch started to use them more frequently as a means of increasing executive power. The Bush-Cheney administration had used them with unprecedented frequency and aggression, breaking all records. Its practices brought wider attention to the device. (I wrote a series of articles about Bush's use of them in the *Boston Globe*.) Many legal critics agreed that there was a problem, but they disagreed about what the problem was.[89] The American Bar Association said *the device itself* was illegitimate because the Constitution gives the president only two options: sign a bill and obey all of it, or veto it and give Congress a chance to adjust the bill or override the veto.[90] But others — mostly veterans of the Clinton-era Office of Legal Counsel, who had prepared signing statements for Clinton — argued that it was unrealistic for a president to veto large and important bills just because a provision might be constitutionally flawed. They maintained that the problem was Bush misusing the device to advance false theories of executive power.

Senator Obama straddled these camps. In his written answers to my December 2007 *Boston Globe* survey, Obama said Bush's use of signing statements was an "abuse" because they made "implausible or dubious constitutional objections to the legislation." But he also said the device was an "appropriate way to protect a president's constitutional prerogatives" and that he would use it, too, but with greater restraint.[91] However, a few months later, when Obama was asked about signing statements at a campaign event and answered off the cuff, he said, "Congress's job is to pass legislation; the president can veto it or he can sign it," and, "We're not going to use signing statements as a way of doing an end-run around Congress."[92]

Ten months later, on March 9, 2009, President Obama issued a policy memo instructing the executive branch not to rely on any of Bush's signing statements to bypass a law, while laying out standards for how he would use them.[93] His memo made a subtle but important adjustment to what it meant to use them with restraint. In the *Boston Globe* survey, Obama had defined *restraint* as not using them "to nullify or undermine congressional instructions as enacted into law." But his March 9 memo defined *restraint* as invoking only "well-founded" legal theories, thereby opening the door to nullifying the unambiguous intent of Congress after all.

This memo was the source of early tensions inside the administration that have never been reported. It was primarily the handiwork of four elite law professors who had taken sabbaticals to serve on Obama's legal team and who saw rehabilitating signing statements as part of the effort to restore regular order in government lawyering. Daniel Meltzer, the number-two White House lawyer, and an aide, Trevor Morrison, drafted it, working closely with David Barron and Marty Lederman at the Office of Legal Counsel. All of them but Meltzer had worked in the Office of Legal Counsel in the Clinton years. Notably, the professional litigators on the legal team, like Greg Craig, Obama's first White House counsel, were not interested in such an abstract endeavor.

But the Office of Management and Budget, an arm of the White House that helps presidents manage executive agencies and prepares bill-signing packages, found out about this policy memo late in the process. Its deputy head, Rob Nabors, and chief counsel, Preeta Bansal, believed that the White House and Justice Department lawyers had gotten out of their lanes. Nabors, who had previously worked for David Obey as the staff director of the House Appropriations Committee, was also suspicious of the practice of presidential signing statements.

Nevertheless, over the course of the spring, Obama issued dozens of signing statements. None of Obama's claims were particularly controversial as a matter of legal theory, but the fact that he was using the device at all began to upset the Democratic leaders in Congress who had criticized Bush's signing statements. Then came the International Monetary Fund dispute.

At the time, White House political and legislative affairs officials were trying to shepherd major pieces of legislation, like the Affordable Care Act, through Congress. The last thing they wanted was to be poking their own congressional allies in the eye. Rahm Emanuel, the White House chief of staff (and a former congressman), blew up. Nabors and Phil Schiliro, the White House legislative affairs director — who just a few months earlier had also been a senior congressional staffer — pushed Meltzer to back off. Meltzer agreed to suspend the use of signing statements unless a very high standard could be met.

For the next fifteen months, Obama issued no signing statements challenging new laws. When I eventually noticed this and pressed the White House for an explanation, a spokesman said the administration had a new policy of not repeating challenges that it had previously expressed, although it still considered itself free to bypass new iterations of such provisions.[94] When I was reexamining the topic for this book, a former official told me that the idea that this rose to the level of a "policy" had been "face-saving bullshit," since what had really happened was the legislative affairs staff had outmuscled the legal staff. Throughout the second half of 2009 and through most of 2010, the Office of Legal Counsel had continued to send comments on bills to the White House raising constitutional concerns — the language that usually becomes signing statements — but the deal held, and Obama issued none.

Finally, in October 2010, when Congress passed a major intelligence bill, Obama issued his first new signing statement since the International Monetary Fund debacle. One of the provisions he challenged required the executive branch to tell congressional overseers "the legal basis" for covert intelligence actions; Obama said he could not be compelled to give confidential Office of Legal Counsel memos about covert actions to Congress.[95] Notably, by then, Congress had finished work on Obama's health-care law and a major Wall Street reform law. Moreover, Obama had raised no challenge of this type in his early 2009 signing statements.

Obama would slowly ratchet the practice back up as his legal team evolved — and, in particular, as Congress tied his hands over the handling of terrorism detainees.* Obama let early Guantánamo transfer restrictions pass without comment or with only political complaint. Then, in December 2011, for the first time, he suggested that they raised constitutional concerns. In May 2014, Obama acted on that threat in order to carry out the Bergdahl-Taliban prisoner exchange.† The White House pointed to his signing statement as part of its justification for bypassing a restriction requiring thirty days' notice to Congress before moving detainees, and a new cycle of controversy over the legitimacy of signing statements erupted.

"When President Bush was in the White House, he had, gosh, hundreds of signing statements, and there was, I believe, a correct amount of outrage amongst many that those signing statements were put out there as a way to simply avoid the law," said Representative Adam Smith of Washington, the top Democrat on the Armed Services Committee. "If it wasn't right for President Bush to do it, it's not right for President Obama to do it."[96]

Like the dispute among liberals about what it meant to "act like Bush" on post-9/11 issues — violate the rule of law, or infringe on civil liberties — Smith's comment raised the question about what it was that Bush had done with signing statements that "wasn't right." Was it *always* illegitimate for a president to sign a bill into law while declaring that the Constitution empowered him to bypass one or more statutes created by that bill, as the American Bar Association had argued? Or was it illegitimate for a president to do that *only when he bases his objections on extreme theories* that most legal scholars rejected, as the Clinton legal team had argued? A June 2015 Supreme Court ruling provided some ammunition to the latter camp.

The case had started with Bush. In 2002, Congress included a provision in a State Department bill requiring the government to say, in the passports of Americans who had been born in Jerusalem, that their

---

* See chapter 7, section 12, and chapter 10, section 2.
† See chapter 10, section 15.

place of birth was Israel. This contradicted executive branch diplomatic policy, dating back to the Truman administration, that the United States would not recognize any state as having sovereignty over Jerusalem because its status should be resolved through negotiations between the Israelis and the Palestinians. Bush claimed in a signing statement that his executive power to conduct the nation's foreign policy trumped Congress, and the State Department, at his instruction, disobeyed the statute when issuing passports. This set up a rare separation-of-powers case in which there was someone with legal standing to file a lawsuit: the American parents of a child born in Jerusalem shortly after Bush signed the bill, and who wanted his passport to say "Israel."

The case took a long time to reach the Supreme Court. In the meantime, Obama succeeded Bush. The executive branch's legal position remained essentially unchanged. And in June 2015, a majority of the Supreme Court sided with the executive branch, voting six to three that the Constitution had indeed empowered Bush — and Obama after him — to disregard that particular statute, even though Bush himself had signed the bill that enacted it.[97] Supporters of signing statements argued that this ruling implicitly showed that it is valid for presidents to use signing statements and bypass provisions of bills they are signing into law, so long as their legal theories are credible ones.

11. The Coup Cutoff Law

Back on June 28, 2009, six months into the Obama administration, Honduran army soldiers burst into that country's presidential palace, seized its democratically elected and pajamas-clad president, Manuel Zelaya, and flew him to abrupt exile in Costa Rica. Zelaya's ouster raised a host of diplomatic issues for the Obama administration, but underlying them was another legal question about control of American foreign policy.

For many years, under American Congresses controlled by both parties, lawmakers had included in appropriation bills a provision requiring the United States to cut off foreign aid to any country whose duly elected head of government has been "deposed by military coup or decree." The statute gave the president no power to waive this require-ment. Its absence suggested that Congress intended the cutoff to be automatic and mandatory, thereby serving as a strict warning to democracies that received American assistance. Honduras received tens of millions of dollars of American foreign aid, including anti-poverty and economic development grants through the Millennium Challenge Corporation.

Hours after the Honduran army deposited its now ex-president in Costa Rica, the Honduran Congress installed a lawmaker from a differ-ent political party as interim president to serve out the remainder of the term, which was almost over. Over the next two months, what had hap-pened gradually became clearer. Zelaya, who had shifted to the left once elected and developed close ties to Venezuela's Hugo Chavez and Cuba's Raúl Castro, had been attempting, as part of the forthcoming election in Honduras, to hold a referendum on rewriting the country's constitu-tion. His critics feared that meant he was planning to cement a perma-nent hold on power. When he ignored a court order to desist, the Honduran Supreme Court had issued a secret warrant for Zelaya's arrest, although its existence took several days to come to light. Noth-ing in the Honduran constitution permitted this forcible removal from power and exiling; indeed, its constitution lacked any impeachment mechanism.

The Obama administration denounced the events in Honduras as "illegal" and a "coup," but as summer turned to fall, some American foreign aid continued to flow to that country. This approach led to criti-cism from some on the left, who thought Obama should have immedi-ately cut off all aid, and from some on the right, who thought that Zelaya was dangerous and that the United States should celebrate what had happened as lawful rather than labeling an illegal coup of any kind. Among the latter was Senator Jim DeMint, Republican of South Caro-lina, who in October visited Honduras and then wrote a *Wall Street Journal* opinion piece about it. It said Koh had written a legal opinion that was key to how the executive branch had viewed the events.[98] DeMint called for its release, but the memo has remained secret and its contents have never been reported in detail.

This is what happened. In July and August, the State Department had sought more information about what had happened — who had been behind the coup, what it all meant — even as it worked, ultimately without success, to broker a deal in which Zelaya would be brought back to finish out his term as part of a "unity" government. Meanwhile, the Senate had confirmed Koh as the State Department's top legal adviser just days before the coup. Now a government official, Koh worked with subordinate lawyers in the department to assess what the options and requirements were regarding the foreign aid cutoff law.

Koh and his team had started by going through dozens of old State Department memos about previous ousters of elected leaders, from Africa to the Western Hemisphere, including Haiti and Ecuador. Each had its own fact pattern: from coups led by the military to coups in which the military arrested the old leader but did not install itself in power afterward. There were cases when the successor was a general, cases where it was a random civilian, and cases where a vice president had succeeded a president who was removed, in accord with the official line of succession. Often, there had been a period of flux in which it was not clear what was happening, or when the United States was trying to use the *threat* of a cutoff in aid as leverage with the people who had just taken power to try to get the old government restored. The two questions raised by each instance were how much discretion the executive had about *when* to make a determination about the cutoff law and *whether* the cutoff requirement had been triggered.

Koh and his subordinates, drawing on that body of executive-branch precedents, first concluded that it would be lawful not to make a determination about Honduras for the first few weeks or even months as the United States tried to develop a better understanding of what had happened. This was because the coup cutoff law imposed no specific deadline to decide whether it had been triggered. But that period could not last forever because a separate law, related to the Millennium Challenge program, specifically required the secretary of state to provide a list of countries that were ineligible to receive foreign aid, including because of the coup law, by September 10, 2009.[99] Since Honduras was one of the countries receiving Millennium Challenge funding, Hillary Clinton had to make a determination about the coup law by that date.

About two weeks out from the deadline, on Friday, August 28, Koh relayed some additional analysis to Cheryl Mills, Clinton's chief of staff, who in turn e-mailed Clinton at 6:20 the next morning to set up a call with Clinton to go over her options.

"Ok — i should be free after 2. email when you want to talk," Clinton wrote back at 7:28 a.m.[100]

Clinton would end up not removing Honduras from the list of countries eligible for aid. She was able to do so because Koh concluded that it was a legally available option to decide that the transition of power in Honduras did not fall into the category of a *military* coup. His rationale was that even though the military had arrested Zelaya, civilian parts of the government had directed his removal and a civilian replacement succeeded him in power; the Honduran military had neither acted on its own nor installed a general in his place. Nearly four years later, after he had left office, Koh discussed this aspect of his analysis in public at an international law conference.

"The key statutory phrase was actually 'military coup,'" Koh said. "The statutory language on its face requires that (1) a duly elected leader (2) be deposed (3) by a coup that was actually done by the military, not just an interruption of democracy where one leader came in for another without military involvement. And it turned out that when we looked back at the facts of the Honduran case, and the many executive-branch precedents interpreting the statute in analogous situations, we found that the military had not undertaken the kind of measures that appeared to be required by the statute when a true 'military coup' has occurred. When we saw that there was a long series of precedents, we asked the harder question, which is: Was there truly a 'military coup,' or was there a transition of power that was not in fact accomplished by the military?"[101]

Koh's legal analysis developed for the Honduras coup became a new executive-branch precedent about what the cutoff law did and did not require. But it would turn out that the first half of his analysis — that it was acceptable not to make a determination for some weeks or months, because the cutoff law imposed no deadline — became the more important part. In 2013, the Obama administration would ratchet that precedent out to a new extreme in response to a coup in Egypt. By then, John Kerry was secretary of state and Mary McLeod was serving as acting State Department legal adviser.

In June 2013, Egypt's military ousted its first democratically elected president, Mohamed Morsi of the Muslim Brotherhood, amid protests against his policies. The Egyptian army chief, General Abdel Fattah el-Sisi, installed a civilian head of an interim government but remained the leader of the army as well as assuming the title of first deputy prime minister. After leading a bloody crackdown on protesters supporting Morsi, Sisi ran for president himself in May 2014 and became the official ruler thereafter.

The ouster of Morsi once again raised the question of whether the coup cutoff law had been triggered. The United States had been giving about $1.5 billion a year to Egypt. Obama did not want to cut off aid to Egypt because the money preserved some American influence with a key Arab government, counterterrorism partner, and neighbor of Israel. Congressional leaders did not want to cut off all foreign aid to Egypt either, including because Morsi and the Muslim Brotherhood were Islamists. In future years, Congress would modify aspects of the cutoff rule to permit making an exception for Egypt. But no one seemed to think that Congress, in its period of sustained gridlock, could swiftly enact legislation creating an exception right away. So the Obama legal team stretched its previous executive-branch precedents to get around the cutoff law.

It was much harder to say that what had happened in Egypt was not a *military* coup. But they sidestepped that issue by instead deciding they could simply not make a formal determination if a military coup had taken place — *ever*. Unlike Honduras, Egypt was not part of the Millennium Challenge program, and its foreign aid programs did not come with any reporting requirement that would independently trigger a determination. So, they reasoned, it was legally available to the executive branch simply to postpone indefinitely asking itself the question, in any formal way, whether the cutoff statute had been triggered. It fell to Jennifer Psaki, a State Department spokeswoman, to be the public face of this theory.

"The law does not require us to make a formal determination — that is a review that we have undergone — as to whether a coup took place, and it is not in our national interest to make such a determination," Psaki said, adding that she rejected the notion that they were "flouting" the spirit of the law because "our legal team was an important part of this process."[102]

This legalistic solution solved the immediate problem in Egypt, permitting the United States to delay some military aid, like a shipment of F-16 fighter jets, but keep other forms of assistance flowing, like funding for Egyptian schools, as it tried to figure out what it wanted to do with el-Sisi. But it also established a new and sweeping executive-branch precedent, one that would make it easier for future presidents to simply look the other way in order to get around all kinds of automatic legal triggers that Congress had enacted.

But lawmakers of both parties agreed with the specific outcome in Egypt, so the maneuver never became much of a political controversy.

12. Executive-Branch Lawyering

It was one thing for an administration to *threaten* to bypass a statute in a signing statement, or to *narrowly interpret* a law while purporting to obey it. It was another thing for it to proclaim that the president had the constitutional power to override a statute and then *actually proceed to disobey it* without even offering an argument for why its conduct somehow comported with it. The Obama administration rarely claimed that the president's executive powers could override statutes and acted on such claims even less often, especially compared to the Bush-Cheney administration.

But on September 19, 2011, Virginia Seitz signed an Office of Legal Counsel memo that simply nullified a law restricting Obama's power.

The legal question was a relatively small one: whether the Constitution permits Congress to constrain the president's choice of diplomats. But the dispute — and its broader context — is worth scrutinizing in greater detail for what it shows about how executive-branch lawyers, working across administrations of both parties, can establish and expand presidential powers without a court ever weighing in.

Obama had signed the disputed statute in April 2011. It provided funds to the White House's Office of Science and Technology Policy but barred the office from conducting diplomatic relations with China. Several Republican lawmakers added that limit because they were concerned about Chinese espionage. The head of the technology office, John Holdren, asked the Justice Department for permission to ignore the statute, received that permission, and spent $3,500 to host a dinner and buy gifts for some Chinese officials who were visiting to attend a conference.[103] (Krass was running the Office of Legal Counsel when it provided oral advice to Holdren; Seitz was in charge by the time the office completed the written memo.) The executive branch could bypass the statute, Seitz wrote, because there was "ample precedent" that the Constitution gives a president "absolute discretion" to choose "whomever he considers most suitable" to be his diplomatic agent.[104]

I decided to do a little legal archaeology, digging backward in time to unearth what lay beneath this sweeping claim. The results surprised me.

The most recent precedent Seitz's memo cited was a June 2009 Office of Legal Counsel memo signed by David Barron when he was running the office.[105] It challenged a law barring State Department employees from attending United Nations meetings chaired by nations deemed to be sponsors of terrorism, like Iran.[106] Congress had enacted versions dating back to at least 2004; the Bush-Cheney White House had issued several signing statements declaring these previous iterations unconstitutional, and it had permitted the State Department to send a delegation to at least one such meeting on that basis. The Obama White House had flagged the latest version of that provision in a signing statement, too. Noting that the State Department existed to practice diplomacy, Barron said the department could again attend an Iran-chaired meeting, and it did so. (Notably, the White House science office does *not* exist to practice diplomacy. When Seitz's 2011 memo drew on the Barron precedent, this factor in his analysis disappeared.)

Barron's memo in turn looked back to older executive-branch precedents. In 1991, Congress had enacted a passport law effectively preventing the State Department from sending the same diplomat to both Israel and Arab countries. George H. W. Bush issued a signing statement declaring the law unconstitutional because the president has "exclusive authority...to choose the officials who will negotiate on behalf of the United States," and the Office of Legal Counsel, then led then by Timothy Flanigan, wrote a memo fleshing out that conclusion.

Finally, I came to the original precedent. In 1990, Congress had passed a budget law funding a certain diplomatic delegation on the condition that it included a representative from a congressional panel. The Bush-Quayle administration issued a signing statement challenging it, and the Office of Legal Counsel, then led by William Barr, wrote a memo saying that the Constitution gave the president the exclusive power "to choose the individuals through whom the Nation's foreign affairs are conducted. That responsibility cannot be circumscribed by statute."[107]

Before those precedents, there was nothing. Barr padded out his memo with discussion of precedents relevant to other types of disputes regarding a president's foreign-affairs powers, like whether Congress could regulate *what he says* when he is conducting diplomacy — the same issue behind Obama's 2009 International Monetary Fund signing statement. But there was no precedent on point for the proposition that Congress could not influence *which government officials* the president selected to use as diplomats. In that vacuum, Barr, who expressed extremely sweeping views of executive power throughout Office of Legal Counsel writings,[108] explained that it was "self-evidently true" that Congress was powerless in this area.[109]

In short, the twenty-one-year chain of executive-branch claims, culminating in a declaration that "ample precedent" existed showing that presidents enjoy an "absolute" power that Congress may not encroach upon, was missing any anchor.[110] And there was something more. The four memos and their associated signing statements proposed a world in which the constitutional system could not tolerate any congressional constraint on the president's choice of the officials through whom the nation's foreign affairs were conducted. But none grappled with a bad fact for this analysis: the Constitution explicitly envisions situations in which the Senate will refuse to consent to presidents' nominees to be ambassadors to other countries.

To be clear, the Bush-Quayle, Bush-Cheney, and Obama lawyers were not necessarily *wrong* about this selection-of-diplomats power. The Constitution doesn't say anything explicit about the issue beyond its requirement for Senate confirmation of ambassadors. The Supreme Court has never analyzed the question and probably never will, since it is unlikely that anyone will ever have legal standing to file a lawsuit about it. Much of the law dividing the power of the president from the power of Congress is like that.

"This is a realm of many questions and few answers," said Harold Bruff, a University of Colorado law professor who worked at the Office of Legal Counsel in the Carter administration and is coauthor of a casebook on separation-of-powers law.

The current system of executive-branch lawyering, a pressure point in the American system of government and the rule of law, is a relatively new phenomenon. The White House Counsel's office and Justice Department's Office of Legal Counsel evolved into their modern form as sizable and influential players run by presidential appointees only in the 1970s.[111] As post-9/11 issues have placed greater attention on the system, it has attracted criticism.

For example, in his 2010 book *The Decline and Fall of the American Republic*, Yale Law School's Bruce Ackerman, who has never worked in the executive branch, argued that the modern system of executive-branch lawyering incentivizes lawlessness. He called for creating an independent tribunal within the executive branch to replace them.[112] When I contacted him and explained my archaeological dig into the source of the president's selection-of-diplomats power, he said it showed why he finds the whole enterprise dubious.

"This is a bipartisan project of executive aggrandizement," Ackerman said. "Law is a disciplined conversation between lawyers and judges. But without any judges, law is a conversation between lawyers and other lawyers — and they're all on the same side, building upon one another."

But Trevor Morrison, the former Obama White House lawyer who later became dean of New York University Law School, wrote an essay rejecting Ackerman's critique as overwrought and Ackerman's proposed solution — the executive-branch tribunal — as unworkable and overly simplistic. Morrison maintained that having swaths of the law that are not decided by courts is a normal part of the American system and that it is legitimate for a president "to pursue policies he thinks are constitutionally defensible, even if he has not determined they are consistent with his best view of the law." This is especially so "where conventional sources of legal meaning suggest a number of plausible answers to a particular question but do not readily identify any one answer as clearly best, and where the area is one in which the practice of the executive branch may give some content to the law over time."[113]

I have not found anyone who has worked in government who thinks that it is realistic to force the president to go to an independent tribunal for legal advice; in practice, things just move too quickly for that, they say. The only answer I can think of is transparency: subjecting the legal analysis of executive-branch lawyers, many of whom come from and will return to private sector and academic communities, to the check of public scrutiny.

13. Treaties and the Iran "Agreement"

In 2015, as Republicans took majority control of the Senate, Obama's conflicts with Congress over control of foreign policy sharpened. One of the most important disputes concerned his effort to negotiate an agreement with Iran intended to prevent it from obtaining a nuclear weapon. The deal involved the United States — along with Britain, France, Germany, Russia,

China, and the European Union—lifting economic sanctions against Iran in exchange for several steps that country would take to curb its nuclear program. Supporters saw it as a way to avoid war; opponents saw it as dangerous and flawed. Whatever the merits of the deal, it also raised a separate legal question: Was it necessary for Congress to approve it?

The Founders, in writing the Constitution, said that contracts negotiated by the president between the United States and other countries—treaties—required the consent of two-thirds of the Senate to be ratified. Over time, however, presidents began calling international deals "agreements" instead and sidestepping that procedure. Sometimes they submitted these agreements to Congress for approval by simple majorities in both chambers, like an ordinary federal statute. Sometimes they did not submit the deal to Congress in any form.[114] Like so much else in the world of separation-of-powers law, the rules were ill-defined. As recently as 2008, some Democrats complained when Bush unilaterally signed a status-of-forces agreement with Iraq that suggested, in a nonbinding way, that the United States would come to Iraq's military defense if it was attacked—as in fact the United States did when the Islamic State attacked it in 2014.[115]

Now, Obama asserted that he could commit the United States to a major arms-control agreement with Iran without Congress. Obama's reasoning was that a statute previously enacted by Congress explicitly gave him the power to suspend sanctions against Iran. His critics noted that he was leaving in 2017. Only Congress could lift sanctions permanently, yet Obama was offering to a longtime adversary the repeal of sanctions beyond his time in office in exchange for its pulling back from developing a nuclear arsenal. Technically, the agreement was not legally binding on the United States, but in practice it would be very hard for a future present to renege.

In early 2015, Boehner invited the Israeli prime minister, Benjamin Netanyahu, to denounce Obama's still-incomplete deal with Iran in a speech before Congress. And forty-seven Republican senators—all but seven of them—signed an unusual letter, organized by Senator Tom Cotton, to the government of Iran; it warned that the United States might not live up to any deal Iran struck with Obama alone.[116] These efforts alienated Democrats. But after emotions cooled, Corker, now the Republican chairman of the Senate Foreign Relations Committee, forged a compromise with Democrats on the committee, led by Senator Benjamin Cardin of Maryland, for a bill requiring Obama to submit the final deal to Congress. Lawmakers would have sixty days to debate the deal and then could pass a resolution approving it, do nothing (in which case it would still happen), or pass a resolution disapproving it (which Obama could veto, meaning it would still happen if he held on to enough votes to prevent Congress from overriding his veto).

"We have to be involved here," Cardin said. "Only Congress can change or permanently modify the sanctions regime."[117]

Under pressure from Democrats, Obama eventually agreed to sign the bill, accepting a role for Congress where he had previously said there should be none. Stripped of hype, this arrangement did not change much. It was essentially the same thing as Congress trying to enact a bill removing the presidential waiver provision from the sanctions statute, which would also mean overriding Obama's certain veto. Still, by setting up a way to vote on the agreement itself, Congress gave itself, atmospherically, a more direct role in foreign policy. The episode suggested that when even Democrats thought Obama was overreaching, creating a rare bipartisan consensus, Congress could still uphold its institutional dignity. My colleague Peter Baker wrote that the concession by Obama suggested that after years of asserting executive power "to advance his agenda in an era of gridlock," Obama was "approaching the outer boundaries of his authority with 21 months left in office."[118]

Forever War

14. Ending the 9/11 War

Back in late 2012, at the end of his tenure as Pentagon general counsel, Jeh Johnson flew to Britain to deliver a speech before the Oxford Union Society. His topic was how the 9/11 war—the longest war in American history, and one in which no formal armistice seemed possible—might end.

"On the present course, there will come a tipping point at which so many of the leaders and operatives of al Qaeda and its affiliates have been killed or captured, and the group is no longer able to attempt or launch a strategic attack against the United States, such that al Qaeda as we know it, the organization that our Congress authorized the military to pursue in 2001, has been effectively destroyed," Johnson said.[119]

At that point, he said, law enforcement and intelligence agencies would continue to take action against individual threats, but "we must be able to say to ourselves that our efforts should no longer be considered an 'armed conflict.'" Johnson did not say that day was near. But after more than a decade of grinding ground wars in Afghanistan and Iraq, Guantánamo, surveillance, torture, drone strikes, military commissions, and all the rest, this was a remarkable thought.

Five months later, shortly after Koh stepped down from the State Department, he picked up on that theme in his own Oxford Union Society speech. Quoting Johnson approvingly, Koh maintained that ending the "Forever War" could be done. But the hard part, he said, would be drawing a line between al-Qaeda and new Islamist groups that spring up.

"Make no mistake: if we are too loose in who we consider to be 'part of' or 'associated with' al-Qaeda going forward, then we will always have new enemies, and the Forever War will continue forever," Koh said.[120]

That was the opposite of the thinking of some in Congress, like Lindsey Graham, who sincerely believed that Western civilization — like it or not — was engaged in a multigenerational, existential war with radical Islam. They believed that it was time to replace the creaky legal basis for the war — the 2001 Authorization for Use of Military Force against the perpetrators of 9/11 — with a new, more open-ended authorization calibrated to how the war had evolved.[121]

But Obama was clearly hoping that he could wind down the atmosphere of war before he left office. In his May 2013 National Defense University speech, he talked about getting the United States off the "perpetual wartime footing" it had been on since 9/11. He observed that "core al-Qaeda is a shell of its former self," that the war in Iraq had ended, and that the war in Afghanistan was scheduled to end soon.

Groups like Yemen's al-Qaeda in the Arabian Peninsula "must be dealt with, but in the years to come, not every collection of thugs that labels themselves al Qaeda will pose a credible threat to the United States," Obama said. "Unless we discipline our thinking, our definitions, our actions, we may be drawn into more wars we don't need to fight, or continue to grant presidents unbound powers more suited for traditional armed conflicts between nation states....Our systematic effort to dismantle terrorist organizations must continue. But this war, like all wars, must end. That's what history advises. That's what our democracy demands."[122]

In light of this need to glide back to normalcy, Obama said, he would engage with Congress "in efforts to refine, and ultimately repeal," the mandate of the 2001 Authorization for Use of Military Force, but "I will not sign laws designed to expand this mandate further."

But new troubles were developing in Syria.

15. Extending the 9/11 War

In the summer of 2014, one of the jihadist groups battling Assad's government in Syria abruptly swept into Iraq, conquering large swaths of Sunni territory and declaring itself the caliphate, meaning the start of a global theocratic government. Calling itself the Islamic State, its members committed atrocities, including large-scale massacres of people with the wrong religions and beheadings of Western hostages, whom they dressed in orange Guantánamo-style garb for the occasion. Thousands of radicalized Muslims from Europe, and at least dozens from the United States, traveled to the war zone to join up, and the American-trained Iraqi army fled before its advance.

The Islamic State was a rebranded descendant of al-Qaeda in Iraq, the franchise that had led a bloody insurgency during the American occupation there. Its current leader, Abu Bakr al-Baghdadi, and the new leader of core al-Qaeda, Ayman al-Zawahiri, had feuded. In February 2014, al-Zawahiri had excommunicated al-Baghdadi's group from al-Qaeda.[123] Al-Zawahiri kept the brand name, but al-Baghdadi saw himself as Osama bin Laden's true heir. In August 2014, as the Islamic State wreaked havoc in Iraq, Obama launched air strikes to help Kurdish and Iraqi forces push it back.

The Obama national security team also discussed sending American ground troops — beyond Special Forces "spotters" who helped coordinate air strikes from the ground — to dislodge the Islamic State. But there was deep caution about getting more involved. In internal deliberations, one official told me, General Martin Dempsey, the chairman of the Joint Chiefs, repeatedly argued that ground occupations did not work because sooner or later, American forces always had to leave, and if the locals had relied upon the Americans to put down insurgents, everything would fall apart at that moment.

We can help them, but we can't do it for them, he said.

By the end of September, the United States had begun bombing the Islamic State — as well as yet another branch of al-Qaeda, which the American government dubbed the Khorasan Group, inside Syria, too. While Obama vowed not to "get dragged into another ground war," he announced that the United States would use air power and its partners on the ground "to degrade, and ultimately destroy," the Islamic State, a campaign that would clearly outlast his presidency. His hope of getting the United States off its "war footing" was gone.

The bombing raised a pressing legal question: What was Obama's authority to carry it out? As a matter of international law, the administration maintained that the bombing was lawful as part of the collective self-defense of Iraq. Baghdad had asked for American help, consenting to strikes on its own territory, and the strikes on Syrian territory were lawful, it said, because Assad was "unable or unwilling" to suppress the Islamic State's threat to Iraq himself. As a result, no Security Council resolution was necessary, they argued.[124]

The domestic law question, though, was tougher to answer. Several senior administration officials — only one of whom, Ben Rhodes, was on the record — told me how the deliberations had played out, a sequence that has not previously been reported.

Before the first bombs fell in early August 2014, Eggleston and the top lawyer on his National Security Council, Brian Egan, along with the other members of the interagency group, developed two theories. Each one, they said, was viable but had its own downside. One was to treat this intervention as a new phase in existing wars Congress had already authorized. That would solve the domestic legal problem, but critics would doubtless criticize it as a stretch. After all, while the Islamic State used to be al-Qaeda's Iraq affiliate, the organization was at odds with the current version of core al-Qaeda. This complicated their ability to call the Islamic State part of or an associated force of the enemy against whom Congress had authorized force after 9/11. The government could argue that the Islamic State problem was part of the continuing security fallout from the original 2003 invasion of Iraq, another armed conflict that Congress had authorized. But that was also awkward in its own way, since the United States military had pulled out of Iraq at the end of 2011, and Obama had taken credit for ending the Iraq war.

The other theory was to treat this as a brand-new conflict. But then Obama arguably would need to seek congressional authorization to keep it going beyond sixty days because of the War Powers Resolution, or face another Libya-style dispute.

In a Situation Room meeting, Eggleston and Egan put those choices before Obama, saying each was a legally available option. The pivotal issue came down, as it so often did in the Obama era, to the administration's perception that Congress was unable to function as a competent governing partner. A conflict against the Islamic State was very likely to last longer than two months, and Congress was already wrapping up its work to head home and campaign for the midterm election. Nobody thought it was realistic to expect Congress to vote on anything before the War Powers Resolution's sixty-day clock ran out in October, and Obama did not want to repeat the experience with Libya. So Obama went with the "Islamic State war equals al-Qaeda war" theory. (The administration kept the "Islamic State war equals Iraq war" theory in its back pocket, saying when asked that the Iraq war authorization supplied redundant legal permission but that it was not relying on this authority and still thought the 2002 war authorization should be repealed.[125])

Obama announced this theory in September.[126] It came as a surprise — many had been expecting him to ask Congress to authorize the new conflict — and provoked an angry response. Several prominent critics maintained that Obama was stretching his existing war authorization too far. Jack Goldsmith argued that "the President's gambit is, at bottom, presidential unilateralism masquerading as implausible statutory interpretation."[127]

Evaluating the administration's claim turned on the baseline. If the comparison point was what Congress had thought it was authorizing back in September 2001, the critics were on solid ground. No one could say with a straight face that lawmakers back then could have envisioned that they were voting for a war against the Islamic State in Iraq and Syria in 2014.

But if the baseline was instead what the 9/11 authorization had come to mean by 2014, the claim was not absurd. With acquiescence and ratification from Congress and the courts, the executive branch had interpreted the act to encompass detaining people without trial, drone strikes and commando raids in a proliferating array of countries far from the hot battlefield, and war against mere supporters and associated forces of al-Qaeda — even organizations that had not yet existed on 9/11. It took only a small additional tug to stretch the interpretation to encompass a war against a group that *formerly* was aligned with al-Qaeda — or, put another way, to say that the splintering of the bin Laden–era al-Qaeda did not terminate the war against any of its successor factions.

"The name may have changed, but the group we call [the Islamic State] today has been an enemy of the United States within the scope of the 2001 AUMF continuously since at least 2004," said Stephen Preston, Johnson's successor as Pentagon general counsel, in an April 2015 speech. "A power struggle may have broken out within Bin Laden's jihadist movement, but this same enemy of the United States continues to plot and carry out violent attacks against us to this day. Viewed in this light, reliance on the AUMF for counter-[Islamic State] operations is hardly an expansion of authority."[128]

In late September 2014, Boehner declared that House Republicans would not vote on *any* Islamic State war authorization until the next Congress was seated, thereby ensuring that the bombing campaign would continue for many months on Obama's premise.[129] In February 2015, Obama proposed a limited Authorization for Use of Military Force tailored to the Islamic State conflict. It would authorize an air war, would expire after three years if Congress did not vote to renew it, and would cover not just the Islamic State but also any unidentified associated forces or "closely related successor." In unveiling this plan for a war authorization that would outlast his presidency, Obama managed to insist again, "I do not believe America's interests are served by endless war, or by remaining on a perpetual war footing."[130]

Democrats worried the new Islamic State proposal gave the executive branch too much power, Republicans thought it would tie the military's hands, and Congress once again did nothing. By March 2015 — eight months after the Islamic State military campaign had begun, or resumed, Goldsmith pronounced the fight over. Congress, he wrote, had acquiesced to Obama's stretched interpretation of his existing powers.[131]

Even as the idea of a separate authorization to fight the Islamic State faded away, it was notable that Obama had not called for repealing and replacing the 2001 authorization as part of this proposal. An official told me that the government still needed it to keep fighting the original al-Qaeda, and the administration had not trusted Congress to take on both the Islamic State and al-Qaeda war questions at the same time.

Indeed, even though Obama repeatedly said America's war in Afghanistan had "ended" after 2014,[132] because the "combat mission" there had officially shifted to training Afghan forces and conducting counterterrorism raids aimed at al-Qaeda, the reality was that the United States was still fighting the Taliban, too. In 2015, the American military continued to attack Taliban units deemed to directly threaten American forces or to support al-Qaeda, and, increasingly, militias in Afghanistan who now swore allegiance to the Islamic State. [133]

By his April 2015 speech, Preston acknowledged that "the fact is that active hostilities continue. As a matter of international law, the United States remains in a state of armed conflict against the Taliban, al-Qaeda, and associated forces, and the 2001 AUMF continues to stand as statutory authority to use military force."[134] Underscoring the point, a Yemeni detainee at Guantánamo, accused of being a Taliban militia member, asked a judge to release him, citing Obama's words and the doctrine that when wars end, wartime prisoners are supposed to be released. But in July 2015, Judge Royce Lamberth ruled that the government still had authority to detain the man as long as there was fighting in Afghanistan, in order to prevent him from returning to that fight — even if Obama's rhetoric suggested that the war was already over.

"A court cannot look to political speeches alone to determine factual and legal realities merely because doing so would be easier than looking at all of the relevant evidence," he wrote. "The government may not always say what it means or mean what it says."[135]

Looking back from this point, the Islamic State's sudden eruption in the summer of 2014 echoed the dynamic of the failed underwear-bomb attack on Christmas 2009. Obama had been moving in a direction of wind-down and scale-back, but the world as it was did not cooperate. One way of looking at this is that Obama entrenched the Forever War. Another is that the Forever War ensnared him.

16. The Lawyerly Administration

"The stunning rise of the Islamic State is yet another reminder that turning the page on war is easier said than done," wrote Rosa Brooks, a Georgetown University law professor who had worked from 2009 to 2011 as a top counselor to Obama's undersecretary of defense for policy, which made her yet another lawyer in an Obama policymaking role. "Today it has become virtually impossible to draw a clear distinction between war and not-war — not just because of bad-faith legal and political arguments made by U.S. officials (though we've seen plenty of those), but because of genuine and significant changes to the global geopolitical landscape." Brooks called for those who worried about the expansion of state power and the erosion of rights that occurs in wartime to "abandon the Sisyphean effort to 'end' war and instead focus on developing norms and institutions that support rights and the rule of law, but are not premised on sharp lines between war and peace."[136]

That, in fact, was a pretty good description of what the Obama administration had tried to do. It kept a surveillance state designed for the post-9/11 war but added dozens of NSA officials to police its adherence to court-imposed rules. It kept the institution of indefinite law-of-war detention for untriable but unreleasable Guantánamo detainees but created parole-like periodic-review-board procedures that went beyond what was required by the laws of war.[137] It relied heavily on targeted killings of terrorism suspects in lawless badlands whose capture was infeasible but added the more stringent targeting rules Obama put forth in 2013, with their stated ideal of near certainty of no civilian casualties. All of these reforms were imperfectly applied in practice and slow to take root, but they represented a lawyerly response — adding an additional layer of rules, standards, and procedures — to the unsettling premise that the United States was still at war and would, of necessity, remain so with no end in sight.

That was a premise that human rights advocates yearned for Obama to abandon. Daphne Eviatar argued that the continued chaos in Afghanistan and Yemen "doesn't support the assumption the American public and U.S. lawmakers seem to make that picking off suspected terrorists with targeted attacks — which, as we've long known, kill hundreds if not thousands of innocent civilians — is doing anything to restore order or reduce the terrorist threat to the United States. On the contrary, we know that U.S. drone strikes and their constant threat have sparked strong anti-American sentiment in Pakistan and Yemen, and terrorists have repeatedly claimed they're targeting Americans because of them."[138]

To the Obama national security team, however, this sort of critique offered no real answer for what to do when a twenty-three-year-old zealot, sent by terrorists hiding in the badlands of Yemen who are likely already plotting their next attack, tries to blow up a plane full of Americans over Detroit. As Obama said in his Nobel Peace Prize acceptance speech, the creed of nonviolence preached by leaders like Mahatma Gandhi and Martin Luther King Jr. (the latter of whom observed in his own Nobel speech that "violence never brings permanent peace") was powerful. But, Obama said, "As a head of state sworn to protect and defend my nation, I cannot be guided by their examples alone. I face the world as it is, and cannot stand idle in the face of threats to the American people....Negotiations cannot convince al Qaeda's leaders to lay down their arms....And yet this truth must coexist with another — that no matter how justified, war promises human tragedy." To reconcile those clashing truths, Obama looked to law: "Where force is necessary, we have a moral and strategic interest in binding ourselves to certain rules of conduct."

These remarks by Obama — bringing up the best arguments against his own position and not rebutting them so much as acknowledging their strengths and looking for procedural rules to resolve the tensions — exemplified his lawyerly approach and the mind-set of his team. Earlier, I talked about some of the ways that lawyers are trained to think and how that mapped onto the strengths and weaknesses of the Obama team's decision-making process.* This theme resonated in another way, reflected in many of the episodes recounted through this book: lawyers prize rigorous adherence to process. Confronted with ambiguous situations where the right *outcome* may not be clear, lawyers tend to look at whether the right *procedures* were followed and take satisfaction if they were. To illustrate in a slightly simplistic way, consider what an activist, a journalist, and a lawyer each might ask about a convict sitting on death row. The activist, depending on his or her stripe, asks, *Is the death penalty immoral?* or *What is the holdup when the victim's family needs closure?* The journalist asks, *Is it true that he committed the crime for which he was convicted?* The lawyer asks, *Did he receive due process at trial?*

---

* See chapter 2, section 9.

A respect for process and deliberation would have been an Obama administration governing tendency under any circumstances. But coming after the Bush-Cheney years, it was almost dogma. A core lesson the Obama administration took from the Bush years, multiple officials told me, was that fully airing interagency deliberations was crucial, reducing the potential for reckless or otherwise ill-considered policy mistakes. As noted, the Bush-Cheney administration had been notorious for violating norms of the decision-making process. It was against the backdrop of such tales that Donilon, helping to design the National Security Council decision-making process, revived a central role for the interagency lawyers group, which he portrayed as an antidote to what had gone wrong with their predecessors. More broadly, although it fell short on occasion, the administration pursued the ideal of making sure that every agency with "equity" in a decision had a chance to weigh in on substantive policy grounds. The same lawyerly commitment to process, as I have argued, explains why many of his key advisers found fault with Bush's post-9/11 record on rule-of-law grounds rather than on civil liberties grounds; the problem was not warrantless wiretapping, per se, it was the president's violating FISA instead of getting Congress to modify the statute to permit warrantless wiretapping. And it illuminates why the Obama administration was comfortable bringing the tools of war to bear on the problem of al-Qaeda, despite all the ambiguities and contradictions raised by applying rules created for traditional armed conflicts to a fight against a transnational, nonstate network of terrorists. In the end, Congress had said it was a war, and the Supreme Court had agreed it was a war, so it was a war.

An irony of the Obama commitment to process was that in some ways it contributed to the ratcheting effect, or continuity, across the two administrations. The Bush-Cheney administration's approach of plowing over or circumventing internal objections and potential voices of caution had succeeded in bringing about dramatic changes to government policy. The Obama administration's restoration of a slow and careful decision-making process made it harder to dislodge the new status quo Bush had created — from big-picture items, like whether to scrap military commissions, to small decisions, like whether to approve the transfer of any particular Guantánamo detainee. The bureaucratic system for deliberations was set up to require consensus in most cases, giving any agency the power to slow or even veto a proposed change. This served to heighten the already considerable influence of the national security establishment, which prized counterterrorism powers, stability, and secrecy over openness with the public and protections for individual rights.[139] Moreover, because of the post-9/11 reforms to the structure of the executive branch, such as the creation of the Office of the Director of National Intelligence, the Department of Homeland Security, and the Justice Department's National Security Division, the security bureaucracy literally had extra seats at the table and extra votes or vetoes in those internal deliberations.

Obama began his presidency by issuing his sweeping executive orders, written during the transition, to ban torture, shutter CIA prisons, and order Guantánamo closed. But it was no accident that after his administration settled in and its internal deliberative processes were fully in place, there were no comparable episodes of such dramatic, top-down policy change. Arguably, the closest thing to that kind of change was Obama's decision in January 2014 to require the NSA to get the FISA Court's permission each time it wanted to query its bulk phone records database.* Not coincidentally, this was a rare decision in which the White House short-circuited the formal deliberative process. The national security agencies thought they had beaten that proposal back. Then, on the eve of Obama's surveillance-reform speech, Obama's key policy advisers on that issue, Kathy Ruemmler and Lisa Monaco, decided that his reforms needed beefing up and added that one to the list anyway.

Instead of rethinking basic premises of the national security state, then, Obama accepted them but sought to find a stronger legal framework for carrying out its policy prescriptions. His team waded into murky, ambiguous situations where the rules were written for twentieth-

---

* See chapter 11, section 12.

century premises that did not perfectly fit twenty-first-century problems, and they tried to update a Cartesian framework of authorities and
constraints. Yet at the same time Obama had to protect the country in
an era of blurry lines, from cross-border attacks by nonstate actors plotting from lawless badlands to a polarized Congress that increasingly
struggled to act. Obama's impulses and responsibilities created irrecon-
cilable tensions that could be managed, but not resolved.[140]

17. A New Normal?

Back in September 2008, as George W. Bush's presidency was drawing
to a close, Koh had testified before a Senate Judiciary Subcommittee
hearing entitled "Restoring the Rule of Law." In his remarks, Koh
warned that the coming years could be crucial in determining whether
the post-9/11 security state the Bush-Cheney administration had
erected stayed in place or faded away.

"As difficult as the last seven years have been, they loom far less
important in the grand scheme of things than the next eight, which will
determine whether the pendulum of U.S. policy swings back from the
extreme place to which it has been pushed, or stays stuck in a 'new normal' position under which our policies toward national security, law
and human rights remain wholly subsumed by the 'War on Terror,'"
Koh said. "To regain our global standing, the next president and Congress must unambiguously reassert our historic commitments to human
rights and the rule of law as a major source of our moral authority."[141]

By Obama's seventh year in power, he had assembled a record against
which Koh's question could be evaluated. Yet the marks were ambiguous and inextricably entangled in whether the observer thought particular counterterrorism policies were necessary or bad ideas.

Civil libertarians and rights advocates, who had voted for Obama in
hope of dramatic changes to the post-9/11 security state, were deeply
disappointed in him. He had closed the door on torture, but compromises complicated many other parts of his policy record. Obama had

willingly done some of the things they disliked, such as keeping broad surveillance activities and expanding drone strikes. He had presided over other things they opposed despite his setting out to do the opposite, as when he announced the closure of Guantánamo but failed to drive the executive branch to overcome bureaucratic and political resistance. Liberals like Yale's Ackerman spoke of the "tragedy of the Obama Presidency—how a candidate pledged to repudiate Bush-era abuses will leave office confirming and extending many of the worst Bush precedents in the conduct of foreign and military affairs."[142]

National security hawks on the right were furious at some things Obama had done, like pulling ground forces out of Iraq and refusing to use Guantánamo for new prisoners. But they also celebrated him, in a backhanded-compliment way, for keeping many other major features of what Bush and Cheney had created. "President Obama has done nothing to change the policies of the Bush administration in the war on terrorism. And I mean practically nothing," said New Jersey governor Chris Christie, with some overstatement. "And you know why? 'Cause they work."[143] Bush's brother, former Florida governor Jeb Bush, seeking the 2016 GOP presidential nomination, praised Obama's stance on surveillance. "I would say the best part of the Obama administration would be his continuance of the protections of the homeland using the big metadata programs, the NSA being enhanced....He's not abandoned them, even though there was some indication that he might."[144]

As they had from the beginning, the Obama team and their defenders rebutted both the left-wing and right-wing critiques as caricatures. They portrayed themselves as belonging to a rule-of-law administration that acted pursuant to congressional authorization rather than in defiance of statutes like Bush had done, which made all the difference, in their view, on those policies they kept. They also portrayed themselves as open-minded pragmatists on substantive outcomes. They banned torture because they saw it as illegal and counterproductive but kept expansive surveillance programs because they saw them as legalized and helpful in protecting the country from genuine threats. They had wound down messy wars of ground occupation, but they still used drone strikes because that was sometimes the only available tool for stopping terrorists who were plotting attacks from lawless regions where they could not be arrested. Congress had impeded their effort to close Guantánamo and pull the 9/11 case out of a military commission, but the administration had developed the Warsame model of interrogating newly captured prisoners aboard ships for intelligence before sending them to trial before civilian courts, because that system works. They had imposed new rules on drone strikes and leak investigations, showing that they were willing to recognize when things were getting off-kilter and adjust their approach rather than dogmatically refusing to change course.

Giving voice to this pragmatist self-evaluation were officials like Rhodes, Obama's longtime national security policy aide. I twice came to the White House to speak to Rhodes while writing this book. In February 2014, we sat with Monaco in her cramped, low-ceiling basement office beneath the West Wing; I remembered being in it once before, when it was still John Brennan's office. Rhodes told me that five years earlier, when Obama was newly inaugurated, "the president believed it wasn't clear what the governing legal philosophy was for a lot of things — detention, drones, the role of Congress in authorizing military deployments, surveillance. I think he would like to leave his successor a sustainable approach, not open questions. Regular order, with appropriate levels of executive branch, judicial, and congressional oversight, so that in 2017 there will be a counterterrorism approach without necessarily being at war, unless we have to."

Almost exactly a year later, I went back to meet with Rhodes again, this time alone in his own, smaller windowless basement office. By then the Islamic State war had begun (or resumed), and Rhodes acknowledged that the United States would still be on a war footing in 2017 after all. Still, he touted Obama's proposed three-year Authorization for Use of Military Force against the Islamic State, which he said could be a model for future time-delineated, organization-specific authorizations as new terrorist groups arose. He said it showed that Obama was trying to do what was necessary to protect national security but in a narrow and legally constrained fashion, repeating his earlier theme but with a tone of lowered expectations. "We are trying to build a legacy," Rhodes said. "We may not be able to solve every legacy issue we inherited, but we are trying to establish frameworks that may be very useful prospectively, while seeing what we can do through force of will and executive actions on legacy issues like Gitmo, though our preference is to resolve this with Congress."

These various critiques and defenses of Obama's legacy seem mutually incompatible, and yet each was true, and each was false, for different policies and at different times. Obama's record was irreducibly messy and complex, not unlike the world in which he tried to govern. The question lurking behind Koh's testimony back in September 2008 — *Will the pendulum swing back?* — had turned out to be too simple. There was not one pendulum, but many, each with its own path. While Obama had largely completed the task of legalizing the counterterrorism powers Bush had created in the immediate emergency, and while Obama had kept some policy approaches and jettisoned others, there was not yet equilibrium. Obama seemed likely to be remembered as less a transformative post-9/11 president than a transitional one — the bridge to a national security legal-policy destination that would be determined by his successor, future Congresses, and the world as it is rather than as one might want it to be.

In the end, Obama, the most lawyerly of American presidents, governed in a very different way than Bush, the gut decider, and Cheney, the master bureaucratic infighter bent on expanding executive power as an end in itself. But Obama was still destined to bequeath to his successor the most significant fact he had inherited from Bush: a country that remained locked in armed conflict with al-Qaeda and its splintering, regenerating, hydra-headed progeny like the Islamic State — a continuing danger Obama had internalized on a nearly horrific Christmas morning back in 2009. Many years later, as the second post-9/11 presidency prepared to give way to the third, much had changed, but as much had not in the United States of America, where the country remained on a war footing, the executive response remained expansive, and the old "normalcy" remained elusive.

Acknowledgments

Power Wars would not exist without my wife, Luiza Ch. Savage. Over the course of the two years it took me to research and write this, most of which came while I was also working full-time for the *New York Times,* Luiza also wrote and produced two television documentaries and then made the transition from the Washington bureau chief for the Canadian newsweekly magazine *Maclean's* to editorial director of events for *Politico.* And, most important, we were raising a family together. Yet despite the constant time demands, Luiza was unwavering in her support of the project, making space in our mutually busy lives for me to write as well as being a sounding board and early reader of drafts of many sections, and her ideas were invaluable. I love you, Luiza.

I thank Dean Baquet, the *Times'* top editor, for granting my request for a book leave of absence that was crucial to completing the project, as well as for his leadership dating back to when he was the *Times'* Washington bureau chief. I am grateful to my editor Rebecca Corbett, who has been a friend since I came to the *Times* and has frequently provided sage advice. Thank you as well to Bill Hamilton, who did a stellar job directing national security coverage for several years of the Obama administration. I also thank my colleagues who have covered national security or legal issues at the *Times,* who are partners in trying to make sense of this world, including Matt Apuzzo, Peter Baker, Elisabeth Bumiller, Helene Cooper, Michael Gordon, Mark Landler, Eric Lichtblau, Adam Liptak, Mark Mazzetti, Claire Cain Miller, Nicole Perlroth, Matthew Rosenberg, Jim Risen, David Sanger, Michael Schmidt, Eric Schmitt, John Schwartz, Scott Shane, Thom Shanker, Benjamin Weiser, and Robert Worth.

Thank you to Jane Harman, Robert Litwak, and everyone else at the Woodrow Wilson International Center for the honor of naming me a Public Policy Scholar and providing me, during my book leave, with an office, access to a research library, a stipend, and — most important — the assistance of a research intern, Keaton Sausman. She helped bring order to my chaotic endnotes and read early drafts of most of the chapters, providing invaluable feedback about making them more readable. Thank you, Keaton. You have a bright future.

Bringing to light what the government is doing in the realm of national security is a team effort, with many reporters and writers at different outlets contributing puzzle pieces. In writing this history I was a beneficiary of the labors of colleagues who work elsewhere, and I thank them, including Spencer Ackerman, Julia Angwin, Josh Gerstein, Adam Goldman, Siobhan Gorman, Shane Harris, Michael Isikoff, Daniel Klaidman, Eli Lake, Jonathan Landay, Jason Leopold, Jane Mayer, Greg Miller, Ellen Nakashima, Carol Rosenberg, Jeremy Scahill, and Marisa Taylor. I also thank the primary recipients of Edward Snowden's leaks: Laura Poitras, Glenn Greenwald, Barton Gellman, and Ewen MacAskill. In particular, thank you, Laura, for sharing certain law-related surveillance documents with me from that archive as we worked together on developing articles about them for the *Times*.

I benefited as well from a community of fellow national security legal-policy nerds online as we grappled together with trying to understand this murky world. In particular I thank my frequent Twitter conversation partner, the estimable analyst Marcy Wheeler of *Emptywheel;* Julian Sanchez of the CATO Institute; and all the contributors to two indispensable national security law blogs, *Lawfare* and *Just Security*.

As I was conceptualizing this book, I had the great fortune of working alongside Michael Davidson, the recently retired general counsel to the Senate Select Committee on Intelligence, as co-teacher of a class on national security legal policy at Georgetown University in the spring semesters of 2013 and 2014. Our collaboration on designing a curriculum and organizing class readings and discussions benefited me as well as our students. Thank you, Mike, for your wisdom and friendship. I also thank the contributors who made possible the Professor Walter I. Giles Endowed Department Seminar in Constitutional Law and Civil Liberties; Judge Robert A. Katzmann for recommending me for that co-teaching position; and Professor Michael Bailey, then the chair of the Department of Government, for taking me on.

During the writing and editing process, I was also the fortunate beneficiary of input from many other people with whom I discussed ideas. Some of them also read drafts of certain chapters and provided invaluable notes. Any errors are, of course, my own. In particular, I thank Steven Aftergood, the director of the Federation of American Scientists' Project on Government Secrecy; Jack Goldsmith, the Harvard Law School professor and former head of the Office of Legal Counsel; and David McCraw, a lawyer for the *New York Times*.

David wrote the legal briefs and argued in federal court for the numerous Freedom of Information Act *Times* lawsuits in which I was a co-plaintiff in recent years, ably assisted by the *Times*' annual First Amendment fellows: Victoria Baranetsky, Stephen Gikow, Dana Green, Jeremy Kutner, and Nabiha Syed. They helped bring to light documents about FBI shootings, the targeted killing of an American citizen, NSA and FBI surveillance, Guantánamo, and other important policy matters that would have otherwise remained secret. I thank you.

This project was shepherded into existence by my justly celebrated agent, Amanda Urban of ICM Talent. Thank you, Binky, for your continued guidance. I also thank John Parsley, my editor at Little, Brown, for his thoughtful comments and criticisms about the draft manuscript. I thank Eric Rayman, an outside lawyer who reviewed the manuscript for Little, Brown, for his excellent suggestions. I also thank the rest of the team at Hachette for their contributions to producing and promoting *Power Wars*. And I thank Geoff Shandler, the editor of my first book for Little, Brown, *Takeover*, for arranging for the publisher to acquire this project as well.

I am also grateful to the marketing team at Hachette for their hard work in getting the word out about *Power Wars*. And I thank my friend

John Musser, of the web development firm Digerati Designs, for building and administering my book website, charliesavage.com.

I give special but necessarily veiled thanks to the more than 150 current and former government officials with whom I spoke in the course of my research, especially those to whom I returned many times as I delved into the details of different episodes and sought to cross-reference memories and reconcile any inconsistencies. Most of you wished to remain unnamed because you are still in the government or may return to the government in the future. But I thank each of you for your generous donation of your time and for your decision to contribute to public understanding of this important period of American history.

Luiza and I were also assisted enormously by our parents, Margaret Chwialkowska and Urich Chwialkowski, and Robert and Sarah Savage, who at particularly busy times came to stay with us or hosted their grandchildren at their homes in Ottawa and Fort Wayne. Our friends and neighbors, Virginia Harrison and Richard Shaw, were always there with a helping hand or a well-timed glass of wine. Each of you helped me write this book, too, and I thank you.

Finally, I dedicate *Power Wars* to my sons, William and Peter. Both of you were born years after 9/11, but its continuing aftermath seems likely to color your lives, as it has my own generation's. As I write these words, you are not yet old enough to read this book, but I hope that someday you will do so. This was my effort to explain a crucial chapter in the shaping of the nation, and the world, that you will inherit.

Notes

Chapter One: The Captive

1. *U.S. v. Abdulmutallab*, E.D. Mich., Jury Trial–Volume 4, Oct. 11, 2011, http://goo.gl/tujtII.
2. Ibid.
3. Simon Perry, Memorandum for the Court: The Level of Danger Posed by Umar Farouk Abdul Mutallab, Jan. 2012, http://goo.gl/Ldvrds.
4. "Transcript: Read Abdulmutallab's Statement on Guilty Plea," *Detroit Free Press*, Oct. 12, 2011, http://goo.gl/UsWVS2.
5. Perry, Memorandum for the Court.
6. Barack Obama, Address to Joint Session of Congress, Feb. 24, 2009, http://goo.gl/VQXonW.
7. Author interview with Greg Craig, Feb. 13, 2009. Excerpts previously appeared in Charlie Savage, "Obama's War on Terror May Resemble Bush's in Some Areas," *New York Times*, Feb. 18, 2009, http://goo.gl/PYqIlX.
8. Savage, "Obama's War on Terror May Resemble Bush's in Some Areas."
9. Glenn Greenwald, "Charlie Savage on Obama's Embrace of Bush/Cheney 'Terrorism Policies,'" *Salon*, Feb. 18, 2009, http://goo.gl/sbxjqV.
10. Glenn Greenwald, "Salon Radio: Charlie Savage on Obama's Civil Liberties Record," *Salon*, July 2, 2009, http://goo.gl/EuRdLx.
11. *U.S. v. Abdulmutallab*, Jury Trial–Volume 4.
12. Perry, Memorandum for the Court.
13. Peter Baker, "Obama's War over Terror," *New York Times Magazine*, Jan. 17, 2010, http://goo.gl/Y9YRaj.
14. Anahad O'Connor and Eric Schmitt, "Terror Attempt Seen as Man Tries to Ignite Bomb on Jet," *New York Times*, Dec. 26, 2009, http://goo.gl/y9OAB9.
15. *U.S. v. Abdulmutallab*, Opinion and Order Denying Defendant's Motion to Suppress Statements Made at the University of Michigan, Sept. 16, 2011, http://goo.gl/3ODiy4.
16. Unless otherwise noted, the information in this section comes from author interviews of Andy Arena, Jim McJunkin, and Art Cummings.
17. *New York v. Quarles*, 467 U.S. 649 (1984).
18. In public reports about this missed opportunity, the Obama administration would say the father had talked to State Department officials, apparently from an instinct to keep secret anything involving the CIA.

19. Walter Pincus, "Christmas Day Bomb Suspect Was Read Miranda Rights Nine Hours After Arrest," *Washington Post*, Feb. 15, 2010, http://goo.gl/Uzjzzg.

Chapter Two: Acting Like Bush

1. As best as we can tell, this threat largely did not come to pass. The CIA torture program was all but shut down following the one-two punch of Congress's enactment of the Detainee Treatment Act in December 2005 and the Supreme Court's June 2006 *Hamdan* decision, which held that Common Article 3 of the Geneva Conventions protected the Guantánamo detainees — meaning that treating them inhumanely was a war crime. The White House may not have believed the rules were binding, but the CIA felt the heat anyway.
2. Arthur Schlesinger Jr., *The Imperial Presidency* (Boston: Houghton Mifflin, 1973).
3. *ABC This Week*, ABC Network, Jan. 27, 2002, http://goo.gl/TN02eY.
4. Jack Goldsmith, *The Terror Presidency* (New York: W. W. Norton, 2007), 124.
5. CIA press release, "CIA Director's Address at Duquesne University Commencement," May 4, 2007, http://goo.gl/HgN0CC.
6. James Risen and Eric Lichtblau, "Bush Lets U.S. Spy on Callers Without Courts," *New York Times*, Dec. 16, 2005, http://goo.gl/dBRBU.
7. E-mail from David Kris to Courtney Elwood, "Re: In Case You Missed It: President Had Legal Authority to OK Taps," Dec. 21, 2005, http://goo.gl/l56vpr.
8. Senate Judiciary Committee, hearing re "NSA III: Wartime Executive Powers and the FISA Court," written testimony of David Kris, Mar. 28, 2006, http://goo.gl/J7LtZl.
9. Transcript, American Civil Liberties Union, town-hall meeting re "Freedom at Risk: Spying, Secrecy, and Presidential Power," Feb. 20, 2006, https://goo.gl/QYBDRT.
10. *ACLU v. NSA*, 6th Cir., "Brief for Amici Curiae Center for National Security Studies and the Constitution Project," Nov. 17, 2006, http://goo.gl/3ulHCR.
11. *Clapper v. Amnesty International*, Supreme Court No. 11-1025 (argument transcript), Oct. 29, 2012, http://goo.gl/KsNm7V.
12. *Congressional Record*, remarks of Senator Obama re "Nomination of General Michael Hayden," May 25, 2006, http://goo.gl/idoMQM.
13. See, for example, "2008: Obama Vows to Reverse Bush Laws," CNN, Mar. 31, 2008, http://goo.gl/ZUm9FS.
14. Barack Obama, remarks at the Wilson Center ("Obama 2007 Wilson Center Speech"), Aug. 1, 2007, http://goo.gl/KZVqGv.
15. Obama 2007 Wilson Center Speech.
16. Charlie Savage, "Barack Obama's Q&A," *Boston Globe*, Dec. 20, 2007, http://goo.gl/RJ3nJ2.
17. Greg Sargent, "Obama Camp Says It: He'll Support Filibuster of *Any* Bill Containing Telecom Immunity," Talking Points Memo, Oct. 24, 2007, http://goo.gl/Q0IMmC.
18. Sam Graham-Felsen, "Barack Obama on Senator Dodd's Endorsement," *Daily Kos*, Feb. 26, 2008, http://goo.gl/pfkB75.
19. See, e.g., Glenn Greenwald, "Congress Votes to Immunize Lawbreaking Telecoms, Legalize Warrantless Eavesdropping," *Salon*, July 9, 2008, http://goo.gl/CVR4uX; Charles Krauthammer, "The Ever-Malleable Mr. Obama," *Washington Post*, June 27, 2008, http://goo.gl/Pav9Tz.
20. Barack Obama, "My Position on FISA," *Huffington Post*, July 11, 2008, http://goo.gl/2hHmXq.

21. Barack Obama, remarks at rally against the Iraq War, Oct. 2, 2002, NPR, http://goo
.gl/ohRwtO.
22. White House transcript, "Remarks by the President on National Security," May 21,
2009, http://goo.gl/W7NaTP.
23. White House transcript, "Remarks by the President at the Acceptance of the Nobel
Peace Prize," Dec. 10, 2009, http://goo.gl/Fh37DM.
24. Bob Woodward, *Bush at War* (New York: Simon and Schuster, 2002), 137.
25. Condoleezza Rice, *No Higher Honor: A Memoir of My Years in Washington* (New
York: Crown, 2011), 104–6.
26. Dick Cheney, speech before the Center for Security Policy, Oct. 22, 2009, https://goo
.gl/UwtpzJ.
27. Leon Panetta, *Worthy Fights: A Memoir of Leadership in War and Peace* (New York:
Penguin, 2014), 442–43.
28. Abram Chayes, *The Cuban Missile Crisis* (New York: Oxford University Press, 1974), 103.
29. Eric Holder, speech before the American Constitution Society, June 13, 2008, https://
goo.gl/b77A3i, http://goo.gl/Lx9AyG, and http://goo.gl/NfsnlG.
30. Tom Brune, "Military Courts to Vary on Rules," *Newsday,* Dec. 1, 2001.
31. Lois Smith Brady, "VOWS: Jeh Johnson and Susan DiMarco," *New York Times,*
Apr. 10, 1994, http://goo.gl/YpHFrK.
32. Andrew Rosenthal, "Legal Breach: The Government's Attorneys and Abu Ghraib,"
New York Times, Dec. 30, 2004, http://goo.gl/FcWxv5.
33. Senate Judiciary Committee, hearing re "Nomination of Alberto Gonzales to be the
Attorney General of the United States," Jan. 6, 2005.
34. Harold Hongju Koh, remarks before the American Constitution Society, June 17,
2011, http://goo.gl/OjVYVo.
35. Peter Baker, "Obama's War Over Terror," *New York Times Magazine,* Jan. 17, 2010,
http://goo.gl/O7NPMJ.
36. "Remarks by the President at the Acceptance of the Nobel Peace Prize."

Chapter Three: Things Fall Apart

1. White House transcript, "Statement by the President on Attempted Attack on Christmas Day and Recent Violence in Iran," Dec. 28, 2009, http://goo.gl/rskeaV.
2. Peter Baker, "Obama Challenges Terrorism Critics," *New York Times,* Feb. 8, 2010,
http://goo.gl/YJ41Z9.
3. Mike Allen, "Dick Cheney: Barack Obama 'Trying to Pretend,'" *Politico,* Dec. 30,
2009, http://goo.gl/Y9MGjr.
4. Brian Mooney, "Brown and Coakley Clash Over Terror Suspects' Rights," *Boston
Globe,* Jan. 5, 2010, http://goo.gl/1nTR9I.
5. Josh Gerstein, "Brown a Game Changer on Terrorism?," *Politico,* Jan. 20, 2010, http://
goo.gl/0wsMuJ.
6. Fred Thys, "Coakley and Brown Debate One Last Time," WBUR, Jan. 12, 2010, http://
goo.gl/Ia4A7L.
7. Letter from Republican lawmakers to Obama, Jan. 8, 2010, http://goo.gl/YFO3nG.
8. State Department cable, "General Petraeus's Meeting with Saleh on Security,"
10SANAA4, Jan. 4, 2010, http://goo.gl/NMG5U6.
9. In 2008, there were 2,500 people, including 250 Americans, on the no-fly list; by
2013, the number had swelled to 47,000 and included 800 Americans. See Jeanne

708   Notes

Meserve, "Terrorist Watch Lists Shorter Than Previously Reported," CNN, Oct. 22, 2008, http://goo.gl/B2tFju; Jeremy Scahill and Ryan Devereaux, "Barack Obama's Secret Terrorist-Tracking System, By the Numbers," *Intercept*, Aug. 5, 2014, http://goo.gl/WcTIUb.

10. Letter from Holder to McConnell, Feb. 3, 2010, https://goo.gl/dpvS1w.
11. Scott Shane, *Objective Troy: A Terrorist, a President, and the Rise of the Drone* (New York: Crown, 2015), 19–20.
12. White House transcript, "Remarks by the President on Security Reviews," Jan. 5, 2010, http://goo.gl/uay1x3.
13. Holder's letter is quoted in a letter from Senator Wyden to Holder, Mar. 26, 2010, http://goo.gl/hKLy4L.
14. Scott Lewis, "FBI Agents Reveal Underwear Bomber Abdulmutallab Wore Explosive Underwear for Three Weeks," WXKZ, Sept. 27, 2012, http://goo.gl/3JEP8I.
15. White House transcript, "Background Briefing by Senior Administration Officials on Umar Farouk Abdulmutallab," Feb. 2, 2010, http://goo.gl/KOW9i6.
16. Gerstein, "Brown a Game Changer on Terrorism?"
17. Senate Homeland Security Committee, hearing re "Intelligence Reform: The Lessons and Implications of the Christmas Day Attack," Jan. 20, 2010.
18. Letter from Republican senators to President Obama, Jan. 27, 2010, http://goo.gl/i5u5Cu.
19. Scott Shane and Benjamin Weiser, "Administration Considers Moving Site of 9/11 Trial," *New York Times*, Jan. 29, 2010, http://goo.gl/whUkFY.
20. For another reconstruction of this meeting, see Daniel Klaidman, *Kill or Capture: The War on Terror and the Soul of the Obama Presidency* (Boston: Houghton Mifflin Harcourt, 2012), 6–10.
21. Mitch McConnell, "War on Terror," remarks before the Heritage Foundation, Feb. 3, 2010, http://goo.gl/1piKlM.
22. Manu Raju, "Mitch McConnell Attacks President Obama's Terrorism Policies," *Politico*, Feb. 3, 2010, http://goo.gl/F8FXPc.
23. Perry, Memorandum for the Court.
24. Because no plea deal was reached, Abdulmutallab's case went to trial on October 11, 2011. Under the agreement with the defense team, prosecutors could not use statements he made from January to April 2010 as evidence in the trial and were left only with Abdulmutallab's initial fifty-minute interview on the day of the attack, which a judge had deemed admissible. As a result, in an opening statement to the jury, prosecutor Jonathan Turkel told the story of the defendant saying someone named Abu Tarek was behind the attack. Only later, at sentencing, did Abdulmutallab's subsequent statements about al-Awlaki become part of the court record. A transcript of the proceedings shows that Turkel carefully avoided telling the jury that the parts about Abu Tarek were true; rather, he continually put it in Abdulmutallab's mouth, such as "That's what he told the FBI on December 25, 2009."
25. "America and the Final Trap," available at http://goo.gl/28Hz5P, starting around 8:53.
26. "Epic Battles for Sharia and the Sacrifices of the Leaders Part 1," available at https://goo.gl/vuma1N, starting around 10:40.
27. "'The Factor' Examines Obama's Anti-Terror Policies," Fox News, *The O'Reilly Factor*, Feb. 2, 2010, http://goo.gl/9SSFM8.
28. Senate Selection Committee on Intelligence, hearing re "Current and Projected Threats on the United States," Feb. 2, 2010.

29. White House transcript, "Background Briefing by Senior Administration Officials on Umar Farouk Abdulmutallab," Feb. 2, 2010.
30. McConnell, "War on Terror."
31. Sarah Palin, remarks to National Tea Party convention in Nashville, Tennessee, Feb. 6, 2010, http://goo.gl/5Ng6bt.
32. *Meet the Press*, NBC, Feb. 7, 2010, http://goo.gl/tfWeOX.

Chapter Four: Look Forward, Not Back (Captives 2009)

1. *This Week with George Stephanopoulos*, ABC News, Jan. 11, 2009, http://goo.gl/MLMvwk.
2. Carol Rosenberg, "Mohammed, Four Others Offer Confessions to 9/11 Attacks," *Miami Herald*, Dec. 8, 2008, http://goo.gl/142pZp.
3. George W. Bush, *Decision Points* (New York: Crown, 2010), 180.
4. Senator John McCain, "Campaign Event" at Hotel Fort Des Moines, Feb. 17, 2007, http://goo.gl/KqHhnj.
5. White House transcript, "Remarks Following a Meeting with Retired Military Officers," Jan. 22, 2009, http://goo.gl/n38b3e.
6. *Hamdi v. Rumsfeld*, 542 U.S. 507 (2004).
7. Bob Woodward, "Guantánamo Detainee Was Tortured, Says Official Overseeing Military Trials," *Washington Post*, Jan. 14, 2009, http://goo.gl/gTvhie.
8. State Department cable, "Counterterrorism Adviser Brennan's Meeting with Saudi King Abdullah," 09RIYADH447, Mar. 22, 2009, http://goo.gl/NixXtA.
9. Alissa J. Rubin, "Afghans Detail Detention in 'Black Jail' at U.S. Base," *New York Times*, Nov. 28, 2009, http://goo.gl/g256l5; Marc Ambinder, "Inside the Secret Interrogation Facility at Bagram," *Atlantic*, May 14, 2010, http://goo.gl/TfKC.
10. *Boumediene v. Bush*, 553 U.S. 723 (2008).
11. "Kaffee vs. Jessup II?: Obama and McCain Square Off on Habeas Corpus Rights for Accused Terrorists," ABC News, June 14, 2008, http://goo.gl/kjdVNx.
12. Charlie Savage, "Obama Upholds Detainee Policy in Afghanistan," *New York Times*, Feb. 22, 2009, http://goo.gl/JTCfVn.
13. Charlie Savage, "Judge Rules Some Prisoners at Bagram Have Right of Habeas Corpus," *New York Times*, Apr. 3, 2009, http://goo.gl/XcJpyK.
14. *Hamdan v. Rumsfeld*, 548 U.S. 557 (2006).
15. Savage, "Barack Obama's Q&A."
16. *Al-Marri v. Pucciarelli*, 534 F.3d 213 (4th Cir. 2008), http://goo.gl/KUoDb9.
17. Justice Department press release, "Ali Al-Marri Indicted for Providing Material Support to Al-Qaeda," Feb. 27, 2009, http://goo.gl/0XMMXO.
18. *Al-Marri v. Spagone*, 555 U.S. 1220 (2009).
19. *USA v. al-Marri*, "Plea Agreement and Stipulation of Facts," Apr. 30, 2009, http://goo.gl/mNmSyn.
20. White House press release, "Readout on the President's Meeting with Family Members of the Victims of the Attacks of September 11th and the Attack on the USS *Cole*," Feb. 6, 2009, http://goo.gl/mttbOC.
21. Mark Mazzetti, "C.I.A. Destroyed 2 Tapes Showing Interrogations," *New York Times*, Dec. 7, 2007, http://goo.gl/eeq9xZ.
22. CIA press release, "Message from the Director: New Review Group on Rendition, Detention, and Interrogation," Mar. 16, 2009, http://goo.gl/ljwA51.

710   Notes

23. Jason Leopold, "The CIA Paid This Contractor $40 Million to Review Torture Documents," *Vice*, July 27, 2015, https://goo.gl/DuzsvN.
24. This reconstructed quote first appeared in Klaidman, *Kill or Capture*, 58, and I confirmed with meeting participants that Obama had said this.
25. "Respondents' Memorandum Regarding the Government's Detention Authority Relative to Detainees Held at Guantánamo Bay," Mar. 13, 2009, http://goo.gl/eQWXwm.
26. *Haitian Centers Council, Inc. v. Sale*, 823 F. Supp. 1028 (E.D.N.Y. 1993), vacated by Stipulated Order Approving Class Action Settlement Agreement (Feb. 22, 1994).
27. Indeed, Koh would face a rocky confirmation battle. While he was endorsed by a prominent legal conservative, Ted Olson, other conservatives, hearing rumors that Koh might be an eventual Supreme Court nominee, mobilized to attack him. In particular, Ed Whelan, a former Bush-Cheney administration attorney now working at a conservative advocacy group, scoured Koh's scholarly writings in which the professor described with approval how national courts internalize and comply with international law; Whelan argued that Koh would undermine American autonomy by making the United States obey rules it had not enacted through its own democratic process. See Ed Whelan, "Harold Koh's Transnationalism," *National Review Online* Bench Memos, Apr. 6, 2009, http://goo.gl/wYVzrh.
28. *Gherebi v. Obama*, Memorandum opinion, DDC, Apr. 22, 2009, http://goo.gl/Lr5P4d.
29. Letter from Wolf to Obama, May 1, 2009, http://goo.gl/zgoSko.
30. *Congressional Record*, "Floor Statement of Rep. Frank Wolf," May 4, 2009, http://goo.gl/gyIKDp.
31. Peter Finn and Anne E. Kornblut, "Guantánamo Bay: How the White House Lost the Fight to Close It," *Washington Post*, Apr. 23, 2011, http://goo.gl/uomdv.
32. "Three Years After Gitmo, Uighurs Prisoners in Paradise," *New York Post*, Sept. 30, 2012, http://goo.gl/k4wiPY.
33. Grace Chung, "Gingrich Comments on Uighurs Don't Sit Well with Some in GOP," McClatchy, June 18, 2009, http://goo.gl/9yJc5y.
34. Richard B. Cheney, "Foreign and Defense Policy," remarks delivered at American Enterprise Institute, May 21, 2009, http://goo.gl/5XeKse.
35. White House transcript, "Remarks by the President on National Security," May 21, 2009, http://goo.gl/W7NaTP.
36. HR 2346, Supplemental Appropriations Act of 2009, http://goo.gl/IqDsth.
37. White House transcript, "Remarks by the President to the City Club of Cleveland," Mar. 18, 2015, http://goo.gl/mvxO5m.
38. Memorandum from Wiegmann and Martins for the attorney general and the secretary of defense, re preliminary report, July 20, 2009, http://goo.gl/0Q8hi7.
39. Department of Justice and Department of Defense unsigned memo, "Determination of Guantánamo Cases Referred for Prosecution," undated, http://goo.gl/0Q8hi7.
40. Mark S. Martins, "National Forums for Punishing Offenses Against International Law: Might U.S. Soldiers Have Their Day in the Same Court?," *Virginia Journal of International Law* 36 (1996): 659.
41. Lindsey Graham, "Key Elements of a Guantánamo Detainee Disposition Plan," Aug. 5, 2009, https://goo.gl/LwQIZ1.
42. Charlie Savage, "Senator Proposes Deal on Handling of Detainees," *New York Times*, Mar. 4, 2010, http://goo.gl/zs3vs0.

43. Justice Department press release, "Special Task Force on Interrogations and Transfer Policies Issues Its Recommendations to the President," Aug. 24, 2009, http://goo.gl/pFHCvl.

44. See, for example, Jeffrey Kaye, "Contrary to Obama's Promises, the US Military Still Permits Torture," *Guardian*, Jan. 25, 2014, http://goo.gl/mMvQUc.

45. Charlie Savage, "U.N. Commission Presses U.S. on Torture," *New York Times*, Nov. 14, 2013, http://goo.gl/DVe4yS.

46. Eric Lichtblau and Scott Shane, "Report Faults 2 Authors of Bush Terror Memos," *New York Times*, Feb. 20, 2010, http://goo.gl/doiMxD.

47. Ali Watkins, "Meet the Only Person Being Punished After the Senate Torture Report," *Huffington Post*, Apr. 28, 2015, http://goo.gl/e9Xx8i.

48. *Garrity v. New Jersey*, 385 U.S. 493 (1967).

49. This factor complicates the cases of some of the detainees whose names the task force added to the list of those recommended for transfer, since the task force made those calls at a time when federal district court judges were frequently siding with detainees. In 2010, after the task force had completed its work, the federal appeals court in the District of Columbia issued a series of rulings that made it much harder for detainees to win habeas cases. See chapter 7, sections 3, 7, and 10.

50. *Mohammed v. Obama*, D.D.C., "Respondents' Brief in Response to the Court's Order of Sept. 4, 2009," Sept. 29, 2009, https://goo.gl/km56r4.

51. Charlie Savage, "Appeals Court Sides with Detainee," *New York Times*, July 4, 2010, http://goo.gl/jU52GS.

52. *Bensayah v. Obama*, 610 F.3d 718 (D.C. Cir. 2010), http://goo.gl/KOl1IS.

53. *Padilla v. Yoo*, 9th Cir., "Brief for Appellant," Nov. 9, 2009, http://goo.gl/jtnFUD.

54. *Padilla v. Yoo*, 9th Cir., "Brief of the United States as Amicus Curiae," Dec. 2, 2009, http://goo.gl/Ah3tWh.

55. *Lebron v. Rumsfeld*, 4th Cir., "Brief of the United States as Amicus Curiae" and "Brief of Appellee Leon E. Panetta," July 18, 2011, http://goo.gl/cQ7vRO.

56. Lichtblau and Shane, "Report Faults 2 Authors of Bush Terror Memos."

57. Charlie Savage, "Accused 9/11 Mastermind to Face Civilian Trial in N.Y.," *New York Times*, Nov. 14, 2009, http://goo.gl/xWXyvD.

58. Senate Judiciary Committee, hearing re "Oversight of the Department of Justice," Nov. 18, 2009.

59. Klaidman, *Kill or Capture*, 147–48.

60. Ibid., 167.

61. Department of Justice transcript, "Attorney General Announces Forum Decisions for Guantánamo Detainees," Nov. 13, 2009, http://goo.gl/RUSGSd.

62. *U.S. v. Mohammed et al.*, (S14) 93 Cr. 180(KTD), S.D.N.Y., Indictment, Dec. 14, 2009, http://goo.gl/u5Cshj.

63. Jack Healy, "Obama Says Guantánamo Won't Close by January," *New York Times*, Nov. 19, 2009, http://goo.gl/6kWNVN.

64. Charlie Savage, "U.S. Said to Pick Illinois Prison to House Detainees," *New York Times*, Dec. 15, 2010, http://goo.gl/IVd8QW.

65. "Remarks by the President at the Acceptance of the Nobel Peace Prize."

Chapter Five: Stellarwind (Surveillance 1928–2009)

1. While I learned additional details about this meeting, its existence was first reported by Ryan Lizza, "State of Deception," *New Yorker*, Dec. 16, 2013, http://goo.gl/Fes57H.

712   Notes

2. John F. Harris, Mike Allen, and Jim Vandehei, "Cheney Warns of New Attacks," *Politico*, Feb. 4, 2009, http://goo.gl/ZWYUr4.
3. NSA report, "Business Records FISA NSA Review," June 25, 2009, http://goo.gl/ C6zU0l.
4. "In re Production of Tangible Things from [redacted], F.I.S.C.: Order Regarding Preliminary Notice of Compliance Incident Dated Jan. 15, 2009," Jan. 28, 2009, http:// goo.gl/OseG70.
5. *Smith v. Maryland*, 442 U.S. 735 (1979).
6. "In re Production of Tangible Things from [redacted], F.I.S.C.: Memorandum of the United States in Response to the Court's Order of Jan. 28, 2009," Feb. 17, 2009, http:// goo.gl/sOqb92.
7. "Business Records FISA NSA Review."
8. "In re Production of Tangible Things from [redacted], F.I.S.C.: Order," Mar. 2, 2009, http://goo.gl/OWih8B.
9. Glenn Greenwald, "NSA Collecting Phone Records of Millions of Verizon Customers Daily," *Guardian*, June 6, 2013, http://goo.gl/zNiDGN.
10. House Judiciary Committee, hearing re "NSA Data Collection and Surveillance Oversight," July 17, 2013.
11. Barton Gellman and Greg Miller, "'Black Budget' Summary Details U.S. Spy Network's Successes, Failures and Objectives," *Washington Post*, Aug. 29, 2013, http:// goo.gl/YikPif.
12. In a landmark 1928 case involving wiretapping evidence against bootleggers, the Supreme Court ruled that the Fourth Amendment creates no reasonable expectation of privacy over one's phone calls. This, ironically, led to *less* wiretapping because in 1934 Congress responded to the ruling by prohibiting wiretapping. Nevertheless, during the run-up to World War II, the FBI director, J. Edgar Hoover, persuaded President Franklin D. Roosevelt to authorize wiretapping against suspected Nazi agents. Executive-branch lawyers secretly interpreted the ban as not applying to wiretapping for the national defense as long as the executive branch did not use the information in court or otherwise divulge it to outsiders. This sequence was an early example of recurring themes: the tendency of technology to outpace legal regulation, the creation of a wall between national security and criminal investigations, and the propensity of presidents and their legal teams to employ stretched interpretations to get around apparent limits.

In 1967, the Supreme Court overruled its 1928 precedent and held that Fourth Amendment privacy rights applied to phone calls after all. This led to *more* wiretapping because in 1968 Congress responded to the ruling by legalizing wiretapping. It enacted procedures — known as *Title III* warrants — that normalized and legitimized wiretapping so long as criminal investigators followed the new rules, and permitted the information to be used in court. But that law did not regulate the president's claimed inherent constitutional authority to wiretap on domestic soil on his own to defend against suspected foreign agents, spies, and terrorists, and it remained unclear whether the Constitution required a warrant for that kind of surveillance. See *Olmstead v. United States*, 277 U.S. 438 (1928); *Katz v. United States*, 389 U.S. 347 (1967); see also Neal Katyal and Robert Caplan, "The Surprisingly Stronger Case for the Legality of the NSA Surveillance Program: The FDR Precedent," *Stanford Law Review* 60, no. 4 (February 2008): 1023, http://goo.gl/Y3BSpf.

13. Congress imposed the new FISA warrant rule on only a narrow slice of that activity. If the NSA wanted to *specifically target* the communications of an American inside the United States for acquisition, it needed a warrant. But FISA did not stop the agency from intercepting an American's international telegram or phone call without a warrant if the American happened to be talking to a person overseas whom the agency had instead targeted. And FISA did not stop the agency from conducting dragnet acquisition of *all* communications entering and leaving the United States over a particular satellite link or undersea cable in international waters without specifically targeting anybody, a technique that permitted it to sift through them later using conceptual search terms, like *Soviet, gold,* and *antisubmarine warfare.* Indeed, the bill included an obscure provision — suggested by the executive branch, one of the congressional staffers who helped write the bill told me — that used roundabout language to *exempt these techniques* from domestic-communications privacy laws when the government used them for gathering foreign intelligence. It is recorded at 18 U.S.C. § 2511(2)(f), https://goo.gl/5zUKPq.

14. Among other regulations, the executive branch created a rule that the NSA could search for an American's name in its storehouse of communications that had been vacuumed up under 12333 only under very restrictive conditions. If the American was located inside the United States, the government would get a FISA Court warrant. If the American was located abroad, the attorney general had to decide whether the American was likely an agent of a foreign power — the same standard the FISA Court used; United States Signal Intelligence Directive 18, Oct. 20, 1980, http://goo .gl/pCyAdf.

15. Julia Angwin, Charlie Savage, Jeff Larson, Henrik Moltke, Laura Poitras and James Risen, "AT&T Helped N.S.A. Spy on an Array of Internet Traffic," *New York Times,* Aug. 16, 2015, http://goo.gl/d1Y7in.

16. "1st Transpacific Fiber-Optic Cable Links U.S., Japan," Associated Press, Apr. 18, 1989, http://goo.gl/3x2aln.

17. Memorandum from Lawton to Levin, re "Possible Amendments to FISA," Nov. 1, 1990, http://goo.gl/khmCEW. (This memo was partially declassified and obtained with redactions due to a Freedom of Information Act request by David Kris in 2007, when he was out of government and working on his book.)

18. Leaked NSA document, "Some Key (SSO) Cyber Milestones Since 2005," http://goo .gl/0FuI2K.

19. "Classified Annex to Department of Defense Procedures Under Executive Order 12333," http://goo.gl/QmAf3w.

20. Julia Angwin, Charlie Savage, Jeff Larson, Henrik Moltke, Laura Poitras and James Risen, "AT&T Helped N.S.A. Spy on an Array of Internet Traffic."

21. An obscure provision in federal law, created by Section 201 of the original FISA, provides the authority for such letters. It reads: "Notwithstanding any other law, providers of wire or electronic communication service…are authorized to provide information, facilities, or technical assistance to persons authorized by law…to conduct electronic surveillance…if such provider…has been provided with…a certification in writing by…the Attorney General of the United States that no warrant or court order is required by law, that all statutory requirements have been met, and that the specified assistance is required," 18 U.S.C. § 2511(2)(a)(ii)(B), https://goo.gl/ 5zUKPq.

22. 50 U.S.C. § 1809.
23. Understanding transit authority is probably the key to solving a surveillance mystery that arose in the fall of 2007, after the warrantless-wiretapping program came to light. Joe Nacchio, a former chief executive officer for Qwest International, a Denver-based phone and network company, told a court that on February 27, 2001, he had attended a meeting at the NSA's Fort Meade headquarters in which the agency had asked Qwest to participate in an unidentified government program that he believed was illegal. He refused to go along after asking the government to "provide him with proper legal authority for what was being asked of Qwest," which it could not do, as he repeated in a 2015 court filing related to a tax dispute; *Nacchio v. USA*, Fed. Cl., No. 12-20 "Joint Motion for Entry of Stipulated Final Judgment," Apr. 21, 2015, http://goo.gl/Mj3gMt. Back in 2007, Nacchio's vague account led some people to jump to the conclusion that he was talking about the NSA's warrantless-wiretapping program and that the Bush-Cheney administration must have started setting it up even before 9/11, even though it justified that program by citing the attacks. But nothing that has come out since then corroborated that theory. What instead probably happened was that Qwest—which had just been founded in 1996 and rapidly grew into a major fiber-optic network operator—was relaying enough foreign-to-foreign traffic by early 2001 that the NSA had asked it to join the transit authority program, which would involve voluntarily installing filtering and collection equipment on its switches. But the lack of any affirmative statutory authority to cite for this proposal left the Qwest executive doubtful about its legality. In 2015, I asked Nacchio if my speculation was accurate. He told me that because of his security-clearance obligations he could neither "acknowledge or deny it was on transit monitoring, but I would say that I specifically asked about 'where is the FISA warrant' and the answer was 'we don't need one.'"
24. Leaked "ST-09-002 Working Draft," Office of the Inspector General, National Security Agency (Draft NSA IG Report), Mar. 24, 2009, 28, http://goo.gl/K2OoXf.
25. Draft NSA IG Report, 3–4.
26. When I spoke with William Binney and Thomas Drake, a former senior NSA official and another Thinthread proponent turned NSA whistleblower, each maintained that using Thinthread on Americans' data would have been legal. I had difficulty understanding their theory for why this was, but Binney said he thought it could be done under a provision of FISA that permits, in an emergency, the government to wiretap an American's phone calls right away, so long as it applies to the FISA Court for after-the-fact approval within seventy-two hours. Drake told me, "Thinthread was fully FISA-compliant, and I know because I was there, and I was executive program manager for Thinthread."
27. Draft NSA IG Report, 4–5.
28. Cyrus Farivar, "The Executive Order That Led to Mass Spying, as Told by NSA Alumni," *Ars Technica*, Aug. 27, 2014, http://goo.gl/R6wZyH.
29. Charlie Savage, *Takeover: The Return of the Imperial Presidency and the Subversion of American Democracy* (Boston: Little, Brown, 2007); Goldsmith, *The Terror Presidency*, 124.
30. Inspector General of the Department of Justice, "A Review of the Department of Justice's Involvement with the President's Surveillance Program," ("DOJ IG Report on Stellarwind"), July 2009, 30, http://goo.gl/eMBhKm.

31. Ibid., 29.
32. Draft NSA IG Report, 10.
33. Memo from Yoo to Ashcroft, [subject line redacted], Nov. 2, 2001, http://goo.gl/wxTg5Y.
34. DOJ IG Report on Stellarwind, 111.
35. Sheldon Whitehouse, "Remarks to the American Bar Association's 18th Annual Review of the Field of National Security Law Conference," Nov. 6, 2008, http://goo.gl/PRtrOM.
36. Draft NSA IG Report, 11, 29.
37. Julia Angwin, Charlie Savage, Jeff Larson, Henrik Moltke, Laura Poitras and James Risen, "AT&T Helped N.S.A. Spy on an Array of Internet Traffic."
38. Ibid.
39. Draft NSA IG Report, 15.
40. "A Review of the Department of Justice's Involvement with the President's Surveillance Program," 71–78.
41. Stewart Baker, *Skating on Stilts: Why We Aren't Stopping Tomorrow's Terrorism* (Stanford: Hoover Institution Press, 2010), 39–60.
42. See, e.g., Elizabeth Goitein and Faiza Patel, "What Went Wrong with the FISA Court," Brennan Center for Justice, http://goo.gl/Xq02l0.
43. "In re Sealed Case, F.I.S.C., Opinion," May 17, 2002, http://goo.gl/n3cbAS.
44. The FISA Review Court ruling permitted law enforcement agents and prosecutors to tell intelligence investigators to get a FISA wiretap on a criminal suspect, even in a situation where their evidence that the suspect was engaged in wrongdoing was insufficient for a criminal wiretap order. See "In re Sealed Case, F.I.S.C., Opinion," Nov. 18, 2002, http://goo.gl/3Rb5Ig.
45. Draft NSA IG Report, 25.
46. Charlie Savage and Laura Poitras, "How a Court Secretly Evolved, Extending U.S. Spies' Reach," *New York Times,* Mar. 12, 2014, http://goo.gl/XE24zU.
47. Charlie Savage, "Government Declassifies Surveillance Court Documents on 'Raw Take' Sharing," *New York Times,* Mar. 3, 2015, http://goo.gl/ASwjIN.
48. For now, the sharing between agencies of raw FISA Amendments Act–gathered communications applies only to information collected from Internet companies like Google or Yahoo via the NSA-FBI Prism system, not via the NSA's "upstream" system for collecting data as it travels across network switches.
49. Savage, *Takeover,* 183–88.
50. Daniel Klaidman, "Now We Know What the Battle Was About," *Newsweek,* Dec. 12, 2008, http://goo.gl/un208a; Draft NSA IG Report, 37–38.
51. Charlie Savage, "Redactions in U.S. Memo Leave Doubts on Data Surveillance Program," *New York Times,* Sept. 7, 2014, http://goo.gl/tlkgA1.
52. Charlie Savagae, "Bush Made Retroactive N.S.A. 'Fix' After Hospital Room Showdown," *New York Times,* Sept. 22, 2015, http://goo.gl./dRaavl.
53. Savage, "Redactions in U.S. Memo Leave Doubts on Data Surveillance Program."
54. See, e.g., 18 U.S.C. § 2702(c)(4).
55. There is another potential legal problem with the collection of e-mail metadata stemming from the way that the Internet works on a technical level, but it appears to be one that neither Goldsmith nor the FISA Court understood or addressed in 2004, unless it is hidden under some redaction in the recently declassified documents. The best analysis of this is by Julian Sanchez. The issue is that in *Smith v. Maryland,* the

Supreme Court concluded that the police could obtain, from a phone company, information about a suspect's calls without a warrant, because the suspect had revealed the fact of those calls to the phone company in the course of placing or receiving them. Similarly, the government can take a picture of a postcard or the outside of a snail-mail letter at the post office, because the sender has revealed that information to the postal service. This is called the *third-party doctrine:* if you reveal something to a third party, you have no Fourth Amendment expectation of privacy over it. The government reasoned by analogy that it could obtain without a warrant, from a network company, e-mail header information revealing the fact that someone was e-mailing someone else. But unlike phone companies, network companies do *not* know who is e-mailing whom. Internet data is broken up into packets, which have layers—rather like envelopes contained in other envelopes. The network company normally only looks at the top layer or outer envelope, which says move this packet from Server A to Server B. It is only after the data arrives at Server B—say, the mail server for a recipient—that additional envelopes are opened, revealing instructions that permit the server to reassemble the message and place it in the right user's inbox; see Julian Sanchez, "Are Internet Backbone Pen Registers Constitutional?" *Cato At Liberty* blog, Sept. 25, 2013, http://goo.gl/wj12F5.

56. See also Julian Sanchez, "Reading Jack Goldsmith's Stellarwind Memo (Part I)," *Just Security,* Sept. 10, 2014, http://goo.gl/l52yYX.

57. *Youngstown Sheet & Tube Co. v. Sawyer,* 343 U.S. 579 (1952).

58. Another component of the Justice Department, the Drug Enforcement Administration, had been relying on a similar interpretation of "relevant" for a secret program that was collecting bulk metadata records of outgoing telephone calls from the United States to certain countries linked to narcotics trafficking. This program dated back to the Bush-Quayle administration, and the Obama administration shut it down in 2013 and declassified its prior existence in 2015. (See chapter 11, section 11.) To obtain the records, the DEA was using administrative subpoenas to phone companies based on a statute permitting the agency to get records "relevant" to a narco-trafficking investigation without court oversight. It is not clear whether the officials involved in the development of the brief submitted to Kollar-Kotelly in 2004 were aware of the DEA program and the theory behind it, or whether they reinvented the theory. Several officials from that era told me they did not remember it playing a role, but cautioned that it had been a long time.

59. [Redacted case name], F.I.S.C., "Memorandum of Law and Fact in Support of Application for Pen Registers and Trap and Trace Devices for Foreign Intelligence Purposes," [date partly redacted], 2004, http://goo.gl/aZJIdv.

60. [Redacted case name], Docket No. PR/TT [redacted], F.I.S.C., "Opinion and Order," July 14, 2004, http://goo.gl/ju2WtY.

61. DOJ IG Report on Stellarwind, 205.

62. [Redacted case name], Docket No. PR/TT [redacted], F.I.S.C., "Declaration of George J. Tenet, Director of National Intelligence," [date partly redacted], 2004, http://goo.gl/VYfqgg.

63. The program was generating numerous tips to the FBI about suspicious phone numbers and e-mail addresses, and it was the job of the FBI field offices to pursue those leads and scrutinize the people behind them. (The tips were so frequent and such a waste of time that the field offices reported back, in frustration, "You're sending us

garbage.") But the agents did not know about Stellarwind and were not sure of the provenance of these mysterious tips — which they were told never to mention in legal documents — or of how they fit into their rules for preliminary and full investigations, both of which require some kind of factual basis to suspect someone of wrongdoing. Responding to these worries, the Justice Department in 2003 created a new kind of low-grade investigation, called a "threat assessment," to permit agents to pursue tips that had no established factual basis. A 2008 revision changed the name to an "assessment" and developed a more elaborate set of rules and permissions for them. By 2009, agents were using this kind of investigation about 40,000 times a year to scrutinize persons or groups, usually finding nothing worthy enough to elevate it to even a preliminary investigation. But until 2015, it was not known that this relaxation in the rules limiting the power of FBI agents stemmed from the dilemma of what to do about Stellarwind tips. See, e.g., DOJ IG Report on Stellarwind, 300–305; Charlie Savage, "F.B.I. Focusing on Security Over Ordinary Crime," *New York Times,* Aug. 24, 2011, http://goo.gl/npo0A3.

64. Risen and Lichtblau, "Bush Lets U.S. Spy on Callers Without Courts."
65. Lesley Cauley, "NSA Has Massive Database of Americans' Phone Calls," *USA Today,* May 11, 2006, http://goo.gl/1bwEi, but see "A Note to Our Readers," *USA Today,* June 30, 2006, http://goo.gl/YEEVoI.
66. [Redacted case name], Docket BR 06-05, F.I.S.C., "Memorandum of Law in Support of Application for Certain Tangible Things for Investigations to Protect Against International Terrorism," May 23, 2006, http://goo.gl/uq9Q0G.
67. "In re Application of the Federal Bureau of Investigation for an Order Requiring the Production of Tangible Things from [redacted], Docket No. BR-05, F.I.S.C.: Order," May 24, 2006, http://goo.gl/fZBc00.
68. "In re Application of the Federal Bureau of Investigation for an Order Requiring the Production of Tangible Things from [redacted], Docket No. BR-08, F.I.S.C., Order," Aug. 18, 2006, http://goo.gl/nJafbA.
69. "In re Application of the Federal Bureau of Investigation for an Order Requiring the Production of Tangible Things from [redacted]," Docket No. BR-12, F.I.S.C., "Order," Nov. 13, 2006, http://goo.gl/1pdZ4K.
70. Charlie Savage, "Extended Ruling by Secret Court Backs Collection of Phone Data," *New York Times,* Sept. 18, 2013, http://goo.gl/4JfYze.
71. Charlie Savage, "N.S.A. Used Phone Records Program to Seek Iran Operatives," *New York Times*, Aug. 13, 2015, http://goo.gl/flWw75.
72. *ACLU v. NSA*, E.D. Mich., "Summary judgment opinion," Aug. 7, 2006, http://goo.gl/NFjXds.
73. *ACLU v. NSA*, 493 F.3d 644 (2007), http://goo.gl/6h6pxe.
74. DOJ IG Report on Stellarwind, 238–39.
75. Letter from Gonzales to Leahy and Specter, Jan. 17, 2007, http://goo.gl/BiJZil.
76. "In re [redacted], F.I.S.C.: Memorandum of Law in Support of Application for Authority to Conduct Electronic Surveillance of [redacted]," Dec. 13, 2007, http://goo.gl/dL3eHm.
77. Charlie Savage, "Documents Shed New Light on Legal Wrangling over Spying in U.S.," *New York Times*, Dec. 13, 2014, http://goo.gl/XHFlkQ.
78. If the Justice Department inspector general staff was aware of this wrinkle, they wrote the Justice Department inspector general report on Stellarwind in a way that

obscured it. Their report, on page 245, said the department had offered to submit the application to Kollar-Kotelly but she said it should be filed in normal fashion, meaning to whoever happened to be on duty, and Howard was on duty the week they filed it. It does not delve into why the department chose to file it that particular week, nor does it mention the FISA Court's angry response.

79. While Howard did not rule for several weeks and asked for a supplemental brief, under FISA Court rules, once the application was submitted to a judge, it stayed with him.

80. "In re [redacted], F.I.S.C.: Order," Jan. 10, 2007, http://goo.gl/dL3eHm.

81. "In re [redacted], F.I.S.C.: Order and Memorandum Opinion," Apr. 3, 2007, http://goo.gl/dL3eHm.

82. It was around this time that Krass left the Office of Legal Counsel for a different Justice Department job; she would return to the center of things in 2009 when DeRosa hired her as her top deputy.

83. DOJ IG Report on Stellarwind, 255.

84. Charlie Savage, "Documents Show N.S.A.'s Wiretap Moves Before Congress's Approval," *New York Times*, Jan. 28, 2015, http://goo.gl/swWK7S.

85. One of the most striking Snowden revelations was that the NSA stores raw global Internet data gathered under 12333 authority in a rolling buffer, accessible through its XKEYSCORE system, for three days. This feature lets analysts go back in time and find recent messages sent by a target before he was targeted; see Glenn Greenwald, "XKeyscore: NSA Tool Collects 'Nearly Everything a User Does on the Internet,'" *Guardian*, July 31, 2013, http://goo.gl/j1uzZu.

86. Charlie Savage, "N.S.A. Said to Search Content of Messages to and from U.S.," *New York Times*, Aug. 8, 2013, http://goo.gl/FkCYiK.

87. See, e.g., "In re [redacted], F.I.S.C.: Supplemental Memorandum of Law in Support of Application for Authority to Conduct Electronic Surveillance of [redacted]," Jan. 2, 2007, 6, http://goo.gl/dL3eHm.

88. "In re [redacted], F.I.S.C.: Declaration of [redacted], NSA Senior Manager for Counterterrorism Projects," Jan. 2, 2007, http://goo.gl/dL3eHm.

89. Julia Angwin, Charlie Savage, Jeff Larson, Henrik Moltke, Laura Poitras and James Risen, "AT&T Helped N.S.A. Spy on an Array of Internet Traffic."

90. Even though the government did not appear to be doing the filtering and selection of all the messages after all, there remained a legal question to be answered about whether that initial step of copying and sifting of everything by the firms violated the Fourth Amendment. Sometimes, if private sector people or organizations do something they would not otherwise do because the government directed them to do it, courts have said they count as agents of the government. For example, police cannot get around search warrant requirements by directing a plumber, when he goes into a suspect's house to fix a pipe, to clandestinely look through the suspect's filing cabinet for them.

91. Charlie Savage, "U.S. Declassifies FISA Court Documents about the Protect America Act," *New York Times*, Aug. 1, 2015, http://goo.gl/sry4rn.

92. Chris Roberts, "Transcript: Debate on the Foreign Intelligence Surveillance Act," *El Paso Times*, Aug. 22, 2007, http://goo.gl/Nvfck9.

93. Department of Justice Inspector General, "Review of the Federal Bureau of Investigation's Activities Under Section 702 of the Foreign Intelligence Surveillance Act Amendments Act of 2008," Sept. 2012, http://goo.gl/FWQSMb.

94. Senate Select Intelligence Committee, hearing re: "The Foreign Intelligence Surveillance Modernization Act of 2007," May 1, 2007, http://goo.gl/CYc1TN.

95. Office of the Director of National Intelligence, "National Intelligence Estimate: The Terrorist Threat to the Homeland," July 17, 2007, http://goo.gl/qGRlpg.

96. The NSA says it does not use its power to steal trade secrets and give them to American firms for competitive advantage.

97. "In re Directives to Yahoo! Inc. Pursuant to Section 105B of the Foreign Intelligence Surveillance Act, F.I.S.C.: Memorandum Opinion," Apr. 25, 2008, http://goo.gl/U18TEW.

98. "In re Directives to Yahoo! Inc. Pursuant to Section 105B of the Foreign Intelligence Surveillance Act, F.I.S.C., Government's Motion for an Order of Civil Contempt," May 9, 2008, https://goo.gl/Rvr2dA.

99. "In re Directives to Yahoo! Inc. Pursuant to Section 105B of the Foreign Intelligence Surveillance Act, F.I.S.C.R.," Aug. 22, 2008, http://goo.gl/WO4FYP.

100. Barton Gellman and Laura Poitras, "U.S., British intelligence mining data from nine U.S. Internet companies in broad secret program," *Washington Post,* June 7, 2013, http://goo.gl/LREOz; Glenn Greenwald, "NSA Prism program taps in to user data of Apple, Google and others," *Guardian,* June 7, 2013, http://goo.gl/LMeflG; an archived version of the *Post*'s original Prism story—the one the world read, but which underwent many changes later—is preserved at Ed Bott, "The Real Story in the NSA Scandal Is the Collapse of Journalism," *ZDNet,* June 8, 2013, http://goo.gl/AHVJe.

101. Leaked N.S.A. slide, "FAA702 Operations: Two Types of Collection," http://goo.gl/UVv1v1.

102. "In re Directives to Yahoo! Inc. Pursuant to Section 105B of the Foreign Intelligence Surveillance Act, F.I.S.C.: Yahoo! Inc.'s Compliance Report," May 14, 2008, https://goo.gl/Lbxkgj.

103. [Case name redacted], F.I.S.C., "Memorandum Opinion," Oct. 3, 2011, ("Oct. 3, 2011, Bate opinion"), 29, http://goo.gl/re5LNH.

104. Gellman and Poitras, "U.S., British Intelligence Mining Data from Nine U.S. Internet Companies in Broad Secret Program."

105. "Department of Defense Supplemental Procedures Governing Communications Metadata Analysis," http://goo.gl/B0KJPw.

106. Executive Order 13470, Further Amendments to Executive Order 12333, United States Intelligence Activities, July 30, 2008, http://goo.gl/qxtUVU.

107. Baker had told Kris in vague terms about the existence of a classified surveillance program, but Kris was not told its details before leaving for the private sector; DOJ IG Report on Stellarwind, 82.

108. Royce Lamberth, Preface, in David Kris and J. Douglas Wilson, *National Security Investigations and Prosecutions,* 2nd ed. (New York: Thomson/West, 2012), vi.

109. David S. Kris, "On the Bulk Collection of Tangible Things," *Lawfare Research Paper Series* 1, no. 4 (Sept. 29, 2013), http://goo.gl/vnjjws.

110. Office of the Director of National Intelligence and Department of Justice, unsigned white paper re "The Intelligence Community's Collection Programs Under Title VII of the Foreign Intelligence Surveillance Act," May 4, 2012, http://goo.gl/ffKa9w.

111. Charlie Savage, "Battle Looms Over Patriot Act," *New York Times,* Sept. 20, 2009, http://goo.gl/jaey2.

112. Subcommittee on the Constitution, Civil Rights, and Civil Liberties, hearing re "USA Patriot Act," Sept. 22, 2009, http://goo.gl/lflFdm.
113. Kris, "On the Bulk Collection of Tangible Things."
114. Letter from Durbin, Feingold, and Wyden to Holder, Nov. 17, 2009, http://goo.gl/z4lvtG.
115. Described in letter from Wyden to Holder, Mar. 26, 2010, http://goo.gl/tLIrV1.
116. Described in ibid.
117. Ibid.

Chapter Six: Targeted Killing

1. U.S. diplomatic cable 09SANAA1669, from Ambassador Stephen Seche, Embassy Sanaa, "Brennan-Saleh Meeting Sep 6, 2009," Sept. 15, 2009, http://goo.gl/ssG3pY. See also U.S. diplomatic cable 09SANAA1430, from Ambassador Stephen Seche, Embassy Sanaa, "Saleh Tells Petraeus: 'No Restrictions' on CT Cooperation," Aug. 9, 2009, https://goo.gl/FNZybX.
2. For a more detailed reconstruction of this secure video teleconference, see Klaidman, *Kill or Capture*, 210.
3. Republic of Yemen Council of Representatives, "Investigating Committee's Report on Security Events in the Province of Abyen," Feb. 7, 2010, http://goo.gl/fdt6wO.
4. Jennifer Steinhauer, "Open to Both Sides, Homeland Security Chief Steps into Immigration Divide," *New York Times*, Aug. 6, 2014, http://goo.gl/qZeQ9K.
5. Klaidman, *Kill or Capture*, 210.
6. "Investigating Committee's Report on Security Events in the Province of Abyen."
7. State Department cable from Ambassador Stephen Seche, "ROYG Looks Ahead Following CT Operations, But Perhaps Not Far Enough," Dec. 21, 2009, 09SANAA2251, http://goo.gl/9mvcIG.
8. See, e.g., Geneva Conventions Protocol I (1977), articles 51 and 57. The United States has not ratified this protocol but it reflects customary international law.
9. Embassy of the Republic of Yemen, "Press Statement," Office of Media and Public Affairs, Dec. 24, 2009, http://goo.gl/xvy1UJ.
10. Scott Shane and Souad Mekhennet, "Imam's Path from Condemning Terror to Preaching Jihad," *New York Times*, May 9, 2010, http://goo.gl/qM6fY1.
11. Shane, *Objective Troy*, 116–21.
12. House Committee on Appropriations, Subcommittee on Commerce, Justice, Science, and Related Agencies, hearing re "Final Report of the William H. Webster Commission on the FBI, Counterterrorism Intelligence, and the Events at Fort Hood," Aug. 1, 2012.
13. William H. Webster Commission on the Federal Bureau of Investigation, Counterterrorism Intelligence, and the Events at Fort Hood, Texas, on Nov. 5, 2009, "Final Report," http://goo.gl/jZ155k.
14. "Awlaki Calls Fort Hood Attack a 'Heroic Act,'" SITE Intelligence Group, Nov. 9, 2009, http://goo.gl/rNXHE2.
15. Sudarsan Raghavan and Michael D. Shear, "U.S.-Aided Attack in Yemen Thought to Have Killed Aulaqi, 2 al-Qaeda Leaders," *Washington Post*, Dec. 25, 2009, http://goo.gl/3WCcLl.
16. "US Jet Bomber May Have Contacted Yemeni Imam: Lawmaker," AFP newswire, Dec. 26, 2009; "Transcript: Special Report with Brett Baier," Dec. 28, 2009, http://goo.gl/xbKrBv.

17. Jeremy Scahill, *Dirty Wars: The World Is a Battlefield* (New York: Nation Books, 2013), 313.

18. Drones Team, "Yemen: Reported US Covert Actions 2001–2011," Bureau of Investigative Journalism, Mar. 29, 2012, http://goo.gl/HzjOxi ("the first known US attempt to assassinate American-born cleric Anwar al Awlaki"); Bill Roggio, "US Adds Anwar al Awlaki to List of Designated Terrorists," *Long War Journal*, July 16, 2010, http://goo.gl/ls3Rkw ("the US targeted Awlaki and several other top al Qaeda leaders").

19. Dana Priest, "U.S. Military Teams, Intelligence Deeply Involved in Aiding Yemen on Strikes," *Washington* Post, Jan. 27, 2010, http://goo.gl/yBSZw.

20. Morten Stern, "How I Helped Kill Al Qaeda's Terrorist Mastermind 'The Sheikh': The Nerve-Shredding Story of an MI5 Spy Posing as a Fanatic," *Daily Mail*, June 22, 2014, http://goo.gl/mpUAuj.

21. "Corrections," *Washington Post*, Feb. 12, 2010, http://goo.gl/hyKqfe.

22. Panetta, *Worthy Fights*, 266–67.

23. U.S. diplomatic cable 10SANAA4, from Ambassador Stephen Seche, Embassy Sanaa, "General Petraeus's Meeting with Saleh on Security," Jan. 4, 2010, http://goo.gl/BrNamC.

24. White paper, "Principles to Guide the Office of Legal Counsel," Dec. 21, 2004, http://goo.gl/fIkHLP.

25. David J. Barron and Martin S. Lederman, "The Commander in Chief at the Lowest Ebb," *Harvard Law Review* 121, no. 3 (2008): 689, 941.

26. See, for example, Dawn Johnsen, "Outrage at the Latest OLC Torture Memo," *Slate*, Apr. 3, 2008, http://goo.gl/x3PGUf; Dawn Johnsen, "Restoring Our Nation's Honor," *Slate*, Mar. 18, 2008, http://goo.gl/o543iF.

27. Johnsen withdrew her nomination in April 2010. In retrospect, the key moment had come during the Senate's August 2009 break, when Obama used his recess appointment powers to fill several still-pending vacancies but chose not to appoint Johnsen as part of that group. When she withdrew, I asked a White House official why he had not done so, and was told that such a step would have undermined the effort to restore a sense that the Office of Legal Counsel worked above the partisan fray. Charlie Savage, "Obama Nominee to Legal Office Withdraws," *New York Times*, April 10, 2010, http://goo.gl/QAtOXu.

28. See, for example, Elizabeth A. Bazen, "Assassination Ban and E.O. 12333: A Brief Summary," Congressional Research Service report order code RS21037, updated Jan. 4, 2002, http://goo.gl/sWmhua.

29. Report of the National Commission on Terrorist Attacks Upon the United States ("The 9/11 Commission Report"), July 22, 2004, 132, http://goo.gl/i6KLZ.

30. Bob Woodward, "CIA Told to Do 'Whatever Necessary' to Kill Bin Laden," *Washington Post*, Oct. 21, 2001, http://goo.gl/tNAdFC.

31. John Rizzo, *Company Man: Thirty Years of Controversy and Crisis in the CIA* (New York: Scribner, 2013), 173. See also Bob Woodward, *Bush at War* (New York: Simon and Schuster, 2003), 76.

32. *NYT v. U.S. Dep't of Justice*, "Brief for Defendants-Appellees," No. 14-4432, 2nd Cir., Apr. 2, 2015, http://goo.gl/hHicJa.

33. *Aulaqi v. Obama*, D.D.C., No. 10-1469, "Memorandum Opinion," Dec. 7, 2010, http://goo.gl/DphflR.

34. Elliot Ackerman, "Assassination and the American Language," *New Yorker* online, Nov. 20, 2014, http://goo.gl/sWZfcM.
35. *Hamdi v. Rumsfeld*, 542 U.S. 507 (2004). Still, in her plurality opinion, Justice O'Connor also held that the detainee was entitled to some kind of a hearing before a neutral arbiter to review the evidence that he was a part of the enemy force in order to make sure the government was not imprisoning him on the basis of mistaken identity; al-Awlaki—who was, of course, not in custody—would receive no such hearing.
36. *Mathews v. Eldridge*, 424 U.S. 319 (1976).
37. *Tennessee v. Garner*, 471 U.S. 1 (1985).
38. *Scott v. Harris*, 550 U.S. 372 (2007).
39. Harold Hongju Koh, "Can the President Be Torturer in Chief?," *Indiana Law Journal* 81 (2006): issue 4, article 2, http://goo.gl/F0D6f0.
40. There is an additional complexity. The United States has taken the position that members of al-Qaeda who are found on a hot battlefield or in a place where their arrest is infeasible can be targeted, as a legal matter, at any time. But the international legal framework for targeting people who belong to a non-state-armed group involved in an armed conflict is not well defined. Some international law scholars and foreign governments disagree with the proposition that an al-Qaeda fighter should be treated like a soldier in a nation-state army who can always be targeted based on his status. Instead, they think he should be considered a civilian, meaning that he can be targeted only when he is directly participating in hostilities. Going down that road raises additional questions whose answers are not well developed, like what functions count as taking direct part in hostilities, how long the period of targetability lasts, and whether some terrorists' participation is nevertheless so sustained that they can still be targeted at any time.
41. Bill Roggio and Bob Barry, "Charting the Data for US Air Strikes in Yemen, 2002–2015," *Long War Journal*, http://goo.gl/9hpMZE.
42. Bill Roggio, "Charting the Data for US Air Strikes in Pakistan, 2002–2015," *Long War Journal*, http://goo.gl/Wp0eK0.
43. Special Rapporteur on extrajudicial, summary or arbitrary executions, Interim Report, Aug. 23, 2010, http://goo.gl/yQxwm8.
44. William McGurn, "The Contradictions of Harold Koh," *Wall Street Journal*, Oct. 18, 2011, http://goo.gl/nIhLFt.
45. The black-and-white legal bar against torturing prisoners is why the defenders of the Bush-Cheney interrogation program were forced to make evasive, inconsistent, and semantic arguments—for example, that the "enhanced interrogation techniques" were effective, meaning they inflicted sufficient pain and suffering to coerce committed zealots into talking against their wills, and yet were still not "torture." They could not just make the far more straightforward case that in light of 9/11, the government was justified in torturing terrorism suspects in its effort to elicit information that might save innocent lives. By contrast, the comparatively complex and subtle legal rules for targeting enemies and threats meant that any particular proposed strike might or might not meet legal standards.
46. Department of Defense transcript, "Remarks by the General Counsel of the Department of Defense on the Legal Framework for the United States' Use of Military Force Since 9/11," Apr. 10, 2015, http://goo.gl/v4e1Rb.

47. Harold Hongju Koh, remarks before the American Society of International Law, "The Obama Administration and International Law," Mar. 25, 2010, http://goo.gl/Uhxm0L.

48. See, for example, Medea Benjamin, "Help Kill an American by Drone, Get a Promotion: The Case of Lawyer David Barron," AlterNet, May 15, 2014, http://goo.gl/Lodg1n.

49. Jennifer Steinhauer, "Open to Both Sides, Homeland Security Chief Steps into Immigration Divide," New York Times, Aug. 6, 2014, http://goo.gl/Jm0Cb6.

50. Statement of No Confidence in Harold H. Koh, http://goo.gl/MDuie6.

51. "Open Letter in Support of Harold Hongju Koh," http://goo.gl/tCS8MH.

52. Elisa Massimino, "The wrong litmus test for activists," Washington Post, April 30, 2015, http://goo.gl/WnpgWG.

53. Ari Shapiro, "U.S. Drone Strikes Are Justified, Legal Adviser Says," NPR, Morning Edition, Mar. 26, 2010, http://goo.gl/PveKsE.

54. John Brennan, remarks at Harvard Law School–Brookings Institution, "Strengthening Our Security by Adhering to Our Values and Laws," Sept. 16, 2011, http://goo.gl/jwOjYe.

55. Department of Justice white paper, "Lawfulness of a Lethal Operation Directed Against a U.S. Citizen Who Is a Senior Operational Leader of Al-Oa'ida or an Associated Force," Nov. 8, 2011, http://goo.gl/QhNMXC.

56. Naz K. Modirzadeh, "Folk International Law: 9/11 Lawyering and the Transformation of the Law of Armed Conflict to Human Rights Policy and Human Rights Law to War Governance," Harvard National Security Journal 5, no. 1 (2014): 225–304, http://goo.gl/dSKWgf.

57. Brennan, "Strengthening Our Security by Adhering to Our Values and Laws."

58. Glenn Greenwald, "Confirmed: Obama Authorizes Assassination of U.S. Citizen," Salon, Apr. 7, 2010, http://goo.gl/fkizQa.

59. Kevin Jon Heller, "Let's Call Killing al-Awlaki What It Is — Murder," Opinio Juris, Apr. 8, 2010, http://goo.gl/4WvBN1.

60. U.S. v. White, 51 F. Supp. 2d 1008 (E.D. Calif. 1997), http://goo.gl/KL3Vfr.

61. See, for example, Kevin Jon Heller, "Let's Call Killing al-Awlaki What It Still Is — Murder," Opinio Juris, June 23, 2014, http://goo.gl/iXFtxw; but see Deborah Pearlstein, "OLC Memo Redux — the Bigger Picture," Opinio Juris, June 25, 2014, http://goo.gl/Ugl yHF.

62. Mark Mazzetti and Robert F. Worth, "U.S. Sees Complexity of Bombs as Link to Al Qaeda," New York Times, Oct. 31, 2010, http://goo.gl/eBp1Dm.

63. "Awlaki Supports Attempted Plane Bombing," SITE Intelligence Group, Feb. 3, 2010, http://goo.gl/InUcrA.

64. Eric Schmitt and David E. Sanger, "Pakistan Shift Could Curtail Drone Strikes," New York Times, Feb. 22, 2008, http://goo.gl/z2YN0l.

65. David S. Cloud, "CIA Drones Have Broader List of Targets," Los Angeles Times, May 6, 2010, http://goo.gl/xrkQNH.

66. Kathy Gannon, Kimberly Dozier, and Sebastian Abbot, "Timing of US Drone Strike Questioned," Associated Press, Aug. 2, 2011, http://goo.gl/xsi8wk.

67. Salman Masood and Pir Zubair Shah, "C.I.A. Drones Kill Civilians in Pakistan," New York Times, Mar. 13, 2011, http://goo.gl/26MFP8.

68. Adam Entous, Siobhan Gorman, and Julian E. Barnes, "U.S. Tightens Drone Rules," Wall Street Journal, Nov. 4, 2011, http://goo.gl/jGUwoM.

69. Greg Miller, "White House Approves Broader Yemen Drone Campaign," *Washington Post*, Apr. 25, 2012, http://goo.gl/Nkxfm.

70. Jo Becker and Scott Shane, "Secret 'Kill List' Proves a Test of Obama's Principles and Will," *New York Times*, May 29, 2012, http://goo.gl/o89cHV.

71. Greg Miller, "Taliban leader Omar's tale reflects clashing agendas," *Washington Post*, July 30, 2015, https://goo.gl/W0JxYq.

72. In 2015, the veteran investigative journalist Seymour Hersh, who has made many important contributions over his long career, published a sensational article in the *London Review of Books* alleging that nearly everything we understood about the much-scrutinized bin Laden hunt and raid was a lie, covering up a massive, previously airtight conspiracy. His source was "a retired senior intelligence official." Numerous other investigative journalists were unable to corroborate what Hersh's source had told him, and a consensus emerged that he had been bamboozled. I share that assessment for two reasons beyond the various problems with the article that were widely dissected at the time. First, in researching the previously unreported legal-deliberations dimension to the operation, I talked separately and on multiple occasions to more than half a dozen people with knowledge of the pre-raid intelligence and the planning for the operation, comparing and cross-referencing their accounts. Second, there are scattered references to the hunt, raid, and aftermath in CIA records referenced by the Senate Intelligence Committee in their torture report and in NSA documents leaked by Edward Snowden. My interviews with my own sources and all the scattered references in those two sets of internal intelligence community documents dovetailed with the consensus history and clashed with the revisionist narrative offered by Hersh's source. Seymour Hersh, "The Killing of Osama bin Laden," *London Review of Books*, May 21, 2015, http://goo.gl/8bZ3XQ; see also Senate Select Committee on Intelligence, "Committee Study of the Central Intelligence Agency's Detention and Interrogation Program" ("Senate CIA Torture Report"), released Dec. 3, 2014, 134–39, 342–51, and especially 381 (footnote 2147), http://goo.gl/wiy1F9; and "Snowden-leaked Documents Referring to the Bin Laden Operation," a set of various internal NSA documents drawn from a larger group originally published individually by the *Intercept* that I compiled and reposted with annotations on Document Cloud at https://goo.gl/ktpN1f.

73. Panetta, *Worthy Fights*, 311.

74. Nicholas Schmidle, "Getting Bin Laden," *New Yorker*, Aug. 8, 2011, http://goo.gl/YlIUB7.

75. Mark Bowden, "The Hunt for 'Geronimo,'" *Vanity Fair*, Nov. 2012, http://goo.gl/Tvbn9b.

76. Ashley S. Deeks, "'Unwilling or Unable': Toward a Normative Framework for Extraterritorial Self-Defense," 52 VA. J. INT'L L. 483 (2012), http://goo.gl/7PXpli.

77. That attitude may be shifting. When the United States first bombed the Islamic State, also known as ISIS or ISIL, in rebel-controlled Syrian territory, United Nations Secretary-General Ban Ki-moon reacted in a way that suggested support for the notion that it was lawful despite a lack of expressed consent by Syria's government: "I am aware that today's strikes were not carried out at the direct request of the Syrian Government, but I note that the Government was informed beforehand. I also note that the strikes took place in areas no longer under the effective control of that Government. I think it is undeniable — and the subject of broad international consensus — that these extremist groups pose an immediate threat to international

peace and security." United Nations transcript, "Climate Change Summit Not about Talk, but Action," Sept. 23, 2014, http://goo.gl/VI2gg4.

78. Senate Select Committee on Intelligence, "Questions for the Record: Caroline D. Krass," undated, http://goo.gl/Vy5kSZ.

79. See, for example, "As Many as 16 Lawmakers Briefed on bin Laden Operation, Biden Says," *CQ Today*, May 4, 2011, http://goo.gl/NyUQEz. In his memoir, Panetta recounts having unilaterally told the chairs and ranking members of the intelligence and defense appropriations committees, as well as congressional leaders, about the suspicious Abbottabad compound in December 2010 and then having told the new chairman of the House Intelligence Committee, Mike Rogers, and his chief of staff about it in early 2011. This was before the raid was planned and was an earlier example of his propensity to tell Congress things without White House permission. "When the White House learned of those [earlier] conversations, it was incensed," he wrote. Panetta, *Worthy Fights*, 298.

80. Jane Perlez and David Rohde, "Pakistan Pushes Back Against U.S. Criticism on Bin Laden," *New York Times*, May 3, 2011, http://goo.gl/zUDt1q.

81. Panetta, *Worthy Fights*, 321–22.

82. Bowden, "The Hunt for 'Geronimo.'"

83. White House transcript, press briefing, May 2, 2011, http://goo.gl/hZaObV.

84. Mark Owen and Kevin Maurer, *No Easy Day: The Firsthand Account of the Mission that Killed Osama Bin Laden* (New York: Penguin, 2012), 177.

85. Phil Bronstein, "The Man Who Killed Bin Laden…Is Screwed," *Esquire*, Feb. 11, 2013, http://goo.gl/8rkcG; see also, Joby Warrick, "Ex-SEAL Robert O'Neill Reveals Himself As Shooter Who Killed Osama bin Laden," *Washington Post*, Nov. 6, 2014, http://goo.gl/6q4qQx.

86. See, for example, Nicholas Kulish, Christopher Drew, and Sean D. Naylor, "Another Ex-Commando Says He Shot Bin Laden," *New York Times*, Nov. 6, 2014, http://goo.gl/6CwjDo.

87. Owen and Maurer, *No Easy Day*, 235–36.

88. Geneva Convention I of 1949, Article 17.

89. See, for example, "Rules About Burial of the Dead Body," Al-Islam.org, http://goo.gl/966axC.

90. Panetta, *Worthy Fights*, 326.

91. Mohammed Al-Asaadi and Michael Slackman, "Kidnapped U.S. Tourists Are Released in Yemen," *New York Times*, May 26, 2010, http://goo.gl/oHA7bD.

92. Testimony of Farea Al-Muslimi, Senate Judiciary Subcommittee on the Constitution, Civil Rights, and Human Rights, Apr. 23, 2013, http://goo.gl/hzRYVM.

93. See, for example, Margaret Coker, Adam Entous, and Julian E. Barnes, "Drone Targets Yemeni Cleric," *Wall Street Journal*, May 7, 2011, http://goo.gl/xD5F4w; Mazzetti, *The Way of the Knife: The CIA, a Secret Army, and a War at the Ends of the Earth* (New York: Penguin, 2013), 307; Scahill, *Dirty Wars*, 454–57.

94. Harith al-Nadarî, "My Story with Sheikh Anwar Al Awlaki," *Inspire*, Issue 9, May 2012, available in various locations, including: http://goo.gl/0De9Xx.

95. Remarks by Jeh Charles Johnson, Dean's Lecture at Yale Law School, "National Security Law, Lawyers and Lawyering in the Obama Administration," Feb. 22, 2012, http://goo.gl/2gmLAo.

96. Klaidman, *Kill or Capture*, 213.

97. For another version of a reconstruction of this meeting, see ibid., 222.
98. Charlie Savage, "At White House, Weighing Limits in Terror Fight," *New York Times*, Sept. 16, 2011, http://goo.gl/vuAxi4.
99. A video of the speech, with question-and-answer period, is available at http://goo.gl/G1qJwt.
100. Mark Mazzetti, Eric Schmitt, and Robert F. Worth, "Two-Year Manhunt Led to Killing of Awlaki in Yemen," *New York Times*, Oct. 1, 2011, http://goo.gl/gtuHG.
101. Mark Mazzetti, Charlie Savage, and Scott Shane, "How a U.S. Citizen Came to Be in America's Cross Hairs," *New York Times*, Mar. 10, 2012, http://goo.gl/nPZwWA.
102. "Awlaki Family Gives Statement on Killing of Anwar and His Son," SITE Intelligence Group, Oct. 19, 2011, http://goo.gl/4NBabz.
103. "Yemeni Journalist Reports on Forthcoming Awlaki Video," SITE Intelligence Group, Dec. 7, 2011, translating article by the Yemeni journalist Abdul Razzaq al-Jamal, "The New Environment in Abyan Province in which the State has Been Absent and al-Qaeda has Been Present," that had been posted on the website of *al-Wasat*, a Yemeni newspaper, Dec. 7, 2011, http://goo.gl/pyauB9.
104. Press release, "Raleigh-Durham Joint Terrorism Task Force Receives FBI Director's Award," FBI, Sept. 10, 2012, http://goo.gl/LUrs85.
105. Scott Shane and Eric Schmitt, "One Drone Victim's Trail from Raleigh to Pakistan," *New York Times*, May 22, 2013, http://goo.gl/0LgDQ8.
106. Charlie Savage, "In G.O.P. Field, Broad View of Presidential Power Prevails," *New York Times*, Dec. 29, 2011, http://goo.gl/8aKSI.
107. Daniel Klaidman, "Avril Haines, the Least Likely Spy," *Newsweek*, June 26, 2013, http://goo.gl/9osz6Q.
108. Mark Mazzetti and Robert W. Worth, "Yemen Deaths Test Claims of New Drone Policy," *New York Times*, Dec. 21, 2013, http://goo.gl/R6AuSO; Amrit Singh, "Death by Drone: Civilian Harm Caused by U.S. Targeted Killings in Yemen," Open Society Justice Initiative, Apr. 13, 2015, http://goo.gl/gaZcVQ.
109. Mark Mazzetti and Matt Apuzzo, "Deep Support in Washington for C.I.A.'s Drone Missions," *New York Times*, April 25, 2015, http://goo.gl/6jzLGO.
110. Mark Mazzetti and Eric Schmitt, "Terrorism Case Renews Debate Over Drone Hits," *New York Times*, Apr. 13, 2015, http://goo.gl/Xiz3Gw; see also Mark Mazzetti and Eric Schmitt, "U.S. Militant, Hidden, Spurs Drone Debate," *New York Times*, Feb. 28, 2014, http://goo.gl/AATScB.
111. Mazzetti and Schmitt, "Terrorism Case Renews Debate Over Drone Hits."
112. Scott Shane, "Drone Strikes in Yemen Said to Set a Dangerous Precedent," *New York Times*, Apr. 13, 2015, http://goo.gl/r2ZtQZ.
113. White House transcript, "Statement by the President on the Deaths of Warren Weinstein and Giovanni Lo Porto," Apr. 23, 2015, http://goo.gl/6NTz4j.
114. Eli Lake and Josh Rogin, "How the U.S. Tracked Down Al-Qaeda's Yemen Chief," *Bloomberg View*, June 16, 2015, http://goo.gl/kk526Q.
115. Greg Miller, "CIA didn't know strike would hit al-Qaeda leader," *Washington Post*, June 17, 2015, http://goo.gl/RCUSut.
116. Eric Schmitt, "U.S. Airstrike in Libya Targets Planner of 2013 Algeria Attack," *New York Times*, June 15, 2015, http://goo.gl/gGcGNw.
117. Charlie Savage, "Relatives Sue Officials Over U.S. Citizens Killed by Drone Strikes in Yemen," *New York Times*, July 19, 2012, http://goo.gl/8TQBBd.

118. Charlie Savage, "Judge Dismisses Suit Against Administration Officials over Drone Strikes," *New York Times*, Apr. 5, 2014, http://goo.gl/zvo1GW.

119. Charlie Savage, "Relatives of Victims of Drone Strikes Drop Appeal," *New York Times*, June 4, 2014, http://goo.gl/uaT6be.

Chapter Seven: Ratchet (Captives 2010–2011)

1. James Rosen, "Graham Seeks to Block Funding for Civilian Terror Trials," McClatchy, Feb. 1, 2010, http://goo.gl/u85cXx.

2. Brennan, "Strengthening Our Security by Adhering to Our Values and Laws."

3. *INS v. Chadha*, 462 U.S. 919 (1983).

4. *Al-Bihani v. Obama*, 590 F.3d 866 (D.C. Cir. 2010), http://goo.gl/jvxgMG.

5. Charlie Savage, "Obama Team Is Divided on Anti-Terror Tactics," *New York Times*, Mar. 29, 2010, http://goo.gl/PX0JD9.

6. Charlie Savage, "Appeals Court Backs Away from War Powers Ruling," *New York Times*, Sept. 1, 2010, http://goo.gl/o6VKG0.

7. Charlie Savage, "U.S. Frees Last of the Chinese Uighur Detainees from Guantánamo Bay," *New York Times*, Jan. 1, 2014, http://goo.gl/FHQkx0.

8. *Al Maqaleh v. Gates*, 605 F. 3d 84 (D.C. Cir. 2010); see also Charlie Savage, "Detainees Barred from Access to U.S. Courts," *New York Times*, May 21, 2010, http://goo.gl/HgHvsh.

9. Stephen I. Vladeck, "The Unreviewable Executive: Kiyemba, Maqaleh, and the Obama Administration," 26 Const. Commentary 603, Summer 2010, http://goo.gl/ki4j9S.

10. Charlie Savage, "Despair Drives Guantánamo Detainees to Revolt," *New York Times*, Apr. 24, 2013, http://goo.gl/GgMs9.

11. Klaidman, *Kill or Capture*, 191.

12. Charlie Savage, "Holder Backs a Miranda Limit for Terror Suspects," *New York Times*, May 10, 2010, http://goo.gl/RW7WDU.

13. Charlie Savage, "Proposal Would Delay Hearings in Terror Cases," *New York Times*, May 15, 2010, http://goo.gl/MBpX.

14. FBI memo, "Custodial Interrogation for Public Safety and Intelligence-Gathering Purposes of Operational Terrorists Inside the United States," Oct. 21, 2010, http://goo.gl/bASKT.

15. Charlie Savage, "Delayed Miranda Warning Ordered for Terror Suspects," *New York Times*, Mar. 25, 2011, http://goo.gl/PhovpL.

16. Charlie Savage and Carl Hulse, "Bill Targets Citizenship of Terrorists' Allies," *New York Times*, May 7, 2010, http://goo.gl/hc1Eqx.

17. Charlie Savage, "Closing Guantánamo Fades as a Priority," *New York Times*, June 26, 2010, http://goo.gl/sBu6Om.

18. See, for example, Charlie Savage, "House Panel Rejects a Plan to Shift Detainees to Illinois," *New York Times*, May 10, 2010, http://goo.gl/go4zeC.

19. Letter from General Jones to the House Armed Services Committee, May 26, 2010, http://goo.gl/14fLHK.

20. Savage, "Closing Guantánamo Fades as a Priority."

21. Ibid.

22. *Abdah v. Obama*, 717 F. Supp. 2d 21 (D.D.C. 2010), May 26, 2010, http://goo.gl/uKrCgl.

23. Charlie Savage, "Rulings Raise Doubts on Policy on Transfer of Yemenis," *New York Times*, July 9, 2010, http://goo.gl/P4J9RC; Defense Department news release, "Detainee Transfer Announced," July 13, 2010, http://goo.gl/zilJW2.

24. *Al Adahi v. Obama*, 13 F.3d 1102 (D.C. Cir. 2010), http://goo.gl/SMtDHD.

25. Transcript, Hearing Before the Senate Select Intelligence Committee, "Nomination of Lieutenant General James Clapper, Jr., USAF, Ret., to Be Director of National Intelligence," July 20, 2010, http://goo.gl/Q0nG9j.

26. Office of the Director of National Intelligence, "Summary of the Reengagement of Detainees Formerly Held at Guantánamo Bay, Cuba," Oct. 2010, http://goo.gl/TSaEoI.

27. See, for example, leaked memorandum from Buzby to commander, United States Southern Command, re "Recommendation for Continued Detention Under DoD Control (CD) for Guantanamo Detainee, ISN US9YM-000686DP," April 29, 2008, https://goo.gl/octFsb.

28. Leaked memorandum from Hood to commander, United States Southern Command, re "Recommendation to Transfer to the Control of Another Country for Continued Detention (TRCD) for Guantanamo Detainee, ISN: US9&M-000681," Sept. 3, 2004, https://goo.gl/QTLDxc.

29. Although I learned additional details about this meeting, it was first reported in Klaidman, *Kill or Capture*, 194–95.

30. Carol Rosenberg, "On First Day of Khadr's Guantánamo Trial, Attorney Faints," *Miami Herald*, Aug. 12, 2010, http://goo.gl/0kodLz.

31. Charlie Savage, "U.S. Wary of Example Set by Tribunal Case," *New York Times*, Aug. 28, 2010, http://goo.gl/C2dl.

32. Charlie Savage, "Deal Averts Trial in Disputed Guantánamo Case," *New York Times*, Oct. 26, 2010, http://goo.gl/hQA6Zb.

33. Charlie Savage, "Delays Keep Former Qaeda Child Soldier at Guantánamo, Despite Plea Deal," *New York Times*, Mar. 25, 2012, http://goo.gl/MUl8b3.

34. Buzby, "Recommendation for Continued Detention Under DoD Control (CD) for Guantanamo Detainee, ISN US9YM-000686DP."

35. Bertrand Slézak, "Maintenant, c'est terminé," *Le Quotidien*, Sept. 29, 2010.

36. The Obama lawyers kicked around one possible escape to buy more time: Don't use the disputed evidence and concede that the man was not detainable under the March 13 Standard but ask Kennedy to stay his release order for six or nine months because releasing him to Yemen would create a national security threat. That would be novel: a claim that Obama had the legal power to detain someone without trial based on his future dangerousness, not his past associations. But Justice Department litigators would need to give Kennedy something more concrete and individualized about Alhag than mere allegations that the detainee seemed dangerous. Moreover, earlier that year, in a secret seven-page memo entitled "Habeas Litigation Involving Yemeni Detainees," the existence of which has never been reported, the Office of Legal Counsel had written that "it might be very difficult to persuade the court" to grant the presidency the authority to keep holding someone that the same court had already "found is no longer subject to lawful detention because the petitioner is not part of an enemy's fighting forces."

37. *Latif v. Obama*, 677 F.3d 1175 (D.C. Cir. 2012), http://goo.gl/vOvPUc.

38. Senate CIA Torture Report, 419.

39. Opinion, *United States v. Ghailani*, Oct. 6, 2010, 3, http://goo.gl/4SxNtt.

40. Ibid., footnote 182.

41. Adam Klasfeld, "Ghailani Jurors Question Burden of Proof in Terrorism Trial," *Courthouse News*, Nov. 17, 2010, http://goo.gl/5fnT8q.

42. That said, there is also some evidence that the panels of military officers who serve as a jury in a military commission panel can be *more* skeptical of prosecutors' claims in terrorism cases than civilian juries. In 2008, Salim Hamdan, a former driver and bodyguard for Osama bin Laden, received the first trial before a military commission at Guantánamo. As in the Ghailani case, a military judge excluded certain evidence as tainted by coercion. The commission reached a mixed verdict, convicting Hamdan only of providing material support for terrorism. Prosecutors urged a sentence of thirty years to life, but the panel instead imposed just sixty-six months — with sixty-one months credit for time already served. Hamdan was home in Yemen before the end of the year. As a kicker, an appeals court later vacated his conviction because material support is not a war crime and so should not have been prosecuted before a military commission.

43. *U.S. v. Ghailani*, 733 F.3d 29 (2d Cir. 2013), Oct. 24, 2013, http://goo.gl/B6erl4.

44. Charlie Savage, "Holder Denounces a Bill to Ban Detainee Transfers," *New York Times*, Dec. 10, 2010, http://goo.gl/kO9akx.

45. Charlie Savage, "Obama May Bypass Guantánamo Rules, Aides Say," *New York Times*, Jan. 4, 2011, http://goo.gl/K7XCL.

46. White House press release, Statement by the President on HR 6523, Jan. 7, 2011, http://goo.gl/79beu.

47. Haines had previously worked for Koh at the State Department and moved to the White House when DeRosa's first deputy, Caroline Krass, returned to the Justice Department in early 2011 as the number-two leader, and acting head, of the Office of Legal Counsel.

48. Statement by President Barack Obama, "New Actions on Guantánamo Bay and Detainee Policy," Mar. 7, 2011, http://goo.gl/e7UZr4.

49. A fact sheet released by the White House at the same time also announced that the Obama administration supported accepting additional legal obligations in international law about the treatment of wartime detainees "because of the vital importance of the rule of law to the effectiveness and legitimacy of our national security policy."

    This addressed two treaties written in the 1970s to expand the Geneva Conventions, so-called additional protocols, which the United States had never ratified. One regulated wars against nonstate groups; Reagan had unsuccessfully asked the Senate to approve it in 1987, an effort that Obama was now reviving. (It wouldn't happen.) The other expanded rules for regular wars between two nations. The United States had long opposed some parts of it, and Obama did not ask the Senate to ratify it, but he said that the United States would now "choose out of a sense of legal obligation" to obey the part of it that expanded humane treatment rules for wartime prisoners. The fact sheet noted that "an extensive interagency review" had concluded that current American military practices and policies were already consistent with that standard, so they would require no changes.

    For all its modesty, this new international human rights obligation was the only one the Obama administration accepted in its first term. White House press release, "FACT SHEET: NEW ACTIONS ON GUANTÁNAMO AND DETAINEE POLICY," Mar. 7, 2011, http://goo.gl/APmn26.

50. Scott Shane and Mark Landler, "Obama Clears Way for Guantánamo Trials," *New York Times*, Mar. 8, 2011, http://goo.gl/05bDu1.
51. Finn and Kornblut, "Guantánamo Bay: How the White House Lost the Fight to Close It."
52. Charlie Savage, "In a Reversal, Military Trials for 9/11 Cases," *New York Times*, Apr. 5, 2011, http://goo.gl/oX8ic.
53. John Yoo, contribution to "Bin Laden, No More: America's Most Wanted Meets His Maker; What's the Significance of His Death? An NRO Symposium," *National Review Online*, May 2, 2011, http://goo.gl/4nzWvJ.
54. Michael Mukasey, "The Waterboarding Trail to bin Laden," *Wall Street Journal*, May 6, 2011, http://goo.gl/KXSiin.
55. Scott Shane and Charlie Savage, "Bin Laden Raid Revives Debate on Value of Torture," *New York Times*, May 3, 2011, http://goo.gl/sr0Zzk.
56. Charlie Savage and James Risen, "Senate Report Rejects Claim on Hunt for Bin Laden," *New York Times*, Dec. 10, 2014, http://goo.gl/sc0GTd; Senate CIA Torture Report, 134–39, 342–51, and 381 (footnote 2147).
57. Mark Boal, "Zero Dark Thirty: An Original Screenplay," Oct. 3, 2011, 20–21, http://goo.gl/6hXOaH.
58. Ibid., 31.
59. Eric Lichtblau and Eric Schmitt, "U.S. Widens Inquiries into 2 Jail Deaths," *New York Times*, July 1, 2011, http://goo.gl/9TjqmO.
60. Transcript, Senate Armed Services Committee hearing, June 28, 2011.
61. Charlie Savage, "Attorney General and Senator Clash on Where to Try Terror Suspects," *New York Times*, June 17, 2011, http://goo.gl/4a7lvK.
62. Department of Justice press release, "Former Iraqi Terrorists Living in Kentucky Sentenced for Terrorist Activities," Jan. 29, 2013, http://goo.gl/Ykao3D.
63. *US v. Warsame*, 11 crim 559, S.D.N.Y., indictment, April 2011, http://goo.gl/0q5sus.
64. Charlie Savage, "U.S. Tests New Approach to Terrorism Cases on Somali Suspect," *New York Times*, July 7, 2011, http://goo.gl/5xWTA7.
65. "Terrorism and the Law," *New York Times*, July 17, 2011, http://goo.gl/EDNo1I.
66. Three years later, in 2014, Obama appointed Malinowski as assistant secretary of state for democracy, human rights, and labor.
67. Benjamin Weiser, "Terrorist Has Cooperated with U.S. Since Secret Guilty Plea in 2011, Papers Show," *New York Times*, Mar. 26, 2013, http://goo.gl/tcmFpO.
68. Opinion and Order Denying Defendant's Motion to Suppress Statements Made at the University of Michigan Hospital, *United States v. Abdulmutallab*, Sept. 16, 2011, http://goo.gl/RsSaBq.
69. Brennan, "Strengthening Our Security by Adhering to Our Values and Laws."

Chapter Eight: The Leak Crackdown

1. Department of Justice press release, "Former NSA Senior Executive Charged with Illegally Retaining Classified Information, Obstructing Justice and Making False Statements," Apr. 15, 2010, http://goo.gl/9fvhgl; see also *U.S. v. Drake*, D. Md., Indictment, Apr. 14, 2010, http://goo.gl/7o4FkS.
2. *U.S.v. Sterling*, E.D.Va., "Government's Motion in Limine to Admit Certain Statements of James Risen, Dr. Condoleezza Rice, and Human Asset No. 1," Oct. 4, 2011, http://goo.gl/7Qau6s; *In re: Grand Jury Subpoena to James Risen*, E.D. Va., "Memorandum Opinion," Nov. 30, 2010, http://goo.gl/w9NStg.

3. James Risen, "Fired by C.I.A., He Says Agency Practiced Bias," *New York Times,* Mar. 2, 2002, http://goo.gl/xqf6hZ.

4. Philip Shenon, "Times Reporter Subpoenaed Over Source for Book," *New York Times,* Feb. 1, 2008, http://goo.gl/Q8Ljvx.

5. Letter from William Binney et al. to Department of Defense Office of Inspector General, Sept. 4, 2002, https://goo.gl/YpiJ8P.

6. Office of the Inspector General Department of Defense, "Requirements for the TRAIL-BLAZER and THINTHREAD Systems," Dec. 15, 2004. https://goo.gl/wnwpqT.

7. Jane Mayer, "The Secret Sharer," *New Yorker,* May 23, 2011, http://goo.gl/xRYJVx.

8. Siobhan Gorman, "NSA Killed System That Sifted Phone Data Legally," *Baltimore Sun,* May 18, 2006.

9. James Risen, *Pay Any Price: Greed, Power, and Endless War* (New York: Houghton Mifflin Harcourt, 2014), 230–268.

10. Department of Defense Inspector General, "Mr. Thomas A. Drake, Whistleblower Reprisal Investigation," Report on Case No. 20121205-001567, Mar. 19, 2014, Department of Defense Inspector General, http://goo.gl/A48ANv.

11. Mayer, "The Secret Sharer."

12. Case Nos. 07-3839 and 07-3840, D.Md., Affidavit in Support of Search Warrant Application, Nov. 21, 2007, and Dec. 7, 2007, https://goo.gl/VSJ1sZ.

13. For example: "None of them were our sources" (Jim Risen), *The Daily Show with Jon Stewart,* Comedy Central, Nov. 6, 2014, http://goo.gl/iJMSvI.

14. Obama-Biden Campaign website, "Ethics Agenda," http://goo.gl/hJ6Al6.

15. Michael Isikoff, "The Whistleblower Who Exposed Warrantless Wiretaps," *Newsweek,* Dec. 12, 2008, http://goo.gl/5TEx0S.

16. Eric Lichtblau, *Bush's Law: The Remaking of American Justice* (New York: Pantheon, 2008), 191.

17. This conversation was off the record at the time. Sussmann gave me permission to recount the anecdote for this book. As noted, he emphasized that he would never make an unauthorized disclosure of classified information under any circumstances, although he understood that I saw his reluctance in this episode through the lens of the leak crackdown.

18. Scott Shane and Charlie Savage, "Administration Took Accidental Path to Setting Record for Leak Cases," *New York Times,* June 20, 2012, http://goo.gl/2S2BmN.

19. Charlie Savage, "Deal in Senate on Protecting News Sources," *New York Times,* Oct. 31, 2009, http://goo.gl/56Hjqx.

20. Sharon LaFraniere, "Math Behind Leak Crackdown: 153 Cases, 4 Years, 0 Indictments," *New York Times,* July 21, 2013, http://goo.gl/uzOdH7.

21. The Official Secrets Act has three categories of potential defendants, and the damage element works differently for each. For intelligence officers accused of leak information, there is no need for prosecutors to show that the information was harmful. For nonintelligence Crown servants, there is a defense if they did not know or have a reason to believe that the information would be damaging. For journalists, prosecutors have to prove that the information was actually damaging.

22. Drake, though accused of leaking to the *Baltimore Sun,* was charged under an Espionage Act provision dealing with unauthorized retention of secrets, not disclosure of them. In 2012, the Justice Department brought the same charge against James Hitselberger, a Navy contract linguist who was accused of taking classified documents to

his living quarters, some of which were discovered within a collection of rare documents he had donated to the archives in the Hoover Institution at Stanford University. I am not including Hitselberger's case in this chapter because it falls too far outside the (in places hazy) category of someone who makes an unauthorized disclosure to the press for the purpose of bringing information to public light. But Hitselberger also illustrates the use of the Espionage Act to punish nonespionage-related actions, as well as, arguably, the punishment of lower-level officials for actions that higher-level officials seem to get away with.

23. *U.S. v. Russo*, No. 9373-(WMB)-CD (C.D. Calif. filed Dec. 29, 1971), *dismissed* (C.D. Calif., May 11, 1973).

24. *U.S. v. Morison*, 604 F. Supp. 655 (D. Md.), *appeal dismissed*, 744 F.2d 1156 (4th Cir. 1988).

25. Letter from Senator Daniel Patrick Moynihan to President Bill Clinton, Sept. 29, 1998, http://goo.gl/rqaXnu.

26. White House press release, statement by the president, Nov. 4, 2000, http://goo.gl/zqUPWw.

27. *U.S. v. Franklin*, E.D. Va., "Criminal complaint," May 3, 2005, http://goo.gl/RfWIKL.

28. Neil A. Lewis and David Johnston, "U.S. to Drop Spy Case Against Pro-Israel Lobbyists," *New York Times*, May 2, 2009, http://goo.gl/GRYiAR.

29. *U.S. v. Franklin*, E.D. Va., motions hearing transcript, June 11, 2009, http://goo.gl/kAWpgH.

30. See, for example, James Bennet, "Palestinian Urges Defiance; Plan to Grab Arafat Reported," *New York Times*, Oct. 4, 1992, http://goo.gl/tL6jxB.

31. Department of Justice news release, "Former FBI Contract Linguist Pleads Guilty to Leaking Classified Information to Blogger," Dec. 17, 2009, http://goo.gl/P2LbGs.

32. *U.S. v. Leibowitz*, D. Md., sentencing hearing transcript, May 24, 2010.

33. Scott Shane, "Leak Offers Look at Efforts by U.S. to Spy on Israel," *New York Times*, Sept. 5, 2011, http://www.nytimes.com/2011/09/06/us/06leak.html.

34. Richard Silverstein, "AIPAC's Hidden Persuaders," *Guardian*, May 15, 2009, http://goo.gl/nsywip.

35. Complicating matters, Leibowitz, after his release from prison, accused Silverstein of lying. When I spoke to him in April 2014, Leibowitz said the materials he had leaked had something to do with surveillance of Americans and that Silverstein was not the blogger. I spoke to a former law enforcement official about the case as well as to the *Guardian* editor who had worked with Silverstein, and their recollections dovetailed with Silverstein's account. I am not aware of any domestic surveillance revelations that appeared on a blog in the spring of 2009, and I concluded that Leibowitz was likely lying to me.

   In August 2015, as this book was about to go to the printer, Leibowitz reached out to me. He retracted what he had said about surveillance, telling me instead about his anti-war motivation. Leibowitz said that he had been misleading before because he was still on supervised release, and he had agreed in the plea deal not to say what he had leaked about. He said his supervised release had since come to an end, and he had decided he could live up to his end of the deal by just not providing details about what he had leaked and to whom, without the "smokescreen" of making up a "lie about it." Shamai Leibowitz, "Edward Snowden and the Crackdown That Backfired," *The Leibowitz Blog*, June 24, 2013, via Internet Archive, http://goo.gl/UOmLEi.

36. American Bar Association 19th Annual Review of the Field of National Security Law Conference, Panel 1: Executive Update on Developments in National Security Law, Renaissance Hotel, Washington, DC, Nov. 12, 2009, http://goo.gl/6oPFPH.

37. Mayer, "The Secret Sharer."

38. In the 2007 search warrant affidavit for Drake's house, Lawless, the FBI agent, told a magistrate judge that the previous searches of the four other Thinthread proponents had found evidence that they had drafted on Microsoft Word, and shared amongst themselves, a document describing Thinthread, based on their memories of it. (This was apparently in connection with preparing their whistleblower complaint, though he did not mention the context.) While they maintained there was nothing classified in that document, the NSA said it *was* classified, so there was "probable cause" to believe the four had mishandled classified information, he said; Affidavit in Support of Search Warrant Application.

39. Scott Shane, "Former N.S.A. Official Is Charged in Leaks Case," *New York Times*, Apr. 16, 2010, http://goo.gl/qQXZk2.

40. Charlie Savage, "U.S. Subpoenas Times Reporter Over Book on C.I.A.," *New York Times*, Apr. 30, 2010, http://goo.gl/MJnmuB.

41. Ellipses in original, but I have normalized capitalization and punctuation. Kevin Poulson and Kim Zetter, "'I Can't Believe What I'm Confessing to You': The WikiLeaks Chats," *Wired*, June 10, 2010, http://goo.gl/NMFfk2.

42. News release, "15,000 previously unknown civilian deaths contained in the Iraq War Logs released by WikiLeaks," Iraq Body Count, Oct. 22, 2010, http://goo.gl/gpPnR6/.

43. Charlie Savage, "Gates Assails WikiLeaks Over Release of Reports," July 30, 2010, http://goo.gl/sKUeWN.

44. Ed Pilkington, "Bradley Manning Leak Did Not Result in Deaths by Enemy Forces, Court Hears," *Guardian*, July 31, 2013, http://goo.gl/xolBpD.

45. Elisabeth Bumiller, "Gates on Leaks, Wiki and Otherwise," *New York Times Caucus Blog*, Nov. 30, 2010, http://goo.gl/qTGqGa.

46. James Rosen, "NK's Post UN Sanctions Plans, Revealed," FoxNews.com, June 11, 2009. Fox News has deleted the post but it is available at the Internet Archive at http://goo.gl/Tm4uBS.

47. Peter Maass, "Destroyed by the Espionage Act," *Intercept*, Feb. 18, 2015, http://goo.gl/tbQDSc.

48. Scott Shane, "U.S. Pressing Its Crackdown Against Leaks," *New York Times*, June 17, 2011, http://goo.gl/ASxSvt.

49. There were a series of pretrial fights before his guilty plea. Notably, in July 2013, the judge overseeing Kim's case, Colleen Kollar-Kotelly, the former FISA Court presiding judge, issued an important ruling against him. She ruled that prosecutors did not need to show that the information he had allegedly leaked could cause even potential damage; rather, they need show only that the defendant "reasonably believed" that the information could be damaging and "willfully" communicated it. In a subtle way, this ruling—which rejected the tighter standard used in the thirty-year-old *U.S. v. Morison* trial—made it easier for prosecutors to win. Steve Aftergood, "Court Eases Prosecutors' Burden of Proof in Leak Cases," *Secrecy News*, July 29, 2013, http://goo.gl/AmSpiO.

50. Maass, "Destroyed by the Espionage Act."

51. Charlie Savage, "Ex-Contractor at State Dept. Pleads Guilty in Leak Case," *New York Times*, Feb. 8, 2014, http://goo.gl/9eRyPB.

52. It is not just defense attorneys for accused leakers who see the evolving role of the Espionage Act as problematic. Judge Ellis, who presided over the AIPAC leak case, suggested in 2006 that lawmakers needed to reform the law in light of all the changes since it was enacted, writing "the time is ripe for Congress to engage in a thorough review and revision of these provisions to ensure that they reflect both these changes, and contemporary views about the appropriate balance between our nation's security and our citizens' ability to engage in public debate about the United States' conduct in the society of nations." *U.S. v. Rosen and Weissman*, E.D.Va., "Memorandum Opinion," Aug. 9, 2006, http://goo.gl/ZfulAK.

53. News release, "Press Statement by Abbe B. Lowell," Feb. 7, 2014, http://goo.gl/gSD66a.

54. In the matter of the search of [redacted], Case 10-291-M-01, D.D.C., "Affidavit in Support of Application for Search Warrant," May 28, 2010, http://goo.gl/1NUWga.

55. Charlie Savage, "U.S. Gathered Personal Data on Times Reporter in Case Against Ex-C.I.A. Agent," *New York Times*, Feb. 25, 2011, http://goo.gl/8IayB2.

56. *U.S. v. Sterling*, E.D. Va., "Memorandum opinion, In re grand jury subpoena to Risen," Nov. 30, 2010, http://goo.gl/w9NStg.

57. Ibid.

58. While there was no federal shield law, the appeals court overseeing Brinkema's court, the Richmond-based Court of Appeals for the Fourth Circuit, had ruled that there was a qualified reporter's privilege as a matter of federal law, allowing her to invoke a balancing test and decide that in this case his testimony was not needed. She cited *LaRouche v. NBC*, 780 F.2d 1134 (4th Cir.). That case involved whether NBC had to provide outtakes of an interview with a criminal defendant that it had not broadcast. In that case, the Fourth Circuit had gone on to decide that the test tilted the other way in the matter then before it, so NBC had to turn over the materials. Brinkema's decision to quash the grand jury subpoena to Risen was novel because she concluded that the balancing test protected the journalist, and because it involved a national security matter rather than a civil lawsuit or an ordinary criminal matter. I explore the legal issues in greater detail below in connection with the subpoena requiring Risen to testify at Sterling's trial.

59. Charlie Savage, "Ex-C.I.A. Officer Named in Disclosure Indictment," *New York Times*, Jan. 7, 2011, http://goo.gl/ukSQZt.

60. *U.S. v. Sterling*, E.D. Va., "Motion for Bill of Particulars," Feb. 24, 2011, http://goo.gl/sLLuMn.

61. Charlie Savage, "Subpoena Issued to Writer in C.I.A.-Iran Leak Case," *New York Times*, May 25, 2011, http://goo.gl/O5gKkm.

62. Mayer, "The Secret Sharer."

63. "U.S. v. Whistleblower Tom Drake," *60 Minutes*, CBS News, May 22, 2011, http://goo.gl/8zkvL7.

64. *U.S. v. Drake*, sentencing hearing transcript, July 15, 2011, http://goo.gl/UnaZFS.

65. Steve Coll, "The Spy Who Said Too Much," *New Yorker*, Apr. 1, 2013, http://goo.gl/m7biW5.

66. Department of Justice news release, "Former CIA Officer John Kiriakou Charged with Disclosing Covert Officer's Identity and Other Classified Information to Journalists and Lying to CIA's Publications Review Board," Jan. 23, 2012, http://goo.gl/h5Rkdz.

67. *U.S. v. Kiriakou,* E.D. Va., Criminal complaint, Jan. 23, 2012, http://goo.gl/wvha3Y.
68. Charlie Savage, "Ex-C.I.A. Officer's Path from Terrorist Hunter to Defendant," *New York Times,* Jan. 24, 2012, http://goo.gl/iVSl3n.
69. Numbers supplied by the FBI to the Senate Judiciary Committee in 2010 provided a rare glimpse of the scale of leak referrals and investigative activity in this era. In 2005, the FBI said, there were 46 leak referrals to the Justice Department, from which 7 investigations were opened and 1 suspect was identified; in 2006, 29 referrals, 9 investigations, 5 suspects; in 2007, 55 referrals, 5 investigations, 5 suspects; in 2008, 23 referrals, 3 investigations, 1 suspect; and in 2009, 30 referrals, 2 investigations, and 2 suspects. Answers to questions submitted for the record by Robert Mueller to the Senate Judiciary Committee, April 8, 2010, http://goo.gl/87PQAf.
70. Charlie Savage, "Former C.I.A. Operative Pleads Guilty in Leak of Colleague's Name," *New York Times,* Oct. 24, 2012, http://goo.gl/x9Dtzt.
71. *U.S. v. Kiriakou,* sentencing hearing transcript, Jan. 25, 2013.
72. "Whistleblowers," CodePink.org, accessed Mar. 3, 2015, http://goo.gl/KTpp48.
73. See, for example, "Exclusive: Freed CIA Whistleblower John Kiriakou Says 'I Would Do It All Again' to Expose Torture," *Democracy Now!,* Feb. 9, 2015, http://goo.gl/dxv6hH.
74. Richard Esposito and Brian Ross, "Coming in from the Cold: CIA Spy Calls Waterboarding Necessary but Torture," ABC News, Dec. 10, 2007, http://goo.gl/Ib4wMK.
76. For example, David Johnston and James Risen, "Aides Say Memo Backed Coercion Already in Use," *New York Times,* June 27, 2004, http://goo.gl/z5CnSA.
77. Brian Stelter, "How '07 ABC Interview Tilted a Torture Debate," *New York Times,* Apr. 28, 2009, http://goo.gl/V3b8SP.
78. Transcript, *Rush Limbaugh Show,* Dec. 11, 2007, http://goo.gl/CnC5on.
79. Senate CIA Torture Report, 494.
80. Ibid., 423.
81. Coll, "The Spy Who Said Too Much."
82. See, for example, Scott Shane, "Inside a 9/11 Mastermind's Interrogation," *New York Times,* June 22, 2008, http://goo.gl/DZlEUI.
83. Matthew Miller, "Obama Is Right to Prosecute Leakers Who Are Not the Same as Whistle-Blowers," *Daily Beast,* Mar. 10, 2012, http://goo.gl/fe6fZS.
84. Charlie Savage, "U.S. Prosecutors Study WikiLeaks Prosecution," *New York Times,* Dec. 8, 2010, http://goo.gl/61s2yq.
85. Julian E. Barnes and Evan Perez, "Assange Probe Hits Snag," *Wall Street Journal,* Feb. 9, 2011, http://goo.gl/TPBUpd.
86. Charlie Savage, "U.S. Tries to Build Case for Conspiracy by WikiLeaks," *New York Times,* Dec. 16, 2010, http://goo.gl/4szAnX.
87. *Electronic Privacy Information Center v. Department of Justice,* D.D.C., "Memorandum opinion," Mar. 4, 2015, http://goo.gl/42rJcl.
88. *U.S. v. Manning,* Additional Charge Sheet, Mar. 1, 2011, http://goo.gl/TmygI6.
89. Yochai Benkler, "The Dangerous Logic of the Bradley Manning Case," *New Republic,* Mar. 1, 2013, http://goo.gl/lxkjGE.
90. Charlie Savage and Emmarie Huetteman, "Manning Sentenced to 35 Years for a Pivotal Leak of U.S. Files," *New York Times,* Aug. 22, 2013, http://goo.gl/4zQ6D0.
91. Presidential Memorandum, "National Insider Threat Policy and Minimum Standards for Executive Branch Insider Threat Programs," Nov. 21, 2012, http://goo.gl/nLFRqP. Policy text available at http://goo.gl/71V7Iw.

92. Marisa Taylor and Jonathan Landay, "Obama's crackdown views leaks as aiding enemies of U.S." McClatchy Newspapers, June 20, 2013, http://goo.gl/8Gk8Uf.

93. Adam Goldman and Matt Apuzzo, "US: CIA Thwarts New al-Qaida Underwear Bomb Plot," Associated Press, May 7, 2012, http://goo.gl/xgSNS2.

94. Transcript, White House conference call, May 7, 2012. Obtained by Judicial Watch via a Freedom of Information Act lawsuit, http://goo.gl/8tvIY2.

95. Daniel Klaidman, "Drones: The Silent Killers," *Newsweek,* May 28, 2012, http://goo.gl/L0LD95; Jo Becker and Scott Shane, "Secret 'Kill List' Proves a Test of Obama's Principles and Will," *New York Times,* May 29, 2012, http://goo.gl/kag7i.

96. David Sanger, "Obama Order Sped Up Wave of Cyberattacks Against Iran," *New York Times,* June 1, 2012, http://goo.gl/c5ZQQi.

97. News release, "Statement by Senator John McCain on the Obama Administration's National Security Leaks," June 6, 2012, http://goo.gl/GhZjTk.

98. White House transcript, "Remarks by the President," June 8, 2012, http://goo.gl/3OjzTw.

99. Transcript, media availability after Senate Republican luncheon, June 12, 2012.

100. Senate Judiciary Committee, hearing re "Oversight of the U.S. Department of Justice," June 12, 2012; Senate Judiciary Committee, hearing re "Federal Bureau of Investigation Oversight," June 19, 2013.

101. Peter Baker, Charlie Savage, and Jonathan Weisman, "Seeking a Fresh Start, Holder Finds a Fresh Set of Troubles," *New York Times,* June 2, 2013, http://goo.gl/D89KRm.

102. See, for example, letter from Robert Goodlatte and James Sensenbrenner to Eric Holder, May 29, 2013, http://goo.gl/SEgy0q.

103. Baker, Savage, and Weisman, "Seeking a Fresh Start, Holder Finds a Fresh Set of Troubles."

104. Daniel Klaidman, "Holder's Regrets and Repairs," *Daily Beast,* May 28, 2013, http://goo.gl/B5OY5s.

105. Department of Justice, Policy Regarding Obtaining Information from, or Records of, Members of the News Media; and Regarding Questioning, Arresting, or Charging Members of the News Media, 28 C.F.R. § 50.10, Feb. 21, 2014, http://goo.gl/ykubnj.

106. Charlie Savage and Mark Mazzetti, "Cryptic Overtures and a Clandestine Meeting Gave Birth to a Blockbuster Story," *New York Times,* June 10, 2013, http://goo.gl/RxIQ6x.

107. Glenn Greenwald, Ewen MacAskill, and Laura Poitras, "Edward Snowden: The Whistleblower Behind the NSA Surveillance Revelations," *Guardian,* June 9, 2013, http://goo.gl/2kTR1K.

108. *Branzburg v. Hayes,* 408 U.S. 665 (1972).

109. Charlie Savage, "Appeals Panel Weighs Question on Press Rights," *New York Times,* May 18, 2012, http://goo.gl/zQKD6v.

110. Judge Richard Posner surveys much of this ambiguous case law in *Mckevitt v. Pallasch,* 339 F.3d 530 (2003); Posner sided with those who concluded that there was no privilege.

111. Charlie Savage, "Judge Explains Letting a Reporter Protect His Source," *New York Times Media Decoder,* Aug. 23, 2011, http://goo.gl/OIRzav.

112. Charlie Savage, "Prosecutor Who Ran Ethics Unit Leaves Justice Dept.," *New York Times,* Apr. 17, 2012, http://goo.gl/MoTnS4.

113. *U.S. v. Sterling,* 724 F.3d 482 (4th Cir. 2013), http://goo.gl/cGmzLY.

114. Video, NPC Luncheon with Eric Holder, Feb. 17, 2015, http://goo.gl/i1Xoik.

115. Charlie Savage, "Amid Moves on Shield Laws, Journalist Tells of a 2011 Subpoena Fight," *New York Times*, May 30, 2014, http://goo.gl/lf3ktH; Josh Gerstein, "Files Detail Fox-DOJ Subpoena Showdown," *Politico*, Oct. 9, 2014, http://goo.gl/Bt4la6.

116. Charlie Savage, "No Prosecution Seen for Official in N.S.A. Leak," *New York Times*, Apr. 27, 2011, http://goo.gl/m4RbbX.

117. Miller, "Obama Is Right to Prosecute Leakers Who Are Not the Same as Whistle-Blowers."

118. Isikoff, "The Whistleblower Who Exposed Warrantless Wiretaps."

119. Panetta, *Worthy Fights*, 331.

120. Adam Zagorin and David Hilzenrath, "Unreleased: Probe Finds CIA Honcho Disclosed Top Secret Info to Hollywood," Project on Government Oversight Featured Investigations, June 4, 2013, http://goo.gl/mnwyf.

121. Michael Isikoff, "Ex-Pentagon General Target of Leak Investigation, Sources Say," NBC News, June 27, 2013, http://goo.gl/dKcQWm.

122. Gordon Lubold, "Obama's Favorite General Stripped of His Security Clearance," *Foreign Policy*, Sept. 24, 2013, http://goo.gl/HUWWLr.

123. Ellen Nakashima and Adam Goldman, "Leak Investigation Stalls Amid Fears of Confirming U.S.-Israel Operation," *Washington Post*, Mar. 10, 2015, http://goo.gl/LLx28U.

124. Josh Gerstein, "Report: Leon Panetta Revealed Classified SEAL Unit Info," *Politico*, June 5, 2013, http://goo.gl/EWieb.

125. "Statement to Employees by Director of Central Intelligence Agency David H. Petraeus on Former Officer Convicted in Leak Case," Oct. 23, 2012, http://goo.gl/P2UDga.

126. Michael Shear, "Petraeus Quits; Evidence of Affair Was Found by F.B.I.," *New York Times*, Nov. 10, 2012, http://goo.gl/88l6hN.

127. Sheryl Gay Stolberg, "After Scandal, Petraeus Stays Under Radar, but Not Out of the Spotlight," *New York Times*, Feb. 28, 2015, http://goo.gl/6CTDO7.

128. Letter from McCain to Holder, Dec. 2, 2014, http://goo.gl/xqjj2b.

129. Michael S. Schmidt and Matt Apuzzo, "F.B.I. and Justice Dept. Said to Seek Charges for Petraeus," *New York Times*, Jan. 10, 2015, http://goo.gl/8lwgrT.

130. *U.S. v. Petraeus*, W.D.N.C., Factual Basis, filed Mar. 3, 2015, http://goo.gl/4jYeow.

131. Michael S. Schmidt and Matt Apuzzo, "Petraeus Reaches Plea Deal Over Giving Classified Data to Lover," *New York Times*, Mar. 4, 2014, http://goo.gl/2Anf1g.

132. Letter from Lowell to Machen et al., Mar. 6, 2015, http://goo.gl/Qc57TK, uploaded to Document Cloud by Peter Maass.

133. Charlie Savage, "Holder Hints Reporter May Be Spared Jail in Leak," *New York Times*, May 28, 2014, http://goo.gl/PRIrWv.

134. Matt Apuzzo, "Times Reporter Will Not Be Called to Testify in Leak Case," *New York Times*, Jan. 13, 2015, http://goo.gl/wnRRLp.

135. *U.S. v. Sterling*, E.D. Va., United States' Memorandum in Aid of Sentencing, Apr. 20, 2015, https://goo.gl/aAtWlV.

136. *U.S. v. Sterling*, E.D. Va., Jeffrey Alexander Sterling's Memorandum in Aid of Sentencing, Apr. 24, 2015, https://goo.gl/bQIGwn.

137. Matt Apuzzo, "Ex-C.I.A. Officer Sentenced in Leak Case Tied to Times Reporter," *New York Times*, May 12, 2015, http://goo.gl/rcClMT.

Chapter Nine: Secrecy and Secret Law

1. Priest, "U.S. Military Teams, Intelligence Deeply Involved in Aiding Yemen on Strikes"; Greg Miller, "U.S. Citizen in CIA's Cross Hairs," *Los Angeles Times,* Jan. 31, 2010.
2. *U.S. v. Reynolds,* 345 U.S. 1 (1953). *Reynolds* involved a wrongful death lawsuit by widows of three air force contractors killed in a plane crash. The executive branch claimed and won a right to suppress the crash report by saying it contained classified details, and the judiciary accepted that claim without examining the report to see if it was true. In a twist, the crash report became public in 2000 and turned out to contain no classified information, transforming the landmark case, at least in the eyes of its critics, into a symbol of abuse of secrecy powers. But the legal principle it had established remains good law.
3. See, for example, *Halkin v. Helms,* 690 F.2d 977 (D.C. Cir. 1982); *Molerio v. FBI,* 749 F.2d 815 (D.C. Cir. 1984); *Kasza v. Browner,* 133 F.3d 1159 (9th Cir. 1998).
4. "Ethics" page, 2008 Obama campaign website, Nov. 4, 2008, snapshot via Internet Archive, http://goo.gl/YJzM4n.
5. In October 2009, the administration invoked the privilege in a San Francisco lawsuit challenging the NSA's warrantless surveillance program in the Bush years, *Shubert v. Obama,* but it raised identical claims to another case in which the Bush-Cheney administration had already invoked the privilege, so this was not truly new.
6. While we do not know the details of any classified evidence against al-Awlaki, such as what the National Security Agency might have intercepted about him, we can make educated guesses at what some of the state secrets filing put before the judge. For example, we know from the Manning-WikiLeaks cables that the president of Yemen had granted diplomatic permission to the United States to carry out air strikes aimed at al-Qaeda in the Arabian Peninsula on Yemeni soil — a crucial step to making them comply with international law — on the condition that both governments maintain the public fiction that the strikes were made by the Yemeni air force. U.S. diplomatic cable 10SANAA4, "General Petraeus's Meeting with Saleh on Security," Jan. 4, 2010, http://goo.gl/KoevLd. In 2012, Saleh's successor would drop the charade, publicly acknowledging and praising American drone strikes. Scott Shane, "Yemen's Leader Praises U.S. Drone Strikes," *New York Times,* Sept. 29, 2012, http://goo.gl/uQVGO.
7. Charlie Savage, "U.S. Debates Response to Targeted Killing Lawsuit," *New York Times,* Sept. 16, 2010, http://goo.gl/7Nbor4.
8. *Al-Aulaqi v. Obama,* 727 F. Supp. 2d 1 (D.D.C. 2010).
9. White House, Memorandum for the Heads of Executive Departments and Agencies, re Transparency and Open Government, Jan. 21, 2009, http://goo.gl/at4Afd.
10. *Rose v. Dep't of Air Force,* 495 F.2d 261, 263 (2d Cir. 1974).
11. White House transcript, "Remarks by the President in Welcoming Senior Staff and Cabinet Secretaries to the White House," Jan. 21, 2009, http://goo.gl/kVYYpg.
12. John Schwartz, "Obama Backs Off a Reversal on Secrets," *New York Times,* Feb. 10, 2010, http://goo.gl/104xHT.
13. Charlie Savage, "Obama's War on Terror May Resemble Bush's in Some Areas," *New York Times,* Feb. 18, 2009, http://goo.gl/YYfMEm.
14. *Mohamed v. Jeppesen Dataplan, Inc.,* 563 F.3d 992 (9th Cir. Cal. 2009).
15. *Mohamed v. Jeppesen Dataplan, Inc.,* 614 F.3d 1070 (9th Cir. Cal. 2010).
16. As the new Obama team debated internally, there was a related back-and-forth with the House and Senate intelligence committees. The oversight panels demanded to be

allowed to read the classified filings the executive branch made to judges when it invoked the privilege. But the security agencies balked at that idea, too, fearing leaks. Career litigators in the Justice Department pushed back, too. They said that such a process would raise separation-of-powers concerns and it was already hard enough to negotiate with the agencies over what they could tell courts without injecting the prospect of legislative oversight into those confidential consultations. The lawmakers, I was told, then tried a compromise: What about sharing the confidential filings only for cases that were over? The administration refused to do that, too.

17. Charlie Savage, "Justice Dept. to Limit Use of State Secrets Privilege," *New York Times*, Sept. 23, 2009, http://goo.gl/e0oB53.

18. Department of Justice news release, "Attorney General Establishes New State Secrets Policies and Procedures," Sept. 23, 2009, http://goo.gl/ObtgYB.

19. The Obama administration would later repeatedly invoke the state secrets privilege in an attempt to block lawsuits brought by individuals who said they had been improperly placed on the no-fly list, which prevents people from boarding airplanes in the United States or flying through American airspace. The government refused to confirm or deny whether someone was on the list, let alone explain the procedures or specific evidence that placed a person on it. (It did, however, release some data about its broader terror watch-list database in 2011 in response to a Freedom of Information Act lawsuit by the Electronic Privacy Information Center, including the information that Americans charged with but acquitted of terrorism-related crimes could stay in the terrorism-watch database; see Charlie Savage, "Even Those Cleared of Crimes Can Stay on F.B.I.'s Watch List," *New York Times*, Sept. 28, 2011, http://goo.gl/smyQf.)

In court declarations in 2013 and 2014, Holder said invoking the state secrets privilege in the cases was justified and complied with the new policy because even disclosing the abstract rules for putting someone on the no-fly list "would provide a clear road map to undermine the government's screening efforts, a key counterterrorism measure, and thus its disclosure reasonably could be expected to cause significant harm to national security"; *Ibrahim v. Holder*, N.D. Cal., Declaration of Eric H. Holder, Jr., Attorney General of the United States," Apr. 23, 2013, http://goo.gl/RNdpPo; *Mohamed v. Holder*, E.D. Va., "Declaration of Eric H. Holder, Jr., Attorney General of the United States," May 28, 2014, http://goo.gl/IrTMyZ.

Nevertheless, in one case it emerged that an FBI agent had elevated a Malaysian student at Stanford University to the no-fly list by mistake, although the evidence that had resulted in her being placed into a much larger underlying database of people who might be linked to terrorists remained murky; *Ibrahim v. Holder*, N.D. Cal., "Findings of Fact, Conclusions of Law, and Order for Relief," Feb. 6, 2014, http://goo.gl/EvCMN8.

In 2014 someone leaked the watch-listing rules Holder had wanted kept secret to the *Intercept*. And the government's effort to use the state secrets privilege to prevent judicial review of the no-fly-list policy failed. Under pressure from several court losses, which found that its policy violated the Constitution, the administration partially lifted the veil of secrecy over no-fly-list rules and redressed procedures in 2015, saying it would now confirm if an American was on the list; see Charlie Savage, "Over Government Objections, Rules on No-Fly List Are Made Public," *New York Times*, July 24, 2014, http://goo.gl/SQpeJJ; Jeremy Scahill and Ryan Devereaux, "Blacklisted:

The Secret Government Rulebook for Labeling You a Terrorist," *Intercept*, July 23, 2014, http://goo.gl/NlNlyQ; Charlie Savage, "Clashing Rulings Weigh Security and Liberties," *New York Times*, June 25, 2014, http://goo.gl/oFrr7q; *Latif v. Holder*, D. Or., "Notice Regarding Revisions to DHS Trip Procedures," Apr. 13, 2015, http://goo.gl/ibBJEI.

20. *U.S. v. Nixon*, 418 U.S. 683 (1974).

21. Later that day, in response to a question from a *Washington Post* reporter, the White House press office e-mailed a transcript of Craig's answer to my question to the *Post*, which published it first as a "statement" from him.

22. Elisabeth Bumiller, "Defense Chief Lifts Ban on Pictures of Coffins," *New York Times*, Feb. 27, 2009, http://goo.gl/ep8dW2.

23. Rizzo, *Company Man*, 284–88.

24. Ibid.

25. This account is based on interviews with several participants and also draws from Klaidman, *Kill or Capture*, 60–63.

26. Scott Shane, "Waterboarding Used 266 Times on 2 Suspects," *New York Times*, April 20, 2009, http://goo.gl/ceD1C.

27. Jonah Goldberg, "Five Minutes Well Spent," *National Review*, Feb. 15, 2008, http://goo.gl/b87f9F.

28. Jonah Goldberg, "Sounds Like Torture to Me," *National Review*, April 20, 2009, http://goo.gl/Coq08l.

29. *ACLU v. Dep't of Defense*, 543 F.3d 59 (2d Cir. 2008), https://goo.gl/twZop9.

30. Jeff Zeleny and Thom Shanker, "Obama Moves to Bar Release of Detainee Abuse Photos," *New York Times*, May 14, 2009, http://goo.gl/4LR5hg.

31. White House transcript, "Statement by the President on the Situation in Sri Lanka and Detainee Photographs," May 13, 2009, http://goo.gl/9mA5Sz.

32. Panetta, *Worthy Fights*, 233–34.

33. Transcript, Feinstein Senate floor statement, Mar. 11, 2014, http://goo.gl/kl17bT.

34. Jonathan S. Landay, Ali Watkins, and Marisa Taylor, "White House Withholds Thousands of Documents from Senate CIA Probe, Despite Vows of Help," McClatchy, Mar. 12, 2014, http://goo.gl/zaMjlK.

35. Ron Wyden and Mark Udall, "How Can Congress Debate a Secret Law?," *Huffington Post*, May 25, 2011, http://goo.gl/Ctovz.

36. Letter from Wyden and Udall to Holder, Mar. 15, 2012, http://goo.gl/scnJa.

37. *NYT v. U.S. Dep't of Justice*, 872 F. Supp. 2d 309 (S.D.N.Y. 2012), http://goo.gl/Y9loKC.

38. *Al-Aulaqi v. Obama*.

39. Recounted in letter from Wyden to Holder, Feb. 8, 2012, http://goo.gl/Okvid9.

40. Department of Justice white paper, "Legality of a Lethal Operation by the Central Intelligence Agency Against a U.S. Citizen," May 25, 2011, http://goo.gl/ccguP2.

41. White House transcript, "Remarks by the President at the 'Change of Office' Chairman of the Joint Chiefs of Staff Ceremony," Sept. 30, 2011, http://goo.gl/DDK7wD.

42. Scott was also told that the government could neither confirm nor deny the existence of other potentially responsive documents to his request.

43. *Phillippi v. C.I.A.*, 546 F.2d 1009 (D.C. Cir. 1976).

44. Daniel Klaidman, "Obama Team to Break Silence on al-Awlaki Killing," *Newsweek*, Jan. 23, 2012, http://goo.gl/F19nas. See also Daniel Klaidman, "Obama's Drone Debacle," *Daily Beast*, May 10, 2013, http://goo.gl/PIIup2.

45. Letter from Wyden to Holder, Feb. 8, 2012, http://goo.gl/w4nHjz.

46. Charlie Savage, "Pentagon Says U.S. Citizens with Terrorism Ties Can Be Targeted in Strikes," *New York Times,* Feb. 22, 2012, http://goo.gl/pi0MkU.
47. Eric Holder, remarks at Northwestern University School of Law, Mar. 5, 2012, http://goo.gl/96j58B.
48. *NYT v. U.S. Dep't of Justice,* 915 F. Supp. 2d 508 (S.D.N.Y. 2013), http://goo.gl/1E2upb.
49. John Brennan, remarks at the Wilson Center, "The Efficacy and Ethics of U.S. Counterterrorism Strategy," Apr. 30, 2012, http://goo.gl/vyJipf.
50. Letter from Obama to Congress, June 15, 2012, https://goo.gl/RnaThg.
51. Letter from John Conyers, Jerrold Nadler, and Bobby Scott to Eric Holder, Dec. 4, 2012, http://goo.gl/ViGK9.
52. Justice Department Office of Legal Counsel, Memorandum from Seitz to Counsel for the President, re Lawfulness of Recess Appointments During a Recess of the Senate Notwithstanding Periodic Pro Forma Sessions, Jan. 6, 2012, http://goo.gl/lLjBLI.
53. Charlie Savage, "Obama Tempts Fight Over Recess Appointments," *New York Times, Caucus Blog,* Jan. 4, 2012, http://goo.gl/A4EbSM.
54. Senate floor statement, Senator Charles Grassley, Jan. 23, 2012, http://goo.gl/iD4Xf9.
55. Justice Department Office of Legal Counsel, "Memorandum for Attorneys of the Office from David J. Barron, re Best Practices for OLC Legal Advice and Written Opinions," June 16, 2010, http://goo.gl/FNa0LR.
56. *NYT v. U.S. Dep't of Justice,* S.D.N.Y., No. 12-3215, Declaration of Paul P. Colborn, June 14, 2012, http://goo.gl/XrE5IF.
57. Specifically Rakoff decided that we lacked proof that the White House had relied on the older memos, which was needed to establish that they were "working law" and hence must be disclosed. *NYT v. U.S. Dep't of Justice,* 2013 U.S. Dist. LEXIS 7396 (S.D.N.Y. Jan. 4, 2013).
58. See also *Brennan Ctr. for Justice at N.Y. Univ. Sch. of Law v. U.S. Dept. of Justice,* 697 F.3d 184, 187 (2d Cir. 2012); *Elec. Frontier Found. v. U.S. Dep't of Justice,* 2014 U.S. App. LEXIS 4541 (D.C. Cir. Mar. 11, 2014).
59. Letter from Weich to Grassley, Feb. 4, 2011, http://goo.gl/V4VibI.
60. Justice Department Office of the Inspector General, "A Review of ATF's Operation Fast and Furious and Related Matters," Sept. 2012, http://goo.gl/2MsnOP.
61. Letter from Issa to Obama, June 25, 2012, http://goo.gl/lJq5fN.
62. Savage, "Barack Obama's Q&A."
63. Jonathan Weisman and Charlie Savage, "House Cites Holder for Contempt in Gun Inquiry," *New York Times,* June 29, 2012, http://goo.gl/apDZvI.
64. Louis Fisher, "Obama's Executive Privilege and Holder's Contempt: 'Operation Fast and Furious,'" *Presidential Studies Quarterly,* Mar. 2013, http://goo.gl/yJ3ud3.
65. Order, *Committee on Oversight v. Holder,* Aug. 20, 2014, http://goo.gl/NaEvzF.
66. Andy Wright, "Fast and Furious: Mixed Ruling in Oversight Committee v. Holder," *Just Security,* Aug. 22, 2014, http://goo.gl/CN2OFc.
67. E-mail from Holder to Grindler, re "Possible subpoena for cooperating FFL," Apr. 15, 2011, http://goo.gl/6FK7pC; see also Devlin Barrett, "E-mails Show Holder's Anger During 'Fast and Furious' Probe," *Wall Street Journal, Washington Wire,* Nov. 7, 2014, http://goo.gl/TJG2ov.
68. *NYT v. U.S. Dep't of Justice,* 915 F. Supp. 2d 508 (S.D.N.Y. 2013).
69. Michael Isikoff, "Justice Department Memo Reveals Legal Case for Drone Strikes on Americans," Feb. 4, 2010, http://goo.gl/pwtngR.

70. Michael D. Shear and Scott Shane, "Congress to See Memo Backing Drone Attacks on Americans," *New York Times,* Feb. 7, 2013, http://goo.gl/wVeAFw.

71. Letter from Paul to Holder, Feb. 20, 2013, http://goo.gl/WGtRqr.

72. Letter from Holder to Paul, Mar. 4, 2013, http://goo.gl/WGtRqr.

73. Hearing of the Senate Judiciary Committee, "Oversight of the Department of Justice," Mar. 6, 2013, http://goo.gl/gUavzK.

74. *Congressional Record,* S1150-S1226 Mar. 6, 2013, http://goo.gl/myUlWS.

75. "Stand with Rand," Trademark Electronic Search System record, United States Patent and Trademark Office website, screenshot, http://goo.gl/uHtysR.

76. Twitter posting by @Heritage account, Mar. 6, 2013, 9:28 p.m., screenshot, http://goo .gl/VB8i94.

77. Richard W. Stevenson and Ashley Parker, "A Senator's Stand on Drones Scrambles Partisan Lines," *New York Times,* Mar. 8, 2013, http://goo.gl/XnVCi.

78. Letter from Holder to Paul, Mar. 7, 2013, http://goo.gl/WGtRqr.

79. Press release, "Sen. Paul Reaches Victory Through Filibuster," office of Senator Rand Paul, Mar. 7, 2013, via Internet Archive, https://goo.gl/fC5PLL.

80. YouTube clip, "Obama Participates in a Fireside Hangout on Google+," Feb. 14, 2013, http://goo.gl/FLhLJV.

81. Department of Defense press release, "Fact Sheet: Increasing Transparency in the U.S. Nuclear Weapons Stockpile," May 3, 2010, http://goo.gl/uQ3sZw.

82. Presidential Policy Directive 19, "Protecting Whistleblowers with Access to Classified Information," Oct. 10, 2012, http://goo.gl/IsHXgw.

83. ISOO Annual Reports to the President, http://goo.gl/GM68wD.

84. Mark Lander, Eric Schmitt, and Michael D. Shear, "Early E-Mails on Benghazi Show Internal Divisions," *New York Times,* May 15, 2013, http://goo.gl/p94Pzu.

85. In 2013, the Justice Department also took the welcome step of voluntarily publishing a compendium of historic executive branch memos by the office or the attorney general between 1934 and 1975, filling in gaps in the historical record of executive branch precedents. Department of Justice Office of Legal Counsel, "Supplemental Opinions of the Office of Legal Counsel of the United States Department of Justice," Vol. 1, Nathan Forrester, ed., 2013, http://goo.gl/wvKqIm.

86. Citizens for Responsibility and Ethics in Washington news release, "CREW and Obama Administration Reach Historic Settlement on Visitor Records," Sept. 4, 2009, http://goo.gl/2g1PkZ.

87. Judicial Watch news release, "Judicial Watch Statement on Court Ruling on the Secret Service's White House Visitor Logs," Aug. 30, 2013, http://goo.gl/rrFUCF/.

88. John Podesta, "Obama Should Lift Secrecy on Drones," *Washington Post,* Mar. 13, 2013, http://goo.gl/5VVabK.

89. Jeh Johnson, "A 'Drone Court': Some Pros and Cons," Remarks at Fordham University, Mar. 18, 2013, http://goo.gl/SWYsra.

90. White House transcript, "Remarks by the President at the National Defense University," May 23, 2013, http://goo.gl/d6IP22.

91. Charlie Savage and Peter Baker, "Obama, in a Shift, to Limit Targets of Drone Strikes," *New York Times,* May 22, 2013, http://goo.gl/NL0Krr.

92. Charlie Savage, "Intelligence Chief Announces New Rules to Curb Leaks," *New York Times,* June 26, 2012, http://goo.gl/jCosDI.

93. Charlie Savage, "Intelligence Chief Issues Limits on Press Contacts," *New York Times*, Apr. 22, 2014, http://goo.gl/11mpUZ.

94. Charlie Savage, "Intelligence Policy Bans Citation of Leaked Material," *New York Times*, May 9, 2014, http://goo.gl/Rt9B8o.

95. Charlie Savage "Memo Revisits Policy on Citing Leaked Material, to Some Confusion," *New York Times*, May 10, 2014, http://goo.gl/NrgybF.

96. *NYT v. U.S. Dep't of Justice*, 2d Cir., Order, May 28, 2014.

97. Jeremy W. Peters, "Judicial Nominee's Memos on Drones Stirring Bipartisan Concern in the Senate," *New York Times*, May 6, 2013, http://goo.gl/CVafmG.

98. Press release, "Udall: Release of Memo Would Affirm Public Has Right to Know Legal Reasoning Behind Targeting of Americans," May 20, 2014, https://goo.gl/C13hpg.

99. Senate roll-call vote 162, May 22, 2014, http://goo.gl/AtXR0B.

100. Charlie Savage, "Official Backs Marines' Move to Classify Photos of Forces with Taliban Bodies," *New York Times*, June 11, 2014, http://goo.gl/rl0KaT.

101. Letter from Wyden, Udall, and Heinrich to Holder, Nov. 26, 2013, http://goo.gl/3dfrad. The senators, as recounted, were shown the memo in February 2013 and so were reacting prior to its public disclosure. I have changed the spelling of al-Awlaki to be consistent.

102. There was, however, a twist. Our Freedom of Information Act lawsuit also sought other post-9/11 memos discussing the legal parameters of targeted killings in general, based on Shane's 2010 request, and the parallel ACLU lawsuit was also seeking a broader set of memos. It turned out there were ten of them, one of which was a previously unknown March 2002 Bush-Cheney legal-team memo addressing the Executive Order 12333 assassination ban. The Obama Justice Department battled to keep all ten entirely secret. It argued, among other things, that even though the executive branch had chosen not to contest the appeals court's ruling and order about publishing the long al-Awlaki memo, it still disagreed with that reasoning and maintained that "the Court's release" of the memo did not "constitute an independent official disclosure or waiver by the government that would strip protection from otherwise exempt information and material" (*NYT v. U.S. Dep't of Justice*, 2d Cir., "Brief for Defendants-Appellees," Apr. 2, 2015, http://goo.gl/oeTD1e).
    In other words, its argument was that court-ordered disclosure is like a leak and doesn't count. Only the executive branch has the power to decide whether something is classified or amounts to confidential legal advice to the president, and the Obama administration had not voluntarily waived that privilege, so it could still deem the information in the al-Awlaki memo as secret for the purpose of evaluating whether other, similar memos must be made public. This particularly extreme example of the phenomenon of public-but-officially-secret information prompted Jameel Jaffer, the American Civil Liberties Union lawyer, to marvel that "the executive branch creates reality. The rest of us — judges included — can only study it"; Jameel Jaffer, "The Unreal Secrecy About Drone Killings," *Just Security*, Apr. 9, 2015, http://goo.gl/NiIZu9.

103. News release, "Appeals Court Orders Release of Targeted Killing Memo," American Civil Liberties Union, Apr. 21, 2014, http://goo.gl/6Xh6WR.

104. Steve Vladeck, "The Second Circuit and the Vices of Selective Disclosure," *Just Security*, Apr. 22, 2014, http://goo.gl/KBaqZo.

Chapter Ten: Wounds That Won't Heal (Captives 2011–2015)

1. "Interrogation Techniques," leaked, unsigned policy memo by the 2012 Romney campaign national security law subcommittee, circa September 2011, http://goo.gl/XQwS04.
2. Charlie Savage, "Election to Decide Future Interrogation Methods in Terrorism Cases," *New York Times*, Sept. 27, 2012, http://goo.gl/91w1Y.
3. S.1253 — National Defense Authorization Act for Fiscal Year 2012, 112th Congress (2011–2012), https://goo.gl/jdVySA.
4. Jeh Johnson, speech before the Heritage Foundation, October 18, 2011, http://goo.gl/3LY4w5.
5. S.1867 — National Defense Authorization Act for Fiscal Year 2012, 112th Congress (2011–2012), https://goo.gl/yVXQwc.
6. Letter from Mueller to Levin, Nov. 28, 2011, http://goo.gl/VDcNIU.
7. "Statement by the President on H.R. 1540," Dec. 31, 2011, http://goo.gl/0Bsgu.
8. Charlie Savage, "Obama Issues Waivers on Military Custody for Terror Suspects," *New York Times*, Feb. 29, 2012, http://goo.gl/YCHs9p.
9. John F. Burns and Michael R. Gordon, "U.S. Says Iran Helped Iraqis Kill Five G.I.'s," *New York Times*, July 3, 2007, http://goo.gl/QPVII3.
10. Charlie Savage, "Detainee in Iraq Poses a Dilemma as U.S. Exit Nears," *New York Times*, Dec. 12, 2011, http://goo.gl/V0PJQd.
11. David B. Rivkin Jr. and Charles D. Stimson, "Obama and the Hezbollah Terrorist," *Wall Street Journal*, Dec. 7, 2011, http://goo.gl/XsAoiF.
12. Charlie Savage, "U.S. Transfers Its Last Prisoner in Iraq to Iraqi Custody," *New York Times*, Dec. 17, 2011, http://goo.gl/YwXmUZ.
13. Charlie Savage, "Prisoner in Iraq Tied to Hezbollah Faces U.S. Military Charges," *New York Times*, Feb. 24, 2012, http://goo.gl/ZT4ct.
14. Jack Healy and Charlie Savage, "Iraqi Court Acts to Free Suspect in Deadly Raid on G.I.'s," *New York Times*, May 8, 2012, http://goo.gl/dQxpRV; Michael R. Gordon, "Against U.S. Wishes, Iraq Releases Man Accused of Killing American Soldiers," *New York Times*, Nov. 17, 2012, http://goo.gl/PEd4un.
15. Charlie Savage, "U.S. Warns Judge's Ruling Impedes Its Detention Powers," *New York Times*, Sept. 18, 2012, http://goo.gl/hW3vsS.
16. Charlie Savage, "At a Hearing, 9/11 Detainees Show Defiance," *New York Times*, May 6, 2012, http://goo.gl/ANgLWA.
17. Charlie Savage, "U.S. Tells Court That Documents from Torture Investigation Should Remain Secret," *New York Times*, Dec. 11, 2014, http://goo.gl/KTmk1R.
18. "AR 15-6 Investigation, Report on the Facts and Circumstances Surrounding 8 September 2012 Death of Detainee Adnan Farhan Abd Latif (ISN US9YM-000156DP) at Joint Task Force-Guantánamo (JTF-GTMO)," Nov. 8, 2012, http://goo.gl/sVROzb.
19. Adam Liptak, "Justices Reject Detainees' Appeal, Leaving Cloud Over Earlier Guantánamo Ruling," *New York Times*, June 12, 2012, http://goo.gl/RBxyy0.
20. Jennifer Daskal, "Don't Close Guantánamo," *New York Times*, Jan. 11, 2013, http://goo.gl/aixCIS.
21. The existence of this memo was first reported by Daniel Klaidman, "How Gitmo Imprisoned Obama," *Newsweek*, May 15, 2013, http://goo.gl/CfMiQ0.
22. Charlie Savage, "Office Working to Close Guantánamo Is Shuttered," *New York Times*, Jan. 29, 2010, http://goo.gl/gtb5P.

23. Charlie Savage, "In Setback for Military Tribunals, bin Laden Driver's Conviction Is Reversed," *New York Times*, Oct. 17, 2012, http://goo.gl/DA6wl.

24. *U.S. v. Bahlul*, D.C.Cir., Brief on Behalf of Appellee, Oct. 21, 2009, http://goo.gl/UG9YVG.

25. Charlie Savage, "U.S. Legal Officials Split Over How to Prosecute Terrorism Detainees," *New York Times*, Jan. 7, 2013, http://goo.gl/EPa9Si.

26. Charlie Savage, "U.S. to Press Fight of Detainee's Appeal," *New York Times*, Jan. 10, 2013, http://goo.gl/YzgUp.

27. Charlie Savage, "Military Prosecutor Battles to Drop Conspiracy Charge in 9/11 Case," *New York Times*, Jan. 19, 2013, http://goo.gl/x3Q2PQ.

28. Charlie Savage, "A Federal Appeals Court Sidesteps How to Prosecute Detainees," *New York Times*, July 15, 2014, http://goo.gl/JUhdgs.

29. Charlie Savage, "Guantánamo Detainee's Conviction Is Thrown Out on Appeal," *New York Times*, June 13, 2015, http://goo.gl/yVqxPZ.

30. Charlie Savage, "Judge Overrules Censors in Guantánamo 9/11 Hearing," *New York Times*, Jan. 31, 2013, http://goo.gl/IBYXwD.

31. Charlie Savage, "Judge Stops Censorship in Sept. 11 Case," *New York Times*, Feb. 1, 2013, http://goo.gl/BF29Q2.

32. *Dhiab v.* Obama, D.D.C., Case No. 05-1457, Declaration of Colonel John V. Bogdan, June 3, 2013, court filing Aug. 26, 2014, http://goo.gl/j9ppD8.

33. Letter from Jeremy Lazarus to Chuck Hagel, Apr. 25, 2013, http://goo.gl/jwYDHE.

34. *In re Grand Jury Subpoena John Doe v. U.S.*, 150 F. 3d 170 (2nd Cir. 1998), https://goo.gl/oTNPS6.

35. Savage, "Despair Drives Guantánamo Detainees to Revolt," *New York Times*, Apr. 24, 2013.

36. Charlie Savage, "Officials Describe Chaos at Guantánamo in Weeks Before Raid on Prison," *New York Times*, Apr. 17, 2013, http://goo.gl/qv2YvS.

37. Charlie Savage, "Amid Hunger Strike, Obama Renews Push to Close Cuba Prison," *New York Times*, May 1, 2013, http://goo.gl/ZS8E7U.

38. *U.S. v. Tsarnaev*, D.Mass, Motion to Suppress Statements, May 7, 2014, http://goo.gl/x2RyNh.

39. Inspectors General of the Intelligence Community, the Central Intelligence Agency, the Department of Justice, and the Department of Homeland Security, "Unclassified Summary of Information Handling and Sharing Prior to the April 15, 2013, Boston Marathon Bombings," Apr. 10, 2014, http://goo.gl/JxsZ6R.

40. Ibid.

41. Senate News Release, Statement from Senators Graham and McCain, Apr. 19, 2013, via Internet Archive, https://goo.gl/hFakSW.

42. Charlie Savage, "G.O.P. Lawmakers Push to Have Boston Suspect Questioned as Enemy Combatant," *New York Times*, Apr. 22, 2013, http://goo.gl/K3qIib.

43. "Remarks by the President at the National Defense University."

44. There was a subtle but important reason the Red Cross and other international law proponents cared so much about these procedures. In international law, there are technically two kinds of wars — *international armed conflicts*, meaning wars between the two countries whose armies wear uniforms, and *noninternational armed conflicts*, meaning a war against a nongovernment armed group and sometimes called a NIAC. The noninternational kind has traditionally meant internal civil wars against

rebels, but the Supreme Court had ruled that the transnational war against al-Qaeda also fell into this category. Under a strict interpretation of the law, in a noninternational armed conflict, all enemies are considered civilians and they can be detained without trial only if they present a future security threat. Such detainees are entitled to periodic reviews because they may be held only as long as they continue to present a danger. By contrast, in a traditional international armed conflict, enemy soldiers may be held on the basis of their status alone until the end of hostilities and without periodic reviews, because the idea is they would be compelled to return to the battlefield by virtue of being part of the enemy army. One of the big legal moves of the Bush-Cheney administration had been to take the harsher legal standards of wars between two countries and apply them to the war against al-Qaeda, and so far, domestic courts had not objected. The Obama administration was not going to say to the world that it now considered the periodic reviews to be *legally required*. Still, the fact that it was creating them resonated internationally; it was edging the United States into closer alignment with how the rest of the world understood the law.

45. Charlie Savage, "U.S. to Send 2 at Guantánamo Back to Algeria, Saying Security Concerns Are Met," *New York Times*, July 27, 2013, http://goo.gl/ALDg2z.

46. "CIA Comments on the Senate Select Committee on Intelligence Report on the Rendition, Detention, and Interrogation Program," June 27, 2013, http://goo.gl/KVkzgg.

47. Transcript, Udall Senate floor statement, Dec. 10, 2014, http://goo.gl/0yZKOA.

48. Greg Miller, "CIA Finds No Wrongdoing in Agency's Search of Computers Used by Senate Investigators," *Washington Post*, Jan. 14, 2015, http://goo.gl/MbNugK.

49. Senate Select Intelligence Committee, hearing re CIA and State Department Nominees, Dec. 17, 2013, http://goo.gl/AMAJY3.

50. CIA Inspector General, "Agency Access to the SSCI Shared Drive on RDINet," July 14, 2014, http://goo.gl/38omXw; CIA Rendition, Detention, and Interrogation Network Agency Accountability Board, "Final Report," Jan. 14, 2015, http://goo.gl/hUl8WW.

51. Ali Watkins, "Justice Declines to Pursue Allegations That CIA Monitored Senate Intel Staff," McClatchy, July 10, 2014, http://goo.gl/svGUSf.

52. Mark Mazzetti and Carl Hulse, "Inquiry by C.I.A. Affirms It Spied on Senate Panel," *New York Times*, Aug. 1, 2014, http://goo.gl/IOlmKJ.

53. The decision by the board not to recommend the discipline sought by the CIA inspector general fit into a pattern. It is exceedingly rare for the security bureaucracy to impose discipline on its own officials for crossing a line due to overzealousness in carrying out their missions. Other examples in this book include David Margolis's blocking of the recommendation that the Bush-era authors of the interrogation memos be referred to the bar for discipline, and John Durham's decision not to recommend charging anyone for abusing CIA prisoners, even those who had died in custody. To give another notable example, every time an FBI agent fires his gun outside the shooting range, the bureau reviews the incident to see whether he complied with its deadly force policy, which permits firing a weapon at someone only if he presents an imminent danger to the agent or another person. Usually local police defer to the feds, so this is the only official examination of what happened. With the *Times* I filed a Freedom of Information Act lawsuit to obtain copies of every such report dating back to 1993. It turned out that over a 20 year period, there had been about a hundred and fifty episodes in which an agent had intentionally shot someone, and in every single one, the review group had deemed it to be a "good shoot" and recom-

mended no discipline. But one of the "good shoots" was one in which a jittery agent mistook an innocent and unarmed man for a criminal and shot him in the face, and the taxpayers paid him $1.3 million to settle a lawsuit; Charlie Savage and Michael S. Schmidt, "The F.B.I. Deemed Agents Faultless in 150 Shootings," *New York Times*, June 19, 2013, http://goo.gl/jDbjeO.

54. Charlie Savage, "Judge Urges President to Address Prison Strike," *New York Times*, July 9, 2013, http://goo.gl/bNEkkl.
55. Charlie Savage, "Appeals Court Allows Challenges by Detainees at Guantánamo Prison," *New York Times*, Feb. 12, 2014, http://goo.gl/aNSxDN.
56. Charlie Savage, "Judge Orders U.S. to Stop Force-Feeding Syrian Held at Guantá-namo," *New York Times*, May 17, 2014, http://goo.gl/ZkIoix.
57. Charlie Savage, "Guantánamo Inmate's Case Reignites Fight Over Detentions," *New York Times*, May 24, 2014, http://goo.gl/BzszTJ.
58. Department of Justice, "Report Pursuant to Section 1039 of the National Defense Authorization Act for Fiscal Year 2014," May 14, 2014, http://goo.gl/2LydnE.
59. Memo from Rice to Hagel, "Guidance on Guantánamo Bay Detainee Transfers," May 24, 2014.
60. Charlie Savage and Helene Cooper, "Under Pressure, Hagel Promises to Act on Guantánamo Transfers," *New York Times*, May 30, 2014, http://goo.gl/4y0hXZ.
61. Dan Lamothe, "Bowe Bergdahl, in Sparse Prose, Details His Captivity for the First Time," *Washington Post*, Mar. 25, 2015, http://goo.gl/LSAa9S.
62. Charlie Savage, "Negotiations with Taliban Could Hinge on Detainees," *New York Times*, June 21, 2013, http://goo.gl/kYyoCg.
63. "Susan Rice Cites 'Sacred Obligation' in Making Deal for Bergdahl's Freedom," ABC News, June 2, 2014, http://goo.gl/i6M2AK.
64. Transcript, "President Obama Talks to Brian Williams About Bergdahl, Snowden, Putin, and D-Day," NBC News, June 6, 2014, http://goo.gl/h7vVy2.
65. Charlie Savage and David E. Sanger, "Deal to Free Bowe Bergdahl Puts Obama on Defensive," *New York Times*, June 4, 2014, http://goo.gl/RhOJq3.
66. White House release, "Statement by the President on H.R. 3304," Dec. 26, 2013, http://goo.gl/scmyfv.
67. U.S. Government Accountability Office, "Department of Defense-Compliance with Stat-utory Notification Requirement," Report B-326013, Aug. 21, 2014, http://goo.gl/5Xg6uQ.
68. The most detailed legal analysis the Obama administration produced in public was an unsigned document a deputy to Preston e-mailed to the Government Account-ability Office on July 31 and a follow-up letter signed by Michael McCord, the Penta-gon comptroller, on December 5; E-mail from deputy general counsel (legislation) to assistant general counsel for appropriations law, "Administration Views Provided to the Government Accountability Office," July 31, 2014, http://goo.gl/5Xg6uQ; letter from McCord to Dodaro, Dec. 5, 2014, http://goo.gl/5Xg6uQ.
69. Charlie Savage, "White House Fills Top Post at Justice Department," *New York Times*, Mar. 26, 2014, http://goo.gl/NRu75P.
70. Charlie Savage, "U.S. Is Said to Plan to Send 6 Detainees to Uruguay," *New York Times*, July 17, 2014, http://goo.gl/kCO74R.
71. Charlie Savage, "Decaying Guantánamo Defies Closing Plans," *New York Times*, Sept. 1, 2014, http://goo.gl/I1bNZW.
72. Charlie Savage, "Invisible Men," *New York Times*, June 16, 2013, http://goo.gl/685VBh.

73. Damon Winter and Charlie Savage, "Camp X-Ray: A Ghost Prison," *New York Times,* Sept. 1, 2014, http://goo.gl/jFcIgp.

74. Ben Fox, "Window Opens on Secret Camp Within Guantánamo," Associated Press, Apr. 13, 2014, http://goo.gl/9LlELd.

75. Google Maps image, @19.913636,-75.122934,590m, http://goo.gl/MS0AQX.

76. E-mail from Hicks to Kelly, Feb. 25, 2013, http://goo.gl/0q7lmT.

77. Savage, "Decaying Guantánamo Defies Closing Plans."

78. Charlie Savage, "A Practice Goes on Trial: Force-Feeding a Detainee," *New York Times,* Oct. 7, 2014, http://goo.gl/hGqF8d.

79. The tapes were filed under seal, but a group of news organizations, including the *New York Times,* asked Kessler to make them public, and she ordered the military to do so. Preston again urged Verrilli to appeal the order, arguing that the images could be used for anti-American propaganda that would endanger troops abroad. The internal deliberations centered on the argument that the sessions supposedly looked reasonable if watched from start to finish but that isolated moments within them, like when the tube was being inserted and Diyab was resisting, looked bad out of context. This time, Verrilli agreed to appeal. The Court of Appeals, however, rejected the challenge as premature. In July 2015, Kessler ordered the government to complete its proposed redactions of the videos by the end of August, chastising the Obama administration for stalling. "The only thing consistent about the Government's position has been its constant plea for more time. However, as the Court learned at the Status Conference, the Government has failed, after having managed to stall for nine months by filing a truly frivolous Appeal with the Court of Appeals, to use the additional time it has already received" to begin work on the redactions, she wrote. It remained unclear whether the tapes would ever become public. *Dhiab v. Obama,* D.D.C., No. 05-1457, Order, July 10, 2015, https://goo.gl/QTHB3Z.

80. Sloan had been pushing for resettling Yemenis, arguing that it was unlikely that any viable rehabilitation center in Yemen would get set up before Obama left office.

81. This was not a perfect comparison — the Guantánamo budget included the military commissions for the handful of detainees facing charges; the Bureau of Prisons budget did not include the costs of the federal courts.

82. When the six arrived in Montevideo, Mujica went on television and criticized Guantánamo, saying that it would be cowardly not to take in detainees "once there is a president of the United States who wants to undo a miserable injustice that they left for him." Essentially validating the concerns of those in the military who had been cautious about that deal, Mujica stated that Uruguay would not place restrictions on the transfers' mobility, saying that "the first day they want to leave, they can go." But he also released a letter Sloan had signed just before the transfer flight. It listed the former detainees' names and stated: "There is no information that the above mentioned individuals were involved in conducting or facilitating terrorist attacks against the United States or its partners or allies" (letter from Sloan to Mujica, Dec. 2, 2014, http://goo.gl/SlpN5U).

83. Charlie Savage and Graham Bowley, "U.S. to Retain Role as a Jailer in Afghanistan," *New York Times,* Sept. 7, 2012, http://goo.gl/16URxV.

84. Spencer Ackerman, "US Quietly Releases 14 Pakistani Detainees from Afghanistan Jail," *Guardian,* Sept. 20, 2014, http://goo.gl/wRvsHL.

85. Josh Gerstein, "U.S. Sends Two Prisoners to Yemen from Afghanistan," *Politico,* Aug. 26, 2014, http://goo.gl/VqKZdu.

86. Adam Goldman, "Russian Fighter Suspected of Terrorism and Held in Afghanistan to Be Prosecuted in U.S.," *Washington Post,* Oct. 23, 2014, http://goo.gl/r9KbYI.

87. Justice Department news release, "Russian Taliban Fighter Convicted of Terrorism Charges," Aug. 7, 2015, http://goo.gl/WV0dUW.

88. Jenifer Fenton, "How Obama Handed Afghanistan a Prisoner Dilemma," Al-Jazeera America, Mar. 16, 2015, http://goo.gl/xX2ioJ.

89. Charlie Savage, "U.S. Seems Unlikely to Accept That Rights Treaty Applies to Its Actions Abroad," *New York Times,* Mar. 6, 2014, http://goo.gl/xZZEDJ.

90. There were many treaties with similar language, some in odd places. One related to a behind-the-scenes problem that had arisen during the endgame in getting Omar Khadr, the Canadian detainee prosecuted before a military commission at Guantánamo, to plead guilty in exchange for a deal permitting him to serve most of his sentence in Canada. Extradition treaties seemed to cover only those situations where an offender was held "in the territory" of another country, so it was not clear that Canada was required to take Khadr under its treaty with the United States, if Guantánamo was not considered to be "in the territory" of the United States.

91. Charlie Savage, "Peace Prize Laureates Urge Disclosure on U.S. Torture," *New York Times,* Oct. 27, 2014, http://goo.gl/js1jwK.

92. Monika Scislowska, "Poland to Pay $262,000 to Inmates Held at Secret CIA Prison," Associated Press, Feb. 18, 2015, http://goo.gl/zEgT3c.

93. For discussion of the first, see end chapter 7, endnote 45.

94. Senate CIA Torture Report, 82, 115.

95. George J. Tenet et al., "Ex-CIA Directors: Interrogations Saved Lives," *Wall Street Journal,* Dec. 10, 2014, http://goo.gl/3wv2dC.

96. Peter Baker, "Bush and C.I.A. Ex-Officials Rebut Torture Report," *New York Times,* Dec. 8, 2014, http://goo.gl/s20VfW.

97. Transcript, *Meet the Press,* NBC, Dec. 14, 2009, http://goo.gl/NU9ypB.

98. Unless otherwise noted, this section is a synthesis of Senate CIA Torture Report, 134–39, 342–51.

99. In June 2003, John Yoo had produced an unsigned, undated list of legal assertions about the torture program. It declared that sixteen "enhanced" techniques violated no law. It also declared that the Convention Against Torture's ban on cruel, inhuman, or degrading treatment that fell short of torture meant only that which was covered by the Eighth Amendment's ban on cruel and unusual punishment and the Fifth and Fourteenth Amendments' ban on government action that would shock the conscience; the idea was that noncitizens abroad are not covered by the Constitution, and so the cruelty ban did not restrict the CIA's actions as it detained foreigners in its overseas prisons. Goldsmith concluded that this bullet-points list of assertions did not constitute real legal analysis, and he said that, notwithstanding this memo, the Office of Legal Counsel had *never* opined on that issue (unsigned, undated memo, "Legal Principles Applicable to CIA Detention and Interrogation of Captured al-Qaeda Personnel," https://goo.gl/7OsFvC).

100. Goldsmith, *The Terror Presidency,* 160–63, http://goo.gl/zohik1.

101. John P. Mudd, "Memorandum for the Record: Meeting with National Security Advisor Rice in the White House Situation Room, Friday [redacted] 2004, re: Interrogations and Detainee [redacted]," [redacted] 2004, http://goo.gl/OiGFft.

102. Office of Professional Responsibility of the Department of Justice, Report re "Investigation into the Office of Legal Counsel's Memoranda Concerning Issues Relating

to the Central Intelligence Agency's Use of 'Enhanced Interrogation Techniques' on Suspected Terrorists," July 29, 2009 [released in redacted form February 2010], 123, http://goo.gl/vS8HqF.

103. The pressure on the Bush-Cheney officials at this moment was immense. Tenet and the top CIA lawyer, Scott Muller, also both abruptly resigned in mid-July.

104. Letter from Ashcroft to McLaughlin, July 22, 2004, http://goo.gl/ZFEiIp.

105. Letter from Levin to Rizzo, Aug. 6, 2004, http://goo.gl/ZFEiIp.

106. Letter from Levin to Rizzo, Aug. 26, 2004, http://goo.gl/ZFEiIp.

107. There were, to be sure, reasons to suspect that al-Qaeda might be up to something ahead of the 2004 presidential election. For one thing, an al-Qaeda suspect abroad had been found with documents suggesting someone had been casing financial institutions in New York, New Jersey, and Washington. For another, the March 11, 2004, bombing of Madrid's subway system, just ahead of the Spanish election, had influenced its outcome; see George Tenet with Bill Harlow, *At the Center of the Storm* (New York: HarperCollins: 2007), 245–47. But the only reason the CIA had to believe that Gul knew about any such plot was what the dubious informant had said.

108. See also Marcy Wheeler, "How a False Witness Helped the CIA Make a Case for Torture," AlJazeera.com, Dec. 22, 2014, http://goo.gl/5sKpHp.

109. Marty Lederman, "Al-Nashiri Can Now Speak About His Treatment...Plus News About Full SSCI Report," *Just Security*, Feb. 23, 2015, http://goo.gl/z4xAjh.

110. Charlie Savage, "Guantánamo Prosecutor Fights Handing Secrets Over to Defense," *New York Times*, May 4, 2014, http://goo.gl/Pxuk6F.

111. Letter from Ruemmler to Feinstein and Levin, Feb. 10, 2014, http://goo.gl/eyHPQb.

112. Mark Martins, "Remarks at Guantánamo Bay," Feb. 22, 2015, http://goo.gl/NVBNEk.

113. Carol Rosenberg, "Pentagon Scraps Judges' Guantánamo Move Order; 9/11 Case Unfrozen," *Miami Herald*, Feb. 27, 2015, http://goo.gl/5LG9Vv.

114. Carol Rosenberg, "War Court Judge Orders Pentagon to Replace USS *Cole* Trial Overseer," *Miami Herald*, Mar. 2, 2015, http://goo.gl/hcO49o.

115. Masha Gessen, "Boston Marathon Trial Opens with Heart-Rending Testimony on Attack," *Washington Post*, Mar. 4, 2015, http://goo.gl/WeX7STHuffin.

116. Rebekah Gregory, Facebook post, Mar. 4, 2015, http://goo.gl/A6j5HG.

117. Transcript, Barack Obama, State of the Union Address, Jan. 28, 2014, http://goo.gl/llwZ4P.

118. "Statement by the President on H.R. 3979," Dec. 19, 2014, http://goo.gl/Um3upv.

119. *Congressional Record*, S8179, Nov. 19, 2013, http://goo.gl/xqIyn8.

120. Transcript, Senate press conference, Jan. 13, 2015.

121. Transcript, Senate Armed Services Committee hearing, Guantánamo Detention Facility and the Future of United States Detention Policy, Feb. 5, 2015.

122. As of January 2015, the combined suspected and confirmed "recidivism" rate for those transferred after Obama took office was 6.1 percent—7 out of the 115 ex-detainees. Of the 532 ex-detainees transferred under Bush, 110 were confirmed and 68 were suspected of engaging in post-transfer militant activity, for a combined rate of 33.5 percent; "Summary of the Reengagement of Detainees Formerly Held at Guantánamo Bay, Cuba," Office of the Director of National Intelligence, report made public Mar. 4, 2015, http://goo.gl/TSaEoI.

123. Such a move might also violate the Antideficiency Act, which makes it a separate crime for an executive branch official to expend funds Congress has not appropriated.

124. Transcript, Senate Armed Services Committee hearing, The Nomination of Ashton Carter to be Defense Secretary, Feb. 4, 2015.
125. Martin Matishak, "McCain: Pentagon yet to offer plan to close Gitmo," *The Hill*, July 16, 2015, http://goo.gl/9IAM8h.
126. Charlie Savage, "6 Guantánamo Detainees From Yemen Are Transferred to Oman," *New York Times*, http://goo.gl/RIzCXK.

Chapter Eleven: Institutionalized (Surveillance 2009–2015)

1. Adam Liptak, "A Secret Surveillance Program Proves Challengeable in Theory Only," *New York Times*, July 15, 2013, http://goo.gl/iDVfVD.
2. *Amnesty Int'l v. McConnell*, No. 08-civ-6259. S.D.N.Y., Arguments transcript, July 22, 2009, https://goo.gl/QuiUcj.
3. *Amnesty Int'l v. McConnell*, No. 08-civ-6259. S.D.N.Y., Opinion and order, Aug. 20, 2009, https://goo.gl/Oub8K9.
4. Leaked NSA document, "Some Key (SSO) Cyber Milestones Since 2005," http://goo.gl/0FuI2K.
5. Savage, "F.B.I. Is Broadening Surveillance Role, Report Shows."
6. For the date of this change, see NSA Director of Civil Liberties and Privacy Office Report, "NSA's Implementation of Foreign Intelligence Surveillance Act Section 702," Apr. 16, 2014, 7, https://goo.gl/YW5xMX. That permission, however, was limited to Internet data gathered via Prism, not the upstream system that collected e-mails as they moved across network switches; see letter from Walsh to Wyden, June 27, 2014 ("June 2014 ODNI Letter"), https://goo.gl/6ZDMTB.
7. Savage, "F.B.I. Is Broadening Surveillance Role, Report Shows."
8. Charlie Savage, Julia Angwin, Jeff Larson, and Henrik Moltke, "Hunting for Hackers, N.S.A. Secretly Expands Internet Spying at U.S. Border," *New York Times*, June 5, 2015, http://goo.gl/jrNTAU.
9. *Amnesty Int'l v. Clapper*, 638 F.3d 118, (2d Cir. 2011), https://goo.gl/9WvRRB.
10. *Amnesty Int'l v. Clapper*, 133 S. Ct. 1138 (U.S. 2013, https://goo.gl/mDfIMl.
11. Senate roll-call vote 236, Dec. 28, 2012, http://goo.gl/0BojR.
12. *Congressional Record* 158, no. 168 (Thursday, December 27, 2012), S8391-S894, http://goo.gl/5Qn2Le. The *Congressional Record* transcript, however, is inaccurate in places. A C-SPAN video clip of her actual remarks is available at http://goo.gl/A7j9ka.
13. Eric Schmitt, David E. Sanger, and Charlie Savage, "Administration Says Mining of Data Is Crucial to Fight Terror," *New York Times*, June 7, 2013, http://goo.gl/8v9V5W.
14. Ellen Nakashima, "U.S. Revealed Secret Legal Basis for NSA Program to Sprint, Declassified Files Show," *Washington Post*, May 14, 2014, http://goo.gl/t8E9m5.
15. The technical official's objections were first reported in November 2014 by Ken Dilanian of the Associated Press, and I later spoke to several people familiar with it (Ken Dilanian, "Before Snowden, a Debate Inside NSA," Associated Press, Nov. 19, 2014, http://goo.gl/ONPkHM).
16. Indeed, when the program was revealed in June 2013, it initially appeared to be collecting records of literally all phone calls placed in the United States. Over time, it emerged that this assumption was overstated. The NSA was taking in records from the largest providers of *landline* accounts, but supposedly was missing customer data from many, but not all, *cell-phone* providers — not because of any legal hurdle but because mobile-phone data apparently raised additional technical problems.

An official told me that the NSA did not initially draw attention to this gap because it still wanted to overcome those technical hurdles and ingest it all. This remains murky; see Ellen Nakashima, "NSA Is Collecting Less Than 30 Percent of U.S. Call Data, Officials Say," *Washington Post*, Feb. 7, 2014, http://goo.gl/Euwyft; see also Charlie Savage, "N.S.A. Program Gathers Data on a Third of Nation's Calls, Officials Say," *New York Times*, Feb. 8. 2014, http://goo.gl/C7UbzZ.

17. Charlie Savage, "In Test Project, N.S.A. Tracked Cellphone Locations," *New York Times*, Oct. 3, 2013, http://goo.gl/HGf7QB.

18. Leaked NSA newsletter, [redacted], "Mobility Business Records Flow Significantly Increases Volume of Records Delivered Under BR FISA," *SSO News*, Aug. 30, 2011, http://goo.gl/LDpbiP.

19. Memorandum from Bauman to staff directors, House and Senate Judiciary Committees, re "Congressional Notification — NSA Acquisition and Use of Telephony Metadata from Cellular Network Call Detail Records," Sept. 1, 2011; see also Marcy Wheeler, "AT&T Pulled Cell Location for Its 'Mobility Cell Data,'" *Emptywheel*, Aug. 15, 2015.

20. While the dates of these events are redacted, Marcy Wheeler has offered a persuasive theory about the timing by marshaling associated clues; see Marcy Wheeler, "The Five Year Parade of Internet Dragnet Violations," *Emptywheel*, Nov. 20, 2013, http://goo.gl/0nKXQZ, and Marcy Wheeler, "The John Bates Internet Metadata Opinion Probably Dates to July 2010," *Emptywheel*, Nov. 20, 2013, http://goo.gl/2U05CB.

21. Generally in the law, *surveillance* is a term of art that refers to the collection of the *content* of a person's private communications, not collection of metadata records. But because of a complexity in the way FISA is written, when the government installs a device on a wire on domestic soil and uses that device to collect metadata about a communication involving an American for the purpose of a national security investigation, that *does* count as "electronic surveillance" and requires a court order. Of course, the NSA had, under Stellarwind, violated FISA left and right, but it was no longer operating under a president's purported authorization to lawfully bypass the statute. Violating FISA is a felony.

22. A 2011 NSA inspector general report that I obtained in a Freedom of Information Act lawsuit confirmed that Bates's opinion was in July 2010; NSA Inspector General, "Audit Reports on NSA Controls to Comply with the Foreign Intelligence Surveillance Court Order Regarding Business Records," May 25, 2011, http://goo.gl/7u5m2X.

23. [Case name redacted], FISC, Docket No: PR/TT [number redacted], "Memorandum opinion," [date redacted], http://goo.gl/UmVf7c.

24. ODNI press release, "DNI Clapper Declassifies Additional Intelligence Community Documents Regarding Collection Under Section 501 of the Foreign Intelligence Surveillance Act," Nov. 18, 2013, http://goo.gl/aXq0dw.

25. Senate press release, "Wyden, Udall Statement on the Disclosure of Bulk E-mail Records Collection Program," July 2, 2013, http://goo.gl/97W5vF.

26. See, for example, Glenn Greenwald, Ewen MacAskill, Laura Poitras, Spencer Ackerman, and Dominic Rushe, "Microsoft Handed the NSA Access to Encrypted Messages," *Guardian*, http://goo.gl/1hYdNp; July 12, 2013; Nicole Perlroth, Jeff Larson, and Scott Shane, "N.S.A. Able to Foil Basic Safeguards of Privacy on Web," *New York Times*, Sept. 6, 2013, http://goo.gl/sOHxnw.

27. Wheeler, "The Five Year Parade of Internet Dragnet Violations"; see also Marcy Wheeler, "John Bates' TWO Wiretapping Warnings: Why the Government Took Its Internet Dragnet Collection Overseas," *Emptywheel,* Nov. 20, 2013, http://goo.gl/ ANfF8O, and Marcy Wheeler, "SPCMA: The Other NSA Dragnet Sucking In Americans," *Emptywheel,* Feb. 17, 2014, http://goo.gl/M9yrEH.

28. James Risen and Laura Poitras, "N.S.A. Gathers Data on Social Connections of U.S. Citizens," *New York Times,* Sept. 23, 2013, http://goo.gl/eMI3I5.

29. Minimization rules for how the FBI can use data it obtains via the Prism system, for example, authorize it to extract and transfer "all" metadata associated with raw communications and use it for "link analysis" purposes; "Minimization Procedures for the Federal Bureau of Investigation in Connection with Acquisitions of Foreign Intelligence Information Pursuant to Section 702 of the Foreign Intelligence Surveillance Act of 1978, as Amended," July 25, 2014, http://goo.gl/Z6eIvF.

30. Charlie Savage, "U.S. Tries to Make It Easier to Wiretap the Internet," *New York Times,* Sept. 27, 2010, http://goo.gl/0bFU.

31. Charlie Savage, "F.B.I. Seeks Wider Wiretap Law for Web," *New York Times,* Nov. 17, 2010, http://goo.gl/XT4zy.

32. Ellen Nakashima, "Proposal Seeks to Fine Tech Companies for Noncompliance with Wiretap Orders," *Washington Post,* Apr. 28, 2013, http://goo.gl/h86A2.

33. Charlie Savage, "U.S. Weighs Wide Overhaul of Wiretap Laws," *New York Times,* May 7, 2013, http://goo.gl/kO7Zy.

34. Ryan Reilly, "FBI Director James Comey 'Very Concerned' about New Apple, Google Privacy Features," *Huffington Post,* Sept. 25, 2014, http://goo.gl/0yoqZG.

35. James Comey, "Going Dark: Are Technology, Privacy, and Public Safety on a Collision Course?" Oct. 16, 2014, http://goo.gl/K8NRrA.

36. Department of Homeland Security transcript, "Remarks by Secretary of Homeland Security Jeh Johnson at the RSA Conference 2015," Apr. 21, 2015, http://goo.gl/ XsFrxe.

37. Kara Swisher, "Obama: The *Re/code* Interview," *Re/code,* Feb. 18, 2015, http://goo.gl/ uVHnvZ.

38. Letter from Turner to Wyden, July 20, 2012, http://goo.gl/AvP7Rf.

39. Two technical problems caused this issue. First, sometimes a single, wholly domestic Internet message happens to flow outside the country and come back in again, so that it looks like a one-end-foreign message to the filtering system — and thus fair game for FISA Amendments Act warrantless surveillance — even though it is not. When such a purely domestic message contains a targeted foreigner's e-mail address or phone number in its body, the system collects it. Second, sometimes Internet companies bundle groups of messages together and transmit the bundle as a unit. (One example of this: when you log in to a web-based e-mail service, each item in your inbox is considered to be a separate communication, but all of them are listed on the same web page and so flow to your web browser as a single transaction.) If just one of those messages in the bundle contains a targeted foreigner's e-mail address or phone number, the NSA collects all of them — including messages in the bundle that were both wholly domestic and had no link at all to any targeted foreigner.

40. Bates opinion, Oct. 3, 2011.

41. Bates's finding that the NSA was violating the Fourth Amendment was limited to the collection of bundles containing wholly domestic messages that had no link to a

foreign target, which the NSA called Multi-Communication Transactions, or MCTs. He ruled it was lawful for the NSA to intercept and use single messages that contained a target's selector and that were wholly domestic messages but had been routed outside the country and had come back in. His reasoning was that this latter collection — while anticipatable — was incidental and not purposeful.

42. Leaked internal NSA newsletters, reproduced in Ewen MacAskill, "NSA Paid Millions to Cover Prism Compliance Costs for Tech Companies," *Guardian*, Aug. 23, 2013, http://goo.gl/Xw50Vk.

43. E-mail from Mary Ellen Callahan to John Cohen et al., June 17, 2011, obtained under FOIA by Julia Angwin, http://goo.gl/hazkfc.

44. I learned of the existence of this meeting from Julia Angwin, "U.S. Terrorism Agency to Tap a Vast Database of Citizens," *Wall Street Journal*, Dec. 13, 2012, http://goo.gl/dyJCr1.

45. Charlie Savage, "U.S. Relaxes Limits on Use of Data in Terror Analysis," *New York Times*, Mar. 23, 2012, http://goo.gl/mzogn.

46. Savage and Poitras, "How a Court Secretly Evolved, Extending U.S. Spies' Reach."

47. Charlie Savage, "Government Declassifies Surveillance Court Documents on 'Raw Take' Sharing," *New York Times*, Mar. 3, 2015, http://goo.gl/ASwjIN.

48. "Transcript: Senator Dick Durbin on Surveillance, Terrorism and the Constitution," *Irregular Times*, Oct. 5, 2009, http://goo.gl/mryMI8.

49. 157 *Cong. Rec.* S3259 (daily ed., May 24, 2011).

50. Most of his campaign advisers, of course, had no idea that they were offering very misleading policy analysis to Romney, although one member of the campaign subcommittee was Steven Bradbury, who, as head of the Office of Legal Counsel in 2006, had played a crucial role in persuading the FISA Court to accept that secret interpretation of the Patriot Act. (See chapter 5, section 9.) This was all still top secret, however, and I found no evidence that Bradbury weighed in on the Patriot Act memo. But the point is that during an election, secrecy thwarted even an opportunity for meaningful debate about an important public-policy issue.

51. Transcript, Senate Select Committee on Intelligence hearing, "National Security Threats to the United States," Mar. 12, 2013.

52. Transcript, press conference with Dianne Feinstein and Saxby Chambliss, June 6, 2013, http://goo.gl/AQbhSA.

53. Transcript, Andrea Mitchell interviews James Clapper, NBC News, June 9, 2013, http://goo.gl/p2jmc4.

54. Letter from Clapper to Feinstein, June 21, 2013, http://goo.gl/IpDbTQ.

55. Glenn Greenwald, Ewen MacAskill, and Laura Poitras, "Edward Snowden: the whistleblower behind the NSA surveillance revelations," *Guardian*, June 11, 2013, http://goo.gl/7JBfwH.

56. Jonathan Weisman, "House Defeats Effort to Rein In N.S.A. Data Gathering," *New York Times*, July 25, 2013, http://goo.gl/X38cyg.

57. *Face the Nation*, CBS, July 28, 2013, http://goo.gl/2yyv2K.

58. Charlie Savage and David E. Sanger, "Senate Panel Presses N.S.A. on Phone Logs," *New York Times*, Aug. 1, 2013, http://goo.gl/HFJ37f.

59. Ibid.

60. Schmitt et al., "Administration Says Mining of Data Is Crucial to Fight Terror."

61. Charlie Savage, "Door May Open for Challenge to Secret Wiretaps," *New York Times*, Oct. 17, 2013, http://goo.gl/P5A4cO.

62. *ACLU v. U.S. Dep't of Justice,* S.D.N.Y., No. 13-7347, "Declaration of Mark A. Bradley," July 25, 2014, https://goo.gl/GTbjld.
63. Liptak, "A Secret Surveillance Program Proves Challengeable in Theory Only."
64. Charlie Savage, "Federal Prosecutors, in a Policy Shift, Cite Warrantless Wiretaps as Evidence," *New York Times,* Oct. 27, 2013, http://goo.gl/Wl89KF.
65. Charlie Savage, "Warrantless Surveillance Continues to Cause Fallout," *New York Times,* Nov. 21, 2013, http://goo.gl/dBeq8V.
66. Charlie Savage, "Clashing Rulings Weigh Security and Liberties," *New York Times,* June 25, 2014, http://goo.gl/oFrr7q.
67. Letter from Morgan Frankel to Thomas Durkin, Sept. 16, 2013, http://goo.gl/yf9Rwp.
68. Charlie Savage, "Newest Spy Court Pick Is a Democrat but Not a Liberal," *New York Times,* Aug. 20, 2013, http://goo.gl/Hkg05I.
69. McLaughlin was primarily Specter's choice. He was, to be sure, from the moderate wing of the Republican Party. Nine years later, at the end of his career, Specter switched to the Democratic Party in hopes of avoiding a primary campaign loss against a more conservative challenger.
70. Charlie Savage, "Roberts's Picks Reshaping Secret Surveillance Court," *New York Times,* July 26, 2013, http://goo.gl/9P8mXO.
71. Savage, "Newest Spy Court Pick Is a Democrat but Not a Liberal."
72. Neil A. Lewis, "A Nomination Is Withdrawn, and a Deal Is Threatened," *New York Times,* May 28, 1998, http://goo.gl/r7cb7q; Douglas Martin, "Betty Binns Fletcher Dies at 89; Liberal Stalwart on the Bench," *New York Times,* Oct. 25, 2012, http://goo.gl/XnUmKA.
73. Charlie Savage, "N.S.A. Program Gathers Data on a Third of Nation's Calls, Officials Say," *New York Times,* Feb. 8, 2014, http://goo.gl/C7UbzZ.
74. Ibid.
75. Cass Sunstein et al., *Are Judges Political? An Empirical Analysis of the Federal Judiciary* (New York: Brookings Institution Press, 2006); Robert A. Carp et al., "The Decision-Making Behavior of George W. Bush's Judicial Appointees," *Judicature* 88, no. 1 (July–Aug. 2004), http://goo.gl/grLvVJ.
76. Letter from Bates to Feinstein, Jan. 13, 2014, http://goo.gl/0RlujD.
77. Mark Landler, "Obama's Fall Moscow Trip Is Even More in Doubt," *New York Times,* Aug. 2, 2013, http://goo.gl/qr8SzM.
78. S.1551 — Intelligence Oversight and Surveillance Reform Act, 113th Congress (2013–2014), https://goo.gl/FlLP8W.
79. S.1631 — FISA Improvements Act of 2013, 113th Congress (2013–2014), https://goo.gl/4K0NcG.
80. S. Rept. 113–119 — FISA IMPROVEMENTS ACT OF 2013, Nov. 12, 2013, https://goo.gl/PB6Izd.
81. H.R.3361 — USA FREEDOM Act and S.1599 — USA FREEDOM Act, 113th Congress (2013–2014), https://goo.gl/s3zzGu and https://goo.gl/Ue2p6J.
82. Office of Dianne Feinstein press release, "Senate Intelligence Committee Approves FISA Improvements Act," Oct. 31, 2013, http://goo.gl/N59yOc.
83. Brendan Sasso and Bob Cusack, "Patriot Act author: Feinstein's bill 'a joke,'" *The Hill,* Dec. 10, 2013, http://goo.gl/mFvVYR.
84. Office of Senator Wyden press release, "Wyden Statement of Support for the USA FREEDOM Act," Nov. 5, 2013, http://goo.gl/jCeJSr.

85. See, for example, Scott Shane and Colin Moynihan, "Drug Agents Use Vast Phone Trove, Eclipsing N.S.A.'s," *New York Times*, Sept. 2, 2013, http://goo.gl/wgbfhR. Charlie Savage, "C.I.A. Is Said to Pay AT&T for Call Data," *New York Times*, Nov. 7, 2013, http://goo.gl/CrmIkF.

86. Brad Heath, "U.S. Secretly Tracked Billions of Calls for Decades," *USA Today*, Apr. 8, 2015, http://goo.gl/Q59MSC.

87. *Schuchardt v. Obama*, W.D.Pa., "Brief in Support of Defendants' Motion to Dismiss Plaintiff's First Amended Complaint," Oct. 20, 2013, http://goo.gl/qQdtnV.

88. It included Richard Clarke, the former Clinton and Bush-Cheney White House homeland security adviser; Michael Morell, the former CIA deputy director; two prominent law professors Obama had met in his University of Chicago days, Geoffrey Stone and Cass Sunstein, and the technologist Peter Swire. Morell had just stepped down in August, and Sunstein had served as Obama's top regulatory officer until 2012.

89. "Liberty and Security in a Changing World: Report and Recommendations of the President's Review Group on Intelligence and Communications Technologies," Dec. 12, 2013, http://goo.gl/T4IHrf.

90. Charlie Savage, "Judge Questions Legality of N.S.A. Phone Records," *New York Times*, Dec. 17, 2013, http://goo.gl/C6J8Yi. In March 2014, a FISA Court judge — and colleague of Judge Leon's on the Federal District Court for the District of Columbia, Rosemary Collyer — rejected his reasoning and permitted the program to continue. Charlie Savage, "Phone Company Bid to Keep Data From N.S.A. Is Rejected," *New York Times*, Apr. 25, 2014, http://goo.gl/wyuLV2.

91. Adam Liptak and Michael Schmidt, "Judge Upholds N.S.A.'s Bulk Collection of Data on Calls," *New York Times*, Dec. 27, 2013, http://goo.gl/sFKEI1.

92. The board consisted of five members. Three — its chairman, David Medine, Patricia Wald, a former appeals court judge, and Jim Dempsey, a privacy advocate and technology expert — were selected by Democrats. Two — Rachel Brand and Elisebeth Collins Cook, both former Justice Department lawyers in the Bush-Cheney administration — were selected by Republicans.

93. Charlie Savage, "Watchdog Report Says N.S.A. Program Is Illegal and Should End," *New York Times*, Jan. 24, 2014, http://goo.gl/uwGege.

94. Julia Angwin, Charlie Savage, Jeff Larson, Henrik Moltke, Laura Poitras, and James Risen, "AT&T Helped N.S.A. Spy on an Array of Internet Traffic."

95. Presidential Policy Directive/PPD-28, "Signals Intelligence Activities," Jan. 17, 2014, http://goo.gl/Hbl8lv.

96. Siobhan Gorman, "White House Added Last-Minute Curbs on NSA Before Obama Speech," *Wall Street Journal*, Jan. 31, 2014, http://goo.gl/TGVUw0.

97. There was a precedent: Judge Reggie Walton had briefly required judicial review of each new query of the bulk data during the 2009 compliance problems. See chapter 5, section 1.

98. The need to go to the FISA Court and prove that the standard of suspicion had been met later appeared to have had consequences. In 2013, before the change, the NSA queried its bulk phone records database for 423 newly identified suspicious phone numbers (on top of checking up on the old ones). In 2014, after the change, it queried only 161 newly identified phone numbers; Office of Director of National Intelligence, "2013 Transparency Report," June 26, 2014, http://goo.gl/DCL0e5; Office of Director of National Intelligence, "Calendar Year 2014 Transparency Report," Apr. 22, 2015, http://goo.gl/iaOXIw.

99. One change came fast: Ten days later, the Justice Department told larger Internet companies that they would now be permitted to disclose aggregate numbers of the demands they received from the government for customer records. This permitted the providers to show that only a small number of their user accounts were subject to surveillance. Letter from Cole to general counsels of Internet firms, Jan. 27, 2014, http://goo.gl/2eEnyL.

100. "Remarks by the President on Review of Signals Intelligence," Jan. 17, 2014, http://goo.gl/Teh82o.

101. Charlie Savage, "Obama Says N.S.A. Curbs Would Address Worries," *New York Times*, March 26, 2014, http://goo.gl/IhMrtZ.

102. Charlie Savage, "N.S.A. Used Phone Records Program to Seek Iran Operatives," *New York Times*, Aug. 13, 2015, http://goo.gl/2uzFBD.

103. Charlie Savage, "Obama to Call for End to N.S.A.'s Bulk Data Collection," *New York Times*, March 25, 2015, http://goo.gl/i0OoWT.

104. White House transcript, "Press Conference with President Obama and Prime Minister Rutte of the Netherlands," March 25, 2014, http://goo.gl/dsV6Fq; see also Savage, "Obama Says N.S.A. Curbs Would Address Worries."

105. *Twitter v. Holder*, No. 14-448, N.D.Cal., "Complaint For Declaratory Judgment," Oct 7, 2014, http://goo.gl/Ivemht.

106. Julia Angwin, Charlie Savage, Jeff Larson, Henrik Moltke, Laura Poitras, and James Risen, "AT&T Helped N.S.A. Spy on an Array of Internet Traffic."

107. See, for example, Anton Troianovski, Thomas Gryta, and Sam Schechner, "NSA Fallout Thwarts AT&T," *Wall Street Journal*, Oct. 30, 2013, http://goo.gl/yJqqrE.

108. One possibility is an aggressive reconceptualization of the provision from FISA that authorizes the attorney general to send letters to firms certifying that their provision of "information, facilities and technical assistance" without a court order is not just lawful but "is required." This is speculation. See also chapter 5's endnote 23 for more discussion of this provision.

109. H.R.4291 — FISA Transparency and Modernization Act (113th Congress, 2013–2014), https://goo.gl/FujzMb.

110. Charlie Savage and Mark Mazzetti, "C.I.A. Collects Global Data on Transfers of Money," *New York Times*, Nov. 15, 2013, http://goo.gl/LB4FmN; Siobhan Gorman, Devlin Barrett, and Jennifer Valentino-Devries, "CIA's Financial Spying Bags Data on Americans," *Wall Street Journal*, Nov. 15, 2013, http://goo.gl/INYLuK.

111. Charlie Savage, "Rival House Bills Aim to Rein In N.S.A. Phone Data Program," *New York Times*, May 6, 2014, http://goo.gl/xufB5R.

112. Charlie Savage, "House Panel Advances Bill on N.S.A. Collection of Phone Data," *New York Times*, May 9, 2014, http://goo.gl/6acxNJ.

113. Charlie Savage, "Changes to Surveillance Bill Stoke Anger," *New York Times*, May 20, 2014, http://goo.gl/Uo1SE9.

114. Roll call vote 230, 113th Congress, May 22, 2014, http://goo.gl/FIPfZR.

115. They included Matt Owen, an aide to Senator Mike Lee, Republican of Utah; Sam Simon, an aide to Senator Richard Blumenthal, Democrat of Connecticut; and Alvaro Bedoya, an aide to Senator Al Franken, Democrat of Minnesota.

116. S.2685 — USA FREEDOM Act of 2014, 113th Congress (2013–2014), https://goo.gl/GsfVgy; see also Charlie Savage, "Senator's Bill Is Stricter on N.S.A. Than House's," *New York Times*, July 25, 2014, http://goo.gl/HmpFxw.

117. Letter from Holder and Clapper to Leahy, Sept. 2, 2014, http://goo.gl/6Ufce6.

118. Michael V. Hayden and Michael B. Mukasey, "NSA Reform That Only ISIS Could Love," *Wall Street Journal*, http://goo.gl/PK3bRr.

119. There was a way, as my former Georgetown class co-teacher Mike Davidson, Feinstein's former attorney, pointed out, for the program to go indefinitely even if the law expired. A little-noticed part of the Patriot Act said the law did not sunset for investigations that had begun before June 1, but continued into force for them. Since the FBI has wide-ranging, open-ended investigations into groups that pose threats to public safety — like al-Qaeda or the Islamic State — the Justice Department could invoke that grandfather clause and those investigations to justify continued collection of phone records. But Obama administration officials vowed not to use that approach, instead keeping the pressure on Congress to pass the Freedom Act. Charlie Savage, "N.S.A. Phone Data Collection Could Go On, Even if a Law Expires," *New York Times*, Nov. 20, 2014, http://goo.gl/6p7PZ3.

120. Charlie Savage and Jeremy Peter, "Bill to Restrict N.S.A. Data Collection Blocked in Vote by Senate Republicans," *New York Times*, Nov. 19, 2014, http://goo.gl/mlGVCn.

121. There were some shifts. Heather Sawyer was detailed to the Democratic staff on the special committee to investigate the Benghazi attacks, so dropped out of Freedom Act work. Lee's staffer, Owen, was succeeded by Mike Lemon. Lynch was assisted by Jason Herring, a detailee to the Judiciary Committee staff from the FBI.

122. Electronic communications transactional records are Internet metadata — not just who sent an e-mail to whom and when, but the locations where users had logged in and targets' website browsing history. The FBI used to be able to get that information with a national security letter, but in 2008 the Office of Legal Counsel issued a memo saying that these kinds of records fell outside the list of things that could be obtained that way. The FBI believed the problem was a mere drafting error in the statute, and had been trying to get Congress to amend the law — something privacy advocates opposed — since 2010; Ellen Nakashima, "White House proposal would ease FBI access to records of Internet activity," *Washington Post*, July 29, 2010, http://goo.gl/1Jed.

123. S.1123 — USA FREEDOM Act of 2015, 114th Congress (2015–2016), https://goo.gl/3fb6zf; H.R.2048 — USA FREEDOM Act of 2015, 114th Congress (2015–2016), https://goo.gl/5BwjQ1.

124. *ACLU v. Clapper*, Case 14-42, 2nd Cir., May 7, 2015, http://goo.gl/8XSPkH; see also Charlie Savage and Jonathan Weisman, "N.S.A. Collection of Bulk Call Data Is Ruled Illegal," *New York Times*, May 8, 2015, http://goo.gl/dY19AS.

125. Charlie Savage, "Surveillance Court Rules That N.S.A. Can Resume Bulk Data Collection," *New York Times*, June 30, 2015, http://goo.gl/N5tqXS.

126. Charlie Savage, "A.C.L.U. Asks Court to Stop Part of N.S.A.'s Bulk Phone Data Collection," *New York Times*, July 15, 2015, http://goo.gl/ZPTSu6.

127. Dan Froomkin, "Hayden Mocks Extent of Post-Snowden Reform: 'And This Is It After Two Years? Cool!'" *Intercept*, June 18, 2015, https://goo.gl/3fzJ1y.

128. Barton Gellman and Ashkan Soltani, "NSA Infiltrates Links to Yahoo, Google Data Centers Worldwide, Snowden Documents Say," *Washington Post*, Oct. 30, 2013, http://goo.gl/qPFLZZ.

129. Joseph Heller, *Catch-22* (New York: Simon and Schuster, 1999), 25, http://goo.gl/41UB8R.

130. Barton Gellman, Ashkan Soltani, and Andrea Peterson, "How We Know the NSA Had Access to Internal Google and Yahoo Cloud Data," *Washington Post,* Nov. 4, 2013, http://goo.gl/GfSBGG.

131. They recommended two big changes. First, the government should be barred from searching the storehouse of intercepted communications for a specific American's information without getting a court order. And second, even if officials found derogatory information about an American in the storehouse — perhaps while searching through the raw data using a keyword like *drugs* — prosecutors should not be permitted to introduce the intercept as evidence against the American in a criminal trial.

132. "Disclosures Action Tracker as of 1200 on Jan. 24 [2014]," http://goo.gl/M0yDTn.

133. Charlie Savage, "Reagan-Era Order on Surveillance Violates Rights, Says Departing Aide," *New York Times,* Aug. 14, 2014, http://goo.gl/qr1MUz.

134. John Napier Tye, "Meet Executive Order 12333: The Reagan rule that lets the NSA spy on Americans," *Washington Post,* July 18, 2014, http://goo.gl/YJlXvg.

135. The 12333-collected metadata could be analyzed without high-level permission, for any foreign-intelligence purpose, and going out as many links as an analyst wanted to look. By contrast, bulk phone records collected through the Patriot Act program could be analyzed only for counterterrorism purposes and, after Obama's January 2014 reforms, only with the permission of the FISA Court and only to two links from a starting point.

136. The NSA did not share raw 12333 content with other agencies, unlike the raw sharing of Prism-gathered FISA Amendments Act content. And NSA analysts needed the attorney general's permission to query the storehouse of previously collected 12333 content for an American's name, but not to search the FISA Amendments Act storehouse.

137. June 2014 ODNI Letter.

138. An FBI official explained to me how their system for searching the results of surveillance from unrelated investigations works. The FBI commingles, into a database, raw communications it has gathered under traditional FISA wiretaps and communications it has gathered via Prism under the FISA Amendments Act. Agents conducting counterterrorism or counterintelligence investigations may search this repository at will, including using an American's identifier to pull up things to read. Agents working on criminal squads may also search it for anything about someone linked to one of their investigations. However, while criminal squad agents can see any hits from the repository for information gathered from ordinary Title III criminal wiretaps, the FBI computer system does not let them see FISA results right away. Rather, it tells them that the FISA repository has *something* related to their query, and they need higher-level permission to see what it is.

139. House of Representatives roll-call vote 356, June 11, 2015, http://goo.gl/2dGb9V.

Chapter Twelve: The Tug of War

1. Mark Mazzetti, "C.I.A. Study of Covert Aid Fueled Skepticism about Helping Syrian Rebels," *New York Times,* Oct. 15, 2014, http://goo.gl/oOMLxb.

2. Peter Baker, Mark Landler, David E. Sanger, and Anne Barnard, "Off-the-Cuff Obama Line Put U.S. in Bind on Syria," *New York Times,* May 4, 2013, http://goo.gl/mOnmQ3.

3. Michael J. Matheson, "Justification for the NATO Air Campaign in Kosovo," 94 *Am. Soc'y Int'l L. Proc.* 301, Apr. 8, 2000, http://goo.gl/d67nzN.
4. Jason Linkins, "Joe Biden Warned in 2007 That He'd Impeach Bush for Waging War without Congressional Approval," *Huffington Post,* Mar. 23, 2011, http://goo.gl/YpxG7.
5. Savage, "Barack Obama's Q&A."
6. Clinton: "I do not believe that the President can take military action—including any kind of strategic bombing—against Iran without congressional authorization." Biden: "What looks 'limited' to us almost certainly would be seen as something much bigger by the Iranians and could spark an all-out war....It is precisely because the consequences of war—intended or otherwise—can be so profound and complicated that our Founding Fathers vested in Congress, not the President, the power to initiate war, except to repel an imminent attack on the United States or its citizens." Charlie Savage, "Hillary Clinton Q&A," *Boston Globe,* Dec. 20, 2007, http://goo.gl/JiYWpa; Charlie Savage, "Joseph Biden Q&A," *Boston Globe,* Dec. 20, 2007, http://goo.gl/INrlcm.
7. Charlie Savage, "Attack Renews Debate over Congressional Consent," *New York Times,* Mar. 22, 2011, http://goo.gl/RbdWWJ.
8. Letter from Dellinger to United States senators, re "Deployment of United States Armed Forces into Haiti," Office of the Legal Counsel of the Department of Justice, Sept. 27, 1994, http://goo.gl/P5hV3W.
9. Charlie Savage, "D.E.A. Squads Extend Reach of Drug War," *New York Times,* Nov. 7, 2011, http://goo.gl/x3uu7; Charlie Savage and Thom Shanker, "D.E.A.'s Agents Join Counternarcotics Efforts in Honduras," *New York Times,* May 17, 2012, http://goo.gl/jEA090; Damien Cave, Charlie Savage, and Thom Shanker, "A New Front Line in the U.S. Drug War," *New York Times,* June 1, 2012, http://goo.gl/L5PjA; Charlie Savage, "Man Is Killed by U.S. Agent in Drug Raid in Honduras," *New York Times,* June 25, 2012, http://goo.gl/7ddhSf; Charlie Savage and Thom Shanker, "Drug Smuggling Suspect Killed by D.E.A. Agents in Honduras," *New York Times,* July 9, 2012, http://goo.gl/7mdAR.
10. Damien Cave and Ginger Thompson, "U.S. Rethinks a Drug War after Deaths in Honduras," *New York Times,* Oct. 13, 2012, http://goo.gl/eqRoaY.
11. Sanger, "Obama Order Sped Up Wave of Cyberattacks Against Iran."
12. White House report, "Cyberspace Policy Review: Assuring a Trusted and Resilient Information and Communications Infrastructure," May 2009, https://goo.gl/yZZDh2. Its classified annex, leaked by Edward Snowden and published by the *New York Times* and *ProPublica* in June 2015, is available here: https://goo.gl/NMY0VE.
13. Harold Hongju Koh, remarks at Cybercom, "International Law in Cyberspace," Sept. 18, 2012, http://goo.gl/DCirIF.
14. Leaked White House document, Presidential Policy Directive 20, "U.S. Cyber Operations Policy," https://goo.gl/SdjgCv.
15. S. Res. 85, 112th Cong., Mar. 1, 2011, http://goo.gl/hHuAcr.
16. Dan Bilefsky and Mark Landler, "As U.N. Backs Military Action in Libya, U.S. Role Is Unclear," *New York Times,* Mar. 18, 2011, http://goo.gl/uQ3Mya.
17. United Nations Security Council Resolution 1973, Mar. 17, 2011, http://goo.gl/M0MJXG.
18. Senate Committee on Foreign Relations, hearing re "Popular Uprising in the Middle East: Implications for U.S. Policy," Mar. 17, 2011, http://goo.gl/InUIYu.

19. Memorandum opinion from Krass for Holder, "Authority to Use Military Force in Libya," Office of Legal Counsel of the Department of Justice, Apr. 1, 2011, http://goo.gl/ILV0bn.

20. Among the anticipated "facts" submitted to Krass around March 18 and cited in her April 1 memo in support of this conclusion was that "[a]s of March 31, 2011, the United States had transferred responsibility for all ongoing coalition military operations in Libya to the North Atlantic Treaty Alliance." While NATO took over air traffic control in the theater after that date, American aircraft kept bombing pro-Gadhafi forces for defense-of-civilian missions through April 4. By the time the lawyers realized this ambiguity, it was too late to change the memo.

21. Charlie Savage, "Attack Renews Debate Over Congressional Consent," *New York Times,* Mar. 22, 2011, http://goo.gl/ELWWZ.

22. *Congressional Record,* S2110–S2111, Apr. 5, 2011, http://goo.gl/hJcCyk.

23. Although Russia and China had not agreed to permit a war of regime change, and although the United Nations Security Council mandate on its face was limited to protecting civilians, on April 15, Obama and the leaders of Britain and France triumphantly made clear ousting Gadhafi was their aim. The Western leaders wrote in a joint op-ed column that "so long as Qaddafi is in power, NATO must maintain its operations so that civilians remain protected and the pressure on the regime builds.... Qaddafi must go and go for good." Barack Obama, David Cameron, and Nicholas Sarkozy, "Libya's Pathway to Peace," *New York Times,* Apr. 15, 2011, http://goo.gl/GEKrt7.

24. Charlie Savage and Thom Shanker, "Scores of U.S. Strikes in Libya Followed Handoff to NATO," *New York Times,* June 21, 2011, http://goo.gl/Y6N5oF.

25. Inexplicably, it is almost routine to see this empirically false claim put forward as if it were an uncontested fact, including by former high-level government officials, and published in prominent outlets without correction. See, for example, Stephen G. Rademaker, "Congress and the Myth of the 60-Day Clock," *Washington Post,* May 24, 2011, http://goo.gl/gOR3b; Michael B. Mukasey and David B. Rivkin Jr., "Another Obama Collision with the Constitution," *Wall Street Journal,* Feb. 20, 2015, http://goo.gl/k08ZpR.

26. Justice Department Office of Legal Counsel, memorandum opinion from Harmon to attorney general, "Presidential Power to Use the Armed Forces Abroad without Statutory Authorization," Feb. 12, 1980, http://goo.gl/KkYCdh.

27. Justice Department Office of Legal Counsel, memorandum opinion from Moss to attorney general, "Authorization for Continuing Hostilities in Kosovo," Dec. 19, 2000, http://goo.gl/KkYCdh.

28. Charles Krauthammer, "The Obama Doctrine: Leading from Behind," *Washington Post,* Apr. 28, 2011, http://goo.gl/W8eib.

29. On day sixty, Obama sent a letter to Congress expressing support for the Senate resolution McCain and Kerry had developed, but without conceding that it was legally necessary; letter from Obama to congressional leaders, May 20, 2011, http://goo.gl/eFn6YB.

30. John Stanton, "Boehner Seeks Answers on Libya Operation," *Roll Call,* June 1, 2011, http://goo.gl/VzyWx6; David A. Fahrenthold and Felicia Sonmez, "Congressmen Criticize Obama's Stand on Libya," *Washington Post,* June 16, 2011, http://goo.gl/HM0L6h; transcript, "Harry Reid Confident of 'Substantial' U.S. Troop Drawdown

in Afghanistan," *NewsHour,* PBS, June 17, 2011, http://goo.gl/5tRlHB. McConnell was indirect about it; he said he was deferring to McCain. Eleven days earlier, McCain had said publicly that the sixty-day clock was unconstitutional; interview with Mitch McConnell, *Fox News Sunday,* May 22, 2011, http://goo.gl/LDfSTC; transcript, press conference with Senators Joe Lieberman, John McCain, Marco Rubio, and Benjamin Cardin, re "Bipartisan Resolution on the Human Rights Situation in Syria," Federal News Service, May 11, 2011.

31. Charlie Savage and Thom Shanker, "As NATO Claims Progress in Libya, a U.S. Deadline Is Put to the Test," *New York Times,* May 21, 2011, http://goo.gl/1fJIav.

32. Charlie Savage, "Libya Effort Is Called Violation of War Act," *New York Times,* May 26, 2011, http://goo.gl/b24EWX.

33. Jennifer Steinhauer and Charlie Savage, "House Sets Votes on Two Resolutions Critical of U.S. Role in Libyan Conflict," *New York Times,* June 2, 2011, http://goo.gl/Cr5YT; House of Representatives roll-call votes 411 and 412, June 3, 2011, http://goo.gl/1QJBnD and http://goo.gl/1eDpl.

34. Charlie Savage and Mark Landler, "White House Defends Continuing U.S. Role in Libya Operation," *New York Times,* June 16, 2011, http://goo.gl/ucFaMC.

35. Koh had won tenure at Yale Law School on the basis of a 1988 law-journal article, written in the wake of the Iran-Contra scandal, that called for a much stronger congressional role in national security and foreign affairs. Harold Hongju Koh, "Why the President (Almost) Always Wins in Foreign Affairs: Lessons of the Iran-Contra Affair," *Yale Law Journal* 97 (1987–1988): 1255, http://goo.gl/N3sH4b.

    Still, there was another strand running through his intellectual history, less remarked upon. Koh had also long been worried about presidential weakness in matters of foreign affairs — especially the examples of Jimmy Carter and Bill Clinton, both Democrats — a weakness that could prevent them from acting to contain crises, including those with human rights dimensions, before they escalated. In a 1995 essay, Koh wrote that he "advocated not a weak President, but a strong president within a strong constitutional system" because "weak presidents are more dangerous than strong ones." Harold Hongju Koh, "War and Responsibility in the Dole-Gingrich Congress," *University of Miami Law Review* 50 (October 1, 1995): 1–16.

36. Harold Hongju Koh, remarks before the American Constitution Society, June 17, 2011, http://goo.gl/OjVYVo.

37. Charlie Savage, "2 Top Lawyers Lost to Obama in Libya War Policy Debate," *New York Times,* June 17, 2011, http://goo.gl/ZA0eC.

38. Bruce Ackerman, "Legal Acrobatics, Illegal War," *New York Times,* June 21, 2011, http://goo.gl/zWOiq.

39. House of Representatives roll-call votes 412 (June 3, 2011), http://goo.gl/1eDpl; 493 (June 24, 2011), http://goo.gl/LWLasJ; and 494 (June 24, 2011), http://goo.gl/c404Zs.

40. Jennifer Steinhauer, "House Spurns Obama on Libya, but Does Not Cut Funds," *New York Times,* June 25, 2011, http://goo.gl/MUFWb.

41. White House transcript, "Press Conference by the President," June 29, 2011, http://goo.gl/m7ZEa4.

42. Mark Mazzetti, "C.I.A. Study of Covert Aid Fueled Skepticism about Helping Syrian Rebels," *New York Times,* Oct. 15, 2014, http://goo.gl/oOMLxb.

43. White House press release, "Government Assessment of the Syrian Government's Use of Chemical Weapons on August 21, 2013," Aug. 30, 2013, http://goo.gl/st2nsr.

44. Paul Harris, Martin Chulov, David Batty, and Damien Pearse, "Syria Resolution Vetoed by Russia and China at United Nations," *Guardian*, Feb. 4, 2012, http://goo.gl/evgQJK.

45. "Remarks by the President at the Acceptance of the Nobel Peace Prize."

46. White House transcript, "Remarks by President Obama and Prime Minister Reinfeldt of Sweden in Joint Press Conference," Sept. 4, 2013, http://goo.gl/m8p7zP.

47. White House transcript, "Remarks by President Obama in a Press Conference at the G20," Sept. 6, 2013, http://goo.gl/D64EsM.

48. Anthony Faiola, "British Prime Minister David Cameron Loses Parliamentary Vote on Syrian Military Strike," *Washington Post*, Aug. 29, 2013, http://goo.gl/qL0gbJ.

49. Charlie Savage, "Obama Tests Limits of Power in Syrian Conflict," *New York Times*, Sept. 9, 2014, http://goo.gl/y1Y569.

50. Adam Entous and Carol E. Lee, "At the Last Minute, Obama Alone Made Call to Seek Congressional Approval," *Wall Street Journal*, Aug. 31, 2013, http://goo.gl/cmCD7T.

51. "Remarks by President Obama and Prime Minister Reinfeldt of Sweden in Joint Press Conference."

52. Lara Jakes and Jennifer Agiesta, "Most Americans Oppose Strike on Syria, Poll Shows," Associated Press, Sept. 9, 2013, http://goo.gl/BChqWN.

53. Israel's ambassador to Washington at that point, Michael Oren, said in his 2015 memoir, *Ally*, that Israel's intelligence minister Yuval Steinitz first proposed this plan to Russia, although Israel's involvement was not disclosed at the time. A senior American official disputed that account; Eli Lake, "Israel Helped Obama Skirt 'Red Line' on Syria," *Bloomberg View*, June 15, 2015, http://goo.gl/hV8J15.

54. Adam Entous, Janet Hook, and Carol E. Lee, "Inside White House, a Head-Spinning Reversal on Chemical Weapons," *Wall Street Journal*, Sept. 16, 2013, http://goo.gl/6NQfOY.

55. Thom Shanker and Lauren D'Avolio, "Former Defense Secretaries Criticize Obama on Syria," *New York Times*, Sept. 19, 2013, http://goo.gl/zd5LAj.

56. David Cole, "Clogging the War Machine," *New York Review of Books Blog*, Sept. 19, 2013, http://goo.gl/QElgt5.

57. Charlie Savage, "Shift on Executive Power Lets Obama Bypass Rivals," *New York Times*, Apr. 23, 2012, http://goo.gl/DqL7F.

58. Charlie Savage, "Suits on Same-Sex Marriage May Force Administration to Take a Stand," *New York Times*, Jan. 29, 2011, http://goo.gl/LXtde.

59. *U.S. v. Windsor*, 570 U.S. 12 (2013).

60. *Obergefell v. Hodges* (2015), http://goo.gl/13FEOw.

61. Letter from Holder to Boehner, Feb. 23, 2011, http://goo.gl/tRHBPC.

62. Senate roll-call vote 278, Dec. 18, 2010, http://goo.gl/dUcyyx.

63. White House transcript, "Remarks by the President at Univision Town Hall," Mar. 28, 2011, http://goo.gl/RNdf8q.

64. Motoko Rich, "'No Child' Law Whittled Down by White House," *New York Times*, July 6, 2012, http://goo.gl/awD60.

65. White House transcript, "Remarks by the President on the Economy," Jan. 4, 2012, http://goo.gl/fyphb5.

66. Although the Senate was still controlled by Democrats, the Constitution forbids either chamber of Congress from adjourning for more than three days without the assent of the other chamber. House Republicans refused to let the Democratic-controlled

Senate adjourn for more than three days, forcing it to hold pro forma sessions every third day.

67. *NLRB v. Canning*, 134 S. Ct. 2550 (U.S. 2014).

68. The 9–0 rebuke to Obama masked a way in which the court's judgment was actually an executive power victory. Back in January 2013, it looked like Ruemmler's advice to Obama—that there was little downside risk to making his disputed recess appointments because if the courts rejected them, the executive branch would be no worse off than if it acquiesced to the congressional tactic—had been a major miscalculation. A federal appeals court panel in the District of Columbia, taking advantage of a rare justiciable case about recess appointments, struck down Obama's recess appointments in a more sweeping way that anyone had expected. The judges blew past the pro forma session issue and pronounced nearly every recess appointment over the previous two hundred years unconstitutional. The panel ruled that presidents may use that power only to fill vacancies in between formal sessions of Congress—not during vacations in the middle of a session—and only vacancies that arose during that very same recess. Those two requirements would essentially eliminate the authority. The Supreme Court majority, while rejecting Obama's appointments, nevertheless rolled back the court of appeals for the District of Columbia's interpretation and restored the traditional understanding that presidents may use that power to fill vacancies during any lengthy recess, including positions that had come open long before Congress left town. To that extent, Ruemmler's assessment that if they lost, the presidency would be in a status quo situation, was vindicated. Moreover, by challenging the tactic and encountering difficulty in court, the executive branch demonstrated to its allies in Congress, some of whom were reluctant to change traditional rules, that it had done all it could. While the case was being litigated, Democrats changed the filibuster rule in the Senate to make it easier to get to an up-or-down majority vote on executive-branch and lower-court nominees.

69. White House transcript, "Remarks by the President before Cabinet Meeting," Jan. 14, 2014, http://goo.gl/qk9oP8.

70. Charlie Savage, "Justice Dept. Seeks to Curtail Stiff Drug Sentences," *New York Times*, Aug. 13, 2013, http://goo.gl/qxKLEm.

71. Charlie Savage, "Trend to Lighten Harsh Sentences Catches On in Conservative States," *New York Times*, Aug. 13, 2011, http://goo.gl/fZsSy.

72. For the Affordable Care Act, see *Obergefell v. Hodges*, No. 14-556 (2015). For Clean Air Act regulations, see, for example, *EPA v. EME Homer City Generation*, 134 S. Ct. 1584 (2014), and *Utility Air Regulatory Group v. EPA*, 134 S. Ct. 2427 (2014); but see *Michigan v. Environmental Protection Agency*, No. 14-46 (2015).

73. Julia Preston and John H. Cushman Jr., "Obama to Permit Young Migrants to Remain in U.S.," *New York Times*, June 16, 2012, http://goo.gl/4s6PM.

74. Ashley Parker and Jonathan Martin, "Senate, 68 to 32, Passes Overhaul for Immigration," *New York Times*, June 28, 2013, http://goo.gl/mSdZbP.

75. Seung Min Kim, "Conservatives Revolt against Boehner on Immigration," *Politico*, Apr. 30, 2014, http://goo.gl/xtdPNa.

76. Charlie Savage, "White House Fills Top Post at Justice Department," *New York Times*, Mar. 26, 2014, http://goo.gl/NRu75P.

77. They included David Shahoulian, its deputy general counsel and a former aide to Rep. Zoe Lofgren, Democrat of California; Serena Hoy, the former general counsel to

Reid when he was still Senate majority leader and now a counselor to the deputy secretary; and Esther Olavarria, who had been Senator Ted Kennedy's staff lawyer for immigration legislation and who was now a counselor to the secretary.

78. "Hillary Clinton Immigration Roundtable," May 5, 2015, C-SPAN, http://goo.gl/0utLNU.

79. *Crane v. Napolitano,* No. 12-3247, N.D. TX, Order, July 21, 2013, http://goo.gl/zp9KXV; *Crane v. Johnson,* 5th Cir., April 7, 2015, http://goo.gl/or8kKI.

80. *Texas v. U.S.A.,* No. 14-254 (S.D. Tex.), "Memorandum Opinion and Order," Feb. 16, 2015, http://goo.gl/h0v5Ol.

81. Julia Preston, "Obama Plan for Immigration Action Gets a Cold Reception at Appeals Court," *New York Times,* July 11, 2015, http://goo.gl/ge0ERJ.

82. "Debating the Implications If Obama Acts on Immigration," *NewsHour,* PBS, Nov. 19, 2014, http://goo.gl/ucTuD4.

83. *The Colbert Report,* Comedy Central, Dec. 8, 2014, http://thecolbertreport.cc.com/videos/mpmtan/president-barack-obama-pt--2.

84. White House transcript, "Remarks by the President at White House Correspondents' Association Dinner," Apr. 25, 2015, http://goo.gl/J1P1DK.

85. Ezra Klein, "The Joke Was That Obama Wasn't Joking," *Vox,* Apr. 27, 2015, http://goo.gl/QbRm7d.

86. George F. Will, "Containing Iran's Nuclear Intoxication," *Washington Post,* Apr. 10, 2005, http://goo.gl/wSIDbl.

87. "Statement on Signing the Supplemental Appropriations Act, 2009," Daily Comp. Pres. Docs., 2009 No. 00512, June 26, 2009, http://goo.gl/dCl95k.

88. Charlie Savage, "Obama's Embrace of a Bush Tactic Riles Congress," *New York Times,* Aug. 9, 2009, http://goo.gl/UpOEUI.

89. Savage, *Takeover,* 224–49.

90. "Recommendations and Task Force Report on Presidential Signing Statements and the Separation of Powers Doctrine," adopted by the American Bar Association House of Delegates, Aug. 6–7, 2006, http://goo.gl/o46iii.

91. Savage, "Barack Obama's Q&A."

92. "Barack Obama, Campaign Event at Billings West High School, Billings, MT," C-SPAN, May 19, 2008, http://goo.gl/7Bzf5z.

93. Charlie Savage, "Obama Looks to Limit Impact of Tactic Bush Used to Sidestep New Laws," *New York Times,* Mar. 10, 2009, http://goo.gl/Qyjm4x.

94. Charlie Savage, "Obama Takes New Route to Opposing Parts of Laws," *New York Times,* Jan. 9, 2010, http://goo.gl/GXIAM8.

95. "Statement by the President on the Intelligence Authorization Act," Oct. 7, 2010, http://goo.gl/aaNspK.

96. House Armed Services Committee, hearing re "The May 31, 2014, Transfer of Five Senior Taliban Detainees," June 11, 2014.

97. The majority's theory was that because the Constitution says the president shall receive ambassadors, this implies an exclusive power—one Congress cannot encroach upon—to recognize which governments legitimately exist (and so may dispatch the ambassadors the president chooses to receive). *Zivotofsky v. Kerry,* 135 S. Ct. 2076 (U.S. 2015), http://goo.gl/8RTiru.

98. James DeMint, "What I Heard in Honduras," *Wall Street Journal,* Oct 10, 2009, http://goo.gl/npqvpN.

99. E-mail from Koh to Steinberg et al., re Honduras military coup decision, 9:23 p.m., Aug. 28, 2009, https://goo.gl/5GgTZo.

100. E-mail from Clinton to Mills, re Honduras military coup decision, 7:48 a.m., Aug. 29, 2009, https://goo.gl/5GgTZo.

101. Transcript, "Retrospective On International Law in the First Obama Administration," American Society of International Law annual meeting, April 4, 2013, http://goo.gl/uuxOmI.

102. State Department transcript, daily press briefing, July 26, 2013, http://goo.gl/SS21x1.

103. Charlie Savage, "Meeting with Chinese, Official Tests Limits Set by Congress," *New York Times,* Nov. 3, 2011, http://goo.gl/9v3lG.

104. Memorandum opinion for the general counsel of the Office of Science and Technology Policy, re "Unconstitutional Restrictions on Activities of the Office of Science and Technology Policy in Section 1340(A) of the Department of Defense and Full-Year Continuing Appropriations Act, 2011," Office of Legal Counsel of the Department of Justice, Sept. 19, 2011, http://goo.gl/WmMzgo.

105. Memorandum opinion for the acting legal adviser, Department of State, re "Constitutionality of Section 7054 of the Fiscal Year 2009 Foreign Appropriations Act," Office of Legal Counsel of the Department of Justice, June 1, 2009, http://goo.gl/WmMzgo.

106. Charlie Savage, "Ignoring a Law on Foreign Relations," Sept. 15, 2009, *New York Times,* http://goo.gl/baS38T.

107. Justice Department Office of Legal Counsel memorandum, "Issues Raised by Provisions Directing Issuance of Official or Diplomatic Passports," Jan. 17, 1992, http://goo.gl/WmMzgo.

108. Savage, *Takeover,* 57–59.

109. Justice Department Office of Legal Counsel memorandum, "Issues Raised by Foreign Relations Authorization Bill," Feb. 16, 1990, http://goo.gl/WmMzgo.

110. The two Bush-Quayle lawyers who started the sequence embraced broad views about the scope of executive power, while the two Obama-era lawyers were relatively more modest in their tone and philosophy; Barron, for example, went out of his way to acknowledge that "Congress quite clearly possesses significant article I powers in the area of foreign affairs." It is far from clear that Barron would agree with Barr about what is "self-evidently" true in a matter of executive power if both were starting from a blank slate. But Barron was working within existing executive-branch precedents, and, like judges, executive-branch lawyers follow the principle of *stare decisis,* which means respecting previously settled issues and being reluctant to reopen them.

This approach helps presidential power snowball. It gives incoming executive-branch lawyers a principled reason to disassociate themselves from their own previous views about the limits of executive power when the president who appointed them is facing a tough issue.

Back in 1995, for example, Walter Dellinger, a head of the Office of Legal Counsel in the Clinton administration, came under criticism by a group of law professors for writing an opinion declaring that Clinton, without prior congressional authorization, could invade Haiti to restore order following a coup there (letter from Dellinger to United States senators, re "Deployment of United States Armed Forces into Haiti," Office of the Legal Counsel of the Department of Justice, Sept. 27, 1994, http://goo.gl/P5hV3W). (This was a central precedent in developing the idea that presidents may unilaterally launch military operations that fall short of *war* in the constitutional sense, which Krass later cited and applied when blessing Obama's Libya intervention.) The law professors who criticized Dellinger — including a younger Harold Koh and Bruce Ackerman — accused him of taking a different view than he had espoused when he was a Duke University law professor. (Letter from law professors to Clinton, Aug. 31, 1994, reprinted in *The American Journal of International Law* 89 [1995]: 96).

Defending himself, Dellinger explained that the role of an executive-branch lawyer was different from that of an academic: "Unlike an academic lawyer, an executive branch attorney may have an obligation to work within a tradition of reasoned, executive branch precedent, memorialized in formal written opinions," Dellinger wrote. "When lawyers who are now at the Office of Legal Counsel begin to research an issue, they are not expected to turn to what I might have written or said in a floor discussion at a law professors' convention. They are expected to look to the previous opinions of the Attorneys General and of heads of this office to develop and refine the executive branch's legal positions" (Walter Dellinger, "After the Cold War: Presidential Power and the Use of Military Force," *University of Miami Law Review* 50 [October 1995]: 107).

111. Bruce Ackerman, *The Decline and Fall of the American Republic* (Cambridge, MA: Harvard University Press, 2010), 111–14.

112. Ibid., 141–52.

113. Trevor Morrison, "Constitutional Alarmism," *Harvard Law Review* 124 (May 20, 2011): 1688, http://goo.gl/bmnHMN.

114. See, for example, Savage, *Takeover*, 33–34.

115. See, for example, Charlie Savage, "Bush Plan for Iraq Would Be a First," *Boston Globe*, Jan. 25, 2008, http://goo.gl/j6bhIQ; the final text was made more ambiguous: "Agreement between the United States of America and the Republic of Iraq on the Withdrawal of United States Forces from Iraq and the Organization of Their Activities During Their Temporary Presence in Iraq," Nov. 17, 2008, http://goo.gl/ucJNgn.

116. Open letter from Republican senators to the leaders of the Islamic Republic of Iran, Mar. 9, 2015, http://goo.gl/DkiIrG.

117. Jonathan Weisman and Peter Baker, "Obama Yields, Allowing Congress Say on Iran Nuclear Deal," *New York Times*, April 15, 2015, http://goo.gl/pdG74v.

118. Peter Baker, "Congress's Role in Iran Nuclear Deal Shows Limits of Obama's Power," *New York Times*, Apr. 17, 2015, http://goo.gl/aHk412.

119. Jeh Johnson, Remarks at Oxford Union, "The Conflict Against Al Qaeda and Its Affiliates: How Will It End?" Nov. 30, 2012.

120. Harold Hongju Koh, Remarks at Oxford Union, "How to End the Forever War?" May 7, 2013.

121. Charlie Savage, "Debating the Legal Basis for the War on Terror," *New York Times*, May 17, 2013, http://goo.gl/9Rt1jJ.

122. "Remarks by the President at the National Defense University."

123. Liz Sty, "Al-Qaeda disavows Any Ties with Radical Islamist ISIS Group in Syria, Iraq," *Washington Post*, Feb. 3, 2014, http://goo.gl/TS4hxs.

124. As a matter of international law, the administration maintained that the bombing was lawful as part of the collective self-defense of Iraq. Baghdad had asked for American help, consenting to strikes on its own territory, and the strikes on Syrian territory were lawful, it said, because Assad was "unable or unwilling" to suppress the Islamic State's threat to Iraq himself. As a result, no Security Council resolution was necessary; Somini Sengupta and Charlie Savage, "U.S. Invokes Iraq's Defense in

Legal Justification of Syria Strikes," *New York Times,* Sept. 24, 2014, http://goo.gl/Rs89ta.

125. Charlie Savage, "Obama Sees Iraq Resolution as a Legal Basis for Airstrikes, Official Says," *New York Times,* Sept. 13, 2014, http://goo.gl/w7gKVX.

126. Charlie Savage, "White House Invites Congress to Approve ISIS Strikes, but Says It Isn't Necessary," *New York Times,* Sept. 11, 2014, http://goo.gl/BilwK2.

127. Jack Goldsmith, "Obama's Breathtaking Expansion of a President's Power to Make War," *Time,* Sept. 11, 2014, http://goo.gl/PMYqy6.

128. Department of Defense transcript, Stephen W. Preston, Remarks before the American Society of International Law, "The Legal Framework for the United States' Use of Military Force Since 9/11," Apr. 10, 2015, http://goo.gl/Kl6vQJ.

129. Carl Hulse, "Boehner Says New Congress Should Debate Military Action," *New York Times,* Sept. 25, 2014, http://goo.gl/VUbnWL.

130. White House transcript, "Remarks by the President on Request to Congress for Authorization of Force Against ISIL," Feb. 11, 2015, http://goo.gl/9np9pz.

131. Jack Goldsmith, "Why the AUMF for the Islamic State Has Stalled," *Lawfare,* Mar. 20, 2015, http://goo.gl/FEcgQT.

132. White House transcript, "Remarks by the President at Farewell Tribute in Honor of Secretary of Defense Chuck Hagel," Jan. 28, 2015, http://goo.gl/hDUiLJ; White House transcript, "Remarks by the President on Memorial Day," May 25, 2015, http://goo.gl/M0Jiqu.

133. Azam Ahmed and Joseph Goldstein, "Taliban Gains Pull U.S. Units Back into Fight in Afghanistan," *New York Times,* Apr. 30, 2015, http://goo.gl/nIwYi0; Joseph Goldstein, "U.S. Steps Up Airstrikes in Afghanistan, Even Targeting ISIS," *New York Times,* July 16, 2015, http://goo.gl/aww8Qt.

134. Preston, "The Legal Framework for the United States' Use of Military Force Since 9/11."

135. *Warafi v. Obama,* No. 09-2368, D.D.C., memorandum opinion, July 30, 2015, https://goo.gl/z6bFUa.

136. Rosa Brooks, "There's No Such Thing as Peacetime," *Foreign Policy,* Mar. 13, 2015, http://goo.gl/bqQV18.

137. The periodic review boards had a slow start, but as Daniel Meltzer, the Harvard law professor who had served as Obama's first deputy White House counsel, told me in April 2015, about a month before his death: "In an armed conflict in which some detainees might be held indefinitely without civilian or military criminal trial, administration lawyers looked for new legal structures that, even if not plainly required by the current law of armed conflict, might mitigate that problem. The PRBs are a good example. They took far too long to be established and far too long again to become operational. But it is possible — hardly certain, but possible — that new architectures like PRBs may over time shine a light on new pathways to follow in conflicts threatening indefinite detention. Law often changes slowly, and change in the national security area is particularly difficult. For a multitude of reasons, it may be some time before we know if any effort to modify the legal architecture will gain traction."

138. Daphne Eviatar, "US Drone Killings of Western Aid Workers Highlight Problems of Nebulous War," *Just Security,* Apr. 27, 2015, http://goo.gl/7LK1g2.

139. For a powerful (if overstated, in my view) argument that Obama's counterterrorism-policy continuity with Bush is explained pretty much exclusively by this institutional force, see Michael J. Glennon, *National Security and Double Government* (New York: Oxford University Press, 2015).

140. These tensions that were managed but not resolved in Obama's national security legal policy dovetailed with tensions in his foreign-policy doctrine, insofar as he can be said to have had one. As my colleague Ross Douthat observed, Obama's evident strategy, from Libya to Yemen, and from Syria and Iraq to Afghanistan and Pakistan, "with its drones and Special Forces and deliberately light footprint, is open-ended by design, a war of constant attrition that aims just to keep our friends (such as they are) in power and our enemies from gaining ground." Douthat wrote this not necessarily as criticism: "There may be cases where America needs to fight to win, enemies that we need to actually defeat instead of managing. But there are also wars that shouldn't be joined at all, and situations where a kind of frozen conflict really is the best out of our bad options." Ross Douthat, "A Case of Too Many Viennas," *New York Times,* Apr. 25, 2015, http://goo.gl/4xSF0h.

141. Senate Judiciary Subcommittee on the Constitution, Civil Rights, and Property Rights, hearing re "Restoring the Rule of Law," Sept. 16, 2008, http://goo.gl/0jsJTi.

142. Bruce Ackerman, "The Republican Fiasco and the Obama Tragedy," *Balkinization,* Mar. 15, 2015, http://goo.gl/vl9E5m.

143. Jonathan Martin, "Christie Assails Libertarian Shift on National Security by Some in the G.O.P.," *New York Times,* July 27, 2013, http://goo.gl/EaepKv.

144. "Michael Medved Asks Jeb Bush: What Has Been the Best Part of the Obama Administration?" *The Michael Medved Show,* Apr. 21, 2015, http://goo.gl/0xjO8j.

An index for *Power Wars* is available at
charliesavage.com/powerwarsindex.

About the Author

Charlie Savage is a Washington correspondent for the *New York Times.* Originally from Fort Wayne, Indiana, Savage graduated from Harvard College and holds a master's degree from Yale Law School. In 2007, while working for the *Boston Globe,* he received the Pulitzer Prize for National Reporting. He lives in Arlington, Virginia, with his wife, Luiza Ch. Savage, the editorial director of events for *Politico,* and their children, William and Peter. Savage's first book, *Takeover,* a bestselling and award-winning account of the Bush-Cheney administration's efforts to expand presidential power, was named one of the best books of 2007 by the *Washington Post, Slate,* and *Esquire.*